LIVING THE REVOLUTION

LIVING THE REVOLUTION

Italian Women's Resistance and

Radicalism in New York City, 1880–1945

JENNIFER GUGLIELMO

The University of North Carolina Press

Chapel Hill

*This volume was published with the assistance of the Greensboro
Women's Fund of the University of North Carolina Press.*
Founding Contributors: Linda Arnold Carlisle, Sally Schindel Cone,
Anne Faircloth, Bonnie McElveen Hunter, Linda Bullard Jennings,
Janice J. Kerley (in honor of Margaret Supplee Smith), Nancy Rouzer
May, and Betty Hughes Nichols.

The paper in this book meets the guidelines for permanence
and durability of the Committee on Production Guidelines for
Book Longevity of the Council on Library Resources.
   The University of North Carolina Press has been a member
   of the Green Press Initiative since 2003.

Library of Congress Cataloging-in-Publication Data
   Guglielmo, Jennifer, 1967–
Living the revolution : Italian women's resistance and radicalism
   in New York City, 1880–1945 /
Jennifer Guglielmo.
   p. cm. — (Gender and American culture)
   Includes bibliographical references and index.
   ISBN 978-0-8078-3356-8 (cloth : alk. paper)
1. Women immigrants—Political activity—New York (State)—New York—
History. 2. Women in the labor movement—New York (State)—New York—
History. 3. Italians—Political activity—New York (State)—New York—History.
4. Italian American women—Political activity—New York (State)—New York—
History 5. Working class women—Political activity—New York (State)—New York—
History. 6. Radicalism—New York (State)—New York—History. I. Title.
   HQ1439.N6G84 2010
   320.53082'097471—dc22
                                        2009039645
   14 13 12 11 10   5 4 3 2 1

To Grace and Angelo Guglielmo,

with great love and admiration

A story is not *just a story. Once the forces have been aroused and set into motion, they can't simply be stopped at someone's request. Once told, the story is bound to circulate; humanized it may have a temporary end, but its effects linger on and its end is never truly an end.*

—TRINH T. MINH-HA, "Grandma's Story," in *Woman Native Other*

Contents

Introduction 1

1 Women's Cultures of Resistance in Southern Italy 9

2 *La Sartina* (The Seamstress) Becomes a Transnational Labor Migrant 44

3 The Racialization of Southern Italian Women 79

4 Surviving the Shock of Arrival and Everyday Resistance 110

5 Anarchist Feminists and the Radical Subculture 139

6 The 1909–1919 Strike Wave and the Birth of Industrial Unionism 176

7 Red Scare, the Lure of Fascism, and Diasporic Resistance 199

8 Community Organizing in a Racial Hall of Mirrors 230

Conclusions 266

Notes 271

Bibliography 325

Acknowledgments 385

Index 389

Illustrations

Women of Carloforte, Island of San Pietro, Sardinia, 1913 10

Women washing clothes in Lago di Piediluco, Umbria, ca. 1890 19

Women dancing, Naples, ca. 1870–90 28

Sant'Agata (Saint Agatha), 1896 31

Girls learning to sew, Sicily, 1921 46

Italian immigrant woman at Ellis Island, ca. 1906–14 67

Mrs. Mary Rena and neighbors shelling nuts, 1911 71

Women making feathers, ca. 1907 73

Women weavers, ca. 1913 74

Italian immigrant woman carrying garment piecework, 1910 80

Sicilian girl, 1914 84

Lombroso's "Homicidal Women," 1897 85

Frank and Dolly Sinatra, 1945 112

Census taker at 332 East 112th Street, 1930 123

Antonia (Zullo) and Francesco Porcelli, ca. 1930 137

Roda and Esteve family, ca. 1916 140

May Day Picnic, Haledon, New Jersey, 1915 146

Guabello, Gallo, and Baronio families, Haledon, New Jersey, 1921 152

May Day, New York City, 1916 178

Women in garment shop, ca. 1900 184

Angela Bambace with her mother Giuseppina, ca. 1930 185

IWW headquarters in New York City after police raid of 15 November 1919 200

Antonino Capraro following kidnapping by KKK, 6 May 1919 208

Betty Marandi, Laura Douglass, and Emma Polcari lead strike march, East Paterson, New Jersey, 1926 211

Antifascist rally, New York City, ca. 1930 222

East Harlem, ca. 1939 232

Margaret Di Maggio with other delegates, ILGWU Convention, Atlantic City, New Jersey 1937 247

Women celebrate victory in sanitation campaign, East Harlem, New York, ca. 1935 259

Women march for cleaner streets and better housing, East Harlem, New York, ca. 1939 262

Italian Americans watching a flag-raising ceremony, New York City, 1942 268

LIVING THE REVOLUTION

Introduction

At the close of the nineteenth century, a visionary movement began to take shape in the New York–New Jersey area. It was led by those on the margins: impoverished, semiliterate, Italian immigrant women who worked in the many sweatshops and mills scattered across the urban-industrial landscape. Inspired by dreams of international working-class solidarity, they came together to leave their mark on the historical record. In venues ranging from newspapers and pamphlets, to theatrical performances, festivals, and community-wide meetings, they exposed the exploitation they experienced as low-wage workers within the expanding capitalist world system. They made visible their daily struggles with family members, bosses, priests, labor leaders, politicians, and the ladies in "perfumed drawing-rooms."[1] They organized alongside men but also on their own, in women's groups—what they called *gruppi femminili di propaganda*. Such groups first formed in New York City and across the Hudson River, in Paterson and Hoboken, within the anarchist movement. They quickly spread to Philadelphia, Boston, New Haven, Chicago, and the mining communities of Illinois, Pennsylvania, and Vermont. Because the network of groups reflected patterns of Italian labor migration and political exile, they also extended across oceans, to connect with similar groups in Buenos Aires, Paris, Milan, Rome, and beyond.[2]

Out of this diasporic working-class movement, a cast of characters emerges: Maria Roda, Maria Barbieri, Ninfa Baronio, Ernestina Cravello, and Angela Bambace are just some of the dozens of women whose stories are chronicled here. Each devoted her life to radical political movements because revolutionary activism generated a sense of hope in the face of despair. Such activism opened their lives to a rich intellectual and cultural milieu, in which to form new kinds of relationships and develop their own ideas about capitalism, nationalism, racism, colonialism, militarism, religion, feminism, socialism, anarchism, and love. Each infused the labor movement and their own communities with collectivist values that grew out of their distinct experiences as migrants, peasants, industrial workers, and women. As a result, they provided a point of entry for other working-class women to join the revolutionary movement for social change.

This commitment came at great risk. Activists faced continual harassment and surveillance from the state, employers, family members, and others. They also lived through beatings, arrests, and the loss of loved ones. Yet, they argued that a world without exploitation, oppression, and coercive authority, and without extremes of rich and poor, required fundamental societal transformation on all levels. It necessitated dismantling the existing governing political institutions and methods of economic production. It also demanded a new consciousness. As a result, they focused much of their energy on their sister workers, on teaching women how they internalized and propagated oppressive ideologies of subservience, self-sacrifice, prejudice, and victimization. As Maria Barbieri, a member of a Hoboken anarchist group wrote in 1905, "A struggle continues each and every day, to pull out the deep roots that a false education has cultivated and nourished in my heart."[3] They called on men in the movement, too, to fully practice what they preached and to do so in their most intimate relationships. In the process, they learned to trust their own experiences and to refute the many disparaging projections they received from all directions. In this way, they came to recognize the power they had to emancipate themselves, to embody and *live* revolution. Revolution was not something they worked toward; it was a new way of being.

Participation in the anarchist movement was just one of many ways that Italian immigrant women and their daughters survived the challenges of the early twentieth century with their spirits intact. This is a story about how these two generations confronted the colossal dislocations of this period, including the Industrial Revolution, transatlantic labor migration, and the violence of state formation. The methods of survival and resistance described here include a wide range of practices, both formal and informal, and a spectrum of activism from the left to the right. In this way, we can begin to understand how these two generations of marginalized immigrant and working-class women claimed space, resources, and political and social identities and possibly learn from their choices.

This history has long eluded scholars. Italians constituted the largest group to immigrate to the United States during the mass migrations from Europe at the turn of the past century. Hundreds of thousands of Italian immigrant women also participated in and led some of the most historically significant labor strikes of this period. But, as historians Donna Gabaccia and Franca Iacovetta recently noted, the "least understood aspect of Italian women's diasporic lives is their role as resisters, protesters, and activists."[4] Scholarship on Argentina and Brazil has more effectively demonstrated the significant role Italian immigrant women played in local labor struggles and in building a transnational revolutionary workers' movement in Buenos Aires, São Paulo, and beyond.[5] In the United States, feminist labor historians have for several decades documented immigrant and working-class women's political activisms in the early twentieth-century. Yet, Italian women's histories of resistance are few and far between, especially when we consider how much scholarship exists on eastern European and Russian Jewish immigrant women, whose migrations and activisms occurred simultaneously.[6]

What explains this invisibility? First, many historical documents affirm an image of Italian immigrant women as apolitical. The writing of male leaders filled entire runs of Italian radical newspapers, with only occasional essays by women. Men held most of the formal leadership positions in neighborhood and labor organizations, and many believed that they were best suited to teaching labor radicalism to women. Indeed, most union leaders and social reformers considered Italian immigrant women to be "ignorant," "hopeless," "absolutely under the dominance of men in their family," and "heavily shackled by old customs and traditions."[7] Other European American women in the labor movement tended to echo such sentiments, to declare that Italian immigrant women were not active because they were "unorganizable."[8] One classic example is that of Elizabeth Gurley Flynn, radical labor organizer and child of Irish immigrants, who proclaimed in her autobiography, "There were practically no women in the Italian movement—anarchist or socialist. Whatever homes I went into with Carlo [Tresca] the women were always in the background, cooking in the kitchen, and seldom even sitting down to eat with the men."[9] Yet, I discovered that Italian immigrant women established anarchist women's groups in precisely the same locales where Flynn organized workers, and on at least one occasion, she even ate in the home of a woman who organized such groups.

Italian women might have appeared in the background to Flynn, but they were absolutely central to early twentieth-century labor movements in cities such as New York, Hoboken, Paterson, Newark, Lowell, Passaic, Little Falls, Boston, Hopedale, Rochester, Lawrence, Lynn, Chicago, Tampa, Cleveland, and Providence. Indeed, the Italian-language radical press often referred to them as "the most passionate in the struggle."[10] They not only entered politics in the United States via labor militancy but became pivotal to workplace actions, where they drew on communal protest traditions from Italy and the urban female neighborhood networks they developed upon resettlement. Clearly, we must look into the kitchen and see what these women were doing in the background spaces to which Flynn was not privy. This book enters such spaces and moves them to the forefront of analysis.

The chapters that follow explore the numerous ruptures and contradictions embedded in the stereotypical myths about Italian women: "silent" women ignored employers' threats and took to the streets; "ignorant" women smashed factory windows with rocks while on strike; and "hopeless" women created revolutionary political cultures to birth a new world. Italian immigrant women and their American-born daughters were in fact far from invisible or hidden in their own day, though their particular methods of resistance often confounded or eluded political and labor leaders. While a great deal of public discourse perpetuated stereotypical images, there existed another world where Italian women formulated strategies of resistance and survival that called into question systems of power and authority within their families, communities, and the larger society.

This history becomes visible only when we expand our understanding of early twentieth-century feminism to include diasporic, working-class activisms that were not produced in English. Such a lens is necessary for southern Italians, most of whom were mobile laborers who traveled to Argentina and Brazil with almost as much frequency as the United States. Most also returned to Italy and few naturalized as U.S. citizens. While women did not repatriate with as much frequency as men, their lives, families, identities, communities, and social movements reflected these patterns of labor migration. As a result, Italian immigrant women's activism differed markedly from traditional models of "first wave" feminism, including many documented forms of labor feminism. For one, they generally did not seek inclusion or authority within the modern nation-state. Moreover, unlike Jewish working women, they did not immediately rely on the established trade-union movement or cross-class alliances with middle-class women to assert working women's power, especially before the Great Depression. Rather, they turned most often to strategies of mutual aid, collective direct action, and to the multiethnic, radical subculture that took shape within their urban working-class communities. This political world was deeply transnational or, even more accurately, *diasporic*. It was rooted in the lived experiences of labor migration, political exile, and high rates of repatriation and thus reflected the intimate, enduring connections between homelands and communities abroad. It was also opposed to the oppressive power of the nation-state and refuted nationalism. Rather, it encouraged participants to imagine themselves as *lavoratori nel mondo* (workers of the world) and actively traversed national and other boundaries.[11] Some of the women in this movement used the word *femminismo* to describe their work, but most preferred *emancipazione*, because it distinguished their activism from bourgeois feminisms while capturing the all-encompassing nature of the freedoms they desired.

In fact, the image of southern Italian women as docile and apolitical emerged at precisely the same time as their mass-based participation in revolutionary social movements. The middle and upper classes in both Italy and the United States invoked such ideas to reinforce popular assumptions about the backwardness of rebellious southern Italians. Northern Italian elites justified their domination and exploitation of southern Italy by racializing the peasant women they encountered there as sexual and political deviants and as beasts of burden.[12] Such ideas informed how the United States greeted Italian immigrants, the vast majority of whom came from the South. Italians quickly learned that to be "dark," "swarthy," and "kinky-haired"—as the U.S. press often called them—was to be despised and degraded.[13] Although Italians arrived in the United States as poor, migrant peasants from a racially suspect area of the globe and were popularly conceived of as innately uncivilized and inferior, they were simultaneously situated as whites and therefore as deserving of rescue, reform, and inclusion.[14] As a result, the image of Italian immigrant women as victims persisted, in contrast to middle-class white women, who became the marker of liberated womanhood, but also against Italian men, whom most Americans imagined largely as victimizers, in the form of criminals, lazy indigents, and violent patriarchs.[15]

Such attitudes served to justify material inequality and labor discipline. They also established the need for Italian immigrant women's rescue and protection without having to indict the state, employers, or others in the middle and upper classes. Most important, this shift marked a journey that southern Italian immigrant women underwent, from the bottom of the racial hierarchy in Italy, to a position above various groups in the United States, especially African Americans, Chinese, Mexicans, Puerto Ricans, and others who were routinely imagined as agents rather than victims of social disorder.[16] The charge of deviance would reemerge however, whenever Italian immigrant women "rejected the condescension and the stigma of impoverishment" to organize for social and economic change.[17] In these moments, they would again be stigmatized as dissolute and dangerous.

I explore this history of racialization in more depth in the pages that follow, but brief mention is necessary here because it helps to explain an additional reason for Italian immigrant women's political invisibility: the historical amnesia that resulted from the political project of whiteness. To American and Italian authorities, labor radicals were not visionaries but terrorists, loose women, and unruly subversives who threatened the very fiber of the nation. The transnational discourses on race that constructed southern Italians as biologically inferior to northern Italians and other white Europeans focused on their supposed natural inclination toward both menial labor and crime, especially in the form of anarchism and the mafia. Admission into the nation was therefore contingent on

Italians embracing U.S. nationalism, including whiteness and negrophobia.[18] This "price of the ticket," as African American writer James Baldwin termed it, was made abundantly clear during the Red Scare of the First World War, culminating in the state's execution of Italian anarchists Nicola Sacco and Bartolomeo Vanzetti in 1927.[19] This "triumph of nativism," coupled with the criminalization of dissent, profoundly crippled Italian immigrant radicalism.[20] As a result, Italians increasingly sought to reconcile their position as unwanted foreigners by abandoning revolutionary social movements and embracing nationalism and whiteness. Ironically (and tragically), they did so to satisfy the same desires for economic justice and dignity that inspired enthusiasm for anarchism, socialism, and communism. The next generation of Italian American labor activists would borrow and co-opt key elements of the radical immigrant subculture. But the kinds of coalitions and identities that had given rise to women's anarchist feminism would diminish substantially in the coming years.

BETWEEN THE closing decades of the nineteenth century and the midpoint of the twentieth century, Italian women embarked on a remarkable journey. They led peasant and worker rebellions, imbued their daily lives with their own priorities and dreams, and helped to organize a revolutionary industrial labor movement worldwide. They also witnessed the complete shift of their political cultures as a result of the Red Scare and the rise in coercive nationalisms ignited by the First World War. As a result, many came together to support Mussolini in the mass-based profascist movement, and by the 1940s many joined efforts to keep people of color out of "their" families, neighborhoods, schools, and workplaces. Embracing whiteness meant the ability to avoid many forms of violence and humiliation. It meant preferential access to citizenship, property, higher wages, political power, and social status, among other privileges. It also meant, as Baldwin noted, that Italians had to "look with loathing upon everything that native whites loathed." Many did so by embracing "the delusion of white supremacy" as it was enacted all around them, through violence, segregation, and other forms of disassociation.[21] This book seeks to explain this trajectory, to assess how these two generations of women not only confronted but also implicated themselves in power relations during this period.

Uncovering this history is especially significant now, as antiglobalization and immigrant rights movements are again exploding, and workers, their activist allies, academics, policy makers, and others are analyzing the human costs of globalization and the politics of inclusion and exclusion within nations. The proliferation of transnational feminisms in recent years has inspired a renewed interdisciplinary commitment to documenting the impact of globalization, nationalism, and the feminization of labor on women's lives.[22] Rooted in the confrontations of working-class women of color with globalizing capitalism since the late 1980s, these activisms have inspired historians to reinterpret the past with a transnational lens. Yet these histories often maintain a focus on elite women's lives. We have learned, for example, how early twentieth-century middle- and upper-class feminisms were international in scope and often pivotal to the success of the British and U.S. empires. We know more about the ways Anglo-American Protestant elite women drew on dominant ideas of race to position themselves as the measure of civilization and thus as the protectors and civilizers of "primitive" women at home and abroad. We also now have a rich body of scholarship documenting how race, class, and imperialism informed white feminisms in the early twentieth century and compelling analyses of how power operated within these movements.[23] What remains largely absent, however, is an understanding that transnational feminism has a past that is also radical and working class.[24] Just a few years ago, historian Nancy Hewitt expressed her frustration at how this impacts younger generations' understandings of feminism: "I am sort of appalled, at the seeming ease with which the dynamic, diverse, internationalist, conflicted, antiracist, socialist, and anarchist strains that defined women's liberation for me and for so many others have been erased."[25] This has occurred despite more than three decades of compelling feminist labor history that has challenged hegemonic notions of feminism and revealed all that is lost when we think of feminism as occurring in just two waves.[26]

Mapping this history requires close attention to class and race hierarchies. The experiences of Italian immigrant women and their American-born daughters differed markedly from women of color because they were not "denied basic political and legal rights and hemmed in by almost impermeable 'color' barriers to mobility."[27] Therefore, a central concern of this book is to ask how white working-class women's lives are shaped by race.[28] It attempts to explore, as Toni Morrison has advised, "the impact of notions of racial hierarchy, racial exclusion, and racial vulnerability and availability on nonblacks who held, resisted, explored, or altered these notions."[29] In doing so, I hope to participate in a developing understanding of the ways gender shaped how European immigrants learned, internalized, and enacted race, from their particular histories of labor, migration, and nationalization.

The act of recuperating repressed, submerged histories is deeply significant because, as feminist theorist M. Jacqui Alexander has written, it provides an "antidote to alienation, separation, and the amnesia that domination produces." It offers a way of excavating "the costs of collective forgetting so deep that we have even forgotten that we have forgotten."[30] My tracing of this history is thus intended not only as an act of recovery but as an attempt to unearth a valuable lesson: far from being backward in comparison to their more Americanized daughters, as the racializing (il)logic would argue, Italian immigrant women were in many ways more complete in their critique of power than later generations. Moreover, this history reminds us that some of the most inclusive and visionary ideas of human liberation have historically been formulated by those on the margins, those excluded from formal political power, the stigmatized, semiliterate, "backward," and "illegal."

Women's Cultures of
Resistance in Southern Italy

Si viju lu diavulu non schiantu (If I see the devil I do not run).
—Calabrese women's song

A wave of popular unrest washed over Sicily at the close of the nineteenth century. In town after town, peasants mobilized labor strikes, occupied fields and piazzas, and looted government offices. While the island had a long history of revolt, this marked a new era of social protest. For the first time, women led the social movement and infused the struggle with their own mixture of socialism and spiritualism.

The activity began in the autumn of 1892, in the towns surrounding Palermo, in the northwestern part of the island. In Monreale, women and children filled the central piazza shouting "Down with the municipal government! Long live the union!"[1] After attacking and looting the offices of the city council, they marched toward Palermo crying "We are hungry!" waving banners with slogans connecting socialism to scripture. In Villafrati, Caterina Costanzo led a group of women wielding clubs to the fields where they threatened workers who had not joined the community in a general strike against the repressive local government. In Balestrate, thousands of women dressed in traditional clothes and also armed with clubs marched through the streets, demanding an end to government corruption. In Belmonte, Felicia Pizzo Di Lorenzo led fifty peasant women through the town and then gathered in the *palazzo comunale*, demanding the abolition of taxes, the removal of the mayor, and the termination of the city council. Three days later, when the crowd had grown to six hundred women and men, the mayor and his police broke up the demonstration and arrested the most vocal protestors.

In Piana dei Greci, thirty-six women were arrested after they occupied and then destroyed the municipal offices, throwing the furniture into the streets.

Women with amphorae, Carloforte, Island of San Pietro, Sardinia, 1913. Alinari Archives, Florence, Italy.

Soon after the uprising, close to one thousand women there formed a *fascio delle lavoratrici* (union of workers). The word *fascio*, "meaning bundle, or sheaf (as in sheaf of wheat)," in this case referred to "a sodality of peasants, miners, or artisans."[2] They celebrated the founding of the group as they would a religious festival, with music and food, and wove their political and spiritual ideologies together in their speeches. In the words of one woman, "We want everybody to work as we work. There should no longer be either rich or poor. All should have bread for themselves and their children. We should all be equal. . . . Jesus was a true socialist and he wanted precisely what we ask for, but the priests don't discuss this."[3]

News of the uprisings traveled quickly. Within days, government officials and newspaper reporters arrived from the mainland to witness the disturbances. Adolfo Rossi, a government official who would become the Italian commissioner of emigration, was one of the first to appear on the scene, and his observations circulated in the Roman newspaper *La Tribuna* in the fall of 1893. From Piana dei Greci, an epicenter of activity, he wrote: "The most serious sign is that the women are the most enthusiastic. . . . Peasant women's *fasci* are no less fierce than those of the men." In some areas, "women who were once very religious now believe only in their *fasci*," and "in those areas where men are timid against authority, their wives soon convince them to join the movement of workers."[4] When the government accused the newly formed Italian Socialist Party of orchestrating the rebellion, party leader Filippo Turati argued that the movement was indigenous and rooted in popular solidarity: "The women, whose role in igniting the insurrection is well known, have abandoned the church for the *fasci* and it is they who incite their husbands and children to action."[5]

The Italian government responded swiftly. On 3 January 1894, Prime Minister Francesco Crispi (a Sicilian himself) called for a state of siege and sent forty thousand military troops to the island to "contain the socialist threat."[6] Movement leaders and participants were arrested, beaten, and gunned down in the streets or executed in prison. Yet agitation continued to spread across the island and to the mainland. As popular unrest moved from the South to the North, women continued to play a critical role, leading street demonstrations and riots in small villages and towns throughout Calabria, Basiciliata, and Puglia and in the cities of Rome, Bologna, Imola, Ancona, Naples, Bari, Florence, Milan, and Genoa. Across Italy, workers in the emerging industrial cities joined with peasants to demand a complete restructuring of society based on socialist principles and filled streets chanting "Long Live Anarchy! Long Live Social Revolution!"[7] In October, Crispi ordered the suppression of all socialist and anarchist groups. A four-year repressive campaign culminated in the *fatti di maggio* of 1898—the massacre of eighty demonstrators in Milan.[8] By 1900 most of Italy's peasantry and workers had experienced or heard of this kind of revolutionary struggle. It was in this climate that mass emigration from Italy took place.

THIS HISTORY of women's revolutionary activity was foundational to Italian women's cultures of resistance in early twentieth-century New York City.

Scholars often label this activity as prepolitical and "primitive" because it began outside of the formal political spaces of trade unions and political parties.[9] Yet it was this kind of activity that launched modern working-class movements in Italy and throughout the diaspora. When women turned to building anarchist women's groups, industrial labor unions, and grass-roots neighborhood coalitions, they drew upon traditions of civil disobedience and community-wide revolts that were independent of formal organizations yet firmly rooted in popular solidarity. In fact, these methods remained fundamental to how Italian women expressed their discontent during the first half of the twentieth century, at home and abroad.

This chapter explores the social and cultural worlds that gave shape to this kind of collective consciousness and action. As with other impoverished women around the world, their politics emerged from daily struggles to care for family, friends, and neighbors. It grew out of daily confrontations with authority and the many indignities brought about by industrial expansion, mass emigration, and national centralization under northern Italian rule. But it also emerged from female social worlds that provided women with a certain autonomy to craft methods of subterfuge.

This new era of peasant women's political activism occurred at precisely the same time that emigration from Italy began to reach mass proportions. As large numbers of men left in search of work, women's responsibilities expanded. The female worlds that developed during men's prolonged absences provided women with the space to articulate grievances, critique authority, and challenge oppressive conditions in new ways. While women continued to struggle with one another and with returning men over issues of power and authority, they also asserted for themselves more autonomous roles in their families and communities.

The peasant uprisings of the 1890s grew out of these worlds and provided a basis from which women crafted a distinctly antinationalist, socialist, and anarchist movement that was informed by their own unique blend of class consciousness and spiritualism. To the northern elites attempting to quell such resistance, southern Italian peasant women came to symbolize the changes they feared the most: as unruly peasants, relatively independent women, and political subversives, southern Italian women routinely challenged the attempts by landowners, state officials, religious leaders, and other authorities, to control and subdue them into model subjects. This struggle occurred not only in their piazzas and fields but also in places they had little access to—in the writings and exhortations of the upper classes, who worked tirelessly to cast the women in disparaging ways in order to justify their repression, dispossession, and poverty. The now familiar tropes of Italian peasant women as submissive, ignorant victims can be traced directly to Italian bourgeois attempts to possess such insurrectionary women in order to secure their own social and economic position.

Transnational Lives

In 1915 the British travel writer, Norman Douglas, reflected on his journey to the southern Italian province of Calabria: "A change is upon the land," he wrote, "the patriarchal system of Coriolanus, the glory of southern Italy, is breaking up." He attributed this rupture to mass emigration, noting that across the region there was "a large preponderance of women over men, nearly the whole male section of the community, save the young and the decrepit, being in America."[10] His words echoed the concerns of the new state, which reported that throughout the province of neighboring Caserta, the population consisted only of women, infants, and the very old.[11] Two decades later, when Carlo Levi was banished by the fascist government to an impoverished agricultural village in Basilicata for his resistance to the regime, he similarly noted, "The men have gone and the women have taken over . . . a matriarchal regime prevails."[12]

The rising numbers of women living on their own drew attention precisely because transnational migration was dramatically transforming life in southern Italy. Between 1870 and 1970, more than twenty-six million Italians migrated to other lands. As many as 60 to 80 percent of the migratory population were young men—peasants, artisans, and unskilled workers—who moved regularly in search of work. Several decades of internal movement from rural areas to cities and at least four centuries of migration throughout the Mediterranean and across the Alps into Switzerland, France, and Germany preceded the mass migrations. But by the 1890s, such movement stretched across continents and oceans, as Italians traveled to and from urban centers such as New York, Philadelphia, Chicago, Boston, Montreal, Marseilles, São Paulo, and Buenos Aires, as well as mining and agricultural regions, where they could earn enough cash to send wages home. The years between Italian national unification in 1861 and the First World War witnessed the largest exodus, as fourteen million people emigrated from Italy.[13]

The majority of Italy's migrants came from the poorer and more agricultural southern provinces of Sicily, Campania, Basilicata, and Calabria and from Veneto in the northeast. Most of those who found their way to the United States came from the South, and they migrated for many of the same factors that fueled their revolutionary movements. In their own testimonies, migrants spoke of intense poverty when reflecting on their motivation to leave.[14] Yet Italians had lived amid poverty, a stagnant economy, unsustainable population growth, devastating diseases like malaria, and natural disasters such as drought and earthquakes for most of the nineteenth century. The formation of the Italian nation and its unjust system of taxation on the South's peasantry and violent repression of resistance movements compelled migration. But the movement of industrial capitalism from northern Europe to the United States was the primary reason southern Italians crossed the Atlantic. Most went to the United States, with smaller numbers going to South America (mostly Brazil and Argentina), Africa, Australia, and the rest of Europe. Many men crossed the Atlantic several times and worked in different locales and countries in one lifetime, and at least half of those who went to the United States ultimately returned to Italy.[15]

Because migrants depended on their families and friends for advice and help about work opportunities abroad, they often traveled the beaten paths of kin and friends from their hometown. Most migrants could not afford to bring their families and sustain them abroad because their jobs were too marginal and precarious. Rather, they sent a portion of their wages home. These earnings not only enabled whole families to survive but were also essential to the economic development of the Italian state. Records show that "remittances to Italy soared from 13 million lire in 1861 to 127 million lire in 1880 and then to 254 million yearly after 1890 and 846 million yearly after 1906. So large was the cash inflow that it ended Italy's negative balance of foreign trade by 1912. Emigration had become one of Italy's largest industries."[16]

Women and Migration Culture

During these years of mass exodus, women participated in transatlantic migration in fewer numbers. Between 1896 and 1914, women composed only 20 to 28 percent of Italian emigration.[17] Italian women's experience of migration was thus most often in the homeland, especially in the years before World War I. But the mass departure of men profoundly altered women's lives as they took over more responsibilities to sustain the home base in Italy. Anna Parola's memories of her childhood confirmed impressions of female-dominated village life: "Many women were like widows, with husbands far away," she recalled. "Eh, our need for bread ruled us."[18] Sociologist Renate Siebert writes that for the women of this generation, transatlantic migration caused "a tragic breaking." In the interviews she conducted with dozens of women from Calabria and Basilicata, she heard of long separations from fathers, husbands, brothers, and lovers and the pain women experienced when contact was lost or when men died abroad and were laid to rest without family present. "I wish I could've been a bird," one woman recalled, "so I could have flown back and forth between here and there, to be with everyone."[19]

Because seasonal labor migration was the primary strategy in which Italians confronted the emergence of a capitalist world economy, transnational families, cultures, and identities became a way of life even for those who never left the homeland. For several generations, kin networks, political cultures, friendships, budgets, and dreams transcended national borders and connected continents. Even though women were separated from the men in their families for long periods, they remained linked to those abroad. In fact, in the years between 1870 and 1914, some "male work camps and rural Italian villages had more communication with each other than with the national societies that surrounded either."[20] Both women and men viewed migration as a temporary but necessary measure to improve a family's economic and social position. As a result, women came to occupy a central position in the international family economy by maintaining the transatlantic household and the many social networks that facilitated migration.

While women experienced loss, longing, and even desperation, the mass exodus also provided new incentives "to carve out new social, economic and civic spaces in the community, the nation and beyond."[21] In the absence of men, women took over all household responsibilities, including the hiring and firing of workers, wage earning, and making decisions and preparations about when or if it was time for the rest of the family to migrate. Oral testimonies are filled with such evidence: Concetta Pancini's father migrated to Philadelphia three times (each period lasting several years) when their crops started to fail, "to make money, but not to stay." While he was gone, her mother and grandmother ran the farm in Italy with the children, "cultivating and planting," canning food for winter, and selling it at the market. It was not until the end of her father's third trip (which lasted more than five years) that her mother decided the family should join him. Philamina Cocozelli's father also migrated several times back and forth across the Atlantic, first for close to seven years, and then for almost three years. While he was away, her mother "managed the land, hiring workers to assist in the harvest."[22] Cecilia Ferrari supported herself and her child for six years by selling her weaving in markets throughout the hill towns surrounding Naples, while her husband worked on the canals and railroads in the United States.[23]

For many women who were born at end of the nineteenth century, *la fatica* (exhausting labor) only increased with mass emigration. Often, a life of intense labor began when girls were ten or eleven years old, the age when many assumed the responsibilities of their household while their mothers worked in the fields. As one woman recalled, "I worked since I was a child, until my arms wouldn't lift anymore."[24] Most women engaged in some form of agricultural labor; tending their own gardens, working as farm hands for neighbors, and hiring out to earn wages on larger commercial farms. One investigator in New York City who interviewed Italian immigrant women garment workers about their lives in Italy in the 1910s found that "whether they had worked as farm hands for their own families or elsewhere, they all agreed in their stories of heavy work, long hours, and child labor."[25]

Women's agricultural work differed by region because geography helped to define the subtle differences between local economies. Larger wheat estates (known as *latifundia*) with highly concentrated landownership tended to dominate the interior hill towns, valleys, and plateaus, as did a rigid system of sharecropping. Mountainous villages were more amenable to goat and sheep herding, whereas coastal towns were characterized by the small-scale cultivation of commercial crops (nuts, citrus, olives, and grapes) and fishing. In many areas, especially in the regions of Campania and Calabria, where people lived close to the fields, women completely replaced men in agricultural work once mass emigration was underway.[26]

The absence of men also led women to develop new relationships with the nation-state. Women in Sicily, for example, turned to bureaucratic officials in new ways with the absence of men: they began to list their newborns with the registry office, went to the mayor's office when they lost track of their husbands abroad or when remittances failed to arrive, and filed complaints against steamship companies when they or their children were denied entrance at U.S. customs. Women dictated letters to city officials, sometimes to convey to emigrant husbands their willingness to endure temporary separation but their refusal to join them overseas. They also learned to read and write, and women's literacy rates began to climb beginning in 1900.[27]

Because women customarily controlled the household budget they also made decisions about which family members would migrate and when. Husbands and all children routinely turned their wages over to wives and mothers at the end of the week or after the harvest, and women budgeted for daily purchases. Even major expenses, "from buying land and mules to purchasing boat tickets to the Americas," generally required the consent of both partners.[28] It was also women's responsibility to save enough cash over the year to pay taxes, which helps to explain their spirited presence in the 1892–94 peasant uprisings and other actions against the state. The pressures of capitalism and mass emigration required that those women who remained in Italy negotiate divisions of labor within families and communities in ways that often called for their increased participation in the economic, social, and political life of their *paese* (homeland).

Faccimu Curtigghiu: Women's Social Worlds

As can be expected, women increasingly turned to each other to deal with the many changes wrought by mass emigration. At the turn of the century, most women in Italy had several things in common: grueling labor, little formal educa-tion, illiteracy, poverty, and the persistent authority of their husbands, brothers, employers, and police, as well as church and government officials. At the center of this world was the family, which formed the heart of Italian social structure, and from which most mediated the struggles in their lives. The proverbs gathered by Giuseppe Pitrè in nineteenth-century Sicily reveal, however, that Sicilians did not have a word to describe the nuclear family (mother, father, and children). Rather, the concept of *la famiglia* was a malleable social ideal, and the signifi-cance of "blood ties" actually took on greater meaning during migration and resettlement.[29] Across southern Italy, the lines between kin and friends were less dramatic, especially because a single *famiglia* could embrace the entire popula-tion of a village owing to the large size of most families.[30] As a result, many people developed the strongest social ties to those they saw on a daily basis: friends, neighbors, and close relatives. The closest words to "friend" were *comare* and *co-pare*, which mean godmother and godfather, or literally co-mother or co-father. Proverbs told, for example, that the child inherits from the mother the blood and from the godmother the bones.[31]

Comari became particularly significant in this period as women relied on one another more intensely in the absence of men. Women in the South used this term not only to identify those friends they assigned as godmothers to their chil-dren but also to honor a close bond of mutual assistance. Some expressed that friends should be found only among kin because they were bound by customary codes of duty and honor.[32] To many, however, friendship outside of kinship was highly prized. As one woman who grew up in Messina in the 1910s noted, "I like to have friends. . . . They help me lead a more complete life than I would if I were isolated and lived only within the family circle. They stimulate my interests — while my immediate family would only teach me things that pertain to family life."[33] Similarly, Renate Siebert found that the "relationships of affection and soli-darity" that developed between *comari* were often the strongest bonds women experienced in their lives, stronger than their marriages.[34] Women crafted their social circles with those they could trust and rely on the most, which were often a combination of kin and neighbors. Carlo Levi described it this way: "It was not that they [peasants] venerated family relationships as a social, legal, or sentimen-tal tie, but rather that they cherished an occult and sacred sense of communality. A unifying web, not only of family ties . . . but of the acquired and symbolic kin-ship called *comparaggio*, ran through the village."[35]

Class and gender shaped daily life, so they profoundly affected how women socialized and developed ties to one another. For example, people made use of their living spaces in ways that revealed the complexity of their social worlds. In most agricultural villages and towns, houses were built close together on narrow winding streets that opened onto a small *cortile* (the semienclosed courtyard at the center of adjoining houses), larger piazzas, and the main town square, and women's daily relationships unfolded in these communal spaces. The surrounding houses most often included a mixture of close and more distant relatives as well as unrelated families. Depending on the town, these spaces could also be somewhat heterogeneous: sometimes "rich and poor, peasant and artisan, kin and nonkin lived in close physical proximity in Sicilian agrotowns. They could easily observe one another; they could mingle easily if they chose to do so." The quality and the size of homes varied widely, however, and only landowning peasants, artisans, and petty merchants owned multiroom and two-story houses. Instead, the "average peasant family and all renters occupied the simplest one-room and two-room stone buildings."[36] In Sutera, Sicily, for example, "it was easy to identify the gentry, professionals and artisans; they were the only men in town, apart from the unemployed, elderly and infirm." Even the men who had not migrated and worked as day laborers or sharecroppers "were gone for days on end."[37]

A few decades later, Carlo Levi also noted the significance of class to a small town in Basilicata: only the *americani* (returned migrants) owned the fancier two-story homes with varnished doors and brass doorknobs—a daily advertisement of the riches that might be waiting across the Atlantic. Levi described the central town square as a place where only the "gentry" gathered before supper to stroll arm-in-arm, occasionally stopping to sit. Peasant women and men, on the other hand, often gathered outside their homes at this hour, when they returned from the fields and prepared the evening meal.[38] Class consciousness was also revealed in proverbs: "The peasant sows and the owner reaps"; "The poor feed the rich"; "Sooner or later even the rich need the poor"; "Don't bother having a peasant for your godparent."[39]

Most women, regardless of social position or region, stayed close to their homes, "their status reflected in their daily chores of making the family's clothes, hauling water, cooking or cleaning."[40] Women of the middle and upper classes were less visible in southern Italian villages because they observed customs regarding female seclusion more often and had servants to perform labor that might have brought them into the public. Peasant women's lives, on the other hand, were by necessity more public. Because there was no running water in most of their homes, women accompanied each other to the public fountain or to the nearest river or lake, to collect water and wash clothes. They also made trips to the woods to gather firewood and edible greens. They worked in their gardens, took care of animals, and performed domestic labor for the local gentry. In more

Women washing clothes on the banks of Lago di Piediluco, Umbria, ca. 1880–90. Photograph by C. Benvenuti, Alinari Archives, Florence, Italy.

populated areas, such as Naples, Palermo, or Cosenza, neighborhoods were organized more strictly according to class. The very poor lived in certain districts that were largely separate from those of the middle and upper classes. But in both settings, communal areas immediately outside the doors to homes were most often female, and the mass emigration of men further encouraged women to make these spaces their own.[41]

"During the day," Levi wrote, "when the peasants are far away in the fields, the villages are left to the women, queen bees reigning over a teeming mass of children."[42] Women gathered in the *cortile* each day, especially in the warmer months. Emmanuele Navarro della Miraglia, a Sicilian writer of short stories and novels in the 1870s and 1880s, called the *cortile* "a kind of shared living room."[43] Here women prepared food together. They roasted peppers, artichokes, and fish on open fires, ground wheat, and baked bread in outdoor ovens; and in midsummer, they spent several days making the *astratto* from tomatoes. Literary critic and memoirist Edvige Giunta writes of this tradition, as she experienced it in the 1950s and 1960s: "The tomato ritual took place primarily in the gardens and orchards in the periphery of the town, but it went on even in the dusty streets and narrow alleys of Gela, a stubborn clinging to a vanishing past. It was a collective enterprise. It was exhausting physical work that started in the early hours of the morning and went on under the boiling Sicilian sun until the early evening, only to start again the following morning. The women labored for days."[44]

The *cortile* was also the space where women came together to do spinning, weaving, and needlework and to teach young girls these crafts. Covello noted that in Sicily, when girls joined the work in their *cortile* (generally at age eleven), they were honored with the title *cummaredda* (little godmother). This rite of passage included changing her dress, hair, and participating in women's songs and storytelling.[45] As women worked, they told stories, shared information about conditions overseas, and helped each other to determine whether to migrate themselves or send other family members. They told stories not to just pass time or entertain but to teach, assist transformation, heal, and remember. There were often several women in a village, town, or neighborhood, who were especially well known for their storytelling style and ability.[46] Agatuzza Messia, a domestic worker and quilt maker in Palermo, was a typical Sicilian storyteller. "Messia is in her seventies," folklorist Giuseppe Pitrè noted, "a mother, grandmother, and great-grandmother; as a little girl she heard stories from her grandmother, whose own mother had told them, having herself heard countless stories from one of her grandfathers. She had a good memory so never forgot them. . . . Her friends in Borgo [a section of Palermo] thought her a born storyteller; the more she talked, the more they wanted to listen. . . . She can't read, but she knows lots of things others don't, and talks about them so picturesquely that one cannot help but appreciate her."[47]

Women's oral tradition often countered narratives of female powerlessness. One of Messia's favorite stories was "Catherine the Wise," which told of a young woman, "known the world over for her vast wisdom," who refused to submit to her husband and instead outsmarted him to ultimately win his respect.[48] Stories of women's resistance were often a part of a storyteller's repertoire, helping female rebels in particular to become folk heroines.[49] Calvino writes that Messia, like most women storytellers, "always brings to life feminine characters who are active, enterprising, and courageous, in contrast to the traditional concept of the Sicilian woman as a passive and withdrawn creature." He then noted, "This strikes me as a personal, conscious choice."[50]

Women's daily labors necessitated strong social networks, which also upset narratives of female passivity and isolation. The significance of these daily connections is especially present in their testimonies: "Mamma used to tell me, you have to keep the neighbors closer than the relatives."[51] It is also present in Sicilian dialect: women say "facimmu curtigghiu"—literally, let's make a *cortile*—to create an intimate space for dialogue. Those women who immodestly gossip risk becoming known to all as *la curtigghiera*, which also signifies a vulgar and irascible woman who makes a habit of picking fights.[52] In the dialect of the Piedmont region, "'ndé a cumare" means literally to go to the godmothers, but also to gossip.[53]

Living in such close proximity had mixed consequences of course. It could strengthen networks of reciprocity and mutual assistance and foster a shared sense of camaraderie, but it was also conducive to surveillance and policing. Irene De Bonis De Nobili, an Italian feminist who interviewed emigrant wives during the early twentieth century, noted how they were "invariably prey to the malice of village gossips" because they were often "young, strong, healthy . . . pregnant or with small children" and alone.[54] Siebert adds, "Social control—envy, gossip, and the maligning of one's character—was the other face of a close neighborhood." One of her informants recalled, "In our neighborhood everybody knows everything; all is known between one family and another. What trouble there was when a woman or a girl spent time on her a balcony! There was too much criticism and envy between neighbors."[55] Women also closely monitored young girls, who often used chores such as collecting water or washing the laundry as opportunities for some freedom from the familial sphere.[56]

Because local surveillance could be so intense, women saw paid employment outside of their villages as an opportunity for more freedom. Lucy Sevirole was strictly guarded by her father in Italy, and when she married and her husband emigrated, her father-in-law took over the job, requiring that she stay near him at all times. When she finally joined her husband in New York City, she immediately found work outside the home where, she noted, "I was freer. . . . I was not so closely watched as a woman." Emma Barruso explained that she migrated because "There was nothing for us there. . . . We were kept too strict. . . . [Father] used to scream at us. If we were outside, he call us. . . . Over here, I figured, it's more free, you can do anything you want, there is more money." Mary Tropiano remembered that it was difficult to leave her grandparents when she emigrated, but she preferred life in the United States because "I was out of the pressure from the small town."[57] Another woman, who went north to work as a servant in Liguria, fell in love and ran off with a circus performer and became a trapeze artist herself. She recalled, "Ah, it was a huge scandal to marry someone in the circus, and to travel in a caravan, but I loved the liberty. Yes, for me it was a challenge, a rebellion against the closed, sanctimonious, and arrogant atmosphere of my village."[58]

Indeed, life in the *cortile* was not always voluntary. In the testimonies that Siebert collected, many women stated that their lives were centered there because of household labor but also because the men in their families prohibited them from leaving.[59] When she reflected on her life as a *contadina* (peasant) in her eightieth year, Maria Einaudi noted, "Ah, it would've been better to have been born a goat than a woman, because goats can live according to the sun, they can walk in the countryside, they are free."[60]

While close quarters were at times confining, Siebert writes that "the impression that one has when listening to women's testimonies and memories, is that most women depended upon such close communal relations for the daily practical concerns of life."[61] It is also not entirely clear that the absence of men strengthened women's policing of one another. Stories of the devastating effect of women's gossip against those with husbands abroad, and other potentially transgressive women, are numerous. But so are stories of women who developed a newfound liberty in the absence of men. One example of many is that of Carmela Cagliari, who was able to pursue an education only after her father migrated. He had disapproved of her studies, stating, "Women have to stay in a corner of the house." But, once he was gone Carmela's grandmother encouraged her to study and become a teacher.[62]

Carlo Levi also found that emigration from Basilicata led women to loosen customary parameters regarding appropriate social behavior. "There were many unmarried mothers," he noted, "and they were neither snubbed nor pointed at with scorn; at worst they might have difficulty finding a husband within the village and have to look elsewhere." Moreover, he recalled, almost all the priests had children, "and no one sees in this fact any dishonor reflecting upon their calling." One letter carrier in Grassano, "a spry old man with a slight limp, and a fine handlebar moustache, was renowned and revered in the village because . . . he was said to have fifty children" with many different women. Yet, the peasants of Basilicata also worked hard to prevent women from talking to men, "except in the presence of others, particularly if the man is unmarried." "This taboo," Levi noted, "is extremely rigid; the most innocent violation is tantamount to sin. The rule applies to all women, because love is no respecter of age." Yet, he pointed out, "The rule does not exist that can stand up against necessity or overwhelming passion. Hence custom, in this instance, was reduced to a mere formality. Still the countryside was wide, life was fraught with unexpected turns, and intriguing chaperones and accommodating friends were not hard to come by."[63]

Women's Power and Men's Authority

The predominance of women in villages profoundly reshaped kin and neighborhood relations at the turn of the century, revealing that social systems in southern Italy tolerated many contradictory positions for women. A proverb that women probably enjoyed recounting to ethnographers went, "The husband is like the government at Rome, all pomp; the wife is like the Mafia, all power."[64] Similarly, Pitrè summarized his research on Sicilian families by noting that they were based on principles of both matriarchy and patriarchy.[65] Scholarship has also documented the ways peasant women "exercised considerable indirect social power, arranging marriages, assigning reputations, helping one another to give birth, and when necessary, to abort."[66] However, much of the literature published on Italian women in the United States has often emphasized the conservative and repressive nature of Latin patriarchal culture and ignored or underestimated the ways in which women carved out spaces to express their own power.[67]

In Italy, patriarchal systems and ideologies shaped social relations, and gender ideals clearly identified appropriate female and male behavior in opposing and hierarchical ways: ideal men were assertive, independent, and authoritative, while women were modeled on the Catholic Madonna, which called for submission and selflessness. Yet, as for all women, actual behavior often transgressed and subverted these ideals, especially at the turn of the century, when gender ideologies and practices underwent dramatic change. The demands of industrial capitalism—labor migration, cash economies, factory work, the dispossession of peasants from land, urbanization, and the movement and resettlement of families and communities across continents—challenged patriarchal relations in myriad ways. With the long-term absence of men, women learned to live and act autonomously; they strengthened their ties to other women, and they assumed new responsibilities in their families and communities. Many of these changes directly challenged patriarchal relations. For example, migration caused a greater separation between and autonomy within "female" and "male" spaces, and women often occupied the center of the family, which was the heart of community. Maria Einaudi recalled that "my mother was in charge since my father was always away," working in Marseilles or the United States.[68] Leonard Covello grew up in Avigliano (Basilicata) with his mother and two brothers, while his father worked for extended periods in New York. His uncles shared responsibility for his upbringing, but he recalled that "all major decisions had to receive the blessing of my paternal grandmother, Nonna Clementina—matriarch by right and personality."[69] Similarly, Margherita Lemasson, who came from a long line of wool spinners, said that in her family, "era nonna che commandava" (it was grandma who commanded).[70]

Yet, as the domination of men over women became less of a reality, it seems to have assumed a greater public appearance. Scholars have explored how men have historically attempted to exert more control over the women in their lives as power relations and social systems are shifting and women are gaining more independence.[71] In Italy, the "idealization of male domination helped compensate for its absence," especially during the period of mass emigration.[72] With men abroad, women gained more power in their households, but this made many men more obsessed with controlling women's behavior, even from afar. As a result, a woman often had to promise an emigrant husband that she would never leave the *cortile* in his absence. Domestic violence was also pervasive. Renate Siebert discovered that women she interviewed often pointed out that their husbands were *not* abusive, to reveal "how exceptional they considered themselves."[73] Similarly, other testimonies and oral histories tell of husbands and fathers who beat women within an inch of their lives.[74] Danilo Dolci's portrait of "Grandma Nedda," a Sicilian woman born in 1877, begins with her words: "Of course a husband can beat his wife. At least when he's right. That's fair, no? Like if she gabs or talks back. . . . But what about a woman raising a hand to her husband? Born to walk the streets, they say." She then told how her own father beat her mother to death because she did not make the bed fast enough.[75] Rosa Cavalleri also spoke of the sanctioned violence against women as formative in her childhood. As a girl, she witnessed a neighbor who, for selling pieces of her hair, was beaten by her husband "so hard we thought he would kill her," and another woman whose arm was broken by her husband "for talking back."[76]

Judging from women's recollections, it appears that the beating of women was often a public spectacle. It occurred in the *cortile* or *piazze*, and often in front of many others in the community, suggesting that the abusive man's intention was not only to enforce the subordination of the woman but to make a public statement. Such demonstrations even assumed a certain bravado: the man who broke his wife's arm did so in the center of town and paid the doctor for her other arm too, announcing that he was paying in advance for the next time she spoke back.[77] Such public posturing was connected to men's anxiety about their status as patriarchs of honorable families.[78] This is not to say that the element of terror that infused such public performances was not also present in private relations. Women and children endured rape, sexual assault, beatings, and other forms of brutality and humiliation behind closed doors. In fact, in their testimonies, women often expressed how little control they had over their own sexual lives: "I had to submit, I didn't have much desire"; "it was submit or fight"; "I didn't want ten children"; "I was married too young"; "it [sex] made me feel sick." Many also grew up, as one woman recalled "Sempre tenjo nu grammofono nelle orecchie: attenzione che l'uomo è vile" (always hearing like a gramophone in the ear: beware, men are vile), and Siebert notes that "fear of men was routinely passed from mother to daughter, and from woman to woman."[79]

In order to understand how women responded to violence, political theorist James Scott's analysis of power relations is helpful: "An element of personal terror invariably infuses these relations—a terror that may take the form of arbitrary beatings, sexual brutality, insults, and public humiliations." While a person may not have to endure such treatment, "the sure knowledge that it *could* happen to her pervades the entire relationship."[80] Often both men and women believed (and taught children) that it was a man's right to beat and rape the women in his family. For example, when, as a child, Cavalleri witnessed numerous disturbing acts of violence by men against women, she asked those around her, "Why are the men always so mean?" She heard from both women and men that "the man is the boss and he has the right to beat his wife," "God gave the man the right to control the woman when He made him stronger," and "when the women can no longer talk back the husbands will stop fighting." Yet children also learned other lessons. After hearing countless justifications for such violence, Cavalleri noted to herself that "no man of the poor ever was the boss of Mamma Lena!"[81]

On occasion, women also retaliated. A man from a village near Foggia in Apulia recalled "an ancient custom which offered us boys much entertainment. When a young husband would beat his wife and curse her family, everybody knew what would happen. The young wife would run to her parents complaining about the husband. In a short while a crowd would gather around the girl's parents' home. Shortly after, the brothers, cousins, and other male relatives of the beaten girl would go, led by the old mother, toward the home of the girl. And there they pounced upon the husband and beat him up. In a kind of procession the mother and her kin returned home." It is, however, unclear if such an action was taken because the new husband beat the young wife or because he cursed the family. Testimonial evidence also tells of husbands who retaliated against insubordinate wives by going to their fathers. A woman from Reggio Calabria recalled, "My husband complained to my father about my being disobedient. One day my father came over and, in the presence of my husband, gave me a severe beating with his cane. In all my life I will never forget it; the brutal looks of my father and the feeble protestations of my husband. Never will I forget how my husband later looked pleasantly at me, and said; 'I am sorry. I see now what fine folks your family are.'"[82]

In order to fully understand the particular cultural dynamics of Italian women's resistance to male authority, it is important to look beyond the public realm. As Scott argues, the rituals and practice of denigration are never the entire story because "the dominant never control the stage absolutely." Rather, in relations of domination two performances take place—the "public transcript," which is the open interaction, and the "hidden transcript," which is the "social space in which offstage dissent to the official transcript of power relations may be voiced."[83] Women commonly acted deferential in public in order to exercise power in private. A young man from southern Calabria remembered the role of disguise in his family's power relations: "When my father got old, we obeyed our mother more than before. . . . My brother, who became the head of the family, had to take orders from her. But that was done only in our home. On the street he tried to impress everybody that he was the boss of the family." His mother also kept up this charade and made a habit of announcing in public that she had to "first ask Rocco" before making any decisions.[84] Similarly, a woman from Potenza (Basilicata) noted the following: "As a young wife I was no angel. I was obstinate and revolted against my husband, whose ideas seemed to me crazy. I was much stronger than he was. Whenever he tried to hit me I was ready to hit him back. This was in our home. But he had it on me for he fixed me many a time on the street. There on the street I didn't even think of resisting him. If I did that I certainly would disgrace him."[85]

Women taught their daughters the intricacies of negotiating power within intimate relationships. They advised girls, "pigghiari cu bonu"—play the fool and act submissive in order to get what they wanted. The lesson was clear: in the art of diplomacy with men, women could wield power if they performed acquiescence. Such a lesson, Covello recalled, "was never overlooked by the mother and was openly taught to the daughter."[86] This skill formed the foundation to women's strategies of resistance. A few decades later, Ann Cornelisen noted of the women in Basilicata, "Somehow they are the ones that understand the intricacies of local bureaucracy. . . . They sense who can be tricked, forced, or cajoled. . . . They teach their children, and it is often the soundest teaching they will receive [about] the 'proper ways' of the community."[87]

Mysticism as a Source of Power

Living in a world that demanded their subordination taught women complex lessons about power and defiance. It is in the realm of popular culture that we find Italian women's "hidden transcript"—the ways they subverted conditions of subordination behind the backs of those in power. Scott argues that "the rumors, gossip, folktales, songs, gestures, jokes, and theater of the powerless [act] as vehicles by which, among other things, they insinuate a critique of power while hiding behind the anonymity or behind innocuous understandings of their conduct." These patterns of insubordination are connected to those strategies that "thwart material appropriation of their labor, their production, and their property: for example, poaching, foot-dragging, pilfering, dissimulation, flight." "Together," he argues, "these forms of insubordination might suitably be called the infrapolitics of the powerless."[88]

The world of mysticism and spiritualism was a space where Italian women confronted power most directly by creating spaces where a dissident subculture could flourish. Both the political theorist Antonio Gramsci and the anthropologist Ernesto De Martino brought international attention to the revolutionary possibilities of southern Italian popular culture, arguing that it was "a potential basis of an autonomous culture for the 'proletariat' struggling for hegemony."[89] Gramsci theorized that the successful domination of one group over others depended not only on physical coercion or economic supremacy but also on the imposition of a system of moral, political, and cultural values.[90] To Gramsci, expressive culture had the potential to embody a worldview that countered the hegemony of the elite (e.g., the state, the Catholic Church, landowners). Inspired by Gramsci, De Martino examined the limitations of modern, bourgeois, Western culture by exploring how southern Italian peasants, and particularly women, confronted the "condition of psychological misery" in their lives.[91] Women responded to poverty, exclusion from formal political arenas, and communal regulation of their sexuality by crafting their own cultural expressions. In particular, they used ritualized weeping, ecstatic dancing such as the *tarantella* or *pizzica*, contained psychological collapse, song, herbal and medicinal healing, and other techniques such as magic, divination, and sorcery "to alleviate self-destructive impulses unleashed by grief."[92] In this way, they created a counterideology, an alternative way of understanding the world that permitted their own expression, power, and self-determination. Folk culture was not only "a view of the world and of life" among the "subaltern classes"; it was also "a weapon of social and political struggle."[93]

While there is not the space to delve fully into the female worlds of healing and sorcery here, it is necessary to examine briefly this aspect of southern Italian popular culture because it was a primary place where women commanded and confronted power. The dominant belief system among peasants at this time was based on the natural world, and the belief that spirit pervaded everything. Belief and ritual centered on unifying the community to facilitate physical survival; as historian Rudolph Vecoli has written, "The margin of survival was always paper thin; an illness, a drought, or a dead mule spelled disaster. . . . For the peasants, religion and magic merged into an elaborate ensemble of rituals, invocations, and charms by which they sought to invoke, placate, and thwart the supernatural."[94] Leonard Covello, too, captured this history of blending: "The people of the Italian peninsula, having adopted Christianity by decree rather than through a process of cultural evolution, retained many pagan rituals and beliefs."[95]

This mixture of popular beliefs and practices provided women with the space to create a worldview that challenged the institutional power of the church, the

Women dancing, Naples, ca. 1870–90. Michael Maslan Historic Photographs/Corbis, IH121256.

nation-state, the men in their families, and others, because the arts of healing and magic were largely women's preserve. When a friend or family member was suffering, peasant women commonly chose a wide range of remedies, such as lighting candles to various saints, visiting the sanctuary of the Blessed Mother, invoking protection with amulets, and visiting the local *maga* or *strega* (witch or healer).[96] Such practices came under increased scrutiny by the Catholic Church, but most communities continued to rely on women's remedies as their primary source of practical medicine. When the devout Catholic Bartolo Longo arrived in Naples in 1872 to manage the estates of a local countess, he remarked not only on the extreme poverty of the area and "endemic brigandage" but also on the people's reliance on "witches to cast and undo spells."[97] The American folklorist Charles Leland noted in 1892, "The witches of Italy form a class who are the repositories of all the folklore."[98] He also noted that most were "of a family in which her calling or art has been practiced for many generations."[99] The travel writer Norman Douglas wrote of a "saint" near Naples "who was so successful in the magics that the Bishop of Pozzuoli, among hundreds of other clients, was wont to drive up to her door once a week for a consultation." In Calabria, he found "wise women and wizards abound" but that the "foreigner is at an unfortunate disadvantage; if he asks questions, he will only get answers dictated by suspicion or a deliberate desire to mislead."[100] Similarly, anthropologist Charlotte Gower Chapman admitted that it was difficult for her "to draw a sharp line between real witches and the wise women who heal by means of charms and secret remedies." But she claimed that thirteen "living witches" were active in the Sicilian town of Milocca in 1928. Some of these women were sisters, or mothers and daughters; all of them practiced cures and had "magical power [which] set them in a class apart from ordinary persons." Moreover, she noted, "The respect which outsiders and practitioners have for witchcraft and charm-healing is in last analysis a tribute to [their] knowledge."[101] Levi counted twenty female "witches" in his small village in Basilicata; all were "exempt from the general rule" governing female propriety and "had many children of unidentified fathers, who, although they had not embraced prostitution (no such trade existed in the village), displayed a tendency to be free and easy, and who were concerned with all that pertained to love, above all the means of obtaining it."[102]

Ethnographic accounts such as these were often steeped in the perspectives and attitudes of their authors, who were almost invariably outsiders to and often mystified by the cultures they studied. Yet there is corroboration in a wide range of sources—oral histories, songs, stories, and spiritual practices—that attest to the ways traditional healing practices enabled women to build community with each other, maintain an oppositional stance to the Catholic Church, and subvert or manipulate the images and teachings of Christianity to reflect their own worldviews. After all, women controlled many of the church's most important communal ceremonies: they conducted fertility, childbirth, and funeral rites; built and maintained altars; and introduced younger generations to the many divine beings who assisted and protected. They shaped Catholicism to reflect their own concerns and practices, most notably by centering their devotion on the divine feminine.

Italian popular Catholicism was (and is still) characterized by the premise that the saints and the Madonna are as powerful as Christ. The Madonna represents more than simply the Mother of God; she has independent power and is considered a "divine patroness" and "miracle worker." Covello writes, "The introduction of the Madonna cult gave the southern Italians what the early Christian Church could not give them—a female element in religion, something that the people had possessed since the early Greek times. . . . [they] adorned the Madonna with virtues that were closely associated with the people's everyday life."[103] One woman from Calabria told him that "the Madonna was just like other women"; she embodied their sorrows, joys, and pains.[104] Because of this, she has many names: Santa Maria Addolorata, Madonna del Carmine, Santa Maria del Consiglio,

Santa Maria Regina, and Nostra Signora della Pellegrina are just some of her many aspects. Often, relationships with her were personal in nature, and at the turn of the century, stories of visitations and miracles abounded.[105]

Unlike the fair, blue-eyed Virgin of the North, the Madonna of the South looked like her devotees and reflected the hybrid cultures of the Mediterranean: she was often olive, brown, and black. Norman Douglas noted that the saints and Madonnas in Calabria were "Byzantines or Africans who, by miraculous intervention, protected the village or district of which they were patrons."[106] Throughout the South, *la madonna nera* (the black madonna) was revered and cherished in her many forms—La Madonna di Loreto (Milicia, Sicily), La Madonna Nera (Tindari, Sicily), La Madonna di Seminara (Calabria), La Madonna Bruna (Naples), La Madonna Mora (Padua), Maria Santissima dei Miracoli (Sicily)—as were black saints such as San Filippo Nero and San Benedetto.[107]

The most popular female saints tended to embody the resistance and martyrdom of women under patriarchy. In Sicily, for example, Santa Rosalia, the protectress against famine, earthquakes, fire, and war, fled an arranged marriage and hid in the hills west of Palermo before her bones liberated the city from the plague and other disasters. Santa Lucia, an early Siracusan Christian martyr under Diocletian's persecutions, who was forced into prostitution, protects vision. Sant'Agata of Catania refused the advances of a senator, who then tortured her, in part, by cutting off her breasts; she protects against Etna's volcanic eruptions, fire, and lightning.[108]

Spiritual practice was central to women's collective consciousness and sense of community. Sunday mass and feast days were often the only time that women took a break from work. To the women interviewed by Siebert, church was a place where women came together once a week to sing, pray, and talk.[109] Revelli found the same: "For the women it was relaxing, a diversion, to go to church," recalled one woman. Another noted that "my moment of freedom was on Sunday." For many, mass was an opportunity "to see some of the folks in the village, to talk with the other women. Sunday was fun for us women because we dressed up a bit. . . . After mass we'd have a coffee together."[110] Rosa Cavalleri also remembered that women built a sense of community by gathering daily in their *cortile* to pray together.[111]

Women routinely incorporated religious ritual into their lives without a priest or any other male authority or mediator through the tradition of home altars. In the vast majority of homes across southern Italy, women set aside a special place (or places) for the sacred. Here they placed images of the Madonna, Christ, and various saints; photos of loved ones who worked abroad or who had died; their own lace and embroidery; votive candles; and other significant items. The altar

Sant'Agata (Saint Agatha), 1896. Source: Giuseppe Pitrè, *Sicilian Folk Medicine* (Turin: Carlo Clausen, 1896), trans. Phyllis H. Williams (Lawrence, Kans.: Coronado Press, 1971).

was an "instrument of creation" that was continually changing.[112] Indeed, women's altar traditions in Italy and elsewhere served "as the tangible inheritance of a woman's relationship—past, present, and future—to her matrilineage," because altar making "embed[s] the elemental forces that long ago came to be associated with reproduction and mothering" and is passed down through the women in a family.[113] Women also made altars with each other in memoriam, to honor seasonal change, and to celebrate the saints. Fatima Giallombardo's research on the feast to San Giuseppe in Salemi reveals that women in Trapani (Sicily) have historically used communal altar-building ceremonies to strengthen their relationships to each other. Such practices have historically provided a space "for women to exhibit their power in the community—their manual skills and more generally their organizing abilities." Today, this "collaboration" functions as it has for many generations. It enables participants "to build a certain joyous and celebratory solidarity" and "reconfirms women's function as the cohesive element in the family."[114]

Women's autonomous spiritual practices also enabled them to critique the hierarchies and exclusions upon which Catholicism was predicated. They not only challenged the precept that they should submit to a male image of God but fought back against oppressive church leaders and practices and nurtured an anticlerical tradition. The high rates of civil marriages and burials throughout southern Italy dramatize the widespread rejection of the formal church doctrine and practice. But women's own recollections and testimonies offer the most detailed evidence of their feelings. Romea Cimma grew up in Italy during the 1910s and related with bitterness, "The priests were the richest people in the parish. They deliberately resisted educating the people so that their corrupt power could continue. It was well-known that an unbeliever or someone the church considered a sinner couldn't be buried within the church, but it was also known that a gangster whose family paid enough could be given the rites of the church."[115] Women's critiques would become explosive toward the end of the nineteenth century, as they connected their grievances against the church with those they held against the state.

Peasant Women Mobilized

When women took to their piazzas and fields in Sicily in 1892–94, they focused their anger on those who directly challenged their ability to subsist. Many considered the nation-state, large landholders, and those priests who were allied with such interests to be the most egregious offenders. After the Italian nation was formed in 1861, many members of the urban bourgeoisie and middle classes supported the national project, but most of the poor actively revolted against it. For the vast majority of Italy's residents—the peasantry—the new state meant excessive taxation, forced conscription, dispossession from land, widespread poverty, police brutality, and government repression.[116]

When a government-appointed commission traveled throughout the country in the 1880s, it "documented both the irrelevance of the nation to Italy's peasants and the growing popularity of migration among them."[117] Peasants told investigators that they despised the rich and state officials because they were "without exception, thieves." They explained, "To what have we been reduced? The servant of every master. We cultivate lands, and plant them, but the fruits are not ours."[118] As a consequence, the popular classes did not come to identify with the nation or its leaders for several generations. Rather, their primary connection was to family, friends, neighbors, and those from the same towns or villages of origin. Those who formed allegiances with political groups were generally drawn to anarchist and socialist groups, which were fundamental to their mobilizations in this period. Moreover, "Italians" did not speak the same language but dozens of mutually incomprehensible dialects. Migration patterns strengthened these ties as people chose particular jobs and destinations according to the well-worn paths of their *paesani* (those from the same village, town, or region). For migrants, a regional identity among Sicilians, for example, emerged long before a shared national identity as Italians, and it appears that the process of nationalization was even slower for those who remained in Italy. Indeed, only in the past half century has a national identity united Italians.[119]

The southern middle and upper classes also protested the northern ruling classes' paternalist plan for industrialization, which channeled resources and capital toward the North while preventing the South from achieving self-government and economic growth. But it was peasants and laborers who organized rebellions. The 1892–94 uprisings came after several decades of antinationalist popular struggle, or what the Italian army called *brigantaggio* (brigandage or banditry). In fact, in the years following unification in 1861, "no phenomenon evoked the South more powerfully in the imaginary of the middle and upper classes than brigandage."[120] Throughout the southern countryside—in Calabria, Apulia, Campania, Molise, and Sicily—rebels formed large bands, often with hundreds of members, hid out in mountains and caves, and attempted to unite peasants in armed resistance against the state and the new class of landowners who expropriated peasant lands for nonpayment of taxes. They resisted the draft, intimidated tax collectors, occupied land, and robbed from the rich to give to the poor. Their activities took place during a decades-long period of class-conscious revolt among southern peasants against the draft and new tax policies.[121] Throughout the North as well, peasants "arose in spontaneous protest, converging upon local town halls, and when their pleas fell on deaf ears, they stormed the buildings, burned official records, and destroyed the new counting devices at the mills."[122]

In remarking on this history, one Italian scholar has noted that the Italian socialist movement was "born anarchist."[123] Although some scholars have considered peasant rebels to be merely criminals (as they were seen by the Italian army and elite) and as predecessors to the mafia, others have illustrated how they represented "a well-documented sociopolitical movement."[124] In most towns throughout Sicily, the mafia worked alongside the *gabellotti*, the middlemen who managed the estates for absentee landlords, and thus were not in solidarity with peasants but rather a source of intimidation and terror.[125] Most government officials noted this, seeing instead that peasant resistance represented "a true civil war waged by the poor against the rich."[126] As a result, the Italian state responded with "a full two-fifths of the national military force, as well as carabinieri (a special corps of national police) and national guardsmen, for a total of 250,000 men.

The repression resulted in over 10,000 dead, both in battle and by executions, and 20,000 imprisoned or exiled."[127]

Many of those who joined in the 1892–94 rebellions had grown up during the intense violence of state formation, and it deeply shaped their lives. Carlo Levi noted that the history of peasant resistance to the new nation was "close to their hearts and constantly on their tongues," and "all of them, old and young, men and women, spoke of it with as much passion as if it were only yesterday"—even fifty years later. "The peasants, with a few exceptions, were all on the side of the brigands and, with the passing of time, the deeds . . . [which] entered into their everyday speech with the same ease as animals and spirits, grew into legends and took on the absolute truth of a myth." "The brigands," he continued, "stood for the life and liberty of the peasants against the encroachments of the State," and "they looked on the brigands as heroes."[128]

While it is impossible to know how many women participated in such bands, certain women reached mythic status and provided a model of subversive womanhood.[129] One story told throughout Basilicata was that of Maria'a Pastora, known as the "goddess of the peasant war." Born in Pisticci, a small agricultural town in the heart of that region, Pastora quickly became a folk hero. Locals thought of her as a "beautiful peasant woman who lived with her lover in the wooded mountains, fighting and robbing at his side, clad like a man, and always on horseback." According to one aging rebel, Pastora's lover, the equally famous Ninco-Nanco, was killed but she was never captured. Rather, "she was seen in Pisticci, swathed in black; then she disappeared on horseback into the woods and was never heard of again."[130] Similarly, the story of Maria Nambrini, known as *celebre Brigantessa* (the celebrated bandit), was recorded and circulated in a 1907 chapbook. At only sixteen years of age, Nambrini was immortalized as a *donna del popolo* (a woman of the people).[131]

In the 1890s, women drew upon these traditions of resistance to confront those in power. They used direct action and regularly resorted to the destruction of property and civil disobedience to be heard. Their theater was most often the *piazza*. It "was the crossroads through which all members of the community passed. Markets and municipal buildings both faced these public spaces; fountains were likely to be located there too. In many parts of the country the piazza was also the labor market, as poor wage-earners waited there for potential employers. Crowds inevitably went 'to the streets' or 'to the piazza' whether their intent was to sack the market, attack the mayor, or intimidate their employers."[132] Women's entrance into the piazza was especially symbolic given their exclusion from public political spaces.

The most detailed account of peasant women's activism in this period remains a 1980 study in which historian Jole Calapso examined newspaper and government reports and compared them with the contemporary writing of political leaders and scholars. Calapso documented the wide variety of female mobilization in Sicily during this period to chart how women's political consciousness increased as they participated in popular demonstrations and endured government repression. Often women initially acted in seemingly spontaneous ways, erupting into riot to defend their dignity and care for their families. Yet, quite rapidly, their confrontations with unjust government officials, tax collectors, priests, landlords, police, and the military, politicized women and led them to mobilize against the entire system of exploitation and dehumanization that constrained their lives.

For example, in the years before women in Bagheria and Piana dei Greci embroidered flags with socialist slogans and organized women's groups, they had gathered in their piazzas to protest the government shut down of water facilities during the cholera epidemic. In Bagheria, the movement began when women from one neighborhood marched into the central piazza with rocks in their fists to protest the closing of communal wells, inciting more than five hundred people in the town to demonstrate outside the mayor's house. Similarly, in 1884 women in Corleone organized a protest against food taxes, and in 1891 the women at Misterbianco led a riot against the hearth tax, in which they set municipal offices on fire and destroyed the registries of the state.[133]

This movement among women changed from isolated and sporadic actions to more organized and widespread activity in 1892, after a series of very poor wheat harvests. One of the first actions occurred on 20 January 1893 when close to five hundred women and men in Caltavuturo occupied fields owned by the state and began tilling the soil. By the end of the day, police and soldiers had opened fire on them, killing thirteen and injuring fifty. The memorial service, held in Corleone, attracted more than four thousand "of every age and sex" from the surrounding towns, and it brought thousands more into the movement. Three months later, when Socialist Party leaders gathered for another ceremony, they found that women "were the most enthusiastic supporters." They greeted the party with a shower of flowers, chanting "Long live socialism! Long live the workers' party!"[134]

Up until 1892, women's collective action was independent of any formal organization. Rather, it was embedded in women's own neighborhood and kinship networks and rooted in the tradition of mutual aid that had been established mostly by Sicilian artisans.[135] This basis of popular solidarity provided the foundation to the more formal styles of political mobilization, such as the *fasci*, during and following the 1892–94 uprisings. As a result, the *fasci* were deeply imbedded within village-based social relationships, and these radical mutual aid groups extended throughout the world as Italians migrated. By the end of 1892, at least "two-thirds of western Sicily's 136 rural towns had a *fascio*"—a region that was defined by labor emigration to the Americas. This militancy centered in the western part of the island where peasants labored in large-scale or semicapitalist agriculture, such as wheat estates and sulfur mines. Class antagonism was particularly extreme in these industries because they, "like Marx, divided the world into two antagonistic groups, the rich and the poor." Furthermore, "the newly rich were everywhere visible," and the peasants grew to resent their arrogance.[136]

The *fasci* uprisings also represented an unprecedented alliance among Italy's poor. Artisans, petty merchants, peasants, and industrial workers could all be found in this movement from the beginning. By the end of 1892, almost half of these groups were in contact with the Socialist Party, which formed that same year.[137] In fact, before northern industrial workers joined the party en masse during a wave of strikes from 1898 to 1914, Sicilian peasants were the largest group of party members. Because of this, the party was founded upon revolutionary syndicalist principles—meaning it believed that the organization of workers into collectivities (i.e., labor unions, *fasci*) was necessary in the struggle to supplant capitalism and the state. The *fasci* drew inspiration from the international anarchist movement as well, and through the radical press they connected their struggles to those of other workers and peasants abroad.[138] By 1893 the *fasci* spread beyond Sicily, into the other southern Italian regions of Apulia, Basilicata, Campania, and Calabria. Moreover, uprisings also included factory workers in cities such as Naples, Bari, Rome, Bologna, Imola, and Ancona.[139] As migration to the Americas began to peak, Italy's many workers were coming together in a revolutionary movement in which women were key activists.

Women were active in local groups, but they also formed their own sections and attended the first socialist congress in Sicily in 1893. There, many women, including a woman by the name of Maria Cammarata, who led one of the largest groups from Piana dei Greci with close to one thousand members, spoke out about the centrality of women's activism to the movement. The editor of *Giornale di Sicilia* wrote of his surprise, not only at the presence of women but at their political sophistication: "I could not believe it myself. They spoke loudly and clearly, with ease and astonishing courage."[140] Such stories lured journalists and government agents deep into Sicilian villages, to witness the spectacle for themselves. They found women's groups in Campofiorito (214 members), San Giuseppe Jato (30 members), and Belmonte Mezzagno (between 30 and 70 members), and women's sections in Altofonte, Sommatino, Bisacquino, Corleone, Chiusa Sclafani, Santa Caterina Villarmosa, Casteltermini, Mazara del Vallo, Trappeto, Campofelice di Fitalia, and Marineo. Local economies gave shape to women's protests, whether they were based in subsistence agriculture, market cultivation, or large wheat estates. The tactics of striking and land occupation, for example, were more common in towns dominated by large-scale agriculture and industry. Tax protests typically occurred in places that were market-oriented. Because of this, the movement differed depending on the locale, leading the *fasci* to function in multiple ways—as mutual aid societies, trade unions, agricultural cooperatives, and political parties. In each of these towns, however, the *fasci* included the majority of residents. They might have developed in a single neighborhood but very quickly branched outward.[141]

When Adolfo Rossi traveled to Piana dei Greci in 1893 to witness the founding of a women's group, he wrote a series of essays for the Roman press, to give readers a sense of what was transpiring: a crowd formed a circle and, after singing, the women engaged in a "long collective conversation." One *contadina*, who he noted was married, recounted how the women present had boycotted the annual religious procession to protest the priests' opposition to their movement, and how this was the first time they had ever done such a thing. Another (unmarried, he noted) *contadina* moved to the center of the circle and added, "The *signori* [the gentry, including the priests] . . . insult us socialist women and say we are dishonorable . . . that we are all whores." She continued, "Yet when a crime is committed by someone rich nobody does anything, but when a poor person robs a piece of bread to keep themselves from starving, they immediately go to prison!" Another woman, the mother of five children, rose to speak about the importance of their women's group in preventing the "abuses and arrogance of the gentry, and those who run the local government." She spoke proudly of the quick speed with which the revolutionary movement was spreading across Sicily, stating, "It is enough that one person begins to speak about the union of the proletariat. Up until last spring we also didn't know what *fasci* were. We were silently dying of hunger. We were blind and could not see."[142]

In some towns, women also organized children's groups. In San Giuseppe Jato, where the women's group included approximately eighty members, close to thirty children between the ages of nine and twelve formed their own *fascio*. Such groups suggest the high value parents placed on involving their children in the movement and the way political struggle was a family as well as community affair. One woman who grew up during this period recalled, "I was socialist, my husband was socialist, my father, my cousins, my brothers, all socialists."[143] Bernardino Verro, the founder and leader of the Corleone *fascio* estimated that the group included close to six thousand women and men. "There is no longer distinction in the town between members and non-members," he told Adolfo Rossi in an interview. "It was founded in September of last year and the women have understood the importance of union among the poor, and even teach socialism to their children."[144] At that time, children (often workers themselves, in the sulfur mines or as lace makers, spinners, or seamstresses) were also leading rallies and speaking publicly in Piana and Belmonte, both villages where women were well organized. For example, Marietta De Felice, born in Catania to Giuffrida De Felice, a socialist deputy, accompanied her father throughout Sicily in this period. At only fourteen years old, she spoke at the inauguration of *fasci* in Piazza Armerina, Misterbianco, and Castrogiovanni, among other occasions, and in Castrogiovanni she was the featured speaker at a dinner hosted by women activists. Rossi recalled that she was a young woman "extraordinarily animated by the spirit of socialism, who spoke to the people with a fervor of a missionary, and because of her sex and age, she commanded the fascination of the masses."[145] The Italian government opened a police file on her and kept close watch on her activities, noting that over the next several decades she developed a correspondence with leaders of the Italian socialist movement abroad, received a variety of radical newspapers, regularly spoke to workers on her own lecture tours, and married another socialist activist in the movement, Michelangelo Caruso.[146]

The Italian government watched many of the women in this movement closely. The director of public security filed a report with Rome in which he stated that the *fasci femminili* in Piana dei Greci, Belmonte Mezzagno, and San Giuseppe Jato should be considered some of the most dangerous. In these towns, he noted, women had developed "highly successful propaganda activities and revolutionary agendas, through which they exercised considerable influence on the other fasci in the region."[147]

Italian prime minister Crispi also subjected activists to violent forms of repression. In September 1893 thirty-six women from Piana were arrested and one, Elena Pellitteri, was sentenced to a term of two months.[148] In the villages of Belmonte, Misterbianco, Partinico, San Vito Lo Capo, Trapani, Valguarnera, Villa Floresta, Sutera, Mussomeli, Acquaviva Platani, Cattolica Eraclea, Casteltermini, Lercara, Giardinelli, Marineo, and Corleone, women clashed with police and were gunned down (some with children in their arms), imprisoned (many sentenced to eight to sixteen years), and beaten for their activities (some of whom were visibly pregnant or breastfeeding). While many of these towns did not have formal women's groups, the large numbers of female victims suggests that women distinguished themselves on the front lines of the movement.[149]

The intensity of government repression continued into 1894, despite some successes on the part of demonstrators. After four thousand women and men protested in the piazza of Borgetto, they obtained a reduction in various taxes. Similarly, the mayor in Altavilla suspended the tax on the sale of bread after women threatened him outside his home in a mass demonstration. In 1894, Sambuca's town council also lowered taxes. Indeed, it was often in those towns with active *fasci* that municipal councils lowered taxes and socialists were elected to municipal offices in late 1893 and early 1894.[150]

These years of activity coalesced into a nationwide movement by 1898, when widespread social unrest spread across Italy as agricultural day laborers and industrial workers mobilized mass-based demonstrations. At the dawn of the twentieth century, women across Italy were protesting high taxes and dispossession from the land with mob action, but they also began to experiment with a wide range of political activities. They built women's cooperatives and labor unions through which they launched a series of labor strikes and a movement to collectively lease and farm the land. In 1901, 480 different cooperatives from western Sicily, most of them former *fasci*, joined together to establish the Fratellanza Agricola in Corleone. The socialist newspaper *L'Avanti!* reported that close to fifteen hundred women and men attended the inauguration, which they celebrated with a parade, food, music, and speeches by local anarchist and socialist leaders, under the banner "workers of all lands unite." According to a 1911 Italian government investigation, women made up one-quarter of the cooperative movement, and they composed the majority of members in Calabria.[151]

Women also engaged in other forms of labor resistance, and Sicily remained a central site of such activism. In 1901 more than six hundred female silk-spinners in two factories in Messina struck to abolish the system of fines and other punitive measures developed by employers. Similar strikes took place in the tobacco industry, where women dominated the labor force. One strike, which lasted almost seven years, involved eighteen thousand women tobacco workers from Palermo and Catania and drew support from male maritime workers.[152] In Siracusa, women who harvested and processed almonds were prohibited by managers from talking while working. Still, they critiqued their labor conditions, organized strikes, and subverted managerial control through the use of song, which they disguised by combining a mixture of dialects with the typical melodies of love songs.[153]

In the years leading up to the First World War, women peasants and artisans staged hundreds of marches, rallies, and strikes across the South, in places such as Reggio, Palermo, Catania, Palagonia, Piana dei Greci, Prizzi, Campfiorito, Roccamena, Canicattì, Castelluzzo, Trapani, Bari, and Naples. Almost invariably, the response of the Italian government was to crush these activities by arresting movement leaders, opening fire on crowds, and injuring participants. The 1898 uprisings, which began in Sicily with a hunger demonstration in Messina and spread to Naples, Bari, and other southern cities and villages, culminated in the *fatti di maggio*, a strike among Milan's industrial workers that ended in bloodshed and a state of siege. That movement unleashed a wave of repression just as brutal as in earlier years. And yet, as Italy prepared for war in 1914, women continued to mobilize against militarism. The women in Piana dei Greci, which had been a focal point during the 1892–94 uprisings, organized their own section of the Socialist Party by 1914 and led local antiwar demonstrations. Throughout the war, women gathered often in piazzas across Sicily to demand food, bread, and grain from municipal officials.[154] In Agrigento, female antiwar demonstrators took over their churches and used them as meeting centers, and in Sciacca they filled the cathedral chanting "Vogliamo la pace!" and "Abbasso la guerra!" (We want peace! Down with war!).[155] Certainly there were many women who did not become active in these movements, who, as one woman noted, "made the sign of the cross and that's it."[156] However, most witnessed these activities because they were such a prominent feature of village life throughout the South at the turn of the century.

Such resistance also became increasingly transnational. Police and military repression, coupled with massive emigration, led many activists to flee. These exiles often found a sympathetic audience among Italian emigrant workers who were not only anxious for news from home but interested in building movements of solidarity abroad.

Fear of Widows in White

Given the vital role southern Italian peasant women played in the revolutionary social movements at the turn of the century, it seems particularly odd that many scholars have overlooked their histories of resistance. But, as noted earlier, women's revolutionary activity *and* depictions of them as apolitical emerged at the same historical moment. Such ideas were routinely invoked by the middle and upper classes in Italy and the United States to reinforce popular assumptions about the backwardness of southern Italians and to delegitimize their political activity. In fact, those in power—politicians, social scientists, and religious leaders—blamed unrest and rebellion not on corrupt governments, repressive police forces, oppressive landholding practices, and a stagnant economy but on the rising numbers of the so-called *vedove bianche* (widows in white). This term differentiated the wives of migrants from those women who wore black in honor of their deceased husbands. Many contemporary observers grew to see the proliferation of villages composed primarily of women who ran households, took charge of communities, stormed piazzas, and lived lives separately from men as a symbol of the "moral anarchy" caused by mass emigration.[157]

Faced with women's rising radicalism and autonomy, the Italian elite became fixated on female deviance. As one observer noted in a leading Italian journal on emigration, "Modesty is not natural in women but imposed on them. The emigration of fathers, brothers, husbands, lovers, eliminates the coercion and lets their natural and unbridled instincts emerge."[158] A statistician who surveyed the South at this time voiced the concerns of many when he expressed his fear over the "young and beautiful bride who finds herself, only shortly after the wedding, alone, and almost a widow in her marriage bed. It is easy to imagine what happens—and must happen—when 50,000 wives are condemned to forced retirement, while still full of the exuberance of youth, and often also very poor."[159] In a 1908 survey of Calabria, another prominent writer warned, "adulteries, infanticides, and vendettas are the order of the day—manifestations of that abnormal social state brought on by emigration and the consequent disequilibrium of the sexes."[160] Many echoed these sentiments: "It is a sad fact," noted one observer, "but one well known to everyone who knows the regions of heavy migration that the wives and fiancées of the 'Americani' take the place of prostitutes."[161]

Indeed, Cesare Lombroso, the founder of criminal anthropology, published extensively on la donna delinquente (the criminal woman) in this period, to document the "swelling ranks of the so-called dangerous classes" that many in his generation believed resulted from mass migration.[162] Several decades later, Carlo Levi continued to bemoan the collapse of the social order, noting that "emigration has changed the picture. . . . a great part of the children are illegitimate, and the mother holds absolute sway. In the villages the women outnumber the men and the father's identity is no longer so strictly important; honor is disassociated from paternity, because a matriarchal regime prevails."[163] As historian Linda Reeder has noted, while social critics "may have disagreed over whether migration was ultimately beneficial or harmful to the island, they all agreed that when the men left, many of the women who remained behind sunk into poverty, sexual depravity or madness."[164]

Despite middle-class fears over the "powerful and potentially disorderly force" of peasant women's sexuality when not controlled by men, rates of "illegitimate" births in Italy did not rise during this period.[165] Rather, regional variations persisted without substantial change, and in some places the rates declined. Reeder explains that, "since women faced harsher punishments than men for any perceived or actual transgression, most women, especially 'white widows,' scrupulously avoided any activity that could bring dishonor to their families. No amount of American money could redeem her family's honor or reputation once the town labeled her a fallen woman and her husband a cuckold. It would be difficult to arrange prestigious marriages for her children or for her husband to succeed in business once he returned."[166] In most villages, impropriety was complicated by the fact that women often kept a watchful eye on each other. As with men, they valued codes of honor and respect because they used them to compete for limited economic and social resources. Such ideals were embedded in families, where women "were the repositories of honor and the public measure of a family's reputation."[167] Yet, these ideals were also contested and malleable along with other historically constituted ideas about gender and sexuality. By the 1880s, a government-appointed commission noted that migration was causing local values to change considerably. Women migrants were returning from sojourns "with little odor of chastity" but went on "to live a more continent life or become good wives and mothers."[168]

Even so, travel narratives and other ethnographic accounts from the early twentieth century contain a marked preoccupation with the expressive sexuality of southern Italian peasant women. Norman Douglas thanked God for the absence of men in San Giovanni, Calabria, because it enabled him to approach women as his "chief objects of interest." These "attractive and mirthful creatures," he noted, had "too little coyness about what is natural."[169] Levi too was mesmerized: "Behind their veils the women were like wild beasts. They thought of nothing but love-making, in the most natural way in the world, and they spoke of it with a license and simplicity of language that were astonishing. When you went by them on the street their black eyes stared at you, with a slanting downward glance as if to measure your virility, and behind your back you could hear them pass whispered judgments on your hidden charms."[170] In women's own testimonies, however, many emphasized a desire to limit sex because of the lack of reliable forms of birth control, the physical suffering brought on by many pregnancies, and the dangers of bringing many children into poverty. In addition, most women married quite young, without an understanding of sex.[171] What can we make of Levi's encounters then? If we remove the bourgeois lens of "wild beasts" and "mirthful creatures," we see young peasant women boldly occupying public spaces and interacting with others in the village. The degree to which middle- and governing-class opinions were internalized by peasants and workers is hard to detect. Yet proverbs, folktales, songs, poems, daily newspapers, and popular novels did reinforce the image of the emigrant's wife as victim, driven to insanity because of long separations from men or, worse, to infidelity.[172]

Ultimately, transatlantic migration had a profound effect on women's lives, whether they ever actually migrated themselves. It challenged a family's ability to maintain cultural and social ideals and affected women's relationships with everyone in their lives, from their own children to state officials. In many ways, the mass departure of southern Italians for the Americas reflected the failures of the new nation to meet the most basic needs of its subjects. To most in the laboring classes, the formation of the Italian nation-state was an intensely violent, exploitive development that only brought more misery to an already severely impoverished people. But to fully understand the colossal changes that unfolded in this period, it is necessary to also explore how women's lives changed as they themselves entered the global economy as wageworkers. As southern Italian women became labor migrants, they confronted a new set of ideologies and practices that resembled the violence, poverty, and denial of their humanity that they had confronted at home. Yet, at the same time, they brought traditions of everyday rebellion and revolutionary politics, nurtured in female worlds of the household, *cortile*, village, and community. In transplanting this culture, they would face the hostility of social Darwinists, the state, employers, and labor leaders, who were keen to label them as either victims or "radicals of the worst sort."[173]

La Sartina (The Seamstress) Becomes a Transnational Labor Migrant

Tina Gaeta, like most girls, learned to sew from the women in her family. Both her grandmother and mother were seamstresses, though her mother Lucia was particularly skilled. Word traveled fast in their southern Italian coastal city of Salerno, and those who could afford it paid Lucia to make their clothes, giving her the status of *la sartina*—the seamstress. Her daughter Tina recalled, "In Italy in those days women who sewed wore their scissors attached to a special ribbon over their long skirts. When they went home, they wouldn't take it off. The other women who didn't work or who worked as peasants on the farm, used to say 'Oh, she's the seamstress, *la sartina*!' In those days, being a seamstress was a very, very good thing. It was very distinguished."[1]

Sewing would also become Lucia's most important resource. Early in her marriage, her husband left for long periods of time, joining the masses of southern Italian men who crossed the Atlantic to lay tracks for the Long Island Railroad. While this work was dangerous and exhausting, it was plentiful. Railroad companies in particular were hungry for cheap labor and recruited men from across southern Italy by the thousands. In addition to working on the railroad, the men filled jobs in construction, as brick masons, coal heavers, stone crushers, concrete laborers, sewer construction workers, tunnel or building excavators, street graders, and ditch diggers—essentially building the infrastructure of modern industrial capitalism.[2] Lucia's husband sent whatever he could back home to his family, but his wages were meager and sporadic so Lucia supported the family in his absence by working as a seamstress. When she saved enough, she purchased tickets for steerage (the cheapest class on the lowest decks of the ship), packed up her three children, and together they crossed the Atlantic.

Lucia's decision to migrate was strongly influenced by the fact that she could find work immediately in New York City, the very center of the international garment industry. Upon arrival, however, she found that the skilled sectors were closed to her, and like the vast majority of Italian immigrant women in the city, she became a pieceworker, finishing ready-made clothing in her own home. Sewing clothing in her kitchen for mass production was monotonous and paid less, but it was necessary given her husband's low wages. It also enabled her to care for the children, especially because their family continued to grow. When Lucia's husband died suddenly, leaving her alone with their six children, industrial sewing kept the family alive. "At the time," Lucia's daughter Tina remembered, "the only means of getting work from the neighborhood was from the men's clothing, boy's jackets, and men's jackets. So she used to send my brother and my sister to pick up the work and take it home. Then, as my sisters grew up, she started them on making dresses." Working together, Lucia taught her children how to sew the invisible seams by hand, while she did the more complex sewing. As they grew older, she taught them to sew the entire garment on their own; and once they became experienced, they went to work in the factories.

Lucia and Tina's story is not just their own, but the story of most Italian women who migrated to New York City. Like men, women became labor migrants. While men worked as "veritable human steam shovels," women became sweatshop workers.[3] The movement of women from southern Italy into U.S. clothing and textile manufacturing marked an important moment in the developing global economy—a stage in the feminization of manufacturing that required that women (and children) move across national boundaries in order to secure their own and their families' survival. This was an early twentieth-century example of the "localization" of globalization, of "cross-border circuits in which the role of women, and especially the condition of being a foreign woman, is crucial."[4] Yet Italian women have been rarely imagined in historical scholarship as labor migrants. Rather, they are generally depicted as family migrants, migrating only at the directives of the men in their families, to join and reconsolidate family.[5] Although most women migrated as a part of family groups, they did so as workers whose paid and unpaid labor was critical to the survival of their families and to the expansion of industrial capitalism.

Why did Italian immigrant women's labor become invisible at the precise moment that it was so foundational to the global economic restructuring of this period? An answer emerges in mapping Italian women's position within and experience of the emerging transnational political economy of the early twentieth century. By humanizing and historicizing the seemingly abstract economic systems that shape migration, and by understanding the world that these women experienced and gave shape to as they moved through space, we can begin to understand why the political culture these Italian immigrant women would craft

Girls learning to sew, Sicily, 1921. Bettmann/Corbis, U131630INP.

was so deeply rooted in transnational labor radicalism. Such an approach also deconstructs the mythic story of the "up-by-the-bootstraps" European immigrant that is so central to American nationalism and is used as the yardstick by which to measure and demonize more recent immigrants. This highly individualistic narrative not only tends to erase women by positioning them purely as appendages to men but also elides the power relations that gave rise to and shaped their migrations.

Lucia and Tina's story brings the world of women's work into focus. Sewing was many things: grueling, tedious, low-wage labor; an admired craft; an expression of creativity; a tool for survival; a skill developed for a changing marketplace; a source of connection between women; and a means of passing on wisdom from one generation to the next. Tina recalled that when her family did industrial piecework at home, Lucia sometimes "would give us a treat and put the potatoes in the oven, or toast bread with oil and chopped garlic," and "tell us so many stories and proverbs while we were sewing." Her favorite story was of a ninety-nine-year-old washerwoman in the old country who fell ill. The woman's sister called the doctor, who, upon examining her, exclaimed, "What can I do? She is very old." The washerwoman was so weak that all she could do was raise her finger. "What is it that you want to tell me?" the doctor asked. "*Oh Dio*, one more year," she replied. Surprised, the doctor asked, "You have had a good life.

Time comes for all of us to leave each other. What is one year more or less? What are you searching for that you want to live one more year?" The old woman replied, "Ho tanto ancora da imparare!"—I still have so much to learn.[6]

This story within a story captures the essence of women's resistance. The belief systems and narratives generated to support industrializing capitalism and patriarchal nation-states valued southern Italian women's lives only to the degree that they served as low-wage menial workers and caretakers of men (as wives, mothers, etc.). Such a worldview developed to justify their subordination and dehumanization and served to hide employers' and consumers' reliance on and complicity in immigrant women's cheapened work. But this arrangement was never complete. By following the women, we are able to see the many creative ways they developed a sense of dignity and refused the master narrative of their instrumental worth. In this story, after all, the humble washerwoman is wise, and it is *she* who teaches the doctor. Lucia made sure to pass this story to her children. Tina did the same with her daughter, and valued it enough to share it with us. As a story of the old woman's learning for her own sake alone, it can be read as containing the profound truth of women's intrinsic value: the washerwoman's love of life stemmed not from her ability to provide for others but from her desire to nourish herself.

Women and the Feminization of Manufacturing Labor in Italy

Italian women's labor migrations were set in motion by global processes of economic change that women first experienced in their homelands. Globalizing capitalism, including political centralization, nation building, urbanization, the rise of the factory system, and mass emigration, were acutely felt even in the most remote southern Italian villages: "As cities grew, the countryside fed and populated them, and as urban factories produced new and cheap products, the countryside often became an important marketplace for them. Change in the countryside might mean a new crop grown, an old trade abandoned, the search for a cash income, migration, or the loss of kin and neighbors to 'better opportunities' elsewhere."[7] It also meant that women entered the local and global marketplace in larger numbers and with more frequency, as consumers, merchants, workers, and rebels.

To cope with these changes, southern Italian women turned to weaving, sewing, and other "female industries" as a gendered strategy for family subsistence in primarily agricultural settings. These trades also offered the possibility of acquiring the respected status of the artisan. Most learned the craft at home from the women in their families and as apprentices in the workshops of skilled dressmakers and tailors, many of whom were women. With the rise in mass-produced textiles and garments in the late nineteenth century, however, and the shift from custom- to ready-made clothing, sewing changed dramatically. Far from offering women social status or a creative outlet, these industries offered tedious, physically debilitating, repetitive work. Migration to the centers of industrial production, therefore, involved a process of deskilling in which women found themselves not only poorly paid but in workshops and factories that were increasingly controlled and defined by men.[8] This shift was underway before women ever left their homelands, giving rise to the militant labor movement described in the preceding chapter.

In exploring women's changing labor experiences in southern Italy at this time, it is difficult to identify an exact occupational distribution for wage work because census and other state records are notoriously inconsistent, with categories and methods that varied from one year to the next. Moreover, as Italy's national elites collected data on the South, they used their statistics as "the most authoritative mode of knowing and representing" the region. Because the 1890s were a decade of widespread social unrest and economic crisis in Italy, "statistical differentials between northern and southern regions came to be read as the expression of an essential difference, a difference inscribed in the bodies and minds not only of individuals but of whole peoples and that characterized whole societies."[9]

The constitutive power of official data was especially significant with regard to southern Italian women's labor. As their productive work intensified with the absence of male migrants, it was largely erased within census records and other government data. In the first decade of mass emigration, for example, the Italian government reclassified peasant women in official documents as *casalinghe* (housewives) instead of the former *contadine* (farmers).[10] In the Sicilian agrotown of Sambuca di Sicilia, for example, women composed about 40 percent of the agricultural workforce in the early 1880s, but in the 1901 and 1911 censuses they had virtually disappeared. They were now *casalinghe*.[11] In many towns, women's occupations varied depending on the records. A woman listed as a farmer in her marriage records, could be listed in the birth records of her children as a spinner one year and a housewife the next. Or a woman listed as a seamstress in marriage and birth registers could be listed as a housewife in the census. Historian Linda Reeder notes for Sicily in this period that "the occupational categories of women reflected government regulations, changing definitions of work, and the family's economic condition more than they reflected women's daily activities."[12]

The irony of hard work that was largely invisible was not lost on the women themselves. One woman from Calabria recalled of her life in the 1920s that, "right after I was married, I worked in our fields, gave birth in the fields, and it nearly killed me. But I never earned wages like my husband. I worked three times as hard but it wasn't considered work because it wasn't paid. A woman wasn't worth anything because she didn't bring home wages."[13] The absence of women's work in government data was not only the result of a larger societal devaluation of unwaged female labor, however. It reflected the common view that women's work, even when waged, was not legitimate economic activity. Because women tended to dominate the more seasonal jobs in agriculture and manufacturing, and worked within informal sectors of the economy, such as domestic service and prostitution, they were often disregarded and thus were both poorly remunerated and inadequately recorded.[14]

The official reclassification of women from farmers to housewives reflected not only this status but also the growing concern on the part of the Italian elite that the long-term absences of male migrants and the increasingly autonomous women they left behind were endangering patriarchal power arrangements within families and communities. The new categorization of women as dependents thus served to reassert male authority (and the Catholic ideal) by crafting women's role as solely in service of men and children. As many feminist scholars have demonstrated, such a framework served industrial capitalists well. By defining women's productive labor as supplemental, business owners could justify paying women very low wages, as well as hiring and firing them at will. By defining men's labor as breadwinning, they effectively conflated masculinity with being a good worker, which included the ability to withstand dangerous work conditions and exploitive labor practices. As such, this gendered division of labor became the prevailing ideal within most industrializing economies.[15]

The ideology of women's labor as supplementary did not, however, eliminate or lessen women's actual labor. Generally speaking, only women from the middle and upper classes were able to avoid intensive physical labor. The vast majority of southern Italian women categorized as "housewives" tended gardens and livestock, preserved food for winter, fetched water and firewood, cooked, cleaned, sewed, spun, wove, raised children, traded goods in the market, and earned wages as farm laborers, weavers, dressmakers, outworkers for tailors, domestic servants, midwives, and sometimes as prostitutes. With men absent for extended periods of time, women's wages were often necessary for survival. They became responsible for making sure there was enough cash to pay taxes, save for daughters' dowries, settle debts, and when possible, purchase property.[16] Migrants sent home remittances because their wages abroad were often as much as five times greater than those garnered by more prosperous families in the North, much less in the South.[17] But expenses abroad were high and remittances were unpredictable. Many women engaged in some form of wage work because men's wages did not arrive regularly, and they always faced the reality of abandonment.[18] It was women's significant role in sustaining their families that inspired their spirited confrontations with the Italian state in this period.

Ironically, while government statistics situated women's work as supplemental to a presumed male head of household, parliamentary investigations of the South fixated on women's heavy workloads. In Campania, investigators noted that women "work in the fields planting, weeding, harvesting olives, and carry wood and other products back to their homes."[19] In Basilicata, women had "precisely two foci of their life—field and home—and their only purpose in life is to work, work all the time, as much as they can, because in doing so they can survive."[20] In particular, they found that "the most noteworthy fact brought about by emigration is the expansion, even in those municipalities where it was not customary, of the work of women and young children in the cultivation of the soil."[21] They noted the same for Sicily and Calabria and found that women were "the hardest working in the region, which deforms their bodies." Throughout the South, especially in the areas with the greatest out-migration, government investigators found women planting, hoeing, and harvesting olives, lemons, almonds, and other products, as well as spinning, weaving, sewing, and performing other kinds of domestic production.[22]

This preoccupation with peasant women's intense physical labor developed in part because it challenged middle-class notions of propriety and confirmed northerners' and elite southerners' ideas of the South as a site of primitive living conditions and gender relations. The image of peasant women as capable of intense physical exertion was also memorialized in popular culture, including novels by Giovanni Verga and the travel writing of British authors Bolton King, Thomas Okey, and Norman Douglas.[23] It also crossed the Atlantic. The essays of Antonio Mangano, the minister of the First Italian Baptist Church in Brooklyn, circulated in popular American magazines and reproduced the image of southern Italian women as capable of extraordinary physical exertion. "I saw many a field with long rows of women toilers," he reported, "the overseer, the only man in sight. . . . Near Tivoli, I met a sunburned peasant woman coming down the steep stony path, carrying on her head a basket in which slept a little child. And often the poor woman has besides the basket cradle on her head, her *zappa* [hoe], black bread and water jug, a cord tied about her waist by which she draws an unyielding pig or sheep to pasture."[24] Others painted similar pictures for American middle-class audiences in popular magazines, replete with images of the "barefooted, sunburned woman, hobbling down some rocky steep with an immense bag of forage on her head for her cow."[25] By rendering female labor as subordinate to men's but also as physically intense, official and popular discourse effectively situated southern Italian women as especially suited to the particular low-wage labor needs of industrial capitalism.

Indeed, women experienced the feminization of manufacturing labor before they ever migrated, even though factory work was still quite uncommon in Italy. Industrialization developed slowly and centered in the North, in the triangle formed by the cities of Turin, Genoa, and Milan. The North remained predominantly rural throughout the nineteenth and early twentieth centuries, however, and land remained "the most important source of wealth."[26] The desire to own a piece of property to call one's own, with a home and small garden or farm, was passed from one generation to the next, and endured mass emigration. The southern cities, such as Naples, Salerno, Messina, Palermo, Trapani, Catania, Potenza, and Bari, also offered women light-industrial and artisan labor, especially in the clothing and textile trades.[27] Because manufacturers could use the rationale that women's labor was supplemental to pay them at least half the wages they offered men, most turned to female labor to save costs and drive up profits. Using the classic rationale that women and children were desirable workers for their "*dita delicate ed agili*" (delicate and agile fingers), manufacturers relied on biological determinist arguments to justify their exploitation of women workers. By the late nineteenth century, women and children outnumbered male workers in most manufacturing in Italy, including the production of silk, wool, cotton, cigars, matches, gloves, glass, pottery, leather, paper, printing, coral, pasta, and straw hats. In 1894, for example, among 382,131 industrial workers overall, women composed 49 percent of the total, not including girls under the age of fourteen who also composed a large group, and were concentrated in the "light" industries of textile and garment work.[28]

Textiles consistently drew the largest numbers of women. Between 1900 and 1910, textiles were among Italy's chief exports, and while such work varied from region to region, women dominated the industry, in domestic production, cottage industry, and factory manufacture.[29] The census records, however, document a large drop in the number of women working in textiles between 1882 and 1901, from 1,213,978 to 661,774. This was a result of mechanization which shifted textile manufacture from homes to factories, causing a sharp decline in the number of independent artisans. In addition, the liberal trade policies of the Italian state "allowed outside producers to challenge artisans' monopoly on local markets," and women were forced to abandon the domestic production of cloth.[30] As a result, the government began to exclude independent weavers (*tessitrici* or *tessitore*) and spinners (*filatrici*) from the category of textile workers in the 1901 census; two trades that were dominated by women.[31] Even so, as factory production increased, the cottage-based industry declined across most of rural Italy, and women had to find new ways to support their families.

By and large, they turned to sewing. The growth of factory-made textiles in particular led to this rise in *sartine* or *sarte* (more specialized seamstresses, dressmakers, and tailors) and *cucitrice* (less-skilled seamstresses). As "spinning and weaving declined, women applied highly elaborate needlework to this factory produced and commercially distributed cloth" and the needle trades proliferated.[32] The rise of labor-intensive clothing industries at home and abroad further compelled women to take up this craft. When asked why she had learned to sew before coming to New York City, one young Italian immigrant woman noted, "We have to think of the future and not always of the present."[33] Indeed, the U.S. Immigration Commission found in 1911 that 91 percent of all southern Italian women in the U.S. garment trades had previously worked in sewing, lace making, and embroidery in Italy.[34]

Oral histories abound with evidence of the journey women made from apprenticing in Italy to becoming industrial workers in New York City. Women generally learned the techniques of hand sewing, lace making, and embroidery from women—relatives, the local seamstress, and teachers in convent and public schools.[35] Carmela Lizza's training was typical. Her parents sent her to the neighborhood *sarta* in Palermo when she was a child, to learn how to design, cut, and sew dresses, blouses, and coats. Because most of her neighbors were artisans and small shopkeepers, becoming an apprentice to the local dressmaker was a valued part of a girl's education. By the age of fourteen, Carmela was training other girls and working as a dressmaker out of her home. Once she became an adult, she and her brother, a cabinetmaker, migrated to New York City. There she found immediate work in a shop that specialized in custom-made bridal dresses, where she remained for thirty years.[36] Custom-made specialty shops that catered to a middle-class and wealthy clientele were becoming increasingly rare by the early twentieth century, however, and only the very skilled seamstresses had a small chance of entering these better-paying jobs.[37]

The vast majority of women entered the garment industry at the very bottom of the ladder. Maria De Luca and her sister were both sent by their parents to apprentice with the village dressmaker in their town of Spinoza (Basilicata). When Maria turned eighteen, she migrated to New York City, having heard returning migrants' "stories of the great wealth they had accumulated while in the United States." She joined relatives in Greenwich Village, and friends of the family helped to find her first job making corset covers and shirtwaists in a factory. Though she stopped working once she married, her husband soon became ill, so she returned to sewing blouses in a neighborhood factory, where she remained for sixteen years.[38] Maria Santoro learned to sew from her mother, who worked as a seamstress for the tailor in their Sicilian village. Her mother's job kept the family of seven children alive during her husband's long absences, because he migrated five times for work in the United States. The family eventually reunited in Brooklyn, where Maria and the children found immediate work as homeworkers on men's pants, as her husband's wages as a bricklayer could not solely support the family.[39]

Those women who did not apprentice with the local seamstress learned to sew by assembling a trousseau, which consisted mostly of linens for their future household, such as sheets, pillowcases, bedspreads, intimate apparel, napkins, table cloths, and towels, which a young woman completed with the help of the women in her family. Because of this, most women learned simple stitching before they were seven years old, and then the arts of embroidery and lacework in their adolescent years. Some even recalled that many of the games they played as children involved working with needle and thread.[40]

For the daughters of peasant and artisan families, the trousseau was deeply significant. First, it enabled women to develop a craft that could assist the transnational family economy without undermining the family's reputation, because sewing was associated with the virtues of female industriousness and restrained sexuality. This connection between sewing and virginity was also affirmed by the large numbers of religious orders who trained girls in needlework. Second, the trousseau was quite often the only form of property that women brought into adulthood. It was also a resource that was mobile—it could come with a migrant and be easily sold or pawned if necessary.[41] In fact, government officials from Puglia reported a growing phenomenon: peasant men marrying in order to acquire the trousseau, which they pawned for passage to America. Men did this, they noted, in order to enlist a "safe manager" to whom they could entrust their remittances, as they saved to purchase property in the homeland.[42] How many women were willing to take this risk is unknown. But it is clear that by the turn of the century, women valued sewing because it enabled them to produce goods that they could both use and potentially exchange. Sewing was honorable and could generate property and wages.

Comparing women's work experiences in the two regions of Sicily and Campania, which experienced the greatest rates of emigration to the United States, illustrates how gender ideologies and regional economies combined to shape women's experiences of work in this period.[43] Sicily was quite atypical of the rest of the South, but it was home to the largest number of emigrants to New York City. The island's female emigrants were concentrated in two categories within state records—as "workers adept at other industries" (which referred to their absence from agricultural labor) and "housewives without profession," while men were listed primarily as agricultural and unskilled laborers.[44] Despite their classification as nonagricultural workers, most Sicilian women who emigrated did engage in farming. Women often harvested crops, especially on land that was close to their homes.[45] Generally speaking, only the poorest women worked in the island's commercial agriculture because this labor required that workers travel long distances to the fields. Such women typically complemented this labor by gathering wild vegetables, grinding their own grain (to avoid the mill tax), making brooms in a putting-out system, and finding work as servants, laundresses, and merchants.[46]

There were also differences within Sicily. According to the 1871 census, women composed 35 percent of agricultural laborers on the island, with the highest numbers in the more densely populated eastern provinces of Messina and Catania, where the growing of citrus fruit and olives predominated.[47] It was also in these zones that government investigators found Italian women working, not just in the orchards or nearby gardens but also out in the fields.[48] Social taboos against women performing agricultural labor in Sicily led most to labor closer to home, in tasks that were clearly defined as women's work—as seamstresses, lace makers, weavers, midwives, and laundresses—trades that held a higher status than that of agricultural day laborer.[49]

The region of Campania, on the other hand, was the most industrialized in southern Italy, with small inland agricultural towns and denser populations along the coast. Most of the residents in this region, including women, engaged in agricultural labor. But this sector of the economy could not support the dramatic population growth at the turn of the century. As a result, many turned to artisanal labor, especially in communities that were some distance from the larger towns and cities, where "greater local self-sufficiency in industrial production prevailed." In these locales, "a fairly large population of artisans, some in good-sized workshops, still manufactured necessary items for local markets."[50] Seamstresses, along with shoemakers, carpenters, merchants (e.g., grocers, butchers, bakers), and masons, generally formed the largest groups of artisans in any given town or city.[51]

The province of Caserta, just north of Naples, provides a useful case study of women's wage work in this region. In 1913 the Italian Emigration Commission undertook a study of women's and children's labor in the province and noted their presence in multiple settings, including bakeries, paper and cotton mills, garment manufacture, and small factories in the woolen, brick and tile, pasta, furniture, and tobacco trades. One government agent noted that in 1909 "female day laborers actually outnumbered male in one region of heavy male emigration."[52] In some towns they found women working mostly as seamstresses, ironers, and hairdressers, with the poorest women supplementing their wages by gathering greens at night: "They left at night, on wagons, and traveled far to find the places where weeds grow in abundance, sleeping outside on the ground with the wagon as their roof. They would stop for two or three days and then return, to leave again the next day."[53] Another middle-class observer was not as sympathetic in his report, noting "they graze like animals."[54]

In addition to conveying the disdain that middle- and upper-class observers had for women workers, whom many considered to be "scarcely recognizable as human," these reports also reveal a female population that was quite mobile, and not just in the search for edible greens.[55] Survival often required that women travel considerable distances from their villages of origin. Factories in Naples employed large numbers of women from the villages of Scisciano, S. Vitaliano, Margliano, and Mariglianellam, while the silk mills in Sarno (Salerno) drew women from Nola. Young women from Santa Maria di Capua, Caserta, Sala, and S. Leucio migrated to work in the cotton mill Berner di Piedimonte d'Alife. Government reports also noted that the largest number of migrants to the Americas had already migrated within the region before crossing the ocean.[56] This was also true for women in Calabria, the region just south of Campania. One woman noted of her life in this period that "in the village there was nothing. . . . How can you eat? How can you live?" As with many others, she went to the city for work.[57] The transatlantic migrations of southern Italian peasants had their roots in these local patterns of labor migration, which increasingly set women in motion by the early twentieth century.[58]

Migration overseas became necessary in part because the economies of Naples, Salerno, and other coastal cities could not fully incorporate migrants from the interior. In addition to combining various forms of wage work, thousands chose to join the masses of migrants who left daily on steamships for the Americas. Naples in fact would become the port through which the vast majority of Italians emigrated. Between 1902 and 1920, close to 200,000 souls departed each year, for journeys that took anywhere between ten and twelve days for New York, or eighteen and twenty days for Buenos Aires.[59] Naples was not only a center of emigration, however. By the late nineteenth century, it was the largest city in Italy, with close to half a million residents in 1884, and notorious for rampant unemployment and the proliferation of an underground economy.[60]

Facing south in the Bay of Naples, with the volcano Vesuvio rising in the distance, Naples was known among Europeans for its "evil smells and foul water," epidemic diseases, crime, and overcrowded, impoverished "slums." A correspondent for the *British Medical Journal* reflected the views of many when he noted that Naples was "barbarous," "squalid," and "obscene."[61] Many also noted the large transient population of workers who faced abysmal wages, rampant disease, and "the most ghastly human habitations on the face of the earth."[62] In the nineteenth century alone, the city was ravaged by twelve epidemics of typhoid and cholera, causing the loss of forty-eight thousand lives.[63]

Even with this devastating loss of life, Naples's economy could not accommodate its enormous and growing population. The city was largely a commercial center and the doorway through which southern agricultural products of wheat, wine, olive oil, wool, and cheese passed on their way to northern Italy and the rest of Europe. Because of this, the city's economy was "geared to marketing rather than production, to services and the retail trades rather than to industry."[64] There was some manufacturing in silk, linen, cotton, and wool, in what manufacturers, political leaders, and other members of the elite referred to as "the small housewife-industries"—which included spinning, weaving, lace and carpet making, and work with wool and wicker—reinforcing the feminization of these trades.[65] However, an overcrowded labor market meant that these jobs were in high demand because most textile mills and other firms were located in midsize towns rather than in the city. In their report on women's work in Naples, for example, the U.S. Consulate noted that the majority of the city's working-class women labored as cigar makers, with smaller numbers working as seamstresses, vendors, household servants, and prostitutes.[66]

Women's Proletarian Diasporas in the Americas

As transnational labor migration became a way of life, women joined the exodus. In the 1880s they accounted for only 17 percent of all emigrants from Italy, but after 1888 the figure rose to 38 percent. By the First World War, the stream of women and children began to equal and even surpass that of men, and in the years leading up to 1921, women totaled 46 percent of Italian emigration, sometimes accounting for more than 60 percent.[67] The gender ratios of emigration varied considerably by region and were shaped by both work opportunities and local economies in Italy and beyond. As with men, the majority came from southern Italy—primarily Sicily, Campania, Calabria, and Basilicata.[68]

Many female migrants had experienced some degree of autonomy because of men's earlier migration. Some learned, as one woman noted, "A man ain't necessary and how he ain't."[69] With the majority of male kin already abroad, women often made their own decisions and preparations to leave. Often the mother or grandmother in a family would save for the voyage and then inform family members of the impending arrival.[70] Zappira Blondi and her mother "put their heads together and laid a plan where they could earn their passage" when her father wrote to them of his troubles finding work in the United States. Agnes Santucci borrowed money from her sister to migrate, and then sent money home to her mother in Italy when she found work in New York City's garment trades.[71]

When women made the trip across the ocean, it often signaled the decision of a family to settle abroad more permanently. Still, in the years between 1909 and 1928, 20 percent of female emigrants returned to Italy, and male repatriation rates remained over 60 percent.[72] As Donna Gabaccia has noted, "The migration of women allowed reproduction to take place in the diaspora, laying foundations for either diasporic identities or incorporation into the countries where migrants lived and worked. It did not create a single, interconnected or Italian nation unbound, however. Italy generated many proletarian diasporas, and for several generations most had their center in a single paese."[73]

Rather than migrating merely at the direction of the men in their families, women who made the decision to migrate often took several things into consideration: their own needs; their ability to find work; and the needs of their families. The Bambace family illustrates this complexity. Involving multiple generations and migrations, this family's story also dramatizes the significance of women to the transnational family economy. It begins in the village of Leonforte in central Sicily, where life centered on the growing of wheat, olives, fava beans, almonds, peaches, and oranges. Here Maria Gattuso was born and raised. Widowed at a young age, she took her only daughter Giuseppina and migrated to São Paulo, Brazil, after a falling out with her family and others in her village. As she packed her bags, she vowed that no daughter of hers would "marry any of these bastards."[74]

In São Paulo, Giuseppina would meet and marry Antonio Bambace, a Calabrese fisherman and sea captain. In the coming years she gave birth to three children: Angela, Maria, and a third who died in infancy. While Antonio had a successful business in the nearby seaport of Santos with a fleet of three ships, he was often overcome with a deep sense of despair. It clung to him so tenaciously that he urged Giuseppina to return with him to Italy, to his village of Cannitello, in the hopes that it might improve his outlook and overall health. The small coastal fishing community did not ease his suffering, however, and the family soon migrated again, this time to New York in 1904. Angela recalled, "My mother did not want to come to America and they had a lot of talks about this. But my father still had the idea or the fixation he would get well if he came to America. But when he got to America it was no different than in Santos, Brazil or Cannitello, Italy."[75]

While the family did not migrate to New York with the explicit intention to find work in the garment industry, it informed their decision. Still consumed by depression, Antonio was unable to find stable employment and soon returned to Cannitello, sending small amounts of money to his family. Giuseppina joined the majority of other Italian women in her East Harlem neighborhood, and supported her children by taking in piecework from the local garment shops.[76] Even later, when Antonio returned from Italy to live with them again, and after another child was born, Giuseppina remained the breadwinner, taking in sewing while also working all day in a factory trimming plumes for ladies hats and, later, sewing shirtwaists. Angela recalled that her father was "too sick to work. So my mother thought she had better take over managing the care and welfare of the family."[77] Giuseppina made sure her daughters completed school, but once they graduated they too entered the garment industry, as seamstresses in a neighborhood blouse shop, like so many of their generation.

From Sicily to Brazil to Calabria to New York, back to Calabria and then once again to New York, the history of the Bambace family illustrates the contours of the Italian diasporic experience, but also how women's labor was far from supplemental. Another example is that of Concetta Di Meo, whose mother worked as a seamstress in Palermo because her father's wages as a hat maker were insufficient. Together the family migrated to Rome where her mother could find work in a clothing factory. "She supported the entire family," Concetta recalled, "and was responsible for making all family decisions." Eight years later the family migrated to New York City, because her mother could be assured of work. There she continued to support the family by working in a dress factory on Spring Street.[78]

Social scientific and government records from this period also confirm that women's wages were absolutely critical to a family's ability to survive. In one study of forty-eight Italian families in Manhattan, 90 percent of all family members were working for wages.[79] Women's labor migration enabled men to carve out more permanent and stable jobs as boot makers and shoemakers, grocers, barbers, and tailors, occupations that required some investment and commitment to settle in order to develop a clientele and learn the trade. Even so, in 1925, men born in Italy were still primarily working in "unskilled," low-paying jobs, and their representation in the higher-paying skilled, semiskilled, and white-collar trades had not changed since 1905.[80] Even as Italian men made the transition from seasonal labor migrations to settlement abroad, their jobs remained marginal and their wages were rarely sufficient to support an entire family, especially in winter months when seasonal work in subway or building construction went idle.[81] As a result, the wages women earned typically contributed more to the family economy than men's. In one 1919 study of 544 family economies among

Italians in New York City, researchers found that an average of 1.5 men and 2.1 women contributed to the family income. Moreover, in 279 of these families, mothers were the primary wage earners: 94 earned their wages as pieceworkers in the garment industry, 89 in factory work, 61 by keeping lodgers and boarders, 23 as janitors, and the remainder in other occupations, often as midwives and shopkeepers. They noted that "the share of women in maintaining the household is large for the entire group."[82] Women migrated, then, in large part because their families needed their labor to survive.

In their own words, women gave many reasons for migrating: "to live with relatives," "to get married," "to see America," "to make a dowry," "to get away from family," and "to forget my sorrows." But the vast majority came "to get a job" because the "family needed help," "father is unable to support family," or they had fallen on "hard times."[83] Migration did not occur simply out of individual desire. As with men, it grew out of economic necessity but also from a highly organized strategy to provide the industrializing sectors of the world economy with cheap female labor. News of work opportunities came not only through transnational relationships with family, friends, and neighbors but also from manufacturing firms that advertised extensively in Italian newspapers and with postings on village walls, promising "good pay, long season, union shop."[84] The garment trades, along with textile factories, cigar manufacturers, canneries, and many other industries, relied on low-wage female labor, and they were eager to import this largely illiterate and impoverished population. They were also able to provide "wages high enough to draw women out of transnational family economies initially based on somewhat different, but solid, financial expectation of men earning where the wages were high (abroad) in order to spend where prices were low (in Italy)."[85]

Like men, women generally migrated because a particular destination offered better wage-earning possibilities than the options they faced at home. Because of this, women headed to the Americas in greater proportions than men, while men migrated within Europe and to Africa and Australia more than women. For southern Italian women, the preferred destinations were, in descending order, the United States, Argentina, and Brazil. In each nation, women composed close to one-third of the Italian immigrant community.[86] As with men, their migrations to the Americas took place in three waves: 1876–90, primarily to Argentina; 1891–97, primarily to Brazil and Argentina; 1898–1930, primarily to the United States. Migration to Latin America continued to be significant in the later period, and from 1890 to 1915, when more than 4 million Italians went to the United States, almost 2 million migrated to Argentina and 1 million to Brazil.[87] By 1914 the cities of New York, Buenos Aires, and São Paulo each had the largest concentrations of Italian immigrants in the world—370,000, 312,000, and 111,000 respectively.[88]

Situating women's labor migration to the United States within this diasporic context illustrates how different states recruited and incorporated southern Italian women into their processes of economic expansion and nation building. Because both Argentina and Brazil focused their recruitment on agricultural workers, these mass migrations developed earlier than the migration to New York City, before processes of industrialization were fully underway. But by the early twentieth century, Italian women entered manufacturing in all three nations, adapting their methods of resistance and political ideologies to these new industrializing, multiethnic, urban settings.

Argentina

Both Argentina and Brazil were popular destinations for Italian migrants because they offered entire families work in commercial agriculture, independent farming, and industrial labor. From the 1860s to the 1880s, Argentina recruited Italians, along with other European workers, through a network of mostly private labor agencies abroad and by offering immigrant harvest workers their own parcels of land, along with animals, seeds, and tools. In the 1880s the Argentine government went one step further and subsidized workers' passage.[89] Their goal was to import workers (men, women, and children) to tend the *pampas*—the fertile prairies that produced wheat, beef, wool, flax, corn, and other key staples for European markets, and which fueled the rapid economic expansion that took place in Argentina between 1860 and 1914.[90]

The plan was successful, and on the eve of the First World War "Argentina was the country with the highest ratio of immigrants to indigenous population in the world," with Italians constituting the largest group, accounting for close to 60 percent of all immigrants.[91] Italian women were "the largest female group to arrive in Argentina during the years of massive immigration," and the majority migrated with their children and the men in their families.[92] Southern Italians accounted for 42 percent of all immigrants to Argentina, and they arrived primarily from Sicily, Calabria, and Campania, the same regions that supplied laborers for the United States. More northern Italians chose Argentina over the United States, in part because their transatlantic migration began earlier, in the 1860s and 1870s. By 1900 the northern region of the Piedmont, plus the southern regions of Sicily and Calabria, provided the largest number of immigrants, however.[93] In the city of Rosario, for example, which was 28 percent Italian in 1895, southern Italians composed 47 percent of the city's Italian immigrant population, with the largest numbers overall coming from Sicily.[94]

Buenos Aires became the center of Argentina's Italian immigrant community, and by the end of the nineteenth century the city's Italian settlement was "larger than those in New York, Philadelphia, Chicago, Boston, San Francisco, and Toronto *combined*."[95] The tide shifted toward the United States in the first two decades of the twentieth century, however, and by 1920 almost twice as many Italians migrated to the United States compared to Argentina. Still, by the time mass migration to the United States began in the 1890s, Italians had been migrating to Argentina by the hundreds of thousands for three decades. Numerically there were more Italians in New York City than in Buenos Aires by 1910, but they were only 7 percent of the city's population, whereas in Buenos Aires they composed 23 percent. In addition, more than 75 percent of the Italians in the United States arrived in a relatively short period of time, from 1900 to 1914, whereas migration to Argentina occurred over a much longer period, from 1860 to 1920.

This combination of factors—Italians' more gradual process of arrival and incorporation, their numerical predominance in Buenos Aires's working classes, and thus their early presence as union leaders—meant that they played a critical role in the development of the labor movement in Argentina. The same can be said for Brazil, where Italians became the largest group of São Paulo's union members. In New York City, however, Italians remained largely on the margins of the trade union movement until the Great Depression. Italian immigrant women's activism in New York City was therefore far more inconspicuous than that of their contemporaries in Latin America.[96]

Because Argentine landowners recruited Italian families to work in the agricultural sector, most of these immigrants were peasants and rural day laborers before migrating. Once in Argentina, they farmed the *pampas*, but by the 1880s many found work in the expanding manufacturing and service sectors of the more urban economies of Buenos Aires, Rosario, and La Plata.[97] In general, "industries associated with the production of locally consumed food, cigars, shoes, and clothing tended to hire females," and women "also served as the main labor force in the production of *alpargatas*, or jute-soled canvas shoes, burlap bag assembling, shirt and hat factories, tailors' shops, and commercial laundries."[98] In 1895 in Rosario, for example, close to 40 percent of Italian immigrant women were working for wages, with more than 90 percent of single women in their early thirties and more than 60 percent of married women in their late thirties composing the largest groups. Their two most common occupations were seamstresses (21 percent) and maids (34 percent). The remainder found work (in descending order) as cooks, laundresses, dressmakers (more skilled tailors and thus distinguished from seamstresses), and merchants, with a small number turning to prostitution.[99] This was similar for Buenos Aires, where Italian immigrant women worked mainly as seamstresses, with smaller numbers working in the declining textile mills, and as washerwomen, servants, cooks, embroiderers, ironers, cigar makers, shoemakers, merchants, and prostitutes. As would be the case in New York City, a large number of Italian seamstresses, especially those with small children, took in piecework.[100]

The social movements that spread across southern Italy at this time extended to the Americas with mass migration, and Italian women emerged as a significant, vocal, and highly visible presence in the Argentine labor movement. The anarchist movement appears to have drawn more support from women than socialism or institutionalized Catholicism did. Those working as seamstresses, shoe binders, and textile workers formed the majority in at least ten of the trade unions that joined the anarchist Federación Obrera Regional Argentina (FORA) in 1907, and they were also at the forefront of several anarchist-led rent strikes that spread throughout Buenos Aires in the same period.[101] In each of these struggles, women drew upon strategies of collective direct action and community-based protest from southern Italy and applied them to their new circumstances.

For example, Italian laundress Josefina Rinaldi was among several Italian women who organized hundreds of women in their southern Italian working-class enclave of La Boca in 1907 to protest a 47 percent rent increase. Refusing to pay, women marched through the streets, carrying red banners embroidered with the name of their tenant league, Centro Feminista Anarquista. With an eye for irony, they chose their weapon wisely. Italians were routinely derided in the popular culture as idiotic street sweepers, but now landlords and police had to face down mobs of angry women wielding brooms, a popular symbol in the fight against corruption.[102] Whole families became involved, not only in the "broom parades" and marches but also in resisting eviction: women gathered in tenement doorways to block police from entering; they attacked the police with brooms and boiling water; and, when that failed, they moved the furniture of evicted families back into the apartment as soon as police left the scene.[103] Reports in the anarchist daily *La Protesta* proclaimed the success of the insurgency, claiming that landlords "gave up their attempts to collect the rents by force and ran away when the women of the building promised them 'a hot shower.'"[104] In one month, close to 750 tenement buildings joined in solidarity, and by the end of 1907 that number had increased to 2,000.

In total, the yearlong strike would come to include close to one-tenth of the entire population of Buenos Aires and involve not only Italians but Spanish, Russian, French, and Turkish immigrants as well. In the end, it is estimated that more than 50,000 women participated.[105] Two years later, the same numbers of women would turn out in the 1909 general strike in Buenos Aires, to protest state repression against workers' movements, and in 1912 a "ten-year period of rural unrest, strikes, and violence took off" in the *pampas*, as Italian sharecroppers fought for better contracts.[106]

The diasporic radicalism that emerged was both inspired by anarchism and rooted in familial, ethnic, and female networks of mutual assistance. It was constituted through the network of mutual aid societies that Italians established wherever they went, to provide for their collective needs, build community, and confront their marginalized position within the emerging capitalist world order. In Buenos Aires, Italian bakers formed the first anarchist groups, and by 1904 they joined with immigrants from Spain, eastern Europe, and other countries to form a federation of sixty-six anarchist mutual aid societies with 33,000 members, at least 4,000 of whom were women.[107] While women were in the minority of formal members, they were consistently present at anarchist meetings, "where they sometimes outnumbered their male comrades." Because the radical culture involved whole families, children were actively encouraged to participate. Thirteen-year-old Delia Barrozo, for example, "fiercely defended women's emancipation in front of 700 people at a conference organized by the carpenters' union" and became commonly known as the "little Michel" after legendary French anarchist Louise Michel.[108] As historian José Moya and others have persuasively demonstrated, women such as Teresa Marchisio, Maria Collazo, and Teresa Caporaleti "became some of the most popular orators in the movement, drawing crowds of more than a thousand in indoor conferences. Others organized schools, libraries, theater and musical troupes, study groups, labor unions, boycotts, and strikes. Women in Buenos Aires published dozens of propaganda pamphlets and what may have been the first anarcho-feminist newspaper in the Western Hemisphere"—*La Voz de la Mujer*.[109] This was a movement that would greatly inspire Italian immigrant women radicals in the United States.

As in Italy, these movements were met with intense state repression. The Argentine government responded to working-class agitation by calling a state of siege five times between 1902 and 1910, including mass arrests and deportations.[110] By recruiting Italian workers, the Argentine government had hoped, as President Domingo Sarmiento (1868–74) stated in 1853, to "drown in waves of industry the Creole rabble, inept, uncivil, and coarse, that stops our attempt to civilize the nation."[111] By the early twentieth century, Argentine nationalists drew on scientific racism not only to build a case for civilizing the nation with European immigrants but to whiten it.[112] The native-born population they sought to purify "included a large number of ex-slaves and their descendants, seminomadic gauchos, and poor *chinos* (the contemporary term for persons of partial Indian descent), who were exploited and despised by the white *gente decente*."[113]

But the mass immigration of Italians caused only more anxiety. The Argentine government extended its offer of free passage to immigrants from northern Europe in an attempt to dilute what they saw as a "dangerous concentration of Italians in the country."[114] The danger was rooted, they believed, in Italians' inherent criminality, evidenced primarily by their inclination toward anarchism.[115] Argentina's elite routinely denounced Italians as "full of defects," "backwards," "ignorant and indigent." One member of the elite noted that "the only benefit they bring are their hands, always disposed to the most injurious and servile labor."[116] While Italian workers were at times reduced to just one fragment of their bodies, their immigration was never restricted. Rather it led to a "creolization" between Italians and Argentines, yielding "a new ethic and aesthetic order wherein the presence of each group becomes integral to the national whole."[117]

Brazil

Brazil also became home to a vibrant labor movement among Italian immigrant workers. As in Argentina, Italians were recruited by various states to modernize their economies, bring down the cost of labor in both agriculture and the new industrial sector, and "to civilize and 'whiten' a racially mixed nation that was among the last in the West to abandon slavery."[118] Beginning in the 1870s, the state of São Paulo recruited whole families to work the burgeoning coffee plantations by offering them free passage. Italians did not migrate to Brazil en masse, however, until slavery was formally abolished in 1888, out of the fear that they too might be enslaved. Between then and 1902, more than one million Italians arrived in Brazil, including several hundred anarchists (mostly men) from Brescia (Lombardy) who established Colônia Cecília in 1890, a commune in the southern state of Paraná. Most immigrants came first from the northern Italian region of Veneto and then from the southern regions of Campania and Calabria. Italian women and children worked on the plantations alongside men, and their subsistence labor—the growing of rice, beans, corn, and fruit, and the raising of poultry and pigs—would prove especially critical to family survival.[119]

When Italians arrived, they found extremely harsh working conditions on the *fazendas*, and while some returned to Italy, most abandoned their contracts and fled for the city. In fact, more than 70 percent of all Italian immigrants in Brazil made the city of São Paulo their home, where they were as large a presence as in Buenos Aires. Between 1890 and 1920, for instance, they composed close to 35 percent of the city's population and created a lively anarchist subculture, which published more than thirty Italian-language newspapers.[120] By 1920 the city had become a "booming metropolis with a distinctively Italian air," because more than half of its half million residents were born in Italy.[121] São Paulo's largest industry, textile manufacturing, focused its recruitment efforts on Italian women in particular, from both Italy and the coffee plantations, hoping in part to limit the access of Afro-Brazilians to factory labor. Because of this, Italian women constituted the bulk of industrial workers in the city, while Italian men filled jobs in construction, printing, metalworking, stone masonry, shoemaking, street sweeping, and gardening.[122]

Because of their concentration in the industrial sector, Italian women textile workers were consistently in the vanguard of the city's labor movement in the first several decades of the twentieth century. In a series of large strikes, beginning in 1907, they denounced the long hours, low pay, and dangerous working conditions, including sexual harassment and violence at the hands of foremen. They walked out of factories, spoke before large rallies, and negotiated with their employers themselves. Historian Joel Wolfe has documented how "the city's women workers consistently avoided participation in the male-dominated unions and chose instead to organize their own formal and informal associations, such as factory commissions comprised solely of women."[123] When they did align with men, it was with those in the anarchist movement, because they opposed centralized authority within organizations, resulting in a "distinct anarcho-syndicalist ideology that defined São Paulo's labor movement into the 1930s" and beyond.[124]

As they had in Italy, women also turned to more informal methods of resistance. They routinely quit jobs that were especially untenable, and many "returned to the rural sector to avoid harsh work conditions, earn higher wages during the harvest, or help their families who still lived as colonos." Wolfe notes that "this mobility became such a problem for mill owners that bosses attempted to standardize wages throughout the city and state."[125] Italian women were central to the local labor movement in other ways as well: noted Italian anarchist Gigi Damiani commented then that massive participation in strikes and working-class organizations developed only when Italians in São Paulo "had raised families and had abandoned thoughts of returning to their homeland."[126]

As in Argentina, Brazil's planters and industrialists recruited Italians, as well as Spanish and Portuguese immigrants, with that hopes that these Europeans would provide "a transfusion of better blood" and displace newly freed black workers.[127] Italians' "preferred position" had complicated results. Some historians have argued that it did not lead to a racially exclusive union movement and labor market. Yet the industrial labor force was primarily European in the first several decades of the twentieth century, and Afro-Brazilians were not able to enter factory work until the 1930s. Moreover, the Italian-language radical press routinely advanced its view that "ethnic and national cleavages within the working class formed the single most important obstacle to the success of São Paulo's labor movement."[128] The Italian-language socialist newspaper *Avanti!* called upon its readers to renounce "false prejudices and false pride of race," presumably because Italian workers were exhibiting such ideas. The paper also critiqued government policy for pitting workers against one another by excluding Afro-Brazilians from the city's labor market and hiring them only as strikebreakers, and then "presenting the conflict between strikers and strikebreakers as the result of 'color prejudice' among immigrant workers."[129] Yet racism and internationalism "co-existed uncomfortably" for Italian anarchists in the city.[130] In addition, Italian immigrants had gained a reputation among their fellow workers as willing to work under extremely harsh conditions. One incident in 1912 reflected popular ideas: "A black servant on a Campinas plantation, after being given an order which she considered beneath her station, retorted, 'what do you take me for, an Italian?'"[131]

São Paulo's elite, however, grew disappointed with its bargain. To them, these rebellious imported laborers were "parasites," "criminals," and "beggars"; "savages from Europe" who were "disloyal ingrates" and "anarchized labor"; and in 1927 they terminated the program.[132] The subsidized immigration and overall labor practices of the Brazilian government had ensured, however, that regardless of their poor reputation, Italians consistently received preferential treatment as whites over Afro-Brazilians. The Italian state also asserted its expatriates' whiteness when holding Brazilian authorities accountable for their inhumane treatment.[133] How Italian workers in Brazil (and Argentina) viewed themselves is harder to determine, but what is certain is that they were transnational subjects with ties to nation-states that were willing to exploit and criminalize them, while repressing their movements for social justice. But they were also powerful enough to position them in the racial hierarchy above those who were of indigenous and African descent.

New York City

Italian women's cultures of resistance in New York City would also be centered within the revolutionary industrial labor movement for the first two generations and take shape within a vibrant, multiethnic world of working-class political radicalism. The city was a logical destination for Italian immigrant women and men given the widespread availability of work. By 1880, New York was the second-largest city in the world following London with a population of 3.4 million, and a world center for banking, brokerage, railroads, oil, mining, wholesaling, importing, shipping, food processing, publishing, manufacturing, and real estate. Before 1880, most immigrants to New York City came from northern and

Italian immigrant woman at Ellis Island, ca. 1906–14. Augustus Sherman Photographs, William Williams Papers, Manuscripts and Archives Division, The New York Public Library, Astor, Lenox and Tilden Foundations.

western Europe. In the period from 1880 to 1914, however, close to 4 million Italians, and approximately 3 million eastern European and Russian Jews migrated to the United States—the vast majority entering through Ellis Island. These two groups became the largest in the city at this time, accounting for two-thirds of the foreign-born population, which composed close to half of the city's population by 1910. Smaller numbers of immigrants also came from Ireland, Germany, China, Japan, Jamaica, Puerto Rico, and Cuba, among other places, at this time and together transformed the city into one of the largest centers of diasporic radicalism and labor activism in the world. For Italians, New York became home to their largest settlement in North America, as the Italian immigrant population swelled from only 44,230 in 1880 to 145,433 in 1900, to 340,765 in 1910, and 390,832 in 1920.[134]

New York City was the preferred destination for Italian women by the early twentieth century. The production of garments was the city's largest industry, making it the fashion capital of the country and a center of the international garment economy. By 1899 the city was home to 65 percent of the women's clothing market and 27 percent of men's clothing market.[135] The garment industry recruited Italian women heavily, and in the 1900 census the top three occupations listed for Italian immigrant women wage earners in the city were tailoress, dressmaker, and seamstress, with cigar maker and silk mill operative in a distant fourth and fifth place.[136] Those designated as tailoresses worked in the men's clothing trade, while dressmakers worked in women's apparel, and seamstresses were typically pieceworkers (also called homeworkers) in both industries.[137] A wide range of other consumer goods' producers recruited Italian women, including artificial flower, candy, and paper box industries, because they too relied on low-wage labor.[138]

This concentration of Italian women within the city's manufacturing sector would have a profound impact on their consciousness, community formation, and political culture. To begin, it meant that the demographics of the Italian immigrant population in the New York metropolitan area differed from other parts of the country. While the ratio was only one woman to every two men in the rest of the United States, women composed close to half the Italian immigrant population in New York City.[139] The city also attracted a much higher percentage of immigrants who had labored as artisans or petty merchants in Italy because of the kinds of jobs that were available.[140] The Dillingham Immigration Commission reported that more than 90 percent of the Italian immigrant women working in New York City's garment trades by 1911 had worked in sewing, embroidering, or lace making in Italy before migration.[141] Those who had not learned to sew before were easily trained by female relatives and co-workers in the simple work of finishing garments, such as tacking, felling, or basting.[142] Migration to New York City thus offered the promise of acquiring the preferred status of artisan and abandoning the more dependant and stigmatized work of the peasant farmer. While some found work in high-end shops as custom tailors, the vast majority became factory operatives or home finishers, where the work was as menial as that which they had left behind, if not more so. Stories of newly acquired wealth from returning migrants enticed many to migrate, but the realities were far more complicated once they arrived. Maria De Luca, the dressmaker from Spinoza (Basilicata) who left for New York because of the stories of wealth she had heard from returning migrants, expressed the sentiments of many when she noted that had she known the realities and hardships that awaited her, she would have not migrated. Like many, the life she found was one of dilapidated and crowded tenements, and monotonous and poorly paid factory work.[143]

Former divisions between artisans and peasants gave way to new divisions as Italian women were twice as likely to work in manufacturing, and Italian men were four times more likely to work in the service sector.[144] This discrepancy reflected the preference that manufacturers and contractors had for hiring immigrant women and children, whom they could pay far less than men.[145] For example, of the 29,439 workers in U.S. dress and waist shops in 1913, 24,128 were women and 4,711 were men.[146] The proportion of Italian women working in the city's manufacturing sector outpaced other women as well. The 1900 census reported that 78 percent of Italian immigrant women wage earners in New York

City were employed in manufacturing, followed by 69 percent of Russian women, 40 percent of German women, 28 percent of Irish women, and 26 percent of native-born women.[147] By 1905 close to 80 percent of all Italian women working in the United States were employed in the fashion industries, which included garments, millinery, and artificial flowers.[148]

The numbers of women working in manufacturing corresponded to the timing of immigration because the industry relied on the steady displacement of old immigrant groups by the more recent arrivals. During the mid-nineteenth century, Irish and German immigrant seamstresses and tailors worked in the city's first clothing shops. But at the turn of the century, eastern European Jews and Italians entered the garment trades, just as clothing became the city's largest and most significant industry. For many decades, eastern European Jews were the most numerous in the industry. But by the 1920s, Italians became the largest group, though they were still concentrated in the lowest-paid jobs, and their numbers grew through the 1930s and 1940s.[149] By 1925, 64 percent of all Italian women in the United States (first and second generation) worked in the fashion industries; and by 1950, 77 percent of the immigrant generation and 44 percent of American-born generation were factory operatives, the majority in the needle trades.[150] For Italian immigrant women and their American-born daughters, industrial factory work and home finishing was a defining experience.

A Sweatshop in Every Kitchen

The arrival of a large body of workers who were desperate for jobs and familiar with needlework combined with technological advances at the end of the nineteenth century to bring dramatic shifts in production, most notably from custom- to ready-made clothing.[151] As the demand for ready-made garments grew, the industry became highly decentralized because new production processes required very little machinery. What emerged was an elaborate system of subcontracting in which manufacturers contracted work out to ethnic entrepreneurs who were almost always male and often Jewish immigrants themselves. They in turn hired women to finish the garments within their own homes or small tenement workshops. The sexual division of labor reserved the best-paid, high-status jobs for men, and the lowest-paid, most "unskilled" jobs for women, even though few jobs required specialized knowledge, extensive training, or physical strength.[152] As a result, Italian women entered the garment industry at the bottom of the ranks. By 1919, work in both artificial flowers and feathers—the lowest-paid work in manufacturing—had become known as "the Italian women's trade."[153] The Dillingham Immigration Commission noted the same for the garment industry, documenting how a "large number of contractors sublet their work to small groups or families who have one room or more in a house or tenement. These groups do the finishing and buttonhole work. This class of work is done almost entirely by Italian women."[154] Embroidery and lace making also relied heavily on Italian immigrant women. For example, in 1920 the International Ladies' Garment Workers' Union estimated that close to 80 percent of the ten thousand hand embroiderers in the city were Italian immigrant women, the majority of whom labored within their homes, adding elaborate embroidery to high-end clothing and textiles.[155]

Because this was the work that was open to them, Italian women turned their kitchens into factories. Homework was a necessity given how few well-paying jobs were open to them and the men in their families. "We all must work if we want to earn anything," one woman told an investigator. She, her three- and four-year-old daughters, and her mother, all worked together in their tenement on MacDougal Street, assembling artificial violets, while her husband worked as a porter.[156] The story was the same for most women of her generation. They collected bundles of partly constructed flowers, feathers, and clothes from subcontractors, at the agent's warehouse or local factory. Then, with the help of their children and other kin or neighbors, they finished the products at home—lining garments, sewing on buttons, trimming threads, pulling bastings by hand, pasting on petals, inserting pistils into stems—tasks that did not require any particular training or skill.[157] As one 1902 study of the industry noted, "Three-fourths of the women go for the work themselves, and it is common thing in these districts to meet Italian women on the street, balancing twenty pairs of pants on their heads."[158]

The experience of Maria Rosario was typical. She migrated from Naples to Greenwich Village with her large family when she was five years old, in 1909. As a child, she and her eleven siblings helped their mother with piecework by sewing ribbons and buttons on ladies' corsets. For one dozen corsets, they made six cents, and sometimes each child made two dozen corsets before heading to school in the morning. At night, they would pick up where they left off. As an adult, Maria continued to work in the industry, as an operator making slips, nightgowns, and corset covers.[159]

Given the limited range of choices, homework was a preferred option for several reasons. It allowed women to care for young children while they worked and to set their own production pace. The majority (two-thirds) did not speak English even after a full year in the United States, and unlike other jobs, such as domestic service, homework did not require proficiency in English.[160] Moreover, homework represented a "superficial approximation of an elevated social status"

Original caption reads: "Mrs. Mary Rena, 46 Laight Street, 3rd floor front, picking nuts with dirty baby in lap. Two neighbors helping. Girl is cracking nuts with her teeth, not an uncommon sight. Mr. Rena works on dock, New York, N.Y. 1911." Lewis W. Hine, Photography Collection, Miriam and Ira. D. Wallach Division of Art, Prints and Photographs, The New York Public Library, Astor, Lenox, and Tilden Foundations.

because it had been idealized work in southern Italy, where women tended to value artisan labor close to home over agricultural labor. It also "enabled these women to establish and maintain strong contacts with neighboring women who could in turn be a source of support for them in caring for children and securing other forms of aid."[161] It was highly exploitative, however. Women often had to work eighteen hours a day to earn four or five cents an hour. They labored in cramped, poorly ventilated, dimly lit tenement apartments that were often only two small rooms, and home to an average of five people.[162] Because homework was seasonal, "families had to maximize their wages in the rush period," which often meant working around the clock.[163] This was, of course, in addition to all of their unpaid domestic labor, not to mention the work they did keeping boarders, working as janitors, and the other work that occupied much of their day.[164]

Most parents were forced to pull their children out of school, because, as in Italy, their labor was necessary for the family to make ends meet. While many wished for a different life for their children, their meager wages necessitated child labor. American social workers and reformers often told of the many ways Italian families circumvented city officials and factory inspectors who attempted to shut down or regulate homework within their neighborhoods. As soon as an agent appeared on the block, word spread like wildfire through the tenements, and everyone hid their homework while the inspection was made.[165] Many of the legal measures and social movements that developed to regulate homework did not have much appeal to Italian immigrant women because they often restricted their ability to earn wages without providing better options. Informed as it was by middle-class bias, the movement sought not to resolve the problems as they were articulated by homeworkers but to address the needs of all others: to protect more established workers against homeworkers' underbidding and "cheapening" of work; to guard against the perceived immorality and ignorance of immigrant workers; to protect consumers from the contagious diseases many believed passed from immigrant workers through the clothing they produced; and to defend male breadwinning and the middle-class gender ideal of separate spheres. Rarely did social commentators express an understanding that homework was symptomatic of the gendered division of labor under industrial capitalism and a manifestation of women's subordinate position within the family, the labor market, and the nation-state.[166] This critique would come from the women workers themselves.

The Lessons of Factory Labor

Factory work taught women workers a powerful set of lessons, and they would use these to expose the power arrangements and ideological justifications that gave rise to their marginalized position within industrial capitalism. Homework often led to factory work, and children typically graduated from one to the other as they grew older. Theresa Albino's story captures what was common. Born in New York City to immigrant parents, Theresa began helping her mother make artificial flowers in their home when she was five, alongside her brothers and sisters. After completing sixth grade, she entered factory work because the combined wages from the homework and her father's wages as a day laborer were insufficient. At the age of fourteen, she became an errand girl in a neighborhood candy factory, and then a year later, a factory worker in artificial flowers in the same shop that supplied her mother with homework. Theresa wished to attend evening school, but she noted, "It was this way, when it gets busy in the trade we have to take work home, and I knew I would have to stop then, so what was the use of starting?" She also felt strongly that work conditions would improve only with effective unionization. But her most impassioned plea concerned her

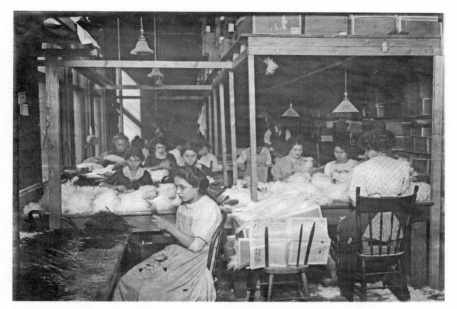

Making feathers, ca. 1907. Lewis W. Hine, Photography Collection, Miriam and Ira D. Wallach Division of Art, Prints and Photographs, The New York Public Library, Astor, Lenox, and Tilden Foundations.

mother. "My mother works all the time—all day, Sundays and holidays, except when she is cooking or washing. She never has time to go out or she would get behind in her work."[167]

For most women, factory work and homework were deeply connected and all consuming. According to the federal government's Dillingham Report, young women entered factories on average at the age of sixteen, and many stayed in the industry, alternating between homework and factory work, and often combining the two, throughout their lives.[168] Yet bosses and workers most likely lied about their ages to inspectors. Women tended to enter the same trades they had come to know as child homeworkers. Others, especially those across the Hudson River in northeastern New Jersey, worked as ribbon and broad-silk weavers, winders, and dyers in the textile industry, which also relied heavily on the low-wage labor of Italian immigrant women and children. Paterson, a city just twenty miles west of Manhattan, with a large Italian immigrant population at this time, became known as the "silk city" because it was one of the most significant capitals of silk production in the world. The ribbons, hat bands, and cloth that workers produced there were shipped to clothing manufacturers in New York City and

Weavers in a modern textile mill, Paterson, New Jersey, ca. 1913. American Labor Museum, Botto House National Landmark.

beyond.[169] In addition, smaller numbers of Italian women and men joined the agricultural labor force that provided the backbone to New Jersey's commercial farming industry.[170]

The conditions of immigrant women's factory labor during this period have been well documented. Whether they worked on sewing machines, looms, or by hand, women experienced the constant pressure to work as fast as possible because employers often compelled them to increase the pace so they might reduce the number of workers needed and generate more profit. In addition, "the materials that Italian women used in the shops were dangerous to their health. In paper box factories glue fumes caused nausea; in the flower factories the aniline dyes irritated throats and skin; and in the feather factories swirling fluff caused bronchitis, asthma, and eye disease. Many of the work materials were highly flammable, yet fire escapes were rickety and inaccessible."[171] Silk mills were not only very toxic places because of the poisonous substances used to dye cloth, but they were also intensely noisy places, with the "crashing, shattering noise of the looms," so that workers had to yell in each other's ears to communicate during work.[172] "I am working on a job that half kills me," one worker noted in the 1920s. "The clash of looms sounds like the gnashing of teeth in hell."[173] Exhaustion from standing, the routine bending over to complete tasks, eye strain from long hours of close work in poor lighting, long-term exposure to unhealthy work environments, and the routine sexual abuse and harassment of some bosses and male workers made factory work extremely dangerous and difficult.[174]

One Italian immigrant sewing machine operator recalled that "workers spent long hours in the shops in those days. They worked from eight in the morning to six o'clock at night, all day Saturday, and sometimes even on Sundays. They had no breaks and were given three-quarters of an hour for lunch. If they went to the bathroom, the boss kept count of how long they took. If they took too long, he would go to the bathroom door and knock. . . . They were not allowed to talk or laugh."[175] While the workday was legally set at sixty hours per week and ten hours per day, many worked much longer hours in these seasonal industries, because of the rush periods.[176] In the silk mills, Italian immigrant weavers and dyers complained of similar challenges. "If you were late five minutes you would be docked," one worker noted. "If you went to the toilet and stayed ten minutes you would be fired."[177]

Employers monitored women closely to maximize production and discourage collective action. Their efforts to prevent alliances among workers were notorious, leading labor economist John Commons to conclude, "The only device and symptom of originality displayed by American employers in disciplining their labor force has been that of playing one race against the other."[178] In addition to engineering ethnic conflict, manufacturers fined workers for being late, for talking, singing, and taking too much time in the bathroom, because these activities were commonly used by workers to organize. When women attempted to unionize, employers found additional methods of surveillance, including sending spies to union meetings to spot the "trouble makers" whose lives they would make "so unbearable, that the worker was forced to leave voluntarily, if not actually dismissed."[179] Italian immigrant women found many ways to contest capitalist labor discipline, or what they termed the *rigorosa sorveglianza* (rigorous surveillance) of employers, including unequal divisions of labor, dangerous work conditions, and the low quality of work they were forced to produce rapidly.[180] When they learned English, they critiqued the system with new words. "They were crooks," Carrie Golzio recalled of the men who ran the ribbon factory in Paterson, New Jersey, where she worked from age nine.[181]

To be sure, factory conditions varied considerably. Some worked in modern brick buildings with hundreds of other girls and women. Others worked in small, crowded tenement workrooms alongside boys and men. Most shops employed between fifteen and fifty workers, but the larger, more modern factories became common in the 1920s.[182] Because the silk and woolen industries were also highly decentralized, the workshops in Paterson, Passaic, Garfield, Lodi, Trenton, Union City, and West Hoboken, New Jersey, were also quite small, employing on average less than twenty-five workers.[183] In some shops "everyone from the owner to the errand girl was Italian, and that was the language of the shop." It was, however, more common for women to encounter workers from other parts of the world in the factory. Before World War One, Italian women in the garment trades most often worked alongside eastern European and Russian Jewish, Irish, and German immigrant women. In candy factories they worked with Jewish, German, Spanish, Hungarian, Swedish, English, and African American workers. In textiles, they shared workrooms with Armenian, Syrian, French, Belgian, and Dutch workers. In the 271 garment factories that Louise Odencrantz investigated, only hand embroiders labored in an ethnically homogeneous setting because Italian women composed 94 percent of that workforce. In garment manufacture, on the other hand, Italian women composed anywhere from 18 to 75 percent of the workforce, depending on the sector, whereas in flower and feathers, cigar, paper box, and textile work, they often composed only 30 to 40 percent of the laborers.[184]

Because most Italian women found jobs through family and friends and worked in factories located within or near their neighborhoods, factories were an important center of informal systems of female networking. Cramped working conditions encouraged women to develop relationships with co-workers, through which they learned transportation systems, how to communicate with employers and co-workers in other languages, and how to find childcare while they worked.[185] Women also relied on these networks to learn the rudiments of the trade, "so she did not feel as 'strange' as if she had been plunged into the midst of work," and "to make her clothes more presentable according to American standards, so she will look less like a new arrival."[186] In fact, some became quite skilled in the art of performance in order to secure work, including taking on new identities and passing for other immigrant groups. When Filomena Macari went for her job interview in a garment shop, she was told by her employer "not to tell anyone she was Italian because everyone in the shop was Jewish and they didn't want other groups there. She worked as an examiner for a whole year before she gave herself away. By that time, she was already known to be a good worker, and it didn't matter to them."[187] The fact that she could pass so effectively suggests her familiarity with Jewish culture and customs.

Overall, wage earning led women to develop new kinds of relationships, whether in factories or their own homes. As one reformer observed, it led "the woman from Naples to take her home work into the rooms of her Sicilian neighbor."[188] Many historians have richly documented the many ways Jewish and Italian women forged new kinds of relationships with each other as co-workers in the garment trades: they learned each other's languages, celebrated birthdays, baby showers, and weddings together, and organized the labor movement side by side. Scholarship on workplace relationships has also documented how prejudice and mistrust were worked out and confronted day-to-day. Rose Gorgoni's older sister lamented the behavior that her sister Rose was learning from the other woman at work: "She is always going into paper boxes or paper bags, and the girls use awful language in them places."[189] At the other end of the spectrum, women in the higher-end custom shops encountered the woman of wealth who "saunters into a shop, puts up her lorgnette, and lisps, 'I'd like to see something in a satin afternoon dress.'"[190] The world of manufacturing work introduced Italian women to new relationships and new experiences of distancing, intimacy, mutual aid, and mistrust.

FOLLOWING THE WOMEN as they became labor migrants reveals their location within globalizing capitalism and the complex, often hidden, processes by which they traversed oceans to enter factories halfway across the world. It also helps answer why Italian immigrant women's labor became invisible at the precise moment that it was so foundational to the global economic restructuring. This "fabricated absence" was the result of the ideological processes that developed to justify and rationalize their incorporation into various nation-states as low-wage, menial labor.[191] In order to redirect profits from the family economy to the pockets of capitalists and in service of middle-class consumers, women's traditional forms of labor were commodified. A wide range of images and discourses then emerged to construct Italian immigrant women as inherently docile yet strong bodies suited for the rigors of manufacturing labor, to legitimate their location as marginalized workers.

This history also reveals the profound contradictions at the heart of women's experiences: labor migration provided women with a chance to earn much-needed wages, contribute to their family economies, and enter new social worlds. But the work to which they were channeled was exhausting, debilitating, and demoralizing. It jeopardized their health and that of their families and subjected them to new, extreme forms of routinization, surveillance, and exploitation. All the while they were, for the most part, slandered in the popular media. In living these contradictions, they would pose a question that remains with us today: economic development at what cost?

The opening story within a story helps us to understand how this question emerged. Women contended with exploitive conditions by developing alternative ethical systems to repudiate, in the words of historian Dana Frank, "capitalist power, employer manipulation, and a largely hostile state."[192] Within these worlds of intensive menial work, a conversation took place, in which women developed a vision of themselves and the world around them that rejected the legitimizing narratives of their oppression. Such a vision developed through stories and discussions. It also resided within actions taken, as in the case of Philomena Cioffari, who flared up at her father when he suggested that she and her sister Flora did not belong in school because they were "stupid and could not learn anything." She exclaimed, "How could I when I had to work all the time?"[193] The radical subculture and union movement that Italian women would form in the New York metropolitan area drew such enthusiastic support because it provided a space for women to educate themselves and collaborate in developing a collective critique of power in all its manifestations. Of course, as Philomena's father's actions make clear, many immigrants also internalized oppressive narratives, and these too would shape their emerging political consciousness and activism. The process by which southern Italian migrant women were positioned within the U.S. racial order further reveals how their location within the emerging global capitalist economy as low-wage workers was justified with biological and cultural explanations that rationalized their subordination but also positioned them above other workers. This too would have a significant impact on their political cultures.

The Racialization of
Southern Italian Women

In Lewis Wickes Hine's classic photo, simply captioned "Italian immigrant, East Side, New York City, 1910," the female subject stands at the center of the frame, dexterously balancing a huge bundle of clothing on her head, heading to or from the garment contractor for whom, we imagine, she works as a home finisher. Off to the side, almost completely shadowed, is another woman; only the shape of her body and the basket balanced on her head are visible. The drama consists of a series of gendered contrasts: woman as manual laborer; woman as solitary in urban-industrial space; woman as present yet anonymous, visible but invisible; woman as the "boundary marker" between the so-called Old World and the New.[1] This photo captures how the U.S. middle and upper classes imagined southern Italian immigrant woman: she was a hardy but downtrodden peasant woman transposed onto the urban landscape, a nameless, faceless woman worker.

Such representations circulated widely through photographs, congressional and social scientific studies, and a wide range of popular culture in this period. Lewis Hine's photos, along with the photographs and journalism of Jacob Riis and others, have become emblematic of early twentieth-century immigration, and as such they continue to inform our collective memory of this past. They were popular because the poverty and supposed dexterity of Italian immigrant women served to assure American audiences not only that these women were uniquely suited for such work but also of *their own* relative freedom from such indignities. Such images also enabled a wide range of actors, including progressive reformers and labor leaders, to position themselves as the saviors and civilizers of such women, thereby absolving themselves of any role in their exploitation.

The position that Mary Kingsbury Simkhovitch took in her 1909 annual report as director of Greenwich House, the settlement house in one of the largest Italian

Italian immigrant woman carrying garment piecework, East Side, New York City, 1910. Lewis W. Hine, Photography Collection, Miriam and Ira. D. Wallach Division of Art, Prints and Photographs, The New York Public Library, Astor, Lenox, and Tilden Foundations.

immigrant communities in the city, illustrates the sentiments that were common for reformers of her generation: "It is the duty of American women, to stretch out their hands to these Italian sisters and welcome them to their coming independence by presenting to them larger ideals of life than those to which they have been accustomed; ideals of common interest, of public welfare, of social responsibility."[2] By identifying Italian immigrant women as deficient in such values and in need of instruction, middle-class and elite white women were able to assert their own superiority, and carve out a role within the U.S. nation-building project. As historian Louise Newman has demonstrated, "freeing themselves from the category of the protected and becoming protectors themselves" were among "the most effective ways that white, middle-class women began to assume political power without transgressing culturally prescribed notions of womanhood and civilized gender relations."[3]

But this was just one reason why these images circulated. By exploring a full range of characterizations that progressive reformers, social scientists, travel writers, journalists, politicians, and the business elite generated, we can trace why an image of Italian immigrant women as docile, dominated, and in need of rehabilitation emerged and understand the material consequences of such depictions. Because ideas concerning Italian women crossed national boundaries, images that emerged out of Italy's nation-building project informed perceptions and practices in the United States, where they changed to fit a different set of economic and political purposes. In Italy, representations of southern peasant women were firmly positioned within a virgin-whore binary. But in the United States, the idea of them as victims would assume primacy, in contrast to middle-class white womanhood, but also against Italian men, and especially in comparison with those working-class women who were racialized as unequivocally nonwhite. The charge of deviance would resurface, however, whenever Italian immigrant women contested their marginalization. While denigrated and exploited, however, Italian immigrant women never occupied the lowest social position in the United States. Rather, they were consistently situated as whites, albeit racially inferior whites, and therefore as deserving of rescue and inclusion in the nation.

In tracing this history, race emerges as relational and shifting, as a culturally defined category of difference that is manifested not only in ideas but in institutions and access to material resources.[4] For most southern Italian women, the categories of whiteness and blackness, northern Italian and southern Italian, civilized and primitive held very little (if any) meaning, as they climbed aboard steamships to traverse the ocean. Those with ties abroad through emigrant family members did receive some lessons about race in the Americas. For example, in the 1910s, Maria Goletto received letters from her husband Andrea, who worked as a miner in the U.S. West before settling in New York with his two brothers. She recalled, "He spoke of America and he always said that the blacks were good people."[5] His (and her) point in noting this suggests that race relations were an important part of the information that migrants relayed back home. But the precise ways in which race fractured life in the United States would become clear only to those who migrated and experienced it firsthand.

This chapter explores how a whole host of actors, on both sides of the Atlantic, racialized southern Italians in the first decades of migration and settlement. In these early years, the immigrant generation experienced the tangible material rewards of whiteness, even though it did not yet consciously embrace this status, and even as those in power adamantly called its assimilability into question. Ironically, the very practices that located southern Italians as inferior to northern and western Europeans *also* established their whiteness, and such practices were deeply gendered. As a result, in the decades following the First World War, Italian immigrants, and especially the first American-born generation, would come to insist on their whiteness and begin to collectively mobilize as whites.

Either Madonnas or Whores

The saying, "Europe ends at Naples. Calabria, Sicily, and all the rest belong to Africa," can still be heard throughout Europe.[6] Beliefs about the inherent racial inferiority of southern Italians infused Italian political debates following national unification in 1861. This preoccupation—also referred to as *la questione meridionale* (the southern question)—resulted in part from the history of subjugation of southern Italy on the part of northern elites and from resistance to that oppression.[7] As northern elites attempted to "make Italians" out of the new nation's subjects, they not only waged war on the South but sought "to separate out those who were incapable of such a conversion."[8] To many of Italy's state builders, the riotous peasantry's resistance to the nation (its taxes, conscription, and violent occupation) was proof of their savagery and backwardness.[9] As such, southern Italy became more than a geographic space with flexible boundaries—it can include or exclude Rome and Sardinia, for example. By the end of the nineteenth century it had become a metaphor for anarchy, rebellion, poverty, and the lack of civilization—all that was anathema to the emergent nation.[10]

As the northern bourgeoisie crafted a national identity from its history of medieval city-states, the Renaissance, and the "glory" of the Roman Empire, it sought to discipline the insurrectionary and "barbarous" South. Many of the government officials who traveled throughout the South following national unification commented on southern Italians' supposed racial inferiority. The senator Eugenio Faina, for example, noted that Sicily was unlike other regions in that it was "inhabited by rough people with primitive instincts."[11] As a result, the Italian state confronted southern resistance movements with martial law, violence, and by stigmatizing peasants "as criminal members of a racially inferior people who preferred the superstitions of religion to civiltà italiana."[12] As one government official wrote in 1861, "What barbarism! Some Italy! This is Africa: the Bedouin are the flower of civil virtue compared to these peasants."[13] Civilization, northern officials believed, would have to be imposed on southern peasants at gunpoint— "otherwise the tumour represented by the Southerners' behavior would grow and infect the rest of the nation."[14]

Government officials found support for these views from the new school of positivist anthropologists, including Cesare Lombroso (1841–1936), Guglielmo Ferrero (1871–1942), Alfredo Niceforo (1876–1960), Giuseppe Sergi (1841–1936), and Enrico Ferri (1856–1929). Together these men founded the field of criminology, providing "scientific proof" to support the ruling elite's beliefs in biological evolution and racial determinism. In particular, they advanced an argument that supported what many northern political leaders suspected: the darker "Mediterranean" southerners were not only racially distinct from the lighter "Aryan" northerners; they possessed "inferior African blood" and demonstrated "a moral and social structure reminiscent of primitive and even quasibarbarian times, a civilization quite inferior."[15] Southern Italy's history of Greek, Roman, Norman, African, and Arab invasions, and its location as a crossroads between Africa, Europe, and the East, they argued, had given shape to "a region that is *a priori* condemned to perpetual inferiority."[16]

Moreover, they posited that race was "fundamental to the etiology of crime in Southern Italy."[17] The father of the Italian school of criminology, Cesare Lombroso, first developed his belief that race could explain the poverty, disease, crime, and rebelliousness of the South while he served voluntarily as a medical doctor in the military campaign to quell peasant resistance in Calabria from 1859 to 1863.[18] In the following decades, his theories would gain international acclaim with the publication of several books and articles that advanced his beliefs in white supremacy, the inherent inferiority of women, and the notion that criminals were born, not made. Using the standard methods of scientific inquiry of his day, Lombroso and his colleagues substantiated their claims regarding racial and sexual difference by measuring crania, ears, foreheads, jaws, arms, vulvae, and other body parts, and by conducting tests on live subjects—including hooking hundreds of women up to electrodes to measure their sensitivity to pain. From such gruesome tests, they built elaborate typologies of deviant behavior based upon a constantly shifting racial classification.[19]

In the end, Lombroso and the other criminal anthropologists inadvertently proved the instability and social construction of race because their classifications were never consistent nor did they ever reach a consensus. Still, their ideas became widely influential. They were disseminated by popular magazines such as *Illustrazione Italiana*, which located "the South's position between Italy and the Orient, between the world of civilized progress and the spheres of either rusticity or barbarism."[20] They were also used to educate students who went on to serve in the prison and police bureaucracies and were often cited by political and labor leaders, as Antonio Gramsci exposed in his famous treatise *La questione meridionale* (The Southern Question).[21] Even southern intellectuals and political leaders essentialized the contrasts between the North and the South, and some of the leading criminologists, including Giuseppe Sergi and Alfredo Niceforo, were

Wilhelm Von Gloeden's portrait of a Sicilian girl, Taormina, 1914. Von Gloeden, a German aristocrat who relocated to Sicily in 1876 to recover from illness, became renowned for his erotic photographs of local girls and boys. They sold throughout Europe and the United States at the turn of the century, as ethnographic portraits of young Sicilian natives, helping to popularize notions of southern Italy as overly sensual and exotic. Alinari Archives, Florence, Italy.

Sicilian. There were some very outspoken opponents to the positivists, such as Gramsci, but most of Italy's political and intellectual leaders portrayed southerners as "culturally homogeneous and unchanging," if not racially distinct.[22]

These popular pseudoscientific racial ideologies were at all times mediated by modern bourgeois notions of gender and sexuality. As Anne McClintock has argued, the invention of race and the project of imperialism were "fundamental aspects of Western, industrial modernity." Because of this, gender, race, and class were (are) not distinct areas of experience. Rather, they "come into existence *in and through* relation to each other—if in contradictory and conflictual ways."[23] Italy's politicians, novelists, scientists, journalists, travel writers, and other popularizers of race discourse routinely made use of sexual idioms to feminize and sexualize the South. One of the most popular tracts on the "two Italies," *Contemporary Barbarian Italy*, published in 1898 by Alfredo Niceforo, called the people of Naples "dissolute and weak by nature," a "feminine people."[24] Similarly, Ippolito Nievo, a writer and member of the nationalist troops during the "liberation" of the South, expressed the opinions of many of his fellow soldiers when he wrote, "The Sicilians are all women; they have a passion for tumult and drama."[25]

The criminologists also argued that women's deviance differed from men's; and

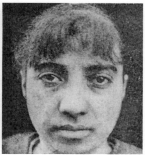

Cesare Lombroso's "Homicidal Women." Source: Lombroso, *Atlante*, 1897.

their studies on female criminal pathology advanced their belief that southern peasant women were naturally inclined toward crime, especially prostitution. To them, sexual deviance (which included homosexuality) was the result of madness, depravity, and poverty, each of which were considered inherent traits. In 1893, the same year the uprisings erupted across Sicily, Lombroso and Ferrero published these arguments in *La donna delinquente* (The Criminal Woman), one of their most influential texts.[26] This work advanced their elaborate typologies of criminal behavior, on the basis of a racial classification that divided Italy into three sections—the Semitic (Arab) South, the Latin Center, and the Germanic, Ligurian, Celtic, and Slavic North—with the South inferior to the rest of Italy.[27] It also proposed that southern Italian men, unlike their northern European counterparts, "were sexually precocious, wasting their lives in the pursuit and enslavement of women, rather than working for the 'advancement of society.'"[28] Thus, they eroticized the entire South and projected onto the region patriarchal power.

In addition, criminologists compared the faces of Italian prostitutes to what they called the "unfeminine faces" of the "savage races" (the "Red Indian" and "Negro beauties") to posit their "lack of maternal affection" because they believed that "sexual promiscuity was the predominant trait of 'savage' women."[29] This obsession with female deviance and its link to racial otherness was, as historian Sander Gilman writes, part of the process by which "The 'white *man's* burden,' his sexuality and its control, [was] displaced into the need to control the sexuality of the Other, the Other as sexualized female."[30] It also erased the violence of patriarchal relations. Instead, these scientists argued that women who murdered their fathers or husbands did so because of "an innate and blind savagery" and "insatiable egotism," rather than for any other reason such as self-defense.[31] Lombroso's comments on the photographs of three such "homicidal women" noted "swollen lips" and "deep furrows in her forehead" as evidence of innate criminality, without considering if this was the result of a lifetime of horrific abuse.

At the other end of the whore or savage trope was the contradictory trope of Virgin, Blessed Mother, or Madonna, which in Italian anthropological literature became the "tragic woman" who was also the selfless but hardworking *mamma*—or, in Lombroso's terminology, the "normal woman."[32] Lombroso's claim that "deviance in women was more often sexual than criminal" had a corollary: the supposed "organic passivity" of women. These two poles—promiscuous and criminal or maternal and passive—were of course foundational within Catholic ideology as well, and they echoed throughout much of the popular culture of the day. For example, northern European travel narratives found southern Italian women to be either "sinewy, indestructible old witches" or "irresistibly seductive."[33] Similarly, newspapers and novels often depicted the emigrant's wife as either a prostitute or a victim (the widow before her time and the mother left alone in her old age).[34]

Many feminist scholars have noted a curious coincidence: findings of anthropologists often reinforced and defended gender ideals just as women were challenging such standards en masse and becoming active within labor, feminist, and other liberatory movements. Philosopher Sandra Harding has illustrated that "the emergence of severe threats to the existing gender order are often followed by new scientific definitions of women's inferiority and deviance."[35] As such, these scientific studies offer a window into the troubled way many elite men greeted social change, including the rise of feminism and the movements for greater freedom among poor women.

These depictions have many historical counterparts, as the emergence of race science was rooted in the formation of nations in the eighteenth and nineteenth centuries. European and American elites built their national identities and crafted policies of expansion and world dominance upon the premise that their economic and political supremacy was not only providential but necessary for the spread of civilization.[36] In Europe and the United States, Africans, Asians, and Indians became "the quintessential zone of sexual aberration and anomaly." Moreover, "women served as the boundary markers of imperialism." The colonial fantasy of subjugation and exploitation was and continues to be premised upon the idea that "women are the earth that is to be discovered, entered, named, inseminated and, above all, owned."[37]

By the late nineteenth century, Lombroso and his colleagues in Italy produced hundreds of studies to support this ideology, arguing that the pathology of the "savage woman" was located in her anatomy. Their publications often included elaborate drawings that compared the "sexual anomalies" in the "primitive genitalia" of Italian prostitutes to African women.[38] In popular culture, these connections were often extended to all southern Italian peasant women. Travel writers routinely argued, for example, that southern Italian women "seem to favour that ideal of the Hottentot Venus which you may study in the Jardin des Plantes; they are decidedly centripetal."[39] The Italian ruling classes also drew these kinds of connections between Africans and southern Italians to justify two simultaneous military invasions—one in southern Italy and the other in Africa. In 1890, the same year that the North launched a brutal campaign to suppress antinationalist sentiment among peasants, Italy prepared to conquer Eritrea and join Europe in the colonization of Africa.[40] One contemporary observer noted, "They [southern Italian rebels] kill and rape like beasts thirsty for blood and booty and not men created in the image of God." Similarly, a government official conducting an inquiry into the southern resistance movement noted that, "in short, this is a country which ought to be destroyed or at least depopulated and its inhabitants sent to Africa to get themselves civilized!"[41]

The elite considered the anarchist movement, in Italy and abroad, to be the most dangerous form of political rebellion. This fear developed not only in response to the willingness of some anarchists to utilize assassination and bombing as political tools but also because adherents sought to overthrow the state and capitalism and thus attracted "a sizeable and militant following among the Italian working classes until the late 1920s."[42] The anarchist movement took hold in Naples and Sicily in the 1860s as a result of government repression and spread quickly because of its compatibility with peasant resistance traditions. Once the island was placed under martial law after the uprisings in the 1890s, those anarchists who did not languish in prison went underground and into exile.[43] Most went to the Americas to nurture a transnational movement in Buenos Aires, São Paulo, New York City, and Paterson, New Jersey, among other locales.[44]

To the criminologists, like most of the Italian elite, anarchism was merely a form of brigandage. Thus, they considered the popularity of anarchism as indicative of the inherent criminality and primitive nature of the southern peasantry. In this way, they helped "to formulate the definition of the political subject by elaborating ever more closely the criteria for political exclusion."[45] Enrico Ferri, for example, declared that it was possible "to delineate good idealist revolutionaries and sick rebels"—one struggled for the nation, the other against it.[46] Lombroso linked the Sicilian peasant rebellions of the 1890s with race, explaining that the epicenter of the movement was in the towns surrounding Palermo, because it was here that "the rapacious Berber and Semite tribes had their earliest and longest-lasting settlements and where anatomical types, customs, politics, and morality retain a clear Arab imprint." He pointed out that "the Arabs are a race of greedy conquerors who are hospitable but cruel, intelligent but superstitious, and always restlessly in movement. Their blood must play a role in fomenting spontaneous and implacable insurrections and perpetuating brigandage."[47] Consistent with his overall ideas about female criminals, Lombroso viewed southern Italian women rebels as the most abhorrent, noting "everyone agrees that the few violent women far exceed men in their ferocity and cruelty."[48] In this way, the Italian criminologists used political radicals as a "foil for defining the boundaries of nationhood and the shared characteristics of 'normal' citizens." Moreover, they offered "a scientific way to understand the failures of unification and a blueprint for disciplining groups that resisted integration into the new national culture."[49]

While this history resembled colonialism in many ways, scholars have illuminated some important differences.[50] For one, these racial theories, though influential, were never converted into a racial caste system in Italy.[51] Moreover, national centralization required mandatory conscription of all citizens, and southern Italians were enlisted to fight the wars of conquest in Africa. Thus, one way that southerners could become "civilized" was through adopting the identity and practice of the "new Roman Empire." This opportunity to participate in the drama of conquest offered southern Italians an even more "barbaric" Other from which to distinguish themselves. Yet this sort of racial positioning among the laboring classes did not fully develop until Mussolini took power in 1922 and used mass culture to popularize racist ideologies as he gained support for the invasion and attempted conquest of Ethiopia in 1935.[52] Before the twentieth century, if Italian peasants used the word *razza* (race) it was meant to signify a common social grouping such as a family, as in the Apulian saying, "Non ha pigghiate de la razza nostra" (She is not one of us), which was used to refer to someone "who rebelled against the established order of family life."[53] However, color and class were clearly connected for most Italians. Rosa Cavalleri, a gifted storyteller from the northern region of Lombardy who immigrated to the United States in 1884, tells of how she met her mother for the first time, an actress, "dressed up like the city" who had left her with nuns. Her mother refused to believe Rosa was her own: "It's impossible!" she cried. "She's got the brown skin of a peasant! *Gesù Giuseppe Maria*! I don't want some other! I want my own!"

Popular folklore, including songs, sayings, and stories, also resonated with such beliefs. Sicilian folklorist Giuseppe Pitrè recalled in this period, "Folk poetry, as an expression of feelings or natural inclinations, always celebrates blond women: and out of eleven cantos about this topic, only one celebrates black hair; the other ten sing the praise of the blonde color. Proverbs, which are formulas of truth and experience, agree with this ideal."[54] The categories of the elite were, however, largely unknown to many southern Italians before they migrated, even though they had profound implications for their daily lives. When asked by

American immigration authorities if they came from the North or South of Italy, many did not know.[55]

Becoming Racially Inferior Whites

At precisely the same time the scientific taxonomies of race collided with Western patriarchal and Christian gender ideologies, the exodus of millions from Italy's South began. As a result, the southern question informed American racial thought and policy. Just as the Italian middle and upper classes wrung their hands over the inability of insurrectionary and "backward" southern Italians to become national subjects, Americans grew equally anxious about their own nation's ability to absorb and assimilate these same people. A range of views emerged, from the paternalistic humanitarianism of social reformers to more "aggressive forms of coercion and racial nativism."[56] Alarmed by the massive influx of what many saw as hordes of "wretched, lazy, ignorant, and criminal dregs of the meanest sections of Italy," American social scientists and politicians turned to Italian positivists to argue that as racial "undesirables," southern Italians were a menace to the nation.[57]

U.S. authorities turned to the Italian criminologists as they crafted immigration policy, and their findings were widely translated and published in many of the most popular American magazines, newspapers, and academic journals. Some also gave speaking tours throughout the Americas to promote their ideas.[58] As early as 1899, the U.S. Bureau of Immigration adopted their framework and began classifying Italians as Northern or Southern on naturalization and census records. By 1907 the U.S. Immigration Commission further codified such distinctions, directly citing the research of Niceforo and Sergi, to distinguish Alpine (North Italian) from Mediterranean (South Italian) peoples. They, however, drew the line far more north than most positivist anthropologists, at the city of Genoa.[59] Moreover, they did not distinguish between women and men, and instead argued simply that while northern Italians were "cool, deliberate, patient, practical, as well as capable of great progress in the political and social organization of modern civilization," southern Italians were "excitable, impulsive, highly imaginative, impracticable," with "little adaptability to highly organized society."[60] This understanding, advanced in the Dillingham Report of 1911, would "become the centerpiece of immigration restriction debates culminating in the Johnson Act of 1921 and the more restrictive Johnson-Reed Act of 1924."[61]

Significantly, however, while the Dillingham Report reinforced the notion that southern and northern Italians were racially distinct, it denied any African origins for southern Italians. In part, this was because the report claimed "Aryan origins for Roman classical culture."[62] The closest U.S. government officials came to recognizing Africa in Italy was to note that southern Italians were "closely related to the Iberians of Spain and the Berbers of northern Africa." Citing Sergi's argument about southern Italian Hamitic stock, they noted that "the Hamites are not Negritic or true African, although there may be some traces of an infusion of African blood in this stock in certain communities of Sicily and Sardinia."[63] Others argued, like University of Chicago anthropologist George Dorsey, that southern Italians had a clear "Negroid" ancestry, and were "of questionable value from a mental, moral, or physical standpoint."[64] But, many of the most famous eugenicists would deny the African presence in Italy, because to assert that Italians were not white meant that "a good deal of Western civilization might not have been either."[65] While these ideas contrasted with the arguments set forth by many of the Italian criminologists, they were in fact compatible with those of Lombroso. He argued that southern Italians were racially inferior to northerners, but classified all Europeans, including southern Italians, as "whites" and argued that "whites were biologically and ethically superior to the darker races."[66]

The U.S. federal government's systems of classification fixed this scheme of southern Italians as racially inferior yet still white, into more concrete form. As historian Thomas A. Guglielmo has shown, on naturalization documents officials marked southern Italian immigrants in three ways: race, color, and complexion. Their race was always South Italian and their color was always white, even though their complexion was often listed as dark.[67] This conceptualization reflected the complexity of race in the early twentieth-century United States, and the way "human differences rooted in biological descent" were used to define the nation.[68] At the point of citizenship, Italians were thus marked as biologically distinct from Anglo-Saxons and other northern Europeans in that they were of the "South Italian" race and for the most part "dark." Yet, they were also "white" even though many Americans saw them, as one journalist noted, as "so swarthy," that their faces "might have been tanned with hemlock bark."[69] This categorization of "white" was not a physical description, however. Rather, it designated social location at a time when the color line was growing more rigid, in the post-Reconstruction period.[70] As historian Martha Hodes has noted, "To qualify for the designation of 'white,' no fractions of blackness were formally permitted."[71]

How did this location as racially inferior yet white at the same time affect Italian immigrant women? For one, the "color" designation of white provided access to citizenship because naturalization laws permitted that only whites and, after the Civil War, that "aliens of African nativity or persons of African descent" could become U.S. citizens.[72] Citizenship conferred to whites especially the ability to vote, own land, marry whomever one wished, and represent oneself in a court of law. Although Italian immigrant women did not have direct access to these privileges as women, they shared in the rewards of citizenship from their fathers, brothers, and husbands. The privileges of whiteness also extended beyond citizenship to inform Italian immigrant women's everyday lives in a whole host of ways. Whether at the job, in their neighborhoods, or in their homes, they encountered a world in which race mattered. A wide range of Americans, including reformers, social scientists, politicians, journalists, and average citizens, referred to each of these spaces as they gathered evidence of southern Italian racial inferiority. But in these same discussions they also established Italians' whiteness, and it was in these very places that Italians began to learn that they were white.

Degraded Labor

The realm of labor offered Italian immigrant women a daily sense of their particular location in the United States social order. Because they entered the city's clothing trades at the very bottom of the ladder, as homeworkers, their work became synonymous with poverty and degeneracy. At the time, the government estimated that Italian immigrants did 98 percent of the homework in the city.[73] Most were married women with young children, between the ages of twenty-one and forty-five, with an average age of thirty-four.[74] Therefore, this widespread concern over sweatshops fixated on Italian immigrant mothers' wage labor as the very epitome of social disorder. As such, homework became "an emblem of workers' foreignness and poverty."[75]

Part of what was so deeply troubling to factory inspectors, social reformers, journalists, politicians, and other observers, was their belief that Italian immigrants lacked the proper boundaries between work and home, public and private, male and female. The treasured middle-class ideal of separate spheres became the measure of a civilized society even though such boundaries were wholly impossible within most working-class families and communities. Because the garment industry had expanded before the extensive development of public transportation, factories sprung up within residential neighborhoods. Manufacturers also relied on the close proximity of workers to fill their factories, and they cut costs even further by sending work into immigrant homes.

Because of this, the early twentieth-century garment district was located below Fourteenth Street, within Italian and Jewish immigrant neighborhoods.[76] Census records reveal that a full 94 percent of Italian immigrant women living in the Italian section of Lower Manhattan (Elizabeth, Mulberry, and Mott Streets) worked as homeworkers in the neighborhood's garment industry.[77] The artificial flower,

feather, and paper box trades were located in the Italian immigrant neighborhood in Greenwich Village, along Barrow, Bedford, Carmine, and MacDougal
Streets. In Italian Harlem and the Upper East Side, Italian women tended to wil-
low plumes and roll cigars in addition to finishing garments.[78] On one block in
Harlem, for example, between Second and Third Avenues, eighteen factories or
shops both employed women and supplied them with homework. As one social
worker noted, "The streets and stoops are full of ostrich feather refuse, the stairways are littered and the air full of feather particles. The houses are filled with
homeworkers, regardless of license."[79]

Those Americans who extolled the virtues of Italian immigrants often objectified them by focusing on two qualities: their attributes as low-wage workers and sexual exotics. In the words of Senator Chauncey Depew, president of
the New York Central Railroad, "their frames are muscular and lithe; they are
black-haired and darkish-skinned; the men are bearded, and the women often
comely."[80] In one of many guided tours of "Italian Life in New York" to appear in
the print media, Charlotte Adams, a regular writer for *Harper's Magazine*, treated
her middle-class audience to tales of the "swarthy Italian" workmen and their
"brown-skinned" wives.[81] Adams was of the opinion that Italian women could become "future citizens of the republic," though this rested on an image of them as
childlike—"a little kindly guidance and teaching can mould them into almost any
form," she noted. Like many others of her generation, Adams identified southern
Italian women's most important virtue as their ability to work. In describing their
labor in low-wage jobs, not only as rag pickers but as embroiders, lace makers,
and seamstresses, she noted that they were "especially fitted for this department
of industry; indeed, their quick instinct for beauty shows itself in every form of
delicate handiwork."[82]

A range of commentators echoed these reports, to argue that Italian immigrant women, when compared to Jewish women, were "less ambitious," more
"ready with their fingers," "quieter and steadier," and more exploited by their own
men.[83] In *McClure's Magazine*, for example, the popular writer Elizabeth Shipley
Sergeant informed her middle-class audience that Italian men put their wives
to work because "the habit of familial labor is ingrained in his race and creed."
Therefore, "the custom persists in spite of changed surroundings and conditions."[84] Factory inspectors also recounted tales of the Italian immigrant wife who
was "busy plying her needle," while her husband was "less energetic" in his search
for work, wasting money on drink while the house and children were "neglected
and filthy."[85] In this way, Italian immigrant women workers were imagined both
as victims of their own cultures *and* as uniquely qualified toward performing the
least skilled and most degraded forms of industrial labor.

By conflating the workers themselves with the conditions of their work, anti-sweatshop language typically naturalized Italians' subordinate location within the labor market, while also positioning them as in need of rescue. The shifting of blame to the immigrants themselves was quite common (and remains so) because it did not require accountability from those in power—business owners, politicians, and others from the middle- and upper-classes who benefited directly from low-wage immigrant labor. Jacob Riis, to cite one very popular example, took his middle-class readers into the garment sweatshop district on the Lower East Side in his classic exposé *How the Other Half Lives*, first published in 1890. Inviting his audience to glance into this sordid world from the safe distance of the Second Avenue elevated trains, he described the following scene: "Men and women bending over their machines, or ironing clothes at the window, half-naked. . . . The road is like a big gangway through an endless workroom where vast multitudes are forever laboring."[86] The image of scantily clad, "swarthy" women and men laboring together in cramped quarters reinforced for many the "moral evils," "promiscuity," "contagious diseases," and other dangers that arose from sweatshop work. Popular magazines such as *Harper's Weekly*, *Charities*, *Nation*, and *McClure's* also supplied a constant stream of similar stories. Together they associated the dangers of the sweatshop with immigrant workers themselves, marking both as sites of disease, filth, racial degeneration, gender disorder, and sexual transgression.[87]

While Italian immigrant women's work generated a great deal of concern and antipathy, it did not provoke the kind of hostility and close scrutiny that white Americans directed toward Chinese immigrant women or African American women, both of whom were concentrated in even lower-paying, lower-status jobs, in domestic and service trades, and were largely excluded from all manufacturing jobs, including the most degraded jobs as homeworkers. Moreover, while Italian immigrant women were constructed as "poor helpless, ignorant foreigners" in desperate need of uplift, African American women, Chinese immigrant women, and other women of color, were more often described as "agents of moral decline and decay."[88] Even in the discourse on Italian criminality, here too there was a marked difference between the ways Italian immigrant women and those women deemed unequivocally nonwhite were cast. This too would have tangible, material consequences.

Crime Stories

In the United States, as in Italy, arguments concerning southern Italian inferiority often rested on claims of their innate criminality. Americans learned about southern Italian resistance to national unification from the elite, in daily news-papers and magazines. Mass migration, many feared, would cause U.S. cities to become "infested" with these "terrorists" and "thieves."[89] The Dillingham Com-mission and local city officials also warned that southern Italian immigrants were "apt to be ignorant, lazy, destitute, and superstitious," with a strong tendency toward "violent crimes."[90]

Such ideas circulated in the most popular daily newspapers, magazines, and academic journals, and by the beginning of the twentieth century Italians were largely depicted in American popular culture as hot-blooded "Latins" who were innately "unruly, violent, dangerous, or anarchistic."[91] In 1890 a well-known Shakespearean scholar, writing for the *Popular Science Monthly*, posed the ques-tion "What Shall We Do with the Dago?" He then painted a cannibalistic picture of "stiletto-wielding dagoes . . . as familiar with the sight of human blood as with the sight of the food [they] eat," who collected bones "and boiled them for their soup! What terror have jails and prisons for such human beings?" He concluded by noting that Italians, as "a people so brutish were unassimilable; they must be excluded from the virtuous American midst."[92]

Likewise, the renowned sociologist Edward A. Ross published a series of ar-ticles for the magazine *Century* in 1913 and 1914 in which he referred to Niceforo's work to argue that southern Italians were by nature "passionate" and "vindictive." They were, he argued, of "the long-head, dark Mediterranean race, with no small infusion of Greek, Saracen, and African blood in the Calabrians and Sicilians," and those from Naples revealed "a distressing frequency of low foreheads, open mouths, weak chins, poor features, skew faces, small or knobby crania, and back-less heads."[93]

Such ideas were further sensationalized in the relentless reporting on orga-nized crime in the city's print media. By the 1890s the most popular newspapers and magazines carried daily stories of the Sicilian mafia, the Neapolitan camorra, and the Calabrese 'Ndrangheta.[94] In just three years—from January 1908 to De-cember 1910—close to six hundred reports of the Italian "Black Hand" appeared in the *New York Times* alone. Thus began America's fascination with Italian mobsters. The city's newspapers turned organized crime into the single-most defining feature of Italian immigrant neighborhoods for outsiders. Several times a week, if not daily, headlines painted a grim picture of life in these communi-ties: "Black Hand Crimes Doubled in Year," "Dynamite Threat in Black Hand Plot," "Wholesale Murders," "Murder in Cold Blood," "Black Hand Bomb Im-perils Scores," "Black Hand Steals Four-Year-Old Girl," "Black Hand Sends Many Recruits Here," and "New York Is Full of Italian Brigands."[95]

Many stories ran on the front page, complete with lurid details of the grisly crimes that were allegedly a common feature of life in these communities. Tales of bomb-throwing, kidnapping, beating, stabbing, murder, arson, blackmail, and extortion marked southern Italians as savage, bloodthirsty, prone to violence, and therefore a peril to the nation. Many were sure, as one reporter noted, that "most of their fights and deeds of violence have been confined among themselves and have been due generally to old feuds and quarrels over the gambling trade."[96] Others pointed to the *padrone* system as an extension of this activity—the system of bosses who advanced emigrants their passage to the United States against their wages with high interest. In this world, they noted, "power was invested not in institutions, but in tough, well-networked individuals."[97] As cultural critic George De Stefano has argued, this "unorthodox route to upward mobility" both terrified and fascinated Americans.[98]

In the vast majority of these stories, the criminals were male while women figured almost entirely as victims or passive bystanders. Even accomplices (the wives or partners of "Black Hand bandits") were imagined as innocent.[99] Such characterizations were reinforced by another set of narratives that reached their apex at this same time—those of "white slavery." Indeed, the two overlapped, and many believed Italian mobsters to be "white slavers."[100] This panic manifested in many ways—in motion pictures, plays, novels, and news stories. But fears of white slavery generally centered on the idea that African American and immigrant men were forcing native-born white or European immigrant women into prostitution. As many historians have shown, this early twentieth-century obsession with coercive prostitution was one way in which native-born white middle-class Americans expressed their anxieties about the monumental changes taking place in this period. Thus, for the most part, the villains were Jewish, French, Italian, Chinese, and African American men.[101] Regardless of the group, however, the narratives "inevitably contrasted the helpless, tricked woman with the heartless, greedy man."[102]

The women in the stories differed dramatically, however. European immigrant women were always "white slaves" (without reference to the internal hierarchy of "Anglo-Saxon," "Teutonic," "Mediterranean," and the like that framed contemporary debates), whose presumed sexual innocence and vulnerability entitled them to both public sympathy and protection from abuse. Chinese immigrant women, on the other hand, were always "yellow slaves." As members of a group formally excluded from the United States on racial grounds, they were subject to particularly virulent forms of repression because all Chinese immigrant women were seen as "a depraved class."[103] As such, they were depicted as savage and viewed with suspicion, even when seen as victims. Moreover, anti-Chinese sentiment was converted into a host of state and federal laws, such as California's "Act for the Suppression of Chinese Houses of Ill Fame" (1866), the Page Law (1875), and the Chinese Exclusion Act (1882). These forms of exclusion and spatial containment were part of the "dense transnational network of surveillance, judgment, and documentation, which would later be applied to monitor and control other Chinese migrants destined for the United States."[104] Similarly, narratives of prostitution almost always constructed African American women as a sexual threat, "the sexually licentious Jezebel," and rarely as victims.[105] Such ideologies materialized into an array of institutions and public policy, including vice commissions, "social hygiene" organizations, the feminist purity movement, reformatories for "delinquent girls," and regulatory laws such as the Mann Act (1910), also called the White Slave Traffic Act.[106] In this way, the race and gender identities, categories, and hierarchies that white slavery narratives produced became concretized to powerfully shape daily life. Because, as historian Kevin J. Mumford has noted, "the worthy fallen woman was coded as white," the white slavery crusade "diverted attention, and resources, away from the social issue of black female prostitution" and cast black women as undeserving of legal protection.[107] As a result, the crusades were central to "making the demarcation between 'colored' and 'white' more absolute."[108]

A pivotal article on white slavery in the city by investigative journalist George Kibbe Turner in a 1909 issue of *McClure's* illustrates the way this discourse constructed Italian immigrant women. Turner argued that the procurer "in the past was almost always Jewish; now the young Italians have taken up the business in great numbers."[109] He told of "young peasant girls" who were induced to migrate from Italy with the promise of marriage, only to be sold to dealers upon arrival. A "no more melancholy feature was discovered," he noted, "than that of the little Italian peasant girls, taken from various dens, where they lay, shivering and afraid, under the lighted candles and crucifixes in their bedrooms. Fear is more efficacious with this class than any other, because of the notorious tendency of the low-class Italian to violence and murder."[110] In response to Turner's article, a special grand jury, headed by John D. Rockefeller, investigated his allegations that local immigrant politicians were facilitating the trafficking of prostitutes from Europe.

As with narratives regarding women's homework, news reports consistently constructed an image of Italian women as oppressed by Italian men, who were both lazy and violent. Indeed, one of the dominant images that would emerge from most of the city's English-language press was that of Italian men who were unwilling to work, abusive, and negligent in their role as providers. A characteristic story is that of the "white slave" Mamie Provenzano, who the *Times* celebrated for killing her "master" Marino Marinelli. As with many of these stories, the paper offered a full description of her as "slender, pretty, with snapping black eyes that defiantly braved the police who arrested her." She told police that she had been betrayed by her lover, who "tried to make me do things I didn't want to do."[111] Another typical story was that of Rosa Graziano, who shot and killed her abusive husband: "Bride of Nineteen says Graziano Wanted Her to Live Shamefully That He Not Need Work."[112] Certainly there were some men who were violent, abusive, and unwilling to work, but news reports and scholarly writing fixated almost solely on this image.

Because of this conflation of Italian men with laxity, those spaces devoted to their leisure, such as the saloon and dance hall, came under attack for enabling transgressive (including interracial and homosexual) relationships and politics and for encouraging laziness and drunkenness.[113] Like the anti-sweatshop movement, which focused on the workplace as a site of transgressive behavior, vice commissions targeted saloons.[114] However, Italian men were never policed in the same way as Filipino, South Asian, Japanese, and Chinese immigrant men or African American men. Rather, popular anxiety focused for the most part on their treatment of the women and children in their *own* ethnic communities.

A story from the *New York Times* captures how these many themes operated together. This fictionalized account, written in 1903 by Minnie J. Reynolds, a suffragist from Colorado and society editor at the *Rocky Mountain News*, began with a tongue-in-cheek title, "A 'Quiet Week' in Rural Italy." Her story centered on a married middle-class white American couple vacationing in a rural Italian farmhouse but was told from the perspective of the husband, a "money-making New Yorker." In addition to finding "great vineyards sweeping all around, orange and fig trees about the house, chestnut and sycamore trees off on the hillside," the husband happened upon "the most beautiful girl; brown velvet skin, black velvet eyes, cameo features, a perfect type of South Italian beauty." Yet, he observed, "She looked rather sad to me." He supposed that it was the result of her "being oppressed or constrained in some way by the old people." Then, he learned that it was because she had fallen in love with a member of the *camorra* who "had no trade, he was never known to work." When the girl had learned of his dark secret, she grew terrified. Her cousin had married a *camorrista*, who "had beaten her frightfully, and forced her to support him in ways that won't bear describing." To lift her spirits, the American couple invited the girl to attend the Feast of the Madonna del Carmine in Naples. While there, a *camorrista* lunged at the girl and slashed her face until she was "absolutely drenched in blood." After taking the girl to the hospital, the vacationing husband and several other American men found and beat the attacker because, he noted chivalrously, "that was what Americans did to people who cut women's faces open with razors."[115] This combination of imagery—the exotically beautiful, innocent, victimized girl who is rescued by the chivalrous white American men and defended against the savage, oppressive, cruel men of her own community—would inform most narratives of Italian immigrants in American popular culture.

The notion that Italians had a propensity for violent crimes extended to women as well, and their criminal activities also appeared in the press.[116] However, these stories generally assured the public that such acts were of a personal nature and not linked to organized crime. Some depicted stiletto-wielding women who were driven to bloodshed at the slightest provocation. Yet most stories told of women turning on one another in acts of revenge or jealousy, reinforcing the notion that southern Italians were a people consumed with drama and passion.

On occasion news stories told of native-born Americans who were the target of Italian women's wrath, and these hint at the ways women asserted their own subjectivity in such encounters. One typical story described a Paterson, New Jersey, judge, James F. Carroll, who allegedly noticed two Italian women gathering dandelions in a lot with knives in their hands as he was driving home. The paper reported that he stopped his car and "spoke sharply to the women" because "there had been several complaints about the Italians picking greens." In response, the paper reported, the women "grew angry and began to brandish their knives menacingly." Before long, a rumor spread that the judge had been attacked by anarchists; perhaps because one of the women, Mary Caminita, shared the same last name as Ludovico Caminita, an anarchist newspaper editor in Paterson.[117] Another example is the reporting on a "riot" that took place in 1911 during a murder trial. Women were apparently a conspicuous presence in the courtroom, and described as "swarthy complexioned Italian women, with flashing eyes, disheveled hair and muttering lips. Many of them gesticulated violently from time to time, making threatening motions."[118] Stories like this suggest how these many images converged: newspapers depicted southern Italian immigrant women both as victimized by their men and as more violent, passionate, and prone to crime than other white women. Overall, the notion that Italians were a vindictive, dangerous people, with a penchant for *vendetta* and anarchism, sold newspapers and captivated the American public.[119]

Swarthy Slums

Crime stories worked to establish the city's moral geography by marking Italian neighborhoods, and therefore Italians themselves, as shadowy, immoral, unsafe, and vice ridden. Other narratives about Italian enclaves supported these assumptions, to further position southern Italians as racially inferior. Many Americans became acquainted with Italians from journalists, novelists, playwrights, photographers, and other social investigators who acted as tour guides and "tramp ethnographers."[120] Jacob Riis was one of many popular writers to regale popular audiences with tales of the "swarthy Italian immigrant" neighborhoods.[121] The Mulberry Street district fascinated his readership because it was one of the largest immigrant "slums" in the city and was synonymous with poverty, overcrowding, crime, filth, disease, and transience. The district was about two-thirds Italian and one-third Irish in the 1890s, but ten years later Italians outnumbered all other groups, composing close to 87 percent of residents. A densely populated neighborhood, 35,420 people called this 104-acre district home (an average of 339 persons per acre) by 1900. Only ten years later, the number had climbed to 110,000.[122] Italian residents also spilled over into neighboring African American, Chinese, and Jewish communities, and into the multiethnic Five Points district (Sixth Ward) to the south; also called the "bloody sixth" by New Yorkers for its reputed gang violence.[123] As with most of the city's working-class neighborhoods of first settlement, the Mulberry district was in constant flux, as many settled here briefly before moving on to the other two large Italian neighborhoods in Manhattan's East Harlem and Greenwich Village.[124]

In *How the Other Half Lives* (1890), Riis described the "Mulberry Bend" district as a "suburb of Naples," a "purgatory of unrelieved squalor" and "an inferno tenanted by the very dregs of humanity."[125] The book went through eleven editions in five years, becoming one of the most significant ways that Americans learned about Italian immigrants.[126] Some took issue with Riis for being too picturesque. In one letter to the editor at the *Times*, a certain J.F.F. argued that Riis too often used "a rose-colored glass." On his own trip into Harlem's Italian neighborhood, he found "reprehensible neglect of the commonest laws of decency. Beer and tobacco, garlic and filth, quarrel and stiletto, noise and noxious odors alternate and fill up the gamut of these people's lives, to the disgust and weariness of soul of all near-by people who have a fractional claim to respectability and culture." He took particular issue at being spat upon from a second story window by "these quasi-savages," suggesting that some of the residents resented his presence there as well. "What can be done to stop the advance of this octopus of sensuality and filth?" he implored his fellow Americans.[127]

Such views were largely the norm in this period as many Americans came to see Italians as "vicious, ignorant, and degraded . . . so vicious, so depraved they hardly seem to belong to our species," and their neighborhoods as a site "where the scum collects."[128] Like the factory inspectors and government officials who condemned workers themselves for the conditions under which they labored, many located the source of degradation in the occupants themselves: "The Italian comes in at the bottom, and in the generation that came over the sea he stays there. . . . [he] is content to live in a pig-sty and submits to robbery at the hands of the rent-collector without murmur."[129]

These stories also conjured the same images of Italian gender relations that commonly circulated in crime stories and sweatshop inspection reports: "Down the street comes a file of women carrying enormous bundles of fire-wood on their heads, loads of decaying vegetables from the market wagons in their aprons, and each a baby at the breast supported by a sort of sling that prevents it from tumbling down. The women do all the carrying, all the work one sees going on in the 'Bend.'" Meanwhile, "the men sit or stand in the streets, on trucks, or in the open doors of the saloons smoking black clay pipes, talking and gesticulating as if forever on the point of coming to blows."[130] Italian men often appeared as "hot-headed" and consumed by "bad passions," while Italian women appeared largely as "faithful wives and devoted mothers."[131]

Such stories also stigmatized interracial relationships in these multiethnic neighborhoods. The murder of an Irish immigrant woman at the hands of her Italian husband was common fare. In one of these many stories, what infuriated the reporter was not the man's history of domestic violence, but that the couple were "living in a dirty, miserable room in the rear of the first floor of No. 95 Crosby Street, which is the joint habitation of filthy Italians and dissolute colored women."[132] Italians themselves would internalize these stigmatized views of their neighborhoods, and it was common for children to tease one another with the statement: "What, are you from Mulberry Street?"[133]

In addition to crime, overcrowding, and filth, Italians were also perceived as extraordinarily "clannish."[134] As with all Italian neighborhoods, the Mulberry district was composed of enclaves of people who came from the same region or village, and sometimes the same *cortile* in Italy. Neapolitans settled along Mulberry Street between Canal and Broome Streets, generally according to village and province. Calabrians lived on Mott between Grand and Broome. Abruzzesi settled on upper Mulberry Street near Spring Street. Immigrants from one particular village in Apulia settled on two blocks along Hester Street between Mulberry and Elizabeth. Those from Basilicata settled on Mott Street between Prince and Houston. Genovesi settled on Baxter Street in the Five Points Area, while Sicilians made Elizabeth and Prince Streets home.[135] The large Italian neighborhood uptown, in East Harlem, was considered the city's "Little Italy." Here, Neapolitans settled from 106th to 108th Street; those from Basilicata lived between 108th and 115th Streets; Calabresi lived on East 109th Street; and some streets, like 112th and 107th, were home to immigrants from specific villages or neighborhoods of Bari, Palermo, and Naples. As many scholars have noted, migration "helped keep alive the localism Italian nationalists sought to overcome."[136]

To most Americans, however, these residential patterns were further evidence of Italian difference; and Italians became famous among sociologists for showing "perhaps the strongest wish to remain in solitary communities."[137] Neighborhoods were not nearly as homogeneous as they imagined. For example, in the mostly Irish and German Hell's Kitchen, on one block, social investigators counted 38 Italian heads of household, amidst 139 Irish and 115 German.[138] However, social scientists obsessed that Italian neighborhoods were too "Old World" and thus perpetuating what they saw as un-American habits and mores. Some considered such patterns as rooted in economic exploitation, because Italian immigrants could afford rent only in the poorest neighborhoods.[139] But most observers saw Italians as among the "lowest class of immigrants" with living standards that were so low, "they have no appreciation of civilization and show little desire to adopt American customs" because "their aim in coming to the United States is to earn enough money to assure them of a comfortable existence after their return home."[140]

The Dillingham Commission confirmed such suspicions when it found that only 23 percent of Italian men and 5 percent of Italian women were able to communicate in English in 1911. Other studies revealed that even by World War I, 75 percent of Italian immigrant men and the vast majority of Italian immigrant women married those of their own nationality.[141] Leonard Covello, an immigrant himself, as well as an educator and community leader in East Harlem, tried to explain this resistance to assimilation, noting that "these ancient customs and practices were survivals, not merely as symbolical residues of the past."[142] Yet, as today, most saw this commitment to the homeland, its languages and cultures, as inconsistent with American values.[143]

Such transnational connections remained strong into and beyond the 1940s and thus became a primary marker of Italian immigrant otherness. One researcher, who in 1920 interviewed two hundred families from Cinisi, Sicily, living along East 69th Street in Manhattan, found that "people do exactly as they did in Cinisi." As with many observers, he centered on the policing of women as indicative of "Old World" ways: "A woman bought a pair of silk stockings and the neighbors talked so much about her that her husband ordered her to take them off." Furthermore, "The town of Cinisi is forever on their minds: 'I wonder if I can get back in time for the next crop?'—'I hope I can get back in time for the fiesta ...' The Cinisi group are more interested in Cinisarian politics than in American."[144]

Italians maintained connections to the homeland through patterns of settlement but also by the high rates of repatriation and low rates of naturalization. A government report in 1911 found that of all the immigrant groups who could become citizens of the United States, Italians were the least likely to naturalize. Even among those who had been in the country the longest (ten or more years), only 17 percent had become citizens. By 1920 another government survey revealed that only 31 percent of Italian-born men and 27 percent of Italian-born women in New York had become citizens.[145] This reluctance to naturalize signifies the complexity of southern Italian immigrant political identity in this period. Donna Gabaccia has argued that "migration probably allowed some immigrants the important illusion that they had successfully escaped the state: gone were the taxes, the draft, and the overbearing elite officeholders of Sicilian towns." It was only when immigrants had an investment—whether personal, economic, or political—that they considered becoming citizens.[146] This would not develop en masse until the migration flows were brought to a virtual halt with restrictive legislation in the 1920s. Moreover, the emergence of the modern welfare state as a result of the Great Depression gave new incentive to becoming a citizen. In earlier years, however, the vast majority of Italian immigrants remained deeply connected to their homelands, culturally and politically. Moreover, their experiences in Italy had taught them to evade the state at all costs. While identities as "workers of the world" would lead to the formation of transnational social movements against global capitalism and the state, it also made Italian workers even more attractive to U.S. business leaders who hoped that their cheap labor and transience would keep them uninvolved in U.S. political parties and labor unions.

Despite widespread opinion that Italians were undesirable, with "disgusting habits and homes," they were classified with other Europeans, even when considered "the lowest class." At the other end of the spectrum were "the Chinese, the negroes, and the Indians," as one sociologist put it. These groups were "forcibly and legally segregated" in separate neighborhoods and on reservations, and considered "non-assimilable" in the eyes of most social scientists.[147] Italians like Jews were criticized for sticking with their own, but their movement outside the ethnic enclave was "hailed as a sign of their Americanization and racial progress."[148] In contrast, the confinement of these other groups led to elaborate forms of policing to keep them contained to particular areas.[149] Because Italians were viewed as assimilable, they became a focal point for social reformers, and many saw immigrant women as central to this process.

Americanization Campaigns

Those who saw themselves in charge of Americanizing Italian immigrants concentrated their efforts on women and children, because they considered them to be overly, even dangerously, rooted in the traditions, rituals, and communities of their homelands, and the primary mediators of cultural change. Thanks to the rich archival materials and published primary sources on this history, many historians have documented how middle-class female reformers challenged Victorian-era gender norms with their commitment to women's education, philanthropy, and professional careers over heterosexual marriage and children. Many formed lifelong partnerships with women, devoted their energies to social service, and became active in the movement for women's rights. In such endeavors, most blended "religious conviction (the ideal of Christian evangelical benevolence) with science (social evolutionary theories) and political ideology (progressivism)." As a result, they created "new roles for themselves that explicitly maintained the racial hierarchies that were based on the presumption that Anglo-American Protestants were culturally, as well as biologically, superior to other peoples."[150] While some reformers related to immigrant families with admiration and empathy, the vast majority sought to instill the sense of scientific modernity that was the hallmark of Progressive Era activism, and therefore "a higher form of civilization," upon immigrant women they perceived as childlike or, in their own words, "ignorant and without any training."[151]

Social reformers carried out this "civilization work" in settlement houses but also in schools, workplaces, and a variety of other settings. Generally speaking, the movement in New York City sought to inculcate Protestant values such as homemaking (which included lessons on proper diet, cleanliness, and childrearing) and to educate women for labor in the garment industry through courses on needlework. Such efforts were carried out through settlement-run factories such as the Brooklyn Neighborhood House Embroidery Industry or the Scuola d'Industrie Italiane on MacDougal Street in Manhattan. While reformers typically imagined themselves as rescuing immigrant women from sweatshops and preserving their artistic traditions, they saw such women as naturally inclined for such work. Many considered Italian women's ability to produce fine lace and embroidery for upper-class homes as the primary "gifts" that Italian women brought to the United States.[152] They also argued that factory labor could rescue women from oppressive family relationships. As Mary Kingsbury Simkhovitch, director of Greenwich House noted in her annual report: "We must regard then the entrance of the Italian girl into industry as the first necessary step in the growth of her independence which cannot but result favorably in the end for the Italian-American group as a whole."[153]

In the effort to liberate Italian women through industrial labor, the settlement houses provided more spacious and airy workrooms, but the women were still subjected to discipline and surveillance. One reformer writing on the Scuola d'Industrie Italiane painted a cheery portrait of women working together, without time cards or a forewoman shouting demands. Yet she also noted the women's tendency toward "chattering in Italian as fast as their fingers can fly—that is the chattering limit—when their tongues outstrip their needles; then, and only then, is restraint placed upon them."[154]

For all their efforts, however, many social workers continually worried that Italian immigrant mothers were not fully responding to their programs. The settlement house reformers at Greenwich House tried to no avail to devise programs that might attract Italian women but discovered that it was "extremely difficult to establish social clubs among Italian girls." They attributed such challenges to the girls having "little feeling of comradeship" and "no interest in classes that involved particular mental effort."[155] Some argued that their reluctance stemmed from the exhaustion of long workdays. But most considered their absence to be evidence of their isolation and imagined them as cloistered with very little interaction outside of their homes. As one social worker wrote in the profession's premier journal, the *Survey*, "The Italians are a domestic people; their women rarely leave their homes and so come into contact with American ideas much less than the men do."[156] In 1918 the New York Association for Improving the Condition of the Poor opened its doors to the Italian women of Mulberry Street in the hopes of changing their nutritional habits, only to report the "indifference" of immigrant mothers and their general uncooperative or "ungrateful" attitudes to such educational programs.[157] Because their participation was far less than that of Jewish immigrant women, many settlement house workers attributed this difference only to Italian family strictness and male dominance.

Some reformers tried other strategies to reach immigrant women, as in the case of labor investigator Cornelia Stratton Parker, who posed as a worker in order to understand "the life of a working girl." Her hope for transcending class barriers was fulfilled when she met Pauline, an Italian immigrant woman on her way to work in the factory where Parker was passing for a worker. As Parker approached the factory, she was met by "little Pauline." She writes, "[She] ran up to me, put her arm through mine, and caught my hand. So we walked to work. Neither could say a word to the other. Each just smiled and smiled. For the first time in all my life I really felt the melting pot first hand. To Pauline I was no agent of Americanization, no superior proclaiming the need of bathtubs and clean teeth, no teacher of the 'Star-spangled banner' and the Constitution. To Pauline I was a fellow-worker, and she must know, for such things are always known, that I loved her."[158] Parker's sentiments were shared by many in this generation of middle-class and elite women who saw in immigrant women a chance to connect to the "bigger, more emotional and freer lives of working people," to escape what social settlement pioneer Jane Addams called "incorrigible bourgeois standards."[159] As a result of cultural distances and class antagonisms, however, Italian immigrant women rarely built solid political alliances or relationships with native-born Anglo-Saxon women. This was in marked contrast to working-class Jewish immigrant women, who were able to rely on middle-class Jewish institutions to mobilize on their behalf and mediate these cross-class relationships.[160]

While Italian immigrant women did not often frequent their local settlement houses, their lives did bring them into daily contact with a variety of people. When Italian women devoted their energy to educational projects, they were most often in the context of revolutionary activism or industrial unionism. Indeed, it was their very reluctance to adopt Anglo-Saxon Protestant values *and* the appeal of radical movements that most concerned reformers. Union Settlement in East Harlem was one of the only settlement houses in the city to routinely open its doors to local anarchist groups and socialist labor unions.[161] This was uncommon, however, and in the end, the Americanization movement inadvertently taught Italian women to be suspicious about reformers, teachers, social workers, and preachers in their midst who sought to inculcate a new system of values and cultural ideals. To many immigrant women, American institutions such as schools and settlements were not a source of greater family cohesion. Instead, as one Italian immigrant woman protested, "the schools made of our children persons of leisure—*signorini* (little gentlemen)—they lost the dignity of good children to think first of their parents." In his interviews with residents of Italian Harlem in the 1920s and 1930s, Leonard Covello recalled a common refrain: "America took our children."[162] He also recorded his own mother's frustration when he came home from school each day and seemed as if he was moving farther and farther away, always with the refrain, "You just don't understand!" She replied, "Will you stop saying that! I don't understand. I don't understand. What is there to understand? Now that you have become Americanized you understand everything and I understand nothing."[163]

Few Italian immigrant women joined settlement house meetings or courses. But they nevertheless were affected by the Americanization movement, which fixated on the particular "barbarity" of Latin Mediterranean patriarchal culture. This concern contrasted markedly with the dominant discourse concerning African American women in the city. In fact, the "domestication" of Italian (and eastern European) women occurred in part through distinguishing them from black women. In imagining and treating Italian immigrant women as victims in need of rescue, social reformers positioned them as entitled to protection and the rights of citizenship, whether through educational programs or labor legislation. For example, Tennessee Claflin, noted suffragist activist and writer (and also Victoria Woodhull's younger sister), traveled to Naples in 1910 to "see something of

Italian women and study the country from which so many thousands are now on their way to America." While she considered American women to be "the most independent women in the world," she noted, "Italy is furnishing America with citizens. I want to study the conditions of the mothers of these future citizens and improve them if I can, and thereby improve the citizens. To expand somewhat to a truism, 'Good mothers make good sons,' and therefore good citizens."[164]

African American women, Asian immigrant women, and other women of color were subjected to an entirely different logic. Most white Americans felt that evolutionary progress toward active participation in civic life was possible for impoverished and "uncivilized" European immigrants but not for non-Europeans.[165] In this way, the Americanization movement taught Italian immigrant women not only that they were different from African American and Asian immigrant women but that they were their opposite. They became the beneficiaries of a whole host of labor laws that sought to protect working women against the abuses of industrial factory work, while domestic and service work—where the vast majority of African American and Asian immigrant women were employed—remained unregulated and of little concern to the movement for protective labor legislation. Such inconsistency affirmed a particular rationale that southern and eastern European immigrants were unlike working-class women of color in that they could be trained for citizenship and were entitled to protection from the state.

The "agents of assimilation" were not only embodied in social reformers, teachers, and other representatives of the Americanization movement. Italians confronted American evolutionist ideologies of white racial superiority in all areas of life. At the end of the nineteenth century, New York City had a "wavering color line"—the state legislature guaranteed equal rights for African Americans, but white supremacy governed the city through violence and de facto segregation.[166] Before World War I, African Americans, Chinese, Japanese, and Latin Americans, composed a small percentage of New York City's population (less than 3 percent overall), yet derogatory images still abounded. The covers of popular newspapers and magazines, as well as local vaudeville and minstrel shows, government officials, local police departments, church officials, school teachers, labor leaders, and social workers routinely dehumanized African, Chinese, Indian, and other women and men deemed nonwhite. Southern Italian immigrants also received daily lessons that they were perceived as menial workers who were racially distinct from, and inferior to, northern and western Europeans. Magazines, newspapers, product brochures, and other forms of marketing, focused on teaching all dark-complected women how to disguise their thick, wiry hair and lighten their skin to appear more American and thereby gain social acceptance. Some companies, especially manufacturers of cosmetics and hair products, targeted Italian immigrant women as they did Jewish and Mexican women, "using the foreign language press, posters in immigrant neighborhoods, and local promotions." Some idealized and objectified the "exotic beauty" of darker complexions, but the subtext of their campaigns was almost always that "the true American face was still a white face."[167] Immigrants picked up this message right away. As one Sicilian immigrant recalled, "Real Americans" had "delicate complexions, blond hair, fine clothes! By contrast, our complexion and hair was much darker."[168]

The color line was also everywhere apparent in the geography of neighborhoods. It was visible in those who were excluded or included in certain jobs, schools, settlement houses, parks, restaurants, churches, unions, and other spaces. It was apparent in accounts of the lynching of African Americans, which were regularly published in a variety of Italian-language newspapers, and in the persistent racial violence against African Americans that erupted in New York City in 1900, 1905, and in the years between 1917 and 1921, when working-class whites attacked and terrorized African Americans migrating to the city from the South.[169] Indeed, Italian immigrant radicals in particular often noted how in America "race hatred is a national duty."[170] Ralph Ellison and Malcolm X would note years later that one of the first words that European immigrants learned when they got off the boat was *nigger*: "[It] made them feel instantly American."[171] The historical evidence confirms this. As early as 1903, Italian immigrants like Tito Pacelli mobilized Italian construction workers in the city to protest employers' recruitment of African American workers during a strike by stating, "The niggers won't stay here—we'll scare them off."[172] In response, a mob of Italians, a third of whom were women, reportedly assaulted the African American workers.[173] Certainly, Italian immigrants engaged in many battles, among themselves and with many other ethnic groups as they struggled to adapt to life in America. Employers also "actively cultivated ethnic discord by spreading false rumors about one group and attributing them to the other."[174] Indeed, management regularly and successfully recruited different populations of workers to break strikes and keep them from developing solidarity.

In figuring out how to act, with whom to ally, and other ways of conducting oneself, the color line and intergroup animosities overall were among the first things immigrants learned in America. Often they applied their growing sense of regionalism to such understandings. Louise Bolard More, a researcher from a local settlement house in Greenwich Village, who interviewed one hundred families, noted, "The racial feeling is often very strong. The Irish hate the Italians ('Dagos') and the negroes ('niggers'), and the North Italians despise the Sicilians."[175] In 1919 another social reformer noted: "Much of the small town spirit still clung to them and made this colony like a village set in the midst of a great city. They all knew one another, gossiped about each other, clung to the customs, the language, and the sectional prejudices they had brought with them from Italy, and they perpetuated their strong racial feeling by intermarriage." The narratives of immigrants themselves are also filled with stories like that of the Genoese mother who "was heartbroken because her son was 'keeping company' with a Neapolitan girl," and the man from Naples who became "deeply embittered" when Sicilians moved into his tenement building.[176] As the racialized division between northern and southern Italians became more pronounced in the United States, it provided the lens through which Italians came to understand the color line. For example, Angelina Frignoca, a northern Italian immigrant worker in Haledon, New Jersey's silk mills taught her granddaughter complex lessons about color and race in her family, which intermarried with southern Italian immigrants. When her grandchildren asked about the meaning of "wop," she had a biting response, "From the South!" She also took particular pride in being called *bionda* (blonde), her granddaughter noted: "Throughout my childhood I accepted the notion that somehow fair was better than dark, even though my own southern Italian family gave evidence to the contrary."[177]

BY TRACING THE transnational history of southern Italian racialization, it becomes possible to identify how the African presence in Italy was both debased and erased in order to serve the connected processes of state formation and capitalist expansion. Identifying the particular contours of this history reveals how race has been constituted in the United States but also the process by which Italians could come to see themselves and their interests as white. How did Italians internalize, enact, and disrupt oppressive ideologies and practices as they adjusted their own worldviews and cultures of resistance to life in the United States? As the next chapters reveal, women were not only imagined in ways that differed from men; they also exerted, defended, and subverted power in ways that differed from them as well. Italian American women's sense of themselves as whites would not emerge fully until the 1930s and 1940s, when they were backed by a host of powerful institutions, including the state, their employers, and some of the largest labor unions, in their claims. In the earlier period, however, they "did not need to be openly and assertively white to benefit from its considerable rewards and resources." Many Americans considered Italians to be a national peril on racial grounds, but they were still a "white peril."[178]

The Hine photo, with which I opened this chapter, embodies the disturbing consequences of Italians' racial journey in the United States. In its own day, this image was intended to motivate the American middle- and upper-class public into taking action on the subject's behalf. Yet it also functioned to assuage their anxieties over the kinds of changes taking place in the country. Here was a woman marked by liminality—exotic, foreign, and hardy—and positioned as the threshold and boundary between the Old World and the New. In this way her location as a menial worker upon whose body industrial capitalism would expand was justified: rather than serving the interests of capital, her exploitation could be imagined as necessary for her own liberation. Such a worldview required that she become a victim, so that her assimilation, discipline, and civilization was imagined as serving her own good.

Today this image serves a newfound but equally disturbing purpose. It is an image that continues to circulate in books, exhibits, and other monuments to the American past.[179] In its reinvigorated form, this photograph, and the many others that progressive reformers produced and circulated to document European immigration at the turn of the past century, has become an emblem of the American success story—self-congratulatory proof that the project of assimilation, discipline, and civilization was not only successful but worthwhile. After all, it supposedly transported generations of European peasants from rags to riches, or at least to the white middle classes. As such, these images and their myths affirm the significance of whiteness to American national belonging and power relations. They are central to what historian Matthew Frye Jacobson has termed "Ellis Island whiteness."[180] In the wake of the civil rights movement, Jacobson writes, "a new national myth of origins" emerged, "whose touchstone was Ellis Island, whose heroic central figure was the downtrodden but determined greenhorn, whose preferred modes of narration were the epic and the ode, and whose most far-reaching, political conceit was the 'nation of immigrants.'" Since the 1960s especially, "appeals to the romantic icon of yesterday's European immigrant—downtrodden, hard-working, self-reliant, triumphant—have shaped policy debates about everything from affirmative action and the welfare state to slavery reparations and contemporary immigration."[181] Though celebratory, these images continue to objectify Italian immigrant women as the boundary marker for the nation. The consequences are as dangerous today as they were in their time: they facilitate a national forgetting, one that elides the violence and trauma of industrial capitalism, imperialism, labor migration, and whiteness, past and present.

Surviving the Shock of
Arrival and Everyday Resistance

In no way did Natalia Garavente fit the image of the poor working girl. She was instead "not a lady to be trifled with."[1] She went by Dolly in the solidly blue-collar waterfront town of Hoboken, New Jersey, where she grew up, just across the Hudson River from Lower Manhattan. She immigrated as a child in 1897, with her family of educated and skilled lithographers from a northern Italian village near Genoa. At the time, Hoboken was home mostly to unskilled laborers from southern Italy, with sizable Irish and German immigrant communities, and smaller numbers of other working-class groups. Against her parents' wishes, Dolly fell in love with a young Sicilian immigrant from the neighborhood, a prizefighter with tattooed arms named Anthony who boxed under the name Marty O'Brien. To attend his matches, she went in drag, with her brothers, wearing their clothes, her hair stuffed under a cap, and a cigar dangling from the corner of her mouth.[2]

Soon after they met, Dolly and Marty eloped and moved into a tenement in Hoboken's poorest section. The birth of their first child a year later in 1915 almost killed both mother and son. Dolly was small, weighing only ninety-two pounds at the time, while the baby was over thirteen pounds. Dolly's mother Rosa was the midwife but called in a doctor for help when the birth became life threatening. He "tugged away with forceps, ripping the baby's ear, cheek and neck." But it was even worse: "The newborn did not breathe. Thinking him dead, the doctor turned instead to treat the mother." Rosa turned to the baby. Scooping him up, she held him under cold running water to get his blood moving. To everyone's amazement he began to cry.[3]

Like most working-class families, Dolly and Marty held several jobs to get by. Marty was a shy, quiet man who worked at different times as a shoemaker, a boilermaker in the shipyards, a part-time bootlegger, and a firefighter. Dolly was a chocolate dipper in a local candy factory and studied midwifery on the side. She would follow in her mother's footsteps to become one of the neighborhood's most trusted midwives. Hundreds of babies came into the world through her hands, and she was well known for her ability to perform safe abortions. At the height of Prohibition, she and Marty also opened a saloon together in Hoboken, on the corner of Fourth Street and Jefferson, calling it Marty O'Brien's.

In many ways Dolly was Marty's opposite: outgoing, social, and ambitious. Between the saloon and her work as a midwife, Dolly came to know most everyone in Hoboken. Perhaps most revealing of her popularity is that she was named godmother to eighty-seven children, many of whom she delivered herself. She parlayed her social networks into local political power by the 1920s, when she reputedly ran half of Hudson County as leader of the Democratic Party for Hoboken's Third Ward. As ward boss she was respected for her no-nonsense manner and ability to help Hoboken's Italians in their dealings with the city's largely Irish public officials. In exchange for political favors, she was rumored to deliver six hundred votes at election time to the city's Democratic Party. Dolly also threw her energies behind her son, who had his own dreams of escaping the poverty of Hoboken to become a successful artist. Her son was Frank Sinatra.[4]

In the rich literature on Sinatra, Dolly is remembered as enterprising, smart, and strong willed; a woman "with a stevedore's heart and mouth." She is also depicted as controlling, demanding, and abusive, a woman who never forgave those who crossed her and who alternately "embraced and bullied" her son.[5] As an adult, Frank would remain very close with both of his parents, and he often defended his mother's reputation. "My mother wasn't tough," he would say, "the *neighborhood* was tough. She was firm."[6] Journalist Barbara Grizzuti Harrison has written that disparaging depictions of Dolly result in part from popular misconceptions: "In Italian-American families, tough noisy women are often the rule. And it is almost impossible for an outsider to locate the source of power in these families—the whole canny point being to deceive the outside world."[7]

To Frank, his mother was hardworking, smart, and visionary. "My mother is what you would call a progressive," he told one interviewer. "She was always interested in conditions outside her own home."[8] On another occasion he explained, "My mother influenced me a great deal. She was a self-taught woman, very bright, had good common sense and was a hard worker. . . . My earliest memories of my father, Marty, are in the kitchen. He did much of the cooking, as Dolly, my mother, was a powerful force and dedicated worker in the political arena. She was out there fighting for women's rights long before women even knew they should have them. My pop would stand at the stove cooking the greatest pasta sauce." Frank punctuated his point of seemingly reversed gender roles

Frank Sinatra with his mother Dolly, October, 1945. Hulton Archive/Getty Images.

with a story: "One time in 1940 I called home at the last minute, and my pop cooked an Italian meal for the entire Tommy Dorsey Orchestra. Some of the sax players had to eat in the hallway, but they still loved the meal!"[9] Frank spoke often of Dolly, in part because the public was fascinated with her no-nonsense manner. As cultural critic John Gennari has written, she "sabotaged hackneyed images of ethnic warmth and projected her spirit far beyond the confines of the flowered housecoat of domesticity."[10]

While few Italian immigrant women would become ward bosses or raise legendary performers, the material realities they encountered through their own migration led many to connect with the life of their communities. In doing so, many defied popularized notions of the cloistered, downtrodden, all-nurturing *mamma*. Dolly's story is one of many that take us into the complex humanity of Italian immigrant women. She was anything but a victim. Throughout her life she embodied a full range of possibility. While her actions were at times controversial, she was decisive, savvy, and acted on her own behalf and in service of those in her community. It seems she learned this from her own mother Rosa, whose combined wisdom and ability to act was what saved her grandson's life.

Dolly and Rosa's stories reveal how Italian immigrant women confronted the challenges and traumas of modern urban industrial life by literally taking matters into their own hands. They also point to three common methods that women employed to survive the shock of arrival:[11] building and sustaining everyday networks of reciprocity and mutual aid; engaging in patterns of subterfuge, waged in the most intimate relationships; and pursuing spiritual work, including healing practices, religious devotion, and the transmission of sacred knowledge to the next generation. These strategies were each firmly rooted in female traditions of resistance in Italy, crafted and recrafted again during the violence of state formation, severe economic hardship, and mass emigration at the turn of the century. As women migrated, they carried these practices across the globe, adapting them to new contexts and challenges. Networks of support and mutuality came to include new neighbors and co-workers, as well as formerly distant kin and friends, all of whom helped women to find jobs, housing, childcare, friendship, and romance, as well as spiritual, emotional, and intellectual sustenance. Daily life remained firmly rooted in relationships with *paesani*, family, and friends from the village or region of origin. But women's lives unfolded in urban, multiethnic, working-class communities and through a variety of relationships that increasingly transcended the boundaries of region, language, religion, race, and nation.

In mapping the ways Italian immigrant women translated daily acts of resistance and survival as they adapted to new settings, my intention is to make visible their everyday struggles for dignity and pleasure. As many scholars have demonstrated, the daily acts of working-class people "to roll back constraints, to exercise power over, or create space within institutions and social relationships" that intended to exclude and marginalize are not just foundational to social movements; they make them possible.[12] As women converted daily methods of survival to cope with the intense hardships and alienations of the modern industrial order, they reconfigured the very spaces and relationships that constrained their lives and transformed their own consciousness in the process. Their strategies were of course deeply complex and not necessarily liberating. They could expand but also contract women's lives. They generated new patterns of deference, oppression, and silencing. But they also offered lessons on how to thrive with one's spirit intact. And ultimately, the knowledge and experience that women gleaned from these everyday activities would inform their more organized, formal struggles for widespread, collective change, whether in anarchist-feminist circles, fascist groups, labor unions, or struggles for public housing.

To explore women's everyday patterns of resistance and survival, I focus here on the narratives that they themselves and their families produced to render and make meaning of their own lives. Their words remain with us in memoirs and other written stories, left behind in books, newspapers, and unpublished personal records. They appear, on occasion, in the various studies that social scientists, journalists, and other investigators generated at the turn of the century. They also reside in the many oral histories that curious scholars conducted with immigrant women and their children, to document early twentieth-century life as these generations were aging and passing on.[13] Most of the available memoirs, stories, and interviews, are from immigrants who composed the 1.5 generation—those who were born in Italy but migrated as children. As with all primary sources, each of these materials is replete with limitations, and none alone could paint a complete picture. I bring them together here to tell this story out of their common themes, attentive to the ways the sources diverge from and complicate one another. Together they reveal complex patterns of covert and overt resistance and the wisdom that women used to empower themselves and their children.

Women's Networks of Reciprocity

Like the stories surrounding Dolly Sinatra, Leonard Covello's migration story speaks to the significance of women's relationships with one another in facing upheaval. In 1896 Leonard arrived in New York City with his mother and brothers. They joined his father, who had worked abroad for six years before the family had saved enough for this trip. After a long and difficult journey by train from their village of Avigliano in Basilicata to the port city of Naples, they boarded an old freighter for an even more arduous voyage across the Atlantic that lasted twenty days. Once at Ellis Island they were separated. To his mother's horror, several guards led the boys away without adequately conveying that it was momentary, for the purposes of inspection. He recalled, "When we ran back to her, she clutched us convulsively. Still in her eyes there was the disbelieving look of a mother who never expected to see her children again." After two days and nights in the chaotic, crowded, filthy, and terrifying world of Ellis Island, Leonard's father learned of their arrival and came to claim them.[14]

Leonard recalled his first impressions of their new home, a tenement flat near the East River on 112th Street, in a section of East Harlem populated by other immigrants from his village in Italy:

> The sunlight and fresh air of our mountain home in Lucania were
> replaced by four walls and people over and under and on all sides of

us, until it seemed that all humanity from all corners of the world had congregated in this section of New York City known as East Harlem. The cobbled streets. The endless, monotonous rows of tenement build- ings that shut out the sky. The traffic of wagons and carts and carriages and the clopping of horses' hooves which struck sparks at night. The smell of the river at ebb tide. The moaning of fog horns. The clanging of bells and the screeching of sirens as a fire broke out somewhere in the neighborhood. Dank hallways. Long flights of wooden stairs and the toilet in the hall. And the water, which to my mother was one of the great wonders of America—water with just the twist of a handle, and only a few paces from the kitchen. It took her a long time to get used to this luxury. Water and a few other conveniences were the com- pensations the New World had to offer.[15]

They soon learned that it was a *paesana*, Carmela Accurso, to whom Leonard's father had entrusted his wages to save for the family's migration. She had also "made ready the tenement flat and arranged the welcoming party with relatives and friends to greet us upon our arrival." During the celebration, however, his mother "sat dazed, unable to realize that at last the torment of the trip was over and that here was America. It was Mrs. Accurso who put her arm comfortingly about my mother's shoulder and led her away from the party and into the hall and showed her the water faucet." *Coraggio!* Carmela said, "You will get used to it here. See! Isn't it wonderful how water comes out?' Through her tears my mother managed a smile."[16]

But the promise of modern technology that might lessen the burden of women's labor did little to quell the despair many felt upon arrival. Once immi- grants survived the harrowing journey across the Atlantic in steerage and passed through inspection at Ellis Island, the urban-industrial world that greeted them was a shocking assault on the senses. Many hoped that migration might bring a better life, but most found they were "unable to free themselves from their heavy burdens." Many also felt "deprived of the fresh country air and the wide spaces of their native villages."[17] Maria Forte did not even believe that she had arrived in America when she immigrated in 1920. She recalled, "I ask my husband, I say 'when we gonna get into the America?' My husband, he says, 'Another two step and we get into the house!' Because I hear, 'America! America! It's beautiful!' And when I see Bank Street, I don't know if you ever see South Brooklyn, but I no see no beautiful thing. You want to see the thing here, you know, the America; we were children, somebody come in the town and they show us New York, and I thought soon I'll see New York, I'll see beautiful, and I see a house that look like a little you know *shack*, and I say 'when we get into America!'" Maria recalled her shock with laughter decades later, but confided that it was a *paesana* who helped her to overcome the disappointment in those early years.[18]

While many turned to friends and family to ease the transition, some still suffered tremendously. Edward Corsi recalled his mother's response to their tenement in East Harlem. She "was discouraged by the sight of the apartment the moment she stepped into it, and she never overcame that repulsion." She "loved quiet, and hated noise and confusion. Here she never left the house unless she had to. She spent her days and the waking hours of the nights, sitting at that one outside window staring up at the little patch of sky above the tenements. She was never happy here and, though she tried, could not adjust herself to the poverty and despair in which we had to live."[19] Within three years she grew very ill and returned to her hometown of Sulmona, where she died within a year. Covello's mother also "lived in constant fear from the uncertainty of life." She became sullen, weary, and "lost all desire to go out into the street or to see anything new, as if just keeping alive was problem enough in itself." Shortly thereafter she too died. The youngest children were sent to live with female relatives and the rest of the family moved next door to Carmela Accurso so she could "keep a watchful eye on things."[20]

These stories offer a compelling explanation for why some Italian immigrant women were secluded in their homes—one that was often overlooked by the social investigators who assumed such patterns could be the result only of male control. We cannot know how many women retreated into their homes of their own volition, but it is clear that for most the loss of the natural world "meant the loss of familiar social rituals that had given life meaning and value."[21] When a social worker asked one Italian immigrant woman in 1911 if she liked America, she shrugged her shoulders, "Not much, not much. Good money, good people, but my country—my country—good air, much air, nice air down Italy. Blue sky, the water laugh in the bay. . . . In my country peoples cook out of doors, maka the wash out of doors, eat out of doors, tailor out of doors, maka macaroni out of doors. And my people laugh, laugh all a time. And we use the house only in the night time to maka the sleep. America—it is sopra, sopra (up, up, with a gesture of going up stairs). Many peoples one house, worka, worka, all a time. Good money, but no good air."[22] As historian Robert Orsi has written, the way that the immigrant generation narrated these different worlds reveals a great deal about the anxieties they faced at this time. In their stories, they typically constructed southern Italy as a place of struggle but also of harmony, intimacy, obedient children, and submissive women. "America" became its polar opposite, a place where "the dead were not buried properly, and went unmourned; women and children ran wild; and men were not really men."[23] This nostalgia served several purposes. It consoled immigrants and imbued homelands with dignity, but it also disciplined the next generation. It was a narrative, "born of fear, desire, and denial," and it emerged with particular force in the years after the First World War, when the American-born generation began to come of age.[24] These narratives remind us that "dysfunction, pain, and alienation" were as central to the immigrant experience as support and cooperation.[25]

This complexity is especially evident in women's relationships with one another. Daily activities—caring for children, shopping, preparing food, taking care of relatives and friends, earning wages in factories, caring for boarders, managing tenement buildings, taking in homework, serving as midwives, and running grocery stores—were exhausting and debilitating. These responsibilities also led women to build community with one another in ways that differed markedly from men. By performing such work, women fulfilled cultural roles as caregivers, but they also built relationships between individuals, families, and institutions that extended their lives beyond the scope of their immediate families. As in other locales, the "lattice-work of female exchange and reciprocity operated as a source of community cohesion, identity, and collective power."[26] Indeed, the changes women experienced in their homelands with the mass exodus of men, such as increased autonomy and the strengthening of female networks of mutual aid, only deepened with their own migration. And, as in Italy, this would challenge patriarchal power arrangements within families and communities.

For many, a sense of community began with one's own family since immigrants often followed and settled among kin. As a result, women developed community ties and social networks in conjunction with the men in their lives. Yet, women remained at the center of family groups inasmuch as they were largely responsible for domestic and reproductive labor, which included maintaining relationships throughout the extended family—what anthropologist Micaela di Leonardo has called "kin work."[27] In fact, oral histories on this period often convey women's autonomy in caring for families. Because most men worked several jobs and socialized in the primarily male spaces of bars, hometown social clubs, and mutual aid societies, women recalled being solely responsible for raising children and caring for the home, in addition to earning wages to support their families—what feminists would later call the double shift. Emma Barruso was like many others in that she rarely saw her husband: "He used to be so tired he eat and go to sleep," she recalled. "Sometimes he had to even work at night, he used to come home one or two in the morning and sometime he leave three in the morning." Similarly, Philamina Cocozelli noted, "He'd go to work, he'd come home, he'd eat, and then he'd have to go to another place and he leave me in the house." Another woman's husband "played cards . . . went to the club. . . . He was sitting with the men all the time, you know what I mean?"[28]

While a man's ability to "hustle" a living was a valued trait for this generation (and later generations) of women, many also complained, like Donna Cassado: "He never asked me how the children did, or things like that, no, he just eat, like that."[29] For many women, their sole responsibility for caretaking was a source of grief since it required arduous work that seemed invisible to men. But some also developed a newfound sense of their own abilities with this autonomy. Antoinette Abbatista recalled, "I used to do the dishes and he would go down and play cards with some friends. . . . He always left things to me. He never thought it was any of his business. . . . [laughing] I was the head chef and bottle washer." Others, like Concetta Pancini, struggled with their responsibilities. "I didn't like it," she recalled. "But that was his only pleasure, what could you do? . . . I means we understand, and we always make up in bed!" Even then, she felt frustrated by her lack of options: "Who's going to take you in with four kids?"[30] The centrality of women to their households meant, however, that their children could grow up like Angelo Bertocci, with a sense that "the brains and the heart and the direct genius of our economic enterprise was my mother."[31] As in Italy, women managed their households out of necessity, and their responsibilities were double-edged. It meant constant and unrelenting work, but also a setting in which to develop a sense of their own power.

Without men to assist them, most immigrant women spoke of relying heavily on the networks of mutual support and reciprocity with those who lived closest to them, whether kin or neighbors. Mary Allessandrina recalled, "These friends in my building—upstairs, downstairs, these friends in my building, they were a lot of help for me. When I had my children they came and bathed my other children while I was in bed. When I had Jimmy, my first, one of the mothers helped me from the building where I was living." Nina Benuto remembered, "I wasn't afraid of anything, I had my mother and I had my relatives and I had my people . . . from the same country, the same town that I came from, so I really wasn't worried." Lucy Sevirole also recalled having "a lot of friends; they were *paesane*, friends from Italy. I had one, she christened my daughter. It was a big family. They come to my house and I'd go over there."[32] Principles of mutuality were often learned at a young age. Leonard Covello recalled that the children in his town in Italy shared their food with one another at school, especially with those "whose family was temporarily without bread."[33] In New York City, women adapted this ethos. They became notorious for "begging off" or "jumping" rent, especially because so many worked as apartment building managers and could negotiate with landlords to give families more time to earn money for rent.[34]

One social worker at Greenwich House found that among the Italian immigrant women she interviewed in the first decade of the twentieth century, such behavior was "not considered dishonest" because of their class consciousness: in their view, "the landlord is considered a rich man, who 'can stand the loss,' and is an easy prey."[35]

Such collective methods of survival were so striking to middle-class social workers and other reformers that they often took note of it. Lillian Brandt observed that on Manhattan's Lower East Side, "there are always women to be seen gazing out of the window, sitting on the steps, and standing on street corners engaged in no more fruitful activity than the interchange of ideas."[36] Another social worker wrote about the "spirit of charity and mutual helpfulness" that pervaded the immigrant district in Greenwich Village. "The residents come into very close touch with the daily life of their neighbors, and their intercourse with them is unusually friendly, natural, and responsive."[37] Sociologist Mabel Hurd Willett also noted the "mutual helpfulness" among Italian immigrants in New York City in her 1902 study of the garment trades.[38] Lillian Wald, who founded the Henry Street Settlement on the Lower East Side, wrote in her memoir, "It has become almost trite to speak of the kindness of the poor to each other, yet from the beginning of our tenement-house residence we were much touched by manifestation of it." She also noted how these solidarities occurred between different immigrant groups and recounted many such tales. One typical story was that of "a Jewish woman, exhausted by her long day's scrubbing of office floors, who walked many extra blocks to beg us to get a priest for her Roman Catholic neighbor whose child was dying."[39]

The density of the homes also contributed to women's ability to forge networks with their neighbors. In the areas of initial settlement, such as the Mulberry district, Greenwich Village, and East Harlem, tenement apartments predominated. The most common housing for the working classes in the city was a flat in which two or three rooms were lined up like railroad cars, with windows on only one wall. Narrow, steep, and unlit stairs separated each floor, with the water supply and toilets located in a hallway or outside. Almost all of the housing was rental and most landlords did not live on the premises. Living quarters were intensely cramped, and often several families lived together in only one to three rooms that were dark, poorly ventilated, and gloomy, with no private bath and few beds. One social investigator noted that "rarely did a woman enjoy the luxury and privacy of a room to herself."[40]

Most women did not enjoy such a privilege in their homelands either. However, there they usually had access to the semiprivate outdoor space of the courtyard and gardens. Congested urban living led most to "create a communal life in the streets and other public spaces" and to seek some privacy, anonymity, and freedom from supervision in new ways in the expanding street culture of this period. Women convened on stoops and went to the music halls, amusement parks, and movies. Children played in empty lots, parks, and along the riverfront. Men played *boccie* in alleyways or cards in the café and saloon. Couples met on tenement rooftops and in parks.[41]

In many ways the tenement building became the equivalent of the *cortile* of their homelands, with a combination of kin and other families living in close proximity, often within shouting or calling distance. At least twice as many families lived in a single tenement than in a typical southern Italian courtyard, however. Settlement house worker Lillian Betts found that for many immigrant women, the "tenement house hall in New York is the substitute for the road of her village."[42] Unlike in Italy, however, more families formed households together in order to split rent. These shared households were especially common among younger and recently arrived families, and most often in the dumbbell apartments where entrance to all rooms was from a shared kitchen, thus affording families some privacy. Multiple family households typically occupied a third of the apartments in such buildings. Others cut costs further by sharing household resources and childcare. In all of these cases, the kitchen often became the courtyard—a shared work and social space primarily for women.[43]

Women used their kitchens, but also their stairways, front stoops, windows, and the street, to socialize with one another. As one historian has noted, "The streets of the Lower East Side were constantly filled with women shopping, running errands, and exchanging news and gossip." To them, "neighborhood life was a way of guarding the streets, comparing prices, being informed about who was sick, out of work, evicted or deserted."[44] Whether it was for their daily round in the markets, their work in the local factories, the celebration of feast days, or visits with family and friends, women's work necessitated moving beyond the household into the life of their communities. Moreover, because Italian women were customarily in charge of the family purse and acted as the family's primary consumers, they were familiar with market prices, paid rent, bought food and clothing, and developed relationships with those who ran the local produce stores, butcher shops, bakeries, and restaurants. These relationships helped them to get through "times of dearth," as many sought to "take out a trust with the grocery man."[45] Because southern Italian diets consisted primarily of fresh vegetables, women typically shopped every day.[46] The daily round was also necessary because "little storage space and many mouths to feed made a constant incursion into the marketplace part of the texture of daily life."[47] The role of these daily outings in helping immigrant women learn about their new communities and build networks with other women is especially vivid in the recollections of their children. Filomena Orlando recalled that her mother went shopping with her friends from her hometown in Italy, who had settled in the same area: "They would go out with each other shopping. If one needed the other, if they were sick or needed help, they would go over. There was *something* about my mother and the friends she had."[48]

Because Italians often lived in "relatively homogeneous enclaves" their sense of *campanilismo* deepened with migration.[49] This word stems from *campanile* (bell tower) and refers to the "solidarity among those who heard the ringing of the same church bell."[50] The neighborhood, village, and region of origin, continued to provide a powerful sense of identity. It was, for example, fairly typical that a woman from Palermo "would rather walk five blocks to visit a *paesana* than spend her time across the hall with her neighbor from Sorrento," a village outside of Naples.[51] Densely populated neighborhoods provided for most residents' needs, so immigrants could avoid learning English altogether. One resident, Marie Concistre, noted that many would "shop contentedly in Little Italy without the use of one English word."[52] Although few in the immigrant generation learned English, many began to learn the newly nationalized language of Italian (based on the northern Italian dialect of Florence) and sometimes other regional dialects as well in order to communicate with those from other parts of Italy. One immigrant who arrived in 1906 said, "When I arrived in New York I went to live with my *paesani*. I did not see any reason for learning English. I didn't need it. Everywhere I lived, or worked, or fooled around there were only Italians. . . . I had to learn some Sicilian, though, for I married a girl from the province. Sicilian helped me a great deal in my family and my work."[53]

Of course, daily relationships also crossed into other ethnic communities. Much has been written of Italian relationships with Irish and Jewish neighbors and co-workers, with whom Italian immigrants in the New York metro area had the strongest ties, especially in the years before the First World War.[54] This would change in the decades after the war with the mass migrations of African Americans from the U.S. South, and Puerto Ricans, Cubans, and other immigrants from the Caribbean and beyond. As later chapters attest, these migrations would transform Italian neighborhoods and identities. But before the First World War, Italians were most often in relationship with Irish and Jewish communities, who together composed the three largest ethnic groups in the city. The Irish shared histories of colonialist subjugation, poverty, and Catholicism with southern Italians and were also racially stigmatized when they arrived in the United States. But their wave of mass migration began in the decades preceding; and as with most marginalized white immigrants, in their efforts to secure their own status, they often distinguished themselves from similarly stigmatized groups, including Italians. As a result, Italian immigrant women's oral histories reveal a closer identification with eastern European and Russian Jews. Italian and Jewish women not only immigrated at the same time but tended to work in the same manufacturing jobs and live in the same neighborhoods. There were of course important differences—differing rates of class mobility and religion most notably. Working-class political cultures offered a space for women and men to cross divisive lines, though, but as with all relationships, they were also rife with conflict and difficulty. Indeed, those who were drawn to border-crossing movements, whether those borders were racial, ethnic, regional, or national, tended to cross such lines in their daily lives. One typical example is that of Ginevra Spagnoletti. She regularly brought her children on excursions throughout the city, to introduce them to the world beyond their Italian neighborhood. Ginevra's son would recall that these lessons were an extension of her teachings at home: "My house, you'd never Jew-bait, red-bait, color-bait. It was never allowed."[55]

Though Ginevra was unique in many ways, most children of immigrants reflected on or simply noted the significance of interethnic relationships to their daily lives.[56] Lillian Cicio's grandmother offers another example. She worked as a midwife in Williamsburg, Brooklyn, and went by the name Mama Vita. Lillian recalled that she "knew all these people who came and went, all these women who talked over coffee cups at the big square table in the kitchen. . . . all these people had come from many different places. Not all of them spoke Italian with Mama Vita; some spoke a curious mixture of Yiddish and English, to which Mama Vita would respond in her broken English."[57] While the services of a midwife often necessitated these relationships, such ties were common in poor, working-class neighborhoods where mutual exchange and assistance were necessary for survival. Anna Valenti recalled that her mother formed close relationships with the Jewish women in the neighborhood, noting that "they would exchange the way they knew. And then the heart would speak, they would understand each other."[58] In addition, the daughters of immigrant women were often acutely aware of the "girl on the lower floor" or those they worked alongside in the factories and developed a desire for the independence they perceived her to have.[59] It is now well documented how the consciousness of immigrant women and their daughters expanded in the multiethnic relationships that animated the urban industrial landscape, whether it meant learning to challenge unequal divisions of labor in households, obtaining information on birth control, experimenting with new styles of fashion, or attending union meetings.[60] Italian immigrant mothers watched their children live entirely different lives, as they increasingly "played sports, went to school, listened to the radio, bobbed their hair,

Census taker Marie Cioffi in modern attire, collecting census data from Margaret Napolitana at 332 East 112th Street in East Harlem, while her daughter looks on, 1930. Bettmann/Corbis, BE048829.

went to the movies," married whomever they chose, and worked better jobs.[61] Immigrant mothers resisted and adjusted to these changes, often with the refrain, "What you gonna do?"[62]

Many also drew upon strategies of survival that had been honed for generations. Lillian Cicio documented this in her story of young Leda, whose family had immigrated from Sicily, and her neighbor Rosalie, a young immigrant from Romania, who pretended to be sisters. "The kitchen walls of the two flats came together and she and Rosalie signaled to one another by a series of knocks on the wall whose meaning was known only to themselves." Leda knew only a few words in Yiddish, but Rosalie spoke Sicilian fluently, and Leda celebrated the Sabbath each week with Rosalie's family. Leda recalled that she "could not decide which she liked best—the hot Sicilian bread soaked with sweet olive oil, seasoned with salt, or the fresh Jewish *kallah* spread with sweet butter." The girls' friendship led their mothers to become friends. Yet, when Leda's brother announced his engagement with a Jewish girl, Leda's grandmother expressed her concern: "What will people say? . . . and the Church?" In the end, she had them pass through the neighborhood in a carriage as if they had been married in a church, "to help her save face with the neighbors."[63] Immigrant women confronted change by drawing on a method of survival that had been a crucial part of their repertoire in southern Italy: they found ways to mask their own and their children's insubordination with public performances that attested to their deference to communal expectations.

Such practices often extended into formal political activities. Angelina Frignoca's story is especially revealing. She and her husband Frank migrated from Biella in northern Italy to work in Haledon, New Jersey's silk mills at the start of the twentieth century. Both had been politicized in Italy during the worker uprisings of their youth and continued to support the anarchist- and socialist-inspired labor movements that extended from their hometown to New Jersey and New York. But Americanization meant that their son repudiated their values. Instead, he would serve as vestryman in the Haledon church, become a tax collector and assessor for the town, and support conservative, right-wing politics. At election time, he would go to his mother's house with a ballot, and instruct her to vote straight Republican. Her granddaughter recalled, "Dutifully, she listened, indicating her intention to follow the party line from local through county, state, and national candidates. It wasn't until 1952 that I realized the charade that had been conducted in Grandma's kitchen each November." For decades she pretended to vote as he suggested, all the while supporting the Socialist Party candidate.[64]

"On the Sly": Everyday Resistance and Subterfuge

This tension between the public and hidden transcript is especially present in women's own narratives, revealing the complex ways they challenged or thwarted communal and patriarchal control over their lives. As one woman noted, "[Wives] might have been in the background, but we weren't dominated. Like we would go along with husbands [in public] but once we got home, things changed, you know. . . . My husband didn't care what went on. He really never cared. No. . . . My husband never cared, never even knew how much money I made or whatever."[65] The innumerable contradictions in women's oral histories reveal how power worked in their families. For example, many women remarked "I didn't go no place," "you've got to stay home because you're a woman," or "he want me cooped in the house," but then recounted regular visits with relatives and friends, and daily trips to shops, museums, and parks beyond the boundaries of their neighborhoods.[66] In part, this exposes women's own sense of the limitations that shaped their lives, but also their consciousness about what constituted home. Home, as they often articulated it, included the public spaces of the stoop, the block, local shops and parks, and the homes of kin and *paesani*. It was a dynamic and shifting space, both public and private; and its fluidity afforded women some flexibility in redefining its boundaries.

While women spoke often of the ways husbands, fathers, and brothers attempted to control their activities, most also discussed challenging patriarchal ideologies in their families, and the ways mothers nurtured such behavior in the next generation. Mary Pappa recounted the following of her immigrant husband: "He is the type, you know Italian men—they got to be the king all the time. And that's what he believes. But I, I don't believe that. If he's wrong, I got to give that he's wrong, and he's got to accept it, but he don't accept. . . . That's the problem." It is not possible to know when she developed this sense that patterns of male dominance were not only cultural but a defining feature of Italian masculinity. But a large portion of oral histories contain women's frustrations with and opposition to such authoritarian behavior. When an interviewer asked Carmela Cagliari if she missed her deceased husband, she did not hesitate: "No, I'm very content." She had developed a severe case of asthma after she married from the stress of her husband's violent temper. Once he passed away, her asthma subsided and she began to enjoy life. "I don't want to live with nobody," she said. "I want to be independent. I want to go, I go. If I want to come over here, I come here. . . . I like to do something but not compulsory." When asked if she had raised her daughters along these same lines, she noted, "No, they don't ask to have any lesson from me because they used to see. And now they are the boss, not the men. Especially with the little one, her husband is a piece of bread. Sometimes she toss so many words and I tell her, if you father was alive and I say words like that *bang*, my teeth would be on the floor." With a detectable sense a pride in her voice, she recounted her daughter's response: "Hey Ma, it's how you train them. You train them this way they go straight this way. If you don't want to put your foot down in the beginning it's too bad for you."[67]

Mothers also taught daughters how to undermine male authority through their role as mediator between husbands who sought to preserve customs of honor and subservience and the children who desired more freedom.[68] For example, girls were customarily forbidden to go out without a chaperone in southern Italy. However the realities of urban life tested such practices. Social investigators commonly noted, "In some families, especially those of south Italian origin, tradition was still so strong that the girls were not permitted to go out unless accompanied by the father or mother. Even if the parents did not seriously object, the girls were afraid of neighborhood gossip if they should be seen out alone after dark." However, because "the mother was usually too tired to accompany them and the father did not want to 'bother,'" some parents permitted girls to go out with siblings and friends; "moving-picture shows, the Fourteenth Street Theater, and an occasional dance sometimes at a nearby settlement, were the chief means of amusement."[69] Some girls made a practice of going out every week, while others did so only rarely. But all studies and testimonies suggest that women and girls found ways to have lives of their own, even if it required negotiation and subterfuge. Most recalled having subverted the authority of their male family members or being aware that this was common practice among other girls and women. Grace Gallo recalled that her mother was "more modern" than her father, and helped her to go out "on the sly" with her fiancé.[70] Caroline Colombo's mother was easier on her than her father and let her leave the house in the early evening with the warning, "Get back before your father gets back."[71] Many spoke of strict fathers, but also how they and their sisters routinely avoided close supervision by sneaking out to meet boys and by protecting each other. Filomena Orlando recalled, "When my little sister went out, we would say that she went out with one of the two older sisters and not mention that she went out with a boy."[72]

Girls also applied such strategies in their relationships with boys their own age. Grace Billotti Spinelli's brother forbade her from reading newspapers, but she noted, "I resolved the problem by having the paper reserved for me at the corner cigar store. The minute my dear brother left the house for the evening, I rushed down to get it, read it from cover to cover and then destroyed it. . . . Once I heard him discuss with a girl an article in *True Magazine* entitled 'Forbidden Fruit,' the title which I remember to this day. I knew he had the magazine hidden in his room; when he was out, I searched his room until I found the magazine and read the article." Still, in time, she became frustrated with secrecy, claiming that, "unlike my girl friends who used to meet boys on the sly, I never did. . . . I wanted to do openly what others were doing covertly."[73]

Some continued such activities into adulthood. Caroline Colombo and three of her friends, all of whom lived in the same apartment building, "joined an all-woman poker game and used it as an excuse to get out and explore." She recalled, "We used to say we were going to play cards at a girlfriend's house," but instead went out on the town without their husbands, to the movies and dance halls. "We took our wedding rings off and just want to have a good time that night. And we start dancing and some boys pick us up, we gave them the wrong address," she recounted while laughing. "We had a wonderful time."[74] Annunziata Macaluso's older sister also grew tired with gendered restrictions. She "opened her pay envelope, attended balls until midnight, and asked her mother to board, which her mother agreed to." Such a privilege was often reserved only for sons, but on occasion girls demanded this as well, "exercising their new entitlement as workers."[75] Macaluso remembers that her mother tried to convince her otherwise, but "it did no good. It went in one ear and out the other."[76]

As many historians have documented, young working women often "carved out spaces in their lives for privacy, independence, and unsupervised social interaction."[77] They dealt with the lack of privacy in overcrowded tenement apartments and the close supervision in factories by crafting a social life that took them out onto their stoops and into the city's streets, dance halls, parks, theaters, and movie houses. Furthermore, the emergent consumer culture they encountered and the popular culture they created in such spaces challenged parental authority because they often affirmed female sexual expressiveness and independence.[78] Such practices were the source of a great deal of tension between foreign-born parents and their American-born children. Indeed, "local police identified generational conflict as the major source of disturbance in Italian homes" in this period.[79] Some parents even institutionalized their daughters for disobedience.[80] As later chapters attest, these tensions would become especially salient in the years after World War One when the American-born generation became numerically larger than the immigrant generation because of immigration restriction legislation.

The Sacred as Antidote

Immigrant women and their daughters also turned to sacred realms for sustenance. Their spiritual practices most often took place outside of formal religious spaces and included devotion to the Madonna and saints, commemoration of ancestors, and folk healing. Scholars often note the pull that Catholicism had for Italian immigrant women because they outnumbered men in devotional practice, and gender conventions dictated that women were responsible for the spiritual labor of the family.[81] Historian Robert Orsi has offered a compelling explanation for this in his study of the largest Italian *festa* (feast) in early twentieth-century

New York City—the Neapolitan devotion to the Madonna del Carmine (Our Lady of Mount Carmel) in East Harlem. He found that women flocked to the *festa*, turning it into "a public celebration and acknowledgement of the power and authority of women." However, while "the devotion offered women this consolation, it reaffirmed those aspects of the culture which oppressed them: the source of their comfort was also the source of their entrapment."[82]

While many activists then, and scholars today, have considered Catholicism as antithetical to revolutionary activism, women's devotional practices contained a full range of possibility. It was above all else a space where women grappled with power in many different forms. To consider these practices as purely regressive is to forget, as feminist theorist M. Jacqui Alexander writes, that "the personal is not only political but spiritual."[83] Any analysis of Italian immigrant women's relationship to Catholicism must account for its complex place in their lives. It was a site where they learned ideologies of female subservience and inferiority. But it was also a medium through which they came to know their own innate power. This was especially true for the immigrant generation, who for the most part considered their devotional practices to be "more important than the doctrines of the church." As historian Rudolph Vecoli has demonstrated, "Italians were generally indifferent to religious doctrine and were distrustful of the institutional Church."[84] As a result, by the early twentieth century, Italian immigrants had earned a reputation among Catholics for being distinctly anticlerical.[85] When Nicholas Russo, the pastor of Our Lady of Loreto in Manhattan's heavily Sicilian neighborhood of Elizabeth Street went on pastoral calls he noted, "We were oftentimes received with the coldest indifference; not seldom avoided; at times greeted with insulting remarks."[86] Most Italians considered themselves Roman Catholic, but as one social investigator noted, of the 1,095 Italian immigrant women she interviewed in New York City, "the church was not an important factor in their lives. The older generation seldom went to services."[87] Carmela Cagliari's response to questions about her Catholicism are typical for women of her generation. She migrated from Palermo at the age of fourteen in 1912 to join her father and work as a seamstress. "We were Catholic and we never go to church," she noted, chuckling. When the oral historian prodded, Carmela explained: "Look darling because we didn't go to church I adore God. I got a God in my house in every room and I don't go to sleep at night if I don't pray all the saint I got in my room. In the morning, when I get up at night, when I go to bed, if I wake up in the middle of the night, I keep on praying. If I walk from my house to here I tell God, God please walk with me."[88]

As in Italy, immigrant women's own daily spiritual practices were more important than church attendance. This was especially true in the New York metro area, where Irish immigrants and their descendants dominated the Catholic Church and often looked upon Italian popular spirituality with disdain. Indeed, during the first decades of the twentieth century, the New York Archdiocese popularized the notion that Italians were a "problem" for the church.[89] Into the 1940s Irish Catholic priests were known for admonishing Italian immigrants for having "the luxuries of religion without its substantials." They saw their elaborate pilgrimages, feasts, shrines, holy cards, and home altars not only as devoid of "the great truths of religion" but as sacrilegious. Moreover, they complained that Italian immigrants "didn't attend mass, didn't receive the sacraments, didn't support the church financially, didn't patronize parochial schools, didn't respect the clergy or contribute to their numbers, and didn't realize they should have been doing these things."[90] Such exasperation was often shared by Irish parishioners. In the words of one Irish immigrant, the Italians "we were sure . . . were the people whom the Lord had chased from the temple."[91] As a result, one resident in East Harlem remembered that in 1886 most Italians in the neighborhood lived within a quarter of a mile from the church but those who attended mass were allowed to worship only in the building's basement, "a fact which was not altogether to our liking."[92]

Italian immigrant women's spiritual practices were, of course, deeply rooted in the traditions of their homelands: they fused Catholic and pre-Christian imagery and ritual in a manner that was largely independent of institutionalized religion. From this syncretism came the devotion to the saints who "served primarily the role of local protectors."[93] Sicilian immigrants from near Palermo continued to honor Santa Rosalia, while those from the eastern part of the island brought their devotion to Sant'Agata, and Neapolitans venerated San Gennaro. Celebrations to San Rocco, San Antonio, San Mauro, San Pasquale, San Donato, San Martino, San Giovanni, and Santa Lucia, among many other saints, also became an important part of Italian immigrant life.[94] Often recently arrived immigrants formed village-based mutual aid societies named after their patron saint, commissioned statues, and transported them across the Atlantic to watch over their communities. Orsi has noted that "these interwoven themes of protection, mutual support, and faithfulness to the values and history of the *paese*" formed the basis of these societies.[95] The devotion to the saints occurred largely outside of clerical control, in whatever spaces were available—basements, kitchens, storefronts, and even saloons.[96]

Makeshift sites of worship did mean, however, that devotees inscribed everyday spaces and activities with transgressive meaning. One particularly revealing example comes from Williamsburg, Brooklyn. In the summer of 1906, several police officers representing the city's Tenement House Squad arrived at 359 Metropolitan Avenue with orders to evict the tenants for "unsanitary conditions." As the police tried to enter the building they faced an angry Italian woman who blocked their entry, shouting "Death to the first man who desecrates our shrine!" A group of Italian women had built a community shrine for the Virgin Mary on the top floor. The first group of officers promptly left, the *New York Times* reported, because "one of them was Italian." The second group of officers arrived to find the women "praying for their destruction, so back to the street they went." It was not until the police convinced the women that "the law provided for their eviction to some cleaner place" that the women carried their shrine out and vacated the building.[97] As in southern Italy, women created their own relationship to the divine, without male intercessors. They also relied on their own sense of spiritual authority to confront adversaries.

Such a strategy was successful in large part because it was affirmed in their faith. Italian immigrant Catholicism continued to borrow from earlier pagan practices in which women were both central and powerful, including devotions to the goddesses Ceres, Demeter, Melaina, Diana, Isis, Cybele, Artemis, and Rhea, because throughout much of southern Italy "the institutional church never penetrated the hinterland."[98] Covello found that this profoundly shaped the religious practices of his East Harlem neighbors in the first decades of the twentieth century: "The popular traditions and the ancient beliefs changed but little, except that the names of deities legally established by the Church were substituted for those of ancient deities, and the manner of their worship was to some extent altered. Otherwise, every mountain, river, fountain had its presiding divinity just as in classic times; specific occasions and situations demanded the invocation of certain deities or magic forces."[99] As a result, pre-Christian cosmologies informed expressions of Catholic ritual. For example, the baptism of a child was valued because it was considered an effective method of protection from *mal'occhio* (the evil eye). A priest might be invited to sprinkle holy water in the four corners of a new home as a blessing. All Souls Day, officially celebrated on November 2 by the Roman Catholic Church, had special significance in southern Italy as Le Notte dei Morti (The Day of the Dead), the day when the veil between the living and the dead is the thinnest, and ancestors are honored with treats, incantations, and trips to their graves in a celebratory spirit. In addition, feast days were occasions not only for the veneration of patron saints but for divination. As Covello noted, during the Great Depression, on the night before the annual Feast of San Giovanni Batista, "every Italian girl on Mulberry Street tells her fortune with the white of an egg" because such powers were considered available only on this saint's day.[100]

The Divine Mother also remained the central figure, a goddess, the embodiment of the earth itself, and a protector with extraordinary power. She knew women's suffering intimately, migrated across the seas to be with her devotees, and performed miracles. It was to her that many Italian immigrant women turned daily, with their hopes, fears, and most desperate concerns. Whether lighting candles in a home altar, making the sign of the cross while passing the neighborhood shrine, sharing stories of divine intercession and healing with neighbors, beginning each day with prayer, or walking barefoot in penitence with hundreds of other women during the annual procession, Italian immigrant women very often had an intimate, daily, personal relationship with the Madonna in all her forms, whether as Madonna dell'Arco, Madonna dell'Assunta, Madonna delle Galline, Madonna dei Bagni, Madonna Addolorata, Madonna di Pompei, Maria Ausiliatrice, and Madonna del Carmine.[101]

Moreover, once a year, devotees took over the streets of their neighborhood, and the public transcript was released: all that was "usually expected to be kept hidden, was publicly proclaimed."[102] This annual rite resembled the *tarantate* in parts of southern Italy—the peasant women who flocked to their chapels on feast days to thank or beseech the saints for healing and to exorcise suffering in a collective ritual of dance that pulsated with the rhythm of the tambourine. The ethnographers who studied these traditions in Italy found them fascinating for many reasons, including how they "signaled certain halts in the process of Christian civilization's expansion."[103] But also because feasts to the Madonna were typically a woman's devotion, a chance for them to publicly and collectively express their suffering as women.[104]

During the feast of Our Lady of Mount Carmel in East Harlem people came (and to this day continue to come) from all over New York City, New Jersey, and beyond for the week-long celebration of "eating and talking and visiting."[105] In the first decade of the twentieth century, newspapers estimated that between 30,000 and 100,000 attended the event.[106] On the feast day itself, the men carried the Madonna, a "young Mediterranean woman holding a small child," through the streets, while women carried "huge and very heavy altars of candles arranged in tiered circles" balanced on their heads and ex-votos (sculpted waxen or silver body parts) representing the grace they received or desired.[107] The women walked together, chanting and shouting entreaties, some barefoot on the searing summer pavement. Still others "crawled up on the steps on their hands and knees, some of them dragging their tongues along the stone."[108] Such penitence was "governed by the vows people made to la Madonna" and if women insisted, men would join them as well.[109] After the procession, people gathered in the streets, richly decorated with lights and crepe. Women hung their finest linens and lacework from their windows to cover dingy and drab fire escapes and windows, to create a sacred space for the procession. Vendors lined the sidewalks with refreshments—peppers, sausages, cheese, bread, and sweets such as the Neapolitan *zeppoli* (fried and sugared dough)—and sold protective amulets, including horns to ward off *mal'occhio*, rosaries, candles, and holy pictures.[110]

While East Harlem's feast to Our Lady of Mount Carmel was the largest in this period, hundreds of smaller feasts occurred throughout the year, though typically in the summer months. Devotees erected elaborate shrines, sometimes five stories in height, in front of their tenements, as well as smaller shrines on window ledges and in their homes. Such practices extended from daily rituals. Social workers, journalists, and other investigators often commented on these practices, noting that, while the homes of Italian immigrant women were sparsely furnished, they were often filled with "images or pictures of the saints," before which were "frequently placed artificial flowers or candles."[111]

Women's daily labor to cultivate, procure, prepare, and share food constituted another type of feast. Food is often associated with women in Italian immigrant families, "as food preparers and organizers of the family's emotional life." As a result, "immigrants and their children glorified their mothers as 'feast makers' and culinary artists, in words that emphasized the warm sensuality that linked food to maternal love."[112] Popular narratives also tend to indulge in sentimentality and essentialism. However, scholars and writers have recently begun to explore the significance of food to women's power within Italian American families, to resisting assimilation, and to building community. The politics of food is, of course, central to women's history and literature, and it figures prominently in Italian immigrant women's own narratives and those of their children.[113] Literary critics Louise DeSalvo and Edvige Giunta write that, "at the heart of a family's emigration story, there is a story about food, or rather, about the lack of food, a story about devastating poverty, malnutrition, disease, starvation, famine."[114] We cannot, then, understand Italian immigrant women's daily forms of survival and resistance without reflecting on how relationships to food might have informed political activisms. Anna Valenti identified food as the central motivating factor in her ability to stand up to the bosses of the garment factories where she and her family worked: "I was always aggressive," she noted. "I always wanted to make more money for the simple reason when you make more money you can buy better food. You can live better."[115] Recall as well the story of Tina Gaeta. One of her fondest memories was how her mother Lucia made piecework more bearable for her children: she "would give us a treat and put the potatoes in the oven, or toast bread with oil and chopped garlic," and "tell us so many stories and proverbs while we were sewing."[116]

While life in the so-called New World was filled with hardship, it provided many with a way out of the famine their homelands. Caroline Colombo recalled that "things were bad in this country the beginning when we came. I would turn back and say at least I can go out and buy myself a piece of meat, butter, everything which over there you couldn't eat—the only thing you would have in the morning maybe a little vegetable soup left over from the night before or maybe a piece of cheese or a piece of food but I mean at least you say here we always ate good in this country. As much as we struggle and work hard we always had a good meal."[117]

Overall, Italian immigrant diets were generally more substantial than in their homelands.[118] Yet social workers still tried in vain to encourage Italians to change their patterns of consumption. Food was particularly contentious because it became a marker of Americanization: "There were constant campaigns to promote the eating of American food in order to transform ethnic culture. Ideas of 'nutrition' and 'food value' were scientific euphemisms that degraded ethnic cooking and sought to replace it with Anglo-American tastes."[119] Some social workers admired Italian diets, which favored an abundance of fresh fruit and vegetables, but most observers decried the strong tastes, including the heavy use of olive oil and garlic and what they saw as unhygienic practices, like drying tomatoes for paste outside in the open air.[120]

The preparing and sharing of food was, like most practices in this period, a double-edged sword. It offered a medium to resist assimilative pressures, to express oneself, experience pleasure, and build community. Yet it was also labor intensive for women. Sunday meals offered the chance for family and friends to convene but also extended women's workweek, giving them little respite. These gatherings did, however, become central to Italian immigrant political cultures. The homes of almost all the activists who animate the remaining chapters were typically filled on Sundays, and during labor strikes, workers turned Sunday meals into organizing meetings.

Food nourished activists in other ways as well. When Angela Bambace moved from New York to Baltimore in the 1930s to become an organizer with the International Ladies' Garment Workers' Union, she had her brother-in-law Nino Capraro, also a radical labor leader, deliver cases of olive oil and canned tomatoes to her new home on a regular basis. The foods of her family and community were especially important in these years. She was not only far from New York but without her children, whom she lost in a custody battle because of her refusal to be limited to a life centered on the kitchen.[121]

Indeed, kitchens emerge as complex spaces in the narratives of immigrant women and their children—as confining and labor intensive, but also as restorative and autonomous. The activities here are rarely visible in histories of Italian immigrant political cultures, especially those that focus on men. In the oral history that Paul Buhle conducted with Vito Magli in 1983 about his activism in East Harlem as a young man, a curious thing happens. They speak at length about Magli's participation in radical congressman Vito Marcantonio's political campaigns, his editing the communist Italian-language newspaper *L'Unità del Popolo*, and his involvement in other local neighborhood movements. As they speak in what appears to be Magli's kitchen and reflect on Italian women's supposed absence in local movements, the careful listener can make out another voice—that of Magli's wife, on the phone, in the background, carefully planning an upcoming event. She is concerned about inviting people who will relate to each other, the tensions that might arise between various individuals, and adequately organizing the preparation of the food. She is networking, literally behind the scenes, doing the kind of kin work that feminist scholars and social historians have shown is foundational to all social movements. In order to see Italian women's participation in community politics, we must enter this world.

The words of prominent labor organizer Elizabeth Gurley Flynn are worth revisiting here because they are so instructive. "There were practically no women in the Italian movement—anarchist or socialist," she stated in her memoir. "Whatever homes I went into with Carlo [Tresca] the women were always in the background, cooking in the kitchen, and seldom even sitting down to eat with the men." She added, "Some were strong Catholics and resented me very much; they were very disapproving of my way of life."[122] Historians would heed her words, as they did social reformers, journalists, and labor leaders, to argue that Italian women were distinct from other European immigrant women in their curious absence from politics. Yet, as the next chapter details, Italian immigrant women established anarchist women's groups in the same cities and movements where Flynn organized workers. Sometimes those same women were preparing the meals for Flynn and her comrades! Why then was Flynn unaware of their activism? Tresca's daughter, who often accompanied them on such visits, offers a clue. She recalled that Flynn never did "get off her fat behind" to help.[123] She chose not to enter the female world of the kitchen but to operate largely in male social worlds.

Another strategy related to food took on both spiritual and subversive dimensions—that of cultivation. Much has been written about the significance of gardening and foraging to Italian immigrants, who worked hard to produce and gather their own food and to create space in their lives for the natural world. These practices figure prominently in the narratives of immigrants and their descendants because they were central to their ability to survive on both practical and spiritual levels. Whether they planted gardens in backyards, on roofs, in pots on windowsills, or wherever there was idle land, Italian immigrants produced and sometimes sold a great wealth of vegetables and herbs, including lettuce, escarole, chicory, cabbage, tomatoes, eggplant, onions, artichokes, asparagus, squash, beans of all kinds, potatoes, broccoli, celery, peas, figs, thyme, basil, mint, parsley, and garlic. As in Italy, they also went out into the nearby woods and fields to gather what grew wild, such as dandelion greens, nettle, and chamomile.[124]

The women gathering dandelions in Paterson, New Jersey, whom the local judge happened upon and reprimanded, responded with a mixture of both anger and self-defense, especially when the local papers branded them as anarchists.[125] Foraging was politicized because it was a survival strategy for Italians, but also because it revealed immigrants' willingness to disregard and contest American ideologies regarding private property. As anthropologist Phyllis H. Williams noted in the 1930s, Italians survived the persistent poverty of recurrent economic depressions by passing on these skills: "[The immigrant] can, however, wander into American fields and woods and return with a burden that includes a bewildering array of mushrooms and other foods as well as of plants, berries, and barks for his medicine cupboard. Wild fennel, deadly nightshade, wild mallow, mullein, dock, and sorrel are all grist to his mill." Moreover, she noted, "Plants that do not grow wild, like basil and rue, are cultivated either in his garden or in little wooden boxes and pots that he sets on his porch or fire escape. Such herbs, dried and mixed with powdered palm leaves or salt, are worn as amulets or, soaked in that powerful repellent of evil, olive oil, are used to massage dislocations and rheumatism, and for worms in children." Though Williams assumed a male subject, women shared this labor with men. Men typically cultivated the gardens, but women did on occasion as well; and they were especially involved in the harvest. They also planted small herb and flower gardens and became experts in folk remedies. In fact, some women employed homeopathy, including "treat[ing] spider and snake bites by feeding a part of the creature itself to its victim."[126]

One typical story is that of Leonard Covello's grandmother, Nonna Clementina, whom he described as "the family matriarch" and "the focal point around which all life revolved." Her wisdom included extensive healing knowledge: "She knew all the herbs and remedies for every ailment. She could set a broken bone and apply the splints. I rarely saw a doctor in our home. And when there was a problem, she found the answer in the wisdom of her years and everyone listened to her. Nonna Clementina had a way of placing her hand upon my forehead that was like a benediction."[127] Film maker and writer Kym Ragusa has told of her immigrant grandmother Luisa, who was also known as a root woman in early twentieth-century East Harlem: "She knew the medicinal—and the magical— properties of many different kinds of plants: asphodel to ward off impotence, mallow to relieve toothache, chamomile to calm frayed nerves and upset stomachs. These she grew in pots on her fire escape. Other herbs she kept dried in paper bags in her closet, the secret herbs that she used to help women—bundled as charms to keep men from straying, packed into poultices to relieve a black eye, steeped into potent teas to ease labor pains or to end unwanted pregnancies."[128] Traditions of folk healing persisted because of their efficacy, but also because they cost very little. And while there were those who were respected for their healing knowledge and abilities, most women received and passed down some wisdom concerning diagnosis, everyday remedies, and other methods of healing and magic.[129] Such practices were transmitted despite the many efforts of American social workers, teachers, and politicians to dispose of what they saw as archaic and superstitious practices.

There is a story in Phyllis Williams's text that is especially revealing. She tells of an Italian immigrant family living on the third floor of a building with a "luxuriant vine that spreads over their old wooden porch." The plant was "coaxed from a bit of ground not more than a foot square, far below, by deft pruning and cultivation."[130] This serves as an apt metaphor for this chapter, because this "luxuriant vine" was not simply Italy transplanted. The city was its means. It hugged the side of the building, adorning the windows of neighbors along the way, a small invocation of the natural world amid a seemingly endless landscape of concrete. In much the same way this family nurtured this little plant, immigrants and their children summoned the natural world even in the smallest of ways, to cope with both the daily difficulties of urban industrial life as well as moments of great despair. My grandmother, the daughter of immigrant gardeners from the countryside just beyond Naples, turned her own small backyard into a lush garden to heal from a nervous breakdown in her fifties. She had raised eleven children, three of whom were in diapers at the same time, while my grandfather worked two and sometimes three jobs to put food on their table. The commitment to her own creative life apart from the family began with the garden.

This theme is deep in the narratives of immigrants and their children. Maria Forte farmed with her husband's family just outside of Naples, while he was away, working as a peddler and construction worker in New York. This helped her through their long separations, and once she crossed the Atlantic to join him, she turned again to gardening to overcome her disappointment that their "shack" in impoverished South Brooklyn was "in the America" she had longed for as a girl. She created a large garden on the roof of their building, and like the luxuriant vine that thrived from careful cultivation, her squash, beans, and other vegetables, transformed the dingy roof into a verdant sanctuary.[131]

We know too that Nicola Sacco found solace in the memory of his childhood

The author's great-grandparents Antonia (Zullo) and Francesco Paolo Porcelli, immigrants from Apice (Campania) in their garden in the Bronx, ca. 1930. They owned a small produce store, had fourteen children, and the author's grandmother Grace (Maria Grazia) was their youngest. She too was a gardener.

garden while he awaited execution and hoped for a miracle. In 1920 he and Barto-lomeo Vanzetti, both activists in the Italian immigrant anarchist movement, were arrested for a robbery and murder for which there was no conclusive evidence. After a trial now notorious for its anti-Italian and antiradical sentiment, the state of Massachusetts executed the two men in 1927. "What power does a garden have that a condemned man can turn from anguish to rapture in remembering it?" Patricia Klindienst writes, noting the shift in Sacco's prose from "anguish to peace, from despair to joy," when he wrote about his family's garden from prison.

His letters go into great detail: "We have fig trees, cherry trees, apple trees, pear trees, apricot trees, plum trees, peach trees, rhubarb shrubs, and three hedges of grapes—two lines of black and one line of white." The garden, he wrote, encompassed far more than the cultivated fields. It included the "grassy paths and the meadows beyond," a whole world of delight that filled his prose. "Hundreds of grass leaves of wild flowers witness there the almighty genius of the universal architect—reflecting the sky, the sun, the moon, the stars, all of its lights and colors. The forget-me-nots are nations there, and nations are the wild daisies."[132] Klindienst notes that "the energy in the details" suggests not just the power of gardens, but of the earth itself: "A moral universe is mapped here, one that transcends intolerance and injustice." Here, this man who was called a "dirty dago" and "anarchistic bastard" by the judge who ordered his execution was a "citizen of the land."[133] This consciousness would infuse the anarchist movement about which Sacco and many other Italians felt so passionate in this period. Indeed, Sacco's garden in Medford, Massachusetts, fed many poor families in the community.[134]

All of the daily forms of resistance described here animated and inspired the movements to which I now turn. The relationships, networks, and identities that women developed in their daily activities gave shape to an intricate pattern of association that served them well in their political work. The next four chapters turn to four different arenas of political struggle—anarchism, industrial unionism, fascism and transnational resistance, and the grass-roots neighborhood movements that arose during the Great Depression. That daily activities could lead to multiple forms of activism, both progressive and regressive, should not surprise us. Everyday resistance could be marshaled to protest desegregation and buttress emerging identities as whites, or to craft anarchist movements committed to *living* revolution—the embodiment of radical change by ending patterns of oppression in the everyday. In order to understand the significance of the ordinary to mass-based social movements, we must appreciate the everyday worlds that gave birth to and supported formal politics. We must become aware of the countless, often-invisible ways that immigrants and their children not only coped with dramatic upheaval and change but found ways to thrive, sometimes in luxuriant ways.

Anarchist Feminists
and the Radical Subculture

By the time Maria Roda immigrated to Paterson, New Jersey, from Italy in 1893 she was already a local hero. Only two years earlier, at the age of fifteen, she had gained notoriety when Italian authorities accused her of singing seditious songs and carrying on "like she was possessed" at a labor rally in Milan among silk weavers. News of her trial traveled throughout the international anarchist movement, not only because of her youth and the harshness of her sentencing (she served three months in prison) but for her "defiant attitude" toward the judge, to whom she gave a piece of her mind.[1]

A self-described anarcho-socialist at a young age, Roda had been forced to grow up fast. She entered the textile mills as a child, in the northern Italian city of Como, upon the premature death of her mother. She found solace in the local anarchist scene, and her commitment to revolutionary activism only deepened as she grew older. At nineteen, she joined her father and three sisters and migrated to Paterson, located about twenty miles west of Manhattan. All became immediately active in the Gruppo Diritto all'Esistenza (Right to an Existence Group), one of the largest and most influential Italian anarchist groups in North America.[2] Soon thereafter, Maria and several other women in the movement formed a Gruppo Emancipazione della Donna (Women's Emancipation Group). They did so, Roda stated at the time, "because we feel and suffer; we too want to immerse ourselves in the struggle against this society, because we too feel, from birth, the need to be free, to be equal."[3]

News of the Paterson women's group traveled quickly via one of the most popular Italian-language anarchist newspapers in the United States, *La Questione Sociale*.[4] Through the press, Roda invited women throughout Italy's many proletarian diasporas to meet on their own as well.[5] Within a short time, similar groups sprouted up in Italian immigrant neighborhoods in New York City, Hoboken,

Maria Roda, Pedro Esteve, and their eight children, ca. 1916. Personal archive of Federico Arcos.

Philadelphia, Boston, New Haven, and Chicago and the mining communities of Illinois, Pennsylvania, and Vermont. They also developed ties to working-class feminist groups in Buenos Aires, Paris, Milan, Rome, and beyond.[6] Although activism differed according to locale, the women in this network shared a common purpose—to create a place for women from the working classes to come together and develop their own visions for revolutionary change.

This chapter and the next explore Italian immigrant women's many interventions in working-class politics between 1880 and 1919, and the emergence of their own distinctive feminism and industrial unionism. As in South America, Europe, and beyond, Italian women's political activism in the United States centered on labor militancy. While they rarely held positions of leadership in unions, strike committees, or other formal organizations before the 1930s, their ability to organize co-workers and neighbors often proved critical to winning labor struggles, especially in the clothing, textile, and cigar-making trades where they often outnumbered men in the rank and file.[7] The anarchist movement offers an important doorway into this history because it was so significant to Italian immigrant labor activism. It also makes visible the diasporic, radical subculture that was foundational to Italian American working-class politics at this time.

All of the social movements to which Italian immigrant women and their daughters devoted their energies emerged from, or were profoundly shaped by, the radical subculture. As the nineteenth century drew to a close, a network of Italian immigrant women devoted to working-class revolution emerged from this world. Indeed, the Italian-language radical press from the 1880s to the 1920s contains the names of hundreds of women active in this movement, as writers, performers, organizers, and subscribers. Some described their activism with the word *femminismo* (feminism), but more often they used *emancipazione*, because this distinguished their activism from bourgeois feminisms and signified their commitment to freedom from oppression in all forms. Some did not call themselves feminists, but their actions directly challenged gender conventions and patriarchal power relations. This chapter explores this history by focusing on a core group of women active in the international anarchist movement, to trace the networks, relationships, and visions for change they created. Together, they remind us of the radical, working-class, and diasporic roots of modern feminism. To them, liberation meant the radical restructuring of society in which pleasure was primary, not just for some on the backs of others but for all.

The Radical Subculture

Because the vast majority of Italian immigrant women and men were concentrated in menial, low-wage jobs, they were not initially recruited by mainstream U.S. labor and political organizations. Rather, American labor and political leaders organized to restrict Italian immigration on the grounds that Italian workers undercut wages, were unorganizable, and racially undesirable. As would be the case for other marginalized workers, Italians responded by forming mutual aid societies, what they called the *società di mutuo soccorso*.[8] This method of self-help and survival was fundamental in Italy, and migrant workers continued this strategy as they traveled to Argentina, Brazil, France, England, Spain, Belgium,

Switzerland, the United States, and other locales. Much like the hometown associations among immigrants today, workers from the same village or region formed these societies to offer health insurance, loans, death benefits, medical services, and a cooperative social setting.[9] They typically centered on male social networks, but it appears that women were active in the socialist and anarchist societies, which Italians called *circoli politici* (political circles) and *circoli di studi sociali* (social studies circles). In addition to providing mutual aid, these *circoli* sought to extend the anarchist and revolutionary socialist movements then spreading across Italy and its many diasporas. Members met in one another's homes and businesses, rented storefronts, gathered in parks, and meeting halls. They also established an impressive network of collectively run libraries, schools, food cooperatives, theater troupes, independent presses, and some of the earliest union locals of the Industrial Workers of the World (IWW) and other industrial unions, through which they built a radical counterculture to the religious, patriotic, or apolitical societies.[10] It was here that Italian immigrant women created spaces for feminist activism, especially in the years before the First World War.

From the 1880s through the 1930s, hundreds of these radical circles formed across the New York metro area. They found ready support among Italian workers whose hopes of finding dignified work and decent wages in the United States were often dispelled upon arrival. Armando Pelizzari, an organizer for the United Mine Workers of America, echoed the sentiments of many when he wrote to the socialist newspaper *Il Proletario*, "America is a land where demoralization, poverty, and slavery reign in abundance, and where our enchanted dreams from across the ocean become disillusions as soon as we set foot upon this land."[11] Carlo Tresca, anarchist writer and publisher who achieved iconic status in the movement, similarly noted, "we sought only bread that was less hard, work less exhausting. . . . [Instead] they gave us bullets, only bullets and handcuffs, as in Italy. Not royal bullets but republican bullets."[12]

By the 1910s, dozens of anarchist groups had formed in the Lower East Side and Mulberry districts alone, and at least one anarchist group coalesced in every other Italian neighborhood. They flourished in Harlem, Brooklyn, and the Bronx, as well as across the Hudson River in Paterson, Bayonne, Orange Valley, Union Hill, West Hoboken, Passaic, Newark, Atlantic City, and Clifton. Intended as nonhierarchical and grass roots, most of these groups were grounded in daily relationships among kin, neighbors, and *paesani*. For this reason they were often small, with anywhere from just a handful to several hundred members.[13] While self-avowed *sovversivi* (subversives), as they called themselves, always constituted a minority in Italian immigrant communities, their influence was much larger than their numbers because they established quite visible alternative cultural and political spaces in their neighborhoods, which became popular centers for immigrant education, political discussion, labor organizing, and recreation. These groups also drew support from their communities because they were the first to successfully mobilize the masses of Italian immigrant workers before the First World War.[14] For example, while only close to a dozen members regularly attended meetings in one of Brooklyn's more active groups, thousands of men and women from the community participated in the frequent dances, festivals, lectures, and picnics they sponsored.[15] In some places, most notably Paterson, group membership grew into the thousands, but in most communities Italian anarchists and socialists became "a ready and relatively visible reference point."[16]

The most popular circles were anarchist because, as Nunzio Pernicone has written, they "rejected electoral politics and espoused direct revolutionary action, [which] had a natural appeal for immigrants eager to transform the world as soon as possible."[17] Paul Avrich has also emphasized that Italians "comprised one of the largest and most militant of the ethnic groups which made up the immigrant anarchist movement" in the United States, and "they came from every corner of Italy (including Sardinia and Sicily)."[18] Many Italians were somewhat familiar with radical ideologies because the popular movements in their homelands were often inspired by a mixture of anarchism and revolutionary socialism. But it was the experiences they faced in the United States as workers in sweatshops, mines, construction, and other low-paid, dangerous, and dirty work that affirmed for many that revolution was not only desirable but of urgent necessity. One Sicilian immigrant anarchist explained the appeal of the movement: "For the most part the anarchists were young immigrants who acquired their anarchism through contact with others. It was mostly by word of mouth and personal experience of the injustice of the system. Then they began to read the anarchist press and to attend meetings. Their hopes for a better life, a better society in America, were disappointed. It was just as ruthless and cruel a society as the one they had left." Remilda Ramella offered a similar explanation for why she was drawn to anarchism as a young mill worker in Paterson; she told of the unrelenting poverty and how the movement ignited her desire for freedom.[19]

Many immigrants came to first know the movement via Italy's most popular anarchist organizers. Errico Malatesta, Luigi Galleani, Pietro Gori, and Francesco Saverio Merlino all became folk heroes as the labor movement exploded across Italy in the last quarter of the nineteenth century. They were, as Rudolph Vecoli has written, "inspired orators, vigorous polemicists, dedicated idealists, who had aroused the Italian working class and imbued it with revolutionary spirit. Now they bent their efforts on awakening the Italian plebes in America."[20] In the decades preceding the First World War, each of these men traveled regularly to

Italian immigrant enclaves, to mobilize workers, inspire revolutionary consciousness, encourage the formation of radical groups, and found radical newspapers. For the majority of Italian workers who had come from rural regions, migration made possible their encounter with such figures. Caterina D'Amico joined the movement soon after she emigrated from Sicily in 1899 when she heard Galleani, one of the most popular, militant, and magnetic anarchists, speak at an open-air meeting in Brooklyn: "I was a teenager, and I liked what he had to say and the way he said it. He spoke directly to my heart. I became an anarchist and took part in picnics, amateur theatricals, and other activities."[21]

Anarchists were not a particularly unified group, of course. Those most active in the movement often split over strategy, constantly debated whether retaliation through violence was consistent with their ideals, and questioned whether they should seek mass-based formal organization among workers. However, they united in their belief that the government, the church, and private property were harmful because they required that people live under a system of inequality and surrender their own power.[22] As Neapolitan anarcho-syndicalist theorist and activist Errico Malatesta explained in his widely popular treatise *L'Anarchia*, anarchists sought "the destruction of all political order based on authority, and the creation of a society of free and equal members based on a harmony of interests and the voluntary participation of everybody in carrying out social responsibilities."[23] They argued that no one was free until all were free. Or, in the words of Mikhail Bakunin, one of the intellectual founders of anarchism: "No individual can recognise his own humanity, and consequently realise it in his lifetime, if not by recognising it in others and cooperating in its realisation for others."[24] Rather than hand over collective power to the state, they advocated a society "in which the exploitation and domination of man by man is not possible; in which everybody has free access to the means of life, of development and of work, and that all can participate, as they wish and know how, in the organization of social life." They called for the free social organization of people into a "community of comradeship," through the very *circoli* that formed the heart of their political culture.[25]

Branded as terrorists, bloodthirsty criminals, and enemies of the state, anarchists embodied the state's worst fears when it came to Italian immigrants. This fear reached a fevered pitch in 1900 when Gaetano Bresci, an Italian immigrant silk weaver from Paterson, who was active in an anarchist group in Hoboken, assassinated the Italian King Umberto I to avenge the 1898 massacre of workers in Milan. A year later, Polish immigrant and self-avowed anarchist Leon Czolgosz, assassinated U.S. president William McKinley.[26] In the aftermath, the media and public officials depicted all anarchists as murderous and vile, even though only some in the movement advocated assassination and many opposed such acts.[27] The wholesale nature of antianarchist sentiment is captured in the words of President Theodore Roosevelt, in his 1908 statement justifying the suppression of all anarchist materials from the mail: "The anarchist is the enemy of humanity, the enemy of all mankind, and his is a deeper degree of criminality than any other."[28] Beginning in 1901, the federal government passed a series of laws barring immigrants with anarchist ideas from entering the country, and aggressively targeted those who resided within U.S. borders, with the aid of foreign consular officials.

Even so, the New York metropolitan area offered a dynamic setting for the movement. It was, after all, one of the largest centers of diasporic radicalism in the world, not only for Italians but for immigrant workers from Poland, Lithuania, Hungary, Russia, Ireland, Germany, Holland, Belgium, England, China, India, Spain, Turkey, Puerto Rico, Cuba, Jamaica, and Trinidad, among other places.[29] Revolutionary socialist and anarchist immigrant workers from all over the world came together in jointly sponsored rallies, picnics, and other gatherings, to build solidarity, raise consciousness, and collect funds for political prisoners, strikers, and their presses, among other causes.[30] In the handmade cigar, textile, and garment industries, mutual aid societies coalesced into multiethnic unions and jointly published radical newspapers. Indeed, the radical subculture provided many with a point of entry into a revolutionary working-class movement that crossed lines of region, language, ethnicity, religion, race, and gender.

For the most part, Italian anarchist groups reflected the overall demographic of their communities. Most were composed of southern Italians, but they included others as well. In Brooklyn, Italian shoe and garment workers organized with their Cuban, Spanish, Puerto Rican, and Russian co-workers and neighbors in a *circolo* called Club Avanti. Founded by Sicilian anarchists, Club Avanti "supported education, sponsored lectures on peace, religion, and sexual and family questions, on women's emancipation, nationalism, imperialism, major immigrant strikes, the Mexican Revolution, the problems of political prisoners in Italy, and, more generally, current events."[31] In East Harlem, Sicilian anarchists collaborated with the Lower East Side Gruppo Il Risveglio to organize events that included Spanish, Bohemian, French, English, Russian, and other immigrant anarchists, as well as native-born Americans.[32] Some groups, such as the Gruppo Diritto all'Esistenza in Paterson, was composed mostly of northern Italian textile workers, with smaller numbers of French, German, Dutch, Spanish, Greek, Austrian, and Belgian immigrants, most of whom worked in the city's silk mills.[33]

Italian anarchist circles from New York City and New Jersey also came together for the annual Festa della Frutta, a secular harvest festival (which translates inelegantly as "Fruit Feast") and Primo Maggio (May Day). Such radical

May Day Picnic, Haledon, N.J., 1915. American Labor Museum, Botto House National Landmark.

holidays were honored with food, music, dance, political speeches, recitations of poetry, theatrical performances, and, in the case of the *festa*, elaborate decorations (some of which were decidedly altarlike) of fruit and vegetables to celebrate the abundance of the season.[34] A photograph of the 1915 May Day picnic in Haledon, a suburb of Paterson, offers another way of understanding the appeal of the movement: it was a source of pleasure, a place to relax, have fun, dress up, and meet others with a passion for social justice. Given how intensely employers exerted control over workers' bodies and lives, such gatherings offered a space to express oneself, recuperate from the long workweek, and build the type of group solidarity that was essential to mass-based action.

The radical press was another important source of community cohesion, especially for such a mobile readership as Italian workers. As Pernicone has written, "The Press—not political parties, federations, or trade unions—was the institutional base of the Italian immigrant left, linking thousands of comrades spread across the country and abroad."[35] Often immigrants published the newspapers in their homes or businesses, with a printer that was purchased by pooling resources. While much smaller in budget and circulation than the more mainstream Italian-language newspapers, like *Il Progresso Italo-Americano*, the radical press still reached significant numbers because they circulated through everyday networks and were read aloud in factories, homes, and other places.[36] In fact, scholars have identified a total of 190 Italian-language radical newspapers published in the United States between 1870 and the end of World War II. While some lasted no more than several issues, a few achieved circulations of close to 15,000 readers and were in print over several decades.[37] Each provided a forum for activists to share and debate a full spectrum of revolutionary ideologies, publicize events, and stay in contact with one another.

The outbreak of the Mexican Revolution in 1910, for example, was front-page news in the Paterson-based Italian-language anarchist newspaper *L'Era Nuova* for many months. Italian radicals in North America stayed in close contact with and kept comrades apprised of this mostly peasant and anarchist revolutionary movement. *Regeneración*, the newspaper of the Partido Liberal Mexicana, and one of the most important papers of the revolution, also included an Italian-language column, as well as graphics and cartoons by Ludovico Caminita, a Sicilian anarchist writer, printer, and member of the Paterson Gruppo Diritto all'Esistenza. Such connections would become especially significant during World War I, when Italian American men fled across the U.S.-Mexico border to avoid military conscription.[38]

These newspapers, many of which remain with us today in a number of archives, hold a key to understanding Italian immigrant women's participation in social movements. They reveal that women were not well represented among the *Galleanisti*, those anarchists who followed the most popular antiorganizationalist (or "individualist") agitator Luigi Galleani. He advocated the overthrow of the government and capitalism by violent means, including the use of dynamite and assassination. He also distrusted all forms of organization, including labor unions, which he believed were likely to turn hierarchical and authoritarian. Rather, women were more often drawn to the *organizzatori*, the organizationalist wing of the anarchist movement. The *organizzatori* were syndicalists who advocated the use of direct action, such as the general strike or sabotage, and industrial unionism, to generate revolutionary consciousness and solidarity.[39] The lines between these two camps were not always entirely clear, however, as most in the movement tended to blend different strategies and change their convictions over a lifetime.[40] Often adherents of Errico Malatesta, who advocated organizing workers into collectivities, admired Galleani, who many described as a great writer, speaker, and philosopher.[41] The newspapers, however, generally identified with one camp or the other, depending on the editor, and these debates were a central part of the movement culture.

Given the preponderance of women in manufacturing, the *organizzatori* had good reason to create a movement that resonated with women. In their newspapers the voices of women are consistently present. Similarly, the only other radical newspapers to accentuate women's voices were those published by the newly formed Italian sections of the garment unions—*L'Operaia*, *Giustizia*, *Il Lavoro*, and *Lotta di Classe*—where women constituted the majority of the rank and file. These papers were an exception, however, and the print culture of the Italian American Left was largely centered on male voices. This reflected the power dynamics in this movement: most of the more prominent male radicals routinely positioned *themselves* as the center of revolutionary culture and relied on language, practices, and identities that celebrated male virility, paternalism, and sexual bravado.[42] They also founded and presided over the institutional culture of the Italian immigrant Left, in organizations that were central to the labor movement, such as the Federazione Socialista Italiana (FSI), the Italian Chamber of Labor, the socialist newspaper *Il Proletario*, and the Anti-Fascist Alliance of North America (AFANA).[43] As historian Michael Miller Topp has documented, the "pervasive masculinist ethos" of these leaders meant that they "paid little attention to women's involvement in the labor movement, much less questioned patriarchal notions in the Italian immigrant community."[44] These same men would administer over the largely female rank and file in the Italian-language union locals of the International Ladies' Garment Workers' Union, formed in 1916 and 1919. These locals would become some of the largest and more politically powerful labor organizations in the nation during the 1930s and 1940s. As a result, scholars often center analyses of the Italian American Left upon a collection of male leaders and networks to conclude that women were largely absent from the radical subculture and the union movement more generally. Moreover, when historians examine Italian anarchists, they are most often drawn to the *Galleanisti* whose adherents included some of the more famous activists, like Nicola Sacco, Bartolomeo Vanzetti, and Gaetano Bresci. By contrast, very little scholarship has documented the history of those anarchists who advocated industrial unionism, the *organizzatori* or anarcho-syndicalists. Yet it is here that we find women, in body and spirit.[45]

Two newspapers represented the discourse and activity of the anarcho-syndicalists: *La Questione Sociale* and *L'Era Nuova*. Both were published in Paterson (and on occasion in Manhattan) successively from 1895 to 1915 by the Gruppo Diritto all'Esistenza to promote the position of the *organizzatori*. This group, to which Maria Roda belonged, consisted mainly of a collective of highly politicized workers from the northern Italian textile districts of Biella, Vercelli, Prato, and Como. The core group had come to know one another through labor struggles and mutual aid organizations in their homelands. Some had even worked together in the Rivetti Mill in Biella, which employed seven thousand workers and "stretched over hundreds of acres and encompassed the entire process of woolen weaving from the arrival of the unwashed sheep skins to the finished cloth."[46] Workers in this mill and the surrounding areas launched some of the largest strike movements among Italy's industrial workers in the decades following national unification, and textile workers throughout the regions of Lombardy and Piedmont became well known for their radicalism.[47] Italian labor leader Rinaldo Rigola, who came of age in this movement, noted that "to identify oneself as a weaver was to be marked as an agitator, so widespread was the agitation against the transformation of the industry."[48] This reputation would expand with migration and labor battles overseas, but the culture of resistance changed. The Gruppo Diritto all'Esistenza grew to include workers from southern Italy and many different countries. Indeed, the government informant who successfully infiltrated the group from 1917 to 1920 (during the Red Scare) did so as an Algerian.[49]

Because Paterson was home to a vibrant anarchist scene and close to Manhattan, it was connected to labor movements and radical subcultures not only in New York City but in northeastern New Jersey as well, through the network of anarchist mutual aid societies. The largest *circoli* in New Jersey were formed by Italian workers in the urban, industrial centers of Newark, Jersey City, Paterson, and Trenton. But sizable groups also emerged in Camden, Hackensack, Elizabeth, Hoboken, Union City, and Passaic, many formed by southern Italian workers in the cement, linoleum, rubber, electrical, garment, and construction industries.[50] *La Questione Sociale* and *L'Era Nuova* were at the center of this network of groups, and both grew to become some of the most important anarchist newspapers in the world at the time.[51]

La Questione Sociale preceded *L'Era Nuova* and was founded in 1895 by several men, including the popular anarchist poet, playwright, and lawyer Pietro Gori, who came to the United States from Italy in 1895 to speak before workers' assemblies and assist in spreading revolution. Because *La Questione Sociale* was already quite popular in Buenos Aires and Italy, Gori, along with Errico Malatesta and a Catalan anarchist and typesetter by the name of Pedro Esteve, established the paper in North America with the headquarters in Paterson. Both *La Questione Sociale* and *L'Era Nuova* would reach thousands across North America and beyond, in Italy, France, Spain, Venezuela, Argentina, and Mexico.[52] Both identified as "*socialisti-anarchici*": they called for the abolition of the state and capitalism, and for "the organization of workers into leagues of resistance" that were "independent from any political party."[53] *La Questione Sociale* ran until 1908, when the federal government revoked its mailing privileges under the obscenity statute.[54]

The newspaper would reappear briefly during the First World War in Manhattan and then vanish with the repression of the Red Scare. *L'Era Nuova* picked up where it left off. It too was published by the Paterson Gruppo Diritto all'Esistenza (now calling itself the Gruppo L'Era Nuova) and ran from 1908 to 1915, when it was also suspended from the mail for containing politically subversive material.

While both papers centered on male voices, women were present, as were their interpretations of anarchism, feminism, and many other aspects of working-class struggle. These newspapers are therefore especially important to reconstructing women's activism, not only because of their significance to the Italian immigrant Left but because so few records have survived. The *circoli* were raided repeatedly by federal officials in the first several decades of the twentieth century. Surveillance and suppression peaked during the First World War, as the federal government criminalized any activity that opposed American domestic or foreign policy, including reading, writing, or speaking against the government. Federal agents focused their contempt on supporters of the Bolshevik Revolution, but especially on anarchists, socialists, black nationalists, antiwar activists, and any others who called the status quo of capitalism, imperialism, militarism, and white supremacy into question.[55] Federal agents routinely raided the offices and homes of those affiliated with the *circoli* and confiscated materials to prosecute activists, such as correspondence, mailing lists, photographs, pamphlet literature, books, and newspapers. The federal government declassified these materials in the early 1980s, but much was destroyed. Moreover, the personal records of Italian women active in the movement were very rarely preserved, either by their families or by libraries.

As a result, scholars have relied on scant records and the memories of prominent figures in the movement to argue that Italian women played a minimal role. Dominick Sallitto, a Sicilian immigrant anarchist in New York City (and gardener by trade) whom Paul Avrich interviewed, echoed many in the movement when he noted, "The women seldom participated."[56] Yet, as we have seen with Elizabeth Gurley Flynn's recollections, there are often ironies contained within such statements. Sallitto's wife Aurora Alleva, who was born in Philadelphia to an anarchist family from Ascoli Piceno, was in fact a well-known anarchist and popular speaker at radical events in New York City during the 1920s and 1930s. Even Italian consular officials watched her activities closely, noting that she was "an anarchist teacher" and "very well known in America for her organizing activity."[57] Yet Sallitto does not mention her activities, and Avrich did not interview her, though he did note that she prepared for them "an excellent Italian lunch, complete with freshly picked fruit and vegetables from their garden."[58]

Certainly there were fewer women in the movement than men. But only a handful of scholars have explored why this was the case or analyzed the lives of those women who were active.[59] The contradictions between oral histories and memoirs that proclaim women's absence and the anarcho-syndicalist press, police records, and other materials that document their presence in this movement suggest that women's activism was not only distinct from men's but also largely invisible or insignificant to them. Most *circoli* publicly encouraged women to participate in events, through such gestures as free admission to events and direct appeals in the newspapers for their attendance at certain meetings and activities.[60] However, it appears that women were rarely present at the regular meetings. Rather, their participation followed familiar patterns of the gendered division of labor. Meetings typically centered on male social networks, but women were engaged in other activities: they helped to organize the lectures, festivals, dances, picnics, and theatrical performances that were sponsored by the *circoli*; and when there were urgent issues at stake, they went to meetings.[61]

Overall, the distinctions between male and female social worlds that defined daily life for most Italians were replicated in the radical subculture. The recollection of William Gallo, the son of Ninfa Baronio and Firmino Gallo, all life-long activists within the anarchist movement, workers in the silk mills, and members of Paterson's Gruppo Diritto all'Esistenza, is useful here: "The Italian anarchists in Paterson started a *cooperativa*, a cooperative grocery store with a club upstairs, a little building. They met every Saturday and practically every evening. They played cards, had a drink of wine or beer, but not too much liquor. Every Saturday there was a dance, with music played by a little orchestra. I played the guitar, [my brother] Henry the violin. My brother-in-law Spartaco ("Spot") Guabello played the mandolin. . . . Father and Mother, especially Mother, did quite a lot of acting at the club, which had a small stage. . . . All the plays were about the life of the poor, and how they were oppressed."[62] As he reveals, the anarchist movement was centered on families. Ninfa and Firmino's five children, Ninfa's sister Anetta and brothers Egisto and Abele, and Firmino's two brothers Louie and Andrea were among the thousands active in Paterson's anarchist milieu.[63] The men typically gathered in the evenings and socialized, while the women attended and organized events and acted in the theatrical performances.

Women also helped to run the stores, publishing houses, boarding homes, and other spaces that knit together the community and provided the foundation for the movement. Indeed, the store that Ninfa and Firmino ran at 77 Ellison Street in Paterson was at the center of Paterson's anarchist world.[64] Like many newsstands, it sold candy and soft drinks, but the store was also home to one of the largest anarchist bookstores in the United States. Called the Libreria Sociologica (sociological bookstore), and formed by four anarchist circles (Gruppo I Risorti,

Family reunion of the Guabello, Gallo, and Baronio families, all of whom were active in the anarchist movement. Ninfa Baronio is fifth from the left, in the second row. Firmino Gallo is sixth from the left, in the third row. Adalgisa Guabello is first from the right, in the third row. Alberto Guabello is fourth from the left, in the last row. Haledon, N.J., August 1921. American Labor Museum, Botto House National Landmark.

Gruppo Verità, Gruppo Pensiero e Azione, and Gruppo Diritto all'Esistenza), it sold pamphlets and books by many of the most popular radical intellectuals of the day.[65] It was also a major distribution center for radical newspapers in North America. It was at Ninfa and Firmino's home that Elizabeth Gurley Flynn would stay for several weeks, when she came to Paterson with other IWW organizers to assist the twenty-five thousand striking silk workers who shut down three hundred silk mills and dye houses in 1913.[66]

Firmino Gallo, or "Old Gallo" as his comrades in the movement called him, was one of the most active anarchists in Paterson. Described by his son as "a very quiet type," the federal government watched him closely and arrested him at least three times—once for displaying antiwar posters in his store window—before a major raid on the community in 1920. He and two of his brothers were central to the activities of the Gruppo Diritto all'Esistenza. The undercover operative who penetrated the Paterson anarchist movement spent many an afternoon in Gallo's shop and came to realize that Gallo's *compagna* Ninfa was also an anarchist.[67] To the Department of Justice, the store was a "seething nest of reeking red anarchy."[68]

But to Ninfa and Firmino's son William, it was an intellectually rich and inspired environment made up of "gentle souls." He would remember his parents' activism with great fondness: "I recall that mother did a lot of reading and a lot of deep thinking, said that the church was dogmatic and authoritarian, cardinals living like princes, crusaders stealing and looting and raping—all in the name of the Vatican. Father felt the same way. He was also a great reader and in fact ran a little *libreria*, a bookstore. People wrote in from all over the country to order books (in Italian) by mail. To my parents anarchism meant honesty and respect for others. Money was the last thing to be considered. Honest work and freedom—that's all they wanted. They didn't aspire to riches, to have bank accounts or wealth. They criticized exploitation of every kind. I remember that Mother respected the Bill of Rights. 'This is wonderful reading,' she said."[69]

Growing up in this atmosphere, William felt able to fully indulge his passion for learning and reading. For most, the radical movement was an important source of education, especially because so many had left school as children to help support their families. The *sovversivi* also distrusted conventional schools, seeing them as an "instrument of domination and enslavement," a way for the state "to fabricate docile citizens, respectful of laws, authorities, and pre-established orders."[70] The children of anarchists often met on their own in youth groups, "to educate ourselves, to read, and study." They attended one of the three Ferrer schools in the country, inspired by Catalan anarchist educator Francisco Ferrer, in Paterson, Boston, and Philadelphia.[71] Much has been written about the ways Italian immigrants undervalued formal schooling, especially when compared with Jewish immigrants; but it is important to expand our notion of what constitutes educational practice to include not only apprenticeships and workplace experiences but also activism in the labor movement, all of which were significant to many Italian immigrants and their children.[72] The radical subculture encouraged children to think critically and familiarized them with a whole host of writers and intellectuals, such as Dostoevsky, Artsybashev, Turgenev, and Nietzsche. William Gallo recalled that his parents taught him to question whether the United States lived up to its ideals of freedom and democracy: "When you talk about the Constitution and the Bill of Rights I'm skeptical and disappointed," he would note as an older man. "We stole the land from the Indians, killed them off, put them on reservations. Is this democracy? Is this Christianity? Is this civilization?" During the First World War, William would join other Italian American anarchists who fled to Mexico to avoid serving in the infantry. "I refused to kill anyone or to shoulder a gun," he asserted. Spartaco Guabello joined him in Mexico—the son of Alberto and Adalgisa Guabello, all of whom were also active in Paterson's anarchist movement.[73]

The Guabello and Gallo families were especially close and here too we get a glimpse into the gender dynamics of the movement. Spartaco Guabello and Lena Gallo (Ninfa and Firmino's daughter) would fall in love and spend a lifetime together. Ninfa also came to the defense of Alberto's brother Paolo during a labor strike, when he was clubbed to the ground by police. She was beaten by police as well, and both were arrested.[74] At one point, Alberto and Adalgisa Guabello ran a print shop behind the bookstore, where they printed many of the radical periodicals, newspapers, and pamphlets that Ninfa and Firmino circulated through the store. Alberto also gained notoriety as a labor organizer for leading several strikes against local silk companies and for helping to bring the newly formed IWW to Paterson.[75] His grandchildren would recall, however, that when it came to earning an income he was "lazy" and his wife Adalgisa "did all the work."[76]

Some of the women in this movement fared better, and like Ninfa, formed loving, mutually sustaining partnerships with men who fully supported their ideals. These relationships offered the next generation an entirely new model of companionship. As anarchists, they did not believe in marriage before the church or state, and unless coerced by the federal government (as some were), most did not legally marry. Ninfa's son William noted proudly that while neither his parents nor any of his aunts or uncles married, "none of them ever separated or divorced, none of them."[77] While anarchists worked to redefine marriage, they struggled with fully enacting their beliefs, however. Many women found that while men in the movement supported women's freedom in principle, it was harder to get them to practice what they preached. Many were, as one man aptly put it, "anarchists by conviction but not by behavior." They supported the principles, but were "an authoritarian at home."[78]

This disjuncture was so widespread that it became the site of much contention within the movement, with some of the more popular Italian theorists weighing in from abroad. Camillo Di Sciullo, a noted anarchist newspaper editor and labor organizer from the southern Italian province of Chieti (Abruzzo), wrote the following to the anarchists in North America through *La Questione Sociale*: "We anarchists are predicated on the emancipation of women. . . . But how many of us consider the women free, as our comrades? I believe very few, or none! It is a cruel truth."[79]

While fewer women were active in the *circoli* than men, those who were active often questioned the power relations that kept women from joining in larger numbers. They also developed a commitment to *l'emancipazione della donna* (women's emancipation), educated themselves, and built community with similarly idealistic and visionary comrades. For example, Italian immigrant women in an anarchist *circolo* in the Bronx hosted lectures on women and labor radicalism by inviting speakers such as Bellalma Forzato Spezia, who ran a radical bookstore at 416 Spring Street in West Hoboken. She was also one of the few women whose writing on such topics as syndicalism, feminism, and education, was widely published in the Italian American radical press.[80] A teacher by trade, Spezia migrated to the United States in 1906, at the age of twenty-nine, from the small village of Mirandola (Modena). Before long, she became well known in radical circles as a "cultured educator and revolutionary," who wrote "brilliant, clear and elegant poetry that one can read in one breath."[81] Perhaps because she was educated, sophisticated, and northern, she was one of the few Italian women to rise to prominence in the movement. Her work circulated more than any other woman's in Italian-language radical newspapers, and she became a regular speaker on the lecture circuit. But there were others. In Newark, for example, local women invited another skilled orator, Concettina Cerantonio, to come from Italy to help mobilize women workers, though little is known of her.[82] Women also hosted benefits to honor their martyrs, such as the anarcho-syndicalist activist Maria Rygier, who was imprisoned in Apulia in 1912 for her radical activities.[83]

The education in radical political theory and practice that Italian immigrant women received in the *circoli* led some to become speakers and organizers themselves. Angela and Maria Bambace both turned to the anarchist and socialist groups in their East Harlem neighborhood as young women, while working in the garment industry alongside their mother Giuseppina. Thus began their lifelong commitment to the labor movement. There they met labor leaders in the IWW and learned the direct-action strategies they would use as organizers in New York City's 1919 uprising of garment workers and later in many other strikes.[84] Reflecting on her life, Angela recalled, "It was difficult to separate the organization of workers from the attempt to reorganize society. The two went hand in hand."[85] Similarly, Tina Cacici, a Sicilian immigrant who would become the leader of a radical faction in the Lawrence textile strike of 1919 and an organizer for the ACWA (and, later, a supporter of Mussolini), first became known for her fiery speeches on women's emancipation at an anarchist *circolo* in Brooklyn.[86]

Given these levels of female activism, why did men consider women to be inactive in the movement? In fact, this was something that women addressed most directly.

Enter Maria Roda

When Maria Roda announced in *La Questione Sociale* in 1897 that she and several others in Paterson were organizing separate activist circles for women, she spoke for many women who had grown frustrated with their invisibility and marginalization within the movement. "It is time that we also agitate and organize," Roda stated, "to prove to the world that accuses us, that we too are capable of something." She addressed herself to "*le operaie*," her sister workers: "Men say we are frivolous, that we are weak, that we are incapable of supporting the struggle against this intolerable society, that we cannot understand the ideal of anarchism. . . . But they are the cause of our weakness, our undeveloped intellects, because they restrict our instruction . . . and ignore us."[87] The solution she proposed was for women to educate themselves and organize their own autonomous groups.

Over the next decade, dozens of women would write to *La Questione Sociale* to express similar sentiments. Writing under the name *La Sartina* (The Seamstress), one woman exposed how men in the movement consistently dismissed women's opinions with such statements as "you are a woman, you must be silent!" and "you are a woman, you must obey!" Exasperated, she called on men to "undo the old concept that we women must always be humiliated" and recognize that "women also have a heart and brain; a soul that must be free."[88] Many of the authors concealed their identities, presumably to enjoy greater creative and political license and to evade harassment, the loss of employment, and deportation, which always plagued the movement. One woman, using only the name Titì, wrote of "the many men who call themselves free thinkers, socialists, anarchists, men who have reached the height of development within humanity . . . who attend our meetings, conferences, and write in our newspapers," but who were authoritarian at home. "They spend their lives at work, in the café or tavern, with little curiosity about the moral education of their wives and children. They never offer a newspaper to their wives, never invite them to attend the lectures, and never care to interest them in the social question."[89]

Another woman, writing under the name Alba expressed similar frustrations. She described a meeting at a Manhattan *circolo* in which a woman had voiced her opinions regarding freedom. "Naturally, the spirit of masculine contradiction was not lacking," she recalled, "and a man rose to say that a woman, for all her efforts, can never elevate herself from subservience." She then explained the position of the women present: "You believe that a woman, who takes care of the entire home and the children, is not concerned with education, that she cannot find the time in her long day, to dedicate herself to her emancipation?"[90]

Maria Roda formed the anarchist women's group in Paterson in response to this collective frustration, just as she was becoming a well-respected presence in the international anarchist movement. Italian and American authorities kept a close watch on the entire Roda family, because Italian authorities considered her father Cesare, a weaver by trade, to be "one of the most dangerous anarchists," with connections to the labor movement not only in their hometown of Como but in Milan and Paris as well. Of Maria, they noted that she was an enthusiastic anarchist, who "was assiduously attending public and private gatherings during her stay in Milan in 1891." But government officials blamed her radicalism on Cesare, who they feared had raised his four daughters, Elisabetta, Regina Paolina, Adele, and Maria, with his "pushy ideals." Each had a reputation for labor radicalism, including singing anarchist songs loudly in the streets. Once the family migrated in 1893, their home at 138 Tyler Street in Paterson became "a meeting place and place of refuge for the anarchists of Como and others passing through," according to the informants who tracked them. Moreover, they feared, "many seditious demonstrations in the Como area in recent years were hatched in this house."[91]

Their concern, however, centered largely on Maria, and the Italian government file on the Roda family contains documents pertaining mostly to her activities. She had been active in anarchist circles in Como as a teenager, and studied with Ada Negri, known widely among Italian anarchists as the "ardent poetess of revolt."[92] Government officials grew especially concerned with Maria's activities when her schoolmate Sante Caserio, a baker reputed to be of quiet temperament, assassinated Sadi Carnot, the president of France, on 24 June 1894.[93] This, combined with Maria's infamous arrest as a young woman and courage during the court proceedings, contributed to her growing reputation among European labor radicals. Her notoriety continued to expand once she arrived in the United States, in part because of her charisma and power as a public speaker.

Maria Roda spoke often before large assemblies of workers, where she impressed seasoned radicals and rank-and-file workers with her ability to rouse audiences. Just a few months after she immigrated, Roda spoke at a large rally to celebrate the release of legendary anarchist Emma Goldman from prison in 1894. The reporters who covered the event, held at the Thalia Theater in Manhattan, observed, "Men, women, and children kept trooping in. Every seat was taken, and the aisles were being filled until the firemen and police objected, and the order was given not to sell any more tickets." The crowd, made up of "Italians, Russian Jews, Hungarians, Frenchmen, Cubans, and Spaniards," grew enthusiastic and boisterous as Roda appeared on the stage. Described as "dark-complexioned" and holding a red handkerchief as she spoke, Roda delivered a "fiery speech in Italian," emphasizing, as the *Times* put it, that "women had even more cause than men to complain."[94]

Goldman never forgot Roda's speech. In her memoir, she would recall that evening with great affection: "The voice electrified me and I was eager to see its owner. I stepped to the door leading to the platform. Maria Rodda [*sic*] was the most exquisite creature I had ever seen. She was of medium height, and her well-shaped head, covered with black curls, rested like a lily of the valley on her slender neck. Her face was pale, her lips coral-red. Particularly striking were her eyes: large, black coals fired by an inner light. Like myself, very few in the audience understood Italian, but Maria's strange beauty and the music of her speech roused the whole assembly to tensest enthusiasm. Maria proved a veritable ray of sunlight to me."[95] Goldman wrote that Roda's power helped her to find the strength to speak that evening, and later, at a small gathering, Roda asked Goldman to be her teacher, telling her that she had immigrated because she "felt that she had work to do among her countrymen in the United States." Goldman then pledged to be her "teacher, friend, comrade."[96]

Goldman's rapture with Roda's "strange beauty" was shared by her companion Edward Brady, who also found Roda "ravishing." Yet Goldman remembered that Brady quickly noted that Roda's "beauty would not endure, much less her enthusiasm for our ideals. 'Latin women mature young,' he said; 'they grow old with their first child, old in body and in spirit.'"[97] While Goldman and Brady had different reactions to Roda, they resonated with contemporary preoccupations with the sexuality of Italian working women, on both sides of the Atlantic. Brady's remarks in particular remind us how such representations worked to delegitimize and diminish Italian women's presence within the U.S. labor movement. Zo d'Aza, a French anarchist writer and newspaper editor, indulged in similar preoccupations when reporting on Roda's trial in Milan. Like the *Times*, he first saw her darkness, calling her "dark Maria," and was surprised by her boldness. He noted that she had a "strange charm, with the decisive air of a rascally young man, with her short curly hair, and her dark, fiery eyes. She had a way of looking at the messieurs of the court that was a form of silent, indefinable insolence."[98]

These stories also reveal how Roda's activities brought her into contact with many of the more renowned activists in this international, diasporic movement. Soon after she migrated, Roda fell in love with Pedro Esteve, the multilingual Catalan anarchist who helped to found *La Questione Sociale*. The two had met a few years earlier at an anarchist gathering in Milan, just as Esteve was becoming one of the more respected leaders of the movement. Born in Barcelona in 1866 of humble origins, Esteve worked as a printer, typesetter, and newspaper editor. He arrived in Paterson in 1892, via Paris and Cuba, to become a prolific writer and labor organizer among Italian, Spanish, Cuban, and Puerto Rican immigrant workers.[99] In the words of one Spanish immigrant anarchist, Esteve was "an educated man who could speak in simple terms," well respected for his eloquence as both a writer and a speaker.[100] Some considered Esteve not radical enough because he disagreed with the individualists and argued against the use of bombs, assassination, and other forms of violence.[101] But many in the movement remembered him as deeply inspiring, "quiet, soft-spoken, dignified, thoughtful, never violent," with a warm sense of humor.[102] His son would describe him similarly, as a kind man who was "the embodiment of his beliefs, idealistic and gentle." Esteve edited and published several anarchist newspapers in the United States in addition to *La Questione Sociale*, including the popular Spanish-language *El Despertar* and *Cultura Obrera*.[103]

Italian women's writing was most voluminous in *La Questione Sociale* when Esteve served as editor, in the years from 1899 to 1906, so it appears that Roda and Esteve's collaboration was the main reason Italian women's voices found publication in the radical press in this period. They also had ten children together and endured the death of two. Like many anarchists, they chose creative and unconventional names for their children: Violet, Sensitive, Sirio, Iris, Flora, Pedro, Helios, and Zophys.[104] Their son Sirio would later recall that their home was always open to a steady stream of foreign radicals. Sundays were particularly festive, as the house would fill with family and an assortment of anarchists, IWW organizers, and other comrades in the movement. Errico Malatesta appears to have lived with them for several months from 1899 to 1900, when he came to help build the anarchist movement in North America. All three had met at an anarchist meeting in Milan years prior, and Esteve and Malatesta had toured Spain together, to meet with workers and learn about their struggles.[105] Over the years, Roda would travel with Esteve as well, to assist and support the collective struggles of Spanish, Italian, Cuban, Puerto Rican, and African American workers in the maritime, cigar-making, and textile trades. While they were based in Paterson until at least 1908, they also lived for different periods in Tampa, Brooklyn, and Weehawken, New Jersey, to connect the diasporic revolutionary labor movements in these communities.[106] In Tampa, for example, Esteve was paid by Spanish and Cuban cigar makers to serve as the *lector*, to sit high on a stool and read radical literature aloud while workers rolled cigars. Both he and Roda conducted their organizing work at great risk, and Esteve especially faced routine threats of lynching and other forms of violence. Tragically, their ten-year-old son died in an explosion that they were convinced was an attempt on Esteve's life.[107]

Their grief only strengthened their commitment to the movement. Over the years, while moving between cities, Roda focused her energies on organizing women workers, because, as she stated at the time, "Chi conosce la miseria più della donna?" (Who knows misery more than women?)

Il Gruppo Emancipazione della Donna

When Maria Roda formed the Gruppo Emancipazione della Donna (Women's Emancipation Group) in 1897, Ninfa Baronio was at her side, along with another young woman who was becoming popular in the movement—Ernestina Cravello. Together, they worked to create a space for women to join the movement and develop their own philosophies and strategies. They met regularly over a period of at least seven years, with close to a dozen other women in Paterson. They also developed connections to radical women abroad, and inspired others to form similar groups. As one female comrade stated, writing from a Spring Valley, Illinois, coal town, where another sizable anarchist movement was underway, Italian immigrant women there formed a group, "for the emancipation of women, together with those struggles that must occur in order to attain the rights that all of oppressed humanity demand." She continued, "A woman must struggle with great zeal to emancipate herself from the tyranny and prejudice of men, and from those who foolishly consider women inferior, and often treat her like a slave."[108]

Because Paterson was a center of the international anarchist movement and the focus of much government investigation, there is more archival material pertaining to these activists. But women's groups developed throughout the New York metropolitan area, involving immigrants from all over Italy. There are few records on women's activism in many of these groups, however, and only scattered references to their activities in the press. It is clear, however, that beginning in 1900, the Paterson women's emancipation group met regularly with a similar group across the river in Manhattan, at Maria Raffuzzi's home at 338 East 22nd Street. One year later, Raffuzzi, Cravello, and fourteen other women, announced the formation of the Manhattan-based group called Il Gruppo di Propaganda Femminile (Women's Propaganda Group) which included southern and northern Italians.[109] They stated clearly their reasons for organizing: "to defend the large number of women workers in the city," "to contribute to the cause of women's emancipation," and "to educate the new generation in the sublime principles of anarchism."[110]

Most of the women who became active in these anarchist women's groups came from families and communities that were already quite active in the movement. Maria Raffuzzi was involved in a *circolo* that included her brother Louis as well as some of the more vocal and prolific writers of the movement.[111] Ernestina Cravello's success in establishing ties between anarchist women in Manhattan and Paterson developed from her own notoriety in the movement. She became active as a young woman, and her two older brothers, Antonio and Vittorio, and her companion Paolo Ferre (with whom she would have five children), were all active in the Paterson Gruppo Diritto all'Esistenza. Italian state security officials watched her family closely from 1900 to 1940, considering Ernestina in particular to be a "militant and very active anarchist."[112]

Such surveillance began when Ernestina appeared in the daily English-language press at only nineteen years of age, with a title that was usually reserved for Emma Goldman: "Queen of the Anarchists."[113] Her claim to fame resulted from comments she made to the press regarding Gaetano Bresci's assassination of King Umberto in 1900. After Bresci's deed, a wave of repression and anti-Italian sentiment washed over the anarchist movement, and the press descended on Bresci's community in Paterson, labeling it "the capital of world anarchism." In its search for a conspiracy, the press fixated on Cravello, an outspoken anarchist. Reporters came across her at a local meeting, where she spoke passionately about her beliefs to an enthusiastic crowd. They followed her to the Paragon Mill where she worked and noted that, as she emerged from the factory with a group of young women, she was immediately recognized by a crowd of reporters who rushed to speak with her. A group of curious onlookers gathered, some of whom greeted her with cheers. One reporter noted: "A bright red scarf was wound round her sailor hat and she carried a bundle of newspapers in her hand, which she waved to friends in the crowd. She was immediately pursued by several camera fiends, but escaped down a side street."[114] Another described her as "young, pretty, and spirited," and then indulged curious audiences with more detail: "Her dark brown hair was carried back in pompadour fashion from her face. Her mouth was red and laughing. Her big purple eyes were full of fire. She looked like a merry, roguish school-girl—not a woman who hated and plotted and encouraged a crowd of fanatics to murder."[115]

Reporters would discover that Ernestina, having migrated with her family of radical textile workers when she was fifteen from Valle Superiore in northern Italy, had been in the United States for four years. Despite her youth, and what the Italian authorities called "a rudimentary education," Cravello was one of the few bilingual activists in the movement willing to speak openly with the American press. As she spoke, reporters noted a crowd of men at her side, many of whom "muttered an occasional word in their own tongue and glanced at her admiringly. They were evidently proud of their spokesman."[116] Reporters also quoted her as saying that, while she did not know of Bresci's intention to kill the king when he returned to Italy, she was "happy that someone had done so." News of her response traveled across the United States and the Atlantic.[117] Outraged at being misquoted and depicted as fanatical, Cravello wrote to the popular Italian-language daily *Il Bolletino della Sera* to clarify her position: "They are only right in the fact that I am an anarchist, this is because I am moved by the suffering of hundreds of millions of workers and I struggle for a world in which such exploitation is no longer possible."[118]

In the months that followed such media attention, Cravello made the best of her notoriety by traveling regularly between Paterson, Hoboken, Brooklyn,

Manhattan, and New London, Connecticut, with her brother Vittorio. Paid informants from the Italian state followed them closely as they worked in different mills and "spread anarchist propaganda among women." Both Italian and American authorities became particularly concerned over Cravello's developing friendship with Ersilia Cavedagni, whom they considered a "very dangerous anarchist," of "limited formal instruction but much audaciousness." In the 1890s, when Cavedagni was in her thirties, she was active in a large *circolo* in Bologna and corresponded regularly with anarchists in Italy and abroad. Through the movement's networks, she met and fell in love with Giuseppe Ciancabilla, an anarchist from Rome and friend of Malatesta's. After she served seven months in prison for her political activities, they were forced to flee Italy during the police repression of workers' movements in the 1890s. They traveled to Switzerland, Belgium, and then France, before coming to New York. By the time they arrived, however, both had become extreme in their antiorganizationalism, and Ciancabilla soon earned a reputation among comrades for his "uncompromising, contentious, acerbic temperament." His letters reveal an uncharacteristic tenderness toward Cavedagni, however, whom he described as a "sweet, strong and wise companion."[119] In fact, some believe that his passionate disagreements with Malatesta over syndicalism may have derived more from his jealousy over Malatesta's closeness with Cavedagni, than from ideological differences.[120]

Cavedagni arrived in Paterson just as Cravello was gaining media attention. Cravello was probably drawn to Cavedagni, sixteen years her senior, for the content of her essays and letters, which were published in *La Questione Sociale* during her exile from 1897 to 1899. In an early letter, Cavedagni critiqued her comrades in the United States for not discussing "the woman question" sufficiently: "We must imitate the priests," she wrote, "who know how to mobilize those of our sex. If we were to have many anarchist women, oh, believe me, the movement would grow substantially." After all, she pointed out, "who does not remember the teachings of our mothers?"[121] In 1902 Cravello heeded her call and participated in organizing a large *festa* with the Paterson and Manhattan women's groups, to "begin a new era of stimulating activity among the female element."[122]

Feminist Theory from the Bottom Up

A central component of the radical culture these women created was to produce their own feminist theory. Through their *circoli* they had access to a wide range of pamphlet literature from the most popular male revolutionary theorists, but to read women's writing they had to print and distribute it on their own. In Italy, the literature of the emerging socialist-feminist movement only very rarely reached rural, peasant women and instead remained firmly rooted in urban political cultures. However, it traveled across the Atlantic to reach women abroad. Because Maria Roda had access to a printing press, and Ninfa Baronio ran the bookstore in Paterson, they were able to publish and widely circulate such texts. In early 1902 they initiated "the publication of a series of simple, short, and popular pamphlets, relative to the condition of women in present society, her aspirations, and role in the society of the future."[123]

They began with the work of Anna Maria Mozzoni, one of the most popular Italian feminist theorists and activists of the nineteenth century.[124] In a 1895 pamphlet, Mozzoni encouraged women to critique patriarchal power arrangements: "You will find that the priest who damns you is a man; that the legislator who oppresses you is a man, that the husband who reduces you to an *object* is a man; that the libertine [anarchist] who harasses you is a man; that the capitalist who enriches himself with your ill-paid work and the speculator who calmly pockets the price of your body, are men." Mozzoni then called on women to join the movement for "justice and liberty," not only for themselves but for the sake of a future without oppression: "See in your sons and daughters all of the children of humanity," she beckoned.[125]

They also distributed texts by Spanish anarchist Soledad Gustavo, who was also popular among women anarchists in Barcelona and Buenos Aires.[126] They translated and published at least two of her pamphlets, *To Women Proletarians* and *Dialogue between a Bourgeois Man and His Daughter*. Gustavo, like many anarchist writers, did not mince words: "The society that has condemned us to be flesh for pleasure, to be indispensable fixtures, to be a hygienic necessity, to be an exploitable thing, is our enemy and as such we should combat it and procure its total and speedy ruin."[127] The New York and New Jersey anarchist women's groups circulated these pamphlets far and wide, and they turned up across the Americas and Europe, including Buenos Aires and São Paulo, where working-class Italian immigrant women were also meeting and publishing their own writing in radical newspapers and pamphlets.[128]

This literature inspired debates and maintained the transnational connections between women in this movement. But many also sought to write from their own hearts, and between 1897 and 1908 Italian immigrant women across North America filled *La Questione Sociale* with their treatises. After 1908, when Roda and Esteve moved to Tampa, such writing continued in the newspaper's successor, *L'Era Nuova*, but not with nearly as much frequency. For close to a decade, however, Italian immigrant women had access to one of the most important anarchist newspapers of this period, and they used it.

Most of the authors were women with little formal education, who had been taught to read and write by comrades in the movement. As one essayist wrote, "I am not an intellectual, but the daughter of a discredited and oppressed people."[129] They valued their experiential knowledge as workers, peasants, mothers, and migrants to argue that revolutionary activism required their visions for change. They "disdained both Catholic feminism's claims of female spiritual superiority and liberal feminism's demands for politico-legal equality."[130] Rather, their feminism emerged from a materialist analysis of power. "We are not feminists in the manner of the bourgeoisie," they declared, "who claim the equality or supremacy of our sex, and would be satisfied with the realization of these dreams." Rather, theirs was a feminism informed by working and poor women's struggles: "Being women, we believe that feminist action is essential, just as we believe that as workers we must take action in unions, congresses, and strikes."[131] Virginia Buongiorno was one of many who added her voice to the discussion: "It is not enough to struggle for the vote (as do the bourgeois women in this hardly free America). We want to tear down all the false prejudices that infest the world. It is not with changing certain laws that we can call ourselves free. . . . You see, my sister workers, these laws are made by the bourgeoisie for their interests."[132] They sought revolutionary change to end all systems of oppression and hierarchal authority, whether in the form of industrial capitalism, the government, the church, or the men in their families and communities.[133]

In much of their writing, women gave voice to the exploitation they endured as a source of cheap labor within the expanding capitalist world system. They addressed themselves most often to other women workers: "We have become human machines," wrote Maria Barbieri in 1905, "who stay locked in the immense industrial prisons where we lose our strength, our health and youth, where our rights are shattered before the greed of the bourgeoisie. And we don't rebel against these abuses to our right to live? We don't shake with rage before the pompous and contemptuous lady, who because of us wears a silk skirt from our humble labor?" Many bemoaned the irony of laboring long and arduous hours to produce material they could never afford: "While we tire ourselves from morning until night with few pleasures from all that is beautiful and comfortable in life; bent over our work, seized with a torrent of grief over the uncertainty of the health of our children, the ladies are in perfumed drawing-rooms, conversing, proposing banquets, balls, theater, vacations . . . gold and more gold they bleed from us and our children."[134]

Alba Genisio echoed these sentiments. Writing from a mining community in Kansas, where she was active in an anarchist *circolo*, she addressed herself to her *sorelle di fatica* (sisters of drudgery): "We who produce all the social riches . . . the silk, the lace, and the embroidery of great luxury, must skimp in our own lives just to wear cotton. . . . Why is it that this life, which should be a paradise, is for us a torment?"[135] Maria Roda captured such sentiment well with a simple but pointed question: "Why does the pleasure of some have to create misery for many?"[136]

Many women expressed an understanding that their exploitation was directly tied to the emergence of industrial capitalism and the attendant forces of imperialism, racism, and nativism. They denounced U.S. imperialism in Asia and Latin America, and the aggression of the Italian government in Africa. They called these "civilizing missions" into question by drawing on the rhetoric of American nationalism to expose how "liberty" and "freedom" were elusive for many in the United States.[137] The multiethnic nature of New York City and New Jersey's radical subcultures meant that they heard firsthand about the effects of U.S. imperialism abroad, and their writing linked these policies to the violence of European colonialism. In 1907, for example, amid a flurry of essays on women's emancipation, Titì wrote an essay titled "Il Congo" (The Congo) in which she reminded readers how Belgian King Leopold disguised policies of violent brutality in Africa with the language of benevolent paternalism.[138] Italian anarchists believed deeply that nationalism was at the root of the problem. In describing what it was like to be an immigrant, Ersilia Cavedagni wrote, "How evil is this, a society in which its members have developed a stupid aversion to others who do not speak the same language, or are born under another sky, and wear different clothes. . . . Ah, this damned and miserable concept of country separates those who nature intended to be brothers, so stupidly, uselessly, and ferociously."[139]

The women also focused their energies on challenging the abuse of authority within their families and communities, believing that to change the larger world they had to transform themselves and their most intimate relationships.[140] They were committed to industrial unionism and direct action, but they argued that revolution began at home.[141] In 1906 Titì began a series of essays with the title "Alle Donne, Emancipiamoci!" (To Women, Let's Emancipate Ourselves!) in which she argued, "We should take a glance not only at the bourgeois society but at ourselves, workers who are part of the anarchist family."[142] On occasion, men voiced their public support, like Camillo Di Sciullo, who reminded his comrades, "Don't you know that the first campaign to do is that of the family? Build a little anarchist world within your family and you will be able to see how it strengthens, how it becomes easier to launch other campaigns!"[143] But Titì, like many of the women writing to *La Questione Sociale*, placed responsibility not only on men but on herself. She called on other women to become aware of their own complicity in patriarchal relations and to disrupt expectations that they be "humble and obedient."[144] Titì explained that "parents, teachers, everyone who has contributed to our education and to our physical and mental development, have made us into cooking and sewing machines, young girl workers." She recognized, however, that many of these parents and teachers were women and that change required raising girls in a new way. "The axiom of domination," she argued, "begins at birth when a girl learns her place in life." She then described her own childhood, how she witnessed fathers ordering daughters not to leave the house without an escort. "If we were very brave and risked asking why, the answer right away would be 'It is not right; *the people will talk*.' And the response satisfies us." After a series of scenarios, ending with "*the people will talk*," Titì asked, "Who are these people, these absolute masters of our happiness and our life? *We* are these people, because we approve of everything that enslaves us."[145]

The solution, she argued, was "to let daughters rebel against our authority." In this way, "it will be much better for her and for all of humanity." She also warned, "If we do not do this she will be weak, without intelligence, without the ability to reflect, without the will of reason, and she will subdue herself blindly, suffocating her rebellious attitudes in order to develop passivity." She asked mothers to discard conventional parenting practices that "limited women's world to a life between the kitchen and the conjugal bed." Young girls, she wrote, were being raised "to sew clothes and mechanically recite the *Ave Maria*." Even so, "the desire to read is manifested in this tiny creature, but she is not allowed to read. She is scolded because she wants to become *literary*, and is forced, with violence, to learn needlework and to forget books." As a result, "a grave crime has been committed; the work of nature is destroyed within the little girl and she is infused with ideas that are different from those that we want to teach, ideas that will lead her to be an illiterate and poor seamstress as an adult." She advised having girls "explain the meaning of the *Ave Maria* before reciting it. It is with reproach and a slap that we ordinarily recite the prayer . . . without discussion or debate."[146]

Most women's writing in *La Questione Sociale* supported this revolutionary vision of motherhood, because many women believed, as Ida Merini Catastini noted, that "it is the woman who guides the household."[147] They wrote how becoming mothers changed their consciousness—one, for example, pointed out that "so many mothers suffer when they see the mean treatment, suffering, deprivation, and danger to which their children are exposed." This was especially difficult, Maria Roda noted, "when it is in joy that they are consecrated."[148] A woman going only by the name Alba was among the many who addressed herself to other mothers, calling on them "to educate our children and raise them to understand the origins of their poverty and deprivation." In this way, they would develop "the noble and generous sentiment of equality, love for one another, reciprocal respect, the right of all to life, joy, and happiness, and contempt for lies, tyranny, and exploitation." Such practice would lead to a new world: "In a short time we will create a new society, where men's supremacy over women will cease to exist and human solidarity will reign supreme."[149]

Many also wrote of enduring the early death of their children. Maria Barbieri lost her young son in 1903, when a pot of boiling water fell on him while she was working in Hoboken's textile mills. She would write about his death as she grieved and call on other "proletarian mothers" to unite against the entire system of capitalism, which not only took mothers away from their children but also valued profit over human well-being and filled one with prejudice.[150]

Many Italian immigrant women in the anarchist movement actively reached out to the younger generation, to inculcate revolutionary principles and encourage rebellion. Some of the more visible women in the movement, including Ersilia Cavedagni, Maria Roda, Maria Barbieri, and Bellalma Forzato Spezia, all wrote treatises addressed to young women. Anna Maria Mozzoni did so as well, in part because she believed that the spirit of curiosity, idealism, and resistance was still alive in them and that therein lay the hope for a new era. Bellalma Forzato Spezia gave a popular lecture "For the New Generation" across the New York metro area in this period and then circulated the talk as a pamphlet. She addressed teenage girls because she believed they were fundamental to revolutionary social change.[151] Cavedagni also wrote to young women workers: "O young woman that suffers . . . I believe that if you knew the cause of this you would rebel. . . . Look at the well dressed, well fed, well educated, well instructed woman, that spends her life happy and joyful; why do you think she has the privilege to live happily while you suffer? It is nothing else but money that her parents make with exploitation, rape, violence, and force. . . . Don't let the word anarchy scare you. It is an idea . . . a remedy in the struggle for liberty and the suppression of every system of authority." Cavedagni also urged women to action: "If your parents do not know true anarchy," she wrote, "it is you that must contribute your thoughts and actions."[152] Titì also believed it was crucial that young women learn "the great difference between the woman and the female." "Woman," she wrote, "lives not only within the body, but also within the spirit. . . . [She] studies her thoughts and culture, is interested in the social world, preoccupied with the world of her children, and also seeks to be useful to humanity and elevated to the same level as men. A woman is, in the end, she who knows how to think with her own mind and operate according to her own convictions." The female or feminine, on the other hand, was "She who does not care to know, and runs from that which would elevate and instruct her; she limits her functions to knowing how to make a potato stew, a good tomato sauce, or mend socks: She is always obeying her husband, committed to being a passive instrument of pleasure for him, incapable of thinking with her own head or act with her own initiative, believing that it is a luxury to interest herself in public life, in which men only have rights; She is incapable of rebelling against social injustices."[153]

In delineating how gender shaped behavior and by identifying what she believed was the naturally liberated spirit in women, Titì hoped to empower readers to "become women who are capable of understanding or reflecting," rather than "ignorant females" who "obey the priest without questioning" and "avoid politics because it does not interest us."[154] This support for women's education was at the core of their philosophy. They not only advocated that women educate themselves and their daughters but also questioned popular "scientific" ideologies that argued that women became physically frail from intellectual pursuits.[155]

Their feminism was also deeply rooted in the philosophy of free love (*amore libero*)—the basis of which was "the need to feel love."[156] Historian Jesse Battan has demonstrated that while scholars have studied women's struggles for sexual autonomy, intimacy, and satisfaction in the late nineteenth and early twentieth centuries, they have often overlooked those who advocated free love, especially from the working classes.[157] For these women, however, independent and radical newspapers were the primary medium through which to publicly discuss the significance of eroticism to their lives and challenge systems of hierarchy and authority in marriage. Their language reveals "the conflicts that grew out of women's pursuit of reproductive self-control, emotional intimacy, and erotic pleasure," and serves as evidence of the "profound shift in the emotional texture of married life" that was occurring in this period.[158]

As with other anarchists, Italian immigrant women active in the movement believed that the institution of marriage often deprived women of desire, a true sense of partnership, and self-determination. None wrote of erotic relationships with other women, to my knowledge, though many of the most prominent leaders in the anarchist movement defended the right of individuals to pursue same-sex relationships.[159] Instead, they focused their contempt on the patriarchal ideal (and legal institution) of marriage, which, as Maria Roda wrote, was "a hateful noose" that corrupted "the pure and natural love of two united hearts."[160] They argued that marriage gave husbands the legal right to dominate and control their wives and publicly exposed the pain they experienced in such a system. Titì directed her critique at the southern Italian tradition of arranged marriage: "Is he beautiful? Ugly? Healthy? Sick? Good? Evil? We know nothing of these things and we are not allowed to ask. Our fathers and mothers have the last say. If we don't love him, it is worse for us. Isn't it necessary to love our husbands?" Upon marriage, she argued, women were forced to "obey him *in everything*. What rights do we have in love? Marriage for our parents meant that the husband was in control, and it is this way for us. To us, they say, 'love will come later.' We enter into a family in which we are slaves to our husband."[161]

Women's lack of choice and power in marriage was a recurrent theme, and many expressed anger at being "used and abused" by husbands who demanded their submission. Some even wrote of men's passion as "a death sentence."[162] Anna De Gigli explained, "Men have the right to betray the women they love, and can even shoot them in the back . . . with the classic justification: I killed her because I loved her." She pointed out that "the physical act cannot be the only basis for union. . . . The man who desires the woman like an appetizer to sleep is a brute. The lamentations of a woman are absolutely useless."[163] In exposing domestic violence and rape, they made visible abusive practices that were profoundly naturalized. In doing so, they argued for their entitlement to emotionally, sexually, and spiritually satisfying unions and called on women to "cast off these servile chains that a family, a society, a church have made us drag from remote eras."[164]

This trinity of oppressive instructions included the church in large part because of women's experiences with repressive church officials in Italy and the United States. Some scholars of the Italian American Left have argued that while men were faithful radicals who scorned organized religion, women's devotion to Catholicism kept them from joining the movement en masse. Some believe that it was women's religiosity that inhibited the revolutionary movement from expanding.[165] Such convictions are reflected in oral histories too. "Many of the Italian women kept to their old beliefs even when their husbands were anarchists," Concetta Silvestrini recalled. Others also remembered that women were "devout Catholics" while men were the anarchists and atheists.[166] In the radical newspapers of that era, men often complained that women "live under the rein of the moon" and were therefore sporadic in their devotion to the movement.[167] These various statements also reveal, however, that women did not just blindly adopt the beliefs and commitments of the men in their families. The view that women were conservative Catholics while men were revolutionaries also tends to flatten the very complex relationship that Italian immigrant women had with Catholicism.

Interestingly, much anarcho-syndicalist feminist writing was oppositional to organized religion, yet also infused with religious language. The women writers understood the immense significance of sacred beliefs and rituals to the women in their communities, and they did not ask that they discard these practices. Instead, they encouraged women to develop a more conscious spiritual life. For example, Titì did not ask women to stop praying to the Blessed Mother. She suggested that they discuss the meaning of such practice with their daughters, rather than force them to pray blindly. Others echoed these sentiments, while arguing,

"When we are free of all the social and religious superstitions inculcated in us, we will be redeemed." Spiritual practice was so deeply woven into women's sense of themselves that even those drawn to the anarchist movement invoked the divine on occasion. For example, a woman by the name of Angelica wrote to *La Questione Sociale* expressing her thanks to another woman from New York, who had written about her free love beliefs. She concluded by saying "Beata lei! Che la Madonna di Pompei la salvi da ogni pericolo!" (Good for you! May the Madonna of Pompei save you from every danger!)[168] Maria Roda's son Sirio recalled that, unlike his father, his mother "had a mystical streak." Later in life she would develop a spiritual practice, in which she sought to connect with the divine through deep meditation and contemplation. This was not incongruent with her anarchism, her son argued, and her combination of spiritualism with anarcho-syndicalism inspired her children. "I too consider myself an anarchist, with a mystical streak like Mother's," he would tell Paul Avrich, shortly before he published a spiritual book on Jesus in 1974, titled *The Experience*.[169]

Similarly, Antonino Crivello, a labor activist in New York City's radical subculture, recalled that his mother Francesca was "an admirer of St. Francis of Assisi, whose teachings she followed from her birth in Palermo to her life in New York." She was also a woman who "never lost the opportunity to speak out on behalf of her christian socialism." Her obituary would note that she was the "exemplary teacher to the family, and taught her son Antonino a love for literature and Latin." A skilled storyteller, her favorite tales were from her childhood during the last years of the Italian Risorgimento, and her own activism in the peasant uprisings of the 1890s. Antonino recalled, "Her narratives of that history assumed an extraordinary vividness. Her graphic descriptions of the Sicilian people's heroic episodes opened the eyes of her listeners and were always rendered in a way that was animated, impressionistic, picturesque, and full of light."[170] He also remembered that his mother "wanted him to prepare for priesthood," while his father took him to socialist meetings as a child in Sicily. When the family migrated to the United States, his mother brought him to her union meetings in the garment trades and encouraged his activism in the anarchist circles in their Lower East Side neighborhood.[171] In this way, Francesca Crivello combined the spiritual with her vision of working-class revolution.

Most anarchist feminists focused their criticism not on eliminating spirituality from women's lives, but on questioning the Catholic Church's abuse of power and corrupt policies. Many Italian immigrants were bitter toward the church, "which they believed had abused its power and amassed extravagant wealth while workers were hungry."[172] Many raised their children in much the same manner as Angelina Frignoca, who told her granddaughter of "the bejeweled Madonna in her local church in Biella, Italy, which shone in splendor while villagers didn't have enough to feed their families."[173] In an open letter to the priest at the Church of San Michele in Paterson, published in *La Questione Sociale*, Cristina Melone wrote of the church as "a huge store, where they sell saints and miracles at expensive prices." What most appalled her was that priests pressured parishioners to donate their precious earnings: "You don't even work," she wrote: "All of your work can be reduced to singing psalms for a half hour mass every morning. . . . You are born lazy and you will die lazy. . . . I don't have any children, but I hope to have them, and when I do I will educate them to rebel against all the laws of oppression and obscurantism. If all mothers were to open their eyes and imitate me the Catholic Church would have to close and you would have to earn an honest living like my husband."[174] In 1907 *La Questione Sociale* reported that a young girl had been raped by a priest in Milan, from whom she had contracted syphilis, and that another priest in Sicily had been condemned to seventy days of seclusion for breaking and entering into the home of a "buxom young woman."[175] Similar stories caused women to write in with comments, "better the mafia, better the *camorra*, better the morals of the thief and assassin," than the church. Others proclaimed their distaste for religion, "because its function is to protect those in power from the righteous rebellions of the oppressed," and called on other women to "stop these merchants of madonnas."[176] Some spoke of their own upbringing within the church, and how parents and clergy used Catholic teachings to legitimize female obedience. They wrote how their desires for freedom were admonished with the demand that they be "good and obedient," and with threats that "there would be no heaven" and "the devil would take me and make me his wife." Yet, this same woman noted that, for all her disobedience, the devil never showed up. "Instead, a young boy, a good boy, whom I met here in America, only spoke to me of God, the devil, hell, or heaven, in order to laugh." They fell in love, she wrote, and "united, freely like birds in the sky, sweetly like butterflies in the fields and meadows."[177]

In addition to writing, women in the anarchist movement lived by example, choosing their own lovers, and celebrating their unions and births without the authority of the church or the state. Most in the movement chose not to marry, though some remained with their partners for a lifetime. In 1907 three women who wrote under the names Susanna Zannotti, Aurora, and Angelica, debated free love in *La Questione Sociale*. Zannotti argued, "To me it signifies the freedom to unite with another person that you love, to live with them and not think of others." To Aurora, free love meant the ability to choose lovers freely, without commitment or monogamy. Angelica agreed with Zannotti but argued that not all could find soul mates and that it was necessary to have the courage and ability to leave an unhappy union.[178] While the exact meaning and practice of free love was subject to debate, Italian anarchist women developed a feminist discourse and practice of free love as part of their revisioning of society based on nonauthoritarian relationships.

Many women in the movement challenged gender conventions with their behavior. Gemma Mello, for example, was one of many remembered for her daring behavior. After working for several years in the Paterson silk mills, she and her cousin Milly moved for work, first to New London, Connecticut, and then to Brooklyn in the 1910s. In each place, they were among the most active in local anarchist circles. Jenny Paglia, another anarchist in New London, recalled that Gemma was "not pretty, but intelligent. She went to the group, to the men, crossed her legs and smoked."[179] Emma Goldman offered a new model of womanhood, as one of the most visible women in the movement. She spoke regularly to Italian audiences in Manhattan, Paterson, and other locales across the New York metropolitan area (and United States) in this period, to "denounce capitalism, militarism, organized religions, and the state, and to defend women's right to sexual freedom and birth control."[180] Many, like Concetta Silvestrini, an immigrant from Abruzzo, traveled to hear Goldman speak and noted, "She was a woman who made you think. Her words went into your brain and you couldn't forget them."[181] The countercultural atmosphere of the radical world offered Italian immigrant women and their daughters a context to challenge gender ideologies and practices, at a time when women were beginning to experiment with new gender roles and public behavior en masse. No venue provided more license for such experimentation than the world of theater.

Performing the Revolution

Italian women in the anarchist movement concentrated their energies on theatrical performance because it was a relatively safe space to enact new ways of being. The collaborations that took place through their staged productions provided a vitally important space for women and their children to develop their own styles of political activism. In 1899 those active in the women's emancipation groups, including Ernestina Cravello, Ersilia Cavedagni, and Ninfa Baronio, formed the Teatro Sociale, a radical theater group based in Paterson. For the next decade, they took to the stage often in plays with titles such as *Emancipata*, in which they performed their ideas on women's emancipation.[182] Maria Barbieri also joined such performances, often singing a *canto delle tessitrici* (song of the women weavers) and reciting revolutionary poems in between acts.[183] Several anarchist women in the Paterson area also formed the Club Femminile di Musica e di Canto (Women's Club for Music and Song) and performed at numerous radical events.[184]

Elvira Catello, an anarchist who migrated to New York from the southern Italian city of Bari (Apulia) when she was nineteen, also founded and ran a popular theater group in East Harlem that produced plays written and performed by women. She immigrated in 1910 with her companion, noted anarchist Paolo Perrini. The two would raise five children while Catello ran a radical bookstore called *La Libreria Elvira Catello*, which served as another major distribution center for anarchist books and periodicals. The store was popular among the *sovversivi* until at least the 1940s and by then had become a publishing house as well, called *Editrice Lux*. Both Elvira and Paolo were members of an East Harlem anarchist *circolo*, and Catello's theatrical troupe often performed at fund-raising events for anarchist groups across the city.[185]

The theatrical productions that women wrote, produced, and performed created images of women that were political and outspoken and exposed audiences to the central issues that women faced in their everyday lives. Their plays included *Il Ribelle* (The Rebel), which was structured around a conversation about free love between a mother and daughter in which the young woman protests traditions of arranged marriage, and *La Figlia dell'Anarchico* (The Anarchist's Daughter). Written by Nena Becchetti, an immigrant woman worker in Jessup, Pennsylvania, *La Figlia* centered on a cast of eight women—four mothers and their daughters—and was celebrated by Italian radicals for its realistic depictions of poverty and suffering but also because it "shouted with the spirit of hope."[186]

Theater was an important vehicle through which women introduced the next generation to the movement. Ninfa Baronio, Ernestina Cravello, Elvira Catello, Maria Roda, and others encouraged their own children and those of their comrades to participate in their dramatic productions.[187] Jenny Salemme's story, though from Boston, mirrors the experiences of others from her generation. After emigrating from Naples with her mother, Jenny went to live with her aunt, because her mother "couldn't take" life in America. Her aunt was an actress, Jenny recalled, "and took me to the club on Maverick Square for rehearsals of the *filodrammatica* [theater group]. They put on *Primo Maggio*, *Tempeste Sociali*, and other radical plays." She began to act in the plays herself and remembered, "We went all over—New London and other cities."[188]

Many women were drawn to radical theatrical productions because they were one of the few female-dominated spaces in the movement. They also provided a sanctioned way to move somewhat freely beyond their families and communities. In 1914, for example, Ninfa Baronio and two other women, Pierina Boffa and Rosalia Forgnene, along with their children, performed to a packed house at Riverside Hall in Paterson during a snowstorm. In the following weeks, they went on the road together, performing in Clifton, Newark, Hoboken, Jersey City, and Manhattan, among other places.[189] Similarly, women and children often performed at the annual Festa della Frutta each autumn, which brought together radical families from the tristate area of New York, New Jersey, and Connecticut.[190]

Theater was popular because it was one of the more practical ways to circulate revolutionary ideologies among a largely illiterate or semiliterate population. For most immigrants who worked grueling jobs for long hours, theater offered a momentary respite and a chance to commune with neighbors and friends. Performance has historically been an important method of revolutionary political struggle among the poor, according to Colette Hyman: "Precisely because it is able to present scenarios of empowerment in which marginalized, disenfranchised social groups can see themselves otherwise."[191] At the turn of the century, theater in the form of vaudeville, musical revue, and comedy were the most popular forms of entertainment in the United States. Moreover, as Susan Glenn has written of these years, "female performers became agents and metaphors of changing gender relations." She writes: "On stage and off, turn-of-the-century women were increasingly drawing attention to themselves, asserting their rights to education, to political participation, to employment, to sexual expressiveness, to a voice as cultural critics."[192] While Italian immigrant women rarely made it to the stages of Broadway, those in the anarchist movement performed often in their neighborhood meeting halls, parks, and beyond.

Women also infused labor parades, rallies, strikes, and other workplace actions with a flair for the dramatic. Whether it meant marching through town with their anarchist banners held high, singing the *Internazionale* or *Bandiera Rossa* at the top of their lungs as they paraded past an employers' home, speaking from the heart before hundreds of fellow workers on a stage or soapbox, or hurling rocks through factory windows, Italian women workers chose many different ways to dramatize and publicize the dangerous conditions under which they labored and lived.[193]

They brought theater to their strikes, and they brought their strikes to the theater. In June 1913, for example, Italians joined with other workers in Paterson's silk mills in a pageant at Madison Square Garden to generate public support for a labor strike that remained deadlocked and without an end in sight. After four months of solidarity among the workers and violent resistance on the part of the mill owners, people were beginning to starve and grow desperate. They turned to performance to raise money and their spirits. Though few knew it then, the strike and pageant would mark a crucial transition in the history of Italian immigrant women's radicalism and labor activism.

As the next chapter reveals, the Paterson strike and pageant were among the many dramatic moments in which the radical subculture moved to the forefront of working-class politics to influence hundreds of thousands. While Italian immigrant women's anarcho-syndicalist feminist culture was quite small in the early 1900s, by the 1910s it would play a central role in the emerging industrial union movement. The masses of Italian immigrant women who labored in textile mills and garment shops erupted into widespread protest in 1913, across New York City and northeastern New Jersey, with a series of labor strikes that shook their industries. This strike movement was inspired by the same forces that had set the anarchist movement in motion. As one older Italian woman recounted, she joined the 1913 strike wave because "me sick of the boss, me sick of work, me sick of go hungry most time." She then raised her deformed finger, the bone worn down into the shape of a hook, and smiled to reveal the space where her front teeth had once been. With her body damaged from decades of quickly twisting cotton and biting button holes to save time and keep her factory job, she concluded, "me sick, me tired, me can stand no longer, that's why me all strike."[194]

The 1909–1919 Strike Wave
and the Birth of Industrial Unionism

On a cold winter evening in January 1913, more than four thousand Italian women garment workers gathered at Cooper Union in New York City with great anticipation. The meeting was the culmination of a mass organizing campaign in the waist and dress industry that had launched an impressive strike wave among garment workers in New York City and New Jersey. Unprecedented numbers of Italian women had joined the strike, alongside Russian, Lithuanian, Polish, German, Greek, Irish, Spanish, Hungarian, and other immigrant workers. By January, the strike had gathered considerable steam. More than 150,000 workers in four sectors of garment production had walked off their jobs, paralyzing the industry and forcing manufacturers into negotiation. Italian women had been pivotal to the success. In hundreds of shops spread across the city, they had organized picket lines, convinced others to walk off their jobs, and withstood arrest and beatings at the hands of employers and police. But on that January evening at Cooper Union, it appeared the union, the International Ladies' Garment Workers' Union (ILGWU), had sacrificed their needs. Not only did the union sign an agreement with manufacturers without their approval, but the agreement did not even include most of the shops that employed Italian workers. With loud jeers and stomping feet, the Italian women present rejected the union leaders' instructions to return to work. Several rushed the stage, forcing speakers off the platform with cries of a frame up, and urged workers to abandon the ILGWU in favor of the more militant Industrial Workers of the World (IWW).

This "storm of protest," as the *New York Times* termed it, spread to the streets. Several women smashed the windows of a nearby shirtwaist factory with rocks and others sat in the center of Third Avenue, bringing traffic in lower Manhattan to a halt. Dissent spread throughout Brooklyn and Harlem as more workers learned of the settlement and gathered in the streets to defy the court injunction forbidding them to picket garment shops. The next day, in an icy snowstorm and subzero temperatures, twenty thousand workers, most of them Italian women, marched through the city's garment districts in opposition to the union, the state, and their employers. A week later, close to one thousand Italian immigrant women in twelve factories across New York City abandoned the ILGWU and declared a strike for better pay and shorter hours under the auspices of the IWW.[1]

As the second largest group of workers in the garment trades, Italian women's solidarity and militancy were crucial to the union's ability to orchestrate the 1913 uprising. Yet, at the height of the strike, it appeared that the ILGWU sold them out.[2] As workers in the most poorly paid and dangerous jobs in the city's dress and shirtwaist factories, they had the most to lose. Many were not covered by the settlement, and those who were faced a more deeply entrenched and institutionalized sex-based division of labor that continued to assign women to the lowest-paid jobs, and set their minimum wage lower than men who held the same jobs. The agreement had won some union recognition, but Italian women had not gained a voice in union affairs. Rather, it appeared as if the leaders of the ILGWU "preferred to deal with the employers rather than with their own members."[3]

The 1913 uprising encapsulates several compelling themes in the history of Italian immigrant women's activism in the United States. As with others in the clothing trades, they faced low wages, dangerous working conditions, and inhumane treatment. Yet, unlike the Jewish women who dominated the rank and file of the industry at the turn of the century, Italian women did not join the garment unions en masse until the Great Depression. While the press, union leaders, and some other workers considered hurling rocks through factory windows as riotous and as evidence of Italian immigrant women's inability to organize, this was a direct-action strategy firmly rooted in the struggles of their homelands. The American-born generation would eventually turn to reformist unions en masse, but the immigrant generation remained deeply skeptical of these organizations. Those who became active in the labor movement most often devoted themselves to transnational anarchist and revolutionary socialist circles and to the militant industrial union movement embodied by the IWW. And while Italian immigrant women were marginalized within most American labor organizations and often dismissed or derided because their actions confounded those around them, they were in fact creating a movement. They were drawing on communal protest traditions, and turning urban networks of mutual exchange into avenues of activism. As a result, in the decade from 1909 to 1919, they participated in some of the

Italian and Jewish women at May Day parade in New York City, 1916, which drew more than 40,000 participants. At the time, close to 120,000 garment workers were on strike. The women hold a banner fashioned out of a nightgown with the word "purity" in Italian. Corbis, IH134464.

largest labor strikes of this period and entered the industrial union movement in force, to create union cultures that were all their own.

Beyond the 1909 Uprising of 20,000

Stories of Italian immigrant women's activism on the front lines of U.S. labor struggles were numerous in the Italian-language radical press during the early twentieth century. Often they highlighted women's audacity, courage, and inventiveness in confronting abusive and demeaning labor conditions. Such stories are largely absent from scholarship on garment workers' labor struggles in New York City in this period, however, which has for the most part portrayed Italian women as nonmilitants.[4] Indeed, this history has almost exclusively focused on the first major garment strike, the 1909 "Uprising of 20,000" shirtwaist workers, which began in the city in July and quickly spread to Pennsylvania and Connecticut.

The details of this five-week strike have in fact become legendary. Young Clara Lemlich, a Jewish immigrant whose family had fled a pogrom in the Ukraine, led her mostly Jewish women co-workers with the rallying cry, "We are starving while we work; we might as well starve while we strike!" A self-proclaimed socialist and member of the union's executive board, Lemlich was a seasoned activist who had been beaten badly on the picket line at her shop. Defying the directives of male union leaders, she called for a general strike to the thunderous applause of the crowd. Jewish women workers also responded to the recalcitrance of the ILGWU's male leadership, by aligning with white Protestant middle-class progressives and feminist activists in the Women's Trade Union League (WTUL), who helped to organize the masses of women who showed up at union halls during the strike.[5]

The 1909 strike captured the imagination of a generation of women's historians for many reasons. It brought tens of thousands of working-class immigrant women into the union movement and strengthened the garment unions overall. It was also an inspiring example of working-class immigrant and middle-class native-born women aligning against men of all classes. Yet, much of this scholarship advanced the idea that Italian women in the garment trades were unorganized and unsympathetic to the union movement because they composed only 6 percent (approximately two thousand) of the strikers, while they were almost 34 percent of the shirtwaist industry labor force at the time. But those who drew such conclusions relied exclusively on English-language source material and uncritically accepted the opinions of many in organized labor. As a result, the reputation that Italian immigrant women were often submissive workers and scabs was passed down from one generation to the next.[6]

The popular Italian-language daily newspapers in New York City, such as *Il Bollettino della Sera* and *Il Progresso Italo-Americano*, covered the shirtwaist strike only briefly. But they gave considerable attention to another strike occurring that same month, just across the Hudson River in Hoboken, New Jersey. There, Italian women textile workers engaged in a month-long strike for livable wages, shorter work hours, and improved working conditions, and they did so alongside Italian men, and Armenian, Russian, German, Polish, and other immigrant women and men.[7] As a result of their success, the ILGWU and WTUL recruited Arturo Caroti, an IWW organizer of the strike, manager of a cooperative store owned by the Hoboken silk workers, and administrator for the Italian socialist newspaper *Il Proletario*, to organize Italian women garment workers in New York City.[8] But while Caroti gained public notoriety as the leader of the Hoboken strike, it was the *pinzettatrici* (pinchers) — Italian women in the worst-paid and most monotonous jobs as pieceworkers in the silk industry — who had formed the most militant core of strikers. Their successful efforts at forging cross-ethnic alliances with other textile and clothing workers under the IWW banner before and during the strike explains, in part, why immigrant workers in West New York, Hackensack, Passaic, Paterson, North Hudson, Jersey City, and New York City, walked off their jobs in solidarity with the Hoboken movement.[9]

Nor was this the first time Italian immigrant women launched a strike in the New York metro area. As soon as they arrived, they began protesting the conditions under which they labored. In early 1897, the Italian immigrant anarchist newspaper *La Questione Sociale* reported that several thousand Italian garment workers — women and men — had walked off their jobs in Brooklyn and Manhattan to protest their fifteen- to eighteen-hour workday and starvation wages. The women, the newspaper noted, were particularly enthusiastic in the movement. Later that year, several hundred Italian women and men joined together again in a strike against Paterson's silk mills. The same newspaper noted the "tight bonds of solidarity" that existed between the "workers of both sexes." Two years later, close to ninety Italian women workers in those same silk mills held a meeting on their own "to address the situation of over work and to discuss joining a labor union." When they showed up to work, however, the factory manager refused to let three of the most active women work. *La Questione Sociale* noted, "With the example of utmost solidarity, all of the other women workers walked off in a voluntary strike in support of their comrades, and demanded that they reinstate the three women and raise all of their pay by $1.25 a week. . . . The strike continues."[10]

Such actions were regular occurrences, though the English-language press rarely reported on them. Indeed, Italian women working in the textile, garment, and cigar-making trades participated in many workplace actions across New

York City and northeastern New Jersey in the years before 1909. In 1903 hundreds struck in Paterson, Passaic Falls, and Astoria (Queens). In 1907, more than 250 Italian and Jewish garment workers (male and female) came together in Harlem to form a labor union. When the factory owner attempted to "inspire antagonism" by threatening to fire the Italian workers, the entire group, including large numbers of women, struck under the auspices of the IWW. Among the most important of their stated demands was that "bosses and foremen respect the women workers." That same year, Italians in West Hoboken issued a "boycott" of a certain silk mill, which refused to bargain with its employees. The strike committee included both women and men.[11] A year later, a group of mostly Italian male weavers at a Plainfield, New Jersey, silk mill sent a committee to the boss to demand higher wages, and Italian women workers at the same mill "applauded from the windows. All of them sympathetic to the strike."[12]

These are just some of the many stories recounted by the Italian-language radical press. They challenge the conventional wisdom that Italian women did not join the 1909 shirtwaist workers' uprising because, unlike Jewish women, they were isolated from radical political and social movements, lacked a revolutionary tradition, or suffered from weak community networks and restrictive families.[13] Rather, Italian women did not join the 1909 strike en masse for several reasons. First, Italian workers were wary about the ILGWU, an affiliate of the conservative American Federation of Labor (AFL). The AFL typically limited its membership to skilled white men and had not only excluded most Italian workers (as well as other semiskilled and unskilled laborers) but also lobbied to restrict their immigration. At the time, the IWW was garnering far more support from Italian workers and their mutual aid societies than the AFL was and actively working to recruit Italian immigrant women in both the textile and garment trades. This was in sharp contrast to the ILGWU, which did not make a significant effort to recruit Italian women before or during the 1909 strike. Rather, the strike was initiated and organized by Jewish workers in Local 25, a shirtwaist local of the ILGWU and United Hebrew Trades. The movement was immersed in Jewish working-class culture and meetings were conducted in Yiddish. Italian workers also tended to transfer "their antagonism for Jewish bosses to Jewish union organizers," and many resented Jewish workers for earning higher wages for the same jobs.[14] In addition, the ILGWU had only several hundred members at the time of the strike and thus had few resources to recruit Italians. Nor did the WTUL reach out to Italian immigrant workers. Within days of the 1909 uprising, the IWW, the Federazione Socialista Italiana (FSI), and the Socialist Party hastily sent out teams of organizers to mobilize Italian women garment workers because this work had not occurred. As a result, several thousand Italian women did walk off their

jobs in solidarity with Jewish women, but organizers noted that the vast majority were deeply skeptical of the strike because very little effort had been made to
include them.[15]

In fact, most social reformers and labor organizers were unable to relate to
Italian immigrant women workers. As with scholars of this history, they often
compared Italians to Jews, to find Italians sorely lacking. When reformers observed relations on the shop floor, they noted, "Italian girls are seen as 'more
tractable'" by their fellow workers, while Jewish women were "seen as 'agitators.'"
Overall, Italians were "seen by other workers as undercutting wages" and to have
"cheapened the whole trade." Moreover, they argued, "when an Italian girl exhibits an interest in her trade it is an interest in craftsmanship or in her own wages
rather than in general trade conditions. The Jewish girl, on the contrary, has a
sense of her social responsibility and often displays an eager zest for discussion
of labor problems." Some expressed awareness that Italian workers' lack of interest might have stemmed from the fact the garment unions were fully immersed
in the extensive network and culture of Jewish working-class mutual aid societies. But still they argued that "the Italian girl is more willing than the Jewish girl
to accept conditions as she finds them."[16] Such ideas circulated freely between
the shop floor, the union hall, and social reform circles and were often couched
in the racial ideologies of the day. As a Jewish woman labor organizer told a
social reformer of the Italian women workers in her midst, "If they were more
civilized, they wouldn't take such low pay. But they go without hats and gloves
and umbrellas."[17]

Few Italian women could afford these symbols of American middle-class ci-
vility and leisure. This woman's comment reveals, however, her awareness that a
different set of priorities was operating for Italian immigrants. This generation of
women was compelled to work for the most basic food, shelter, and clothing; and
their wages rarely allowed for anything beyond. As historian Nancy Carnevale
has written of the garment trades, "The unions saw in homeworkers—and home
finishers, in particular—a threat to factory workers, who could not compete with
the low wages home finishers accepted. Out of self-interest, they chose to oppose
homework at every turn, rather than attempting the difficult task of organizing the overwhelmingly non-English-speaking Italian home finishers and other
homeworkers in the garment industry."[18] As unions took up an antihomework
agenda, they alienated Italian immigrant women workers, making it especially
hard for them to join Jewish workers under the banner of the ILGWU. The leftist press did little to inform the public about these complexities, and the Italian
prominenti did not help much either. As one noted northern Italian writer explained, "Those at the head of the movement for better conditions saw all their

efforts about to be nullified by this brown, ignorant, silent woman who would not listen, and when she did could not or would not understand."[19]

Everyday Resistance on the Shop Floor

As in their homelands, Italian immigrant women's forms of protest and resistance were independent of formal organizations but embedded in their own neighborhood and kinship networks. Because most found jobs through family and friends and worked in factories located within or near their neighborhoods, the workplace was an important place where women built a sense of community. Women's conversations, songs, jokes, complaints, and shared dreams of a life without backbreaking work and never-ending struggle reinforced their sense of collective identity. Ginevre Spagnoletti's dress shop in the Bowery was "full of Italian women bending over their machines and peering at the needles," as the El trains roared by. But it was also a place where the women were always "singing and joking together to escape the monotony and beat back the gloom."[20] Even in shops where singing or talking was prohibited, it was common that "some girl, unable to endure the silence any longer, would begin humming a tune which would be taken up by others near her."[21] As with other workers, Italian women also colluded to steal time for themselves on the job by slowing down the pace of work and finding ways to talk about their families, neighborhoods, work conditions, and politics.[22] Ginevre Spagnoletti's son, Ralph Fasanella, worked as a steam iron operator, among other jobs, before becoming an artist. His painting *Dress Shop* (1970) depicted the factory in New York City where his mother worked as a buttonhole maker in the 1910s and 1920s. In the painting, he placed newspaper headlines on the walls of the factory to signify the women's worries, noting how the women "did not go through their days in a state of narcosis, but carried the news of the day with them, and worried about their families in the context of current affairs."[23]

Women's networks also facilitated dramatic episodes of resistance, and strikes often began when one woman was harassed or insulted and her co-workers walked off the job in protest. Familial experiences in the peasant and worker rebellions in southern Italy sometimes shaped and inspired their actions. Anna Valenti learned the power of collective action from her parents' stories of peasant uprisings in their *paese* at the turn of the century. As a teenager, she took action in her garment shop after listening to the women she worked alongside discuss their continual struggle to feed their families. "I was a fighter," she recalled of the day she shut off the power in her shop in the 1910s, and signaled workers to leave their machines and hold an outdoor meeting. When the owner came after her with an umbrella, demanding she leave, all the women operators walked out with Anna.[24] Carrie Golzio recalled the Paterson ribbon mill where she worked as a child in the early twentieth century: the supervisors "were tough. But I was tough too. My father always said, 'no matter where you work, don't let them step on you.' That was instilled in me when I was a kid and I always fought. . . . I used to fight like hell. . . . If there was a strike I was the first on the line."[25] Angela and Maria Bambace were also politicized by women's everyday struggles in the garment shops where they worked. There they met others committed to challenging the power of the bosses and became active in the radical milieu in East Harlem. When they became labor organizers themselves, they did so with their mother Giuseppina's blessing. She even accompanied them on their union rounds with a rolling pin tucked under her arm, in case they encountered trouble.[26]

Stories of women's everyday resistance on the job fill oral histories, but they are also visible in the radical press. On occasion, some English-language labor newspapers reported on these episodes to illustrate that, while Italian women might not be sympathetic to certain labor unions in the United States, they were adept at collective action and therefore capable of organization. In one story, an Italian labor organizer in the ILGWU told of several Italian women finishers who grew impatient with a demanding forelady after she continually screamed at them to

Women in garment shop, ca. 1900. International Ladies' Garment Workers' Union Archives, Kheel Center for Labor-Management Documentation and Archives, Cornell University.

Angela Bambace with her mother Giuseppina, ca. 1930. Bambace Papers, Immigration History Research Center, University of Minnesota.

quicken their pace. When an older worker who "could not stand the nagging any longer" got the "courage to tell the forelady to 'Shut Up,'" the forewoman, "with one hand, snatched the garments from her and with the other gave her a good strong push and told her to 'Get out of the shop.'" In response, "every worker walked out of the shop in a body, in protest against the action of the forelady and in defense of the abused finisher."[27] Italian-language labor newspapers regularly chronicled such stories to encourage oppositional activism. One such story is that of Rose Alagna, who wrote about the indignities that she and other women were forced to endure, in a shop on West 27th Street. She announced their plans to strike against the boss who demanded, among other things, that they stay late without compensation to gather stray pins on the floor.[28] Women also shared stories of resistance on the shop floor, around kitchen tables, and on tenement stoops, and such tales passed from one generation to the next. These daily, un-organized, seemingly spontaneous actions formed an important part of Italian immigrant women's political culture, as they did for all workers.[29]

Building the Industrial Union Movement

Italian immigrant women's labor agitation increased dramatically after the found-ing of the IWW in 1905.[30] As a "militant organization that made unskilled workers the primary subjects of its revolutionary program," the IWW immediately appealed to Italian immigrants.[31] As one of the nation's largest pools of underemployed and exploited industrial workers, Italians were pivotal to the IWW's goal of creating a revolutionary alternative to the AFL. Founded by a variety of socialists, anarchists, and trade unionists, the "Wobblies" (the nickname for those active in the IWW) sought to organize workers who were excluded from the craft unions—women, migrant workers, people of color—into "One Big Union." Together they hoped to take over the means of production and distribution through workplace actions that would cripple capitalism and end the class system. Included in their founding statement was the line, "There can be no peace so long as hunger and want are found among millions of working people, and the few, who make up the employing class, have all the good things of life." They argued that "by organizing industrially we are forming the structure of the new society within the shell of the old." The IWW quickly became notorious for "its revolutionary tactics of direct action, its dynamic leaders, and its inspiring songs and graphics."[32]

The IWW also became known for its courageous and dramatic strikes. Between 1905 and 1914, as economic conditions worsened among America's working classes from a series of depressions, widespread unemployment, and declining wages, the IWW helped some of the most vulnerable workers—those in mining, textile production, lumbering, construction, agriculture, dock work, and marine transport—in a series of strikes that "shook the nation."[33] From the very beginning, Italian immigrants were a critical force within this movement. The anarchists in Paterson's silk mills were among the first to create a foreign-language local of the IWW, and they remained active during the critical period from 1905 to 1908 when the leadership of the IWW shifted from socialists to direct actionists.[34] In the years leading up to 1905, Italian silk workers in New Jersey had tried numerous times to organize a labor union, often employing strategies the IWW would later encourage and celebrate, such as parades, mass picketing, workplace sabotage, and threats against those workers who did not honor strikes. Indeed, the Italian anarchists were key activists in many workplace revolts, and both Paterson and West Hoboken became home to a strong, vocal IWW movement. The IWW "came the closest of any American leftist organization to paralleling the syndicalist movement in Italy," and was therefore the movement that Italian workers turned to en-masse once it was formed.[35] The IWW's direct-action philosophy and revolutionary socialist platform, in particular, made it appealing to those Italian immigrants who arrived fresh from the mass protests in Italy. But the IWW had broad appeal because it backed Italian immigrants' labor struggles, unlike any other organization in the period. Following the famous 1909 uprising of shirtwaist workers in New York City, for example, it was the IWW that demanded that the ILGWU make all of its decisions in mass meetings rather than in committees where Italians were absent or underrepresented.[36]

For all of these reasons, some of the earliest IWW locals formed out of the anarchist circles described in the preceding chapter and many Italian immigrants active in the radical subculture became leaders in the major organizing drives among Italian shoemakers, hotel workers, barbers, piano makers, and textile, garment, construction, and dock workers throughout New York City and New Jersey.[37] Italian anarchists and socialists brought the IWW into their communities by inviting charismatic Wobbly speakers such as Elizabeth Gurley Flynn, Big Bill Haywood, and Carlo Tresca to speak before large audiences. But it was during the 1909–13 strike wave that the IWW achieved its greatest notoriety, and it was largely thanks to Italian radicals that the "birth of unionism" occurred among Italian immigrant industrial workers. As Paul Buhle has observed, among "Italian clothing and garment workers of the 1910s, anarchist and syndicalist militants had an importance all out of proportion to their numbers. Without them, craft and industrial unionism might not have happened for another generation." While in Italy anarchist "insurrectionary strategies and egalitarian slogans disappeared into Communist political and ideological functions," in the United States they entered the industrial unions.[38] Italian immigrant women and their American-born daughters would play a crucial role in this movement.

Creating a Radical Feminist Culture in the Industrial Unions

One can mark the beginning of the 1909–13 strike wave in Hoboken, or as many historians have done, with the famous uprising of twenty thousand shirtwaist workers. Italian women did not join their Jewish co-workers in large numbers that year, but they became visible and active participants in the "Great Revolt" of sixty thousand cloak makers one year later that helped to make the ILGWU the third largest member of the AFL. More than twenty-eight hundred Italian workers—many of them inspired by the gains made in the 1909 uprising—joined the ILGWU in the first three days of the 1910 strike.[39] Several men active in Italian socialist circles, such as Salvatore Ninfo and Arturo Caroti, were central organizers in the strike. Less known is the role of women, like strikers Catherine Valenti, Anna Canno, and Sadie La Porta, who mobilized the unprecedented numbers of Italian women that began attending union meetings and joining picket lines, often with their children at their side. Their names suggest that they had either immigrated very young or were the daughters of immigrant women, but unfortunately they left few additional traces in the historical record. We do know, however, that within the next three weeks, an additional twenty thousand Italian workers walked out on strike, including large numbers of women home-finishers who went on strike in solidarity with the mostly male cloak makers.[40]

Italian women's move from scabs to strikers in one year speaks less to their sudden politicization than of an important change in strategy that was taking form. First, Italian women were willing to join a strike orchestrated by the ILGWU because it was becoming increasingly impossible to organize separately from them. As historian Annelise Orleck has argued, the 1909 uprising produced mixed results, but it "breathed new life into a struggling immigrant labor movement and transformed the tiny ILGWU into a union of national significance."[41] In the next decade, the ILGWU would become more effective than the IWW in forcing garment employers to the bargaining table. As a result, the union began to attract Italian workers who hoped that building alliances with Jewish workers might bring access to higher wages, shorter hours, and safer working conditions. They also joined because the ILGWU began to actively recruit Italian workers.[42] They hired Arturo Caroti, hoping that his role in the Hoboken movement would enable him to mobilize Italian women workers in New York. His first step was to form a *circolo*, called the Italian Women's Mutual Benefit Society, open to "any girl of working age, and any female member of a workers' family." In addition to receiving "free medical care during illness," the women "were required to attend bi-monthly meetings held at two New York settlement houses."[43] Caroti's tactics also included buying off the strikebreakers and enlisting the support of fathers and husbands. But he failed to generate substantial union membership and returned to Italy in 1913. It was clear: neither the needs of the union nor the support of certain Italian male leaders were enough to coax Italian women into the ILGWU. Once the union trained Italian women to organize and granted them financial support and self-governing spaces crucial to developing the movement and building internal leadership, Italian women began to enter the union en masse.[44]

Such institutional support developed just as Italian immigration was peaking. Between 1900 and 1910, the numbers of Italians in the United States tripled. By the 1910s, "Italian associational networks had grown in leaps and bounds, and their presence within the American industrial apparatus had consolidated." In the next decade, Italians would play a central role in "one of the most sweeping organizational drives ever to take place in one single industrial sector"—the garment trades.[45] As the IWW and the ILGWU competed for Italian immigrant workers' allegiance, both became central to Italian American labor activism and radicalism. Many of the Italian men who rose to prominence in the radical subculture, such as Arturo Giovannitti and Antonino Crivello, would become officials in the ILGWU. But it was Italian women who at all times composed the majority of workers in the garment industry, the majority of union members, and the most successful organizers.

After the 1910 strike, women formed the majority of the newly formed Organizational Committee of the Italian Branch of the ILGWU, which became the Italian Branch of Local 25 after the 1913 strike. As one male ILGWU official would note years later, "You needed women to approach the women."[46] From the outset, women such as Angela and Maria Bambace, Grace De Luise, Margaret Di Maggio, Millie Tarantino, Lucy Guida, Mary Sanfilippo, Clara Zara, Minnie Lero, Rose Grassa, Almerinda Castellucci, Rosalia Conforti, Mary Lamantia, Anna Cassio, Alma Varanelli, and countless others—many of whom were also active in anarchist or socialist circles in their neighborhoods—created the first organizing teams that brought thousands of Italian immigrant women into the union.[47] From isolated shops spread across the city, Italian women workers contacted the Italian Branch daily, reporting on their struggles, methods of resistance, and need for assistance. Organizers met with workers through community meetings and by finding work in garment shops that were nonunion. They listened to women's grievances, brought them into the union, and encouraged them to shape and direct the movement.

Women organizers faced almost constant harassment from police and employers, and many endured arrest and violent beatings. "There isn't a tougher job a woman can take than being an organizer," Angela Bambace would note. "This is a hard job." For much of her life, she spent every waking hour consumed by the movement. As a young woman she was often at the union hall late into the night after a full day of work as a seamstress in a shirtwaist shop. On her organizing rounds, she was regularly roughed up or thrown down stairs by employers, and on several occasions she was incarcerated, once for thirty days.[48] Most women active in the union during this period spoke of the picket line as if they were "in battle."[49] As historian Nan Enstad has documented, "Police violence, mass arrests, and harsh sentences were standard fare for workers who sought a political voice through strikes. Because the striking women were working class and mostly immigrants, police and thugs did not feel compelled to treat them with the deference due to white, middle-class women." She continues, "The women also faced tactics that capitalized on the historic association of unescorted women in public space with disorder, including sexual disorder."[50]

Margaret Di Maggio was beaten up and arrested several times while working to bring Italian women into the ILGWU in the 1910s. Described as both "crass and aggressive" and "talented" by others in the movement, she became well known for her courage as an organizer and power as an orator.[51] Grace De Luise was her organizing partner, and she recalled that "in those days, when we picketed, they thought it was a horrible thing for young girls. They called us all sorts of terrible things and said that we were terrible people just because we were picketing to earn a better living." Organizing nonunion shops was particularly dangerous, De Luise recalled: "They would throw things at you, and you had to be ready to go running down the stairs." Once while on a picket line, a woman twice De Luise's size kicked her in the stomach in order to cross the picket line, sending De Luise to the hospital. Employers also hired enforcers from the mob to threaten and harass young women who picketed their shops, and many women recalled being thrown down stairs and hurled across rooms "like a football" by such men while on their organizing rounds. Such work also cost activists their lives. Willie Lurie, a close friend of De Luise and Di Maggio's, and fellow organizer, was shot dead by gangsters during a strike in the 1940s; and Giuseppa Maresca and Anna Lo Pizzo were two of the more publicized female strikers who were killed by police while walking picket lines in this period.[52]

Even in this climate, Italian women were able to generate support for the garment unions through a variety of strategies, including workplace committees, house visits, educational programs, community-wide publicity, cultural activities, demonstrations, strikes, picket lines, soup kitchens, and theater troupes, which often involved entire families.[53] The culture they sought to create is partly evident in the Italian-language weeklies that the ILGWU published during the 1910s to recruit and educate workers. As with some of the anarchist newspapers, these periodicals provided women with a space to articulate their own visions of industrial unionism. The audience of these newspapers was much broader, because it included the thousands of women union members who were regular subscribers by 1914.[54] But the union newspapers played an important role in bringing the radical subculture into many new homes. Some newspapers like *L'Operaia* (The Woman Worker) were directed at an entirely female audience of Italian dressmakers, and while edited by Italian men, reprinted articles and poems by popular female authors from the anarchist and revolutionary socialist press. They also enlisted the more active and vocal female union members to write essays. In such writing, women worked to create a community of *lavoratrici coscienti* (conscious women workers), and they drew heavily upon the model offered by newspapers like *La Questione Sociale* and *L'Era Nuova* to do so. Other newspapers, like *Lotta di Classe* (Class Struggle)—the official newspaper of the Italian section of the Cloak and Skirt Makers' Union of the ILGWU in New York City—reserved a page for women's writing called *La Pagina della Donna*. Here various women active in the union shared stories from their experiences as organizers, and analyzed capitalism as well as patriarchal work and family relations. The paper also included the writing of well-known anarchists such as Leda Rafanelli, Pietro Gori, and Luigi Galleani, and routinely announced the lectures, dances, picnics, and other events of the radical circles.[55]

These union newspapers reveal the importance of Italian women's radical political ideologies and practices, including feminism, to their emerging industrial union culture. Women authors conveyed the message that "the inferiority of women is not physiological or psychological, but social."[56] They also advocated a "*femminismo*" (feminism) that was based on "the spirit of solidarity between women." This feminism, they asserted, was "not a movement against men, but one that is primarily interested in developing intelligence among women. . . . Feminism is the belief that the woman is exploited doubly, by capitalism and by her companion." Moreover, they contended, "In the labor movement women can find the opportunity to become a militant force for humanity with a clear vision of the world."[57] As in the anarchist newspapers, their feminism was transnational. Organizers continually publicized women's struggles in Italy and in factories across the United States, as evidence of their ability to fight oppression. Yet, unlike the anarchists, the union culture of the ILGWU drew upon Italian cultural codes of honor and respect, and an emergent Italian nationalism, to refute the reputation that plagued them: "You are not Italians," wrote Clara Zara, a labor organizer and factory operative, "you who trample on our revolutionary traditions; you are not Italians who dishonor and betray the holy and sublime cause of our work. . . . You have massacred our reputation, our dignity, our honor, [and created] the suspicion that Italian immigrant women workers have inherited."[58]

To dismantle this reputation, organizers sought to build a union movement in the garment trades that welcomed both immigrants and the American-born. In fact, union meetings, demonstrations, and picket lines were often multigenerational. Tina Gaeta learned labor activism from her immigrant mother: "My mother was always against homework and she encouraged my sister . . . to carry the picket sign when her shop went on strike." She "used to make me take hot coffee to [my sister] when she was picketing." On one occasion Tina joined the picket line as a child, "took the sign and put it on, and started walking with it so proudly." When her mother learned that she had participated, she "just smiled."[59] Francesca Crivello often brought her son Antonio to union meetings and picket lines. When he was a teenager, he organized an anarchist circle on the Lower East Side with other young immigrants from Italy and later became a union organizer in the ILGWU himself.[60] Ginevre Spagnoletti joined the union after she started reading the newspapers and pamphlets of an Italian anarchist group in her Greenwich Village neighborhood. Each evening after work, she read them aloud to her five children and encouraged political debate at the kitchen table.[61] Families thus remained a central site where Italian immigrant women developed oppositional ideologies, and the union culture they created would be grounded in such relationships.

The Italian women who composed the first organizing teams for the ILGWU differed from their rank-and-file counterparts in one significant respect: most did not have children. Still, they worked in the same "women's jobs" as operatives, drapers, finishers, hemstitchers, and examiners. They became radicalized by the deteriorating labor conditions in the factories, exemplified most dramatically by the devastating fire at the Triangle Shirtwaist Factory near Washington Square on 25 March 1911, which claimed the lives of 146 garment workers—the vast majority Italian and Jewish women and girls. The Triangle Fire was particularly devastating because it had been cited during the 1909 strike for hazardous working conditions. Moreover, the nightmare of dozens of workers—almost entirely young women in their teens and early twenties—jumping from the eighth and ninth floors of the factory and hitting the sidewalk with such force that they shattered the cement was horrific. Those who survived revealed that employers had locked the doors to keep workers from taking breaks and to prevent petty theft. They had disregarded rusty fire escapes and carelessly kept highly flammable oil close to bundles of fabric. Rage deepened. Many Italian immigrant women marked the fire as the critical moment when they committed themselves to the labor movement, believing that unionism was their most powerful recourse.[62]

In addition, the highly publicized and violent labor uprisings between 1910 and 1913, in Lawrence, Paterson, Chicago, Tampa, and other cities where Italian women were major components of the labor force, further politicized Italian immigrant women in New York City and New Jersey. These events also helped to unify Italian immigrant communities. Workers across regional and craft differences came together, and for the first time the mainstream Italian-language press, the *prominenti*, and local parish priests joined together in defense of labor.[63] In New York and New Jersey, Italian immigrant workers launched their own mass movement in 1913, in the hopes of building on the successful 1912 strike in Lawrence, to launch a series of general strikes that would change the face of the American labor movement.

The Turning Point of 1913

With tens of thousands of Italian immigrant women joining in labor uprisings, 1913 unfolded as a year of dramatic activity. One mother of six children who joined the 1913 garment workers' strike in New York City spoke for many when she explained her rationale for joining the movement: "It's all for my childs. I fight them again. I no care."[64] Stories of Italian women's militancy appeared in leftist and mainstream newspapers daily because disturbances and confrontations became regular fare. In the first days of the strike, a group of several hundred Italian women stormed a large factory in lower Manhattan wielding umbrellas as weapons and lunging at police officers who tried to keep them from entering. Once inside the shop, "the women, fighting like furies, jabbed right and left with their umbrellas and in their excitement sometimes jabbed strikers."[65] Such demonstrations culminated in a meeting at Union Square on 14 January in which newspapers estimated that 100,000 attended. The *New York Call* reported, "There were Jews, Italians, Russians, Lithuanians, Poles, Germans, Americans, Spaniards, Hungarians, and others."[66] Four days later, however, Italian women would gather in Cooper Union to learn that the union had sacrificed their demands and settled without the women's approval.

In the following weeks, Italian women launched a movement of their own, confronting workers who crossed their picket lines. Angelina Bruno, Marguerite Cololito, and Rosie Cereida were just a few of the many young women arrested daily for disorderly conduct, when they tried to persuade other workers outside the factory to ignore the settlement and defy the union; their last names suggest they were not all Italian.[67] The union and manufacturers were forced to meet again, as a result of the unrest, to work out a new settlement. But the union also issued a statement expressing its disbelief that the women were acting on their own. Rather, they announced "that there was no real discontent among the workers, only a plot by the rival Industrial Workers of the World to destroy the union," and declared that the Italian women had been "easily pacified."[68] ILGWU officials focused their contempt on the IWW because many of the disgruntled workers turned to the revolutionary industrial union as they grew frustrated with the ILGWU's accommodationist strategy. What the ILGWU leaders failed to see was that Italian women were using a strategy of resistance that was proven in its effectiveness. As in their homelands, they deployed mass-based street demonstrations, civil disobedience, and the direct action of female mobs to assert their voices. The Italian-language press came to the defense of the strikers, and almost $1 million in funds was raised by Italian mutual aid societies.[69]

This spirit of resistance spread across the city and into northeastern New Jersey. By February workers in Paterson were also inspired to launch what they hoped would be a duplication of the 1912 Lawrence strike. Immigrant textile workers, joined in solidarity across lines of ethnicity, led by a largely female rank and file, and supported by the IWW, hoped to force mill owners to meet their demands. Moreover, for the IWW the strike provided an opportunity to challenge the growing power of the AFL unions. From the beginning, Italian immigrant radical circles constituted the heart of the movement. They provided the meeting halls, enlisted inspiring speakers to address the crowds of strikers, and formed a core group of organizers and picketers.[70] Paterson was particularly well suited for such a movement because the anarchist movement was strong and more than nine thousand of the city's residents were IWW members. As historian Steve Golin has noted, "In this fluid atmosphere, in which capitalism itself was open to question and revolution seemed a real possibility, the IWW thrived."[71] While the IWW was able to serve the workers of Paterson at this time, the strike was entirely immigrant directed—"the workers created their own unity."[72]

The strike began from below, from the most unskilled sectors of the city's textile trades. Southern Italian and Jewish dyers' helpers and broad silk weavers, many of whom were women, united out of a shared experience of oppression. Their sense of collective identity emerged not just from being confined to the worst-paid and most dangerous jobs but from all areas of life. One young Jewish woman from Poland "noticed—and never forgot—how her first-grade teacher, who was Irish, singled out the Jewish and Italian children, putting a plaster across their mouths when they made a noise."[73] In addition, throughout the strike, Paterson's predominantly Irish police force routinely referred to the strikers as the "Wops and Jews."[74] By the second week of the strike, twenty-four thousand workers had walked off their jobs. Sympathy strikes spread throughout New Jersey, to Summit, Hackensack, Carlstadt, Pompton Lakes, Lodi, Stirling, Phillipsburg, Hoboken, West New York, Weehawken, Union Hill, and North Bergen, and beyond, across Brooklyn, Queens, and Manhattan. The strike spread even further away, to Norwalk and New London, Connecticut; Buffalo, New York; and Pennsylvania. Paterson's mill owners moved production to the eastern part of Pennsylvania during the strike, where the IWW was not yet established, to reassert their power over workers. This tactic, in the end, would prove decisive in the strike. Unlike Lawrence, the Paterson movement was not able to completely halt production and force employers to meet their demands.[75] In addition, Paterson's manufacturers had two other things on their side: a repressive police force and hunger. During the first months of the strike, the police responded to the mass picket lines and meetings with extreme aggressiveness. They arrested speakers and pickets and attempted to discourage activism with violence. Ninfa Baronio was one of many arrested on the picket line. Her son recalled the mayhem that ensued: "Paolo Guabello was on the picket line and was ordered to move by the police. He didn't move fast enough and was clubbed to the ground. Mother had come to get me and saw Paolo fall. She got down to help and the police clubbed her too. They threw them in a police wagon pulled by a horse. I ran after it crying, 'Mama, Mama!' Paolo was bleeding all the way to the jail."[76] Mary Gasperano was not as well known in the community as Ninfa for her radical activities, but during the strike she and many other women became local heroines. In one month she was arrested four times, for her speeches before the pickets, for biting the hand of a police sergeant during one arrest, and for slapping a woman strikebreaker across the face.[77]

Most employers, as well as outside observers, were unprepared for and surprised by women's militancy during the strike. While the strike included seasoned activists like Ninfa Baronio and other anarchists, it radicalized many young women. Teresa Cobianci's experience was somewhat typical. She was only fifteen years old and working as a ribbon weaver in Paterson when the strike began. She was born in southern Italy but had come to Paterson with her parents when she was four years old. Although she returned to Italy with her mother who contracted tuberculosis and died soon after, she came back to Paterson at the age of twelve. Suffering from chronic stomach trouble and an injury she sustained when a fire hose came loose in the factory and struck her head, "she was badly underweight but 'with a face like a flower,'" Elizabeth Gurley Flynn recalled. Encouraged by Flynn, she delivered speeches at the largest meeting halls during strike meetings, to speak out about the terrible working conditions she endured. The experience changed her: "I want always to go back to Italy, but since the strike I am more happy here. We are all together. We stand solid. My father says there will always be bosses. I say 'Yes? Then we shall be the bosses.'"[78]

Carrie Golzio also began speaking publicly during the strike, often with her four-year-old sister by her side. As with many other young women, she attended the daily mass meetings that took place first thing in the morning and the shop meetings in the afternoon. While her husband protested, she justified her actions: "I can't stay home, I got to go out and fight." For many, the strike suspended the prohibitions that normally governed female behavior. Years later, Golzio would recall, "Ah that was a strike. I had a lot of fun. I'd go around and laugh and carry on. They had meetings with singing and dancing. . . . It was exciting."[79]

As the strike wore on, the regular meetings helped workers to stay united, inspired, and focused. In May, Pietro and Maria Botto offered their home in nearby suburban Haledon as a center for meetings when workers were barred by local authorities from assembling in Paterson. Their home was situated on a hill overlooking a large lawn, and included a small porch on the second floor that served as a platform for speakers. For the first time, strikers could meet in one large gathering. On Sundays, thousands took trolleys from surrounding towns to gather on the front lawn for rallies that included music, speeches, and a picnic. Estimates of thirty thousand participants were made by a wide range of sources.[80] To Eva and Adele, the Botto's young daughters, the transformation of their home into an amphitheater was spectacular. It was also exhausting. The home served as a boarding home to many speakers, and the women all worked around the clock to maintain the household. On Sundays, hundreds and sometimes thousands of strikers gathered to hear well-known Wobbly leaders such as Elizabeth Gurley Flynn, Carlo Tresca, Antonio Guabello, and Hubert Harrison speak from the second-floor balcony after a hearty meal downstairs. Less known, however, is that, as the strike wore on, Maria Botto's health steadily declined and within two years of the strike she was dead. "I'm certain the work contributed to her death," her granddaughter would later lament.[81]

To those in attendance, however, such gatherings were exhilarating. "To speak at such meetings," Bill Haywood, a founder of the IWW and strike leader, would later recall, "is worth a lifetime of agitation."[82] The gatherings provided visible evidence of the power of workers' solidarity. The weekly women's meetings were also among the most popular. Six hundred women attended the first meeting held on 5 March, about a month into the strike, but three thousand showed up for the second meeting, held only five days later. Steve Golin writes, "Not only did these meetings build confidence in the women, they also broke down the resistance of male strikers to the equal participation in the strike. They allowed women to show how much they cared."[83] They also created the setting where women strikers could develop leadership skills and learn about political radicalism. Because women's activism had been so crucial to winning the Lawrence strike, IWW leaders encouraged women's activism in Paterson and beyond, and they trained them to become organizers and public speakers, to address the crowds alongside the more seasoned activists.

As in the meeting at Cooper Union across the river in Manhattan that January, the women in the crowd at Paterson played an active role and voiced their opinions freely. Flynn reported on one women's meeting in Paterson, where she, Bill Haywood, and Carlo Tresca spoke at the invitation of the strikers: "Tresca made some remarks about shorter hours, people being less tired, more time to spend together and jokingly he said: 'More babies.' The women did not look amused. When Haywood interrupted and said: 'No Carlo, we believe in birth control—a few babies, well cared for!' they burst into laughter and applause."[84] Haywood seems to have considered women's role in the movement as more central than Tresca or many of the other male leaders of the Italian syndicalist movement. The women, he wrote in the strike's fifth month, "have been an enormous factor in the Paterson strike. Each meeting for them has been attended by bigger and bigger crowds." Speaking before a large audience of male strikers, he made sure to remind them of the significance of women to a successful strike: "One woman is worth three men—I never knew it to fail."[85]

In the end, the defeat of the 1913 Paterson strike forced the IWW to retreat from the East Coast. Without the funds to continue organizing, especially during the

1914–15 period of economic downturn and unemployment, the IWW turned its attention to organizing miners in the Midwest and to antiwar activism. Most of the women in Paterson who were active in the strike were blacklisted and unable to find work in the local silk mills. The six-month strike had, however, shown many what it was like to conceive of a world run by workers, and what it might mean to create such a society. The radical subculture had become a part of the daily lives of not just several thousand but hundreds of thousands. It would not be until the 1918–19 strike wave that workers would rise up again with similar devotion to each other. By then, they would find themselves the target of a federal campaign to eliminate all opposition to the status quo.

The 1919 Strikes and the Birth of the Italian Locals

In reflecting on the early years of labor organizing in New York City's garment shops, Angela Bambace recalled working all night on strike activities after a full day of sewing in the factory and dealing with abusive employers who resorted to all kinds of tactics, including physical violence, to keep organizers out of the shops. But one thing especially stood out for her: "The women played a very big part in the union and saved a lot of lives because they got the employer and the employees to sit down and talk instead of a lot of commotion and fighting."[86] Angela and her sister Maria joined the ILGWU during the 1919 strikes, where they witnessed firsthand the effectiveness of women organizers.

During the 1919 strike wave, four million workers walked off their jobs in thousands of strikes nationwide. In Manhattan, Brooklyn, Passaic, Paterson, and other locations, Italian immigrant women led the effort to organize the textile and garment trades. As with other workers across the country, they momentarily found themselves in an unprecedented position of power because strikes could block war production and force employers to the bargaining table.[87] Massive wartime inflation and the rising cost of living amid low wages and deteriorating working conditions led workers to come together to demand change. The feeling that capitalism could be successfully challenged from the bottom up grew particularly strong in November 1917, when the Bolshevik Party staged a successful communist revolution in Russia. Yet workers not only drew inspiration from the possibilities offered by developments in Russia. They also insisted that the United States live up to its own promises of democracy, freedom, and justice.

While the 1918–19 strikes were largely unsuccessful in the garment and textile trades, they provided a stage for Italian immigrant women to publicly demonstrate their commitment to the U.S. labor movement. Tens of thousands joined the walk-out and several hundred endured arrest on picket lines. They were "exceedingly energetic and bellicose, as the police rolls showed," and "distinguished themselves on picket lines, at strikers' meetings, and on organizational committees."[88]

What distinguished this from earlier strikes was that following the 1919 strike Italian women workers achieved their first significant institutional space within the American labor movement—the ILGWU granted Italian dressmakers their own "language local," the Italian Dressmakers Local 89, with headquarters at 8 West 21st Street in Manhattan. At the head of the organization department was Margaret Di Maggio, with Grace De Luise, Maria Bambace, Laura Di Guglielmo, Anna Fama, Lina Manetta, Angelina Limanti, Maria Prestianni, Anna Squillante, and Millie Tirreno serving on the local's first board.[89] Almost all had been active in the movement since 1913. Italians also established two other large locals in the aftermath of strikes—Local 63 of the ACWA and Local 48 of the ILGWU.[90] Each of these locals cemented the presence of Italians in U.S. labor politics, and with a combined membership of more than twenty thousand, they became a center of Italian American working-class political activity from the 1920s through the 1970s.

The Italian locals of the ACWA and the ILGWU included many anarcho-syndicalists and revolutionary socialists who responded to the devastation of the 1913 strikes by infusing these new labor organizations with the kind of ideology and strategy that had defined the prewar movement. But these radicals faced a reformist leadership, not a revolutionary one, which continually opted to institutionalize hierarchy to maintain their own autonomy and power in the union. Rather than build an international, multiethnic movement to dismantle capitalism, the leadership of these locals focused on including their members in the U.S. polity. As a result, they cultivated ethnic nationalism in their members, encouraging them to identify as both Italians and Americans. As we will see, such a strategy created a sense of community, but it also reinforced ethnic antagonism and segmentation within the union. In the 1930s, the Italian Dressmakers Local 89 would become the single largest union local in the nation and a powerful institution through which Italian American workers could assert identities and mobilize as whites. We cannot understand why and how this developed without first attending to the dramatic upheavals of the 1920s, however. The rise of coercive nationalism in the form of the Red Scare, 100 percent Americanism, the hugely popular Ku Klux Klan, immigration restriction, and fascism would forever change American politics. The Italian immigrant Left turned increasingly to the new unions to build a meaningful political culture that could survive the pervasive antiradicalism in the United States. Italian immigrant women's powerful role in the 1909–19 strike wave would ensure their centrality in this emerging world and usher in a new era of struggle over the meanings of emancipation.

Red Scare, the Lure of Fascism, and Diasporic Resistance

Valentine's Day 1920 was a day few in Paterson, New Jersey, would ever forget. The events surrounding that day would reverberate for generations, transforming Italian immigrant political cultures across the New York metropolitan area and far beyond. In the middle of the night, "over one hundred federal agents, assisted by volunteers from the American Legion, descended on Paterson and raided the homes of more than thirty members of *Gruppo L'Era Nuova*," the group formerly known as Gruppo Diritto all'Esistenza (The Right to an Existence Group). Those arrested also came from another anarchist group, the Galleani-inspired Gli Insorti (The Insurgents), and the Ferrer School, "an anarchist-inspired place for the children of workers to study, which was directed by the workers themselves."[1] With warrants in hand and several large suitcases, the agents arrested whomever they could find, confiscated over a ton of documents, and brought the suspects to Ellis Island's detention cells to await possible deportation.

Among those arrested were Firmino Gallo, Ludovico Caminita, Alberto and Paolo Guabello, Pietro Baldisserotto, Serafino Grandi, and Severo Espi—all active anarchists. Agents gathered all the printed material they could find, as well as several revolvers.[2] The next morning the *New York Times* announced: "Terrorists Caught in Paterson Raids." In a rudimentary fashion, the reporter translated and published selections from various anarchist texts to illustrate that these men were "anarchists of the worst type, not philosophical anarchists," who "seek their ends . . . through the use of bombs and other engines of destruction to create terror and fear."[3] Police raids had occurred in the past, but 1919 and 1920 witnessed a massive wave of government repression. Fueled by a heightened fear of political dissent during World War I, the U.S. Department of Justice launched a nationwide operation to crush the labor movement and working-class radicalism in all forms. Attorney General A. Mitchell Palmer led the charge, and in January

iww headquarters in New York City after police raid of 15 November 1919. Labadie Collection, University of Michigan.

1920 alone he oversaw the arrests of "six thousand alleged radicals in thirty-three cities. Many were held without warrants, were never formally charged, and were not allowed to contact lawyers or relatives. Some had no connection to radical activities; others signed coerced confessions. Six hundred of them were eventually forced to leave the country."[4]

This wave of government-sanctioned repression against the Left taught Italian immigrants a powerful lesson: admission into the U.S. nation was contingent on their rejection of anarchism and other forms of opposition to capitalism, imperialism, and white supremacy. The state's execution of anarchists Sacco and Vanzetti in 1927 was further proof that American fear of foreign radicalism, cast in racist and nativist language, could put Italian immigrants' lives in jeopardy.[5] Labeled as "lazy, criminal, sexually irresponsible, and emotionally volatile," Italians remained "one of the most despised immigrant groups" well into the 1940s.[6] Popular images of them as "illiterate, harmless organ grinders," circulated alongside images of "stiletto-wielding criminals drunk on vino . . . [and] bomb throwing revolutionaries motivated by Marx and Malatesta."[7] In 1921 and 1924, Congress affirmed these ideas with the passage of immigration restriction legislation, to "shut the door" and to preserve "the pure, unadulterated Anglo-Saxon stock" that supposedly made the United States "the foremost nation in her progress."[8] As a result, Italians increasingly sought to reconcile their position as unwanted foreigners by turning away from revolutionary social movements and toward a politics that embraced nationalism and, along with it, whiteness and negrophobia.[9] During the 1920s, revolutionary activism persisted, especially in the transnational antifascist movement, and in labor struggles. But the spaces where Italian American women could organize collectively to challenge oppressive power in all its forms became severely circumscribed.

This chapter and the next examine the impact of these dramatic changes on working-class politics to explore how Italian immigrant women and their American-born daughters journeyed from waging oppositional struggles from the margins to acquiring institutional power in the single largest union local in the nation by the 1930s and 1940s. As Italian American workers sought the acceptance of mainstream labor and political institutions, they accommodated to the pervasive antiradicalism that defined U.S. politics. In the garment unions, this meant the development of a virulent anticommunism. It also meant new forms of ethnic nationalism, including mass-based support for the aggressively masculine, nationalist, racist, and imperial project of Italian fascism. In fact, the political culture that developed in the interwar period gave rise to collective identities that were deeply contradictory. Support for nationalism in the form of fascism *and* "100 percent Americanism" challenged diasporic, class-based identities, and threatened the kinds of political consciousness working-class revolutionaries had worked so hard to develop since the 1890s. But fascism also persisted in maintaining transnational ties, even as immigration restriction and the Red Scare forced Italians in the United States to turn away from their homelands and fully engage in American politics.

Red Scare

It seemed the Justice Department's worst fears concerning foreign radicals were confirmed when a series of bombs exploded in seven cities on the night of 2 June 1919, including New York, Paterson, Boston, Pittsburgh, Philadelphia, Cleveland, and Washington. Two of the bombs detonated almost simultaneously outside the homes of both Attorney General A. Mitchell Palmer and a Paterson silk mill president. The bomber killed by the premature explosion at Palmer's house was Carlo Valdinoci, "one of Luigi Galleani's closest associates."[10] There was little evidence that the explosions were an organized anarchist conspiracy or the work of anyone in Paterson's Gruppo Diritto all'Esistenza. But in the aftermath of the

Russian Revolution and the 1919 labor strikes the "fear of revolution gripped public opinion. Citizens and congressmen alike lumped all radicals—anarchists, communists, iwws—into a single 'red menace' and demanded appropriate action'" in the form of police raids, detention, and execution, "to trace them to their hiding places, to destroy them."[11]

Women were generally not targeted for arrest, but the Palmer raids threw their lives into chaos as federal agents hauled their lovers, brothers, fathers, and other male comrades to jail and shut down community centers. Every Sunday, often in subzero weather, women made the pilgrimage to console their loved ones, bringing with them food, cigars, cigarettes, and clean underwear. Ludovico Caminita would write about the raid and incarceration in his memoir *Nell'isola delle lagrime: Ellis Island* (On the Island of Tears: Ellis Island). There he recounted one of the women's first visits, when the men were transported from the city jail to Ellis Island's detention center. As the men appeared outside, Ninfa Baronio, Fiorina Grandi, and Anna Baldisserotto struggled to break through the police line, after waiting over eight hours in the freezing cold. The crowd that gathered beside them "expressed its sympathy for these poor women by hurling taunting remarks and cutting insults at the agents." When one police officer withdrew a blackjack to threaten the women, "the women became furious. But they were three against a group of strong men, armed with every weapon, including the most powerful: the certainty of going unpunished."[12] One of the accused men waved to the crowd and yelled "Goodbye! Goodbye!" An agent turned to him and shouted "Shut Up!" The man, "drunk on his quarter of an hour of sudden popularity," shouted back, "Shut up you!" The agent punched the man in the face and went for his blackjack, but was restrained by another officer fearful of the crowd. "When we get to the island I'll kill you," the agent seethed to the accused man. Caminita recalled, "The poor man didn't understand, but when I translated the threat into Italian, the color drained from his face, he bent his head, and remained silent."[13]

When the women returned from these desperate sojourns, they did what they could to reassure their children, some of whom would later recall the many "hushed conversations" that transpired in those dark days. They would also remember that it was hard not to internalize popular perceptions and that many in the American-born generation wanted to distance themselves from this movement, deemed shameful, violent, and fanatical.[14]

But the women did more than bring supplies to the men, worry over their fate, and care for the children in their absence. The Justice Department would later discover that as soon as the raids began, bundles of radical pamphlets and newspapers turned up in the hands of women, who took responsibility for hiding and distributing the material. As men were forced to go underground to escape arrest, women assumed new roles in the movement.[15] In Paterson, federal agents centered their attention on a certain B. Emilio, who was receiving large quantities of foreign-language newspapers at a small Italian grocery store in the weeks following the Valentine's Day raid.[16] Upon further investigation, agents realized that B. Emilio was in fact Gemma Mello: a thirty-year-old broad silk weaver in Paterson's mills who had migrated seven years earlier from a small town outside of Novara. She was, they argued, "a dangerous idealist and anarchist, one who would not hesitate to do anything to accomplish an end."[17] They issued a warrant for her arrest and apprehended her on 19 March 1920 for the distribution of radical materials. This was punishable under the 1918 Immigration Act, which authorized the deportation of any alien who "opposed all organized government (anarchism); advocated the overthrow of the government 'by force or violence'; or belonged to any organization teaching these ways."[18]

They were right that Mello was very active in the movement and that she had become a major distributor of radical materials, especially after the arrest of Firmino Gallo, whose radical bookstore had been raided. She was also a member of the militant antiorganizationalist group Gli Insorti. As Galleanisti, members advocated the use of violence and were behind several bombings, including an explosion that shook the corner of Wall and Broad Streets in Manhattan on 16 September 1920.[19] The Wall Street bomb exploded just days after indictments against Sacco and Vanzetti were handed down. Because their conviction occurred amid the raids, arrests, and deportations, most in the movement believed they were set up. It is now known that the explosion on Wall Street was in retaliation for the Sacco and Vanzetti conviction, and it had grisly consequences.

The blast occurred at noon in one of the busiest sections of the city: "Glass showered down from office windows, and awnings twelve stories above the street burst into flames. People fled in terror as a great cloud of dust enveloped the area. In [J. P.] Morgan's offices Thomas Joyce of the securities department fell dead on his desk amid a rubble of plaster and glass. Outside scores of bodies littered the streets. Blood was everywhere." Thirty died immediately and "more than two hundred were injured seriously enough to be taken to the hospital."[20] Those in the movement would recall the deep remorse that many felt over the numbers of innocent people who suffered as a result of the blast. "The victims of the blast, far from being the financial powers of the country, were mostly runners, stenographers, and clerks."[21] Anarchists had always debated whether such acts of retaliatory violence were productive. Some believed in an eye-for-an-eye and that the violence and power of capitalism could be challenged only by force. But many others in the movement were certain that such practices only lead to greater violence and suffering.[22] One thing was certain, however, and that was the growing power of the state to retaliate against the movement.

The antiradical and anti-immigrant crusades of this period were part of a much larger effort on the part of the U.S. federal government and business elite to limit the growing power of the labor movement. In 1919 alone, four million workers, a full one-fifth of the nation's workforce, went on strike "to make good on the war's democratic promise."[23] This included garment and textile workers, but also theater workers, telephone operators, coal miners, iron and steel workers, police officers, and shipyard workers. Workers' demands focused on bread-and-butter issues, such as hours and wages, but working-class radicalism and a revolutionary spirit were central to the movement. For this reason, federal authorities focused their campaign not only on anarchists but on working-class activism as a whole. Special Agent Frank Stone, who was in charge of the Paterson raid, considered it a huge success because he believed he had crushed one of the major centers of labor activism in the country. In an interview with the *Evening Mail* following the raid, Stone speculated that his agents had thwarted the move of the IWW headquarters from Chicago to Paterson. Particularly revealing, he noted, were the "bulky membership rosters and ledgers showing financial transactions all over the eastern half of the country" found in the house of IWW organizer Andre Graziano. Such an observation suggests the significance of the Paterson anarchists to the IWW, but it reveals much more: the fear on the part of the federal government that a multiethnic, revolutionary industrial union movement was gathering strength on the East Coast.[24]

Another grave consequence of the federal government's crusade against radicalism was that it sought to eradicate a critical antiracist politics that was emerging within Italian immigrant anarchist circles. As Salvatore Salerno and others have demonstrated, the Justice Department had a particular virulence for those radicals who publicly challenged the practices of American racism and imperialism.[25] FBI director J. Edgar Hoover singled out the same two Paterson-based anarchist newspapers that most often published women's writing, as the worst offenders. They hired translators to go through *La Questione Sociale* and *L'Era Nuova*, and fixated on essays with titles such as "The Crimes of the White Race" and "Race Hatred." They were particularly concerned with a series of articles that ran in 1919 that called attention to the irony that African Americans were serving in the war for a country that would not guarantee them basic human rights. Even patriotism, the essays argued, did not protect them. They documented how lynching and other forms of terrorism against African Americans increased dramatically during and after the war. Indeed, 1919 witnessed some of the most violent white rioting against African Americans in the early twentieth century.[26] "They call this a free country!?" the Italian anarchist press bellowed, as they detailed how American citizens who actively defended the nation were not safe from racist violence, and how activists who sought to uphold the principles of democracy and freedom were deemed "un-American" and subject to arrest, harassment, and murder.[27] In this way, Italian anarchists argued that citizenship and nationalism offered little protection to those who did not have economic or political power in the United States. The government agents who infiltrated the movement fixated on this critique in their reports, citing folks like Nicola Pirozzi, an anarchist active in the Paterson scene, as saying aloud to a group of friends, "Citizen papers are only good to wipe my ass on."[28]

Some Italian immigrants and their children responded to the mass arrests, deportation, and surveillance in their communities by returning to Italy. But the vast majority of those who stayed sought greater inclusion, which meant rejecting diasporic identities as "workers of the world" and embracing nationalism. The Red Scare had "dealt the first debilitating blow to Italian radicalism," as Rudolph Vecoli has written; "Smashing their presses, shuttering their offices and meeting places, and arresting thousands, federal and state agencies instituted a reign of terror against the *sovversivi* [subversives]."[29] Demographic changes were also significant. With Italian immigration to the United States drastically limited by the restrictive legislation of the 1920s, the economic strategies of many Italian families shifted from seasonal labor migrations and temporary settlement to the expansion of permanent communities and support systems. As a result, the migration of women increased right after the war. Their arrival often marked the moment when Italian immigrant families could move out of the "slum" to areas of second settlement, not only because women desired better housing quality and safer neighborhoods but because women's additional wages (and sometimes also children's) made such moves possible.[30] Moving to the more residential, less transient, but still urban and heavily working-class neighborhoods in Brooklyn, Queens, Staten Island, and The Bronx, also offered women the opportunity to develop more lasting ties to their neighbors and a greater sense of investment in their homes and surroundings. Such a shift impacted social movements, as regional loyalties and diasporic identities began to give way to American nationalism, but also to Italian nationalism, as "ethnic identity, class-consciousness, and workers' demand for respect as 'citizens' fused."[31] Paul Miceli echoed the sentiments of many children of immigrants: "As we grew older and became more attached to America, we resented more and more the stigma of being called 'foreigners.' We prided ourselves as being Americans, and tried to obscure by devious subterfuge the circumstances of our foreign birth."[32]

The most dramatic way Italians could assert an American identity was to distance themselves from any practices that justified and perpetuated their political and economic marginality. The Italian-language locals of the garment unions offered a relatively safe space to unite around a common sense of ethnic nationalism and class struggle, especially because the unions responded to the Red Scare by moving toward a more reformist socialist or social democratic stance. Radical groups had typically coalesced among those from the same region or town of origin in Italy, even as they participated in a political culture that continually transcended such attachments. But the ethnic nationalism of the interwar period was a significant departure from the *campanalismo* or regionalism of the radical subculture because it was less dependent on interethnic and transnational methods of organizing. The rise of ethnic nationalism was not necessarily a tale of assimilation, however. Rather, as Vecoli has argued, "the 'deradicalization' of Italian American workers was as much due to transnational influences as it was to domestic developments. The Bolshevik and Fascist revolutions had profound impacts upon the Italian labor movement in America."[33] In addition, in the aftermath of the Red Scare, unionism was at a low tide on the national level. The number of women in garment unions plummeted by almost 40 percent between 1920 and 1927.[34] The strategy of sustaining ethnic autonomy within a reformist union was thus prompted by a variety of cultural, economic, and political exigencies.

But Italian immigrant women's transition from revolutionary industrial unionism to the reform socialism of the garment unions was neither straightforward nor immediate. They struggled over shifting strategies, and, as many scholars have noted, the transition was as much characterized by the "ideological and organizational cleavages that had marked the development of the leftist movement in their home country," as it was by the divided and fractured labor movement in the United States.[35] The Italian-language radical press is one place where we can see these struggles unfold, as those in the movement wondered, "Is it compatible for an industrial socialist to also become a propagandist for the AFL?"[36] Women were at the very center of these struggles, because they composed the majority of workers in the AFL-affiliated garment unions, and they made themselves highly conspicuous in these debates. When, for example, Pasquale Di Neri, an organizer for the ILGWU, attempted to speak before a group of Italian women garment workers before the 1913 strike, he was met with the "loud cynical laughter" of an older Italian woman, who yelled out, "Ha! Ha! you want more 15 cents to pay you fakers!" She then proceeded to "make [him] look ridiculous in the presence of the other finishers." Several weeks later, the same woman led an independent strike in her shop when employers demanded an impossible work pace.[37] In fact, Italian immigrant women and their daughters did not turn to the reformist unions en masse until repression against the Left eliminated the more radical alternatives.

Even then, many combined union activism with strategies, ideologies, and practices that drew on more radical traditions.

The Bambace Family

The lives of sisters Angela and Maria Bambace are revealing of the ways in which activist women experienced the transitions of the interwar years. Born in Brazil to migrant workers from Sicily and Calabria, they grew up largely in Italian East Harlem, in a tenement on East 103rd Street. As teenagers in the 1910s, they worked alongside their mother Giuseppina in a local shirtwaist factory where they became politicized by women's everyday struggles in the shops. As young women, they were committed to challenging the power of the bosses and drawn to the anarchist and socialist groups in their neighborhood. Here they met a community of people in the IWW, studied anarcho-syndicalist theories and tactics, and became labor organizers themselves.[38] While they remained very close over the course of their lives, they approached organizing differently, especially when it came to strikebreakers. Maria believed in talking to them with compassion, while Angela's strategy more often included socking them in the nose.[39] But both believed that the effort to organize workers required not only a deep commitment to such difficult work but also an ability to envision a world where profit did not take precedence over human well-being.

In 1919 not only were both women active on the picket line; they also married. Maria wed Antonino Capraro, a Sicilian immigrant anarcho-syndicalist labor organizer she met at an East Harlem anarchist *circolo*. Angela married Romolo Camponeschi, a waiter from Rome who was not politically active but someone Angela's father had chosen. Together, the two couples moved to Flushing, Queens, into a two-family home, started families, and withdrew momentarily from labor organizing. They had young children, and the Red Scare forced most activists into retreat. Nevertheless, their children all spoke Italian as their first language and grew up surrounded by labor organizers and other radical activists. But the culture of fear and repression against the Left had a huge impact on their lives. In 1919, when Maria was pregnant with her first child, her husband Antonino was kidnapped and beaten by a gang of masked men while organizing textile workers in a Lawrence, Massachusetts, strike. He survived the attack and spoke out against the Ku Klux Klan, which was quickly becoming a popular movement with mass-based support, and a significant form of organized anti-labor and white supremacist intimidation and violence.[40]

Despite this culture of intimidation, fear, and repression, prewar styles of activism persisted through the Red Scare. The Bambace house was like those of

Antonino Capraro on 6 May 1919, after being kidnapped by the Ku Klux Klan from the Needham Hotel in Lawrence, Mass., the night before, for helping to organize the 1919 textile workers' strike. Capraro Papers, Immigration History Research Center, University of Minnesota.

Maria Roda, Ninfa Baronio, Maria Botto, Ernestina Cravello, Maria Barbieri, Elvira Catello, and many other women in the movement: it was a center of radical political activity. Angela's son remembered that it was "usually filled during the weekends with all sorts of interesting people, many of them radical, some of them slightly zany."[41] On Sundays, Angela would cook and everyone would feast on her tomato sauce with meatballs and sausages, breaded chicken and veal cutlets, and pasta piselli. After dinner, there would be more wine, bourbon, coffee, and long, passionate conversations in the smoke-filled dining room.[42] The Bambace household was multigenerational, and in this way was typical of the 1920s: American-raised parents brought up American-born children in households that included diasporic grandparents. They struggled daily with the clash of different cultural values and tried to make sense of them. From the start, Angela resisted her traditional marriage and complained of a life limited to "tomato sauce and home made gnocchi."[43] Soon after giving birth to her two sons, a series of struggles in the fledgling labor movement and an inability to be fully happy at home led Angela to return to activism as an organizer in the garment industry. Her son recalled, "Along with its willingness to admit and exploit immigrants, [the United States] paradoxically also provided [immigrants] with a host of new opportunities and a hornet's nest of freedoms, for women as well as men, and especially for those with the temperament to respond."[44] The choice to respond cost Angela her marriage and the custody of her children. She fought vigorously not to lose her parental rights, but when she lost, she moved into a house only a few doors away from her sons. Those years, her son would later write, were "the saddest and most lonely" of her life.[45] She found solace in activism and in the friendships with likeminded people she met in the radical labor movement. In the late 1920s she fell in love with Luigi Quintiliano, an immigrant tailor and anarchist from Abruzzo who became her companion for the rest of her life.[46]

With Quintiliano, Angela found a kindred spirit. He was a leader in two of the major social movements of the 1920s—antifascism and the defense of political prisoners. As one of Carlo Tresca's most trusted associates, Quintiliano helped to edit the New York–based anarchist antifascist newspaper *Il Martello* through the 1930s and wrote articles under the pseudonym Lucifero. He also served as secretary to the Comitato Italiano Pro Vittime Politiche (Italian Committee for Political Victims), which defended the growing numbers of anarchists and other radicals targeted by the Palmer raids. And he was at the forefront of the Alleanza Anti-Fascista di Nord America (Anti-Fascist Alliance of North America), also known as AFANA. This alliance emerged in 1923 to unite antifascists, to come to the "relief of radical and labor institutions in Italy which have been destroyed or harmed by the *Fascisti*."[47] AFANA also became the site of an intense political struggle among Italians in the garment unions between the remaining radicals, many of whom now identified as communist, and a new breed of labor leaders who distanced themselves from radicalism and identified as social democrats.[48]

To those in the movement, the world was changing dramatically, as Italian American workers and labor leaders increasingly sought to accommodate to capitalism rather than inspire revolution.

Industrial Unionism at Low Tide

The federal government's campaign against dissent meant that employers emerged from the First World War in a powerful position, which they quickly consolidated. Following the lead of Henry Ford, industrialists drew upon their immense economic and political resources to assert their power over labor. They regimented the production process through "scientific management," developed corporate welfare programs that undercut unions, and attempted to control all areas of workers' lives through the establishment of company towns. With the IWW effectively removed from the East Coast, those committed to revolutionary industrial unionism sought new forms of activism. Some joined the Amalgamated Clothing Workers of America (ACWA), a union of workers who broke away from the United Garment Workers of America (UGW) in 1914 to mobilize unskilled and skilled workers alike in the men's clothing trade. Founded in Chicago, the ACWA attempted to recruit Italians who had been active in the IWW. But many anarchists and syndicalists remained deeply skeptical of the union, and the Jewish leadership grew frustrated with Italian workers' continued reliance on their own self-activity in the form of work stoppages and sabotage, rather than the procedures of collective bargaining instituted by the union. Throughout the 1920s, Italian workers continued to rely on these so-called primitive strategies, brought from Italy and honed in the radical subculture and IWW. But most of the unions that survived the Red Scare did so by accommodating to the new power of employers. They adopted practices of red-baiting, repressed dissent in the rank and file, and challenged grass-roots movements for democratization among members. Both of the unions that recruited large numbers of Italian American women—the ILGWU and the ACWA—barely survived the 1920s; membership in the garment unions alone fell from 172,700 in 1920 to 101,400 in 1927.[49] Nevertheless, these unions remained central to the American labor movement, as 40 percent of all unionized women in this period were members of three garment unions—the ILGWU, ACWA, and the UGW.[50]

As employers devised new ways to force higher productivity from their workers through assembly lines, bureaucratization, and divisions of labor, most Italian American women workers found themselves in a movement that was too weak to effectively combat industrialists' attempt to discipline and control them. Drawing on strategies of the prewar era, women continued to strike autonomously from unions, and radicals were still at the forefront of these actions. As historian David Montgomery has noted, "Paradoxically, the importance of revolutionary organizations in strike activity rose as the general level of strike participation subsided after 1922."[51] Even though formal membership in unions was quite low, 1926 was an explosive year. Tens of thousands of workers in the textile factories of Paterson, Passaic, Garfield, Clifton, and Lodi in New Jersey and in New York City's garment trades walked off their jobs in strikes that were orchestrated largely by communists and Wobblies. Italian immigrant women and their American-born daughters made themselves conspicuous at union meetings and on picket lines.[52] Because they occurred in a period of economic downturn, union weakness, and employer strength, the strikes were especially difficult ones. Both workers and employers hired thugs and gangsters to protect their interests, and picket lines grew increasingly violent. The strikes also brought to the surface factional disputes and political tensions that were brewing within the movement.[53]

Betty Marandi, Laura Douglass, and Emma Polcari lead three thousand strikers through the National Silk Dye Company grounds in East Paterson during the 1926 Strike. American Labor Museum, Botto House National Landmark.

Faced with difficult conditions, the leadership of the garment unions sought some measure of stability and as a result emphasized reforming rather than overthrowing capitalism. Many of the women in the union, especially those inspired by revolutionary socialism, anarchism, syndicalism, and communism, found this direction deeply troubling because "stability" often translated into quelling opposition and limiting participation from the rank and file, especially women. In the ILGWU, factional disputes erupted into a full-scale "civil war" in 1920, when the general executive board expelled communists and unaffiliated women activists struggling for more democratic representation. The conflict began in 1919, when female insurgents in Local 25 organized "workers councils" within many locals across New York City, inspired by events in revolutionary Russia and with the intention of challenging the bureaucratization of the union. Denouncing the male leadership as conservative, they also attempted to form shop delegates' leagues to elect a council of delegates to replace the union's general executive board. The movement gained a mass base of support from a wide range of radicals in the union, and it was this moment that pulled Angela Bambace back into activism. The board struck back by declaring the leagues unconstitutional and by dividing Local 25: the shirtwaist makers remained in the old local and the dressmakers were organized into Local 22.[54] In addition, the board passed a rule stating that anyone with less than two years membership in the union could not hold office.

The leadership's reaction to Local 25 was a direct attack on rank-and-file women as they attempted to gain a voice and power within the ILGWU. Referred to as the "girls' local," Local 25 grew dramatically following the 1909–19 strikes. By 1919 it included thirty thousand members, making it "the largest single local in the ILGWU, with nearly 25 percent of the International's total membership." Many joined during the 1918–19 strike wave, and "fired by the idealism the local had nurtured, young women began to agitate for a greater voice in union affairs." Their largest concern was lack of representation. Within the local, "the shop chairladies were virtually all female; local officers, all male." The union encouraged women's participation until they began to develop their own priorities and demand democratic participation.[55]

The 1918–19 strikes had led women to believe that the labor union was not a hierarchical and bureaucratic institution but a liberatory movement that would bring about a new world. The ILGWU leadership, however, sought to inculcate these new members in a reform-style unionism that included procedure, regulations, and a chain of command.[56] The female membership of Local 25 formally declared their intentions at the 1922 convention: they sought to establish a shop-delegate system, "aimed to weld together all workers of an industry into a strongly organized representative unit with many workers participating in the making of decisions rather than leaving it to officers, executive boards and a small group of active members who are responsible to no one but themselves." In response, the ILGWU leadership labeled the women radicals and communists, using the discourse of the Red Scare to exclude them. Historian Alice Kessler-Harris has argued that this labeling "was not so much an indication of their political position (although some were surely communists) as an acknowledgement of their potential power and a fear that oppositional politics of whatever kind would breed disloyalty in a fighting organization."[57]

The International's attack on the insurgents backfired. Support for Local 25 grew as members in other locals began to side with the insurgents and collectively turn to the newly emerging Communist Party for support and guidance. By the end of 1922, the union was polarized so severely that only two sides existed. In August 1923, Morris Sigman, president of the International, disbanded all insurgent groups within the locals. In response, the rank and file elected communists and others seeking more democratic representation to the executive boards of Locals 2, 9, and 22, which represented thousands of cloak makers and dressmakers across the city. On 11 June 1925, Sigman suspended the communist members of these executive boards, charging them with antiunion activity. In turn, the insurgents refused to recognize Sigman's instructions and formed the Joint Action Committee, which functioned independently of the International. By 1925 the union was in chaos, and a special convention was called in Philadelphia to confront the tensions.

Some Italian American workers such as Angela Bambace joined the insurgents, but the leadership of their locals sided with the Sigman administration. At the heart of the conflict were questions concerning the autonomy of locals and the distribution of power within the union. Of central concern to many was the selection of business agents: the insurgents insisted that all business agents be elected by the membership at large, whereas the Italian Dressmakers Local 89 demanded that business agents be elected or appointed only by the local they represented. The leaders of Local 89 took this stand out of the concern that Italian business agents represent Italian workers, and their concerns were understandable: while the percentage of Italian workers in the union was growing steadily, Jewish workers still outnumbered Italians in the industry. Having worked for more than a decade to establish their autonomy in the union, the Italian leadership at the convention was convinced that this position could be preserved only if their ethnic locals selected business agents, rather than the Joint Board.[58]

As a result, the Italian delegates at the convention became central players in the struggle for control over the direction of the union. They voted against the insurgents because they feared their program for democratization and reorganization might threaten Italian workers' autonomy.[59] Italian garment workers had gained the right to organize within their own locals under Sigman's administration, and they repaid this debt with their support. Because the Italian locals were just developing as political and social institutions in this period, their decision to align with the administration also meant that they could more fully consolidate their autonomy within the union. This alliance and preferential positioning would only grow stronger in the 1930s and 1940s.

Conference proceedings do not reveal whether Italian American women workers supported the decisions of the primarily male delegates of Local 89. Organizers, however, were divided in their allegiances. Grace De Luise, who joined Local 89 as a young woman, described her sentiments at the time: "If a shop was called out on strike, the union would ask us to go and help out where the organizers needed. But if the strike was called by the left-wingers we not only went out there, but we became operators in the shops and took the place of the strikers to make sure that the left-wingers lost their strike! The union was fighting the left-wingers more than the employers."[60] As union organizers internalized antiradical ideologies and divisions, it became harder to find common ground. Many women, including Grace De Luise, chose to oppose the insurgents and to ally with men in their own local. Presumably they believed that their interests were best served by defending the autonomy of Italian workers, even though their decision came at the expense of other women in the union. But the trade-off was decisive. By the late 1920s, the Italian Local 89 was heavily bureaucratized, with men in leadership positions over a primarily female rank and file. This "progressive" union (which, unlike other AFL unions, sought to organize women workers) had become even more deeply stratified along gender lines. Although union membership was 85 percent female, the leadership was firmly in the hands of male officers, who imposed "a standard of political, ethnic, and sexual homogeneity" and "created a power structure dominated by anti-communist Jewish and Italian males."[61] In part this reflected the division of labor by gender in the industry. Most of the skilled workers were male, and the overwhelming majority of the semiskilled machine operators or "unskilled" finishers were female. Skilled male workers became the leaders of both the most powerful locals (including those initially organized by women) and the International, whose top officials came from Local 10, the almost completely male cutters' union.[62] Shop stewards were largely women while officers of locals were almost all men. Men also predominated among the delegates at union conventions. As historian Altagracia Ortíz has argued, while the union leadership was mostly Jewish and Italian socialist men, committed to working-class political action, they "had an Achilles heel—sexism—that severely limited their vision of worker solidarity, leading them to take a condescending view of the bulk of the union's rank and file, which was female."[63] Moreover, the intense internal factionalism, which occurred "in the context of a defensive and harassed trade union movement," represented a decisive rejection of the cultural space women had created in the ILGWU the decade before.[64]

Some organizers, such as Angela Bambace, Albina Delfino, and Frances Ribaudo, opposed this direction and became active in Communist Party meetings and strikes, where they formed alliances with Jewish anarchists and communists in the union. For such actions they were denounced by the leadership of the Italian locals. For the rest of the 1920s, Bambace assisted the ACWA's organizational campaigns in Elizabeth, New Jersey, and then accepted a paid organizing position with the ILGWU in Baltimore to mobilize garment workers in Maryland, Delaware, and Virginia, where in the span of a decade she brought more than fifteen thousand workers (mostly women) into the union.[65] Albina Delfino joined the Communist Party dual-union, the Needle Trades' Workers' Industrial Union, and became part of an organizing team that included several African American and Jewish women. Inspired by this experience, and having gained notoriety for her effectiveness, she then became a paid organizer for the Communist Party. In this capacity, she traveled between Lawrence, Providence, Boston, Paterson, and

New York City, with Frances Ribaudo, an Italian American organizer in the party, to assist workers on the verge of striking or already on strike, and especially to combat racial antagonism within working-class communities.[66] All three were also deeply committed to fighting another development, which was rapidly transforming the world: the rise of fascism.

The Rise of Fascism

When Benito Mussolini seized control of the Italian state in 1922, a new transnational struggle emerged that played itself out in the streets of New York, New Jersey, and beyond. The mainstream U.S. and Italian American presses—including everything from the *New York Times* and *New York Post*, to the *Saturday Evening Post*—heralded Il Duce as a heroic savior, "an economic genius who had engineered a 'commercial revolution,'" and "a modern Caesar, the Napoleon of 1925."[67] Few U.S. political leaders questioned Mussolini's violent repression of the Left, his commitment to a corporate state, and his use of military nationalism, in part because his policies closely matched their own.[68] In fact, American fascination with Mussolini often centered on his "embodiment of the traditional American values of duty, obedience, patriotism, and anti-materialist soberness."[69] Even when stories of fascism's violence and antidemocratic politics made their way across the ocean, the *Saturday Evening Post* declared that "desperate diseases need desperate remedies. Italy was a surgical case that called for a major operation." To many in the United States, Mussolini was the "Doctor Dictator."[70]

Representations of the Italian leader as capable and powerful contrasted sharply with popular images of Italians as destitute and uncivilized. The U.S. media and political leadership generated images of Mussolini as the epitome of virile masculinity but also of white civilization.[71] Such images only grew more popular when Italy invaded Ethiopia in 1935, then the only independent African nation, with the claim that Italy's war constituted nothing more than a "civilizing mission." The idea that Ethiopians were barbaric and in need of civilization, and that Italians could best serve them and the rest of the world with conquest, resonated powerfully with white Americans' own ideas of race, nation, and power in this age of imperialism.[72]

Enthusiasm for Mussolini grew very quickly in Italian American communities. Fascist groups emerged in Little Italies everywhere across the United States, and New York City became a key center of Italian diasporic fascism. In an attempt to quantify Italian American sympathy for fascism, historian Gaetano Salvemini estimated that half were indifferent to all forms of political ideology, 10 percent were actively antifascist, 35 percent were susceptible to fascist propaganda, but only 5 percent were actively profascist.[73] The *prominenti*—middle- and upper-class professionals and self-appointed "leaders"—led the vast majority of fascist groups. They shared Mussolini's desire to unite around a national Italian identity, in part because they saw it as a way to quell working-class resistance and advance their own class position.

In New York City, one of the most influential supporters of fascism was Generoso Pope, the wealthy publisher of the largest Italian-language newspaper in the country, *Il Progresso Italo-Americano*. During the 1920s, Pope purchased his competitors' papers to own close to 70 percent of the Italian-language newspapers in the New York metropolitan area. Working closely with the Italian state via consular officials, Pope strengthened ties to other profascist community institutions—including the Catholic Church, Casa Italiana of Columbia University, the Italian Chamber of Commerce, and the largest fraternal orders such as the Order of the Sons of Italy (OSIA)—through hundreds of banquets and social activities designed to develop fascist support among Italian Americans.[74] In 1925 the Italian Fascist government established the Fascist League of North America (FLNA), incorporated in New York, to cultivate the nationalist solidarities of Italian Americans (to both Italy and the United States) and to bring Italian American *prominenti* under one organization. In the attempt to draw in supporters, the FLNA, under direct guidance from fascist authorities in Italy, linked love of homeland with support for Mussolini. The fascist regime clearly stated that objective: "To arouse, conserve, and exalt *Italianità* among the millions of fellow Italians dispersed throughout the world."[75] Yet, as the profascist president of OSIA reminded the public, fascism's goal was not just to strengthen the Italian state; "its aims are inspired by a deep patriotism towards the United States." He echoed the sentiments of a wide array of U.S. officials when he declared in the 1930s that fascism was "an American movement," designed to counteract "the Reds" by teaching Italian immigrants and their children to become American citizens and "take their place of duty and stand by the flag."[76] Even as a wide array of forces—from immigrant restriction, and the coming of age of the American-born population, to wartime nationalism and the Red Scare—were encouraging Italian Americans to focus more intensely on struggles in the United States, the rise of fascism ensured that Italy continued to inform their political culture.

Italian Americans formed hundreds of fascist groups across the New York metropolitan area and throughout New Jersey, in Camden, Garfield, Hackensack, Hoboken, Jersey City, Montclair, Nutley, Orange, Trenton, West Hoboken, and West New York. Italian consular agents, local OSIA lodges, veterans' clubs, parochial schools, newspapers such as the *New Jersey Italian-American* in Newark, cultural organizations such as the Dante Alighieri Society and the Partito Fascista Nazionale (National Fascist Party) of New Jersey, and sympathetic pastors in Jersey City, Lodi, Newark, and Trenton all disseminated fascist propaganda. On 16 August 1936, one of the largest fascist demonstrations in the country was held at the Maestre Pie Filippini religious order in Morristown, with close to ten thousand people in attendance.[77]

Italians also paraded through their neighborhoods in military formation wearing black shirts and clashed violently with antifascists. Such struggles were so common in this period that they became a key part of the political culture. One antifascist rally in Harlem on 21 August 1926 "was interrupted by fascists who threw bottles and bricks at the speakers." At another gathering on 4 July 1925, fascists and antifascists clashed when close to 350 fascist sympathizers marched past a crowd of some 1,000 antifascists who had gathered to hear speeches at the Garibaldi memorial on Staten Island: "As they passed, a woman in a red dress shouted at them and the Blackshirt band began playing 'Giovanezza,'" the Fascist Hymn.[78]

Race was central to these conflicts. In some ways, the Italian-Ethiopian War seemed to unfold in New York City's streets, in those spaces where Italian and African American communities overlapped.[79] Profascist Italians embodied the role of colonizer in multiple ways, including hanging Emperor Haile Selassie in effigy during parades. In doing so, they took on an identity that resonated as white in the United States, especially in a period when the Klan was one of the largest mass-based social movements in the country. Children reenacted the war in playgrounds, on their front stoops, and in schools, to such a degree that Leonard Covello noted the "appreciable effect" the war had upon "the attitudes of Negroes and Italians toward one another."[80] James Baldwin too recalled fighting "every campaign of the Italian-Ethiopian War with the oldest son of the Italian fruit and vegetable vendor who lived next door to us. I lost. Inevitably. He knew who had the tanks."[81] African American opposition to Mussolini's invasion of Ethiopia also took the form of widespread protest against Italian merchants in Harlem especially. Whether they wrote "Italians—Don't buy here," in chalk in front of Italian businesses or stormed markets, African Americans held Italians accountable for the ways they "made thousands upon thousands off our race."[82] In Harlem, Italian anarchists from the Italian Workers' Club joined with local African American groups to organize rallies and other demonstrations against the war in Ethiopia. The Communist Party was also pivotal in uniting Harlem residents for interracial rallies in defense of Ethiopia. One parade, held in 1935, began in two separate contingents—one led by Italian Americans and the other by African Americans. They merged into a unified line at 129th Street and Seventh Avenue and concluded the march with a mass outdoor rally that included more than twenty-five thousand participants.[83] Though the Red Scare and the rise in coercive nationalisms had dealt a crushing blow to the Italian immigrant radical subculture, it was central to the antifascist movement. But first, how did the fascist movement appeal to women?

Women in the Fascist Movement

A rich literature exists on how fascists defined women's roles narrowly, as solely in the service of men, as mothers and wives.[84] Only recently has research emerged on the effect of fascism on Italian women abroad.[85] As Mussolini's propaganda machine stretched across the Atlantic, his regime encouraged women to embrace a new sense of national identity as "mothers of the race."[86] As historian Victoria de Grazia has noted, Mussolini "tried to keep women from viewing work as a stepping stone to liberation. If they held jobs, it had to be out of family necessity or because no men would take them."[87] This was in part because some of the most significant labor actions in Italy during the 1930s were either led by women or dominated by them.[88] In the attempt to recruit working-class women and discourage their resistance, Mussolini established the Section for Factory and Home Workers (SOLD) in 1938. Even so, the vast majority of fascism's female supporters, like men, came from the middle and upper classes—those who could more easily devote themselves to the private life that the fascist order heralded for women.[89]

In the United States, women who became active in fascist groups were also largely from middle-class or upwardly mobile families. But focusing on women who joined fascist groups does not capture the many more women who supported Mussolini without engaging in formal political activity. Mass-based spectacles of Italian American female devotion to fascism, such as the dramatic episode during the height of the Italian-Ethiopian war, when thousands of women in New York City publicly donated their wedding rings to Mussolini's coffers and restated their wedding vows, suggests that fascism's appeal crossed class lines.[90]

For the past several decades, historians have attempted to understand Italian American enthusiasm for Mussolini, citing the financial support that the Italian state provided immigrant institutions in exchange for Italians' loyalty and the sense of pride that Italian immigrants and their American-born children derived from mainstream American adoration of Mussolini and his "New Italy." To a population "deeply scarred by restriction, racialism, and criminalization," many Italian immigrants and their children drew upon this image of the imperialist, nationalist, and masculine leader who "seemed to bring long-overdue prestige and praise to their motherland."[91] Paul Pisicano echoed the sentiments of many when he recalled that to him, "Mussolini was a hero, a superhero. He made us feel special, especially the southerners, Sicilian, Calabrian. I remember the Abyssinian War, about 1935. I was five. It was talked about as a very positive thing. We had the equivalent of your pep rallies for football teams. To us it was a great victory. We never really got down on Mussolini. He was applauded. Then he went to Greece. He wasn't doing too well (laughs) and had to be bailed out by the Germans, remember? We were awfully disappointed by that. It was us against the outside. One block against another block." Playing out the conflict and reenacting the war in the streets was also a way for Italian American men to assert their masculinity. After all, Pisicano recalled, "We were brought up on this great macho crap. Our heroes were Joe DiMaggio and Phil Rizzuto. When the Yankees won the pennant in '41, they were our biggies." War, nationalism, and competitive aggression were celebrated as the way for Italian men to redeem themselves: "We were heavy on the Italian feeling in America. We were more Italian than Italians. We always had a transient sense of our stay here. My uncle never became a citizen until he was in the army. Staying in America was something that you did to make money. You didn't stay in America to lead a good life. Nobody ever confused America with leading the good life. That happened after the war."[92]

Similarly, Agostino De Biasi (an immigrant journalist from Avellino) and most other prominent fascist leaders in the United States embraced the nationalist fervor of fascism out of their own sense of indignation: "Those youths who yesterday were called *dagoes*," De Biasi declared in his New York–based periodical *Il Carroccio* in 1924, "today must be called *Italians*."[93] They hoped, as historian Thomas A. Guglielmo has written, that "the more barbaric Ethiopians appeared the more civilized and desirable their own people would become in the eyes of Americans."[94]

The vast majority of women who became active on behalf of the fascist regime joined the movement in their neighborhoods through events sponsored by pro-fascist groups. The Order of the Sons of Italy, the largest Italian American mutual aid society in the United States, was a primary site of women's fascist activity. As early as 1922, the president of the order, Giovanni Di Silvestro, formally aligned the organization with Mussolini's regime, and local "lodges" began to circulate fascist propaganda. At the time, hundreds of lodges were active in Italian neighborhoods across New York and New Jersey. Beginning in the 1910s, women had begun to play a more active role in the administration of these patriotic mutual aid societies, and by 1916 they formed their own women's lodges in most communities.[95] Among the largest were the Loggia Femminile "La Perla di Savoia," founded in 1926 at Haarlem House (the main settlement house in East Harlem), and the Loggia "Duchessa Elena D'Aosta," both of which were headed by women married to *prominenti*.[96] During the 1930s, the women's lodges played an especially important role in encouraging young women to join the order. On 12 April 1932, the OSIA newspaper *Corriere* reported on the initiation of fifteen hundred individuals in ten new youth lodges, six of which were female, in Manhattan, The Bronx, Queens, and Brooklyn.[97] Most of the women's lodges were named after Italian royalty, and one of the young men's lodges took the name Cesare Lombroso, in honor of the leading proponent of racial determinism in Italy.

In highly ritualized ceremonies of inauguration, the order celebrated the institutionalization of a new generation of "proud" Italian Americans, they stated, "not '*cafoni*.'" The word *cafoni* (pronounced "gavones" by most Italian Americans) meant to be low-class, and in this way the order expressed its upper-class aspirations. As the Supreme Venerable and attorney Stefano Miele announced at the gathering, OSIA was composed of "the future senators and judges, leaders of the nation that has given civilization to the world." This quite clearly meant the men in the lodge. To the women, the OSIA leadership commended their commitment to teach the "principles of americanism" to the next generations. In particular, the role of the women's lodges was to educate the younger American-born generation in high Italian culture, civics, and history.[98] To support this effort, and especially to instruct the younger generation on the virtues of fascist Italy, Mussolini's regime sent funds to OSIA in 1931 and 1932 so that a group of young women and men could make a pilgrimage to the homeland. The group met with Mussolini himself, and while the men were introduced to key state officials, the women met with Itala Loiacono, the wife of a leading fascist official, who organized women's groups.[99] Her job was to help the young women embrace the values of motherhood, to see themselves as reproducers of the white race and Italian nation. Fascism provided women with a role in the modern nation-state but within a masculinist framework.[100]

The activities of the Unity, Nobility, and Ambition Society (UNA) in Brooklyn, offer a view into how the regime affected those Italian American women who joined fascist youth clubs in their neighborhoods. In 1929 a group of young women and men, mostly unmarried and American-born, formed this society "to spread Italian culture among Italian-Americans."[101] It grew from a handful of people in June to about seventy-five in "a few years" and appears to have been composed mostly of women. The group held monthly socials with "well-known Italian speakers," recitations of poetry, and theatrical performances in the meeting hall at St. Rocco's Church.[102] The support of their meetings by the local Catholic Church suggests its important role in normalizing fascism for parishioners, especially after the Lateran Accords between the Vatican and the Italian state in 1929 encouraged fascist supporters to focus their efforts on the system of Catholic churches and schools.

The UNA's weekly newsletter suggests these kinds of connections. Often, they celebrated Mussolini as the "Savior of Society" who "preached the gospel of work, discipline and sacrifice."[103] Writers for the newsletter also reflected the language of the Red Scare, noting that Italy "stood in greatest peril of revolution during the difficult post-war years—to combat this Bolshevism, fascism was born." Writing primarily in English, they focused in particular on Mussolini's imperial project in Ethiopia: "a land of barbarism and slavery which needs a guiding hand will find that the Italians will give her the proper guidance and not exploit them for personal gains."[104]

Mirroring a gendered understanding of empire, the newsletter also regularly announced the many romances that were developing within the group.[105] As with OSIA, this group provided a way for young women and men to come together, socialize, and devote themselves to "the race and nation." Its stated objectives were "to bring together men and women who represent the highest aims and standards of Italian-American life, and who will serve in some substantial way to improve the propriety and stateliness of manner, speech and culture of others." Its name—Unity, Nobility, and Ambition—represented "the three aims of every UNA member."[106] The group was intended as an "intellectual society" with programs in "high culture," which included the staging of Shakespearian plays and trips to the opera. The mostly female members were also especially preoccupied with "when to marry," how to "avoid foods that will increase her waistline," and voluntary activities, such as teaching citizenship and English to adults.[107]

The UNA was not formally affiliated with the fascist regime, but it reflected the kinds of cultural groups that developed in this same period among bourgeois women in Italy, which sought to combine intellectual endeavors with social work in patriotic service. While women's activism seemed to counter fascism's deeply held antifeminist beliefs, the fascist state reconciled this by maintaining women's role as partners in patriarchy and by perpetuating their exclusion and marginalization from the sources of power. Many Italian American women accepted this bargain believing it might bring them a greater sense of dignity and stature in their communities. Yet it meant always having to negotiate tyrannical rule. Even if the nationalist project was inherently contradictory in the demands it placed upon women, it conditioned their thinking and encouraged them to articulate demands for civic participation as mothers.[108]

Antifascist Resistance

As Italian Americans became increasingly sympathetic to Mussolini, those who were active anarchists, syndicalists, communists, and revolutionary socialists

Antifascist rally on Fifth Avenue, New York City, ca. 1930. Banners include the Industrial Workers of the World (IWW), the Italian Antifascist Front, and several antifascist and radical newspapers. Fort Velona Papers, Immigration History Research Center, University of Minnesota.

came together to lead oppositional movements in their homes, neighborhoods, workplaces, and unions. Most women entered the antifascist movement through labor unions or family networks that connected them to the radical subculture. The Red Scare had crippled the organizational bases of Italian immigrant working-class radicalism, but radicals reconsolidated in the movement to fight fascism. Evidence of women's participation in the antifascist movement exists in photographs of rallies, often sponsored by the garment unions.[109] It is also revealed in the Italian-language press. During the summer of 1923, for example, several Italian women snuck into a local fascist celebration and took to the floor during speeches, shouting in Italian "Long Live Italy! Down with Mussolini!" They also lunged at several of the speakers, causing fights to break out and the meeting to end.[110]

Oral histories are also rich with evidence of women's antifascist activities. Margaret Di Maggio, who ran the organizational department of the Italian Dressmakers' Local of the ILGWU in the 1920s and 1930s, was also well known in her

Sicilian family for challenging those who "felt drawn by Mussolini's promise of grandeur to the Italian people." Di Maggio's niece recalled, "She and my grandfather were always arguing. . . . She wanted to buy him a round trip ticket to go back to Italy and see how things were." When the arguments "got worse," Margaret bought him a one-way ticket and "within two months he wrote back here begging her to send him the return ticket."[111] Ginevra Spagnoletti joined an antifascist group in her Greenwich Village neighborhood through her job as a buttonhole maker. There she met organizers for the ACWA, and developed an interest in broadening her social conscience. She joined the union and became fast friends with Pietro Di Maddi, a socialist exile from fascist Italy. A regular contributor to two left-wing antifascist newspapers, *Il Nuovo Mondo* and *La Stampa Libera*, Di Maddi was a well-known figure in the antifascist movement. Ginevra's son remembered that Ginevra and Pietro were drawn to each other "by each other's intelligence and political leanings," and they "struck up a friendship that developed into a close relationship." Ginevra often hosted meetings in her home and became more active in the day-to-day affairs of the antifascist movement. While her son remembered such meetings as a critical part of his own politicization, her "outspokenness" antagonized her husband Joe, who "had no interest in politics and felt threatened by his wife's disposition to voice her opinions." During one heated argument Joe slapped Ginevra, telling her to "keep quiet like a woman should." Ginevra gathered her six children and left him for good that night.[112]

Many women organizing in the garment trades at the time, including Lucia Romualdi, Lillie Raitano, and Josephine Mirenda, became active in antifascist circles and in the movement that coalesced to fight for the release of Sacco and Vanzetti and other political prisoners.[113] The union remained one of many sites of activism, but it was a key place where many women were introduced to these movements. In 1923 Italians active in the ACWA and ILGWU joined together to form the Antifascist Alliance of North America (AFANA) "to rouse public opinion to the terror in Italy as well as to warn against the 'spread of the movement to America.'"[114] Angela Bambace and Luigi Quintiliano were among them. Their collective objective was to bring together communists, socialists, syndicalists, and anarchists into one organization. Only three years later, however, the same kinds of tensions and factions that had caused the civil war in the ILGWU divided AFANA, which basically split into anarcho-syndicalists and communists, who gained control of AFANA, and reformist socialists (leaders of the ACWA and ILGWU), who abandoned the group and set up another rival organization.[115]

It is hard to locate women's voices in the organizational battles of AFANA, but they are present in the radical print culture. Despite the concerted effort of the federal government to shut down the Italian-language radical press, papers continued to reappear under different titles and from new locations. The effects of the Red Scare became more visible in the unwillingness of authors to publicize meeting places, times, or dates, and in the prolific use of pseudonyms. But during the 1920s and 1930s, activists continued to use the radical press to voice their opinions, organize rallies, and fiercely contest the messages of the mainstream, broad-circulation newspapers owned by Generoso Pope and other wealthy fascists. They publicized and circulated stories from Italy about the devastating effects of fascism and connected repression against the Left in Italy with similar antidemocratic practices in the United States.[116] As an anarchist from West Hoboken surmised, "the Klan seeks Americanization, Fascism seeks Italianization."[117] While outnumbered and financially weaker than the fascist papers, antifascists created a visible, vocal culture that enabled them to remain committed to revolutionary politics in a period of widespread repression.

The anarchist newspaper *L'Adunata dei Refrattari* (The Gathering of the Disobedient) was one of the most important and popular centers of transnational antifascist resistance in this period.[118] Published in New York City beginning in 1922, *L'Adunata* included women's letters, essays, and news. It lasted until 1971 to become the longest-running Italian American anarchist newspaper.[119] For more than thirty of those years, from 1922 to 1954, the paper was edited by Osvaldo Maraviglia. Born in Caldarola, a small village in Le Marche, Maraviglia appears to have migrated to Newark with his brother in 1912, when he was eighteen years old, to work as a tailor. He became active in the anarchist movement where he met his lifelong companion Maria Caruso, who was born in Newark to immigrants from Avellino. Together they had six children while Maraviglia ran the newspaper. Both were considered to be dangerous and militant anarchists by the Italian state, and Mussolini's agents kept a close watch on them during the 1920s and 1930s.[120] They were also good friends with renowned anarchist Errico Malatesta and his companion Elena Melli, who were then living in Rome under house arrest with their daughter Gemma. After Malatesta died in 1932 from pneumonia, Elena stayed in close contact with Osvaldo and Maria, who often sent her whatever funds they could raise.[121]

Women's essays in *L'Adunata* often called on women in the movement to oppose fascism as they would any systemic and pervasive form of domination. A letter from one woman in Philadelphia typified much of the writing, with her dramatic call for women to refuse acquiescence to patriarchy: "Uplift yourselves, throw oppression and iniquity into the face of this vile society which imposes them on you. . . . Become women . . . free, not prostitutes, the comrades of men in life and in the struggle."[122] A distinctly anarchist feminist perspective also infused many essays that continued to critique male comrades who refused to see how women were fundamental to the revolutionary movement: "Men should know," wrote another woman, "that humanity cannot elevate itself if women are not elevated and that the emancipation of the proletariat cannot move forward without the emancipation of women."[123] By the 1930s, the anarchists were much smaller in number than they had been before World War I, and greatly outnumbered by communists and socialists, but their circles continued to provide a place for women to develop a critique of power relations.

Radical movements were also reinvigorated by the activism of *fuorusciti*, refugees from the fascist regime. Throughout the 1930s, Italian workers filled meeting halls to capacity to hear Virgilia D'Andrea, an anarchist labor organizer and schoolteacher from Sulmona in Abruzzo. She fled Fascist police in 1928 and settled in Brooklyn with her lover, the noted anarcho-syndicalist writer and activist Armando Borghi.[124] By all accounts, D'Andrea was a woman who had been "raised in pain."[125] Her mother died when she was a child, and as a teenager she and her brother witnessed the murder of their father at the hands of his second wife's lover. After years of work as an elementary school teacher, Virgilia became an organizer for the Italian Socialist Party and was soon assigned the task of establishing a women's section. In one of the first scholarly explorations of D'Andrea's life, Robert Ventresca and Franca Iacovetta note, "Her rebellion may have been nurtured by close contact with impoverished students; she herself endured relative poverty as a self-supporting teacher in one of Italy's poorest regions. She also witnessed the region's great earthquake of 1915, which devastated the capital town of Avezzano where D'Andrea taught and which killed thousands of people—mainly women at home—in the surrounding towns and villages. The state's inadequate response and indifference sharpened D'Andrea's sense of injustice."[126]

While teaching and organizing, D'Andrea became deeply inspired by the anarchist movement, whose leaders would come to consider her "an indomitable fighter." Her skill as an orator and writer drew recognition during the 1910s, and by 1919 the prefect of Bologna expressed his concern to state authorities, describing her as a "morally shameful" woman with "the gift of the gab" and a "loud and violent . . . disposition." They also found her to be "modestly intelligent and cultured" and feared her ability to impress and agitate "the masses" with ease.[127] As with other anarchists, the Italian authorities' concern with D'Andrea's morality stemmed in part from her belief in *amore libero*, and her very public free love union with Borghi. In 1922 D'Andrea published her first book of poems, *Tormento*, and the Italian state immediately seized and banned all copies, charging her prose with the ability to disrupt public order and incite class hatred.

As with the many women active in New York's and New Jersey's anarchist circles, writing enabled D'Andrea to develop her own thinking on the meanings of revolution from below. In her words, anarchism meant "freedom and justice . . . the abolition of suffering, of hate, of superstition; the abolition of man's oppression of man, that is the abolition of government and private property."[128] After several years of labor organizing, Virgilia left Italy in 1922 to escape the continual surveillance and threats of the Fascist government. Together with Borghi, she traveled to Berlin, Paris, and Marseilles, where they stayed with other exiled radicals. In November 1928 she crossed the Atlantic and arrived in New York. An anarchist group in South Brooklyn had paid for Borghi's trip a year earlier and covered her expenses as well. Valerio Isca, a member of that Brooklyn group recalled, "A comrade from New Jersey went to Paris and married her so she could come as an American citizen" and gain entry to the United States.[129] The Italian Embassy in Rome immediately warned Washington of her arrival, noting that she was "a dangerous propagandist and organizer of radical activities," which "she disguises under the cover of antifascism."[130]

To Italian anarchists abroad, however, D'Andrea was a noted organizer and *compagna poetessa* (poet-comrade). They raised funds for a speaking tour and soon after she arrived, she set off across the country to speak before enthusiastic crowds in city after city, as far west as California. She spoke in Italian and urged her audiences to oppose nationalism and imperialism, "based as it is on colonial conquest and the subjugation of peoples of color." Rather, she argued, all should see themselves as a "citizen of the world, a child of father Sun and mother Earth." She told of the metalworkers who took over their factories in northern Italy and of her own imprisonment during the strike. She spoke out against the escalating campaign of violence and physical intimidation against workers in Italy and the United States, and protested the execution of Sacco and Vanzetti.[131] While she commanded great respect from most in the movement, her closest friends were other exiled intellectuals. Unlike most other Italian American radicals who had developed their activism within their neighborhoods and factories, her work tended not to focus on local conditions. Rather, she spoke to "international proletarian struggles, and her approach was historical, argumentative, and theoretical, though the purpose remained essentially educational."[132] Her speaking as well as her writing, while emotionally rich, did not contain personal references but rather conveyed her sense of identity as a political exile. This was also a state of mind shared by her closest friends, many of whom had endured house arrest, imprisonment, and exile during Mussolini's rise to power.

Often in her speeches, D'Andrea challenged her audiences to develop a sense of collective identity that rejected the oppressive nationalisms of the bourgeois nation-state. Rather, she spoke of love for homeland as love for the earth itself, the actual land where one is born and raised. She was always conscious that her audience was composed of many who were long separated from and longed for the land of their birth. Speaking before a large crowd at Cooper Union in 1929, D'Andrea dedicated herself to the crowd in this manner: "To all of you who roam the streets of the world, because you do not have safe refuge in your own country, a country you render great and noble with your work, that you render glorious and admirable with your struggle." Like many anarchists, she defined citizenship not as blind patriotic devotion to a government or as bounded by juridical concepts. Rather, she sought to reconcile the radical internationalism that emerged from labor migration and political exile, with the sense of belonging that was born from the shifting experience of home.[133]

During the eleven years that D'Andrea was in exile, she focused on fighting fascism and imperialism in order, she said, "to feel useful to someone." She did so while suffering chronic depression, periodic blackouts, and continual illness from cancer, which ultimately claimed her life in 1933. When she died, Italian workers in Italy, the United States, and beyond grieved the loss of this *profuga ribelle* (refugee rebel), and celebrated her powerful presence in the movement for social justice. A comrade in Somerville, Massachusetts, noted that "every time she spoke, she left behind seeded ground."[134]

D'Andrea was part of a wave of political exiles escaping fascist repression that rejuvenated New York's radical movement. Albina Delfino was another exiled anarchist (turned communist) who made her way to New York City in the early 1920s and immediately immersed herself in the city's radical political world. After contesting the Italian locals' direction in the ILGWU, and working as a Communist Party organizer in various cities for several years, she returned to Manhattan. There she held open-air meetings, often six days a week, with Frances Ribaudo, the daughter of Sicilian immigrants, who also worked as an organizer for the party. Both were also street orators who drew significant audiences at the corner of 116th Street and Lexington Avenue, the very center of street politics in Italian Harlem. During the Spanish Civil War (1936–39), both worked to bring Italian women into the movement for Republican Spain by canvassing their neighbors. Before long, Delfino recalled, "those women were organizing affairs, going from house to house collecting clothes for the children."[135]

Delfino was not a newcomer to activism. Like D'Andrea, she arrived from Italy with several years of experience in local anarchist circles. She too witnessed firsthand the impact of fascism, which resembled much of what was transpiring in the United States at that time, including "dragnets, closings, and confiscations that befell thousands of working-class reading circles, cooperatives, and trade union halls as the prefects, police, and local party officials cited them in violation of the dictatorship's public safety laws." Indeed, the repressive movement had a powerful affect on working-class women's activity across Italy. As Victoria de Grazia has noted, "It seems no coincidence that the years 1924, 1927, and 1928 registered the highest number of female suicides in modern Italy."[136]

The Italian police archives, especially the files of the Casellario Politico Centrale (CPC), contain dozens of dossiers on antifascist women who fled Italy in the 1930s. Most were suspected anarchists, and many made New York City their home.[137] Ironically, the centralization of Italy under Mussolini, and the collaboration of an increasingly powerful surveillance state in the United States, means that historians have a rich source of confiscated material through which to recreate women's activism against the regime. Such files purport specific details about women's activities, and sometimes include photographs and personal letters. They are of course problematic because police informants frequently confused communists with anarchists and were paid for the evidence they passed to the police, so they had a strong incentive to manufacture information.[138] Because sources on Italian women's antifascist activities in the United States are scarce, the police records, combined with the radical press, enable a partial recovery of this history.

Such records reveal that the movement was in many ways dependent on women's ability to effectively canvass their neighbors. The longevity of L'Adunata dei Refrattari, for example, was due in large part to the successful fund-raising activities of women, who customarily held the family purse. During the 1920s, for two years in a row Maria Tomasi and Maria Zaccari went door to door to collect funds for the periodical, sometimes raising thirty-five dollars in an afternoon.[139] Their success undoubtedly stemmed from their familiarity with their neighbors and their ability to politicize female spaces of collaboration. In fact, women were so effective at fund raising that L'Adunata dei Refrattari frequently publicized gratitude for "women's cooperation in keeping 'Adunata' alive to fight the vital battle for liberty."[140] Similarly, in the 1920s an anarchist women's group in West Hoboken raised funds for the legal defense of Sacco and Vanzetti, and their events involved women from Paterson, Brooklyn, and New York.[141] Women were also behind the hundreds of anarchist picnics, dinner-dances, and *feste* held all over the metropolitan area, throughout the 1920s and 1930s. Such events raised consciousness and funds and were often billed as *festicciuola familiare* (informal family parties). While some events were small, including only a few dozen attendees, others were huge, involving several thousand. These were the events where D'Andrea and others found an eager audience. They were also spaces where women continued to develop and perform theatrical productions to dramatize the political struggles they faced. As in the prewar era, women's participation was motivated in part by female responsibilities of mutuality and caretaking, but it also broadened into very public, outspoken, and subversive activities.[142]

When we consider that antifascists constituted only 10 percent of the Italian American population of 4.6 million in 1930, the efforts of Italian anarchist and communist women to build an oppositional movement might seem particularly negligible. Yet, interestingly, the garment unions, whose rank and file was predominantly female, had more success in repelling fascist agents from recruiting supporters than the male-dominated trades of longshoremen and barbers.[143] In the next decade, Italian American women active in the garment unions would once again occupy central stage in the city's working-class political culture. But life in America during the interwar years had taught most Italians and other European immigrant workers to demand social change not through revolutionary, internationalist, working-class solidarity but through asserting identities as whites. The shifting racial order would fracture working-class politics just as leftist movements commanded the attention of millions hungry for an alternative to the devastations of capitalism during the Great Depression.

Community Organizing
in a Racial Hall of Mirrors

Among those who lived in Harlem during the 1930s and 1940s, a common story is recounted—that of young people confronting each other with hostility and violence when racial boundaries were transgressed.[1] The stretch of Lexington Avenue from 104th to 112th Streets was one of many such battlegrounds. Johnny Rodríguez, a musician who came to the city from Puerto Rico in the 1930s, recalled that even Third Avenue was claimed by Italians in the neighborhood: "If I crossed Third Avenue by mistake, I barely escaped getting killed."[2] Writer Piri Thomas remembered that when his Puerto Rican and Cuban parents moved the family into "Italian turf" in East Harlem during the Great Depression, he experienced a daily onslaught of anger. Taunts of "Hey, you dirty fuckin' spic," and getting beaten up by Italian kids who spoke in heavily accented English with their elders only a few feet away, were formative in his childhood. On one occasion, one of the kids shouted, "Hey you got any pretty sisters? We might let ya stay onna block." Another replied, "Aw, for Chrissake, where ya ever hear of one of them black broads being pretty?" Yet another said, "Fuck it, we'll just cover the bitch's face with a flag an' fuck er for old glory."[3]

These were not just working-class boys fighting over turf or scarce resources. As their disturbing taunts reveal, they were asserting white American identities through the specter of gendered and racial violence. As their taunts also reveal, these struggles involved women. In Harlem, a principal at a girls' high school that was 40 percent African American, 25 percent Italian, and 25 percent Puerto Rican, noted that by the 1930s, the school was "a keg of dynamite" where "girls lived among prejudices and discriminations every hour."[4] In fact, among the generation of Italian Americans who came of age in this period there is a striking self-consciousness about how engaging in violent acts of racial terror made one American. As one Italian immigrant noted of this process, "acquiring a 'white man's' attitude toward a Negro or Jew was motivated by the desire to identify themselves as Americans."[5] Another resident of the neighborhood, who grew up in a Sicilian immigrant family, remembered that during the Second World War he and many of the other men in his East Harlem neighborhood resented the ways Italians were depicted as "chumps" in the movies and media and felt they had "something to prove." "It was very painful to live in America," he added, "You sorta wanted not to talk about it." During the 1945 race riot in Harlem, he recalled a man in the neighborhood who rounded up others "to get in the riot" with the call, "Let's beat up some niggers." He explained, "It was wonderful. It was new. The Italo-Americans stopped being Italo and started becoming Americans. We joined the group. Now we're like you guys, right?"[6]

This chapter explores why and how Italians began to mobilize as whites and the consequences of this emerging consciousness on women's activisms in the 1930s and 1940s. One of the lessons of this history is how increased despair, fear, and militarism led to practices of violent disassociation. But this was also a period when Italians came together with their neighbors in new ways, to mobilize in defense of social justice and challenge the reactionary politics and violence within their own communities. This chapter, then, is as much about the power of fear to mobilize people as it is about the ways people were able to transcend and transform their many fears. I explore three sites of neighborhood activism—labor, schools, and housing—to examine how women negotiated the shifting meanings of race in their daily lives at this time. Beginning in the 1930s, hundreds of thousands of Italian American women entered the labor movement and built some of the largest union locals in the country. Thousands also joined in mass-based grass-roots coalitions around housing and education that completely transformed their neighborhoods. Some drew upon the radical immigrant subculture in order to build coalitions to fight fascism and racism, confront poverty, and mobilize in defense of civil rights. But the vast majority moved toward institutionalizing their own power, hoping that this would safeguard against further calamity.

Recalling her Depression-era childhood in an Italian section of Brooklyn, poet Diane di Prima noted the following: "This pseudo 'white' identity . . . was not something that just fell on us out of the blue, but something that many Italian Americans grabbed at with both hands. Many felt that their culture, language, food, songs, music, identity, was a small price to pay for entering the American mainstream. Or they thought, as my parents probably did, that they could keep up these good Italian things in private and become 'white' in public."[7] But such worlds blurred, and the costs were heavy.

"America became white," James Baldwin has written, "because of the necessity

Street scene in East Harlem, ca. 1939. New York City Housing Authority Photograph Collection, The La Guardia and Wagner Archives, La Guardia Community College/The City University of New York.

of denying the Black presence, and justifying the Black subjugation. No community can be based on such a principle—or, in other words, no community can be established on so genocidal a lie." The "price of the ticket" for Italians and all immigrants was to learn how to demonize and reject. "And in the debasement and defamation of Black people, they debased and defamed themselves."[8] Assimilation into whiteness brought a whole host of material privileges and rewards, but it required distorting and disowning that which most resembled the dark other. It was often those active in the radical subculture who struggled to point this out, because embracing whiteness severely limited Italian Americans' ability to dismantle the systems of inequality that threatened their very lives. By the 1940s, though, this world was greatly diminished.

It is only in tracing this history that we can begin to understand the violence of this period. Daily taunts, beatings, rape, and other forms of racial and gendered violence escalated at this time because of the many different worlds that supported this, not only in the streets but in workplaces, union halls, classrooms, parks, playgrounds, and kitchens, among other spaces, powerfully buttressed by a national political culture deeply invested in both patriarchy and white supremacy.

Fear of Racial Stigma

Harlem was one of many neighborhoods plagued by racial strife during the Great Depression and Second World War. The intensifying violence was in part a consequence of the culture of aggression generated and legitimated by war. But it also signaled that the U.S. racial order was shifting. As African Americans, Puerto Ricans, and other people of color migrated to cities for jobs in the expanding war industries, they challenged the nation to live up to its wartime democratic propaganda, and whites of all classes resisted, expecting the state to defend their "rights" as whites.[9]

In New York City, the dramatic increase in racial violence alarmed public officials. They responded by launching a campaign to discipline and reform what they saw as wild youth, especially after such tensions erupted into a riot reportedly involving five hundred students at East Harlem's high school in 1945.[10] The explosion of tension in the school mirrored the racial hostilities that increasingly shaped everyday life for the city's residents. Battles between youths "occurred primarily in New York's borderlands, where neighborhoods touched, and Euro-American gangs defended their turf while African-American and Puerto Rican gangs formed to contest their control."[11] The gangs were part of a male-dominated street life that included social and athletic clubs, racketeers, and politicians. Each "defined East Harlem's public space as a masculine, defended, segmented, and bounded domain," historian Eric Schneider writes. "Not every individual had to belong to such groups, but everyone owed them deference."[12] By the 1930s the gangs "exacerbated deepening racial tensions" and, along with these other male arenas, "utilized violence to preserve their community."[13] For Italians, regional identities were giving way to allegiances rooted in neighborhood, ethnic nationalism, and race. While ethnic and racial tensions had shaped community relations in the city for generations, for the first time, Italians were uniting with other European Americans to defend "their" neighborhoods, schools, and jobs as whites.

Why this shift? First, the federal government's repression of civil liberties during and following the First World War heightened popular concern over "drawing and defending boundaries—between us and them, white and black, Protestant and Catholic, American and foreign—and the idiom most often used to build the reassuring partitions was a specious science of race."[14] As discussed in the preceding chapter, patriotic fervor was ignited by the Red Scare, "100 percent American" campaigns, the rapid growth of white supremacist vigilante groups such as the Ku Klux Klan, and fascism. At precisely the same time, Harlem emerged as the nation's most visible black metropolis, as African Americans migrated en masse from the South, hoping to find a better life and reprieve from "lynchings, police brutality, rape, inferior education, and political disfranchisement."[15] Harlem had long been a space that whites imagined and depicted as "both a squalid, dangerous slum and a mythic kingdom of illicit erotic delight."[16] This, combined with the economic collapse of the Great Depression and rising competition for scarce resources, intensified the desire among Italians, especially the American-born, to distance themselves from the racial stigma of their largely working-class and interracial neighborhoods. In 1946, for example, *Time* magazine described the residents of Harlem as "hordes of Italians, Puerto Ricans, Jews and Negroes" living in a "verminous, crime-ridden slum."[17]

News of the escalating tensions among Harlem's residents only solidified many whites' convictions that all of these groups were racially undesirable and uncivilized. Local community leaders received a constant stream of letters from whites, some from as far away as the Midwest, expressing their opinions as to the source of the violence. One example among many came from a woman who in 1945 wrote to Salvatore Pergola, an Italian American dean of the interracial Benjamin Franklin High School in East Harlem: "You are what I class the Yellow Race and your own kind no doubt started this trouble among the students. I am a white woman well on in years, in the U.S. City of New York, and while the odor of the Negro race is somewhat different from the odor of the wop (of which you are one), I much prefer the negro to the wop in odor and company. The section of NY City where your school is located is classed as Little Italy, hence the trouble."[18] Beliefs in Italian racial inferiority persisted throughout this period and beyond. They were also supported on occasion by government agencies, which began to classify the city's Italian neighborhoods alongside Puerto Rican and African American areas as unworthy of investment. Neighborhoods like East Harlem were particularly undesirable to government, bank, and real estate officials for their "mixture of low grade races."[19] The struggle of Italian Americans to distinguish themselves from their darker neighbors was deeply rooted in the painful messages they received about their own racial inferiority. Many who grew up in Harlem lied about where they lived to get jobs and drew sharp lines between "their" neighborhood in East Harlem and the African American and Puerto Rican communities.[20]

Such strategies were common among Harlem residents, whose lives unfolded in what historian Robert Orsi has termed a "racial hall of mirrors."[21] For decades,

Harlem was a diverse, interracial and multiethnic community, home to African Americans and immigrants from Italy, Ireland, Germany, Russia, Poland, Greece, Finland, Spain, China, India, Brazil, Cuba, Puerto Rico, Jamaica, and other islands in the Caribbean. Those from the same town and region of origin tended to settle alongside one another, but communities overlapped. In 1902, for example, there were approximately seventy African American families living in the heart of the Italian section of Harlem.[22] As discussed earlier, Italians struggled primarily with their Irish and Jewish neighbors in the decades before the First World War, because these were the two largest groups with whom they competed for jobs, housing, and political presence. Kids battled in the streets and schools, and tensions flared up between adults over everything from jobs and housing to religion, labor relations, politics, and intergroup romance. But by the 1930s, many of the Jewish and Irish residents had moved out of the neighborhood to the Bronx and Queens.[23]

In the span of a decade, Harlem became home to the largest Puerto Rican, African American, and Italian communities in the city. Italians came to the neighborhood directly from Southern Italy but also from the Mulberry Bend area downtown, in search of less congested neighborhoods. Jobs in construction for men and the garment trades for women lured them as well, and by the 1930s Italian Harlem extended from about 96th to 125th Streets and from Lexington Avenue to the East River. Eighty-nine thousand Italians, immigrant and American-born, called the neighborhood home at this time, making the community three times the size of the Mulberry Bend enclave, and the largest Italian community in the United States. But even at its peak, Italian Harlem was not entirely homogeneous, as Italians constituted anywhere between 79 and 84 percent of residents. Even in the late 1930s, there were at least thirty-four different groups living in that section of Harlem.[24]

Puerto Ricans had been settling in New York since at least the 1860s, and migration increased once they were granted U.S. citizenship in 1917, though the largest migratory waves occurred after World War II. Spanish Harlem or "El Barrio" as it came to be known, grew steadily into one of several thriving Puerto Rican communities in the city, with anywhere between 45,000 and 100,000 Puerto Rican residents by 1930.[25] Bernardo Vega, an immigrant cigar maker and socialist labor organizer who migrated to the city from Puerto Rico in 1916, documented the neighborhood in his memoir: "The ghetto of poor Jews extended along Park Avenue between 110th and 117th and on the streets east of Madison. It was in this lower class Jewish neighborhood that some Puerto Rican and Cuban families, up to about fifty of them, were living at the time."[26] Catalino Rolón also recalled how the neighborhood was divided when he arrived in 1926: "The blacks were over in the area of 125th Street. . . . In those times they didn't come below Lenox Avenue. Lenox Avenue was completely Jewish. . . . They had their sections around 125th and Eighth, Sixth, and Fifth, and they didn't want blacks around there then. . . . The Italian neighborhood of that time [extended] . . . from 120th and Madison and Fifth till Second and Third Avenue. The Latino neighborhood was from 100th and 102nd till 96th. Past 96th they didn't want Hispanics there."[27]

A pan-Latin sense of identity had developed in the first decades of the twentieth century, as "occupational and revolutionary activities brought Cubans, Puerto Ricans, and even some Spaniards and Sephardic Jews together."[28] This world included Italian immigrants through the network of anarchist, socialist, and communist mutual aid societies that made up the radical subculture. The economic devastation of the Great Depression also encouraged residents to come together in new ways, as all "were brought together and forced to confront each other by the logic of shared social, economic, and geographical circumstances."[29] James Baldwin recalled, for example, that in this period of economic collapse, Harlem was a neighborhood where "the white people who lived there then were as poor as we." He continues, "We could all be found eating as much as we could hold in Father Divine's restaurants for fifteen cents."[30]

While stories of cooperation, mutual assistance, and friendship emerge in this period, narratives of disassociation predominate. By the 1930s, Italian Harlem was a community "acutely conscious" of its borders. Orsi notes that "there was no doubt in the 1930s, for example, that Lexington Avenue marked the boundary between Italian and black Harlem; if the boundary was crossed, it was done intentionally."[31] Indeed, race governed all community relations: African Americans from the North differentiated from those migrating from the South; Spaniards, Cubans, Italians, Jews, and Irish tended to look down on Puerto Ricans; while light-skinned blacks, Puerto Ricans, and Cubans distinguished themselves from those who were darker.[32] Of course, this was not a level playing field. Some groups won acceptance as whites and therefore had access to privileges not afforded those deemed nonwhite. In the 1930s Italians were successful in their claims to whiteness in part because the state recognized them as white. But it was also because of the political and economic power they acquired in the 1930s and 1940s, through labor and housing struggles, which enabled them to assert themselves as whites. In addition, Italians acquired preferential access through the denigration and exclusion of racial others. In this way, "whiteness functions as a form of capital."[33] How Italians acquired that access and the ways they asserted such privileges were not similar to other whites, however, as they did so against their own transnational history of racial stigmatization and class oppression.

These particularities are evident in much of the correspondence that community leaders in Italian Harlem received from local residents in these years and offer an important backdrop to women's activisms at this time. A man by the name of Joseph Spada was one of dozens of residents who wrote to Leonard Covello, the principal of Benjamin Franklin High School (and the first Italian American high school principal in the city) in the aftermath of the 1945 riot at the school.[34] He wrote to express his gratitude that Italian youth were acting violently against African American students: "A race riot has finally come to a reality to your school," he wrote. "I have been expecting this to happen. I am very glad there is still some red blood Americans of the White race who don't give a damn for niggers." He then demanded that African American students be removed from Benjamin Franklin High School in East Harlem. After chastising Covello for his commitment to racial integration, he concluded, "I don't think you would like to have your daughter, if you have one, to marry a nigger. I wonder."[35]

Viola Mellone, who lived just around the corner from Spada, on East 117th Street was one of several Italian American mothers to echo these sentiments:

> I feel the same as thousands of White mothers in this section of Harlem in having their children attend this school where their lives are in peril by this Negro element who are beyond control in their viciousness toward the White Race. Why are they allowed to mingle with the White Boys teaching them besides stealing, using vile language, no respect for elders, disobedience, not abiding law and order, and going so far as being taught to smoke and rape if given the chance, using narcotics and go out and do mugging and possible murder if necessary. . . . no matter how much we do for the negroes an exorbitant larger percentage don't appreciate or cherish their growth into civilization, they are still too young from savagery and cannibalism to be inserted into civilization.[36]

While the immigrant generation had often attributed the loss of control over children to the forces of Americanization, the American-born generation often felt it could not afford the same strategy, lest they be seen as anti-American, especially during the Second World War, when Italian Americans struggled with the federal government's classification of Italians as "enemy aliens." Many turned instead to blaming and demonizing those with relatively little political and economic status and to projecting onto *them* the stigma of criminality and racist violence. As Mellone's letter illustrates, women in particular also drew upon fascist ideologies of white supremacy *and* virtuous motherhood to disassociate from their darker "uncivilized" neighbors and to align with other whites.

But this letter also reveals that cultural exchange was occurring among youth, even as they were battling in the streets. Mellone's fear derived from her observation that Italian American and African American children were befriending one another. Italian men in the neighborhood shared these concerns, which helps explain why some elders just stood silently by or expressed their approval while the youth attacked Puerto Ricans and African Americans. Many admonished their children for their friendships across the color line, believing instead that they should, as one parent noted, "stay away from them because they learn the habits of the black people and that's no good. Most of the black people are not civilized, and they should not be together with us people."[37] Luigi Criscuolo, editor of the *Rubicon*, whose subtitle read "An American Publication," was also among the many Italian Harlem residents who wrote to Covello in these years to express his opposition to a local school's practice of racial integration: "It has been related to me that Negro girls have often been a disturbing influence there, attacking white girls with knives, and the result was many fights in which boys of both groups joined. . . . Fraternization between Whites and Blacks is entirely out of order. I believe that the Negroes are entitled to a good common school education [but] they should be segregated in the public schools."[38]

Criscuolo and many others also wrote letters to protest Benjamin Franklin High School's dean, Salvatore Pergola, after he issued a public statement decrying racial violence in the aftermath of the 1945 riot. "We don't want Bilboism here," Pergola had declared at a mass public meeting in the neighborhood.[39] In response, some residents contested Pergola's denunciation of the segregationist and white supremacist Mississippi senator Theodore Bilbo. An Italian American man in the neighborhood wrote that "a man like Bilbo is our only savior from a complete Mongrelization of the human race." He supported the senator despite the fact that Bilbo had recently become notorious in the neighborhood for his racism against Italians. In response to a letter written by an Italian American woman from East Harlem (who had written Bilbo to castigate him for his opposition to the Fair Employment Practices Commission), the senator opened his response with "My dear Dago." When East Harlem's congressman Vito Marcantonio demanded a public apology, Bilbo refused, noting, "You are a notorious political mongrel." But when the controversy became highly publicized, Bilbo insisted he was motivated by "the respect and love that I have for the Caucasian blood that flows not only in my veins but in the veins of Jews, Italians, Poles and other nationalities of the White race, I would not want to see it contaminated with Negro blood."[40]

By the 1940s, East Harlem's Italians were not only referring to themselves as whites but were more often referred to as "whites" by American political leaders and the mainstream media, even as they were described as "swarthy" and "unstable," with "un-American" tendencies toward "strict supervision of women," "criminality," and "taking the law into their own hands."[41] As World War II unfolded, and the U.S. government proclaimed "Don't Speak the Enemy's Language" in signs that were posted throughout Italian neighborhoods, embracing whiteness seemed the most viable way to assert a patriotic American identity. Whiteness also guaranteed access to government protection and benefits. As many scholars have recently demonstrated, both the social democratic reforms of the New Deal era and the subsequent neoconservative reactions to liberalism, gave Italians and other European Americans a powerful reason to assert a white identity. Beginning in the 1930s, policies including the Wagner Act, the Social Security Act, the Federal Housing Act, the Fair Labor Standards Act, and other welfare, housing, and job programs, excluded agricultural and domestic workers from coverage, sectors of the economy that were disproportionately occupied by people of color. Rather, New Deal programs channeled benefits and protection to white industrial workers, helping to subsidize the development of a "modern white middle class."[42] They guaranteed whites access to federally subsidized housing loans, which they would use to abandon the inner city for segregated suburbs, and empowered industrial trade unions.[43] At the same time, people of color were routinely denied access to workforce protections, housing loans, and other material rewards of these reforms and subjected to occupational and residential segregation. Beginning in the 1940s, slum clearance, highway construction, and public housing reinforced practices of racial segregation. In many cities, including New York, such projects confined the poorest families—who were most often newly arriving African Americans and Puerto Ricans—to isolated high-rise buildings, further distancing them from whites.[44]

Once the United States entered the war against fascism, "racialist ideologies lost their official credibility," however, and the federal government instead "promoted a pluralist vision of nationhood that emphasized integration rather than inherent difference."[45] While the rhetoric was becoming more race neutral, government policies continued to entrench racial hierarchies, and the assimilationist vision of unity excluded people of color. The labor movement would mirror this tension and combine a discursive commitment to unity with policies that more deeply embedded practices of racial segregation and discrimination.[46] Moreover, because the federal government promised workers that the state would protect them, a new era of rights consciousness emerged. The "rights discourse" catalyzed "new conceptions of racial identity and its meaning, new modes of political organization and confrontation, and new definitions of the state's role in promoting and achieving 'equality.'"[47] Because New Deal policies were preferential to whites, they encouraged white workers to articulate their rights *as* whites.[48] As a result, struggles over jobs, housing, and education became vehicles through which Italians (and other European Americans) asserted identities as whites, and women were central actors in all three arenas.

Before exploring women's activism, it is first important to note that, while this larger context redefined political struggle in this period, Italians applied their own shifting cultural values and class consciousness as they navigated the color line in their daily lives. James Baldwin recalled that in the 1940s, the Italian owners of the San Remo, a restaurant on the corner of MacDougal and Bleecker in Greenwich Village, threw him out every time he entered. But they let him stay when he arrived one day with the president of the publishing firm Harper & Brothers. Baldwin made a point to return later that evening on his own, to sit on a bar stool in the window, and announce what he called the "desegregation of the San Remo." From that point on, he wrote, the owners and workers at the San Remo, and most of the Italians in the neighborhood, never bothered him. It is unclear if the San Remo was indeed fully desegregated and other African Americans were permitted full entry, but Baldwin's story suggests how individual transgressions can become the building blocks of interracial solidarity. For example, one night, when a mob of menacing white tourists threatened Baldwin, the owners of the San Remo offered him sanctuary. They closed the place, turned out the lights, and sat with him in the back room for a couple of hours before judging it safe to drive him home. "Once I was in the San Remo," Baldwin noted,

> I was *in*, and anybody who messed with me was *out*—that was all there
> was to it, and it happened more than once. And no one seemed to remem-
> ber a time when I had not been there. I could not quite get it together, but
> it seemed to me that I was no longer black for them and they had ceased
> to be white for me, for they sometimes introduced me to their families
> with every appearance of affection and pride and exhibited not the re-
> motest interest in whatever my sexual proclivities chanced to be. They
> had fought me very hard to prevent this moment, but perhaps we were
> all much relieved to have got beyond the obscenity of color.[49]

Baldwin's story reveals the complex ways Italians in his neighborhood treated him as a gay African American writer. While fear of racial stigma generated an intense desire to disassociate from African Americans, such practices were not rigid and fixed. They could and did break down.

Popular Front Womanhood

This fluidity is especially apparent when we focus on Harlem's vibrant political culture.[50] As tensions erupted, community organizers and activists crossed divisive lines daily, to build coalitions and a shared sense of community. Ella Baker, one of the most influential grass-roots organizers of the civil rights movement, was transformed by Harlem's Depression-era social movements. The neighborhood was, she would recall, a "hotbed of radical thinking." The suffering brought on by the Great Depression inspired an explosion of socialist- and communist-inspired protest activity, drawing thousands who were deeply disillusioned by capitalism into radical politics.[51]

Bernardo Vega also described Harlem as a "Socialist bastion" in this period. "The center of assemblies and great indoor events was the Park Palace, a relatively large auditorium. The public forum was the corner of 110th Street and Fifth Avenue . . . every night . . . more than a half a dozen orators expressed their point of view with the active participation of the public."[52] The space that Vega referred to was the northeast corner of Central Park, which lay at the crossroads between the African American, Puerto Rican, and Italian neighborhoods of Harlem. The American Communist Party, founded in 1919, was at the forefront of this activism, as it became a vital part of working-class resistance during the Great Depression. All across the country, rebellions of the unemployed and impoverished gave shape to a new social movement often referred to as the Popular Front (after a 1934 redirection of policy in which the party sought to develop a broad alliance against the spread of fascism). The movement coalesced out of the crises of the 1930s, including the massive 1933–34 strike wave and the uprisings of the unemployed, which involved millions. But the movement also included socialists, anarchists, unaffiliated community organizers, industrial unionists, and unemployed workers, as well as others active in the labor, civil rights, antiracist, and antifascist movements.[53]

In one of the more sweeping accounts of this era of working-class activism, Michael Denning's *The Cultural Front* reminds us that the "symbolic center of Popular Front womanhood was the garment industry."[54] It was at this precise moment that Italian women became the largest group of workers in both the garment industry and unions. Yet, it is one of this period's great ironies, that just as mass mobilization at the point of production offered new opportunities for coalition, the labor movement was becoming more firmly structured by racial and gendered hierarchies than ever before. New York City's garment unions entered the 1930s deeply divided. The reconsolidation of capitalism, together with the Red Scare, dealt the first major blow to the labor movement, and the Great Depression crippled it further. The membership of the ILGWU fell from 105,400 in 1920 to only 40,000 in 1932, as most members simply could not afford to pay dues. Of the strikes that mobilized to fight wage decreases in 1932, over half ended in failure.[55] Part of the problem was that employers exploited the out-of-town labor market when workers struck, as they had done in the 1913 Paterson strike. The ILGWU was not strong enough to stop such employment practices, and workers often considered themselves fortunate if they worked seventy or eighty hours a week.[56]

Change came in 1933. That year, newly elected president Franklin Delano Roosevelt instituted the National Industrial Recovery Act (NIRA), an act designed to revive industry and business, and increase employment. For the labor unions, the most important provision was section 7(a) of the act, which stated that workers had a right to organize in unions of their own choosing. The ILGWU leadership responded quickly to this development by calling for mass mobilization. Under the new legislation, Roosevelt invited both employers and union leaders to come to Washington to write "fair competition" codes for the industry. Union leaders hoped that mass mobilization of workers in preparation for a general strike would ensure a strong place for their demands at the bargaining table.[57] After four long years of economic depression, garment workers had suffered huge wage reductions, deteriorating sweatshop conditions, and chronic unemployment. By the summer of 1933, they were more than ready to come together.

At that time, Italian women and some men worked in virtually every dress factory in New York City, and they constituted large majorities in many of the biggest shops.[58] Italian women organizers were thus crucial to the union's success, and they assumed primary responsibility for organizing workers in preparation for the strike. On 16 August 1933, they witnessed the fruit of their labor when an estimated seventy thousand dressmakers walked off their jobs and into the streets in New York, New Jersey, and Connecticut.[59] Italian women were joined by Jewish women, but also the newest members of the industry, African American, Puerto Rican, and other women from the Caribbean. Together, they filled strike halls to capacity and stormed nonunion shops calling workers to join them. As they marched through the streets, they distributed thousands of handbills stating, "This general strike is being called to make an end to the misery and chaos in the dress shop, to introduce union concerns in the entire industry, and to enable the dressmakers to work like human beings and live like human beings."[60]

The Italian American women dressmakers who helped to orchestrate the strike were both veterans from earlier labor struggles and new recruits. They were both immigrant and American-born, though most were the first generation born in the United States.[61] Together they ushered in a new era, one that Italian garment workers would long refer to as *l'alba radiosa* (the radiant dawn).[62] The American labor movement, which had for decades reinforced women's institutional marginality and relied on an image of the worker as male, was flooded with tens of thousands of women with their own theories and methods of working-class insurgency.[63] Following the strike, Italian American women immediately set to work, building the union movement by devising strategies that could not only mobilize workers but provide them with a sense of community and a vision of solidarity that could sustain them through the Depression.

The sheer drama of it all—seventy thousand mostly female workers leaving factories en masse, filling streets, calling for economic justice, and organizing this mass movement—captured the attention of journalists. Several reporters were especially struck by what they saw as the new role of Italian women in this great uprising.[64] Their prominent role was unmistakable: they often greeted the thousands of strikers who filled the union halls, staffed the membership booths, handed out leaflets, assigned strikers their picketing locations, and helped workers bring out their shops.[65] One reporter noted, "A grey haired Italian mother, chairlady of a shop, was emphatically explaining picket duty to a group of girls who had never struck in their lives. 'An I wanna see everybody face on the picket tomorra morn',' she concluded. All agreed quickly, as though their own mother had given the instruction."[66] This particular report, appearing in the Communist Party's *Daily Worker*, disrupted popular images of passive, apolitical, "Old World" Italian women by linking their perceived maternalism with their ability to successfully transmit unionism and labor radicalism to the next generation. Italian American women's significance to the strike remained hidden in the *New York Times*, however, whose front page pictorial showed only men, and whose text on the strike kept the thousands of women invisible behind the gender neutral term "strikers."[67] Women workers were still largely excluded from the language and iconography of labor in the mainstream media.

Regardless, the five-day strike signaled the new importance of Italian garment workers to the American labor movement, as they became the overwhelming numerical majority within both the industry and the union. The Italian Dressmakers' Local 89 became the largest local in the nation with 40,000 members, and women constituted more than 80 percent of the membership.[68] Indeed, Local 89 and the Italian Cloakmakers Local 48 both became important centers "around which Italian American life in New York City revolved."[69] They also became a space where Italian American workers sought to consolidate their power, not only with employers but with the state as well, which appeared to support their organizational appeals for economic justice. In fact, union members and organizers marked this strike as the moment they became American. As Frank Liberti, a Sicilian immigrant who joined the union in 1910, recalled, "Before I became a Citizen of this Country I became a Citizen (considered my self) of the ILGWU. In fact I became Citizen of the United States during the 1933 Strike."[70] Such sentiments were affirmed by the rhetoric of the union, which fashioned itself as "the portal through which masses of immigrants have integrated into America."[71] In March of the following year, some of the main organizers of Local 89, including Margaret Di Maggio, Minnie Badami, Dorothy Drago, Yolanda Liguori, and Angelina Farruggia, traveled to Washington, D.C., to present Eleanor Roosevelt with a bronze plaque and pledge the support of Italian American garment workers to the National Industrial Recovery Act.[72]

The acquisition of institutional authority in the U.S. labor movement reconfigured Italian American women's activism in several significant ways. Following the uprising in 1933, the garment unions became one of the most important community institutions, not only in Italian neighborhoods but also to the American labor movement overall. Because women composed the majority of the rank and file, they were called upon by the union leadership to consolidate the gains of the strike and run the organizational drives. As tens of thousands of women workers poured into ILGWU offices across the city, they worked with veteran organizer Margaret Di Maggio, who was in charge of training and mentoring the new recruits. She had migrated with her family from Palermo as a child, and like most in her generation, she went to work in the garment industry when she was thirteen. She joined the labor movement as a teenager, and ILGWU organizers quickly took note of her militancy, intelligence, and oratorical skills.[73] The union honored her work in the 1919 strike by offering her a post as officer in the newly formed Italian Dressmakers' Local 89. She, too, was the one who challenged her father to return to Italy to see fascism for himself. Margaret's niece, Diane Romanik, often attended union meetings at Margaret's side as a child and recalled that she was "self-educated, an orator if there ever was one, and she helped organize shops, was beaten up many times, was jailed several times, once for a period of three months for her labor activities."[74] After the 1933 strike, Margaret was asked to run Local 89's organization department, and she threw all of her energies into the movement.

For many women who became organizers in this period, the union was a home away from home. "In the 30s and 40s you couldn't get through the halls for the mobs that were there," Romanik recalled. "They would work on their lunch hours. They would run to the union at 5:00. At 8:00 the halls would still be mobbed. . . . You become so involved, it's home."[75] Some of Di Maggio's only surviving letters are those she wrote to Frank Liberti, who became an organizer in this period, and they offer a glimpse into the culture of Local 89 at this time.[76] In 1928 Liberti was organizing in Cleveland, and Di Maggio described the Local 89's main office at 36 West 28th Street in Manhattan to him this way: "We still have the same gang kicking, flirting, eating, swearing, sleeping, snoring, snorting, yelling, talking nonsense, doing nothing, but all looking for money and not finding it (including myself).”[77] In another letter on the state of things in the New York office, she concluded, “In closing let me say that the whether [*sic*] is crazy and money is scarce, but love and hunger including babies and trouble are abundant.”[78]

The local became a social, cultural, and political center as a result of the flood of new members, and this demanded a new level of commitment from women organizers like Di Maggio. Most “worked until the wee hours of the morning” and on weekends, and “few knew whether they had families.”[79] Such a choice was possible because many organizers came from union families. Most also delayed marriage and left organizing or took a break during child-rearing years. Some women did their union work in defiance of their families and spoke of being disowned by parents and suffering broken marriages. But those who did marry often chose partners from within the movement. Albina Delfino put it this way: “You cannot be active, unless your mate has the same opinion.”[80] Always painfully aware that her activism had cost her the custody of her children, Angela Bambace would later recall: “The women who worked in our industry in the beginning were great people. They went out, they fought, and they worked very hard to organize. They gave so much of themselves, they completely threw themselves into this—as much as the men—and they were more effective than the men. The key people weren’t even thinking of themselves, of marrying and building a family. They just threw themselves into this hope they had of building a better world, a better place for everybody.”[81] While activism exacted a heavy price in women’s intimate relationships, the massive Depression-era organizing drives led more women than ever to devote their lives to the movement and to redefine their responsibilities to kin in ways that included community organizing.

For a generation of women who entered the workforce as children, became young mothers, and were inculcated with a debilitating ideal of female self-sacrifice, the revitalized labor movement offered a radical space, as it had in the past. It provided a setting to witness and cultivate their own intellectual and creative abilities and to devote themselves to a larger social purpose. Most of the women who became organizers in the 1930s were like their predecessors in that they were not formally educated, but relied instead on informal lessons and strategies honed in their daily lives. Tina Gaeta had learned from her mother the important lesson that she was “never too old to learn.” To her, intuition and an ability to think on her feet were crucial to effective organizing. “We used to go into the shop,” she remembered, “we used to walk in with a committee, spontaneously, and just pull the switches. We used to take a lot of chances. When you are really working hard for a cause, you do a lot of things automatically that would not be considered right, if you went by the book . . . you take chances not because you want to corrupt the rules, but you do things so spontaneously that it works out very well."[82]

Most of the women who became labor organizers also had extensive personal knowledge of the garment industry as workers. Tina Catania's story captures what was typical. She migrated from Sicily in 1929 at the age of fourteen, and settled with her brother and father in East Harlem. In 1931, at the age of sixteen, she married and began working as a finisher in a shop on Seventh Avenue. "The conditions were terrible!" she recalled. "I was making about $15 a week and I had to work until 7 o'clock at night. Later, the boss would come and he would say, 'Listen, things are very bad. We're going to have to cut your check.' There was nothing you could do about it." Catania joined the union and her experience as an operator, finisher, and sample maker caught the attention of Local 89's officers. It was clear she was smart and a fast learner. "Anywhere I went to work," she explained, "people saw I was a good worker. When I went to work for Emmet Joyce, the chairwoman there, Margaret, liked me, and she made me a forelady. She taught me the hemstitching machine and other machines. After I left, I could work as an operator anywhere. I worked on 48th Street and 5th Avenue on a very expensive line. The forelady was a friend of mine. Then I went to 400 Broadway as a sample maker. I cut my own patterns, and my own fabric. I made the sample."[83]

In 1934 Carmelo Iandoli, an official in Local 89, invited Catania to become an executive board member of the local. For the next two decades she worked alongside Antonetta Lazzaro, an organizer who had also migrated from Sicily with her family as a child. She was so young when she became a garment worker she had to sit on top of pillows to reach the sewing machine. She also drew the attention of Local 89's officers, and they invited her to join the union as a shop chairlady, which involved collecting union dues and serving as a liaison between the boss and the workers. Catania and Lazzaro worked together to organize women in Harlem, and their experiences formed a bond that lasted a lifetime.[84]

Both learned a great deal from other women in the movement, especially Margaret Di Maggio and veteran organizer Grace De Luise.[85] Di Maggio and De Luise, close friends themselves, left a lasting impression on the women they trained. "She was an organizer," Lazzaro recalled, "she was wonderful. She was a dress operator at first, but I don't remember her then. I remember only from when I started in the union. I was about 18 years old then, and she was already active. She had been arrested for organizing."[86] Catania also described Di Maggio as "a fantastic organizer," noting her strong personality: "She was very eager, and things had to be done her way, just like she said. Everybody knew Margaret. We were young, me and Antonetta [Lazzaro] and we were under her and we had to

Margaret Di Maggio (*to the left*) with other delegates (*left to right*) Rose Pesotta, Sadie Reisch, Jennie Matyas, [unknown], and Aida Rose at ILGWU Convention, Atlantic City, N.J., 1937. International Ladies' Garment Workers' Union Archives, Kheel Center for Labor-Management Documentation and Archives, Cornell University.

do what she said. If we were going to organize a shop, she would tell us to be there at a particular time in the morning, or at lunch time, or when we had to picket a shop during a strike. She would give us our assignment and we were there."[87] Di Maggio's influence extended beyond her teams of organizers, as she was invited often to address workers at meetings, picket lines, ceremonial occasions, and charitable events across the city and at the national ILGWU conventions.[88]

Howard Molisani, vice president of the ILGWU and president of the Italian American Labor Council, recalled that Di Maggio "was absolutely fearless," especially when it came to dealing with gangsters.[89] She taught other women organizers the art of dealing with such situations. Her niece remembered: "Gangsters would infiltrate the picket lines in the 30s and they were trying to protect the firms and the bosses. If anybody on the picket lines had trouble, they would call the office, and she would come down. She wasn't afraid of gangsters, she wasn't afraid of a thing. She was a very strong woman."[90] Grace De Luise also developed a reputation for being "tough." Lazzaro recalled, "She organized a lot of shops at the risk of being killed, like Margaret."[91] Both women offered the new recruits a courageous model of womanhood.

Under their direction, Catania and Lazzaro organized women across the city, but centered their work in the East Harlem office at 143–145 East 103rd Street. This was one of the five new branches that Local 89 opened in the city in the aftermath of the 1933 strike.[92] The office was run by Antonetta Barbera, Millie Forte, Paolina Bruno, Mary Marchesi, Nettie Salandra, Silvia DeCaro, Peggy D'Agnese, Carolina Giuliani, Sarah Pirrone, Rose Prosetto, and Fannie Emanuele, with Joseph Piscitello as district manager. Most of the women lived in the neighborhood, within blocks of the union office, and focused on organizing neighbors and co-workers.[93] By 1935, after two years of organizing, thousands of garment workers were regularly attending district meetings in the neighborhood.[94] Two years later, membership grew large enough that Local 89 opened a new East Harlem headquarters with facilities for meetings, educational, and athletic activities.[95]

Lazzaro remembered that East Harlem "was really dangerous because there was a lot of organized crime. When we were organizing in downtown around 1937, they killed one of the organizers who was working with us."[96] Racketeering had been endemic to the industries for decades, because antiunion employers relied on gangsters to keep unions out of their shops.[97] According to Di Maggio's niece, this only made organizers more determined.[98] "Oh, I don't even want to say this," Grace De Luise noted, "but how many times did they threaten to slice my ears off! I was threatened several times. They'd put you in a sack if you didn't do what they said. But I never let it stop me."[99] To carry out their work as safely as possible, they organized in teams: "There was a big group of us," Tina Catania remembered. "We would go to the shops early in the morning, sometimes at 6 o'clock before everyone else got there and talk to the workers."[100] In addition to facing gangsters, organizers also had to contend with shop owners. On one occasion, Catania and Lazzaro faced down an employer who prevented them from entering her shop by wielding a pair of scissors, shouting, "Get out of here, or I'll kill you!" Catania recalled, "I pulled Antoinetta away and said, 'Come on Antoinetta, don't be a dead hero.' So we went downstairs and picketed downstairs."[101]

When they successfully overcame such obstacles, organizers still had to convince other women that activism in the union was in their best interests. Even with the enthusiasm of the 1933 strike, most organizers had experienced in their own families how southern Italian gender conventions could inhibit women from joining the movement. Grace De Luise's immigrant father publicly disowned her because of her union activities and announced his denunciation in the local newspapers. We can presume he did so to protect his own honor in the eyes of the community, which judged women harshly for disobedience. De Luise also witnessed daily how bitter family clashes erupted when women joined the union. She recalled that an organizing meeting on Staten Island was fairly typical, noting that "some of the husbands and some of the parents actually came and dragged out their wives and daughters who were attending the meeting because they were against the union."[102] Tina Catania found that "the families of those girls who had just immigrated from Italy were much stricter with them. They had to be home at a certain time, and they couldn't join in union activities even if they wanted to. This was very true especially of the young girls."[103]

In addition, between 35 and 50 percent of Italian women working in the garment trades were married, and their familial obligations made it especially difficult for them to engage actively in the union movement. To complicate matters further, Antonetta Lazzaro noted that women worked in local garment shops on schedules that coincided with their children's schooldays.[104] Bosses often exploited this concern, warning women that if they joined the union they would have to travel far from home to work in union shops. Even when women did join the union, their ability to fully participate was severely constrained as in earlier periods. Although Lazzaro's husband could not prohibit her activism, his constant concern for her safety stopped her from attending certain strikes.[105] The archival records of Local 89 are also filled with letters from women resigning from activities because of the birth of a child, the opposition of a husband to their activism, and other family constraints.[106] Italian family authority was not absolute, however. Women resisted and defied these pressures, as the women who were dragged out of the union meeting suggests. Catania's husband was like most in that he expressed opposition to the long hours she dedicated to union activities. But she found ways to convince him to accommodate her needs. "I used to explain to my husband that I wanted to be somebody, and that was how it went."[107]

Indeed, the union expanded so dramatically in this period in part because of what it offered women workers. It gave them bargaining power with their bosses, but many were drawn by the same factors that inspired them to join anarchist and socialist groups: the union was a unique space where women could work for social justice, pursue their own intellectual development, and socialize with others committed to challenging narrow gender conventions. It offered a rich social world, including dances, theater, summer camp, and athletic teams, as well as vocational and technical training, and classes in political strategy, including Marxist theories of working-class revolution.[108] Tina Gaeta was one of thousands of women who took advantage of these opportunities. "I remember in 1935, when I was supporting my daughter and my mother, a course was offered during the course of the winter and we had an awful lot of snow and I still made an effort. I also used to take parliamentary courses. My family background was union, and to me it's a loyalty, to me it's like a career. I wanted knowledge, to take advantage of every opportunity to go to classes and learn. Like my mother would say, 'You're never too old to learn.' With all my experience, I still wanted my school. As long as they had the classes, I wouldn't miss them."[109]

While the union offered women the opportunity to develop new friendships, transgress gender mores, redefine the meanings of family loyalty, and gain an education, women struggled for a voice in the male-dominated union hierarchy. Tina Gaeta was an organizer for ten years before she was appointed business agent in 1958, and her experience was typical. Most did not wait a decade, however. They resigned themselves to marginal roles, fought bitterly for appointments, or left the union altogether. Tina Catania also attended the International School, and passed all the exams to become an officer, but was still not placed. After observing that men who had joined the union after her had received appointments, she marched into the local's administrative offices and warned that if she was not given a position she would immediately leave the union. Soon afterward, she was appointed to business agent.[110] Women were invited to serve on the executive board of the local, but it was especially difficult for them to become business agents, which gave them the power to vote on key administrative decisions. Although Local 89 was more than 80 percent female, men always dominated these positions. In 1934, for example, only four women held such positions among twenty-three men—Margaret Di Maggio, Lucia Romualdi, Grace De Luise, and Lillie Raitano. This pattern held through the 1940s; and from 1947 to 1950 only three women served as business agents, among twenty-eight men.[111] Similarly, Italian women were rarely appointed to the male-dominated positions of price adjuster and district manager. At no point during the 1930s and 1940s were women proportionally represented in the hierarchy of Local 89.[112]

Power in the Garment Unions

As Italian American women became the largest proportion of workers in the garment industry, African American and Puerto Rican women began to enter in greater numbers. Italian American women's most common response to their own marginalization was not to unite with them to democratize the union. Rather, they most often chose to align with their co-ethnic men around the practice of racialized exclusion. This choice reflected a growing consciousness among Italian Americans about the politics of their own racial identity. Union records show that the national origin of women workers in New York City's garment industry in 1936 was 51 percent Italian, 32 percent Jewish, 5 percent African American and 2.5 percent Latin American (primarily Puerto Rican). In the period from 1938 to 1958, the percentage of Latinas grew to 10 percent.[113]

Puerto Rican and African American women entered the industry during the 1920s, and they were often able to find jobs only as pieceworkers. Following the 1933 strike, both groups were admitted to the second largest local in the ILGWU, Local 22, which included twenty-eight thousand members, most of whom were Jewish. This local, having been shaped by communist insurgency in the 1920s, was renowned for its "international" composition, and included smaller numbers of forty-three other ethnic groups, including Chinese, German, French, Polish, Greek, Austrian, British, Syrian, non-Jewish Russian, Hungarian, Turkish, Japanese, Scandinavian, and Lithuanian workers.[114] In the aftermath of the 1933 strike, Local 22 incorporated four thousand African American women and four thousand Puerto Rican women into its ranks for the first time.[115] But Puerto Rican and African American workers were still almost entirely excluded from the best-paying jobs in the industry and from leadership positions in the union. The ILGWU was also silent on the issue of wage discrimination, and both groups consistently received lower wages than Jews or Italians.[116]

While Italian women had also entered the industry below other workers in the early twentieth century, they had done so before foreign competition and the relocation of businesses to lower-wage areas had begun to erode key sectors of the industry. The union failed to prevent the acceleration of deskilling, job contracting, and relocation, all of which adversely affected those entering the industry in this period. As a result, African American and Puerto Rican women bore the brunt of industry contractions during and after the Second World War. By then, Italians held a relative monopoly over the higher-paying jobs, the result of their shared political leadership with Jewish men in the union's hierarchy, and their special status as the *only* workers granted autonomy in their own "language locals." The union leadership was unwilling to significantly redistribute power in the union and instead established exclusionary electoral processes that prevented the newest recruits from occupying important decision-making positions. They also did not allow political groups or caucuses to convene until three months before the annual convention, which made it difficult for contending candidates to meet with the rank and file to present their platforms. Those in office, however, could meet with the members as often as they wished. Exclusivist appointment methods also prevented Puerto Rican and African American women from becoming local managers or agents in the lower ranks of the union, and the union leaders deliberately gave vacancies, transfers, or new appointments to Jewish and Italian members of the union.[117]

Even in East Harlem, where most Puerto Rican garment workers lived and worked, the union did not alter its policy. An Italian American, Joseph Piscitello, was appointed district manager in Harlem in 1933, even though could not speak

Spanish. Instead, he relied on his assistant Carlotta Rodríguez to communicate with Puerto Rican women union members. He admitted: "This is a problem, you see, because they can't understand English, a lot of them, and we can't make them understand about the things they should have and why they should have a vision." He continued, "But, you see, the Puerto Ricans, they don't have the education that we have. . . . mostly they're backward."[118] In suggesting that the problem lay with Puerto Ricans, rather than with his own shortcomings or the union's structural inequality, Piscitello echoed the many union leaders who had levied the same charge against Italian workers. He also had the full weight of U.S. imperialist discourse to support his role as civilizer of Puerto Ricans. As historian Altagracia Ortíz has noted, "Perhaps if Piscitello had been able to communicate directly in Spanish with the Puerto Rican workers, rather than through Carlotta Rodríguez, the workers may not have seemed so 'backward.'"[119]

The newest recruits were also not permitted the autonomy of their own locals, a privilege that the union bestowed only to Italians.[120] Rather, Puerto Ricans were assigned a Sephardic Jewish organizer, Saby Nehama, who organized them into a "special department" of Local 22. African American dressmakers were organized into a "Colored Department" headed by another Jewish organizer and Russian immigrant, Charles Zimmerman. Under the rationale and rhetoric of worker unity, the ILGWU officially banned the establishment of language locals by 1937, just as Puerto Ricans and other Spanish-speaking workers were entering the union in greater numbers. Puerto Rican and African American women confronted their marginalization within the union by forming their own autonomous organizations, such as the Spanish Left Opposition Group, the Union Local Hispana, and the Negro Labor Committee. In this way, they addressed those issues not adequately taken up by the ILGWU leadership, such as job discrimination, sexual harassment, and the need to build leadership within their own rank and file.[121]

Overall, Italian and Jewish women experienced much more solid bases of organizational power, grounded in their longer history in the union, their numerical majority, and the support of their co-ethnic men in positions of authority. While the ILGWU sought to instill a sense of socialist international class solidarity, its structural organization did not necessarily encourage workers to identify shared interests. Many of the Italian American men who occupied positions of leadership over the female rank and file in the union—such as Luigi Antonini and Arturo Giovannitti—had assumed these roles after years of participation in the radical culture, which as we have seen, often excluded and ignored women. Many also held a deeply masculinist interpretation of revolutionary activism.[122] They presided over organizations and newspapers that did not value women's voices, downplayed women's activities in their publications and speeches, and defined radical politics and leadership as largely the preserve of men. The language of Italian male union leaders in the 1930s reflected an ongoing commitment to these beliefs. For example, Arturo Giovannitti, who became the educational director of the Italian Local 89 in 1922, and a leader in the union during the 1930s and 1940s, entered the ILGWU via the radical subculture, having worked as an organizer for the FSI (Italian Socialist Federation) and editor of the popular Italian-language syndicalist newspaper *Il Proletario* in the 1910s. He rose to prominence in 1912, when his arrest and trial during the Lawrence strike led to a yearlong mass-based organizational campaign on his behalf. Soon after the 1933 strike, Giovannitti published a poem, widely distributed by the local, commending the women for their success: "The Italian Seamstress! Sartina! The sweet, impudent, petulant, darling young thing! . . . For though she has grown considerably since the days I used to spank her (oratorically, of course), across my knee at the week-end meetings, to me she is still the cross and peevish little girl of fifteen years ago."[123] Underneath this paternalistic discourse there existed great tensions, as women were in fact leading the union's organizational drives on their own.

Indeed, the Italian locals mirrored power dynamics in families, and even referred to themselves as a *grande famiglia* (large family). They did so to recruit women but also to offer an alternative to fascist nationalism. One of the local's most prominent male officials described the local to its membership in an anniversary publication this way: "Local 89 in this foreign land is the most complete manifestation of the collective greatness of our emigrants. It is the most faithful guardian of our civilization. It is Italy."[124] In the imaginations of Local 89's male leadership especially, the union and not the fascist state was the medium through which Italian workers could defend their homelands.[125] In fact, they sought to construct a nationalism that was directly oppositional to both Italian fascism and American nativism, but one still rooted in male authority and power.

The rhetoric of the union in regard to race is equally revealing. Italian and Jewish male union leaders frequently espoused the ideology "We are all minorities," or they sought to avoid the issue of race altogether by focusing on the "culture of unity" offered by a multiethnic socialist union.[126] In both choices, they made invisible their complicity in the union's structural inequality, which limited the role of people of color and thus translated into harsher working conditions for them on the shop floor. In 1934 Local 89's anniversary booklet published an essay by Arturo Labriola titled "Le Razze di Colore e il Socialismo" (The Colored Races and Socialism) in full text for the rank and file, in commemoration of the ideologies they felt informed the local. Labriola, a prominent antifascist and revolutionary syndicalist leader in Italy, wrote eloquently of the history of slavery, the persistent exploitation of African labor, the insidiousness of racist ideology, and the contours of an evolutionary theory in which he traced the birth of civilization to Africa. Labriola indicted "quelli che hanno la pelle bianca" (those with white skin) for the atrocities of racism, slavery, and colonialism. White people, or "son di stripe europea" (those of European stock) counted for only a fraction of the world's population, he argued, while "at least 15,000,000 of the world's population are NOT from European races: black, yellow, olive, mixed. Together, this accounts for the majority of the world population." After positioning Italians among the "olive" and non-European races, Labriola connected racist ideology with class, and the atrocity of European "robbery" of black labor. In doing so, Labriola reminded Italians of their position in an international system of labor exploitation based on race and called upon socialists to attack racism directly.[127] But the fact that this essay appeared in a publication, distributed to Local 89's entire membership, at a time when Italians were acquiring institutional power *over* people of color, reveals how differentiating from whiteness could be used to mask the role of Italian American workers in perpetuating structures of domination.

Italian American women did not possess the same type of formal power as men to exclude workers from the union, but the evidence suggests that they worked actively to exclude women and men of color in informal ways. One way was to oppose granting membership to Puerto Rican women and thus keep them out of union shops.[128] Luisa López, who worked in a dress shop in East Harlem in this period, recalled, "I was working in a shop called El France Dress Company in El Barrio, on 104th Street. The Italian girls didn't want us to sit down. The rest of the girls refused to work, ah, because they didn't want to work with Puerto Ricans. So, ah, when I saw that, I went to the union and I spoke to the manager and I told him what happened. . . . I explained to him, you know, that after all, I'm also an American. I told him I am more American citizen than some of these people are that don't even know how to speak English."[129]

This story is similar to many recounted by Puerto Rican and African American women in the industry who experienced these kinds of "hate strikes" when trying to enter shops that were predominantly Italian.[130] Elsie Hunter and other African American garment workers brought Local 89 to court in the 1940s, forcing the Italian local to enter an agreement with the New York State Commission against Discrimination "that it would not bar Negroes, Spanish-speaking or other persons from membership in the all-Italian locals."[131] The action was intended not only to desegregate the union but to gain access to the higher-paying jobs in the industry. Using their rights as citizens to equal treatment, Puerto Rican and

African American women called into question Italian Americans' attempts to marginalize them in the industry. In the end, few ever gained entrance into the Italian locals, which lasted until 1977.

The policies of the emergent American welfare state encouraged such practices (especially with the combined rhetorical avowal), because whiteness (including patriarchal authority) was held out as the most valuable asset Italian Americans had in their struggle for a better life. But Italian American working-class politics coalesced in multiple ways in the 1930s and 1940s, and neighborhood coalitions offered Harlem residents opportunities to come together in ways that were increasingly difficult in the garment unions. For a moment, it appeared as if Italians might see their everyday struggles as intimately connected to and bound up with their African American and Puerto Rican neighbors, rather than against them.

Neighborhood Coalitions

Another important center of neighborhood activism in Harlem during the Depression was the Harlem Legislative Conference (HLC), a Popular Front coalition that included more than one hundred groups. Founded on 19 November 1937 by local progressive leaders, including the Italian American congressman Vito Marcantonio and the African American reverend Adam Clayton Powell Jr., the HLC sought to bring together Harlem's labor unions, settlement houses, parent-teacher associations, and religious, fraternal, youth, and political groups under one umbrella organization, to "foster unity among the area's three major communities"— Italian Americans, African Americans, and Puerto Ricans. Their platform involved fighting to improve Harlem's housing, medical, and educational facilities, ending police brutality, fighting fascism, combating racial discrimination, establishing independence for Puerto Rico, and condemning "persecution of the foreign born, of minority groups; lynching, or mob violence of any form; and anti-semitism."[132] The headquarters was located at 147 East 116th Street, at the crossroads between each of these communities but firmly within Marcantonio's congressional district in East Harlem, which comprised mostly Italian and Puerto Rican constituents. Meetings were often held at the Park Palace Casino on 110th Street and 5th Avenue, which was "more centrally located" for Harlem's African American and Puerto Rican residents.[133]

The HLC was effective in Italian Harlem in large part because it was spearheaded by Marcantonio, whose office at 247 East 116th Street, on the main thoroughfare in Italian Harlem, was a hub of community organizing. Annette Rubinstein, a longtime socialist activist, educator, and adviser to Marc (as he was affectionately called by many of his friends, colleagues, and constituents) first met him in 1934. She recalled, as many have, that he was beloved by those in his district: "He couldn't walk a block without being stopped thirty times. He took care of the community."[134] The voluminous letters that fill twenty-nine large boxes in Marcantonio's archival records at the New York Public Library attest to how most in the neighborhood looked to him not just for congressional representation but to solve the most immediate problems in their lives. Whether it meant finding a job, dealing with a difficult landlord, accessing free school lunch programs for children, helping a relative to immigrate, applying for citizenship, or confronting police brutality, the residents in East Harlem turned to Marc for help.[135] Rubinstein writes, "Inside his headquarters there would usually be 100 to 150 people sitting there with problems about the toilet, about the landlord, or an immigrant might be having some difficulties. Everybody whose number was called would come up and sit down at Marc's desk. In about two and a half minutes he would know what the problem was."[136] The child of southern Italian immigrants from Basilicata, Marcantonio was born and lived his entire life in East Harlem, just a block from high school principal Leonard Covello, who would become his close friend and collaborator. As historian Gerald Meyer has written, "The two men frequently headed the speakers' list" at East Harlem rallies and events.[137] Marcantonio died suddenly from a heart attack in 1954, but held political office for fourteen years. In those years, he ensured that Italians had a pathway into interracial, radical working-class politics.

The HLC was one such doorway, and Marcantonio served as chairman from its inception in 1937 until its demise in 1943. In those years, women were largely responsible for the successful day-to-day operation of this coalition. They participated on many levels—as union members, social workers, mothers, teachers, radical activists, and artists—and they came from a wide range of Popular Front groups such as the United Council of Working Class Women, the Communist Party's International Workers' Order, the Italian Social Workers Association, parent-teacher associations, and anarchist circles, one of which called itself Nosotras and appears to have included Italian, Spanish, Cuban, and Puerto Rican women.[138]

Esta Pingaro, the daughter of Italian immigrants, emerged as a key activist in the HLC during the 1930s. She worked alongside Helen Vásquez, a Puerto Rican woman who was one of the leading organizers in Harlem's Communist Party. Together, the two ran the Lower and East Harlem Youth Congress, a HLC-affiliated group. Combining their commitment to both the community's youth and antifascism, they used the medium of radio broadcasting to reach the community.[139] In a letter to Marcantonio, Pingaro stated her reasons for this work: to "fight against discrimination because of race, color and creed," and "establish amicable relations" between Italians and their neighbors.[140]

While the Communist Party did not draw as many Italians in Harlem as it did Puerto Ricans, African Americans, or Jews, it provided one of the most important sites for antiracist activism in this period. In fact, the Italian American communist newspaper *L'Unità del Popolo* (Unity of the People) became a mouthpiece for such interventions. One example among many is a letter that Aurora De Gregorio wrote to John Williams, one of nine African American young men from Scottsboro, Alabama, who were falsely accused of raping two white women in the spring of 1931 and sentenced to death.[141] Her name Aurora (Dawn) was one that anarchists typically bestowed upon their children, though it is unknown if she was a child of this movement. But in her published letter to Williams, she sought to remedy the historical amnesia she witnessed sweeping over her community and link the struggles of Italians and African Americans. "Your people and mine rarely get the decent jobs, and have to work in pick and shovel gangs," she wrote. "Many of us are forced to live in the same rat-infested slum houses." Moreover, she argued, the same people "who deny your people the right to vote, who would doom your Youth to the poverty and lynch mobs of the South, are the same fellows who brand us Italian-Americans as 'Fifth Columnists,' 'Trojan Horses,' and 'Gangsters,' and are fingerprinting our parents."[142]

It was out of this political consciousness that Pingaro and Vásquez came together to work closely with Fausta Mercado. She was chair of a local parent-teachers' association, a leader in the campaign for bilingual and nondiscriminatory education, and one of Marcantonio's close collaborators. Mercado came to the city from Puerto Rico in the 1920s, and during the Depression many in the community turned to her for assistance. Mercado found ways to resolve her neighbors' requests for relief by appealing to local politicians and by mobilizing community-based protest movements directed at city officials. She was active in the antifascist movement, fought layoffs and budget cuts in the National Youth Administration (NYA), and led a grass-roots coalition to confront the racial violence and animosity that plagued these communities.[143]

If Esta and Helen did not meet Fausta through these networks, they would have met through the HLC, because all were active in the coalition.[144] The three came together to focus their energies on several crises with the schools, including violence between students, overcrowding (students often had to sit two to a seat), lack of resources, and racial discrimination. For example, in the 1940s, they joined with local parents and teachers to introduce intercultural educational programs to encourage respect among youth. Their work led schools across Harlem to revise their curricula and investigate racial tensions between students. The studies that grew out of this effort documented intricate systems of protection and allegiance among girls and boys. For example, teachers reported that in one all-girls school, the toughest student was an African American girl with family from the Caribbean. She was well known among teachers and students for her "sensitivity" to racism. A teacher noted, "Some of the other Negro girls bring stories to her and she does the fighting. All the other girls seem to be very much afraid of her."[145] In response, the women joined with others in the community to work with the girls by encouraging them to write and perform plays that exposed and critiqued the race relations in their neighborhoods. The girls explored romance across the color line and intergenerational struggles, while also teaching one another their cultural traditions.[146]

But tensions between children were just one aspect of the problems that women in East Harlem sought to alleviate through collective action. Another pressing and shared issue was housing. Hundreds of women from East Harlem attended a mass meeting in January 1938 to address the dilapidated tenement buildings that dominated the neighborhood. A group called the East Harlem Housing Committee formed as a result and met regularly over the next two years. Its early goal was printed on the hundreds of petitions to the mayor and the New York City Housing Authority that circulated throughout the neighborhood: "We, the undersigned tenants of East Harlem, living in one of the worst slum areas in the city, urge you to allocate funds for a low-cost housing project." The first rally occurred on 22 March 1938. Billed as a "monster mass meeting," hundreds jammed the streets of East Harlem, singing, cheering, and chanting, moving in parade fashion, with colorful banners and placards. The neighborhood's churches, schools, labor unions, settlement houses, political organizations, and social clubs all participated. Prominent neighborhood residents such as Leonard Covello, Edward Corsi, Union Settlement director Helen Harris, Congressman Vito Marcantonio, Assemblyman Oscar García Rivera, and Silvio Battini of the Cement and Concrete Workers' Union gave speeches, in Italian, Spanish, and English, urging all residents and community organizations to cooperate in the movement for low-cost housing. The mass rally was the first of its kind in East Harlem.[147] This was not the first time women in the neighborhood had organized to demand better housing or services in their neighborhoods, but never before had the movement included so many different people from the community. The crisis conditions created by the Great Depression had forced Harlem residents to organize on an unprecedented scale.

The committee's activism, like that of every other group of Americans during this period, was influenced by Franklin Roosevelt's New Deal. In the first years of the Depression, their focus had been on self-help—setting up neighborhood

Women celebrate victory in sanitation campaign on East 114th Street, East Harlem, ca. 1935. The Historical Society of Pennsylvania, Covello Photograph Collection, Balch Institute for Ethnic Studies.

councils and working for better housing tenement by tenement. In the late 1930s, the tactics and arguments reflected an acceptance of Roosevelt's corporatist vision: poor and working-class women had begun to see themselves as a group that could, by organizing and lobbying, force the New Deal state to respond to their needs.

From the start, Fausta Mercado, Esta Pingaro, and Helen Vásquez played a vital role in mobilizing women in the community. They also turned to another local organizer for help: Layle Lane, the perfect ally. Lane was a well-respected teacher in Italian Harlem and an African American activist who brought considerable experience to the movement. She served as vice president of the American Federation of Teachers and was a key organizer, alongside A. Philip Randolph, in the March on Washington Movement, which ultimately forced the federal government to prohibit racial discrimination in the armed forces in 1941.[148]

While the meetings of the East Harlem Housing Committee initially attracted those who were already quite active in the neighborhood, new faces began to appear at meetings after the march in the spring of 1938.[149] Fifteen Italian American women joined to form a core group of active members, including Mary Bassano, Mary Cammorota, Adoneta Cuoco, Anna Russo, Cammilla Pagano, Rose Di Geronimo, and Angelina Perrone, all of whom were married with children. Their activism symbolized a major shift. At first, those new to the movement followed the lead of those with more experience. But as the movement gathered strength, and women began to join the committee in larger numbers, they gained the confidence to take a leadership role in initiating rallies, organizing delegations to lobby state and federal government officials, and building alliances within and across racial boundaries. At this point Pingaro, Vásquez, Mercado, and Lane attended meetings with less frequency, and appear to have served mainly as advisers. Meanwhile, Mary Bassano, Mary Cammarota, Adoneta Cuoco, and Anna Russo, focused on mobilizing their neighbors. Using their extensive neighborhood and kin networks, they directed a petition drive, organized an advertising campaign, and placed housing posters in retail shops and community organizations throughout East Harlem. They canvassed their neighborhoods and organized petition stands on street corners, outside grocery stores, drugstores, political organizations, and subway stations. Each woman was assigned to a post, and throughout the day she engaged passers-by in conversations regarding the condition of the dilapidated tenements and the need for low-cost, federally funded housing projects. In the first year, the women collected twenty thousand signatures in support of a new housing project in East Harlem.

Their ability to generate mass support for public housing grew out of the neighborhood setting itself. Women could join with their neighbors in protest without even leaving the streets that were well known to them. They could act in close proximity to their homes and children. While their activism might have stemmed from a division of labor that assigned issues of housing to women, it had the potential to generate a more radical consciousness because it politicized everyday networks and relationships.[150] As a result, their vision went beyond building housing projects. In December 1938 the East Harlem Housing Committee organized a forum on housing at Benjamin Franklin High School, in which Marcantonio, Covello, and students responded to questions from community residents about the problems confronting the community. Hundreds of residents attended the forum and learned the central objectives of the Housing Committee: to obtain the demolition of useless buildings, to recondition usable buildings, and to retain the East River frontage for low-rental housing units, to be made available to current residents of Harlem. The women present also demanded that two additional resolutions be adopted: that a youth council be initiated and that a petition be circulated to establish nurseries in Harlem. The committee adopted both resolutions.[151]

The women in the housing movement also ventured out of their neighborhoods to pursue their demands, and as a result the movement expanded its base of supporters. At the time, they had the support of East Harlem's labor unions, political parties and clubs, social welfare agencies, and settlement houses, as well as citywide organizations such as the State County and Municipal Employees of America, the Welfare Workers Federation of America, and the American Labor Party. In early 1939 they used such widespread support to lobby city officials. A delegation composed of Anna Russo, Mary Cammarota, Mary Bassano, and Adoneta Cuoco made regular trips to the mayor and the chairman of the New York Housing Authority, armed with their petitions.[152] They approached city officials as mothers, arguing for their rights to safely house their families. On their petitions, rather than stating organizational affiliations, women identified only as mothers, hoping this would legitimate their demands upon the state. Soon thereafter the same delegation made repeated trips to Washington, D.C., to lobby for the new housing projects.

Their demands of the government reflected a complex understanding of the marketplace and the potential uses of the growing New Deal government bureaucracy. The direct involvement of the federal government in public housing construction began in 1933 with the passage of the National Industrial Recovery Act. This act authorized the Public Works Administration (PWA) Housing Division to construct low-income housing projects on land acquired for the government by condemnation or purchase. Between 1934 and 1937, the Housing Division of the PWA was replaced by the United States Housing Authority (USHA), which began building twenty-one thousand units in forty-nine separate projects costing a total of $129 million. It was to this government agency that the residents of East Harlem focused their appeals.[153]

In March 1939, however, tragedy struck. First, a five-alarm fire broke out at the Star Casino on East 107th Street. Within the week, another fire erupted in

Women of East Harlem march for cleaner streets and better housing, ca. 1939. The Historical Society of Pennsylvania, Covello Photograph Collection, Balch Institute for Ethnic Studies.

a tenement on East 112th Street, killing four children. Residents expressed their outrage in hundreds of letters of protest to the Housing Committee.[154] On 25 March, one week after the children's deaths, thousands of residents filled the streets for another march. Italian women, who constituted the bulk of the demonstrators, stated their demands simply and directly: "We refuse to die like rats, in dirty old tenement flats! Make East Harlem a model town, tear the old-time tenements down!"[155] The HLC helped to mobilize the rally, and as a result it included representatives from the Stone Masons' Union, the Teachers' Union, the Carpenters' Union, the Excavators' Union, the Cement and Concrete Workers' Union, the Plasterers' Union, the East Harlem branches of the American Labor Party, Haarlem House, Union Settlement, the La Guardia Club, the Workers Alliance, the International Workers Order, the Union of Italian Associations, and the Italian Social Workers Association.[156] Protesters demanded not only safe and sanitary low-rent housing but adequate fire protection by the strict enforcement of the multiple dwelling law and increased facilities for recreation, playgrounds, and parks.[157]

This mass protest attracted new supporters to the movement. An additional twenty-four women from East Harlem joined the Housing Committee that spring, and the numbers of women attending meetings regularly doubled.[158] The sense of urgency created by the fires, along with the influx of new members, changed the character of the movement. It was only at this point that Italian American women began to seek consciously to develop alliances across the lines of race and class. Covello states, "It was decided that since the Housing Problem knows no creed, color or political denominations, the Housing problem must be presented throughout the entire community. It is very important that the people of Harlem be made housing conscious."[159] The women in the movement turned to Fausta Mercado, along with Beatrice Velasco, both of whom were active in Madres Unidas, a left-wing organization of Puerto Rican mothers in the neighborhood that was part of the HLC.[160] As a result, several Puerto Rican women from the neighborhood joined the movement. Italian Americans continued to predominate, however. They presided over meetings and set the agenda. On 28 April 1939 the committee held another mass meeting in the Verona Theater on Second Avenue and 108th Street, in the heart of Italian Harlem. At no point in the movement's history were meetings ever held in the Puerto Rican section of East Harlem, nor did the Puerto Ricans present at meetings or mass rallies ever equal or surpass the numbers of Italians present. At mass meetings, Italian and Puerto Rican community leaders joined together to stress the need for collective action. But the audience continued to be predominantly Italian American, and speeches were given only in English and Italian.

On 18 September 1939 Congressman Vito Marcantonio announced that the allocation of funds for the low-rent housing project had been granted by the Federal Housing Authority (FHA) and that the low-rent housing unit would be located between 102nd and 105th Streets near East River Drive. East Harlem had won its housing project. The FHA allocated up to $7,638,000 for the construction of fourteen six-story buildings with 2.5 to 6.5 rooms in each unit. The buildings would be located from the north side of 102nd Street to the south side of 105th Street, and from the east side of First Avenue to East River Drive. The apartments would house 1,326 families at approximately five dollars per room. Each unit contained a refrigerator, gas stove, and modern plumbing. The city also created a forty-two-thousand-square-foot park surrounding the projects and made plans for gyms and recreational areas.[161]

On 15 October 1939 the Housing Committee staged a parade to celebrate its victory. Yet the years to follow would be difficult ones. The apartments went primarily to low-income African American and Puerto Rican families, and most Italians were unable to gain access to the apartments because of their relatively higher incomes. In the next two decades, eleven public housing projects were constructed in the neighborhood, displacing the local Italian population with more than twelve thousand low-income African American and Puerto Rican families.[162] Many Italians from East Harlem would blame the new residents and Marcantonio for the loss of the community. As Robert Orsi has written, "The arrival of the Puerto Ricans was woven in this way into the familiar southern Italian epic of political treachery and malfeasance, and even though in this case it was not true, the tale of Marcantonio's betrayal and the coming of the Puerto Ricans allowed Italians to deny what was really happening in their community—Italian Americans were finally well-off enough to get out."[163] In addition, few residents expressed an awareness of how their displacement was rooted in the way federal agencies conceived of and implemented "urban renewal" programs.[164] As many scholars have since demonstrated, such programs decimated poor, urban communities under the guise of "slum clearance" to subsidize the development of racially segregated suburbs.[165] Italians "found themselves caught up in this desperate racial mapping of American identities and they became 'Italian American' on this turbulent and shifting terrain."[166]

To date, close to nothing has been written on the women who animate this chapter. We know that this period of economic collapse and war was a time of massive transition, as the color line was redrawn in the urban north in powerful and lasting ways, in part because of the new power of the federal government to institutionalize and codify racial discrimination and inequality. We also know that the contested terrain for desegregation was not only workplaces but increasingly housing and schools. These were places where women were disproportionately active in their communities, and their struggles here have much to teach us about how women negotiated power in their daily relationships. It was also from these sites of struggle that women created new roles for themselves as community advocates and coalition builders. Those who became activists in Popular Front coalitions like the Harlem Legislative Conference developed innovative ways to build common ground across the color line. They did so within a period of heightened nationalist and racial consciousness among local residents. The ability of community organizers and activists to mobilize their neighborhoods to unite around common concerns was further challenged by the scarcity and fear ushered in by the Great Depression. When the housing units in East Harlem went to thousands of African American and Puerto Rican families, the group of Italian American women in the Housing Committee virulently protested, demanding that the state permit Italians access on the grounds that it should not discriminate against "white families."[167] By the 1940s, Italian Americans had learned to demand change not through revolutionary, internationalist, working-class solidarity but with the terms of interest-group liberalism—relying on a sense of white citizenship to justify their claims upon the state.[168]

In the next decade, Italian American women's neighborhood activism would move further in this direction, toward keeping African American and Puerto Rican children out of "their" jobs, "their" schools, "their" housing, and "their" families. In doing so, they drew upon a growing sense of racialized entitlement that was central to so many of the social movements of this era. Italian Americans would also distance themselves from their darker neighbors and co-workers through a narrative of self-righteousness about their own struggles. Tragically, they began to turn what had once been blamed on them—poverty, joblessness, crime, and other socioeconomic problems—on the supposedly deficient character of African Americans, Puerto Ricans, and other people of color. The demonization of those with relatively little political or economic power would have deleterious effects, as it kept Italians from joining with others to transform the political institutions and methods of economic production that threatened all working-class people's lives.[169]

Conclusions

What is the way back to knowing?

—Cherríe Moraga

Sophie Elwood grew up in a family of Italian immigrant anarchists in Paterson and recalled that after the Palmer raids in 1920 the community was never the same. While she was raised on collectivist values, with some scattered stories of this early radical world, most of this history was discussed in hushed tones or shrouded in silence. Her great-uncle had been among those arrested in the Valentine's Day raid, and after he was released he refused to speak of the experience, only to say that it was "finito"—finished. In the 1980s, as a young woman, Sophie interviewed the elders in her community but found them still unwilling to discuss this history. To the children of the immigrant generation, she noted, "anarchism carried the dread that terrorism does today."[1]

But the silk mills remained central to Sophie's childhood, even after businesses left Paterson for the U.S. South and then overseas in search of lower production costs, less-organized labor, and greater profits. "The evidences we children had of the internal activities of the mills," she writes, "came from the frequent dumping of dyes into Molly Yahn's Brook, a favorite area for games of hide and seek or follow-the-leader. As we sloshed through red, green, or purple water, neither we nor our parents ever thought that we might be endangering our future health nor were any restraints placed upon the dye house owners to stop dumping chemicals into the brook. Today several families whose children played within the tainted brooks of Haledon claim a relationship between the incidence of malignant tumors and birth defects among their adult children and the powerful chemicals which polluted the streams."[2]

In my conversations with families who had been central to the grass-roots and transnational anarchist movement, I found that the grandchildren of these radical immigrants were quite active during the 1960s and 1970s, only they poured their energies into policing their neighborhoods. They set up elaborate neighborhood watch programs to notify one another and local authorities at the first sight of an African American person in the neighborhood. When I probed into their collective memory to see what remained, they too were cautious about sharing their stories, concerned that the public would harshly judge their anarchist relatives. But they spoke with a certain pride about their ability to effectively turn neighborhood networks into a mechanism of control, to keep people of color out.

In the span of just two generations the world had changed dramatically. Because the immigrant generation was largely marginalized from institutional power in the United States, they articulated demands in ways that challenged power at its very foundations. They critiqued systems of class exploitation, and some, especially the women active in revolutionary working-class movements, devoted themselves to analyzing how such oppression was mediated by race, gender, and sexuality. As Italian Americans committed to life in the United States, they increasingly turned to trade unions and government agencies to fight exploitation at work and in their neighborhoods. By the 1930s, many used the Popular Front sense of entitlement as Americans to demand safe housing, dignified work, decent pay, and other rights from the federal government. The majority of those active in Depression-era movements were the daughters of immigrant women who either migrated as children or were the first generation born in the United States. Their coming of age in the 1910s and 1920s occurred amid aggressive antiradicalism, coercive nationalisms, and pervasive xenophobia. This forced a profound change in the focus of their activisms, as they increasingly turned away from revolutionary strategies toward more reformist and accommodationist visions of change.

A host of contradictory lessons accompanied this move away from transnational radicalism. Industrial capitalism encouraged competition among people as they struggled over scarce resources, but the Great Depression also taught people the logic of working-class solidarity and collaboration. Repression against the Left caused many to disassociate with revolutionary movements and from the kinds of political practices and solidarities that were growing organically from daily life. But for some, socialism, anarchism, communism, and feminism continued to provide meaningful ways to imagine and enact a new world, especially in a society so defined by economic disparity, male authority, and racial inequality. Indeed, unity against fascism led the greatly diminished but still vibrant radical subculture to elaborate once more a diasporic vision of freedom. However, the

Italian Americans watching a flag-raising ceremony during the feast of San Rocco, New York City, August 1942. Library of Congress, Prints & Photographs Division, FSA/OWI Collection, LC-USW3-006904-E.

heightened nationalism during both world wars, in Italy and the United States, created its own set of repressive and conformist movements.

Moreover, during the Depression-era, Italian Americans learned the power of the emerging liberal social welfare state to incorporate their demands, whether they demanded control over the workplace or new housing. At the same time, the seemingly race-neutral government programs of "urban renewal" underwrote the development of white suburbs while disinvesting from and decimating immigrant urban neighborhoods. The very urban spaces that had been foundational to early twentieth-century working-class radicalism were "renewed" out of existence and, along with them, the strong networks that women created from

shared neighborhoods, schools, and workplaces. By the 1940s the types of alliances that had been so fundamental to the radical immigrant subculture were no
longer central to the labor movement, even though alliances with Jewish workers
would continue to strengthen into the postwar period. Indeed, as many scholars have argued, differences among European Americans would assume even
less importance in the 1950s and 1960s, and a sense of unity as "white ethnics"
emerged, founded upon "residential segregation, on shared access to housing and
life chances largely unavailable to communities of color."[3]

Yet, alongside this history there are other stories. Sizable numbers of working-
class Italian American (and Jewish) women were active in New York City's radical
subculture from the 1950s through the 1970s and formed an important backbone
to the early women's liberation, welfare rights, and labor movements. Some even
"emerged as leading figures in the revival of the 'woman question,'" historian
Sara Evans writes, by demanding that women participate in shaping the direction and vision of liberatory movements, as their mothers and grandmothers
before them.[4] Film maker Christine Noschese documented how, in the 1970s,
working-class Italian American, Puerto Rican, African American, Dominican,
and Jamaican women in Williamsburg, Brooklyn, effectively built a coalition to
confront racial tensions and the lack of municipal services in their community.[5]
Similarly, a group of Italian American women in the Elmhurst-Corona section
of Queens were pivotal in forming a neighborhood coalition to fight the federal government's withdrawal of funding from the inner city in the 1980s and
1990s—a group that included African American, Spanish, Greek, Chinese, Ko-
rean, Iranian, Turkish, Ecuadorian, Haitian, European American Jews, and other
residents.[6] Both were urban neighborhoods where a sizable Italian American
community remained even after the postwar white flight, often because they
did not have the resources to leave. These were neighborhoods where women's
everyday networks transcended divisions of race and ethnicity, so they were effectively transformed into tools of grass-roots activism. One resident of Elmhurst
compared the neighborhood of the 1990s with the 1930s: "In those days . . . only
the rich had telephones. We had no telephone, and yet I couldn't do anything
and get home before my mother knew about it and met me on the way in the
door with a smack. So my father called it the mothers' union—all the mothers
were plugged into the clothesline, he said. Well the world hasn't changed. . . . the
mothers' union is still alive and working."[7] These networks formed the basis of
collective action in Elmhurst-Corona, and thus women were more effective than
men in organizing coalitions. Moreover, by strengthening local democracy, these
groups provided local residents with a way to recognize each other's concerns

and develop common ground to respond to economic recession, crime, and political misrepresentation. "The basis of inclusion," anthropologist Roger Sanjek writes of this community, "was place, not ethnicity or race."[8]

We are now at the beginning of another century, one hundred years from the days when Maria Roda, Ernestina Cravello, Ninfa Baronio, Angela and Maria Bambace, and others gathered and organized with the intention of emancipating themselves from the disorders of capitalism, imperialism, white supremacy, and patriarchy. The significance of their history is not just in the drama of their lives, the poetry of their prose, or the striking way in which their visions for change are still relevant today. They compel us to remember the infinite possibilities present in every moment, especially in periods of intense repression and despair. While they witnessed the eclipse of their movement within the span of their lives, its retreat was never complete. By embodying and living the freedoms they desired, the seed was planted. Though the meeting halls were shut down, the multilingual rallies and picnics subsided, and an emerging critical consciousness was criminalized and then disavowed, they had their daily lives to remind them that ebb is always followed by flow, even in a country "constructed on forgetfulness" where the amnesia is "so deep that we have even forgotten that we have forgotten."[9]

Notes

List of Abbreviations

BDE   *Brooklyn Daily Eagle*
CPC   Casellario Politico Centrale, Records of the Ministry of the Interior, Archivio Centrale dello Stato, Rome
DOJ   Department of Justice
EN   *L'Era Nuova*
FBI   Federal Bureau of Investigation
HLC   Harlem Legislative Council
IHRC   Immigration History Research Center, University of Minnesota
INS   Immigration and Naturalization Service
IWO   International Workers Order
LMDC   The Kheel Center for Labor-Management Documentation and Archives, Cornell University
LQS   *La Questione Sociale*
NYCILHP   New York City Immigrant Labor History Project, Robert F. Wagner Labor Archives, New York University
NYPL   New York Public Library
NYSDOL   New York State Department of Labor
NYT   *New York Times*
OHAL   Oral History of the American Left, Robert F. Wagner Labor Archives, New York University
RG   Record Group
SSC   Sophia Smith Collection, Smith College
UNA   Unity, Nobility, and Ambition Society, Immigration History Research Center, University of Minnesota
WOMP   World of Our Mothers Oral History Project, Henry A. Murray Research Center, Radcliffe College

Introduction

1. All translations from Italian to English are mine unless otherwise noted. Maria Barbieri, "Ribelliamoci!," *LQS*, 18 November 1905.
2. *LQS*, 10 May 1902, 12, 26 July 1902, 16 August 1902; *L'Aurora*, 22 December 1900; Merithew, "Anarchist Motherhood."
3. Maria Barbieri, "Ricordi? Al compagno lontano," *LQS*, 4 November 1905.

4. Gabaccia and Iacovetta, "Women, Work, and Protest," 176.

5. See essays by José Moya and Angelo Principe in Gabaccia and Iacovetta, eds., *Women, Gender, and Transnational Lives.*

6. Glenn, *Daughters of the Shtetl*; Glenn, *Female Spectacle*; Orleck, *Common Sense and a Little Fire*; Enstad, *Ladies of Labor*; Falk, *Emma Goldman*; Ewen, *Immigrant Women*; Friedman-Kasaba, *Memories of Migration*; Frank, "Housewives, Socialists and the Politics of Food"; Hyman, "Immigrant Women and Consumer Protest"; Weinberg, *The World of Our Mothers.*

7. Glenn, *Daughters of the Shtetl*, 190–93; Fenton, *Immigrants and Unions*, 483–85; Razovki, "The Eternal Masculine," 117; Castiglione, "Italian Immigration," 194; Simkhovitch, *Greenwich House*, October 1911, 14.

8. Glenn, *Daughters of the Shtetl*, 191–94.

9. Flynn, *Rebel Girl*, 333.

10. *EN*, 13 May 1913.

11. Gabaccia, *Italy's Many Diasporas*, chaps. 4 and 5.

12. See, for example, *Atti della giunta parlamentare per l'inchiesta agraria*, vol. 7, fasc. 1, 188; Gibson, "The 'Female Offender.'"

13. T. Guglielmo, *White on Arrival*, esp. chap. 3.

14. Ibid.; Jacobson, *Whiteness of a Different Color.*

15. See my chapter 3, but also Simkhovitch, *Greenwich House*, October 1909, 17, and October 1911, 14.

16. Hunter, *To 'Joy My Freedom*, 154; Kang, *Compositional Subjects*, esp. chap. 3; Gross, *Colored Amazons.*

17. Enstad, *Ladies of Labor*, 86.

18. T. Guglielmo, *White on Arrival*; Orsi, "The Religious Boundaries"; Jacobson, *Whiteness of a Different Color*; J. Guglielmo and Salerno, *Are Italians White?*; Roediger, *Working toward Whiteness.*

19. Baldwin, *The Price of the Ticket*, 667.

20. R. Daniels, *Coming to America*, 265–84.

21. Cunningham, "The Italian," 23; Baldwin, *The Price of the Ticket*, 656.

22. See, for example, "Transnational Feminism: A Range of Disciplinary Perspectives," Roundtable with Ellen Dubois, Nayereh Tohidi, Spike Peterson, Maylei Blackwell, and Leila Rupp, 18 May 2005, UCLA International Institute, transcript at <<http://www.isop.ucla.edu/article.asp?parentid=28482>> (accessed 25 May 2009); Kamel and Hoffman, *The Maquila Reader*; Louie, *Sweatshop Warriors*; Kaplan et al., *Between Woman and Nation*; Mohanty, *Feminism without Borders.*

23. Rupp, *Worlds of Women*; Newman, *White Women's Rights*; Burton, *Burdens of History.*

24. Exceptions are Louie, *Sweatshop Warriors*; and Frank, "Where Is the History of U.S. Labor and International Solidarity?"

25. Quoted in Cott et al., "Considering the State," 156.

26. See, for example, Pérez, *The Decolonial Imaginary*; Ruiz, *From Out of the Shadows*; Lomas, "Transborder Discourse"; Hewitt, *Southern Discomfort*; Castañeda, "Women of Color and the Rewriting of Western Women's History"; Cobble, *The Other Women's Movement*; Hunter, *To 'Joy My Freedom*; Faue, *Community of Suffering and Struggle*; Weigand, *Red Feminism*; Janiewski, *Sisterhood Denied*; V. Green, *Race on the Line.*

27. Glenn, *Issei*, 5–6.

28. Frank, "White Working-Class Women"; E. Brown, "Polyrhythms and Improvisation"; Higginbotham, "African-American Women's History."

29. Morrison, *Playing in the Dark*, 11.

30. M. J. Alexander, *Pedagogies of Crossing*, 14.

Chapter 1

1. Gabaccia, *Militants and Migrants*, 55; J. Schneider and P. Schneider, *Festival of the Poor*, 121.

2. J. Schneider and P. Schneider, *Festival of the Poor*, 121.

3. Calapso, *Donne Ribelli*, 83–103. See also Gabaccia, *Militants and Migrants*, 55–66; Hobsbawm, *Primitive Rebels*, chap. 6; De Stefano and Oddo, *Storia della Sicilia*, 291–93; Gramsci, *La questione meridionale*, 28–30; J. Schneider and P. Schneider, *Festival of the Poor*, 121–31.

4. Rossi, "La situazione in Sicilia," *La Tribuna* (8 October 1893), quoted in Calapso, *Donne Ribelli*, 83.

5. Quoted in ibid., 84.

6. Mansueto, "Blessed are the Meek," 124.

7. Calapso, *Donne Ribelli*, 83–103; Gabaccia, *Italy's Many Diasporas*, 53; Calapso, *Una donna intransigente*; Bortolotti, *Alle origini del movimento femminile*; Bortolotti, *Femminismo e partiti*; Bortolotti, *Socialismo e questione femminile*; Bortolotti, *Sul movimento politico delle donne*; Ravera, *Breve storia*; Zappi, *If Eight Hours Seem Too Few*; Colajanni, *Gli avvenimenti*; Colajanni, *L'Italia nel 1898*; Zaninelli, *Le lotte nelle campagne*.

8. Tilly, "I Fatti di Maggio," 124–60.

9. The classic text is Hobsbawm, *Primitive Rebels*.

10. Douglas, *Old Calabria*, 48–49, 209.

11. Commissariato Generale dell'Emigrazione, "L'emigrazione delle donne e dei fanciulli dalla provincial di Caserta," *Bollettino dell'emigrazione* 12 (1913): 1428–29.

12. C. Levi, *Christ Stopped at Eboli*, 102.

13. Gabaccia and Ottanelli, "Diaspora or International Proletariat?," 65; Gabaccia and Iacovetta, *Women, Gender, Transnational Lives*, 165.

14. Quoted in Siebert, "*È femmina, però è bella*," 200.

15. Gabaccia, *Italy's Many Diasporas*, 5, 74–75; Foerster, *The Italian Emigration of Our Times*, 131–34; Vecoli, "The Italian Diaspora," 114; Castiglione, "Italian Immigration," 186.

16. Gabaccia, *Italy's Many Diasporas*, 92.

17. Commissariato Generale dell'Emigrazione, *Annuario Statistico della Emigrazione Italiana dal 1876 al 1925*.

18. Revelli, *L'anello forte*, 128.

19. Siebert, "*È femmina, però è bella*," 196–200.

20. Gabaccia, *Italy's Many Diasporas*, 83.

21. Reeder, "When the Men Left Sutera," 3.

22. Coser et al., *Women of Courage*, 17, 81–82.

23. Robert Ferrari, "American Immigrant Autobiographies," microfilm pos. 4634, IHRC.

24. Siebert, "*È femmina, però è bella*," 197. See also Bevilacqua, *Breve storia*, 61.

25. Odencrantz, *Italian Women and Industry*, 28.

26. Rogari, *Mezzogiorno ed emigrazione*, 415; Commissariato Generale dell'Emigrazione, "L'emigrazione delle donne," 1423–43; Rossi, "Vantaggi e svantaggi," 1595, 1639.

27. Reeder, "When the Men Left Sutera," 23–24, 11; Bevilacqua, *Breve storia*, 61; Rossi, "Vantaggi e svantaggi," 1595.

28. Reeder, "When the Men Left Sutera," 9. See also Chapman, *Milocca*, 37–38; Pitrè, *La famiglia, la casa*, 33–34; P. H. Williams, *South Italian Folkways*, 77.

29. Gabaccia, *From Sicily to Elizabeth Street*, 4, 115.

30. Covello, *The Social Background*, 149, 175–76.

31. Leonardo Sciascia, "Le zie di Sicilia," *L'Espresso*, 27 January 1974; Covello, *The Social Background*, 187; Williams, *South Italian Folkways*, 80.

32. Covello, *The Social Background*, 189–90.

33. Ibid., 189.

34. Siebert, "*È femmina, però è bella*," 202. For a slightly later period (1920–40), see Francesco Faeta, "Appunti sull'immagine del femminile: In un paese contadino della Calabria, 1920–1940," in Vibaek, *Donne e Società*, 377.

35. C. Levi, *Christ Stopped at Eboli*, 89.

36. Gabaccia, *From Sicily to Elizabeth Street*, 49, 26–27.

37. Reeder, "When the Men Left Sutera," 4–5.
38. C. Levi, *Christ Stopped at Eboli*, 43, 11.
39. Quoted in Gabaccia, *From Sicily to Elizabeth Street*, 7.
40. Reeder, "When the Men Left Sutera," 4–5.
41. Birnbaum, *Liberazione della donna*, 12; Reeder, "When the Men Left Sutera"; J. Schneider and P. Schneider, *Culture and Political Economy*; Gabaccia, *Militants and Migrants*, 87; Covello, *The Heart Is the Teacher*, 10.
42. C. Levi, *Christ Stopped at Eboli*, 102–3.
43. Quoted in Gabaccia, *From Sicily to Elizabeth Street*, 44.
44. Giunta, "The *Giara* of Memory."
45. Covello, *The Social Background*, 231–32.
46. Reeder, "When the Men Left Sutera," 9; Gabaccia, *From Sicily to Elizabeth Street*, 44; Burgaretta, "Il ruolo della donna"; Chapman, *Milocca*, 109; J. Schneider and P. Schneider, *Culture and Political Economy*, 93.
47. Quoted in Calvino, *Italian Folktales*, xxiii.
48. Ibid., 540–46.
49. C. Levi, *Christ Stopped at Eboli*, 71.
50. Calvino, *Italian Folktales*, xxii–xxiii.
51. Siebert, *"È femmina, però è bella,"* 202.
52. Edvige Giunta, phone conversation, 12 June 2001.
53. Revelli, *L'anello forte*, 338.
54. I. De Nobili, *Per il voto alle donne*, 26.
55. Siebert, *"È femmina, però è bella,"* 202.
56. Covello, *The Social Background*, 161; Grace Billotti Spinelli, "American Immigrant Autobiographies," microfilm pos. 4625, IHRC.
57. Coser et al., *Women of Courage*, 19, 86.
58. Revelli, *L'anello forte*, 62–63.
59. Siebert, *"È femmina, però è bella,"* 213–14.
60. Revelli, *L'anello forte*, 219.
61. Siebert, *"È femmina, però è bella,"* 202–3.
62. This name is fictitious to preserve anonymity. Tape 158, Oral History Group 14, New York City Immigrant Labor History Project, Wagner Labor Archives, Tamiment Library, New York University.
63. C. Levi, *Christ Stopped at Eboli*, 103, 101.
64. Quoted in Gabaccia, *From Sicily to Elizabeth Street*, 49.
65. Summarized in ibid., 4.
66. Birnbaum, *Liberazione della donna*, 12. See also Gabaccia, *Italy's Many Diasporas*, 87–99; Reeder, *Widows in White*, 107; Salomone-Marino, *Customs and Habits*, 41–55; Covello, *The Social Background*, 212–13; J. Schneider and P. Schneider, *Festival of the Poor*, 209.
67. Gabaccia, "Italian Immigrant Women in Comparative Perspective."
68. Revelli, *L'anello forte*, 218, 320.
69. Covello, *The Heart Is the Teacher*, 5, 15.
70. Revelli, *L'anello forte*, 14, 16.
71. Gordon, *Heroes of Their Own Lives*, 291.
72. Gabaccia, *From Sicily to Elizabeth Street*, 49; M. Cohen, *Workshop to Office*, 34.
73. Siebert, *"È femmina, però è bella,"* 214–15. See also Reeder, *Widows in White*, chap. 2.
74. Revelli, *L'anello forte*.
75. Dolci, *Sicilian Lives*, 150–54. See also Williams, *South Italian Folkways*, 92.
76. Quoted in Ets, *Rosa*, 28–29.
77. Ibid.
78. M. Cohen, *Workshop to Office*, 33–34; Iacovetta, *Such Hardworking People*, 79–85.

79. Siebert, "*È femmina, però è bella*," 211–17; Revelli, *L'anello forte*, 335.
80. Scott, *Domination and the Arts of Resistance*, xi.
81. Ets, *Rosa*, 80–82.
82. Covello, *The Social Background*, 218–19, 193.
83. Scott, *Domination and the Arts of Resistance*, xi, 4, 16.
84. Covello, *The Social Background*, 214; Siebert, "*È femmina, però è bella*," 216.
85. Covello, *The Social Background*, 193.
86. Ibid., 231.
87. Cornelisen, *Women of the Shadows*, 26.
88. Scott, *Domination and the Arts of Resistance*, xiii.
89. Filippucci, "Anthropological Perspectives," 61.
90. Gramsci, *Selections from the Prison Notebooks*.
91. Filippucci, "Anthropological Perspectives," 61.
92. Ibid. See also De Raho, *Il tarantolismo*; De Martino, *Sud e magia*; De Martino, *La terra del rimorso*; Satriani, *Il folklore*; De Simone, *La Tarantella napoletana*; Di Lecce, *La danza della piccola taranta*.
93. Gramsci, *Selections from the Prison Notebooks*, 189.
94. Vecoli, "Cult and Occult," 26.
95. Covello, *The Social Background*, 103.
96. Ibid., 111; Salomone-Marino, *Customs and Habits*, 13–19; De Martino, *Sud e magia*; De Martino, *La terra del rimorso*; Andrews, "Neapolitan Witchcraft"; Douglas, *Old Calabria*, 247–68; Chapman, *Milocca*, 196–209; Cornelisen, *Torregreca*; Appel, "The Myth of the *Jettatura*"; Prandi, *La religione popolare*; M. Carroll, *Madonnas That Maim*; M. Carroll, *Veiled Threats*; De Rosa, *Vescovi*; De Rosa, *Chiesa e religione popolare*; P. H. Williams, *South Italian Folkways*; Vecoli, "Cult and Occult"; Di Nola, *Lo specchio e l'olio*; Magliocco, *Witching Culture*; Magliocco, *The Two Madonnas*; Orsi, *The Madonna of 115th Street*; Orsi, *Between Heaven and Earth*; Barzman, "Sacred Imagery," 236; Varacalli et al., eds., *The Saints in the Lives of Italian-Americans*; Covello, *The Social Background*, chap. 5.
97. M. Carroll, *Veiled Threats*, 68; Longo, *Storia del santuario di Pompeii*, 33–50.
98. Leland, *Etruscan Magic*, 9.
99. Leland, *Legends of Florence*, 252.
100. Douglas, *Old Calabria*, 58.
101. Chapman, *Milocca*, 196–209.
102. C. Levi, *Christ Stopped at Eboli*, 104–5.
103. Covello, *The Social Background*, 119–21.
104. Ibid., 127.
105. Ets, *Rosa*, 44–49; Douglas, *Old Calabria*, 247–68; Pitrè, *La famiglia*, 22–25; P. H. Williams, *South Italian Folkways*, chap. 9.
106. Douglas, *Old Calabria*, 247.
107. Moss and Cappannari, "In Quest of the Black Virgin"; Moss and Cappannari, "The Black Madonna"; Salerno, "The Black Madonna"; Birnbaum, *Black Madonnas*; Begg, *The Cult of the Black Virgin*; Covello, *The Social Background*, 122–23.
108. Pitrè, *Spettacoli popolari*; Pitrè, *Feste patronali*; Attanasio and Leone, *Il divino e il meraviglioso*; Reeder, *Widows in White*, 107.
109. Siebert, "*È femmina, però è bella*," 198.
110. Revelli, *L'anello forte*, 52, 7, 335.
111. Ets, *Rosa*, 27.
112. Quaggiotto, "Altars of Food to St. Joseph."
113. Turner, *Beautiful Necessity*, 54.
114. Giallombardo, "La donna nelle feste," 276.

115. Elwood, "The Roots and Results of Radicalism," 51; Revelli, *L'anello forte*, 335, 349; Siebert, *"È femmina, però è bella"*; Reeder, *Widows in White*.

116. Gabaccia, *Italy's Many Diasporas*, 52–57; Calapso, *Donne Ribelli*, 71.

117. Gabaccia, *Italy's Many Diasporas*, 52.

118. Ibid., 56.

119. Ibid., 6, 8; D. Smith, "Regionalism"; Levy, *Italian Regionalism*; G. Levi, "Regioni e cultura"; Calcagno, *Bianco, rosso e verde*.

120. Dickie, *Darkest Italy*, 25.

121. Ibid., 25–51; Snowden, *Violence and the Great Estates*; Molfese, *Storia del brigantaggio*; Gaudioso, *Calabria ribelle*; Cingari, *Brigantaggio*; Gabaccia, *Militants and Migrants*, 27–30; Pernicone, "The Italian Labor Movement"; Del Carria, *Proletari senza rivoluzione*, chaps. 1–2; Cerrito, *Radicalismo e socialismo*.

122. Pernicone, *Italian Anarchism*, 33.

123. Dadà, *L'Anarchismo in Italia*, 23.

124. Dickie, *Darkest Italy*, 26.

125. Dickie, *Cosa Nostra*, 131–44.

126. Quoted in Dickie, *Darkest Italy*, 36.

127. Verdicchio, *Bound by Distance*, 24–25; Molfese, "La repressione del brigantaggio," 52.

128. C. Levi, *Christ Stopped at Eboli*, 138–40.

129. Trapani, *Le brigantesse*; De Matteo, *Brigantaggio e risorgimento*; Sangiuolo, *Il brigantaggio nella provincia di Benevento*; Barone et al., *Briganti e partigiani*; Di Giacomo, *Per la storia del brigantaggio nel Napoletano*; Majorino, *Storia e leggende di briganti e brigantesse*.

130. C. Levi, *Christ Stopped at Eboli*, 71–72.

131. Anonymous, *Maria Nambrini*; Dickie, *Darkest Italy*, 46.

132. Gabaccia, "Migration and Militancy," 252.

133. Calapso, *Donne Ribelli*, 88–89.

134. Ibid., 92.

135. J. Schneider and P. Schneider, *Festival of the Poor*, 121; Renda, *I fasci siciliani*, 10–27; De Stefano and Oddo, *Storia della Sicilia*, 291–94.

136. Gabaccia, *Militants and Migrants*, 3, 30–35, 44, 55–66; Calapso, *Donne Ribelli*, 83–103.

137. Gabaccia, *Militants and Migrants*, 61.

138. Cerrito, *Radicalismo e socialismo*, 214–23.

139. Calapso, *Donne Ribelli*, 87; Gabaccia, *Italy's Many Diasporas*, 110.

140. Quoted in Calapso, *Donne Ribelli*, 85.

141. Ibid., 89–90; Gabaccia, *Militants and Migrants*, 56–66; Colajanni, *Avvenimenti di Sicilia*, 13–14.

142. Calapso, *Donne Ribelli*, 86–87.

143. Siebert, *"È femmina, però è bella,"* 226.

144. Quoted in Calapso, *Donne Ribelli*, 96.

145. Ibid., 102.

146. Ibid., 102–3.

147. Ibid., 88.

148. Ibid.

149. Ibid., 83–103; Gabaccia, *Militants and Migrants*, 56–66; Renda, *I fasci siciliani*.

150. Romano, *Storia dei fasci*, 467; Gabaccia, *Militants and Migrants*, 61; Colajanni, *Gli avvenimenti di Sicilia*.

151. Gabaccia, *Militants and Migrants*, chap. 8; Nicolosi, *50 anni di cronaca siciliana*; Fabbri, *L'audacia insolente*; Fabbri, *Il movimento cooperativo*; Sapelli, *Il movimento cooperativo in Italia*; Ministero di agricoltura, industria e commercio, Direzione generale della statistica e del lavoro, Ufficio del lavoro, *Le organizzazioni operaie cattoliche in Italia*; Cappelli, "Le donne in Calabria."

152. The findings of *Avanti!*, 7 September 1901, are summarized and quoted in Calapso, *Donne Ribelli*, 119–38.

153. Burgaretta, "Il ruolo della donna."

154. Gabaccia, *Militants and Migrants*, 153.

155. Calapso, *Donne Ribelli*, 141–72; Gabaccia, *Militants and Migrants*, 153.

156. Siebert, *"È femmina, però è bella,"* 201.

157. Gabaccia, *Italy's Many Diasporas*, 88; Reeder, *Widows in White*, chap. 2; Rogari, *Mezzogiorno ed emigrazione*, 435.

158. Quoted in Harney, "Men without Women," 85.

159. *Inchiesta parlementare sulle condizioni dei contadini*, 5:591.

160. De Nobili, "L'emigrazione in Calabria," 81–82.

161. Quoted in Harney, "Men without Women," 85. See also Ministero degli Affari Esteri, Commissariato dell'Emigrazione, *Bollettino dell'Emigrazione*, 53–54; Caroli, *Italian Repatriation*, 70; Reeder, *Widows in White*, 104–27.

162. M. Gibson, "Editors' Introduction," to Lombroso, *Criminal Woman*, 4.

163. C. Levi, *Christ Stopped at Eboli*, 102.

164. Reeder, *Widows in White*, 55.

165. Gabaccia, *Italy's Many Diasporas*, 85–88; Livi-Bacci, *A History of Italian Fertility*, 69–70; Reeder, "When the Men Left Sutera," 12; Reeder, *Widows in White*, 104–27.

166. Reeder, "When the Men Left Sutera," 12.

167. Ibid.

168. *Atti della giunta parlamentare per l'inchiesta agraria*, vol. 7, fasc. 1, 347.

169. Douglas, *Old Calabria*, 205.

170. C. Levi, *Christ Stopped at Eboli*, 101–2.

171. Revelli, *L'anello forte*, 58, 316, 319, 373, 326; Siebert, *"È femmina, però è bella,"* 215–16.

172. Pitrè, *Proverbi*, 2:414; Pitrè, *La famiglia*, 30, 36; Salomone-Marino, *Costumi e usanze*, 44; Navarro della Miraglia, *Storielle Siciliane*, 130–31; Messina, "La Merica," in *Piccoli gorghi*, 127–37; Chapman, *Milocca*, viii–ix, 46, 108; *Inchiesta parlementare sulle condizioni dei contadini*, 5:591; Gabaccia, *Italy's Many Diasporas*, 88; Harney, "Men without Women," 85; Reeder, *Widows in White*, chap. 2.

173. Cameron, *Radicals of the Worst Sort*, 1.

Chapter 2

1. Tina Gaeta, interview by Colomba Furio, 22 November 1976, now included in the Voices in Feminism Oral History Project, Sophia Smith Collection, Smith College, Northampton, Mass.; abridged transcript of Gaeta interview is reprinted in Furio, "Immigrant Women and Industry," 449–50.

2. Sheridan, "Italian, Slavic, and Hungarian Unskilled Immigrant Laborers," 420; U.S. Department of Commerce, Bureau of Census, *Twelfth Census of the United States: 1900*, vol. 13: *Occupations*, 634–41.

3. Gabaccia, *Italy's Many Diasporas*, 74.

4. Sassen, "Strategic Instantiations," 43.

5. Pessar, "Engendering Migration Studies."

6. Gaeta interview by Furio, 22 November 1976.

7. Gabaccia, "In the Shadows of the Periphery," 167.

8. Gamber, *The Female Economy*, 126.

9. Patriarca, "How Many Italies?," 78, 88.

10. Commissariato Generale dell'Emigrazione, *Censimento* (1882–84); Commissariato Generale dell'Emigrazione, *Censimento* (1902–4); Gabaccia, *Militants and Migrants*, 43; Audenino et al., "Storie di donne che partono," 280–83; J. Schneider, "Trousseau as Treasure," 336–38.

11. Gabaccia, *Militants and Migrants*, 43.

12. Reeder, *Widows in White*, 158; J. Schneider, "Trousseau as Treasure," 335–38.

13. Siebert, *"È femmina, però è bella,"* 201. See also Laudani, "Trasformazioni."

14. Morokvasic, "Birds of Passage Are Also Women," 888.

15. Glenn, *Unequal Freedom*, 74–76.

16. Rossi, "Vantaggi e Svantaggi," 48; *Atti della giunta per l'inchiesta agraria e sulle condizione della classe agricola (1881)*, vol. 7, fasc. 1, 14–16; Siebert, *"È femmina, però è bella,"* 197; Rogari, *Mezzogiorno ed emigrazione*, lxv–lxvi; Gabaccia, *Militants and Migrants*, 24; Reeder, *Widows in White*, 154–67; Covello, *The Heart Is the Teacher*, 10.

17. Gabaccia, *Italy's Many Diasporas*, 90–92; *Annuario statistico*, 1637–45; Cinel, *The National Integration*, 141–44; Bevilacqua, *Breve storia*, 61–62.

18. *Atti della giunta parlamentare per l'inchiesta agraria*, vol. 7, fasc. 2, 331; Siebert, *"È femmina, però è bella,"* 194–204.

19. *Atti della giunta parlamentare per l'inchiesta agraria*, vol. 7, fasc. 1, 188.

20. Ibid., 198.

21. *Giunta parlamentare d'inchiesta sulle condizione dei contadini*, vol. 5, 84.

22. *Atti della giunta parlamentare per l'inchiesta agraria*, vol. 13, fasc. 3, 672; Nitti, *Scritti sulla questione*, 281; *Giunta parlamentare d'inchiesta sulle condizione dei contadini*, vol. 5, 268; Lorenzoni, *Inchiesta parlamentare*, 140–42, 449.

23. Verga, *Tutte le novelle*; King and Okey, *Italy Today*; Douglas, *Old Calabria*; Noether, "The Silent Half," 7–8.

24. Mangano, "The Effect of Emigration upon Italy," 22.

25. Johnson, "The Backwardness of Italian Farming," 640.

26. Elwood, "The Roots and Results of Radicalism," 12.

27. Merli, *Proletariato di fabbrica*, 108–10; Ministero di agricoltura, industria e commercio, "Sul lavoro dei fanciulli e delle donne"; Gabaccia, *Militants and Migrants*, 17–25; D. Smith, *Modern Italy*, 139–42.

28. Merli, *Proletariato di fabbrica*, 90–97, 214, 239; Ellena, "La Statistica di alcune industrie italiane," 29; Ministero di agricoltura, industria e commercio, Generale della Statistica, Censimento della Popolazione del Regno d'Italia al 10 febbraio 1901, vol. 5 (1904), xci.

29. Bull, "The Lombard Silk-Spinners," 26; Noether, "The Silent Half," 7; Noce, *Gioventù senza sole*; "Organizing a women's union, Italy, 1903," in Riemer and Fout, *European Women*, 27; Birnbaum, *Liberazione della donna*, 15–18; Zappi, *If Eight Hours Seem too Few*.

30. Gabaccia, *Militants and Migrants*, 42–43.

31. Merli, *Proletariato di fabbrica*, 88, 95; Ministero di agricoltura, industria e commercio, *Censimento*, lxxxv–lxxxvi; Reeder, *Widows in White*, 157.

32. J. Schneider, "Trousseau as Treasure," 336.

33. Odencrantz, *Italian Women in Industry*, 39.

34. Dillingham, *Reports of the Immigration Commission: Immigrants in Industries*, 376; Odencrantz, *Italian Women in Industry*, 38 and table 7, 314; N. Green, *Ready-to-Wear*, 180.

35. Odencrantz, *Italian Women in Industry*, 38–50; Bernardy, "L'emigrazione delle donne," 168–84; Seidman, *The Needle Trades*, 35; Krause, *Grandmothers, Mothers, and Daughters*, 18; Furio, "Immigrant Women and Industry," 67 and reprinted interviews in Appendix D; Noether, "The Silent Half," 7; J. Smith, "Italian Mothers," 207; Ewen, *Immigrant Women*, 244; Fenton, *Immigrants and Unions*, 469; Williams, *South Italian Folkways*, 26–27.

36. "Mrs. L," interview by Colomba Furio, 2 November 1976, in Furio, "Immigrant Women and Industry," 409–10. See also Siebert, *"È femmina però è bella,"* 198; Ewen, *Immigrant Women*, 52.

37. Gamber, *The Female Economy*, esp. chap. 7.

38. "Mrs. D," interview by Colomba Furio, 20 October 1976, in Furio, "Immigrant Women and Industry," 397–98.

39. "Mrs. S," interview by Colomba Furio, 10 October 1976, in Furio, "Immigrant Women and Industry," 415.
40. "Mrs. M," interview by Colomba Furio, 2 November 1976, in Furio, "Immigrant Women and Industry," 402.
41. J. Schneider, "Trousseau as Treasure"; Silverman, *Three Bells of Civilization*, 198–99; De Clementi, "Gender Relations," 82–87; J. Schneider and P. Schneider, *Festival of the Poor*, 209–10.
42. Rogari, *Mezzogiorno ed emigrazione*, lxv–lxvi; Reeder, *Widows in White*, 147–54; Bruccoleri, *Oggi in Sicilia*, 91; Conte, *Dieci anni in America*, 11.
43. Commissariato Generale Dell'Emigrazione, *Annuario statistico*, 23, 27, 149.
44. Ibid., 178–83, 354.
45. Gabaccia, *From Sicily to Elizabeth Street*, 43; Chapman, *Milocca*, 32.
46. Reeder, *Widows in White*, 154–67; J. Schneider and P. Schneider, *Festival of the Poor*, 210, chap. 9.
47. Laudani, "Trasformazioni agricole," table 1, 120.
48. Franchetti and Sonnino, *La Sicilia nel 1876*, vol. 2, 77.
49. *Atti della giunta per l'inchiesta agraria*, 672; Gabaccia, *Militants and Migrants*, 41; J. Schneider and P. Schneider, *Festival of the Poor*, chap. 9.
50. Gabaccia, *Militants and Migrants*, 23.
51. Merli, *Proletariato di fabbrica*, 108.
52. Gabaccia, *Italy's Many Diasporas*, 89.
53. Commissariato Generale dell'Emigrazione, "L'emigrazione delle donne e dei fanciulli"; Calapso, *Donne Ribelli*, 120–38.
54. *Atti della giunta parlamentare per l'inchiesta agraria*, vol. 9, 327.
55. Ibid., vol. 11, part 1, 786.
56. Ibid., 202, 472–73.
57. Siebert, *"È femmina, però è bella,"* 201.
58. Cinel, "The Seasonal Emigration"; Gibson, *Prostitution and the State in Italy*, 116; Gabaccia, *Militants and Migrants*, 26; Gabaccia, *Italy's Many Diasporas*, 62; De Clementi, "Gender Relations," 98–99.
59. Commissariato Generale Dell'Emigrazione, *Annuario statistico*, 400–30; Baily, *Immigrants in the Lands of Promise*, 52–53.
60. Municipio di Napoli, *Relazione sul V censimento*, 32.
61. "Special Correspondence: Letters from Italy," *British Medical Journal*, 5 April 1884, 693–94; Twain, *Innocents Abroad*, 316; Nitti, *Napoli e la questione meridionale*; Pellet, *Napoli contemporanea*; "La cronaca: Il problema della salute pubblica," *Il Mattino*, 28–29 September 1910; Munthe, *Letters from a Mourning City*.
62. Munthe, *Letters from a Mourning City*.
63. Snowden, *Naples in the Time of Cholera*, 15.
64. Ibid., 30.
65. Rogari, *Mezzogiorno ed emigrazione*, 183–84.
66. Cited in Snowden, *Naples in the Time of Cholera*, 33–34.
67. Commissariato Generale Dell'Emigrazione, *Annuario statistico*, table 5; Favero and Tassello, "Cent'anni di emigrazione italiana," 9–64; Senner, "Immigration from Italy," 652; Willcox, *International Migrations*; Gabaccia, *Italy's Many Diasporas*, 67.
68. Between 1876 and 1914, close to 5,400,000 people left southern Italy, with the largest numbers emigrating from the regions of Campania (1,476,000), Sicily (1,353,000), and Calabria (879,000). Percentage of women migrants: Abruzzo/Molise (19%), Campania (27%), Puglia (21%), Basilicata (30%), Calabria (19%), Sicily (29%), Sardinia (15%). Rosoli, *Un secolo*, 19; Commissariato Generale dell'Emigrazione, *Annuario statistico*, 149.
69. Quoted in P. H. Williams, *South Italian Folkways*, 105.
70. Coser et al., *Women of Courage*, 22.

71. Ewen, *Immigrant Women*, 98, 105.

72. Bacci, *L'immigrazione e l'assimilazione*, 26; Caroli, *Italian Repatriation*; Stella, *Some Aspects*, 34; Gabaccia, *Italy's Many Diasporas*, 8; De Clementi, "Gender Relations," 79.

73. Gabaccia, *Italy's Many Diasporas*, 67.

74. "Notes to interview questions dictated by Angela Bambace to Marian, February, 1975"; Speech, 15 November 1980, Bambace Papers, IHRC; Certificate of Death 2780, Josephine Bambace, 9 April 1941, City of New York, Department of Health, Bureau of Records, Anthony Capraro Papers, box 1, IHRC; Athena Iris (Capraro) Warren, interview by author, 5 December 2005; Scarpaci, "Angela Bambace."

75. "Notes to interview questions dictated by Angela Bambace to Marian, February, 1975," Bambace Papers, IHRC.

76. The family lived at 158 East 103rd Street. Scarpaci, "Angela Bambace," 101.

77. "Notes to interview questions dictated by Angela Bambace to Marian, February, 1975," Bambace Papers, IHRC.

78. "Mrs. Concetta D.," interview by Colomba Furio, 22 September 1976, in Furio, "Immigrant Women and Industry," 407–8.

79. Odencrantz, *Italian Women in Industry*, 18, 170.

80. These figures are derived from the 1905 and 1925 New York State Manuscript Census. M. Cohen, *Workshop to Office*, 44.

81. M. Cohen, *Workshop to Office*, 42–44; Dillingham, *Immigrants in Industries*, 228; More, *Wage Earners' Budgets*; "Immigrants from Italy," *NYT*, 6 October 1895, 25.

82. Odencrantz, *Italian Women in Industry*, 18, 20, 189–90. See also Lillian Cicio, "Mama Vita," 332, *American Immigrant Autobiographies*, part I, Manuscript Autobiographies from the IHRC, microfilm #4634; More, *Wage-Earners' Budgets*; Coser et al., *Women of Courage*; Ewen, *Immigrant Women*, 124, 248; Gabaccia, *Italy's Many Diasporas*, 101–3.

83. Odencrantz, *Italian Women in Industry*; Mathias and Raspa, *Italian Folktales in America*, 272; Ewen, *Immigrant Women*, 52; Coser et al., *Women of Courage*, 69–70, 73–75; Gabaccia, *Militants and Migrants*, chap. 3.

84. Odencrantz, *Italian Women in Industry*, 44, 304; Odencrantz, "The Italian Seamstress," in Stein, *Out of the Sweatshop*, 62–3; Covello, *The Heart Is the Teacher*, 4–5.

85. Gabaccia and Iacovetta, *Women, Gender, and Transnational Lives*, 16.

86. Commissariato Generale Dell'Emigrazione, *Annuario statistico*; Favero and Tassello, "Cent'anni," 16; Gabaccia and Iacovetta, *Women, Gender, and Transnational Lives*, 5; *Altreitalie* 9 (1993).

87. Commissariato Generale dell'Emigrazione, *Annuario statistico*, 74–75, 145, 149, 150–51; Rosoli, *Un secolo*, 19.

88. Baily, "Italian Immigrants"; Moya, "Italians in Buenos Aires's Anarchist Movement," 191, table 6.1.

89. Baily, *Immigrants in the Land of Promise*, 70, 79, 98–99; Baily, "The Italians and the Development of Organized Labor"; Moya, *Cousins and Strangers*, 49–50; Silberstein, "Immigrants and Female Work in Argentina," 198.

90. Moya, *Cousins and Strangers*; Silberstein, "Migrants, Farmers, and Workers"; Molyneux, "No God, No Boss, No Husband," 120.

91. Baily, *Immigrants in the Land of Promise*, 54.

92. Silberstein, "Immigrants and Female Work in Argentina," 196. See also 199, table 1.

93. Baily, *Immigrants in the Land of Promise*, 61.

94. Silberstein, "Italianos en Rosario," table 2.

95. Moya, "Italians in Buenos Aires's Anarchist Movement," 189, 191.

96. Baily, *Immigrants in the Land of Promise*, 54–59, 100–1; Baily, "The Italians and the Development of Organized Labor," 125.

97. Moya, *Cousins and Strangers*, 55–56.

98. Guy, "Women, Peonage, and Industrialization," 77.

99. Silberstein, "Immigrants and Female Work in Argentina," 209–12; Molyneux, "No God, No Boss, No Husband," 125; Moya, *Cousins and Strangers*, 228; Guy, *Sex and Danger in Buenos Aires*, 16.

100. Guy, "Women, Peonage, and Industrialization," 78–80; Guy, *Sex and Danger in Buenos Aires*; Munck et al., *Argentina*, 45–47; Moya, *Cousins and Strangers*, 223–24.

101. Moya, "Italians in Buenos Aires's Anarchist Movement," 201; Molyneux, "No God, No Boss, No Husband."

102. Moya, *Cousins and Strangers*, 357, 382.

103. Baer, "Tenant Mobilization," 359; Moya, "Italians in Buenos Aires's Anarchist Movement," 202–8.

104. Both quotes from Moya, "Italians in Buenos Aires's Anarchist Movement," 203.

105. Baer, "Tenant Mobilization"; Moya, "Italians in Buenos Aires's Anarchist Movement," 203, 210; Bellucci and Camusso, *La huelga de inquilinos de 1907*.

106. Moya, "Italians in Buenos Aires's Anarchist Movement," 210; Silberstein, "Migrants, Farmers, and Workers," 80.

107. Moya, "Italians in Buenos Aires's Anarchist Movement," 208–9.

108. Ibid.

109. Ibid., 189–95.

110. Baily, *Immigrants in the Land of Promise*, 79–83; Baer, "Tenant Mobilization," 350.

111. Sarmiento to Victorino Lastarria, Santiago, Chile, 18 January 1853, in *Correspondencia entre Sarmiento y Lastarria, 1844–1888*, ed. María L. del Pino de Carbone (Buenos Aires, 1954), quoted in Moya, *Cousins and Strangers*, 49.

112. Gabaccia, "Race, Nation, Hyphen," 49.

113. Moya, *Cousins and Strangers*, 219.

114. Ibid., 73.

115. Ibid., 348.

116. Ibid., 347–48.

117. Quote from Cara-Walker, "Cocoliche." See also Gabaccia, "Race, Nation, Hyphen," 48–50.

118. Trento, "Wherever We Work," 102.

119. Alvim, *Brava Gente!*, 62; Holloway, *Immigrants on the Land*, 42; Cenni, *Italianos no Brasil*, 173; Commissariato Generale dell'Emigrazione, *Annuario statistico*, 152. See also Giron, "L'immigrata in Brasile"; Felici, "Gli anarchici italiani"; Felici, *La Cecilia*; De Souza, *O anarquismo da Colônia Cecília*; Rodrigues and Chersi, *Lavoratori italiani in Brasile*; Wolfe, "Anarchist Ideology"; Wolfe, *Working Women, Working Men*; Trento, "Wherever We Work"; Andrews, *Blacks and Whites in São Paulo*; Veccia, "Family and Factory."

120. Trento, "Wherever We Work," 104.

121. Veccia, "Family and Factory," 23; Veccia, "'My Duty as a Woman,'" 102.

122. Wolfe, *Working Women*, 7.

123. Ibid., chap. 1; Veccia, "Family and Factory."

124. Wolfe, "There Should be Dignity," 193; Veccia, "Family and Factory," chap. 2.

125. Wolfe, *Working Women*, 33.

126. Damiani, *I paesi*, 32.

127. Quoted in Andrews, "Black and White," 495.

128. Andrews, "Black and White," 498.

129. Quoted in ibid.

130. Trento, "Wherever We Work," 110.

131. Holloway, *Immigrants on the Land*, 105.

132. Quoted in Andrews, "Black and White Workers," 499, 502; Holloway, *Immigrants on the Land*, 48–49; Lesser, *Negotiating National Identity*, 34, 82.

133. Holloway, *Immigrants on the Land*, 37, 42–43.

134. U.S. Department of Commerce, Bureau of Census, *Twelfth Census of the United States: 1900*, vol. 5: *Population*, 732; *Thirteenth Census of the United States: 1910*, vol. 3: *Population*, 216, 240; *Fourteenth Census of the United States: 1920*, vol. 3: *Population*, 710.

135. Soyer, *A Coat of Many Colors*, 3–7; N. Green, *Ready-to-Wear*, 46–44.

136. U.S. Department of Commerce, Bureau of Census, *Twelfth Census of the United States: 1900*, vol. 13: *Occupations*, 634–41.

137. Dillingham, *Immigrants in Industries*, part 6, 384.

138. Commissariate Generale dell'Emigrazione, *Annuario statistico*, 619; U.S. Department of Commerce, Bureau of the Census, *Women in Gainful Occupations*, esp. chaps. 5, 6; Bernardy, "L'emigrazione delle donne"; Gabaccia and Iacovetta, "Women, Work, and Protest," 168; M. Cohen, *Workshop to Office*, 45.

139. Gabaccia, "Peopling 'Little Italy,'" 47.

140. Gabaccia, *From Sicily to Elizabeth Street*, 63.

141. Dillingham, *Immigrants in Industries*, part 6, 376; and table 57, 546.

142. Willett, *The Employment of Women*, 65; Odencrantz, *Italian Women and Industry*, 43; U.S. Department of Labor, *Regularity of Employment in the Women's Ready-to-Wear*, 18–22; Seidman, *The Needle Trades*, 36; N. Green, *Ready-to-Wear*, 175–183.

143. "Mrs. D," interview by Colomba Furio, 20 October 1976, reprinted in Furio, "Immigrant Women and Industry," 397–98.

144. U.S. Department of Commerce, Bureau of Census, *Twelfth Census of the United States: 1900*, vol. 13: *Occupations*, 634–41. See also Gabaccia, *Militants and Migrants*, 76–97, 127–36; Gabaccia, *From Sicily to Elizabeth Street*, 61–64; Starr, *The Italians of New Jersey*, 12–14.

145. Willett, *The Employment of Women*, 78–79, 90–92, 110–13; Van Kleeck, *Artificial Flower Makers*, 58–89; Carnevale, "Culture of Work," 160–61.

146. U.S. Department of Labor, Bureau of Labor Statistics, *Wages and Regularity of Employment*, 8; Dillingham, *Immigrants in Industries*, part 6, 370, 385; Bernardy, "L'emigrazione delle donne," 9, 22–24, 38–61; Watson, "Homework in the Tenements."

147. U.S. Department of Commerce, Bureau of Census, *Twelfth Census of the United States: 1900*, vol. 13: *Occupations*, 638; Odencrantz, *Italian Women in Industry*, 32; Van Kleeck, *Artificial Flower Makers*, 31–34.

148. Dillingham, *Immigrants in Industries*, part 6, 366–67.

149. U.S. Department of Labor, *Regularity of Employment in the Women's Ready-to-Wear*, 17. See also Dillingham, *Immigrants in Industries*, part 6, 369–73; Willett, *The Employment of Women*, 33–34, 38; Seidman, *The Needle Trades*, 31–36; Bender, *Sweated Work*, 31; N. Green, *Ready-to-Wear*, 30–21; Gamber, *The Female Economy*; and Stansall, "The Origins of the Sweatshop."

150. On men's clothing, see U.S. Congress, Senate, *Report on Condition of Woman and Child Wage Earners*, 2: *Men's Ready-Made Clothing*, 45. For the clothing industry as a whole, see U.S. Congress, Senate, *Report of the Immigration Commission*, vol. 11: *Immigrants in Industries*, part 6, 372.

151. Willett, *The Employment of Women*, 31; N. Green, *Ready-to-Wear*, esp. chap. 1.

152. Dillingham, *Immigrants in Industries*, part 6, 385; NYSDOL, *Report of the Growth*, 88, 93; NYSDOL, *Seventh Annual Report of the Factory Inspectors*, 112–211 (1893); Pope, *The Clothing Industry*, 28; Bender, *Sweated Work*, 23–35; Soyer, "Introduction," in *A Coat of Many Colors*, 4–5; N. Green, *Ready-to-Wear*; M. Cohen, *Workshop to Office*, 47; Glenn, *Daughters of the Shtetl*, 106–22.

153. Odencrantz, *Italian Women in Industry*, 45, 52, 119–20, 178; Van Kleeck, *Artificial Flower Makers*, 38; M. Cohen, *Workshop to Office*, 65.

154. Dillingham, *Immigrants in Industries*, part 6, 385–86.

155. Odencrantz, *Italian Women in Industry*, 45, 52, 119–20, 178; M. Cohen, *Workshop to Office*, 65; N. Green, *Ready-to-Wear*, 203, 351.

156. Van Kleeck, *Artificial Flower Makers*, 94–95; Willett, *The Employment of Women*, 118–133; U.S. Senate, *Report on Condition of Woman and Child Wage Earners* (1911), 2:300.

157. Dillingham, *Immigrants in Industries*, part 6, 385–86; Willett, *The Employment of Women*, 94–8, 109–10, 273–74; Van Kleeck, *Artificial Flower Makers*, 96; Van Kleeck, "Child Labor in New York City Tenements"; Seidman, *The Needle Trades*, 36; Bernardy, "L'emigrazione delle donne," 34–37; Watson, "Homework in the Tenements."

158. Willett, *The Employment of Women*, 106.

159. "Mrs. R," interview by Colomba Furio, 6 October 1976, in Furio, "Immigrant Women and Industry," 399–400.

160. Bernardy, "L'emigrazione delle donne," 9; Willett, *The Employment of Women*, 100; Odencrantz, *Italian Women in Industry*, 44; Carnevale, "Culture of Work," 149–50; N. Green, *Ready-to-Wear*, 184; Fenton, *Immigrants and Unions*, 467–69.

161. Carnevale, "Culture of Work," 151–52; Gabaccia, *From Sicily to Elizabeth Street*, 64.

162. Willett, *The Employment of Women*, 63, 103; Van Kleeck, *Artificial Flower Makers*, 99–117; Bernardy, "L'emigrazione delle donne," 38–47, 168–84; Odencrantz, *Italian Women in Industry*, 106–7, 257; Cicio, "Mama Vita"; Stella, "From Italy's Fields to Manhattan's Sweatshops"; Fenton, *Immigrants and Unions*, 468–69; Furio, "Immigrant Women and Industry"; M. Cohen, *Workshop to Office*, 47–51; Ewen, *Immigrant Women*, 248–49; Gabaccia, *From Sicily to Elizabeth Street*, 92.

163. M. Cohen, *Workshop to Office*, 48; Seidman, *The Needle Trades*, 62–63; Van Kleeck, "Child Labor"; Van Kleeck, "Working Hours"; Sergeant, "Toilers of the Tenements," 239; Van Kleeck, *Artificial Flower Makers*, 40–57; Carnevale, "Culture of Work," 155; Boris, *Home to Work*, 186.

164. Coser et al., *Women of Courage*, 97–98; Gabaccia, *From Sicily to Elizabeth Street*, 59, 80–81, 93; Gabaccia, *Militants and Migrants*, 132; Odencrantz, *Italian Women in Industry*, 226; Bernardy, "L'emigrazione delle donne," 8, 16–17, 168–84; Modell and Hareven, "Urbanization and the Malleable Household."

165. Watson, "Homework in the Tenements"; "Characteristics of Italian Immigrants," *NYT*, 18 May 1902, 12; "Saving the Lives of Babies," *NYT*, 3 July 1910, 11.

166. Boris, *Home to Work*, 2; Boris, "Sexual Divisions," 20.

167. Van Kleeck, *Artificial Flower Makers*, 228–35.

168. Dillingham, *Immigrants in Industries*, part 6, table 66.

169. Golin, *The Fragile Bridge*; Elwood, "The Roots and Results of Radicalism"; Hutchins, *Labor and Silk*, 178–82; Bernardy, "L'emigrazione delle donne," 51–61.

170. Bernardy, "L'emigrazione delle donne," 69; "Picking Berries in Jersey," *BDE*, 17 June 1901, 9; Starr, *The Italians of New Jersey*; Goldberg, *A Tale of Three Cities*.

171. M. Cohen, *Workshop to Office*, 67; Van Kleeck, *Artificial Flower Makers*, 118–43.

172. Hutchins, *Labor and Silk*, 114–25.

173. Ibid., 117.

174. Odencrantz, *Italian Women in Industry*, 54–107; Hutchins, *Labor and Silk*, 114–27; Van Kleeck, *Artificial Flower Makers*, 23–39; M. Cohen, *Workshop to Office*, 66–67; Ewen, *Immigrant Women*, 246–55.

175. "Mrs. R," interview by Colomba Furio, 6 October 1976.

176. Willett, *The Employment of Women*, 73–77.

177. Hutchins, *Labor and Silk*, 106.

178. Quoted in Jacobson, *Barbarian Virtues*, 69.

179. Concetta D., interview by Colomba Furio, 22 September 1976, in Furio, "Immigrant Women and Industry," 408.

180. "Fra i tessitori, Lo sciopero di Hackensack," *Il Bollettino della Sera*, 17 December 1909; Odencrantz, *Italian Women in Industry*, 41; Grace Billoti Spinelli Autobiography, *American Immigrant Autobiographies*, part I, Manuscript Autobiographies from the IHRC, microfilm #4634, 34; Ewen, *Immigrant Women*, 244–47; Gutman, *Work, Culture, and Society*, 13.

181. Carolina Golzio, interview by Steve Golin, 13 June 1983, SSC.

182. Willett, *The Employment of Women*, 35–40, 65; M. Cohen, *Workshop to Office*, 63–64.

183. Hutchins, *Labor and Silk*, 26, 109.

184. Parker, *Working with the Working Woman*, 17, 28; Hutchins, *Labor and Silk*, 141; Odencrantz, *Italian Women in Industry*, 59–60; *Lotta di Classe*, 18 December 1914; reprinted interviews in Furio, "Immigrant Women and Industry"; M. Cohen, *Workshop to Office*, esp. chap. 2.

185. M. Cohen, *Workshop to Office*, 60–64; Scarpaci, "Angela Bambace," 101. See also Gaeta, Lazzaro, and "Mrs. D" interviews in Furio, "Immigrant Women and Industry," 453, 473, 397; Josephine Roche, "The Italian Girl," 95–8; Odencrantz, *Italian Women in Industry*, 273.

186. Odencrantz, *Italian Women in Industry*, 13, 25, 43; Enstad, *Ladies of Labor*, 61–62.

187. "Mrs. M," interview by Columba Furio, 2 December 1976.

188. Odencrantz, *Italian Women in Industry*, 13, 25, 43.

189. Ewen, *Immigrant Women*, 275.

190. Parker, *Working with the Working Woman*, 117.

191. Drukman, "Suzan-Lori Parks and Liz Diamond."

192. Frank, "White Working-Class Women," 83.

193. Parker, *Working with the Working Woman*, 258.

Chapter 3

1. McClintock, *Imperial Leather*, 22.

2. Simkhovitch, *Greenwich House*, October 1909, 17.

3. Newman, *White Women's Rights*, 86.

4. Mumford, *Interzones*, xvii.

5. Revelli, *L'anello forte*, 122.

6. De Lesser, *Voyage en Italie*, 86; Gribaudi, "Images of the South," 87; Verdicchio, *Bound by Distance*, 22; P. H. Williams, *South Italian Folkways*, 1.

7. Gramsci, *The Southern Question*; Verdicchio, *Bound by Distance*; J. Schneider, *Italy's "Southern Question,"* 4–8; Patriarca, "How Many Italies?," 77.

8. Pick, "The Faces of Anarchy," 63.

9. D. Smith, "The Peasants Revolt," 212; Nicotri, *Rivoluzioni*, 126.

10. Patriarca, "How Many Italies?," 81–87; Dickie, "Imagined Italies"; Dickie, *Darkest Italy*; Gribaudi, "Images of the South"; J. Schneider, *Italy's "Southern Question"*; Lumley and Morris, *The New History of the Italian South*; Moe, "Altro che Italia!"; Moe, "'This is Africa.'"

11. Rogari, *Mezzogiorno ed emigrazione*, 427.

12. Gabaccia, *Italy's Many Diasporas*, 52.

13. Quoted in Dickie, *Darkest Italy*, 35.

14. Gribaudi, "Images of the South," 75.

15. Niceforo, *L'Italia barbara*, 181. See also Niceforo, *La delinquenza in Sardegna*; Niceforo, *Italiani del nord e italiani del sud*; Lombroso, *L'uomo bianco*; Lombroso, *L'uomo delinquente*; Lombroso, *In Calabria*; Sergi, *Ari e italici*; Renda, *La questione meridionale*.

16. Renda, *La questione meridionale*, 124.

17. Gibson, "Biology or Environment?," 99.

18. Gibson, *Born to Crime*, 19; Lombroso, *In Calabria*.

19. D'Agostino, "Craniums, Criminals, and the 'Cursed Race,'" 322; Gibson, "Race and 'Deviancy,'" 101; Gibson, *Born to Crime*, 62–64; Gibson, "On the Insensitivity of Women"; Gibson, "Biology or Environment?"; J. Schneider, *Italy's "Southern Question"*; Dickie, *Darkest Italy*; Bongiovani, "The Question of the South," and "Anthology of the Problem of the South," both in Pirovano, *Modern Italy*, vol. 1, 89–98, and vol. 2, 41–61; Stepan, *"The Hour of Eugenics,"* 51, 114–15; Cinel, *The National Integration*, 3, 11–44; Verdicchio, *Bound by Distance*, 21–29; Teti, *La razza maledetta*; Pick, "The Faces of Anarchy"; Rafter, *Creating Born Criminals*; Pick, *Faces of Degeneration*; Horn, *The Criminal Body*; Becker and Wetzell, *Criminals and Their Scientists*; Lombroso and Ferrero, *Criminal*

Woman; Lombroso, *Criminal Man*; Lombroso, "Criminal Anthropology"; Lombroso, *In Calabria*; Lombroso, *L'uomo bianco*.

20. Dickie, "Stereotypes of the Italian South," 135.
21. Gramsci, *The Southern Question*, 20–21. See also Gibson, "Biology or Environment?," 112; Gibson, "The 'Female Offender,'" 158–59; D'Agostino, "Craniums, Criminals, and the 'Cursed Race'"; Gramsci, "Alcuni temi della questione meridionale," 137–58; Forgacs, *An Antonio Gramsci Reader*.
22. J. Schneider, *Italy's "Southern Question*," 11; Gibson, *Born to Crime*, 112; Filippucci, "Anthropological Perspectives on Culture in Italy"; Clemente et al., *Il dibattito sul folklore in Italia*; Colajanni, *Gli avvenimenti*; Colajanni, *l'Italia nel 1898*; Salvemini, *Scritti sulla questione meridionale*; Nitti, *Scritti sulla questione meridionale*; Killinger, *Gaetano Salvemini*.
23. McClintock, *Imperial Leather*, 5.
24. Niceforo, *L'Italia barbara contemporanea*, 6.
25. Nievo, *Lettere* garibaldine, quoted in Verdicchio, *Bound by Distance*, 35.
26. Gibson, *Born to Crime*, chap. 2.
27. Ibid., 105. See also Lombroso, *L'uomo delinquente*, 29.
28. J. Schneider, *Italy's "Southern Question*," 10–11.
29. Quoted in Gibson, "On the Insensitivity," 21.
30. Gilman, *Difference and Pathology*, 107.
31. Lombroso and Ferrero, *Criminal Woman*, 186–87.
32. Gibson, *Born to Crime*, 60–67; Trupia, "La donna e gli studi," 231.
33. Douglas, *Old Calabria*, 206.
34. Reeder, *Widows in White*, 56. See, for example, Mosso, *Vita Moderna*, 13–14; Conte, *Dieci anni in America*, 11.
35. Harding, *The Science Question*, 68.
36. Key texts include González, *Refusing the Favor*; Castañeda, "Sexual Violence"; Castillo, *Massacre of the Dreamers*; Minh-ha, *Woman, Native, Other*; Balce, "The Filipina's Breast"; Sharpley-Whiting, *Black Venus*; Shohat and Stam, *Unthinking Eurocentrism*; Stoler, "Carnal Knowledge"; Stoler, *Haunted by Empire*; McClintock, *Imperial Leather*; Bederman, *Manliness and Civilization*; Briggs, "The Race of Hysteria"; Briggs, *Reproducing Empire*; Kaplan, *The Anarchy of Empire*; Kaplan and Pease, *Cultures of United States Imperialism*; Jacobson, *Whiteness of a Different Color*, esp. chap. 1.
37. McClintock, *Imperial Leather*, 22, 24, 31.
38. Gilman, *Difference and Pathology*, 76–108; Lombroso, *Criminal Woman*.
39. Douglas, *Old Calabria*, 299.
40. Verdicchio, *Bound by Distance*, 27. See also Goglia, *Il colonialismo italiano*; Gramsci, *Il Risorgimento*, 75–81.
41. Bixio, *Epistolario*, 143, quoted in Dickie, *Darkest Italy*, 35.
42. Pernicone, *Italian Anarchism*, 3.
43. Ibid., 40–42; 284–94; Nettlau, *Bakunin e l'Internazionale*, 227–28; Romano, *Storia*, 2: 104–15, 210–11; Buccellato and Iaccio, *Gli anarchici*, 291–97.
44. Pick, "The Faces of Anarchy," 68.
45. Ibid., 76.
46. Ibid., 78.
47. Lombroso, *Criminal Man*, 118.
48. Ibid., 67.
49. Gibson, *Born to Crime*, 2.
50. See, for example, J. Schneider, *Italy's "Southern Question."*
51. D'Agostino, "Craniums, Criminals, and the 'Cursed Race,'" 328.
52. Dickie, *Darkest Italy*, 35; Verdicchio, *Bound by Distance*, 27. See also *Atti della giunta parlamentare per l'inchiesta agraria*, vol. 3, fasc. 2, 611, 615.
53. Covello, *The Social Background*, 181.

54. Pitrè, *La famiglia*, 7.

55. "Only Birds of Passage," *NYT*, 28 July 1888, 8.

56. D'Agostino, "Craniums, Criminals, and the 'Cursed Race,'" 332.

57. "Undesirable Immigrants," *NYT*, 18 December 1880, 4. See also U.S. Immigration Commission, *Dictionary of Races and Peoples* (1911), 81, 82; Ross, *The Old World in the New*, 95–119.

58. For Lombroso's publications in the U.S., see "The Ultimate Triumph of the Boers," "Why Homicide Has Increased in the United States," "Criminal Anthropology," and English translations of his texts: *Criminal Woman* and *Criminal Man*. For his colleagues, see Ferri, *Criminal Sociology, Socialism and Modern Science*, and *The Positive School of Sociology*; and Sergi, *the Mediterranean Race*. See also the following articles in *NYT*: "Scientific Aspects of Crime," 23 January 1893; "Criminal Women," 18 May 1895; "Lombroso's Criminal through Passion," 4 October 1895; "Criminality a Disease," 18 October 1895; "Criminology and Education," 30 December 1897; "Italian Anarchism," 21 October 1900; "Homicide and the Italians," 24 March 1901; "Cesare Lombroso," 20 October 1909. See the following in the *Washington Post*: "Scientific Palmistry," 7 August 1907; "Study of Murderess," 4 July 1908; "Death of Lombroso," 21 October 1909. On the influence of Lombroso and his colleagues in the Americas, see Jones, *History of Criminology*, 81–125; Salvatore, "Criminology"; Dyer, *Theodore Roosevelt*, 13; D'Agostino, "Craniums, Criminals, and the 'Cursed Race,'" 328–39; Gabaccia, "Race, Nation, Hyphen," 52–56.

59. U.S. Immigration Commission, *Dictionary of Races or People*, 9, 81–82; *Annual Report of the Commissioner-General of Immigration* (1899), 5, (1901), 9; D'Agostino, "Craniums, Criminals, and the 'Cursed Race,'" 330.

60. U.S. Immigration Commission, *Dictionary of Races or People*, 82.

61. D'Agostino, "Craniums, Criminals, and the 'Cursed Race,'" 330.

62. Ibid.

63. U.S. Immigration Commission, *Dictionary of Races or People*, 82.

64. T. Guglielmo, *White on Arrival*, 24.

65. Ibid., 30.

66. D'Agostino, "Craniums, Criminals, and the 'Cursed Race,'" 323.

67. T. Guglielmo, *White on Arrival*, 7–10.

68. Gabaccia, "Race, Nation, Hyphen," 51.

69. "Only Birds of Passage," *NYT*, 28 July 1888.

70. T. Guglielmo, *White on Arrival*, 8; DeSalvo, "Color: White / Complexion: Dark," in J. Guglielmo and Salerno, *Are Italians White?*

71. Hodes, "Fractions and Fictions," 241.

72. T. Guglielmo, *White on Arrival*, 30; Haney-Lopez, *White By Law*, chap. 2; Jacobson, *Whiteness of a Different Color*, 223–45.

73. Because most worked illegally, the numbers of homeworkers were notoriously difficult to calculate. For estimates, see Van Kleeck, "Child Labor"; NYSDOL, *Annual Report of the Industrial Commission* (1919), 38; NYSDOL, *Twentieth Annual Report of the Bureau of Labor Statistics* (1903), 65; Carnevale, "Culture of Work"; M. Cohen, *Workshop to Office*, 47–51.

74. *Twentieth Annual Report of the Bureau of Labor Statistics*, 60; Willett, *The Employment of Women*, 102.

75. U.S. Congress, Senate, *Report on Condition of Woman and Child Wage Earners*, 35, 221; U.S. Congress, Senate, *Reports of the Immigration Commission*, 20; Van Kleeck, *Artificial Flower Makers*, 218; Bender, *Sweated Work*, 65.

76. Magee, *Trends in Location*, 72–74; N. Green, "From Downtown," 32.

77. Willett, *The Employment of Women*, 96–97, 115; U.S. Department of Commerce, Bureau of Census, *Twelfth Census of the United States: 1900*, vol. 3: *Occupations*, table 43; Gabaccia, *From Sicily to Elizabeth Street*, 63.

78. Watson, "Homework in the Tenements," 775; Willett, *The Employment of Women*, 260–62; Van

Kleeck, *Artificial Flower Makers*, 92; Bernardy, "L'emigrazione delle donne," 9; Simkhovitch, *Greenwich House*, January 1913, 16; Carnevale, "Culture of Work," 147; Gabaccia, *From Sicily to Elizabeth Street*, 64.

79. Watson, "Homework in the Tenements."

80. *NYT*, 12 May 1901, 22.

81. Adams, "Italian Life in New York," 676.

82. Ibid.

83. Willett, *The Employment of Women*, 89–93, 119–20; Van Kleeck, *Artificial Flower Makers*, 30–37, 93, 113; Seidman, *The Needle Trades*, 36; NYSDOL, *Annual Report of the Factory Inspectors of the State of New York* (1898), 759; Watson, "Homework in the Tenements."

84. Sergeant, "Toilers of the Tenements," 232.

85. *Reports of the Industrial Commission on Immigration*, vol. 15 (1901), 372–73.

86. Riis, *How the Other Half Lives*, 124.

87. Bender, *Sweated Work*, 62–65; "The Slaves of the Sweaters," *Harper's Weekly* 34, 26 April 1890, 335; John De Witt Warner, "Sweating System," *Harper's Weekly* 39, 9 February 1895; E. L. Godkin, "Our Sweating System," *Nation* 50 (June 1890); McKay, "The Effect upon the Health," 88–89; Irwin, "The Story of a Transplanted Industry"; Bernardy, "L'emigrazione delle donne," 14.

88. Quote from speech given by Annie S. Daniel from the New York Infirmary for Women and Children before the annual meeting of the New York City Consumers League, "The Wreck of the Home," *Charities*, 1 April 1905. See also *Fourteenth Annual Report of the Factory Inspectors of the State of New York*, 42; Hunter, *To 'Joy My Freedom*, 154; Kang, *Compositional Subjects*, esp. chap. 3; Gross, *Colored Amazons*.

89. "The Sinister Myth," *Washington Post*, 5 March 1911. For reports in *NYT*, see "Brigandage in Italy," 28 May 1865; "Brigandage: A Traveler's Views of Brigand Life in Italy," 29 October 1865; "Brigandage—Inability of the Government to Suppress It," 6 August 1868; "Brigandage: The Brigands of South Italy," 16 October 1868; "Brigands," 5 March 1871; "Modern Banditti," 18 April 1871; "Filippo, the Bandit," 17 February 1872; "Brigandage: The Latest Evidence of Its Vitality," 8 August 1872; "Sicilian Brigandage," 1 September 1874; "Modern Brigandage in Italy," 27 December 1874; "Brigandage in Italy," 30 August 1875; "Indignant Robbers," 31 August 1875; "The Vendetta," 19 January 1879; "Brigandage," 20 June 1881; "Our Brigands," 1 January 1884; "An Italian Romance: The Mother of Twelve Brigands Robbed by Her Husband," 3 February 1890; "Brigands Thrive in Italy," 15 September 1892; "Sicily and Her Bandits," 24 October 1892; "The Brigands of Sicily," 20 January 1895; "Italy's Increased Brigandage," 31 August 1895; "Italy Hunting Brigands," 19 November 1899; "Raid on the Mafia," 2 May 1900; "Italy and the Mafia," 19 November 1900; "Italian Secret Societies," 27 July 1902; "The 'Black Hand' and Brigandage," 12 April 1908. See also the following in the *Washington Post*: "The Sicilian Bandit," 13 July 1881; "Brigands in Italy," 30 July 1890; "Sworn to Evil Ways," 12 June 1891; "Anarchy Exists There," 4 November 1894; "Terrorized by Italian Mafia," 7 January 1900; "Where Brigandage Still Exists," 18 March 1900; "Robbery Recognized Profession," 20 September 1908; "Life under the Camorra," 2 April 1911.

90. U.S. Immigration Commission, *Dictionary of Races or People*, 82; "Italian Life in New York," in *Harper's Magazine*, New York, 240; Train, "Imported Crime."

91. Senner, "Immigration from Italy," 650. See also *NYT*, 12 May 1901, 22; McLaughlin, "Italians and Other Latin Immigrants"; "Work among Italian Immigrants," *Charities* 10 (7 February 1903); "Latin Element in the United States," *NYT*, 12 May 1901; "The Sinister Myth," *Washington Post*, 5 March 1911. For scholarship on the racialized criminalization of Italians see D'Agostino, "Craniums, Criminals, and the 'Cursed Race,'" 332–34; Higham, *Strangers in the Land*, 66, 90–92; LaGumina, *Wop!*; De Stefano, *An Offer We Can't Refuse*; T. Guglielmo, *White on Arrival*, chap. 4.

92. Morgan, "What Shall We Do with the Dago?," 172–77.

93. Ross, "Italians in America," 440, 445.

94. Higham, *Strangers in the Land*, 160. See also Gabaccia, "Inventing 'Little Italy'"; Pozzetta, "The

Mulberry District," 23. For newspaper articles on the Black Hand, see next note. For articles on the *mafia* and *camorra*, see the following articles in *NYT*: "The Camorra," 23 July 1882; "The Vendetta in New York," 23 April 1883; "A Branch of the Camorra Said to Be Established in New York," 21 February 1885; "A Pupil of the Camorra," 22 February 1885; "The Camorra," 15 March 1885; "Neapolitan Cruelty," 23 July 1885; "The Mafia on Its Own Soil," 27 April 1891; "Two Italian Societies," 4 June 1891; "The 'Mala Vita' Society," 12 June 1891; "Mafia's Code in New York," 16 May 1893; "Ready with a Knife or Pistol," 16 May 1893. See also "Mafia's Bloody Hand," *Washington Post*, 11 August 1895. For magazine articles, see "The Camorra," *Eclectic Magazine of Foreign Literature* 41:3 (March 1885); Morgan, "Secret Societies in the Two Sicilies"; "The Mafia in Sicily," *Littell's Living Age* 189:2449 (6 June 1891); "The Two Sicilies and the Camorra," *American Catholic Quarterly Review* 16:64 (October 1891); "Stories of Naples and Camorra," *Literary World* 28:6 (20 March 1897); Denison, "Black Hand"; "The Growing Black-Hand Problem," *Literary Digest* 37:7 (15 August 1908); "Blackmail and Murder," *Outlook* 91 (27 March 1909); "Undesirable Citizens," *Independent* 66 (1 April 1909); "Black Hand Sway in Italian New York," *Literary Digest* 47 (30 August 1913): 308. See also Hartt, "Made in Italy," 20; Pecorini, "The Italians in the United States"; "To Rid This Country of Foreign Criminals," *Harper's Weekly* 52 (27 June 1908); Watchorn, "Black Hand and the Immigrant"; Bennett, "Immigrants and Crime"; White, "Fostering Foreign Criminals"; White, "Against the Black Hand"; White, "The Black Hand in Control"; White, "How the United States Fosters"; White, "The Passing of the Black Hand"; Warner, "Amputating the Black Hand"; Carr, "The Coming of the Italian"; Train, "Imported Crime"; Reid, "Death Sign"; "Black Hand Scourge," *Cosmopolitan*, June 1909; Turner, "Tammany's Control"; Turner, "The Daughters of the Poor"; Woods, "Problem of the Black Hand"; "Scrubbing Italy's 'Black Hand,'" *Literary Digest*, 15 April 1911; "The Growing Black-Hand Problem," *Literary Digest* 15 August 1908; "Uncle Sam to Fight the Black Hand," *Literary Digest*, 19 June 1915.

95. Mangione and Morreale, *La Storia*, 166–67. See also Pitkin and Cordasco, *The Black Hand*. For reproductions of "Black Hand" letters from New York City, see Fiaschetti, *You Gotta Be Rough* (1930), IHRC Print Collection, 131, 134.

Of the thousands of articles on the subject in *NYT*, see, for example, a sampling of those that appeared in 1905: "'Black Hand' Bomb," 5 January 1905; "True Story of the Origin of 'The Black Hand,'" 8 January 1905; "A Black Hand Band, Maybe," 9 January 1905; "Held as Black Hand Chief," 15 January 1905; "Threatened by Black Hand," 10 March 1905; "Black Hand Throws Bomb," 11 May 1905; "Dynamited by Black Hand," 23 May 1905; "Black-Hand Man Free," 21 June 1905; "Move or Be Blown Up," 24 June 1905; "The Land of the 'Black Hand,'" 2 July 1905; "Killed Black Hand Agent," 7 July 1905; "'Black Hand' Scare," 9 July 1905; "Black Hand Threats," 11 September 1905; "Bomb Explodes on Doorstep," 21 September 1905; "Explosion Injures Three," 21 September 1905; "Threat of More Bombs Scares First Avenue," 22 September 1905; "A Black Hand Haul Afloat," 23 September 1905; "Explosion Wrecks Shop," 29 September 1905; "Traps 'Black Hand' Men," 30 September 1905; "Boy Tells of Woman Held by Kidnappers," 7 October 1905; "A Black Hand Four," 12 October 1905; "New York is Full of Italian Brigands," 15 October 1905; "Petrosino Asks Aid to Catch Brigands," 18 October 1905; "The Black Hand," 29 December 1905.

For a small fraction of those from other years, see the following articles in *NYT*: "The Vendetta in New York," 23 April 1883; "The Mafia in New Orleans," 17 March 1891; "Mafia's Code in New York," 16 May 1893; "Ready with Knife or Pistol," 16 May 1893; "A Mafia in New York," 5 August 1900; "The Italian as a Citizen," 23 June 1904, 8; "Black Hand Scared Mothers," 30 September 1904; "Threat of Kidnapping in Blackmail Letter," 15 January 1906; "Shot in Black Hand Row," 30 April 1906; "Defied Black Hand," 20 July 1906; "Wholesale Murders," 21 August 1906; "Dynamite for Saloon," 16 August 1906; "Wholesale Murders in Watershed Region," 21 August 1906; "Dynamite for Saloon," 26 August 1906; "A 'Black Hand' Haul," 27 August 1906; "Black Hand Leaders Caught," 25 October 1906; "Bomb Wrecks Buildings," 6 November 1906; "A Sicilian Vendetta," 5 December 1906; "Murder in Cold Blood," 12 December 1906; "Shot Down on His Birthday," 13 December 1906;

"Shop Wrecked by a Bomb," 17 December 1906; "A Secret Service Squad to Hunt the Black Hand," 20 December 1906; "Stolen Boy Home Again," 23 December 1906; "Jersey Glassworker Slain," 24 December 1906; "'Black Hand' Agent Caught," 28 December 1906; "Black Hand on Long Island," 1 January 1907; "Shoots Black Hand Agent," 5 January 1907; "Murder in Harlem Street," 20 Jan 1907; "Boy Held for $500 Ransom," 24 January 1907; "Shot a Black Hand," 26 January 1907; "Bomb Thrown at Tenement," 30 January 1907; "Get 15 Years in Sing Sing," 31 January 1907; "Foreign Shotgun Killed Butcher," 11 February 1907; "More Black Hand Threats," 15 February 1907; "'Black Hand' Bomb Wrecks Stores," 25 February 1907; "Girl Fears 'Black Hand,'" 26 February 1907; "Is the Black Hand a Myth," 3 March 1907; "Bomb Outrage on East Side," 17 March 1907; "Bomb Wrecks Store," 21 March 1907; "Black Hand Blamed," 25 March 1907; "Police Dragnet Out for Armed Italians," 16 April 1907; "Gift from the Black Hand," 20 April 1907; "Black Hand Trial," 23 April 1907; "14 Arrested for Black Hand Plot," 7 May 1907; "Black Hand Italians Guilty," 7 May 1907; "Bomb from the Black Hand," 11 May 1907; "Woman and Girl Torn by a Bomb," 4 June 1907; "Black Hand Death Warning," 25 June 1907; "The Black Hand in Passaic," 30 June 1907; "Bomb Exploded in Crowded Street," 16 July 1907; "Black Hand Plants Bomb," 17 July 1907; "Black Hand Threat," 25 August 1907; "Black Hand Steals Four-Year-Old Girl," 2 September 1907; "Led Victim to a Grave," 18 September 1907; "Black Hand Bullet in Heart," 18 November 1907; "Aided Our Black Hand," 8 December 1907; "Big Bomb Wrecks," 22 December 1907; "Black Hand Suspects," 1 January 1908; "Confesses Cortese Bomb Plot," 20 January 1908; "Must Stop Outrages by the Black Hand," 26 January 1908; "Bomb Wrecks a Tenement," 4 February 1908; "Black Hand Shakes Town," 6 February 1908; "Black Hand Letter in Collection Plate," 20 February 1908; "Dynamite Threat in Black Hand Plot," 23 February 1908; "Black Hand Threat," 29 March 1908; "Black Hand Rumor Causes School Panic," 9 April 1908; "Bomb in Tenement Starts Wild Panic," 15 April 1908; "Another Tenement Wrecked by Bomb," 21 May 1908; "Black Hand Leader Caught," 29 July 1908; "Fire in Tenement Black Hand Revenge," 23 September 1908; "Tenement Wrecked," 10 December 1908; "Threat to Blow Up an Italian Church," 23 February 1909; "Black Hand Sends Many Recruits Here," 7 December 1909; "Bomb Wrecks Bank in Black Hand Block," 17 December 1909; "Black Hand Bomb at Italian Bank," 31 December 1909; "Black Hand's New Plan," 23 April 1910; "Held as Black Hand Chief," 21 May 1910; "Black Hand Bomb Imperils Scores," 28 December 1910; "Sure They've Caught Black Hand Chief," 7 September 1911; "Black Hand Terror," 26 October 1911; "Black Hand Crimes Doubled in Year," 31 December 1911; "Black Hand Killing," 15 April 1912; "Murder Revives Black Hand Feud," 10 September 1915. See also "Italians and the Mafia," *New York Daily Tribune*, 23 March 1891.

96. "Immigrants from Italy," *NYT*, 6 October 1895, 25. See also Gabaccia, "The Invention of 'Little Italy,'" 6.

97. Dickie, *Cosa Nostra*, 163; Riis, *How the Other Half Lives*, 92–93.

98. De Stefano, *An Offer We Can't Refuse*, 10. See also Bernstein, *The Greatest Menace*.

99. See, for example, "Detective Accuses Italian Prisoner's Handsome Wife," 30 April 1907; "'White Slave' Raid in Nyack Woods," 11 September 1910; "Mothers Mob City Schools," *NYT*, 20 April 1910; "White Slaver Sentenced," *NYT*, 20 June 1912, 24; "Black Hand Forced Wedding," 4 December 1912; "Whiteslaver Slain Husband Is Sought," 1 December 1913.

100. See the following articles in *NYT*: "White-Slave Dealers Arrested," 25 December 1885; "White Slaver Sentenced," 20 June 1912; "Black Hand Leader Caught," 29 July 1908; "'White Slave' Raid in Nyack Woods," 11 September 1910; "Ruined Her Life," 12 September 1910; "Black Hand Trails Pastor," 2 April 1911; "Witness Sees 'Death Sign,'" 29 March 1912; "White Slave Kills Master," 1 November 1912; "Whiteslaver Slain Husband Is Sought," 1 December 1913; "'Death Sign' Balks Bronx Slave Case," 26 July 1914; "Guilty Plea Stops White Slave Trial," 16 July 1914.

101. Donovan, "The Sexual Basis of Racial Formation," 708. See also U.S. Immigration Commission, *Abstract of Reports of the Immigration Commission*, 342–43. For other scholarship on white slavery, see Donovan, *White Slave Crusades*, 18–22; Langum, *Crossing over the Line*, esp. chap. 2; Johnson, "Defining 'Social Evil'"; Johnson, "Protection, Virtue, and the 'Power to Detain'"; Mumford, *Inter-*

zones; Soderlund, "Covering Urban Vice"; Diffee, "Sex and the City"; Roediger, *Wages of Whiteness*, chap. 4.

102. Keire, "The Vice Trust," 8.

103. An article from *Hutching's California Magazine*, quoted in Caldwell, "The Negroization," 128.

104. Kang, *Compositional Subjects*, 120–22. See also Lee, *At America's Gates*; Lowe, *Immigrant Acts*.

105. Donovan, "The Sexual Basis of Racial Formation," 100; Donovan, *White Slave Crusades*, chaps. 5 and 6. See also Hunter, *To 'Joy My Freedom*, 154; Newman, *White Women's Rights*, chap. 1; Gross, *Colored Amazons*.

106. Donovan, *White Slave Crusades*, 124; Mumford, *Interzones*; Gilfoyle, *City of Eros*, 270–83; Odem, *Delinquent Daughters*; Hobson, *Uneasy Virtue*; Soderlund, "Covering Urban Vice"; Rosen, *The Lost Sisterhood*, 117; Langum, *Crossing over the Line*; Kneeland, *Commercialized Prostitution in New York City*; Gross, *Colored Amazons*.

107. Mumford, *Interzones*, 15–17.

108. Donovan, "The Sexual Basis of Racial Formation," 709.

109. Turner, "The Daughters of the Poor," 57; Donovan, *White Slave Crusades*, 89–91; Langum, *Crossing over the Line*, 18, 24–25; Gross, *Colored Amazons*.

110. Turner, "The Daughters of the Poor," 57–58.

111. "White Slave Kills Master," *NYT*, 1 November 1912, 7.

112. Some examples from *NYT*: "A Woman Murdered," 8 June 1880; "The Mulberry-Street Murder," 9 June 1880; "Mrs. Mangano's Murderer," 8 December 1880; "Accused of Killing His Wife," 9 January 1882; "Murder and Suicide," 25 January 1885; "Shot by Her Husband," 18 January 1886; "Killed in Jealous Fury," 19 January 1886; "Shot in Cold Blood," 16 February 1886; "Her Father Wanted Her," 11 January 1888; "Shot by her Husband," 24 July 1888; "Italian Stabbing Cases," 6 August 1889; "Another Italian with a Knife," 10 August 1889; "Mother and Babe Starve to Death," 19 April 1893; "Murder and Suicide," 2 July 1898; "Killed Woman, Shot Himself," 7 April 1901; "Characteristics of Italian Immigrants," 18 May 1902; "Bride Slashed by Discarded Admirer," 15 August 1902; "Old Man Stabs Wife Twelve Times," 10 June 1904; "Mrs. Di Pietro Is Cleared of Murder," 15 December 1904; "Shot with His Own Pistol," 3 June 1906; "Tried to Stab Policemen," 11 July 1906; "Illario Trial Started," 30 October 1906; "Girl Shoots Man She Had Accused," 28 July 1907; "Killed Husband to Save Her Honor," 16 August 1908; "Double Murder in East Side Family," 9 May 1907; "2 Are Dead, 4 Hurt," 5 September 1910; "Killed by the Man She Tried to Help," 12 May 1912; "Woman Found Shot Dead," 27 January 1913; "Kills Woman and Himself," 27 February 1913. See also Iacovetta and Dubinsky, "Murder, Womanly Virtue and Motherhood"; Pucci, *The Trials of Maria Barbella*. See also the following from *BDE*: "Garlic Always Sells Well," 17 August 1902; "Italian Woman Murdered," 3 September 1900; "Tried to Kill Two Women," 7 April 1899; "Two Women Attacked," 25 May 1890; "Rose Used a Razor," 10 February 1900; "Italian Girl Causes a Fight," 18 September 1900; "Italian Woman Stabbed," 26 September 1900; "Mixed-Up Italian Story," 22 January 1901; "Woman and Boy Destitute," 8 February 1901; "Young Italian Actress Murdered in the Street," 5 March 1901; "Italian's Murderous Attack," 24 March 1901; "At Raines Law Hotel," 7 April 1901; "Killed Woman and Himself," 4 June 1901; "Carmela Accuses Antonio," 15 February 1902; "Didn't Know Why She Wed Him," 1 April 1902; "Shot by Rejected Lover," 16 July 1902; "Jilted Italian Lover," 3 September 1902. These stories filled New York City's newspapers and can be found in others as well, including *New York Journal*.

113. Mumford, *Interzones*, 66–67, 136–37; Chauncey, *Gay New York*; Riis, *How the Other Half Lives*, 95–95; "Italians Make Resistance," *BDE*, 11 January 1902, 2.

114. Langum, *Crossing over the Line*, 25.

115. Minnie J. Reynolds, "A 'Quiet Week' in Rural Italy," *NYT*, 19 July 1903, 8.

116. See, for example, the following stories in *NYT*: "Shooting at Her Countrymen," 26 May 1882; "Stabbed during Services," 12 April 1897; "One Italian Woman Kills Another," 21 October 1898; "Woman Killed for Scrubbing Debt," 24 November 1900; "Knife in Her Rival's Heart," 12 March

1904; "Stone Frank Gould's Auto," 16 August 1904; "Shoots Man to Death in Husband's Presence," 5 March 1905; "Women Mob Autoist," 25 May 1905; "Women in Nun's Garb," 2 July 1905; "Trafficked in Babies," 19 July 1905; "Stabs Man Who Spoiled Her Music," 19 June 1907; "Girl Shoots Man She Had Accused," 28 July 1907; "Judge Fights Armed Women," 3 June 1908; "Mistrial in a Murder Case," 28 November 1910; "Slain by Godmother," 13 April 1911. See also the following in *BDE*: "Two Italian Women Fight in a Tenement," 2 January 1896; "Carved Her Up," 6 April 1891; "Woman Causes Scene in Court," 7 August 1900; "Italian Woman Arrested," 17 September 1900; "One Woman Kills Another," 23 November 1900; "Italian Woman Held," 27 November 1900; "Mrs. Antoinetta Bacacto Arrested," 4 January 1901; "Italian Barber's Wife Attacked City Marshal," 3 September 1902. See also "Italian Girl in Duel," *New York Journal*, 14 January 1898.

117. "Judge Fights Armed Women," *NYT*, 3 June 1908.

118. "Manhattan Italians in Riot," *BDE*, 11 August 1902, 3.

119. "Girl Shoots Man She Had Accused," *NYT*, 28 July 1907.

120. In addition to works by Riis, see also Parker, *Working with the Working Woman*; Hapgood, *Types from City Streets*; Norr, *Stories of Chinatown*; McCabe, *Lights and Shadows*; Brace, *The Dangerous Classes*; Van Vorst and Van Vorst, *The Woman Who Toils*; Anonymous, *Four Years in the Underbrush*; Roseboro, "The Italians of New York"; Hartt, "Made in Italy"; "New York Street Scenes," *NYT*, 4 September 1898; Zoe Anderon Norris, "Seeing Manhattan—The Land of the 'Black Hand,'" *NYT*, 2 July 1905. See also Mumford, *Interzones*, 135–36; Nord, "The Social Explorer," 118–30; Bender, *Sweated Work*, 9; Higbie, "Crossing Class Boundaries"; Pittenger, "A World of Difference"; Gabaccia, "The Invention of 'Little Italy.'"

121. Riis, *How the Other Half Lives*, 95; Riis, *Out of Mulberry Street*.

122. New York State Assembly, Tenement House Committee, *Report* (1895); U.S. Department of Commerce, Bureau of Census, *Thirteenth Census of the United States: 1910*, vol. 3: *Population*, 253–55; Gabaccia, *From Sicily to Elizabeth Street*, 67; Mariano, *Italian Contribution*, 19.

123. Sante, *Low Life*, 197–235; Lord et al., *The Italian in America*, 8; Gabaccia, *From Sicily to Elizabeth Street*, 67; Gabaccia, "Peopling," 50; Zappia, "Unionism and the Italian American Worker," 98; Lui, *The Chinatown Trunk Mystery*, 22.

124. Mariano, *The Italian Contribution*, 19; Orsi, *The Madonna of 115th Street*, 16; Ware, *Greenwich Village*, 152; Tricarico, *The Italians of Greenwich Village*; Mariano, *Italian Contribution*, 19; Riis, *How the Other Half Lives*, 18–19.

125. Riis, *How the Other Half Lives*, 92–93.

126. Irving, *Immigrant Mothers*, 75; Szasz and Bogardus, "The Camera," 422.

127. J.F.F, "Romance vs. Reality," *NYT*, 23 May 1899, 6.

128. Forman, "Italians in New York."

129. Riis, *How the Other Half Lives*, 92–93; "Brooklyn's 'Little Italy' the Largest in America," *BDE*, 20 May 1900, 20.

130. Riis, *How the Other Half Lives*, 98. See also Cosco, *Imagining Italians*, 25.

131. Cosco, *Imagining Italians*, 29–30.

132. "A Crosby-Street Mystery," *NYT*, 12 April 1880.

133. D'Ambrosio, "Ralph Fasanella," 27. See also Kessner, *The Golden Door*, 15; Riis, *How the Other Half Lives*, 41; Brace, *The Dangerous Classes*, 194.

134. "Italian Girls Take Up the Burden," *BDE*, 17 August 1902, 33.

135. *Il Progresso*, 22 June 1893; *L'Eco*, 13 February 1896; *Corriere della Sera*, 15 March 1912; Speranza, "Industrial and Civil Relations," Gino C. Speranza Papers, NYPL; Pozzetta, "The Mulberry District," 18; Gabaccia, "Peopling Little Italy," 50–51.

136. Gabaccia, *Italy's Many Diasporas*, 73; Gabaccia, "Inventing 'Little Italy.'"

137. Park and Miller, *Old World Traits Transplanted*, 146.

138. Herzfeld, *Family Monographs*, 10–11.

139. Castiglione, "Italian Immigration," 201.

140. Simons, "Social Assimilation IV," 400.

141. U.S. Congress, Senate, *Reports of the Immigration Commission*, vol. 26: *Immigrants in Cities*, 1:20, 235; Gabaccia, "Peopling Little Italy," 50; Baily, *Immigrants in the Land of Promise*, 150–52.

142. Covello, *Social Background*, 277.

143. *New York Tribune*, 1 April 1903, 6. See also "Only Birds of Passage," *NYT*, 28 July 1888; "Come and Go," *BDE*, 25 April 1890, 6.

144. Gaspare Cusumano, "Study of the Colony of Cinisi in New York City," quoted in Park and Miller, *Old World Traits Transplanted*, 148–49.

145. U.S. Immigration Commission, *Immigrants in Industries*, 355, 399–400; U.S. Department of Commerce, Bureau of Census, *Fourteenth Census of the United States: 1920*, vol. 2: *General Report and Analytical Tables*, 812, 820–21.

146. Gabaccia, *Militants and Migrants*, 171.

147. Ibid., 386; "The Italian Problem," *NYT*, 4 July 1888, 3.

148. Bender, *Sweated Work*, 10.

149. For these practices in New York City, see Lui, *The Chinatown Trunk Mystery*; and Wilder, *A Covenant with Color*.

150. Newman, *White Women's Rights*, 7. See also Ewen, *Immigrant Women*, chap. 5; Lasch-Quinn, *Black Neighbors*; Briggs, *Reproducing Empire*; Kunzel, *Fallen Women*; Wexler, *Tender Violence*.

151. Razovki, "The Eternal Masculine," 117; Castiglione, "Italian Immigration," 194.

152. Dr. Jane E. Robbins, "Helping Italian Women and Ourselves Also," *NYT*, 9 March 1913, 73; Irwin, "The Story of a Transplanted Industry," 404; "School for Immigrants," *NYT*, 24 June 1908; Elizabeth A. Woodward, "Education of Immigrant Mothers," box 68, file 8, Leonard Covello Papers; Pozzetta, "Immigrants and Crafts."

153. Simkhovitch, *Greenwich House*, October 1909, 17.

154. Irwin, "The Story of a Transplanted Industry," 406.

155. Simkhovitch, *Greenwich House*, October 1911, 14.

156. Quoted in Friedman-Kasaba, *Memories of Migration*, 96.

157. Gillett, *Adapting Nutrition Work*. See also Friedman-Kasaba, *Memories of Migration*, 112.

158. Parker, *Working with the Working Woman*, 30.

159. Addams, *Democracy and Social Ethics*, 38.

160. See, for example, Johnson, "Protection, Virtue and the 'Power to Detain'"; Johnson, "Defining 'Social Evil'"; Glenn, *Daughters of the Shtetl*; Orleck, *Common Sense and a Little Fire*.

161. See, for example, the announcement for the commemoration of anarchist martyr Giordano Bruno by the Gaetano Bresci group to be held at Union Settlement at 231 East 104th Street, *Lotta di Classe*, 19 February 1915. See also Records of Union Settlement Association, Columbia University Rare Book and Manuscript Library.

162. Covello, *The Social Background*, 296.

163. Covello, *The Heart Is the Teacher*, 31.

164. "Lady Cook in Naples," *NYT*, 3 July 1910.

165. Gabaccia, "Italians Everywhere"; Johnson, "Race and the Regulation"; Newman, *White Women's Rights*.

166. Riis, *How the Other Half Lives*; Osofsky, *Harlem*.

167. Peiss, *Hope in a Jar*, 146–49.

168. Miceli, *Pride of Sicily*, IHRC Print Collection, 12.

169. T. Guglielmo, *White on Arrival*; Watkins-Owens, *Blood Relations*; James, *Holding Aloft the Banner of Ethiopia*; Schoener, *New York*; Yu, *To Save China*; Sánchez-Korrol, *From Colonia to Community*; Osofsky, *Harlem*.

170. *Il Proletario*, 4 June 1909; Vecoli, "'Free Country,'" 36.

171. Quoted in Roediger, *Black on White*, 19; West, *Race Matters*, 3; Malcolm X, *Malcolm X on Afro-American History*, 24.

172. Quoted in Pozzetta, "The Italians," 346–49.

173. *Evening Sun*, 18, 22, 29 May 1903; Fenton, *Immigrants and Unions*, 215.

174. Jacobson, *Barbarian Virtues*, 69.

175. More, *Wage-Earners' Budgets*, 11.

176. Odencrantz, *Immigrant Women in Industry*, 166–67.

177. Quoted in Elwood, "The Roots and Results of Radicalism," 60.

178. T. Guglielmo, *White on Arrival*, 10.

179. Jacobson, *Roots Too*, 75–85.

180. Ibid., 7.

181. Ibid., 9.

Chapter 4

1. Sinatra, *Frank Sinatra*, 40.

2. This composite of Dolly Sinatra (1896–1977) comes from the following sources: Sinatra, *Frank Sinatra*; Gennari, "Mammissimo"; Meyer, "Frank Sinatra"; Pignone, *The Sinatra Treasures*; Lahr, *Sinatra*; Fagiani, "The Italian Identity of Frank Sinatra"; Petkov and Mustazza, *The Frank Sinatra Reader*; Hamill, *Why Sinatra Matters*; Pugliese, *Frank Sinatra*; *Rolling Stone*, 25 June 1998, 57; Lowenlfels, "Frankie's Fight"; and the U.S. Department of Commerce, Bureau of Census, *Fifteenth Census of the United States: 1930*, Hoboken, Hudson, New Jersey, roll 1349, 9B, 290, image 819.0; Social Security Death Index 151-32-9978 (1958–59).

3. Sinatra, *Frank Sinatra*, 36; Pignone, *The Sinatra Treasures*, 14. Frank Sinatra was born on 12 December 1915.

4. Lowenfels, "Frankie's Fight," 3.

5. Quotes from Lahr, *Sinatra*, 7.

6. Quoted in Sinatra, *Frank Sinatra*, 40.

7. Barbara Grizzuti Harrison, "Terrified and Fascinated by His Own Life," *NYT*, 2 November 1986.

8. Lowenfels, "Frankie's Fight," 3.

9. Quoted in Pignone, *The Sinatra Treasures*, 36.

10. Gennari, "Mammissimo," 6.

11. Phrasing inspired in part from Meena Alexander, *The Shock of Arrival*.

12. Kelley, "'We Are Not What We Seem,'" 77; Kelley, *Hammer and Hoe*; Naples, *Grassroots Warriors*; Hondagneu-Sotelo, *Gendered Transitions*; Cameron, *Radicals of the Worst Sort*; Ruiz, *Cannery Women*; Blackwelder, *Women of the Depression*; Hunter, *To 'Joy My Freedom*; Glenn, *Daughters of the Shtetl*; Orleck, *Common Sense and a Little Fire*; Payne, *I've Got the Light of Freedom*; Camp, *Closer to Freedom*; Ransby, *Ella Baker*; Orleck, *Storming Caesar's Palace*; J. Smith, "Our Own Kind."

13. This chapter draws on several major oral history collections. First, the New York City Immigrant Labor History Project (NYCILHP) of the Oral History Project of the City University of New York (CUNY), which began in 1973 and is now housed at the Robert Wagner Archives at the Tamiment Library of New York University. This collection includes more than two hundred interviews with residents at the ILGWU Nursing Home and other retirement communities in New York City, whose memories dated back to the early twentieth century. Elizabeth Ewen used these interviews in her book *Immigrant Women in the Land of Dollars*, but the tape numbers are new since they have been recently recataloged by the archive. The collection includes more than a dozen interviews with Italian immigrant women garment workers, all of whom requested that their names be changed to protect anonymity. I have therefore created pseudonyms. The second collection comprises one hundred interviews with Jewish and Italian women who immigrated to New York City in the immediate aftermath of World War I, conducted by Rose Laub Coser, Laura S. Anker, and Andrew J. Perrin for the World of Our Mothers Project (WOMP) at the State University of New York at Stony Brook. The typed transcripts and interview tapes (61 Jewish, 39 Italian) are housed

at the Henry A. Murray Research Center of Radcliffe College in Cambridge, Mass. I have adopted the same pseudonyms that the interviewers assigned to the interviewees to preserve continuity and anonymity. See Coser et al., *Women of Courage*, 147–48. I have also utilized the Oral History of the American Left (OHAL) at the Wagner Archives; and oral histories conducted in the 1970s and 1980s by Steve Golin, with women active in the 1913 Paterson textile strike, and by Columba Furio, with Italian immigrant women garment workers in early twentieth-century New York City, both of which are now housed at the Sophia Smith Collection, Smith College.

14. Covello, *The Heart Is the Teacher*, 19–21.
15. Ibid., 21.
16. Ibid., 22.
17. Odencrantz, *Italian Women in Industry*, 286. See also Williams, *South Italian Folkways*, 146.
18. NYCILHP, tape 157.
19. Corsi, *Shadow of Liberty*, 23–24. See also Orsi, *The Madonna of 115th Street*, 20, 37–42; Lapolla, *Grand Gennaro*, 104.
20. Covello, *The Heart Is the Teacher*, 36, 46, 67.
21. Ewen, *Immigrant Women*, 63.
22. Watson, "Homework in the Tenements," 772.
23. Orsi, "The Fault of Memory," 138–39.
24. Ibid., 140.
25. Ibid., 143.
26. Cameron, *Radicals of the Worst Sort*, 5.
27. Di Leonardo, "The Female World"; Di Leonardo, *The Varieties of Ethnic Experience.*
28. WOMP interviews 25009, 25021, 25005; Coser et al., *Women of Courage*, 61–5; Williams, *South Italian Folkways*, 105; NYCILHP, tapes 157, 167; Kisseloff, *You Must Remember This*, 347.
29. WOMP interview 25005.
30. WOMP interviews 25003, 25028; Coser et al., *Women of Courage*, 61–5, 116–17.
31. Bertocci, "Memoir of My Mother," 9.
32. WOMP interviews 25008, 25030, 25052; Coser et al., *Women of Courage*, 26; Kisseloff, *You Must Remember This*, 353–54.
33. Covello, *The Heart Is the Teacher*, 11.
34. Ewen, *Immigrant Women*, 154–55.
35. More, *Wage-Earners' Budgets*, 12, 31–32.
36. Brandt, "In Behalf of the Overcrowded," 503. See also Foerster, *The Italian Emigration of Our Times*, 390; P. H. Williams, *South Italian Folkways*, 46.
37. More, *Wage-Earners' Budgets*, 12.
38. Willett, *Women in the Clothing Trades*, 131.
39. Wald, *The House on Henry Street*, 17, 21. See also Ewen, *Immigrant Women*, 86, 203–4, 115.
40. Odencrantz, *Italian Women in Industry*, 184–85, 196–97, 225.
41. Covello, *The Heart Is the Teacher*, 28, 36; Chotzinoff, *The Lost Paradise*, 81–82; Herzfeld, *Family Monographs*, 33–35; Chauncey, *Gay New York*, esp. chap. 7; Enstad, *Ladies of Labor*; Peiss, *Cheap Amusements*, 54–44, 106; Ewen, *Immigrant Women*; Orsi, *The Madonna of 115th Street*; Goodman, *Choosing Sides*; Nasaw, *Children of the City*; Coser et al., *Women of Courage*, 41–43. See also NYCILHP.
42. Betts, "The Italian in New York," 94. See also Jones, *Sociology of a New York City Block*, 31–34, 38–39; Gabaccia, *From Sicily to Elizabeth Street*, 80; Peiss, *Cheap Amusements*, 12–16.
43. Gabaccia, *From Sicily to Elizabeth Street*, 74–77, 82.
44. Ewen, *Immigrant Women*, 166. See also Gabaccia, *From Sicily to Elizabeth Street*, 99; More, *Wage-Earners' Budgets*, 13.
45. Odencrantz, *Italian Women in Industry*, 198–99. See also Kisseloff, *You Must Remember This*, 355, 361.

46. More, *Wage-Earners' Budgets*, 218; Kisseloff, *You Must Remember This*, 355.

47. Ewen, *Immigrant Women*, 171–72.

48. NYCILHP, tapes 142, 147, 148, 157, 161, 167, 168, 169, 171; Holloway quoted in Elwood, "The Roots and Results of Radicalism," 58; Ewen, *Immigrant Women*, 162.

49. Gabaccia, *Militants and Migrants*, 127; Covello, *The Social Background*, 135.

50. Ibid., 81.

51. P. H. Williams, *South Italian Folkways*, 46.

52. Quoted in Ewen, *Immigrant Women*, 166.

53. Quoted in Covello, *The Social Background*, 279.

54. Bayor, *Neighbors in Conflict*; Femminella, *The Interaction of Italians and Irish*; Scarpaci, *The Interaction of Italians and Jews*; Fraser, "Landyslayt and Paesani"; Jacobson, *Special Sorrows*; Orsi, *The Madonna of 115th Street*; J. Smith, *Family Connections*; Ignatiev, *How the Irish Became White*; Brodkin, *How Jews Became White Folks*; Kessner and Caroli, "New Immigrant Women at Work"; Coser et al., *Women of Courage*; Ewen, *Immigrant Women*; M. Cohen, *Workshop to Office*; Friedman-Kasaba, *Memories of Migration*; E. Schneider, *Vampires*; Roediger, *Working toward Whiteness*.

55. D'Ambrosio, *Ralph Fasanella's America*, 18. See also G. Guglielmo, "My Antonia."

56. Kisseloff, *You Must Remember This*, 342–80.

57. Lillian Cicio, "Mama Vita," *American Immigrant Autobiographies*, 11, 174, IHRC, mf 4635.

58. Quoted in Ewen, *Immigrant Women*, 162. See also Kisseloff, *You Must Remember This*, 355.

59. Quoted in Ewen, *Immigrant Women*, 68; Speranza, "The Italians in Congested Districts," 56.

60. Coser et al., *Women of Courage*, 49–56, 59; Enstad, *Ladies of Labor*; Danzi, *From Home to Hospital*; Peiss, *Cheap Amusements*; Ewen, *Immigrant Women*; Friedman-Kasaba, *Memories of Migration*; M. Cohen, *Workshop to Office*; Glenn, *Daughters of the Shtetl*; Orleck, *Common Sense and a Little Fire*; Hewitt, *Southern Discomfort*; Vecchio, *Merchants, Midwives, and Laboring Women*; Ware, *Greenwich Village*; Ruiz, *From Out of the Shadows*; Gabaccia, *From the Other Side*; Yung, *Unbound Feet*.

61. Orsi, "The Fault of Memory," 134–35.

62. NYCILHP, tape 158.

63. Cicio, "Mama Vita," 13, 56, 60–61.

64. Elwood, "The Roots and Results of Radicalism," iii–iv.

65. <<http://www.italianamericanwomen.com/story_elena.html>> (accessed 6 May 2008).

66. NYCILHP, tapes 142, 158, 160, 161, 167, 168, 171, and WOMP interviews.

67. NYCILHP, tape 158.

68. Furio, "Immigrant Women and Industry," 23, 26; Ewen, *Immigrant Women*, 134–35.

69. Odencrantz, *Italian Women in Industry*, 204.

70. NYCILHP, tape 160.

71. NYCILHP, tape 142.

72. NYCILHP, tapes 147–48. See also Ewen, *Immigrant Women*, 212–15; M. Cohen, *Workshop to Office*, 69–75; Roche, "The Italian Girl," 95, 112–13; Ware, *Greenwich Village*, 186–87, 405–6; Kisseloff, *You Must Remember This*, 357.

73. Grace Billotti Spinelli, "American Immigrant Autobiographies," IHRC, mf. 4635, 96–98.

74. NYCILHP, tape 142; Ewen, *Immigrant Women*, 212–15; Roche, "The Italian Girl," 112–13.

75. Enstad, *Ladies of Labor*, 63.

76. NYCILHP, tape 167; Ewen, *Immigrant Women*, 200.

77. Peiss, *Cheap Amusements*, 187; M. Cohen, *Workshop to Office*, 69–75.

78. Enstad, *Ladies of Labor*. See also Glenn, *Daughters of the Shtetl*; Ewen, *Immigrant Women*; Coser et al., *Women of Courage*; Friedman-Kasaba, *Memories of Migration*.

79. Orsi, "The Fault of Memory," 134. See also Gordon, *Heroes of Their Own Lives*, 188.

80. See case files of Anna Tercillo, Cecilia Tomasi, Rosa Covello, and others (pseudonyms), Bedford Hills Correctional Facility, Inmate Case Files, 1915–1930, New York State Archives and Records

Administration, State Education Department, Series 14610–77B, Albany, New York; and Alexander, *The "Girl Problem."*

81. Orsi, *The Madonna of 115th Street*; Varacalli et al., *The Saints in the Lives of Italian-Americans*; Covello, *The Social Background*, chap. 5; Vecoli, "The Making and Unmaking"; Johnson, *Growing Up and Growing Old*; J. Smith, *Family Connections*; M. Brown, *Churches, Communities, and Children*, 44–47.

82. Orsi, *The Madonna of 115th Street*, 205.

83. She borrows Lata Mani's phrasing here. Alexander, *Pedagogies of Crossing*, 7–8, 295.

84. Vecoli, *The Italians of New Jersey*, 33–34; Vecoli, "Prelates and Peasants"; Vecoli, "Cult and Occult."

85. In addition to Vecoli's articles, see Orsi, *The Madonna of 115th Street*, xvi–xvii, 83–84; Pozzetta, "The Mulberry District," 21; McBride, "The Italian Americans and the Catholic Church"; M. Brown, *Churches, Communities, and Children*; Gabaccia, *Italy's Many Diasporas*, 120–21; Varacalli et al., *The Saints in the Lives of Italian-Americans*; Covello, *The Social Background*, chap. 5; M. Cohen, *Workshop to Office*, 107–8; Foerster, *The Italian Emigration*, 397; Williams, *South Italian Folkways*, 147; Elwood, "The Roots and Results of Radicalism," chap. 3. See also J. T. Smith, *The Catholic Church in New York*, 471; Testa, "'Strangers from Rome,'" 217; Panunzio, *The Soul of an Immigrant*, 18–19; and Zema, "The Italian Immigrant Problem," 129.

86. Russo, "The Origin and Progress of Our Italian Mission in New York," 139.

87. Odencrantz, *Italian Women in Industry*, 206. See also Zema, "The Italian Immigrant Problem," 129.

88. NYCILHP, tape 158.

89. Orsi, *The Madonna of 115th Street*, chap. 3; M. Brown, *Churches, Communities, and Children*. See also the following essays from the period: Browne, "The 'Italian Problem'"; Tolino, "The Priest in the Italian Problem"; Zema, "The Italian Immigrant Problem"; Di Domenica, "Conditions among Italians in America." See also LaGumina, *WOP*, 116–17; Varacalli, "The Changing Nature"; and Tomasi and Stabili, *Italian Americans and Religion*.

90. First two quotes are from Lynch, "The Italians of New York." The last quote is Mary Elizabeth Brown paraphrasing Henry J. Browne. Brown, *Churches, Communities, and Children*, 28. See also Orsi, *The Madonna of 115th Street*, 57.

91. Orsi, *The Madonna of 115th Street*, 56.

92. Ibid., 57.

93. Covello, *The Social Background*, 122. See also Balzano, *Abruzzi e Molise*, 239–60; Douglas, *Old Calabria*, 147; Riviello, *Costumanze*, 200; Perri, *Enough of Dreams*, 240; Williams, *South Italian Folkways*, 136.

94. *Il Progresso*, 20 July 1890, 13 May 1893, 6, 8, 30 September 1894; *New York Tribune*, 9 September 1900, 10 September 1901, 14 September 1902, 12 July 1903, 18 July 1904; "Italian Festivals in New York," *Chautauquan* 34 (1901–2), 228; P. H. Williams, *South Italian Folkways*, 149. See also the following in the *NYT*: "Child Cured on Feast Day," 17 July 1903; "Feast of Mount Carmel," 17 July 1903; "Thousands do Homage to Our Lady of Mount Carmel," 17 July 1904; "Virgin's Statue in Back Yard," 18 September 1904; "Little Italy Aglow for Good St. Anthony," 14 July 1905; "Thousands of Italians in Illuminated Parade," 16 August 1906; "San Rocco Honored by Rival Factions," 17 August 1906; Riis, "Feast Days." See also Meazza and Bertolotti, "La macchina rituale"; Primeggia and Varacalli, "The Sacred and the Profane." The NYPL holds a substantial collection of photographs documenting these feasts in their digital library under *Photographic Views of New York City, 1870s–1970s*.

95. Orsi, *The Madonna of 115th Street*, 51.

96. Pozzetta, "The Mulberry District," 20; Orsi, *The Madonna of 115th Street*, 51–53; Varacalli et al., *The Saints in the Lives of Italian-Americans*; Gabaccia, *From Sicily to Elizabeth Street*, 50, 105; Covello, *The Social Background*, chap. 5; M. Brown, "Italian-Americans and Their Saints," 46; M. Brown, *Churches, Communities, and Children*, 42–44, 51–52; Riis, "Feast-Days"; and the following articles in *NYT*: "Little Italy's Fete Day," 17 July 1900, 12; "Fire at Church of the Transfiguration," 4 March 1901, 2; "Feast of Santa Maria," 16 August 1901, 12; "Festival of San Donato," 18 August 1902, 7; "Fes-

tival of St. Calogero," 18 June 1903, 6; "Fire Mars a Festival," 16 August 1903, 11; "Virgin's Statue in Back Yard," 18 September 1904, 4; "Shrine Their Sanctuary," 15 June 1906, 9; "San Rocco Honored by Rival Factions," 17 August 1906, 7.

97. "Shrine Their Sanctuary," *NYT*, 15 June 1906, 9.

98. Cappannari and Moss, "In Quest of the Black Virgin," 65, 71; Moss and Cappannari, "The Black Madonna." See also C. Levi, *Christ Stopped at Eboli*; Williams, *South Italian Folkways*, 135; Vecoli, "Cult and Occult"; Covello, *The Social Background*, 117–29.

99. Covello, *The Social Background*, 117. See also Williams, *South Italian Folkways*, 136–37; Pitrè, *La famiglia*, 379.

100. Covello, *The Social Background*, 113–16; Riviello, *Costumanze*, 200. See also P. H. Williams, *South Italian Folkways*, 135–59; Salomone-Marino, *Customs and Habits*; "Quaint Italian Customs of Summer Festal Days," *NYT*, 12 July 1903, 30.

101. *Ricordo della decorazione della chiesa di Maria Ausiliatrice*, 22 May 1921, IHRC Print Collection; *Parrocchia della Madonna di Pompei in New York; notizie storiche dei primi cinquant'anni dall sua fondazione, 1892–1942* (1965), IHRC Print Collection; *Dall'Italia a New York guida dell'emigrante* (1902), IHRC Print Collection. See also Pozzetta, "The Mulberry District"; Orsi, *The Madonna of 115th Street*, 51–53; Varacalli et al., *The Saints in the Lives of Italian-Americans*; Covello, *The Social Background*, chap. 5; M. Brown, "Italian-Americans and Their Saints"; M. Brown, *From Italian Villages*; Tomasi, *Piety and Power*.

102. Orsi, *The Madonna of 115th Street*, 35.

103. De Martino, *The Land of Remorse*, 11, 21–32.

104. Orsi, "The Religious Boundaries," 265; Orsi, *The Madonna of 115th Street*, esp. 204–17.

105. Orsi, *The Madonna of 115th Street*, 2. See also Orsi, "The Religious Boundaries"; McAlister, "The Madonna of 115th Street Revisited." For contemporary *feste*, see Sarah Garland, "A Reunion of Little Italy in East Harlem," *NYT*, 6 September 2006; Barbara Stewart, "The Man Behind the Festival of Our Lady of Mount Carmel," *NYT*, 25 May 1997.

106. See the following articles in *NYT*: "Little Italy's Fete Day," 17 July 1900, 12; "Feast of Santa Maria," 16 August 1901, 12; "Feast of Mount Carmel," 17 July 1903, 2; "Thousands Do Homage," 17 July 1904, 7; "Italian Worshippers in Panic from Fire," 18 July 1905, 2.

107. Orsi, *The Madonna of 115th Street*, 12. See also D'Agostino, "The Religious Life," 74–75; P. H. Williams, *South Italian Folkways*, 139–50.

108. Orsi, *The Madonna of 115th Street*, 4. See also Riis, "Feast-Days," 498–99; Kisseloff, *You Must Remember This*, 376; and the following articles in *NYT*: "Child Cured on Feast Day," 17 July 1903, 2; "Quaint Italian Customs of Summer Festal Days," 12 July 1903, 30; "Feast of Mount Carmel," 17 July 1903, 2; "Thousands do Homage to Our Lady of Mount Carmel," 17 July 1904, 7; "Italian Worshippers in Panic from Fire," 18 July 1905, 2.

109. Orsi, *The Madonna of 115th Street*, 9.

110. Wald, The *House on Henry Street*, 213–14, 252; McLeod, *Heart of a Stranger*, 69; Lapolla, *Fire in the Flesh*, 150; Lapolla, *Grand Gennaro*, 47; P. H. Williams, *South Italian Folkways*, 135–50; Orsi, *The Madonna of 115th Street*, chap. 1.

111. Willett, *The Employment of Women*, 104. See also Riis, "Feast-Days"; P. H. Williams, *South Italian Folkways*.

112. Gabaccia, *We Are What We Eat*, 180.

113. DeSalvo and Giunta, *The Milk of Almonds*; Till, *Loaves and Wishes*, x; Shange, *If I Can Cook*; Shange, *Sassafrass, Cypress and Indigo*; Ehrlich, *Miriam's Kitchen*; Reichl, *Tender at the Bone*; Randall, *Hunger's Table*; Fussell, *My Kitchen Wars*; Kadi, *Food of Our Grandmothers*; Esquivel, *Like Water for Chocolate*; Allende, *Aphrodite*.

114. DeSalvo and Giunta, *The Milk of Almonds*, 1.

115. NYCILHP, tapes 161–161a. See other interviews in this collection as well, such as tapes 142, 146, 168–168a.

116. Tina Gaeta, interview by Colomba Furio, 22 November 1976.

117. NYCILHP, tape 142.

118. Gabaccia, *From Sicily to Elizabeth Street*, 92; M. Cohen, *Workshop to Office*, 103. See also Odencrantz, *Italian Women in Industry*, 198; More, *Wage Earners' Budgets*, 97; Ware, *Greenwich Village*, 191; De Forest and Veiller, *The Tenement House Problem*, 294; Chapin, *The Standard of Living*, 172–79, 240; New York State Welfare Conference, *Report of the Special Committee*, 14; P. H. Williams, *South Italian Folkways*, 61; Covello, *The Social Background*, 295; Pagano, *Golden Wedding*, 12–14.

119. Ewen, *Immigrant Women*, 175.

120. Simkhovitch, *The City Worker's World*, 58; "Italian Housewives' Dishes," *NYT*, 7 June 1903, 28.

121. Nino Capraro to Angela Bambace, 2 October 1954, Capraro Papers, IHRC.

122. Flynn, *Rebel Girl*, 333.

123. Quoted in Pernicone, *Carlo Tresca*, 83.

124. Mangione and Morreale, *La Storia*, 175; P. H. Williams, *South Italian Folkways*, 53–54. See also Klindienst, *The Earth Knows My Name*; DeSalvo and Giunta, *The Milk of Almonds*; Ragusa, *The Skin between Us*; DeSalvo, *Crazy in the Kitchen*; Cappello, *Night Bloom*; Laurino, *Were You Always an Italian*; Cusumano, *The Last Cannoli*; Ets, *Rosa*; Mangione, *Monte Allegro*; Gillan et al., *Italian American Writers on New Jersey*; Ardizzone, *In the Garden*; Italian Immigrant Gardens, Oral Histories, 1985–87, Center for Oral History, Thomas J. Dodd Research Center, University of Connecticut, Storrs.

125. "Judge Fights Armed Women," *NYT*, 3 June 1908.

126. P. H. Williams, *South Italian Folkways*, 175.

127. Covello, *The Heart Is the Teacher*, 15.

128. Ragusa, *The Skin between Us*, 117.

129. P. H. Williams, *South Italian Folkways*, 161. See also Ragusa, *The Skin between Us*; DeSalvo and Giunta, *The Milk of Almonds*; Gillan et al., *Italian American Writers on New Jersey*.

130. P. H. Williams, *South Italian Folkways*, 46.

131. NYCILHP, tape 157.

132. Klindienst, *The Earth Knows My Name*, xx.

133. Ibid., xxi.

134. George T. Kelley interview, Avrich, *Anarchist Voices*, 99.

Chapter 5

1. Maria Roda Balzarini, CPC file 4368; Zo d'Axa, "Little Girls" (1895), available at http://www.marxists.org/reference/archive/zo-daxa/1895/little-girls.htm (accessed 20 November 2008). D'Axa notes that Roda was fifteen at the time. Other state and personal records list her birth date as 1874, 1877, 1878, and 1879; and the trial as 1891. Her birth year was most likely 1877. See also Sione, "Industrial Work, Militancy, and Migrations," 1, 199–200; Salerno, "'No God, No Master,'" 178; Carey, "'La Questione Sociale,'" 292; U.S. Department of Commerce, Bureau of Census, *Twelfth Census of the United States: 1900*, Paterson Ward 8, Passaic, New Jersey, roll T623, 993, 16B, 158; *Thirteenth Census of the United States: 1910*, Tampa Ward 8, Hillsborough, Florida, roll T624 162, 6B, 60, 865; *Fourteenth Census of the United States: 1920*, Weehawken Ward 2, Hudson, New Jersey, roll T625 1050, 1A, 314, 116.

2. Roda-Balzarini, CPC file 4368; "Amministrazione," *LQS*, 26 May 1900; "Ricordi della vecchia Paterson," *L'Adunata dei Refrattari*, 15 October 1932. See also Salerno, "'No God, No Master'"; Salerno, *Red November*, 48–49, 58, 89; Sione, "Industrial Work, Militancy, and Migrations," 1, 199–200; Carey, "'La Questione Sociale,'" 292; Carey, "The Vessel," 51; Avrich, *Anarchist Portraits*, 173; Avrich, *Sacco and Vanzetti*, 55.

3. Maria Roda, "Alle operaie," *LQS*, 15 September 1897; Roda-Balzarini, CPC file 4368. All the translations from Italian are mine unless otherwise noted.

4. *LQS*, 15 September 1897, 6 November 1901, 23 November 1901, 4 January 1902.

5. I borrow this phrasing from Gabaccia, *Italy's Many Diasporas*.

6. *LQS*, 10 May 1902, 12 July 1902, 26 July 1902, 16 August 1902; "Cronaca di Spring Valley, Il gruppo femminile"; and Il Gruppo I Nuovi Viventi, Il Gruppo Femminile Luisa Michel, "La questione della donna," *L'Aurora*, 22 December 1900; Merithew, "Anarchist Motherhood"; Panofsky, "A View," 275–76.

7. Cameron, *Radicals of the Worst Sort*; Golin, *The Fragile Bridge*; Golin, "Defeat Becomes Disaster"; Osborne, "Paterson"; Osborne, "Italian Immigrants and the Working Class in Paterson"; J. Smith, *Family Connections*; Cooper, *Once a Cigar Maker*; Snyder, "Women, Wobblies, and Workers' Rights"; Hewitt, *Southern Discomfort*; Dodyk, "Winders, Warpers, and Girls on the Loom"; Avrich, *Anarchist Voices*, 97, 107, 497; O'Farrell and Kornbluh, *Rocking the Boat*; Sione, "Industrial Work"; Gabaccia, *From the Other Side*; Gabaccia and Iacovetta, *Women, Gender Transnational Lives*; Russell, "The Strike at Little Falls."

8. Davenport, "The Italian Immigrant," 32; Mangano, "Associated Life," 479; Vecoli, "Pane e Giustizia," 57–58; Fenton, *Immigrants and Unions*, 15–16, 50; Pozzetta, "Italians of New York City," 243–45; Pozzetta, "The Mulberry District," 19–20; Gabaccia, *Militants and Migrants*, 136–38; Gabaccia, *Italy's Many Diasporas*, 124; Lapolla, *Grand Gennaro*, 114; Mariano, *The Italian Contribution*, 140; Mormino and Pozzetta, *Immigrants of Ybor City*; Mormino and Pozzetta, "The Cradle of Mutual Aid."

9. R. Smith, *Mexican New York*; Louie, *Sweatshop Warriors*; *The Sixth Section* (DVD).

10. Gabaccia, *Italy's Many Diasporas*; Cannistraro and Meyer, *The Lost World*; Fenton, *Immigrants and Unions*; Topp, *Those without a Country*; Pernicone, *Carlo Tresca*; and Bencivenni, "Italian American Radical Culture in New York City"; Rigazio, "Alberto Guabello."

11. *Il Proletario*, 3 December 1909. Pelizzari was a leader among Italian striking mine workers during the Ludlow Massacre; see "Miners Welcome Federal Troops," *NYT*, 1 May 1914, 4.

12. *Il Martello*, 20 June 1919; Pernicone, *Carlo Tresca*, 102.

13. The activities of these groups were regularly featured in the Italian-language anarchist newspapers, including *La Questione Sociale* (*LQS*), *L'Era Nuova* (*EN*), *Cronaca Sovversiva*, *L'Anarchia*, *Il Martello*, and *L'Adunata dei Refrattari*.

14. Fenton, *Immigrants and Unions*; Gabaccia, *Militants and Migrants*; Vecoli, "Italian Immigrants and the United States Labor Movement"; Vecoli, "Etnia, internazionlismoe protezionismo operaio."

15. Participation can be discerned from the radical newspapers' accounts of these events, and especially from announcements about the number of tickets sold, which often amounted to hundreds and thousands. See, for example, *LQS*, 15 November 1902; "Anarchist Meeting Quiet," *NYT*, 3 August 1900, 3.

16. Gabaccia, *Militants and Migrants*, 128.

17. Pernicone, "Italian Immigrant Radicalism in New York," 78.

18. Avrich, *Anarchist Voices*, 316.

19. Dominick Salitto interview, Avrich, *Anarchist Voices*, 166; Ramella cited in Elwood, "The Roots and Results of Radicalism," 41–43.

20. Vecoli, "Pane e Giustizia," 59. See also Pernicone, "Luigi Galleani"; Fabbri, *Malatesta*; Topp, *Those without a Country*.

21. Caterina D'Amico (aka Catina Willman) interview, Avrich, *Anarchist Voices*, 111; Avrich, *Anarchist Portraits*, 167–71; Pernicone, "Luigi Galleani."

22. Cerrito, "Sull'emigrazione anarchica"; Avrich, *Sacco and Vanzetti*; Vecoli, "'Free Country'"; Vecoli, *The People of New Jersey*; Pernicone, "Anarchism in Italy"; Pernicone, *Italian Anarchism*; Carey, "'La Questione Sociale'"; Carey, "The Vessel."

23. Malatesta, *L'Anarchia*, 13.
24. Quoted in ibid., 27.
25. Ibid., 45. See also *LQS*, 30 December 1897; Guérin, *No Gods, No Masters*.
26. Gremmo, *Gli anarchici che uccisero*; Carey, "The Vessel, the Deed, and the Idea." Ferraris, "L'assassinio de Umberto"; Goldman, *Living My Life*, 271; Galzerano, *Gaetano Bresci*; Rosada, "Gaetano Bresci," 400–402.
27. Carey, "The Vessel, the Deed, and the Idea," 52.
28. "Roosevelt Demands Action," *NYT*, 10 April 1908, 5. See also Halstead, *The Illustrious Life of William McKinley*, chap. 4.
29. Anthony Capraro, interview by Julia Blodgett, 11 September 1969, tapes 4, 6 and 7, Capraro Papers, IHRC; De Ciampis, "Storia del movimento"; Ramirez, "Immigration, Ethnicity, and Political Militance"; Vecoli, "Etnia, internazionalismo e protezionismo operaio"; Vecoli, "The Italian Immigrants in the United States Labor Movement," 274–75; Topp, "The Italian-American Left"; Goldman, *Living My Life*; Gabaccia, *Militants and Migrants*, 139–41; Fenton, *Immigrants and Unions*, chap. 9; Salerno, "I Delitti della Razza Bianca"; Salerno, "'No God, No Master'"; Pernicone, *Carlo Tresca*; Meyer, *Vito Marcantonio*; Ewen, *Immigrant Women*, 259; Glenn, *Daughters of the Shtetl*, 177–83; Vega, *Memoirs*; Sánchez Korrol, *From Colonia to Community*; Rodríguez-Morazzani, "Linking a Fractured Past"; Mirabal, "No Country but the One We Must Fight For"; Yu, *To Save China, To Save Ourselves*; Watkins-Owens, *Blood Relations*; James, *Holding Aloft the Banner of Ethiopia*; Enstad, *Ladies of Labor*; Orleck, *Common Sense and a Little Fire*, 26–27.
30. On connections between different groups, see *LQS*, 24 May 1902, 15 June 1907, 5 June 1910; *EN*, 28 May 1910, 5 June 1910, 3 September 1910, 12 November 1910; on the libraries, see *EN*, 6 October 1913, 15 November 1913, 20 December 1913; on the food cooperatives, see *EN*, 10 September 1910; on benefits and support work, see *LQS*, 11 August 1906, 26 October 1907, 15 January 1910, 10 December 1910, 17 December 1910, 1 April 1911, 8 April 1911.
31. Club Avanti was located at 210 Humboldt Street in Brooklyn. Gabaccia, *Militants and Migrants*, 139–41. See also their regular announcements in *Il Proletario* and *EN*; Subscription Lists for *EN* for New York State, ca. 1920, DOJ, RG 65, file 26049, National Archives.
32. Gruppo Il Risveglio was located at 106 West 3rd Street in Manhattan. *EN*, 15 January 1910, 30 April 1910, 5 November 1910, 10 October 1914, 20 February 1915. See also Galileo Tobia interview, Avrich, *Anarchist Voices*, 137.
33. See *LQS*, 15 April 1897, 15 July 1897, 3 December 1898, 4 February 1899, 26 January 1901, 16 February 1901, 14 March 1908, 2 May 1915; and *EN*, 21 October 1909, 6 November 1909, 15 January 1910, 1 April 1911, 6 December 1913, 24 April 1915; "Special Report of Operative K-K Covering Italian Anarchist Situation in Paterson, N.J. and Vicinity," 12 December 1919, INS records, National Archives, Washington, D.C.; Carey, "'La Questione Sociale'"; Salerno, "'No God, No Master'"; Vega, *Memoirs*, 115.
34. For information on the Festa della Frutta, see *LQS*, 5 September 1903, 3 September 1904, 23 September 1905, 7 September 1909, 28 September 1907, 19 October 1907; *EN*, 12 September 1908, 30 October 1910, 21 September 1912, 28 September 1912, 12 October 1912. For May Day celebrations see, for example, *EN*, 22 April 1911; Vecoli, "'Primo Maggio'"; Foner, *May Day*; Panaccione, *Sappi che oggi è la tua festa*.
35. Pernicone, "Italian Immigrant Radicalism," 83. See also Errico Malatesta on this, quoted in Turcato, "Italian Anarchism," 411.
36. Mormino and Pozzetta, "The Reader Lights the Candle"; Massari, *The Wonderful World*, 56; Flynn, *The Rebel Girl*, 62, 184; Vega, *Memoirs*.
37. Vecoli, "The Italian Immigrant Press," 25; Pozzetta, "The Italian Immigrant Press of New York City"; Cartosio, "Italian Workers and Their Press in the United States"; Hoerder, *The Immigrant Labor Press in North America*.
38. *LQS*, 7 October 1905, 25 May 1907; *EN*, 10 December 1910, 18 March 1911, 25 March 1911, 1 April 1911, 6 May 1911, 3 June 1911, 10 June 1911, 17 June 1911, 24 June 1911, 1 July 1911, 8 July 1911, 15 July 1911;

Ricardo Flores Magón to Pedro Esteve, 30 May 1911, Archivio Electrónico Ricardo Flores Magón, www.archiviomagon.net (accessed 15 July 2008). See also Salerno, "'No God, No Master'"; Salerno, "I Delitti della Razza Bianca"; Topp, *Those without a Country*, 14; Avrich, *Sacco and Vanzetti*; Gallo interview in Avrich, *Anarchist Voices*, 156.

39. Topp, *Those without a Country*; Salerno, *Red November*; Pernicone, *Carlo Tresca*, 29.

40. For example, when Malatesta came to the United Sates from August 1899 to March 1900, he was shot in the leg by a follower of Galleani during a heated discussion. Topp, *Those without a Country*; Pernicone, "Luigi Galleani"; Pernicone, *Carlo Tresca*; Fabbri, *Malatesta*; Galleani, CPC file 2241.

41. Avrich, *Anarchist Voices*, 111, 146, 159, 165, 173.

42. Topp, *Those without a Country*, 51; Pernicone, *Carlo Tresca*; Bencivenni, "Italian American Radical Culture"; Avrich, *Sacco and Vanzetti*; Cerrito, "Sull'emigrazione anarchica italiana."

43. Cartosio, "Italian Workers and Their Press"; Vezzosi, "Class, Ethnicity, and Acculturation."

44. Topp, *Those without a Country*, 51; Topp, "'It is Providential.'"

45. Avrich, *Anarchist Voices*; Avrich, *Anarchist Portraits*; Avrich, *Sacco and Vanzetti*; Salerno, "'No God, No Master'"; Salerno, "'I Delitti della Razza Bianca.'"

46. Elwood, "The Roots and Results of Radicalism," 19.

47. Horowitz, *The Italian Labor Movement*, 37–40; Merli, *Proletariato di fabbrica*, 461–70; Davis, *Conflict and Control*, 202–10.

48. Elwood, "The Roots and Results of Radicalism," 33; Horowitz, *The Italian Labor Movement*, 40.

49. "Brief History of the L'Era Nuova Group of Anarchists at Paterson," ca. 1920, DOJ, RG 65, file 61–4185, National Archives.

50. The Italian population in New Jersey was the third largest, after New York and Pennsylvania. Starr, *The Italians of New Jersey*, 7.

51. Historian Max Nettlau "considered LQS to be among the 17 authoritative organs of anarchist thought in the 1900s. He compared LQS with *L'Anarchie* of Paris and *Freedom* of London." Salvatore, "'No God, No Master,'" 171; Carey, "La Questione Sociale," 289.

52. See subscription lists, 1920, DOJ, National Archives; Carey, "'La Questione Sociale'"; Salerno, "'No God, No Master'"; Cerrito, "Sull'emigrazione anarchica."

53. "Perchè siamo Organizzatori," *LQS*, 30 March 1897; Pedro Esteve, "L'anarchia e gli anarchici," *LQS*, 14 September 1901; and the guide on socialist-anarchism (2,000 copies of which they circulated), *LQS*, 14 March 1908.

54. "Rout Out Anarchy," *NYT*, 24 March 1908, 4; "Ruled Out of the Mails," *NYT*, 27 March 1908, 8.

55. Preston, *Aliens and Dissenters*; and Kornweibel, "Seeing Red."

56. Sallitto interview, Avrich, *Anarchist Voices*, 166.

57. Aurora Alleva, CPC file 73.

58. Avrich, *Anarchist Voices*, 166.

59. These few works include Avrich, *Sacco and Vanzetti*; Salerno, "'No God, No Master'"; Bencivenni, "Italian American Radical Culture in New York City"; Merithew, "Anarchist Motherhood"; Ventresca and Iacovetta, "Virgilia D'Andrea"; and Scarpaci, "Angela Bambace."

60. *LQS*, 5 December 1903; *EN*, 11 March 1911, 25 March 1911, 27 July 1912, 4 April 1914, 19 September 1914, 19 December 1914, 17 July 1915.

61. See minutes for Gruppo L'Era Nuova in Paterson, INS records, National Archives, FBI microfilm roll #706 (OG file # 289493); "Exhibit C" Mailing List for "La Jacquerie," apprehended from Ludovico Caminita by DOJ agents during a raid on Paterson anarchists, 14 February 1920; Acting Commissioner of Immigration, Ellis Island, to Commissioner General of Immigration, Washington, D.C., 25 April 1920, file 54861/362; "An Outing of Members of the L'Era Nuova Group Held at Haledon, N.J.," ca. 1920; and the special reports from informant Joseph Delfine on the activities of the Paterson Group, 1919, INS records, National Archives; "Police Stop Reds' Meeting," *NYT*, 4 April 1908, 7.

62. William Gallo interview, Avrich, *Anarchist Voices*, 154–55.

63. Ibid., 154–55; Guabello/Gallo family reunion photograph, 1921, American Labor Museum/Botto House; Firmino Gallo file, DOJ, RG 65, National Archives; U.S. Department of Commerce, Bureau of Census, *Twelfth Census of the United States: 1900*, Paterson Ward 3, Passaic, NJ, roll T623 991, 3A, 127; *Thirteenth Census of the United States: 1910*, Paterson Ward 4, Passaic, NJ; roll T624 906; 9A; 116; 755.

64. "Brief History of the L'Era Nuova Group," ca. 1920, DOJ, RG 65, file 61-4185, National Archives.

65. Authors included Zola, Tolstoi, Wagner, Stepniak, Mirbeau, Moro, Nordau, Ferrero, Bakounin, Hamon, Lafargue, Novicow, Guyot, Malatesta, Kropotkin, Gino, Rousselle, Gori, Ovidi, Zavattero, Canzani, Roule, Manzoni, Grave, Giaboli, Tolstoi, Most, Merlino, Cafiero, Salvatore, Delasalle, Reclus, Converti, Sivieri, Tcherkesof, Richepin, Esteve, and two women, Anna Maria Mozzoni and Soledad Gustavo. See, for example, *LQS*, 5 September 1903, 10 October 1903, 24 October 1903, 28 November 1903; *EN*, 6 October 1913, 15 November 1913. See also many documents about this store in the Firmino Gallo file, DOJ, RG 65, National Archives.

66. Gallo interview, *Anarchist Voices*, 155. The strike is discussed in my chapter 6.

67. Firmino Gallo file, DOJ, RG 65, National Archives; Firmino Gallo, CPC file 2256.

68. Summary of Gemma Mello hearing, 21 April 1920, file 98767/34, DOJ, RG 65, National Archives.

69. Gallo interview, Avrich, *Anarchist Voices*, 154–55.

70. Bellalma Forzato Spezia, cited and translated by Marcella Bencivenni, "Writing from the Left," 1.

71. *EN*, 17 December 1910, 20 December 1910, 3 June 1911, 19 September 1914, 20 February 1915, 17 July 1915; Quote from Gallo interview, Avrich, *Anarchist Voices*, 155. See also 107–11; Avrich, *Sacco and Vanzetti*, 56; Avrich, *The Modern School Movement*.

72. Kessner, *The Golden Door*; M. Cohen, *Workshop to Office*; Friedman-Kasaba, *Memories of Migration*; Perlmann, *Ethnic Differences*.

73. Sadly, William's own son would die a soldier in the Second World War, ten days after D-Day. Gallo interview, Avrich, *Anarchist Voices*, 153–57.

74. Ibid., 155.

75. A. Guabello, "Un po' di storia," *EN*, 17 July 1915; Carey, "The Vessel, the Deed, and the Idea"; Carey, "'La Questione Sociale'"; Rigazio, "Alberto Guabello." See also the exhibit files at the National Archives, FBI microfilm roll #706 (OG file # 289493).

76. Guabello Family, interview by author, Haledon, New Jersey, 15 July 2001.

77. Gallo interview, Avrich, *Anarchist Voices*, 154.

78. Salitto interview, Avrich, *Anarchist Voices*, 166.

79. Camillo Di Sciullo, "La Donna," *LQS*, 26 October 1907. See also Palombo, *Camillo Di Sciullo*.

80. Topp, *Those without a Country*, 114, 156–57, 167, 169; Bencivenni, "Italian American Radical Culture."

81. *EN*, 11 March 1911, 6 May 1911, 27 May 1911. See also Bellalma Forzato Spezia, CPC file 4908. She was born in 1877 and immigrated to the United States in 1906. For information on her lectures, see *EN*, 15 October 1910, 26 November 1910, 4 December 1910, 31 December 1910, 1 January 1911, 7 January 1911, 14 January 1911; Passenger List, S. S. Liguria from Genoa to New York, 1 March 1906, microfilm serial: T715, roll T715 669, Line 1, Records of the U.S. Customs Service, RG 36, National Archives, Washington, D.C.

82. "Nostre Corrispondenze," *Il Proletario*, 1 December 1907; *EN*, 27 May 1911.

83. *EN*, 31 August 1912, 7 September 1912, 4 January 1913, 14 March 1914; Rygier, *Sulla soglia di un'epoca*; Rygier, *Il sindacalismo alla Sbarra*; Topp, *Those without a Country*, 156.

84. Scarpaci, "Angela Bambace," 101–3. See also "Notes to interview questions," 18–20, February 1975, Bambace Papers, IHRC; and Capraro interview by Blodgett, 11 September 1969, tape 7, Capraro Papers, IHRC.

85. Angela Bambace notes, 15 November 1980, Bambace Papers, IHRC.

86. *Il Proletario*, 17 February 1911; *L'Adunata dei Refrattari*, 25 October 1924, 9 April 1927, 16 April 1927; Capraro interview by Blodgett, 12 September 1969, tape 5, Capraro Papers, IHRC; Cristina Cas-

tagnaro (aka Tina Cacici and Gaetana Cacici), CPC file 1158; *Autobiography of Carlo Tresca*, 1 microfilm reel, IHRC, 195. See also Vecoli, "Anthony Capraro," 14–5; Pernicone, *Carlo Tresca*, 107; Goldberg, *Tale of Three Cities*, 102, 119.

87. Maria Roda, "Alle operaie," *LQS*, 15 September 1897.

88. Una Sartina, "Ma tu sei donna!," *LQS*, 24 August 1901.

89. *LQS*, 23 June 1906.

90. Alba, "Eguali diritti," *LQS*, 15 October 1901. For similar essays by women, defending their right to participate equally in the movement, see Maria Roda, "Alle madri," 7 September 1901; "I gruppi femminili di propaganda," *LQS*, 23 November 1901; Caterina Sebastiani, "L'ultima parola," *LQS*, 8 December 1906; Aurora, "Cose di Paterson," *LQS*, 14 September 1907.

91. Roda-Balzarini, CPC file 4368; U.S. Department of Commerce, Bureau of Census, *Twelfth Census of the United States: 1900*, Paterson, Ward 8, Passaic, New Jersey, Roll T623 993, 16B, 158.

92. Bortolotti, *Sul movimento politico delle donne*, 249; Goldman, *Living My Life*, 150. See also Giovanni Di Nardo, "Sempre Avanti!," *LQS*, 17 February 1900; Titì, "Alle mie sorelle proletarie," *LQS*, 9 June 1906. For Ada Negri's poetry, see "Il Canto della Zappia," *LQS*, 30 July 1896; "Autopsia," *LQS*, 30 October 1896; "Nota di cronaca," *LQS*, 6 May 1899; "Sciopero," *L'Operaia*, 31 January 1914; "Fine di sciopero," *L'Operaia*, 11 March 1914; "Disoccupato," *L'Operaia*, 21 March 1914; "Terra," *L'Operaia*, 2 May 1914; "La tessitrice," *L'Operaia*, 26 September 1914; "La vedova," *L'Operaia*, 5 January 1917; "Sonetto d'inverso," *L'Operaia*, 6 October 1917; "Il Sogno," *L'Operaia*, 12 January 1918.

93. Roda-Balzarini, CPC file 4368; Goldman, *Living My Life*, 150–52; *NYT*, 16 August 1894.

94. *NYT*, 16 August 1894, 20 August 1894.

95. Goldman, *Living My Life*, 150.

96. Ibid., 151.

97. Ibid., 150.

98. Zo d'Axa, "Little Girls" (1895), available at http://www.marxists.org/reference/archive/zo-daxa/1895/little-girls.htm (accessed 12 May 2007).

99. Interviews with Marcelino García and Sirio Esteve, Avrich, *Anarchist Voices*, 390–93; Mormino and Pozzetta, *The Immigrant World*, 150; Halstead, *The Illustrious Life of William McKinley* (1901), chap. 4; Massari, *The Wonderful World*, 107; Goldman, *Living My Life*, I, 150; Vega, *Memoirs*, 13; Carey, "'La Questione Sociale'"; Carey, "The Vessel"; Salerno, "'No God, No Master'"; Fernández, "Migración y sindicalismo"; Dolgoff, *The Cuban Revolution*, 39–40; Fernández, *Cuban Anarchism*, 34; Ealham, "Parallel Lives" (unpublished paper); Olive i Serret, "El movimiento anarquista catalan." See also Esteve's writing, including *Vest-Pocket Essays*; "La Revolución en la Practica" (1958); *Memoria de la Conferencia Anarquista*.

100. García interview, Avrich, *Anarchist Voices*, 390–93.

101. Juan Anido interview, Avrich, *Anarchist Voices*, 396–97.

102. Jacques Rudome interview, Avrich, *Anarchist Voices*, 272. See also 171, 175, 210–13, 229–30.

103. Esteve interview, Avrich, *Anarchist Voices*, 393. See also Maria Esteve, "Pedro Esteve," *Cultura Proletaria*, 14 September 1929. *Cultura Proletaria* succeeded *Cultura Obrera*. Both are available at the NYPL and the International Institute of Social History in Amsterdam.

104. In the census, she is listed as Mary, Marie, and Maria Esteve. U.S. Department of Commerce, Bureau of Census, *Twelfth Census of the United States: 1900*, Paterson, Ward 8, Passaic, New Jersey, roll T623 993, 16B, 158; *Thirteenth Census of the United States: 1910*, Tampa Ward 8, Hillsborough, Florida, roll T624 162, 6B, 60, Image 865; "Brief Historical Sketch of L'Era Nuova Group," ca. 1920, DOJ, RG 65, file 61-4185, National Archives.

105. "Brief Historical Sketch of L'Era Nuova Group," ca. 1920, DOJ, RG 65, file 61-4185, National Archives; Avrich, *Anarchist Voices*, 142, 390–93.

106. They lived at the following addresses, in this order: 350 Clay Street, Paterson; 610 Francis Avenue, Tampa; and 611 Gregory Avenue, Weehawken. U.S. Department of Commerce, Bureau of Census, *Twelfth Census of the United States: 1900*, Paterson, Ward 8, Passaic, New Jersey, roll T623 993, 16B,

158; *Thirteenth Census of the United States: 1910*, Tampa Ward 8, Hillsborough, Florida, roll T624 162, 6B, 60, Image 865; *Fourteenth Census of the United States: 1920*, Weehawken Ward 2, Hudson, New Jersey, roll T625 1050, 1A, 314, 116. See also Vega, *Memoirs*, 13, 24, 113; Massari, *The Wonderful World*, 107; Salerno, "'No God, No Master'"; Avrich, *Anarchist Voices*, 143, 272, 390–93, 398; Mormino and Pozzetta, *The Immigrant World*, 80, 140–50, 167–69; Topp, *Those without a Country*, 14.

107. Avrich, *Anarchist Voices*, 210–12, 143, 393. See also Mormino and Pozzetta, *The Immigrant World*, 80, 140–50, 167–69; Mormino and Pozzetta, "The Reader Lights the Candle"; Ealham, "Parallel Lives."

108. "Cronaca di Spring Valley, Il gruppo femminile," *L'Aurora*, 22 December 1900. See also Merithew, "Anarchist Motherhood."

109. *LQS*, 15 September 1897, 6 November 1901, 23 November 1901, 13 December 1901, 4 January 1902, 11 January 1902, 5 April 1902, 5 September 1903, 2 January 1904.

110. *LQS*, 15 September 1897, 6 November 1901, 23 November 1901, 4 January 1902, 5 April 1902.

111. *LQS*, 14 December 1901, 2 August 1902.

112. Ernestina Cravello, CPC file 1524; Antonio Cravello, CPC file 4849; Vittorio Cravello, CPC file 4851.

113. "Assassin's Lot Fell upon Anarchist Here," *NYT*, 31 July 1900, 1; "Searching among Paterson Anarchists," *NYT*, 1 August 1900, 1; "Paterson Anarchists Quiet," 5 August 1900, 2; "Girl Anarchist Proud of Bresci," *New York World*, 15 September 1900, 6; Gremmo, *Gli anarchici*, 42; Carey, "La Questione Sociale," 292–93.

114. "Searching among Paterson Anarchists," *NYT*, 1 August 1900, 1.

115. "Girl Anarchist Proud of Bresci," *New York World*, 15 September 1900, 6.

116. Ibid.

117. Goldman, *Living My Life*, 271, 289; Ernestina Cravello, CPC file 1524; Antonio Cravello, CPC file 4849; Vittorio Cravello, CPC file 4851.

118. Letter to *Bollettino della Sera*, reprinted in *LQS*, 1 September 1900.

119. Italian Consulate General to Minister of the Interior, New York, 11 September 1903, in Vittorio Cravello, CPC file 4851; Ciancabilla to Jacques Gross, 25 January 1902, quoted in Vecoli, "Giuseppe Ciancabilla," unpublished paper, IHRC. Ciancabilla also edited *LQS* for a short period, from 1898 to 1900, but left the position because of this "acrimonious polemics" with the organizationalist anarchists with whom he disagreed. For more on this, and for the two quotes cited in text, see Vecoli, "'Primo Maggio,'" 62. See also Carey, "'La Questione Sociale,'" 293; Fedeli, *Giuseppe Ciancabilla*; Rosada, "Giuseppe Ciancabilla," in Andreucci and Detti, *Il movimento operaio*, 31–33; Avrich, *Sacco and Vanzetti*, 47; Avrich, *Anarchist Voices*, 503; Pernicone, "Luigi Galleani"; Mapelli, "Giuseppe Ciancabilla."

120. Nunzio Pernicone, correspondence with author, 1 September 2007, 16 July 2008.

121. Ersilia (Cavedagni) Grandi, "Gli anarchici e la donna," *LQS*, 4 April 1897. See also her essays in *LQS*, 15 April 1898, 12 October 1898, 31 December 1898, 29 April 1899, 14 January 1899; Ersilia Cavedagni Grandi, CPC file 1205.

122. *LQS*, 5 April 1902.

123. *LQS*, 4 January 1902, 11 January 1902, 5 April 1902.

124. Mozzoni, *Alle fanciulle che studiano*, 10, IHRC Print Collection.

125. Ibid., 10. Translation by José Moya, in "Italians in Buenos Aires' Anarchist Movement," 344.

126. Soledad Gustavo was a pseudonym for Teresa Mañé i Miravet (1865–1939).

127. *LQS*, 12 July 1902; Soledad Gustavo, *Alle proletarie*, quoted in Moya, "Italians in Buenos Aires' Anarchist Movement," 196.

128. Moya, "Italians in Buenos Aires," 213 nn21, 25; Molyneux, "No God, No Boss, No Husband"; Veccia, "Family and Factory." The essays that were circulating in *La Battaglia* mirrored those that were in *LQS*: "La donna di oggi e quelli di domani," 18 August 1910; "Il femminismo e la donna

nella religione dell'umanita," 18 October 1910; "L'emancipazione della donna," 28 November 1910; "La schiavitu' della donna," 26 June 1904; "Alle donne del popolo," 30 September 1906; "La morale degli uomini e la liberta' della donna," 29 December 1907; "Il problema della donna: Una questione indiscussa," 29 November 1908; "Famiglia ed educazione," 1 November 1908; "Voce di donna," 16 June 1907.

129. Alba Genisio, "Alle donne proletarie," *LQS*, 7 March 1908.

130. Moya, "Italians in Buenos Aires' Anarchist Movement," 341.

131. Luigia Reville, "Ai rivoluzionarii, in nome del gruppo 'L'azione femminile' di Parigi," *LQS*, 5 May 1900. See also Anita Sweedsky, "Femminismo elettorale o emancipazione della donna?," *EN*, 7 June 1913; Mary, "L'emancipazione della donna," *EN*, 3 January 1914.

132. Virginia Buongiorno, "Alle compagne lavoratrici!," *LQS*, 15 October 1895.

133. Moya, "Italians in Buenos Aires' Anarchist Movement," 343.

134. Maria Barbieri, "Ribelliamoci!," *LQS*, 18 November 1905.

135. Alba Genisio, "Alle donne proletarie," *LQS*, 7 March 1908. See also *EN*, 22 February 1908, 24 December 1910.

136. Maria Roda, "Alle madri," *LQS*, 7 September 1901.

137. *LQS*, 30 January 1896, 30 June 1897, 25 February 1899, 12 May 1900, 5 December 1903, 19 January 1907, 15 June 1907; and *EN*, 29 October 1910, 27 January 1912.

138. Titì, "Il Congo," *LQS*, 26 January 1907.

139. *LQS*, 31 December 1898.

140. Una Donna, "Scab!," *LQS*, 12 November 1904; Angiolina Algeri, "A sciopero protratto," *EN*, 18 February 1911; Anna Nigra, "Non uccidere!," *EN*, 14 December 1912; Mary Barsanti, "Per Aldemas," *EN*, 4 January 1913.

141. For example, see Una Donna, "Scab!," *LQS*, 12 November 1904; Angiolina Algeri, "A sciopero protratto," *EN*, 18 February 1911; Anna Nigra, "Non uccidere!," *EN*, 14 December 1912; Mary Barsanti, "Per Aldemas," *EN*, 4 January 1913.

142. Titì, "Alle donne, emancipiamoci!," *LQS*, 7 July 1906.

143. Camillo Di Sciullo, "La donna," *LQS*, 26 October 1907. See also the following in *LQS*; A. Ferritti, "La donna, come era, come è, e come sarà," 29 February 1896; A. Ferritti, "Considerazioni sulla donna," 15 August 1897; "Gli anarchici e la donna," 4 April 1897; Albert Guabello, "Alle donne," 18 February 1899; Evening, "La donna dell'avvenire," 18 February 1899; Giuseppe Corna, "Il martirio della donna," 17 June 1899; See response to Luigia Reville, "Ai rivoluzionarii," 5 May 1900; A. Visalli, "Alla donna," 19 January 1901 and 29 January 1901; "I gruppi femminili di propaganda," 23 November 1901; Il Mefistofelico, "Intorno all'emancipazione della donna," 2 November 1907; Il Gruppo I Nuovi Viventi, Il Gruppo Femminile Luisa Michel, "La questione della donna," *L'Aurora*, 22 December 1900.

144. Maria Barbieri, "Ribelliamoci!," *LQS*, 18 November 1905.

145. *LQS*, 9 June 1906, 16 June 1906.

146. Ibid.; *LQS*, 7 July 1906.

147. Ida Merini Catastini, "La donna nella famiglia," *LQS*, 16 November 1907. See also Merithew, "Anarchist Motherhood."

148. Maria Roda, "Alle madri," *LQS*, 7 September 1901.

149. Alba, "Alle mie compagne," *LQS*, 31 August 1901. For others that shared this vision, see *LQS*, 5 October 1901; Linda Murri, "Come si educano i figli," *LQS*, 2 June 1906.

150. Maria Barbieri, "Alle madri," *LQS*, 8 August 1903.

151. Bellalma Forzato Spezia, *Per le nuove generazioni* (New York: Nicoletti Brothers Press, 1911), IHRC Print Collection.

152. *LQS*, 12 October 1898.

153. *LQS*, 16 June 1906.

154. Ibid.

155. See, for example, *LQS*, 17 May 1902.

156. *LQS*, 16 June 1906. For examples of writing on this philosophy, see *LQS*, 30 September 1897, 30 July 1897, 6 January 1900, 3 March 1900, 28 September 1901, 27 June 1903, 20, 27 February 1904, 5 March 1904, 23 December 1905, 16 June 1906, 7, 14, 28 September 1907, 26 October 1907, 25 June 1910.

157. Battan, "The 'Rights,'" 167.

158. Ibid., 178.

159. Kissack, *Free Comrades*.

160. Maria Roda, "Alle madri," *LQS*, 7 September 1901.

161. *LQS*, 16 June 1906.

162. *LQS*, 26 October 1907; Anna De Gigli, "L'amore, la proprietà e i delitti," *EN*, 31 May 1913.

163. Anna De Gigli, "L'amore, la proprietà e i delitti," *EN*, 31 May 1913; and "La virtù dell'esempio," *EN*, 19 October 1912. See also her other essays in *EN*: "Il colera in Italia," 20 October 1910, "La legalità ci uccide," 12 November 1910; "Mentre imperano le leggi e la morale borghese—La Taglia," 3 December 1910; "Favole . . . ," 17 December 1910; "Al di la' del divino," 21 September 1912; "Sacrilegi," 2 November 1912; "La prostituzione," 8 February 1913; "L'Amore, la proprietà e i delitti," 31 May 1913; "La potenza del danaro," 5 July 1913; "Regime contro natura," 30 August 1913; "Verità antiche" and "Contro dio e lo stato," 27 September 1913; "L'avvenire," 3 January 1914; "Contro il cannibalismo," 21 February 1914; and "A un borghese," 18 April 1914.

164. Maria Barbieri, "Ribelliamoci!," *LQS*, 18 November 1905.

165. See, for example, Vecoli, "The Making and Un-making," 64; Pernicone, *Carlo Tresca*, 138.

166. Avrich, *Anarchist Voices*, 101, 108.

167. *LQS*, 7 April 1907.

168. Maria Barbieri, "Ribelliamoci!," *LQS*, 18 November 1905; Augusta De Angelis, "Redenta," *LQS*, 22 December 1906.

169. Esteve interview, Avrich, *Anarchist Voices*, 393; Esteve, *The Experience*.

170. "In Memoriam Francesca Crivello," box 3, Crivello Papers, IHRC.

171. "Antonino Crivello," box 3, Crivello Papers, IHRC; CPC file 1540.

172. Elwood, "The Roots and Results of Radicalism," iii.

173. Ibid.

174. Cristina Melone, "Lettera aperta: Ai preti della Chiesa di San Michele di Paterson," *LQS*, 20 April 1907.

175. *LQS*, 21 September 1907.

176. Elvira, "L'abbomino della religione," *EN*, 27 July 1912; Titì, "Odio," *LQS*, 14 April 1906; Una Neofita, "Sorelle di fatiche!," *EN*, 3 December 1910.

177. Vanda Caiola, "Via dalla chiesa!," *EN*, 25 May 1912. See also Aurora, "È il sentimento religioso innato nell'uomo," *LQS*, 9 June 1906; Candida M. D'Arcangelo, "Alle donne proletarie," *LQS*, 11 January 1908.

178. *LQS*, 2 March 1907, 25 May 1907, 7, 14, 28 September 1907, 12, 19 October 1907.

179. Avrich, *Anarchist Voices*, 97.

180. Glenn, *Female Spectacle*, 127. For Goldman's lectures before Italian audiences, see *LQS*, 31 December 1898; *EN*, 1 November 1913, 20 December 1913, 16 January 1915.

181. Avrich, *Anarchist Voices*, 108.

182. *LQS*, 18 November 1899, 15 April 1899; *EN*, 3 January 1915.

183. *LQS*, 31 May 1902, 12 September 1903.

184. *LQS*, 3 September 1904.

185. Her store was at 1946 First Avenue. Elvira Catello, CPC file 1182; *EN*, 17 May 1913, 20 September 1913, 20 December 1913, 13 January 1914, 14, 21 February 1914, 29 August 1914, 20 February 1915. See also Catello's husband, Paolo Perrini's CPC file 3875; and U.S. Department of Commerce, Bureau of Census, *Fourteenth Census of the United States: 1920*, Manhattan Assembly District 18, roll T625 1218, 13B, 1227, 30.

186. Nena Becchetti, *La figlia dell'anarchico* (Jessup, Pa.: Gruppo Autonomo, 1928), IHRC Print Collection.

187. *LQS*, 14 January 1899, 7 September 1907, 26 October 1907.

188. Avrich, *Anarchist Voices*, 109.

189. *EN*, 3 January 1915.

190. See, for example, *LQS*, 3 September 1904, 7, 28 September 1907, 10 September 1915; *Il Proletario*, 21 April 1911.

191. Hyman, *Staging Strikes*, 3.

192. Glenn, *Female Spectacle*, 3.

193. Carolina Golzio, interview by Steve Golin, 13 June 1983; and Rose Villano, interview by Golin, 13 June 1983, SSC; Jenny Paglia interview, Avrich, *Anarchist Voices*, 97.

194. Quoted in Malkiel, "Striking for the Right to Live."

Chapter 6

1. *New York Evening Post*, 20 January 1913; *NYT*, 19, 20, 22 January 1913, 2 March 1913; *New York Call*, 30 December 1912, 1, 7, 9, 13, 14, 16, 19, 20 January 1913, 2, 5 February 1913; *New York Sun*, 4 January 1913; *Bollettino della Sera*, 3, 4, 10, 16 January 1913; *EN*, 11, 25 January 1913; *Il Proletario*, 18, 25 January 1913, 1 February 1913; *Il Progresso Italo-Americano*, 1 January 1913 to 3 February 1913; Malkiel, "Striking for the Right to Live"; Women's Trade Union League of New York, *Annual Report, 1912–13*, 22. See also Furio, "Immigrant Women and Industry," 185–204; Orleck, *Common Sense and a Little Fire*, 75–76; Dubofsky, *When Workers Organize*, 83; Levine, *The Women's Garment Workers*, 226–27; Fenton, *Immigrants and Unions*, 515–24; Foner, *History of Labor Movement*, 256.

2. *NYT*, 19 January 1913.

3. *NYT*, 19, 20 January 1913; Orleck, *Common Sense and a Little Fire*, 76.

4. See Susan Glenn's discussion of this historiography in *Daughters of the Shtetl*, 191–94.

5. Kessler-Harris, *Out to Work*; Schofield, "The Uprising of the 20,000"; Seller, "The Uprising of Twenty Thousand"; Dye, *As Equals and as Sisters*; Tax, *The Rising of the Women*; Buhle, *Women and American Socialism*; Glenn, *Daughters of the Shtetl*, 177, 213; Friedman-Kasaba, *Memories of Migration*, 167–69; Enstad, *Ladies of Labor*; Orleck, *Common Sense and a Little Fire*, 41–50, 57–63; Greenwald, *The Triangle Fire*, chap. 1. For first-hand accounts, see Malkiel, *The Diary of a Shirtwaist Striker*; Stein, *Out of the Sweatshop*, 59–86.

6. Marot, "A Woman's Strike"; ILGWU, *Proceedings of Convention* (1910), 91; Van Kleeck, *Artificial Flower Makers*, 37; Spadoni, "The Italian Working Woman," 14; Sarah Comstock, "In the Strikers' Hall," *New York Tribune*, 11 December 1909; *L'Araldo Italiano*, 3, 5 December 1909; *Jewish Daily Forward*, 11, 17 September 1909; Women's Trade Union League of New York, *Annual Report, 1910–1911*, 5; Stein, *Out of the Sweatshop*, 59–86; Fenton, *Immigrants and Unions*, 485; Friedman-Kasaba, *Memories of Migration*, 117, 167–69; M. Cohen, *Workshop to Office*, 76–83.

7. *Bollettino della Sera*, 2, 23, 24, 26, 27 November 1909, 4, 8, 9, 10, 14, 17 December 1909; *Il Progresso Italo-Americano*, 25 November 1909.

8. Women's Trade Union League of New York, *Annual Report, 1910–1911*, 3–5; Spadoni, "The Italian Working Woman," 14–15; *EN*, 10 September 1910; Fenton, *Immigrants and Unions*, 490, 500; P. Buhle and Georgakas, *The Immigrant Left*, 136–37; Topp, *Those without a Country*, 51; Pernicone, *Carlo Tresca*, 22, 28, 92.

9. *Bollettino della Sera*, 2 November 1909, 4, 9, 10, 14, 17 December 1909.

10. *LQS*, 30 March 1897, 30 May 1897, 30 July 1897, 4 February 1899; Hutchins, *Labor and Silk*, 135–37.

11. *LQS*, 7 April 1907, 6 July 1907.

12. *EN*, 12 September 1908.

13. Friedman-Kasaba, *Memories of Migration*, 165–67, 190; M. Cohen, *Workshop to Office*, 77–81.

14. De Gregorio, "'This Is Not Your Union,'" 6; *48 Libro Ricordo: XXV anniversario della unione dei cloak makers italiani, Local 48, ILGWU, 1916–1941*, 76–79; Fraser, "Landslayt and Paesani," 287–88.

15. *Il Proletario*, 3, 24 December 1909; *L'Araldo Italiano*, 23, 24, 26 November 1909; Levine, *Women's Garment Workers*, 156; Fenton, *Immigrants and Unions*, 488–89.

16. Van Kleeck, *Artificial Flower Makers*, 30–39. See also Bernardy, "L'emigrazione," 36; Spadoni, "The Italian Working Woman," 14; *Weekly Bulletin of the Clothing Trades*, 28 February 1908, 6; Sarah Comstock, "In the Strikers' Hall," *New York Tribune*, 11 December 1909.

17. Van Kleeck, *Artificial Flower Makers*, 37.

18. Carnevale, "Culture of Work," 163–65.

19. Spadoni, "The Italian Working Woman," 14.

20. Watson, *Fasanella's City*, 99.

21. Ganz, *Rebels*, 73.

22. Furio, "Immigrant Women and Industry"; Ewen, *Immigrant Women*, 250.

23. Watson, *Fasanella's City*, 99–100. See also Mary Cacchione and Vincenza Cracchiolo, interview by Columba Furio, ca. 1977, SSC.

24. Ewen, *Immigrant Women*, 253–54.

25. Carolina Golzio, interview by Steve Golin, 13 June 1983, SSC.

26. Speech, 15 November 1980, Bambace Papers, IHRC.

27. Pasquale Di Neri, "When Is the Next Meeting?," *Message*, 15 October 1915.

28. *L'Operaia*, 18 April 1914. See also, for example, *LQS*, 31 May 1902; *EN*, 3 September 1910; *Lotta di Classe*, 13 April 1912, 4, 11 May 1912, 19 February 1915, 9 April 1915.

29. See, for example, Kelley, "We Are Not What We Seem."

30. Gabaccia, *Militants and Migrants*, 140; Fenton, *Immigrants and Unions*; Cartosio, "Gli emigrati italiani e l'Industrial Workers of the World"; Ramirez, "Immigration, Ethnicity, and Political Militance."

31. Ramirez, "Immigration, Ethnicity, and Political Militance," 128.

32. Quoted in M. Buhle et al., *Encyclopedia of the American Left*, 356. See also Salerno, *Red November*.

33. M. Buhle et al., *Encyclopedia of the American Left*, 356.

34. Salerno, *Red November*; Salerno, "'No God, No Master'"; Carey, "The Vessel, the Deed, and the Idea"; Vecoli, "'Free Country'"; Rigazio, "Alberto Guabello."

35. Topp, *Those without a Country*, 42.

36. *Il Proletario*, 16, 22 July 1910; *Bollettino della Sera*, 30 June 1910; *L'Araldo Italiano*, 12 August 1910. See also Furio, "Immigrant Women and Industry," 156–57, 242–46; Fenton, *Immigrants and Unions*, 498–99.

37. Salerno, *Red November*, 48–49, 58, 89; Salerno, "No God, No Master"; Cartosio, "Gli emigrati italiani"; Furio, "Immigrant Women and Industry," 156–57, 242–46; Zappia, "Unionism and the Italian American Worker"; De Ciampis, "Storia del Movimento," 154; Gabaccia, *Militants and Migrants*, 117, 140–42; Vecoli, "The Making and Un-making"; Vecoli, "The Italian Immigrants in the United States Labor Movement"; Vecoli, "Italian American Workers," 28–29; Fenton, *Immigrants and Unions*, 479–91; Foner, *The Industrial Workers of the World*, 67; Orleck, *Common Sense and a Little Fire*, 76; Collomp and Debouzy, "European Migrants and the U.S. Labor Movement," 363–73; Ramirez, "Immigration, Ethnicity, and Political Militance."

38. Buhle, "Anarchism and American Labor," 21, 28. See also Fenton, *Immigrants and Unions*, 317.

39. "Cloak Makers Vote to Strike," *New York Call*, 5 July 1910. See also Foner, *The Industrial Workers of the World*, 66; Furio, "Immigrant Woman and Industry," 154; N. Green, *Ready-to-Wear*, 364–65.

40. *L'Araldo Italiano*, 8, 26 April 1910, 13 May 1910, 19 June 1910, 21 July 1910, 18 September 1910; *Il Proletario*, 10 June 1910; *Bollettino della Sera*, 30 June 1910; Furio, "Immigrant Women and Industry," 154–56, 162; Fenton, *Immigrants and Unions*, 495–97; ILGWU, *Proceedings of Convention (1910)*; Levine, *Women's Garment Workers*, 205; Greenwald, *The Triangle Fire*, chap. 2.

41. Orleck, *Common Sense and a Little Fire*, 63.

42. Fenton, *Immigrants and Unions*, 495.

43. Ibid., 501; Women's Trade Union League of New York, *Annual Report, 1910–1911*, 5–6, *1911–12*, 15–16, *1912–13*, 21–22; Spadoni, "The Italian Working Woman," 15.

44. Women's Trade Union League of New York, *Annual Report, 1910–11*, 3–5, *1912–13*, 22; ILGWU, *Proceedings of Convention (1910)*, 74–89; Fenton, *Immigrants and Unions*, chap. 11; Topp, *Those without a Country*, 51; Buhle, *The Immigrant Left*, 136–37.

45. Ramirez, "Immigration, Ethnicity, and Political Militance," 130, 139; Fenton, *Immigrants and Unions*; Vecoli, "The Making and Unmaking"; Montgomery, "The 'New Unionism.'"

46. Ralph Iannanto, interview by Columba Furio, ca. 1977, SSC.

47. *L'Operaia*, 4 April 1914, 16 May 1914, 8 August 1914, 3 September 1914, 27 February 1915; Furio, "Immigrant Women and Industry," 192.

48. "Notes to interview questions," February 18–20, 1975, Bambace Papers, IHRC.

49. Grace De Luise, interview by Columba Furio, 22 September 1978, SSC.

50. Enstad, *Ladies of Labor*, 91.

51. Diana Romanik, interview by Columba Furio, 1 April 1977; and Iannanto interview by Furio, SSC.

52. De Luise and Romanik interviews by Furio; *Lotta di Classe*, 6 July 1912; Haywood, *Bill Haywood's Book*, 249; Scarpaci, "Angela Bambace," 101–2; Cameron, *Radicals of the Worst Sort*, 106.

53. Una Compagna, "Interessi femminili," *Lotta di Classe*, 27 December 1912; *Lotta di Classe*, 13 April 1912; *L'Operaia*, 13 September 1913, 4, 13, 18, 23 April 1914, 13 August 1914, 3 September 1914, 17, 24, 31 October 1914, 2 January 1915, 27 February 1915, 24 April 1915; Angela Bambace, "Notes to interview questions dictated by Angela Bambace to Marion," 18–20 February 1975, Bambace Papers, IHRC.

54. Circulation figures are estimated in the *Message*, 25 December 1914.

55. *L'Operaia*, 4 July 1914; *Lotta di Classe*, 28 August 1914, 22 January 1915, 9 February 1915, 19 March 1915, 30 April 1915, 25 June 1915, 29 October 1915.

56. *L'Operaia*, 4 July 1914.

57. *L'Operaia*, 24 April 1915. See also *Lotta di Classe*, 10 February 1912, 22 May 1912.

58. Clara Zara, "Alle Krumire della Liptzin & Co.," *L'Operaia*, 24 October 1914. See also *Lotta di Classe*, 9 April 1915.

59. Tina Gaeta, interview by Columba Furio, 22 November 1976, SSC.

60. "Antonino Crivello, Operaio-Poeta," *Giustizia*, December 1969.

61. Watson, *Fasanella's City*, 137–40; D'Ambrosio, *Ralph Fasanella's America*, 18–19, 26–27.

62. See, for example, interviews with Antonetta Lazzaro, 29 March 1977; Diane Romanik, 1 April 1977, Grace De Luise, 22 September 1978, Tina Catania, 30 March 1978; and Tina Gaeta, 22 November 1976, by Columba Furio, SSC, reprinted in Furio, "Immigrant Women in Industry"; "In Memoriam Francesca Crivello," box 3, Antonino Crivello Papers, IHRC; *Il Proletario*, 31 March 1911; 7 April 1912, *Lotta di Classe*, 23 March 1912, 27 April 1912; *EN*, 1 April 1911; Ewen, *Immigrant Women*, 260; Glenn, *Daughters of the Shtetl*, 167–73; Greenwald, *The Triangle Fire*.

63. Cameron, *Radicals of the Worst Sort*; Ramirez, "Immigration, Ethnicity, and Political Militance," 134; Fenton, *Immigrants and Unions*, 320–66; Furio, "Immigrant Women and Industry," 191–82; Topp, "The Italian-American Left," 131; Montgomery, *Workers' Control in America*, 93–95; Golin, *The Fragile Bridge*, 2–11.

64. Quoted in Theresa Malkiel, "Striking for the Right to Live," *Coming Nation* 1:124 (25 January 1913).

65. *New York Sun*, 4 January 1913.

66. *New York Call*, 1, 7, 13, 14, 15, 19, 20 January 1913, 2, 5, 13 February 1913; *New York Sun*, 4, 7, 9, 29 January 1913; *Bollettino della Sera*, 3, 4, 9, 10 January 1913.

67. "Girl Strikers in a Fight," *NYT*, 2 March 1913, 3.

68. Orleck, *Common Sense and a Little Fire*, 76; Levine, *The Women's Garment Workers*, 226.

69. *L'Araldo Italiano*, 17, 22, 25, 27 January 1913, 9 February 1913, 8 March 1913.

70. Swanton, *Silk City*; Golin, *The Fragile Bridge*; Golin, "Defeat Becomes Disaster"; Osborne, "Paterson"; Osborne, "Italian Immigrants"; Dodyk, "Winder, Warpers, and Girls on the Loom."

71. Golin, *The Fragile Bridge*, 8, 232.

72. Ibid., 37.

73. Helen Meadow, interview by Rita Isaacs and Jerry Nathans, 17 and 24 August 1982 (on tape in Charles Goldman Judaica Library, YM/YWHA, Wayne, N.J.), paraphrased in ibid., 31.

74. Ibid.

75. *New York Call*, 20, 27 March 1913, 3, 5 May 1913; *Paterson Evening News*, 6 March 1913, 25 April 1913, 14 June 1913; *Solidarity*, 15 March 1913; 10, 31 May 1913; Golin, *The Fragile Bridge*, 44–45.

76. Quoted in Avrich, *Anarchist Voices*, 155.

77. *Paterson Evening News*, 17 April 1913, 9.

78. Flynn, "Contract Slavery in the Paterson Silk Mills," 30; "I Make Cheap Silk," *Masses* 5 (November 1913), 7; *New York Call*, 22 March 1913; Golin, *The Fragile Bridge*, 66–67.

79. Carolina Golzio, interview by Steve Golin, 16 June 1983, SSC.

80. Golin, *The Fragile Bridge*, 154.

81. Quoted in Elwood, "The Roots and Results of Radicalism," 72.

82. William Haywood, "A Rip in the Silk Industry," *International Socialist Review* 13 (May 1913), 788; Flynn, *Rebel Girl*, 165; *New York Call*, 7 April 1913; *Solidarity*, 24 May 1914; Bunny Kuiken and Sylvia Bochese, interview by Robert Kirkman, Haledon, N.J., 19 March 1981, American Labor Museum, Haledon, N.J.

83. Golin, *The Fragile Bridge*, 63.

84. Flynn, *The Rebel Girl*, 165–66.

85. Haywood, "On the Paterson Picket Line," 848; *Masses* 4 (June 1913), 5.

86. "Notes to interview questions dictated by Angela Bambace to Marian, February 1975," Bambace Papers, IHRC.

87. Brecher, *Strike!*; J. Green, *The World of the Worker*.

88. Fenton, *Immigrants and Unions*, 526; Furio, "Immigrant Women and Industry," 95.

89. Furio, "Immigrant Women and Industry," 251.

90. Local 48-ILGWU, *"48" Libro ricordo del XXV anniversario della unione dei cloakmakers italiani* (New York: International Newspaper Printing Co., 1941), 25–30; Crawford, *Luigi Antonini*; Furio, "Immigrant Women and Industry"; Zappia, "Unionism and the Italian American Worker"; Glenn, *Daughters of the Shtetl*; Fenton, *Immigrants and Unions*, 526; N. Green, *Ready-to-Wear*, 366.

Chapter 7

1. Salerno, "'*I Delitti*,'" 114.

2. See DOJ reports, 1919–20, FBI microfilm 706, file 289493, INS, National Archives; "Terrorists Caught in Paterson Raids," *NYT*, 16 February 1920, 1; "Raid Business Booms in Paterson," *New York Call* 1:1, 16 February 1920; "Red Raids Yield Bomb Plot Clue," *NYT*, 17 February 1920, 1; "Paterson Raids," *Evening Mail*, 16 February 1920, 1.

3. "Terrorists Caught in Paterson Raids," *NYT*, 16 February 1920, 1.

4. American Social History Project, *Who Built America?*, 306–7.

5. Ventresco, "Crises and Unity"; Vecoli, "The Making and Un-making"; Vecoli, "Etnia, internazionalismo e protezionismo"; Vecoli, "'Free Country'"; Vezzosi, *Il Socialismo indifferente*; Vezzosi, "Class, Ethnicity, and Acculturation"; Cartosio, "Gli emigrati italiani"; Avrich, *Sacco and Vanzetti*; Preston, *Aliens and Dissenters*; Higham, *Strangers in the Land*, 264–330; Topp, *The Sacco and Vanzetti Case*; Delamater and Trasciatti, *Representing Sacco and Vanzetti*; McGirr, "The Passion of Sacco and Vanzetti"; Davis, *Sacco and Vanzetti*.

6. Orsi, "The Religious Boundaries," 315; Drake and Cayton, *Black Metropolis*, 175; *Public Opinion Quarterly* (March 1940), 95.

7. Diggins, *Mussolini and Fascism*, 12; Higham, *Strangers in the Land*, 65–66.

8. Quotation of Senator Ellison DuRant Smith of South Carolina during a Senate debate on the 1924 Johnson-Reed Act, cited in *Who Built America?*, 322. See also Ngai, *Impossible Subjects*, chap. 1.

9. Daniels, *Coming to America*, 265–84. See also Roediger, *Working toward Whiteness*.

10. Pernicone, *Carlo Tresca*, 115; Frank R. Stone, Special Agent, to J. E. Hoover, Special Assistant to the Attorney General, DOJ, 7 May 1920, file 26049, RG 65, National Archives; "Red Raids Yield Bomb Plot Clue," *NYT*, 17 February 1920, 1; "Palmer and Family Safe," *NYT*, 3 June 1919, 1; "Girl Tells of Italian Near Bombed House," *NYT*, 4 June 1919; Avrich, *Sacco and Vanzetti*, Salerno, "*I Delitti*," 114–15.

11. Avrich, *Sacco and Vanzetti*, 165; Murray, *Red Scare*, 80; Jaffe, *Crusade against Radicalism*, 94; Kornweibel, "*Seeing Red*"; Preston, *Aliens and Dissenters*; *NYT*, 4 June 1919; *Philadelphia Inquirer*, 4 June 1919.

12. Caminita, *Nell'isola*, selection translated and reprinted in Marazzi, *Voices of Italian America*, 129.

13. Ibid., 125–26.

14. Elwood, "The Roots and Results of Radicalism," 82; Salerno, "'*I Delitti*'"; Guabello family, interview by author, 20 August 2001.

15. See Bureau reports, 1919–20, file 89493, RG 65, National Archives.

16. "Continuation of Hearing in the Case of Jemma [*sic*] Mello," 1 April 1920, file 98767/34, DOJ, RG 65, National Archives. See also Salerno, "B. Emilio."

17. Summary of Gemma Mello hearing, 21 April 1920, file 98767/34, DOJ, RG 65, National Archives; Gemma Mello, CPC file 3214, file 54861, INS Records, National Archives.

18. Immigration Act of October 16, 1918, also known as the Anarchist Exclusion Act.

19. Avrich, *Anarchist Voices*, 97, 497 n221; Avrich, *Sacco and Vanzetti*, 205; "Continuation of Hearing in the Case of Jemma Mello," 12–13, 1 April 1920, file 98767/34, DOJ, RG 65, National Archives.

20. Avrich, *Sacco and Vanzetti*, 205; *NYT*, 17 September 1920; *New York Call*, 17 September 1920; Gilligan, "The Wall Street Explosion Mystery."

21. Avrich, *Sacco and Vanzetti*, 206.

22. During the plenary session for "The Lost World of Italian American Radicalism" Conference, City University of New York, New York, N.Y., 14–15 May 1997, a relative of one of the men who orchestrated the bombing told of the remorse many in the movement felt when a child was killed by the tooth of the horse that drove the carriage with the bomb. See also Diva Agostinelli, interview by Rebecca DeWitt, 3 March 2001, at http://flag.blackened.net/ias/9diva.htm (accessed 6 July 2008).

23. American Social History Project, *Who Built America?*, 301. See also Brecher, *Strike!*, chap. 4; Hagedorn, *Savage Peace*.

24. "Paterson Raids Give Clues to Palmer Bomb," *Evening Mail*, 16 February 1920, 1; "Raid Business Booms in Paterson," *New York Call*, 16 February 1920; "Terrorists Caught," *NYT*, 16 February 1920. See also Salerno, "*I Delitti*," 114–17.

25. Salerno, "*I Delitti*," 117–23; Kornweibel, "*Seeing Red*"; Preston, *Aliens and Dissenters*; Norwood, "Bogalusa Burning"; U.S. Senate, *Investigation Activities of the Department of Justice*, 66th Cong., 1st sess., S. Doc. 153 (Washington, D.C.: Government Printing Office, 1919).

26. Tuttle, *Race Riot*; Lentz-Smith, *The Great War for Civil Rights*.

27. For a sample of these essays, see "L'America e' un paese senza pari," *LQS*, 30 January 1896; Ludovico Caminita, "Odio di Razza," *LQS*, 18 May 1906; "Free Country," *LQS*, 19 January 1907; "I delitti della razza bianca," *LQS*, 20 February 1909; "Undesirable," *EN*, 10 September 1910; "Echi e rumori: Free Country," *EN*, 29 October 1910; "Razze superiori, imparate!," *EN*, 27 February 1915; "Questione di razze?," *EN*, 10 January 1915; "Guerra di razze," *EN*, 6 February 1915; "Il rogo dal 'Chattanooga' Tennessee," and "Come fu linciata e sventrata M. Turner," *La Guardia Rossa*, 1 May 1919. See also Salerno, "*I Delitti*," 116–23; Vecoli, "'Free Country.'"

28. Termini Report, 15–27 July 1919, INS Papers, RG 65, National Archives.

29. Vecoli, "Etnia, internazionalismo e protezionismo," 14. See also Vecoli, "The Making and Unmaking," 51–53.

30. Ramella, "In fabbrica"; Ramella, "Reti sociali."

31. Vezzosi, "Radical Ethnic Brokers," 134.

32. Miceli, *Pride of Sicily*, 16.

33. Vecoli, "The Making and Un-making," 52.

34. Furio, "Immigrant Women and Industry," 267.

35. Ramirez, "Immigration, Ethnicity, and Political Militance," 116.

36. *Il Proletario*, 31 March 1911.

37. P. Di Neri, "When Is the Next Meeting?," *Message*, 15 October 1915.

38. Speech, 15 November 1980; Laura Segretti, "Angela Bambace and the ILGWU," n.d.; and "Notes to interview questions dictated by Angela Bambace to Marian, February, 1975," Bambace Papers, IHRC; Scarpaci, "Angela Bambace."

39. Scarpaci, "Angela Bambace," 102; Laura Segretti, "Angela Bambace and the ILGWU," n.d., Bambace Papers, IHRC.

40. See correspondence, clippings, and photographs, boxes 2 and 8, Capraro Papers, IHRC; Capraro interview by Julia Blodgett, 12 September 1969, tapes 6 and 7, Capraro Papers, IHRC; "Nino Capraro," *La Guardia Rossa*, 1 May 1919; Vecoli, "Anthony Capraro and the Lawrence Strike of 1919," 16–17.

41. Speech, 15 November 1980, Bambace Papers, IHRC.

42. See her grandson's recollections at <<http://slimman.com/kitchen.html>> and <<http://slimman.com/pasta_piselli.html>> (accessed 16 October 2008).

43. Nino Capraro to Maria Bambace-Capraro, 12 July 1921, box 3, Capraro Papers, IHRC.

44. Speech, 15 November 1980, Bambace Papers, IHRC.

45. Ibid.

46. Ibid.; "Notes to interview questions dictated by Angela Bambace to Marian, February 1975." Angela Bambace died on 3 April 1975 in Baltimore.

47. *NYT*, 9 April 1923. See also Pernicone, *Carlo Tresca*, esp. chap. 15.

48. Pernicone, *Carlo Tresca*, 105, 116, 119, 175; Avrich, *Sacco and Vanzetti*, 190–91.

49. Mitchell, *100 Years of Women in the Workforce*, 10.

50. Kessler-Harris, "Problems of Coalition-Building," 113.

51. Montgomery, "Nationalism, American Patriotism, and Class Consciousness," 345.

52. General Relief Committee Textile Strikers, *Hell in New Jersey: Story of the Passaic Textile Strike Told in Pictures* (1926), Labadie Collection, Harlan Hatcher Library, University of Michigan, Ann Arbor; Murphy, *The Passaic Textile Strike*; Foner, *History of the Labor Movement*, vols. 9 and 10.

53. Locale 89, Sezione Centrale, *Processo verbale*, 26 October 1926, IHRC Print Collection; Charles Zimmerman, interview by David Gurowsky, ILGWU Oral Histories, 8 November 1976, OHAL; Zappia, "Unionism and the Italian American Worker," 297–301.

54. Levine, *The Women's Garment Workers*, 350–51; Draper, *The Roots of American Communism*, 315–20; Soyer, *A Coat of Many Colors*, 13–14; Bender, *Sweated Work*, 155; Gurowsky, "Factional Disputes"; Nadel, "Reds versus Pinks."

55. Kessler-Harris, "Problems of Coalition-Building," 126–29.

56. ILGWU, *Report and Proceedings to the 15th Biennial Convention* (1920), 29.

57. ILGWU, Report of the Ladies' Waistmakers' Union Local 25 to the 16th Convention of the ILGWU, Cleveland, May 1922, 7; Kessler-Harris, "Problems of Coalition-Building," 129.

58. ILGWU, *Proceedings of Convention* (1925), 304; Zappia, "Unionism and the Italian American Worker," 298–99.

59. Zappia, "Unionism and the Italian American Worker," 299.

60. Grace de Luise-Natarelli, interview by Columbia Furio in "Immigrant Women and Industry," 282.

61. Ortíz, "Puerto Rican Workers in the Garment Industry," 111. See also Kessler-Harris, "Where Are the Organized Women Workers?"; Baden, "Developing an Agenda"; Waldinger, "Another Look"; Leeder, *The Gentle General*; Orleck, *Common Sense and a Little Fire*; Glenn, *Daughters of the Shtetl*; N. Green, *Ready-to-Wear*; M. Cohen, *Workshop to Office*.

62. Zappia, "Unionism and the Italian American Worker," 224.

63. Ortíz, "Puerto Rican Workers," 110.

64. Kessler Harris, "Problems of Coalition-Building," 133. See also Albina Delfino, interview by Ruth R. Prago, 9 January, 1981, OHAL; Scarpaci, "Angela Bambace"; Zappia, "Unionism and the Italian American Worker"; Gurowsky, "Factional Disputes"; N. Green, *Ready-to-Wear*.

65. In 1956 Bambace became the first Italian American woman to serve in the top union hierarchy when she was elected to the general executive board of the ILGWU, a post she held until she retired in 1972.

66. Scarpaci, "Angela Bambace"; Furio, "Immigrant Women and Industry"; Delfino interview by Prago; Ralph Iannantuono and Vanni Montana, interviews with Colomba Furio, ca. 1977, SSC.

67. *Collier's*, 15 September 1923; *NYT*, 8 January 1927, 25 May 1930, 25 August 1935; "The *New York Times* and Mussolini," *Il Mondo*, 15 October 1939. See also Coselschi, *Universalità del fascismo*; Diggins, "Mussolini and America"; Brunetta, "Il sogno e stelle e strisce di Mussolini," 173–86.

68. Diggins, *Mussolini and Fascism*, 27, 30.

69. Bertellini, "*Duce/Divo*."

70. *Saturday Evening Post*, 29 May 1926. See also *NYT*, 15 July 1923; *Cosmopolitan*, January 1927, 145–46; Diggins, "Mussolini and America," 564–65, 579–80.

71. Bertellini, "*Duce/Divo*"; Spackman, *Fascist Virilities*; and Cannistraro, *Blackshirts*.

72. T. Guglielmo, *White on Arrival*, 223; D. Smith, *Mussolini's Roman Empire*; Caponetto, "Going Out of Stock."

73. Salvemini, *Italian Fascist Activities*, 244–45.

74. Cannistraro, *Blackshirts*, 112–13; Cannistraro, "Fascism and Italian-Americans"; Cannistraro and Rossi, "La politica e il dilemma dell'antifascismo italiano."

75. Quoted in Cannistraro, *Blackshirts*, 9. For additional examples, see Il *Carroccio*, April 1921, 368–69; De Biasi, "Il fascismo negli Stati Uniti," 171; Domenico Saudino, "Il movimento fascista fra gli italiani d'America," *La Parola del Popolo*, December 1958–January 1959, 69; Ottanelli, "'If Fascism comes to America,'" 185; Cannistraro, "Fascism and Italian Americans," 51–66; Luconi, La "*diplomazia parallela*."

76. Speech by Giovanni Di Silvestro, 1930, box 11, file 24, Records of Giovanni Di Silvestro, Papers of the Order of the Sons of Italy in America, IHRC.

77. Salvemini, *Italian Fascist Activities*, 68.

78. Cannistraro, *Blackshirts*, 79, 63. See also "La vigliacca," *Il Nuovo Mondo*, 25 August 1926; and "Fascisti and Reds," *NYT*, 5 July 1925. For additional incidents, see "Il processo contro i fascisti aggressori di Princeton, N.J.," *Il Nuovo Mondo*, 27 July 1929; Saudino, "Il processo Greco-Carillo"; "Antonio Fierro assassinato dai neri-camiciati," *La Parola del Popolo* 9 (December 1958–January 1959): 296; Ottanelli, "'If Fascism Comes to America,'" 184; Diggins, "The Italo-American Anti-Fascist Opposition," 584–86.

79. Ventresco, "Italian-Americans and the Ethiopian Crisis"; Venturini, *Neri e Italiani*; Venturini, "'Over the Years People Don't Know,'" 202–10.

80. Leonard Covello, "An Experiment in Building Concepts of Racial Democracy" (c. 1943), box 51, file 6, Covello Papers; *Amsterdam News*, 26 January 1946.

81. Baldwin, *The Price of the Ticket*, 660.

82. Naison, *Communists in Harlem*, 139; quotation from Shankman, "The Image of the Italian," 42–44; *NYT*, 4 October 1935; Greenberg, "*Or Does It Explode?*"

83. *NYT*, 6 May 1936; Ventresco, "Italian-Americans"; Venturini, *Neri e Italiani*; Naison, *Communists in Harlem*, 138–40, 157, 195–96.

84. De Grazia, *How Fascism Ruled Women*; Spackman, *Fascist Virilities*; Pickering-Iazzi, *Mothers of Invention*; Slaughter, *Women and the Italian Resistance*; Giacobbe, *Donne siciliani*; Bortolotti, *Le donne della resistenza antifascista*; and Pickering-Iazzi, *Unspeakable Women*.

85. See essays in Gabaccia and Iacovetta, *Women, Gender, and Transnational Lives*; Pautasso, "La Donna Italiana."

86. Spackman, "Fascist Women and the Rhetoric of Virility," 100.

87. De Grazia, *How Fascism Ruled Women*, 168.

88. Ibid., 199, 247–48.

89. Ibid., 265–66.

90. *NYT*, 8 January 1936, 8; 25 April 1936, 19; 25 May 1936, 21; Ventresco, "Italian-Americans and the Ethiopian Crisis," 18–19; Kisseloff, *You Must Remember This*, 374.

91. T. Guglielmo, *White on Arrival*, 212–13, 218; Salvemini, *Italian Fascist Activities*, 56–57; Diggins, *Mussolini and Fascism*, 92; Cannistraro, *Blackshirts*, 61.

92. Terkel, *"The Good War,"* 138–39, 162–65, 487–90.

93. De Biasi, "Il mio orgoglio," *Il Carroccio*, January 1924, 1–7.

94. T. Guglielmo, *White on Arrival*, 227.

95. Two examples are the Loggia Regina Elena #241 of 140 Second Avenue in Manhattan and Loggia Adelaide Cairoli #294 of 203 Bleecker Street in Manhattan.

96. "L'iniziazione della Loggia 'Perla di Savoia' 1416," clipping in box 6, file 26, Di Silvestro Records. There were also some mixed-sex lodges, such as Loggia Glen Cove and "Fides" Lodge #482 of The Bronx. See the lodge meeting minutes (1941), membership records for 1939–41, and ritual booklet, Records of the Glen Cove Lodge, Papers of the Order of the Sons of Italy, IHRC. /

97. See clippings in box 13, file 6, box 6, files 26 and 31, Di Silvestro Records, including "Le tre logge giovanili femminili," *Bollettino della Sera*, 23 March 1932; "1500 giovani veranno iniziati," *Bollettino della Sera*, 5 April 1932; and "Una conferenza dell'Avv. Giovanni Di Silvestro a New York," *Il Progresso*, 10 November 1922. Some of the women's lodges inaugurated that evening were "Candida Miele" #2 of Brooklyn, "Manhattan" #3, "1.o Settembre 1847" #5 of The Bronx, "Fiume Italica" #8, "Candida Miele" #10 of The Bronx, and "Regina Margherita" #12 of Brooklyn, "Regina Margherita" #114 of Brooklyn, "Principessa Iolanda" #501 of Brooklyn, "Duchessa Elena D'Aosta" #712 of Corona, box 6, file 26, Di Silvestro Records.

98. "Il Fiero Discorso del Cav. Avv. Stefano Miele," box 6, file 26; "L'Iniziazione in massa delle nuove logge giovanili," *Corriere*, 12 April 1932, Di Silvestro Records.

99. See photographs from *Corriere*, 13 November 1932, and *Progresso*, 20 November 1932, box 4, file 5; and "Molti studenti faranno parte questo anno del pellegrinaggio O.F.d'I.," *Bollettino della Sera*, 18 November 1931, box 13, file 6, Di Silvestro Records.

100. De Grazia, *How Fascism Ruled Women*, 251.

101. See box 3, UNA.

102. "Italian Program Presented by the Italian Club of St. Rocco's Church," 7 April 1934, box 3, UNA Papers.

103. John A. Cimino, "Italian Expansion," *Nik Naks* 4:1 (1934), 32, UNA Papers.

104. Cimino, "Italian Expansion," 32.

105. See newsletter *Nik Naks* (1932–35), box 3, UNA Papers.

106. Mary E. Todaro, "'Nik Naks,' a Quarterly for Spreading Italian Culture in the United States," clipping in box 3, UNA Papers.

107. See, for example, "The Tintype of a Girl Editor," *Nik Naks* 4:1 (1934), 22, UNA Papers.

108. De Grazia, *How Fascism Ruled Women*, 246–71.

109. See photographs in the Capraro Papers, IHRC.

110. *L'Adunata dei Refrattari*, 9 June 1923. See also "Labor Groups Clash in Fascist Dispute," *NYT*, 24 November 1935, 19.

111. Diane Romanik, interview by Colomba Furio, 1 April 1977, SSC; reprinted in Furio, "Immigrant Women and Industry," 417–26.

112. D'Ambrosio, *Ralph Fasanella's America*, 26–27.

113. Scarpaci, "Angela Bambace," 104–7; Furio, "Immigrant Women and Industry"; Serafino Romualdi, "Storia della Locale 89," in *Local 89 Fifteenth Anniversary Commemoration Pamphlet*, 1934, IHRC Print Collection; Speech, 15 November 1980, Bambace Papers.

114. Ottanelli, "'If Fascism Comes to America,'" 183.

115. Ibid., 183–86; Diggins, "The Italo-American Anti-Fascist Opposition," 580–81; Dadà, "Contributo metodologico," 203–4.

116. See, for example, the series of letters on this topic in *L'Adunata dei Refrattari*, 16 June 1923; and reports on the "Efferati assassini della 'milizia nera,'" *L'Adunata dei Refrattari*, 4 August 1923.

117. *L'Adunata dei Refrattari*, 15 January 1923.

118. Ottanelli, "'If Fascism Comes to America,'" 183; Pernicone, *Carlo Tresca*, 160, 199–202; Avrich, *Anarchist Voices*, 147, 153.

119. Microfilm for the entire newspaper can be found at the IHRC. The archives for the paper are at the Boston Public Library, Rare Books Department, and the International Institute of Social History, Amsterdam, Holland.

120. Maria Caruso, CPC file 1121; Osvaldo Maraviglia, CPC file 3017. The police files list them as living at 589 8th Street in Newark in 1932. See also Avrich, *Anarchist Voices*, 147, 153, 503 n295.

121. Osvaldo Maraviglia, CPC file 3017; Elena Melli, CPC file 3212.

122. Delie, "Alle donne, L'Italia grande espone i suoi grandi uomini a moralizzare!," *L'Adunata dei Refrattari*, 15 January 1923.

123. Una Donna, "Parole al vento al mio sesso," *L'Adunata dei Refrattari*, 30 August 1922. See also "L'emancipazione della donna," *L'Adunata dei Refrattari*, 15 January 1927.

124. Ventresca and Iacovetta, "Virgilia D'Andrea," 299–326; D'Attilio, "Virgilia D'Andrea."

125. Borghi, *Mezzo secolo di anarchia*.

126. Ventresca and Iacovetta, "Virgilia D'Andrea," 301–2.

127. Virgilia D'Andrea, CPC file 1607. See also Ventresca and Iacovetta, "Virgilia D'Andrea," 302.

128. Virgilia D'Andrea, "Chi siamo e che cosa vogliamo," reprinted in D'Andrea, *Richiamo All'Anarchia*.

129. Avrich, *Anarchist Voices*, 146.

130. D'Andrea, CPC file 1607.

131. Poster from Il Circolo di Cultura Operaia announcing Virgilia D'Andrea's lecture at La Casa del Popolo in Somerville, Massachusetts, 22 February 1929, Fabrizi Papers, IHRC; *L'Adunata dei Refrattari*, 26 March 1932, 3 September 1932, 24 September 1932. The quotations are from her lecture, "I delitti della patria borghese, I diritti della patria umana," Somerset Hall, Somerville, Mass., 3 December 1931, and other cities throughout the U.S., reprinted in D'Andrea, *Richiamo all'anarchia*, 142, 147.

132. Ventresca and Iacovetta, "Virgilia D'Andrea," 308.

133. Ibid., 316–17.

134. Poster from Il Circolo di Cultura Operaia, 22 February 1929, Fabrizi Papers, IHRC.

135. Delfino interview by Prago.

136. De Grazia, *How Fascism Ruled Women*, 240–41.

137. See, for example, CPC files: Anna Teresa Altomare, 80; Emilia Bellardo, 445; Giuseppina Bosco, 780; Maria Teresa Brocca, 845; Maria Caruso, 1121, Matilda Carollo, 1103, Angela Colomba Chini, 1306; Adelina Ciampa, 1317; Beatrice Cigna, 1340; Maria Cigoi, 1341; Maria Ciocca, 1353; Angela Maria Cipriani, 1361; Giulietta Defendi, 1653; Domenichina Del Castello, 1671; Caterina Dall'Olio, 1694; Fioretta De Zolt, 1763; Maria Di Giose, 1788; Assunta Di Pietro, 1814; Elvira Frank, 2162; Rosa Maria Guardabascio, 2556; Carmelina Matarese, 3150; Irena Padovani, 3643; Rina Stramesi, 4968.

138. Morelli, "Nestore's Wife," 332.

139. *L'Adunata dei Refrattari*, 6 October 1923, 24 May 1924.

140. *L'Adunata dei Refrattari*, 21 February 1925.

141. *L'Adunata dei Refrattari*, 3 January 1925.

142. *L'Adunata dei Refrattari*, 17 February 1922, 20 April 1922, 15 May 1922, 15, 30 June 1922, 15 August 1922, 30 September 1922, 30 November 1922, 12 May 1923, 31 March 1923, 16 June 1923, 10 November 1923, 15 May 1925.

143. Diggins, "The Italo-American Anti-Fascist Opposition," 582; Diggins, *Mussolini and Fascism*; Salvemini, *Italian Fascist Activities*; Vecoli, "The Making and Un-making," 22.

Chapter 8

1. Thomas, *Down These Mean Streets*; Mohr, *Nilda*; Lapolla, *Grand Gennaro*; LaPolla, *Fire in the Flesh*; Corsi, *Shadow of Liberty*; Covello, *The Heart Is the Teacher*; Catalino Rolón interview, quoted in Glasser, *My Music Is My Flag*, 95–96; Baldwin, *The Price of the Ticket*; Vega, *Memoirs*, 9–10; Kisseloff, *You Must Remember This*, 253–380; Cimilluca, "The Natural History"; Parkhurst, *Undertow*; "Intercultural Education—Clashes—Miscellaneous, 1938–1940," box 53, file 16, Committee for Racial Cooperation, "Report," box 52, file 20, and D. Di Pino, "Interview with Lieutenant Haas of the 104th Street Station, Re: Italo-Porto Rican Riots," box 53, file 14, Covello Papers, Balch Institute for Ethnic Studies, Philadelphia.
2. Quoted in Glasser, *My Music Is My Flag*, 96; Orsi, "The Religious Boundaries," 319–20.
3. Thomas, *Down These Mean Streets*, 24–27. See also "Adult Whites Push Children Up to 'Revolt,'" *Amsterdam News*, 6 October 1945; E. Schneider, *Vampires*, 91–93.
4. Principal Margaret Bryne quoted in Report of Wadleigh High School (1940), box 30, file 12, Rachel Davis DuBois Papers, IHRC.
5. Leonard Covello, "Italians and Race Prejudice," "Italians, Prejudice I," box 100, file 22, Covello Papers; Cinotto, "Leonard Covello."
6. Terkel, *"The Good War,"* 138–39. See also Di Prima, *Recollections*, 51; Parkhurst, *Undertow*; Vito Magli, interview by Paul Buhle, 15 March 1983, OHAL; Covello, *The Heart Is the Teacher*, 237–58.
7. Di Prima, "Don't Solidify," 27.
8. Baldwin, "On Being 'White,'" 90–92.
9. Wilder, *A Covenant*; Gregory, *Black Corona*; Sugrue, *The Origins of the Urban Crisis*; Hirsch, *Making the Second Ghetto*; L. Cohen, *Making a New Deal*; Jackson, *Crabgrass Frontier*; Biondi, *To Stand and Fight*; Gilmore, *Defying Dixie*; Roediger, *Working toward Whiteness*; MacLean, *Freedom Is Not Enough*; Rieder, *Canarsie*.
10. *NYT*, 10 December 1944, 29 September 1945, 10 November 1945; *Daily News*, 29 September 1945; *New York Sun*, 28 September 1945; *Life*, 8 April 1948; *Amsterdam News*, 10 April 1937, 12 November 1938, 11, 17, 24 March 1945, 21 April 1945, 5, 19 May 1945, 23 June 1945, 13, 28 July 1945, 22 September 1945, 6, 27 October 1945, 10 November 1945; Covello, *The Heart Is the Teacher*, 237–58; Covello, "Notes on the Racial Incident at Franklin," n.d., and "Excerpts from Investigative Bureau Report," box 54, files 4 and 9; "State on the Disturbances," 29 September 1945, box 54, file 20; "Statement of Racial Incident and Recommendations," n.d., box 54, file 20; "Suggested Program for Promoting Desirable Interracial Attitudes at BFHS," 1937, box 56, file 9; "Report of the Committee for Racial Cooperation," November 1938, box 56, file 9, and the following from box 57, file 12: Steve De Salvo, "Ten to One Odds"; Thomas Foudy, "Race Prejudices"; Gaetano Ricci, "White vs. Black," Covello Papers. See also Meyer, "When Sinatra Came to Harlem"; Meyer, *Vito Marcantonio*, 124–25; E. Schneider, *Vampires*, 68–70.
11. E. Schneider, *Vampires*, 33.
12. Ibid., 96–97. See also *New York Herald Tribune*, 26 March 1933; Spergel, *Racketville*, 64–65, 157; Orsi, *The Madonna of 115th Street*, 31–35.
13. Orsi, *The Madonna of 115th Street*, 33; E. Schneider, *Vampires*, 98.
14. Orsi, "The Religious Boundaries," 318.
15. Hunter, *To 'Joy My Freedom*, 235.
16. Orsi, "The Religious Boundaries," 320.
17. *Time*, 4 November 1946. See also "Night on the Beat," *Life*, 21 June 1948; "Our Worst Slum," *American Magazine*, September 1949; "World They Never Made," *Time*, 12 June 1950, 24–26; Padilla, *Up from Puerto Rico*, 233; Meyer, *Vito Marcantonio*, 112–13.

18. Letter from Jane Noel to Salvatore Pergola, 8 October 1945, box 54, file 20, Marcantonio Papers, NYPL.

19. Quoted in Wilder, *A Covenant with Color*, 192. See also "Security Area Descriptions," Section VI, Federal Home Loan Bank Board Records, RG 195, box 58, National Archives.

20. Orsi, "The Religious Boundaries," 321.

21. Ibid., 322.

22. Meyer, "Italian Harlem," 57; Orsi, *The Madonna of 115th Street*, 16; Osofsky, *Harlem*, 85; Gurock, *When Harlem Was Jewish*, 147; Lapolla, *The Fire in the Flesh*, 47–58.

23. Orsi, *The Madonna of 115th Street*, 17; Orsi, "Religious Boundaries," 319–22; Meyer, *Vito Marcantonio*, chap. 6; Kisseloff, *You Must Remember This*, 344–46.

24. "A Portrait of East Harlem," January 1960, Covello Papers; Orsi, *The Madonna of 115th Street*, 17; Meyer, "Italian Harlem," 57; Meyer, *Vito Marcantonio*, chap. 6; Cordasco and Galatioto, "Ethnic Displacement," 302–12; E. Schneider, *Vampires*, 94.

25. Schoener, *New York*, 288; Glasser, *My Music Is My Flag*, 94–107; Meyer, *Vito Marcantonio*, chap. 7.

26. Vega, *Memoirs*, 9–10.

27. Quoted in Glasser, *My Music Is My Flag*, 95.

28. Ibid., 96.

29. Orsi, "The Religious Boundaries," 320.

30. Ibid., 660.

31. Orsi, *The Madonna of 115th Street*, 18. See also Report from Frank Soto to Vito Marcantonio on "racial troubles," box 44, Marcantonio Papers; Leonard Covello, "Developing Racial Appreciation through the School," n.d., box 56, file 11; Pedro Jamesis Orata, "Relative Effects of Various Factors upon Race Prejudice" (1924), box 100, file 22; "Inquiry Focuses Spotlight on Ills of East Harlem," *Tribune*, 15 December 1946, box 75, file 12; "Interethnic Education—Clashes—Miscellaneous, 1938–1940," box 53, file 16, Covello Papers; Cinotto, "Leonard Covello," 53–57.

32. Thomas, *Down These Mean Streets*, 24–38, 119–28; Padilla, *Up from Puerto Rico*, 44–81; Baldwin, *The Price of the Ticket*; Petry, *The Street*; Vega, *Memoirs*; C. Brown, *Manchild*, 167, 291; Mohr, *Nilda*; Covello, *The Heart Is the Teacher*; Abner Berry, interview by Mark Naison, 1974–77; Mother Audley Moore, interview by Mark Naison, 1972, OHAL.

33. Roediger, *Black on White*, 124.

34. Meyer, "When Sinatra Came to Harlem," 162.

35. Spada at 229 East 118th Street to Covello, 2 October 1945, box 54, file 20, Covello Papers.

36. Mellone at 227 East 117th Street, to Covello, 2 October 1945, box 54, file 20, Covello Papers. See other letters by residents in this file.

37. WPA interview with Liberato Dattolo by Vincent Frazetta, 26 August 1939, WPA box 23, 109:13B, reprinted in Stave, *From the Old Country*, 221.

38. Letter from Luigi Criscuolo to Leonard Covello, 3 October 1945, box 54, file 20, Covello Papers.

39. *New York Herald Tribune*, 2 October 1945.

40. Bilbo to Marcantonio, 24 July 1945, and Marcantonio to Bilbo, 24 July 1945, box 1, Marcantonio Papers; *Amsterdam News*, 27 October 1945; Meyer, *Vito Marcantonio*, 134.

41. *Time*, 22 April 1935; "Italian, Prejudice I, 1927–1935 and 1936–1953," box 100, files 21 and 22, Covello Papers.

42. Katznelson, *When Affirmative Action Was White*, 17.

43. Lipsitz, *Possessive Investment in Whiteness*, 5.

44. T. Guglielmo, *White on Arrival*, esp. chaps. 7 and 8; Lipsitz, *Possessive Investment in Whiteness*; Katznelson, *When Affirmative Action Was White*; Roediger, *Working towards Whiteness*; Rieder, *Canarsie*; Bauman, *Public Housing, Race, and Renewal*; Jackson, *Crabgrass Frontier*; Sitkoff, *A New Deal for Blacks*.

45. Sugrue, *The Origins of the Urban Crisis*, 9.

46. Ibid., 10.

47. Omi and Winant, *Racial Formation*, 95.

48. Sugrue, *The Origins of the Urban Crisis*, 10.

49. Baldwin, *The Price of the Ticket*, 687.

50. Gerson, *Pete*, 91; Meyer, *Vito Marcantonio*; Charney, *A Long Journey*; Powell, *Marching Blacks*; B. Davis, *Communist Councilman from Harlem*; C. McKay, *Harlem*; Naison, *Communists in Harlem*; Orleck, *Common Sense and a Little Fire*; Piven and Cloward, *Poor People's Movements*; Biondi, *To Stand and Fight*; Ransby, *Ella Baker*; Davies, *Left of Karl Marx*; Gore, "To Light a Candle in a Gale Wind."

51. Cantarow and O'Malley, "Ella Baker," 64; Ransby, *Ella Baker*, 67.

52. Vega, *Memoirs*, 47.

53. Denning, *The Cultural Front*; Piven and Cloward, *Poor People's Movements*; Naison, *Communists in Harlem*; Kelley, *Hammer and Hoe*; Faue, *Community of Suffering and Struggle*; L. Cohen, *Making a New Deal*; Hutchinson, *Blacks and Reds*; Weigand, *Red Feminism*; Orleck, *Common Sense and a Little Fire*; Gutiérrez, *Walls and Mirrors*; Gilmore, *Defying Dixie*.

54. Denning, *The Cultural Front*, 38, 4.

55. "Il sindacato dell'abbigliamento femminile-ILGWU," *La Parola del Popolo*, 50th Anniversary Publication, 1908–1958; Bernstein, *The Lean Years*, 342; Tyler, *Look for the Union Label*, 169–79; Seidman, *The Needle Trades*, chap. 10; Ross, *Slaves to Fashion*, chap. 3.

56. "Genesi ed attività della locale 89 delle sartine italiane," *La Parola Del Popolo*, 50th Anniversary Publication, 1908–1958, 200.

57. *Justice*, 1 January 1933, 1, 15 August 1933, 1 September 1933; *NYT*, 16 August 1933; Bernstein, *The Turbulent Years*, 34, 37, 84; Danish, *The World of David Dubinsky*, 75; Gurowsky, "Factional Disputes," 343.

58. Serafino Romualdi, "Storia della Locale 89," in *Local 89 Fifteenth Anniversary Commemoration Pamphlet*, 1934, 56, IHRC Print Collection.

59. *NYT*, 16, 17 August 1933; Fannia M. Cohn, "The Uprising of the Sixty Thousand," *Justice*, 1 September 1933; *Daily Worker*, 17–19 August 1933; *Il Progresso Italo-Americano*, 16–20 August 1933. See also materials on 1933 strike in box 28, file 5, Papers of Charles Zimmerman, and in box 69, file 2, Papers of David Dubinsky, ILGWU Archives, LMDC; Danish, *The World of David Dubinsky*, 77; Tyler, *Look for the Union Label*, 178–79.

60. *NYT*, 16–18 August 1933; *Daily Worker*, 17–19 August 1933; *Il Progresso Italo-Americano*, 18–19 August 1933.

61. See following in Zimmerman Papers: "Joint Board Dress and Waistmakers Union, General Strike, 1933, Hall Committee Assignments," box 45, file 1; "Tentative Instructions and Information for Hall Chairmen, Secretaries, and Deputies, 1932," box 45, file 1; Luigi Antonini to Charles Zimmerman, 8 August 1933, box 28, file 5; "Assignments, Strike 1933," box 28, file 5; "Information and Directory of the General Strike Committee, Joint Board Dress and Waistmakers' Union, General Strike, August, 1933," box 28, file 5. See also "Women Speakers List, Strike Meetings, 1932," box 8, file 15, Papers of the Research Department, ILGWU Archives; and *Giustizia*, January 1932, April–May 1932, August 1932.

62. Serafino Romualdi, "Storia della Locale 89," in *Local 89 Fifteenth Anniversary Commemoration Pamphlet*, 1934; Montana, *Amorostico*; O'Farrell, "A Stitch in Time."

63. See, for example, Faue, *Community of Suffering and Struggle*; and Enstad, *Ladies of Labor*.

64. *Il Progresso*, 16 August 1933; *Daily Worker*, 17 August 1933.

65. *Giustizia*, October 1933, 2.

66. *Daily Worker*, 17 August 1933.

67. *NYT*, 17 August 1933.

68. *Giustizia*, April 1934.

69. Zappia, "Unionism and the Italian American Worker," 87.

70. Frank Liberti to David Dubinksy, 1962, Liberti Papers, American Labor Museum, Botto House

National Landmark, Haledon, N.J. See also Romualdi, "Storia della Locale 89"; Antonino Crivello at the Fourth Anniversary of the 1933 Strike, ILGWU Local 144, Newark, New Jersey, 1937, box 1, file 1, Papers of Antonino Crivello, IHRC; "Compagne e Compagni della Local 89!," Address by John Gelo, Ratification Meeting, Madison Square Garden, 2 April 1937, box 15, file 8, Antonini Papers; Local 48-ILGWU, *Libro Ricordo*; "Il Sindicato dell'Abbigliamento Femminile-ILGWU," *La Parola del Popolo*, 50th Anniversary Publication, 1908–1958, 195; Local 89, ILGWU, *We the Italian Dressmakers Speak* (New York, 1944), IHRC Print Collection; *Giustizia*, October 1933.

71. Quoted in N. Green, *Ready-to-Wear*, 228.

72. "Take Plaque to Mrs. Roosevelt," *NYT*, 28 March 1934, 27; *Justice*, 1 April 1934; O'Farrell, "A Stitch in Time."

73. Iannantuono interview by Furio.

74. Romanik interview by Furio.

75. Ibid.

76. Pesotta, *Bread upon the Waters*, chap. 29; Obituary, *NYT*, 12 December 1965, 87, *New York Post*, 12 December 1965.

77. Di Maggio to Liberti, 8 November 1928, Liberti Papers.

78. Di Maggio to Liberti, 12 September 1928, Liberti Papers.

79. Romanik interview by Furio.

80. See Italian Immigrant Women in New York City's Garment Industry Oral Histories, 1976–1978, SSC; Delfino interview by Prago.

81. Angela Bambace, transcript of interview by Shirley Parry of *Women: A Journal of Liberation*, 29 November 1972, file 6, Bambace Papers.

82. Gaeta interview by Furio.

83. Catania interview by Furio.

84. Ibid.

85. Furio, "Immigrant Women and Industry," 341.

86. Lazarro interview by Furio.

87. Catania interview by Furio.

88. Furio, "Immigrant Women and Industry," 281.

89. Molisani interview by Furio, 23 February 1978, in Furio, "Immigrant Woman and Industry," 281.

90. Romanik interview by Furio.

91. Lazzaro interview by Furio.

92. The other offices were located at 17 Montrose Avenue in Williamsburg, Brooklyn; 219 Sackman Street in Brownsville, Brooklyn; 1377 42nd Street in Boro Park, Brooklyn; and 505 East Tremont Avenue in The Bronx. "Amministrazione 1934–35 Consiglio Esecutivo," box 16, Antonini Papers, ILGWU Archives.

93. Tina Catania, for example, lived at 211 East 97th Street; Antonetta Barbera lived at 175 East 101st Street; Silvia DeCaro lived at 110 East 121st Street; Peggy d'Agnese lived at 203 East 114th Street; Rose Prosetto lived at 48 East 107th Street; and Mary Marchesi lived at 1753 Lexington Avenue. See "Amministrazione 1934–35 Consiglio Esecutivo," box 16, Antonini Papers; "Administration of Local 89," in *Local 89 Fifteenth Anniversary Pamphlet*, 1934, 4; "Our March in Time," in *Local 89, 1919–1944: Jubilee—We, the Italian Dressmakers Speak*, 1944, 15, IHRC Print Collection.

94. *Justice*, 1 July 1935.

95. Local 89 of ILGWU, *We, the Italian Dressmakers Speak* (New York, 1944), IHRC Print Collection; *Justice*, 1 January 1937.

96. Lazzaro interview by Furio.

97. Danish, *The World of David Dubinsky*, 190.

98. Romanik interview by Furio.

99. De Luise interview by Furio.

100. Catania interview by Furio.

101. Ibid.

102. De Luise interview by Furio.

103. Catania interview by Furio.

104. Lazzaro interview by Furio.

105. Ibid.

106. For example, see Maria Rosaria Cimato to Luigi Antonini, 9 June 1939, box 16, file 6; Lucia De Stefano to Luigi Antonini, 9 February 1940, box 15, file 9; Lina Richeri to Luigi Antonini, 19 March 1942, box 16, file 7; Lucia Romualdi Lupia to Luigi Antonini, 18 August 1942, box 16, file 7, Antonini Papers.

107. Furio interview by Catania.

108. "Dressmakers on Outing," NYT, 26 July 1936, N5; "'Aida,'" NYT, 25 March 1937, 28; Thirtieth Anniversary, Italian Dressmakers' Union Local 89, ILGWU— "The Spirit of '89," 1950; Commemorative Pamphlet, Local 89, XV Anniversary of the Formation of the Italian Dressmakers' Union, Local 89, New York: ILGWU, 1934; Local 89, 1919–1944, 1944; Jubilee, 1944, IHRC Print Collection.

109. Gaeta interview by Furio.

110. Furio, "Immigrant Women and Industry," 302–3.

111. See, for example, "Amministrazione 1934–35 Consiglio Esecutivo," and "Business Agents," box 16, Antonini Papers; "Administration, Local 89, 1947–1950," in Thirtieth Anniversary, Italian Dressmakers' Union Local 89, ILGWU— "The Spirit of '89," 1950; "Administration of Local 89," ILGWU, Commemorative Pamphlet, Local 89, XV Anniversary of the Formation of the Italian Dressmakers' Union, Local 89, New York: ILGWU, 1934; "Administration, Local 89, 1944–1946," in Local 89, 1919–1944; and Jubilee, 1944, all in IHRC Print Collection.

112. "Administration of Local 89, 1934," in Local 89 Fifteenth Anniversary Commemoration Pamphlet, 1934, and "Administration of Local 89, 1944–46," in ILGWU, Jubilee, 1919–1944, 1944, IHRC Print Collection. See also "New York: Our City–Our Union, 24th Convention of the ILGWU, Fortieth Anniversary" (1940), box 1, Crivello Papers; Catania, De Luise, and Gaeta interviews with Furio.

113. "Il Sindacato dell'Abbigliamento Femminile-ILGWU," La Parola del Popolo, 50th Anniversary Publication, 1908–1958; Corbella, "Storia di un Sindacato Operaio Italiano," 380; Seidman, The Needle Trades, 36, 44–46.

114. Local 22, ILGWU, Our Union at Work: A Survey of the Activities of the Dressmakers' Union Local 22, ILGWU, 1937, 59–62, IHRC Print Collection.

115. Ibid.; Edith Kine, "The Garment Union Comes to the Negro Worker," Opportunity 12 (April 1934): 107–10.

116. Ortíz, "Puerto Rican Workers," 106–7, 111–12.

117. Ibid.; Ortíz, "'En la aguja y el pedal eché la hiel'"; Bao, Holding Up More Than Half the Sky; Hill, "Guardians of the Sweatshops," 387; Laurentz, "Racial/Ethnic Conflict," 186–87; Helfgott, "Puerto Rican Integration"; Wong, The Negro in the Apparel Industry; Ross, Slaves to Fashion, chap. 3; Helfgott, "Puerto Rican Integration"; Michael Meyerson, "ILGWU: Fighting for Lower Wages," Ramparts, October 1969, 54; N. Green, Ready-to-Wear, 230–33.

118. Wakefield, Island in the City, 211.

119. Ortíz, "Puerto Rican Workers," 119.

120. Leaflet, box 33, file 11, Zimmerman Papers; Ortíz, "Puerto Rican Workers," 114; Laurentz, "Racial/Ethnic Conflict," 123–24.

121. La Prensa, 23 December 1933; Strike leaflet, 1934, box 33, file 11, Zimmerman Papers; Ortíz, "'En la aguja y el pedal eché la hiel,'" 58–59; N. Green, Ready-to-Wear, 374–75; Foner and Lewis, The Black Worker, 598; N. Green, Ready-to-Wear, 231–33.

122. Topp, Those without a Country, esp. chaps. 1 and 4.

123. Arturo Giovannitti, "The Italian Seamstress," in Local 89, ILGWU, Ricordo della Libertas, IHRC Print Collection.

124. Romualdi, "Storia della Locale 89," 63.

125. See also *"48" Libro Ricordo*, 12. See also Local 89, *Jubilee, 1914–1944* and *Giustizia*, October 1933, 4.

126. Romualdi, "Storia della Locale 89"; Speech given by Antonino Crivello, organizer and district manager for the Italian Dressmakers' Local 89 at fourth anniversary of the 1933 strike, ILGWU Local 144, Newark, New Jersey (1937), box 1, file 1, Crivello Papers; N. Green, *Ready-to-Wear*, 379; L. Cohen, *Making a New Deal*.

127. Arturo Labriola, "Le razze di colore e il socialismo," in *ILGWU, Local 89 Anniversary, Commemoration Booklet* (1934), 87–89, IHRC Print Collection.

128. Ortíz, "En la aguja y el pedal eché la hiel," 58.

129. Luisa López, interview by Blanca Vázquez, in "Nostras trabajamos en la costura: Puerto Rican Women in the Garment Industry," oral histories, Centro de Estudios Puertorriqueños, Hunter College, New York.

130. "Nosotras trabajamos en la costura" oral histories; Matos-Rodríguez and Hernández, *Pioneros*; Ortíz, "En la aguja y el pedal eché la hiel," 56–59.

131. *Elsie Hunter v. Agnes Sullivan Dress Shop*, 4 September 1946, quoted in Hill, "The ILGWU—Fact and Fiction," 10.

132. Announcement of HLC, 19 November 1937, box 3, file "General Correspondence: HLC," Marcantonio Papers; Meyer, *Vito Marcantonio*, 70–79. See also other archival materials on the HLC in box 3, Marcantonio Papers.

133. Ibid.

134. Gerald J. Meyer, "Annette T. Rubinstein: 95th Birthday Celebration," http://www.monthlyreview.org/annetterubinstein.htm (accessed 4 August 2009); Meyer, "Annette T. Rubinstein"; Kisseloff, *You Must Remember This*, 368.

135. See constituents' correspondence and papers, boxes 6–35, Marcantonio Papers.

136. Kisseloff, *You Must Remember This*, 368.

137. Meyer, *Vito Marcantonio*, 13.

138. Esta Pingaro to Marcantonio, 5 October 1941, box 67, file 6, and John W. Sutter to Marcantonio, 24 October 1938, box 3, file 3, Marcantonio Papers; Buhle interview by Magli, OHAL. See also Natalina Arcangeli to Constantino Lippa, 16 August 1950, box 10, file 14; Constantino Lippa to "Sorella Geraci," 18 April 1950, box 10, file 14; Constantino Lippa to Salvatore Geraci, 22 August 1950, box 10, file 14; Conferenza dei Delegati Sezione Italiana alla Quarta Convenzione Nazionale, 28–29 April 1938, box 10, file 14, IWO Papers, LMDC. For evidence of the anarchist circles see "Communicazioni: New York, NY," *L'Adunata dei Refrattari*, 26, 30 April 1932.

139. "Meeting on Harlem and Defense: St. Martin's Church," 17 January 1942; and Helen Vásquez to Vito Marcantonio, 31 July 1941, box 3, Marcantonio Papers. See the following from Colón Papers, Centro de Estudios Puertorriqueños, Hunter College, New York, N.Y.: "Conferencia Distrital de la Seccion Hispana de la I.W.O.," 24–25 February 1940, box 4, file 5; "Curso de Estudio Para La Escuela Elemental de la Seccion Hispana de la Orden Internacional de Trabajadores," October 1938–February 1939, box 4, file 5; "El Imperialismo Americano en Relación a Puerto Rico y Latinoamérica," Conference at Club Obrero Espanol, n.d., box 2, file 2; Helen Vásquez to Jesús Colón, 29 April 1944, box 1, file 10.

140. Vito Marcantonio to Esta Pingaro, 1941, box 67; Poster "NYA Variety Show," box 67, Marcantonio Papers.

141. Goodman, *Stories of Scottsboro*.

142. Aurora De Gregorio, "Open Letter to a Young Negro," *L'Unita del Popolo*, 13 July 1940.

143. "Directory of Community Resources in East Harlem," prepared by the Family Service Committee of the East Harlem Council for Community Planning, 1 August 1963, box 79, file 3, Covello Papers; "Gen. Corresp.: HLC" file, box 3, Marcantonio Papers; Comite Hispanico Para La Defensa Nacional, 1942, series V, box 1, file 12; Comite de Madres Hispanas flyer, July 1939, series V, box 3, file 8; and IWO minutes, "Libretas para las actas del Comite de la Ciudad," series V, box 4, file 7, Colón Papers.

144. See box 3, Marcantonio Papers.

145. Report in box 17, file 10, DuBois Papers.

146. See plays in box 30, file 12; box 17, files 10 and 11, DuBois Papers.

147. See the following documents from the Covello Papers: Pamphlet, "Harlem Parade for Better Housing," 1938, Housing File, box 43; Leonard Covello, "Building Democratic Ideals through a School-Community Program," *Library Journal* 65 (1 February 1940): 108; Minutes of the First Meeting of the East Harlem Housing Committee of the Harlem Legislative Conference, 15 January 1938, East Harlem Housing Committee Meetings, box 43; "The East Harlem Housing Committee of the East Harlem Legislative Conference Presents a Campaign, 1938," box 43; Petition, East Harlem Tenants, 1939; "Who Wants Better Housing?," 22 March 1938; "Notes from Minutes, 1937–1940," Community Centered School, box 43; Leonard Covello Speech, ca. 1939, Community Centered School, box 43. See also Venturini, "Nascita di un Complesso."

148. Leonard Covello to Layle Lane (1937, 1954–69), box 4, file 25, Covello Papers; Marcantonio announcement on housing victory, 6 October 1939, box 3, Marcantonio Papers.

149. The material on the activities of the committee is culled from the East Harlem Housing Committee Meetings, box 43, file 10, Covello Papers.

150. Kaplan, "Female Consciousness and Collective Action"; Jetter et al., *The Politics of Motherhood*; Glenn et al., *Mothering*.

151. "CAC Report, January 1939," box 43, file 6, Covello Papers.

152. See "Housing—General," box 43, file 6, Covello Papers.

153. Jackson, *Crabgrass Frontier*, 222–23.

154. Speech by Leonard Covello, "Community Centered School, Housing—General," box 43, file 6, Covello Papers.

155. "Harlem Parade for Better Housing," 25 March 1939, box 43, file 10, Covello Papers.

156. "Housing, General," box 45, files 5–6, Covello Papers. I was not able to find estimates of the number of people who marched or watched the parade in the Covello or Marcantonio Papers or the English-language newspapers.

157. Speech by Leonard Covello, "CCS-Housing, General," box 43, file 6, Covello Papers.

158. Minutes of East Harlem Housing Committee, 1938–1940, box 43, file 10, Covello Papers.

159. "CAC Report, January 1939," "CCS Housing-General," box 43, file 6, Covello Papers.

160. Mercado's activism within Madres Unidas and other organizations is also noted throughout Marcantonio's Papers and Meyer, *Vito Marcantonio*, 151.

161. "Housing," box 68, Marcantonio Papers; Marcantonio to Covello, box 5, file 8, Covello Papers.

162. Orsi, "The Religious Boundaries," 326.

163. Ibid., 329.

164. See the following documents from the Covello Papers: Pamphlet, "Harlem Parade for Better Housing" (1938), Housing File, box 43; Leonard Covello, "Building Democratic Ideals through a School-Community Program," *Library Journal* 65 (1 February 1940): 108; Minutes of the First Meeting of the East Harlem Housing Committee of the Harlem Legislative Conference, 15 January 1938, and East Harlem Housing Committee Meetings, box 43, file 10; "The East Harlem Housing Committee of the East Harlem Legislative Conference Presents a Campaign, 1938," box 43, file 10; Petition, East Harlem Tenants (1939), "Who Wants Better Housing?," 22 March 1938, box 43, file 10; "Notes from Minutes, 1937–1940," Community Centered School, box 43, file 9; Leonard Covello Speech, ca. 1939, Community Centered School, box 43, file 10; and "The East Harlem Housing Committee of the East Harlem Legislative Conference Presents a Campaign, 1938," box 43, file 10. See also Venturini, "Nascita di un Complesso."

165. Wilder, *A Covenant*; Gregory, *Black Corona*; Sugrue, *The Origins of the Urban Crisis*; Hirsch, *Making the Second Ghetto*; Jackson, *Crabgrass Frontier*; Biondi, *To Stand and Fight*; Rieder, *Canarsie*; T. Guglielmo, *White on Arrival*, esp. chap. 8; Lipsitz, *Possessive Investment in Whiteness*; Katznelson,

When *Affirmative Action Was White*; Roediger, *Working towards Whiteness*; Bauman, *Public Housing, Race, and Renewal*.

166. Orsi, "The Religious Boundaries," 318.
167. "Notes from Minutes, 1937–1940," Community Centered School, box 43, file 9, Covello Papers.
168. Omi and Winant, *Racial Formation*, 84.
169. Rieder, *Canarsie*, 66.

Conclusions

1. Elwood, "The Roots and Results of Radicalism," 80–83. See also Salerno, "'I Delitti Della Razza Bianca,'" 112–13.
2. Elwood, "The Roots and Results of Radicalism," ii.
3. Lipsitz, *Possessive Investment in Whiteness*, 7. See also Gerstle, "Working-Class Racism"; Roediger, "Whiteness and Ethnicity"; Roediger, *Working towards Whiteness*.
4. Evans, *Personal Politics*, 120. See also Rotolo, *Free Wheeling Time*; Di Prima, *Recollections of My Life*; J. Guglielmo and Salerno, *Are Italians White?*; Capotorto, *Bronx Italian*.
5. Noschese, *Metropolitan Avenue* (VHS). See also Haywoode and Scanlon, "World of Our Mothers"; Carroll, "Grassroots Feminism."
6. Sanjek, *The Future of Us All*, see esp. 280–99, 373.
7. Bill Donnelly quoted in Sanjek, *The Future of Us All*, 372.
8. Sanjek, *The Future of Us All*, 390.
9. Moraga, "From Inside the First World," xxv; Alexander, *Pedagogies of Crossing*, 14.

Bibliography

PRIMARY SOURCES

Manuscript Collections

American Labor Museum, Botto House National Landmark, Haledon, N.J.
  1913 Strike Records
  Botto Family Records
  Frank Liberti Papers
Archivio Centrale dello Stato, Rome, Italy
  Casellario Politico Centrale Records
Balch Institute for Ethnic Studies, The Historical Society of Pennsylvania, Philadelphia, Pa.
  Leonard Covello Papers
Biblioteca Comunale Centrale, Milan, Italy
Biblioteca della Fondazione Gian Giacomo Feltrinelli, Milan, Italy
Center for Migration Studies of New York, Inc., Staten Island, N.Y.
  Luigi Antonini Papers
  Italian American Labor Movement Collection
Centro de Estudios Puertorriqueños, Hunter College, New York, N.Y.
  Jesús Colón Papers
  Joaquín Colón Papers
  Oscar García Rivera Papers
Centro di Studi Storici sul Movimento di Liberazione della Donna in Italia, Milan, Italy
Centro Sociale Conchetta Special Collection, Milan, Italy
Centro Studi Libertari Archivio Pinelli, Milan, Italy
Columbia University Rare Book and Manuscript Library, New York, N.Y.
  East Side House Records
  La Guardia Memorial House (Haarlem House) Records
  Union Settlement Association Records
Immigration History Research Center, University of Minnesota, Minneapolis, Minn.
  Gioacchino Artoni Papers
  Emilio Augusto Papers
  Angela Bambace Papers
  Antonino (Nino) Capraro Papers
  Salvatore Castagnola Papers
  Fred Celli Papers
  Antonino Crivello Papers

Alberto Cupelli Papers
Mario De Ciampis Papers
John P. Diggins Papers
Giovanni M. Di Silvestro Papers
Rachel Davis DuBois Papers
Marie Hall Ets Papers
Oreste Fabrizi Papers
Elizabeth Gurley Flynn Papers
Francis X. Giaccone Papers
Emilio Grandinetti Papers
Clara Grillo Papers
International Ladies' Garment Workers' Union, Local 48 Records
Italian Actors Union Papers
Italian American Miscellaneous Papers
Eduardo Migliaccio Papers
Howard E. Molisani Papers
Order of the Sons of Italy in America, New York Grand Lodge Records
Order of the Sons of Italy in America, Glen Cove Lodge Records
Order of the Sons of Italy in America, Uguaglianza Lodge No. 83 Records
Onorio Ruotolo Papers
Domenico Saudino Papers
George J. Spatuzza Papers
Grace Billotti Spinelli Papers
Carlo Tresca Papers
Unity, Nobility and Ambition Society Papers
Girolamo Valenti Papers
Fort Velona Papers
Albino Zattoni Papers
The Kheel Center for Labor-Management Documentation and Archives, Cornell University, Ithaca,
N.Y.
Amalgamated Clothing Workers of America Records
International Ladies' Garment Workers' Union Records
International Workers Order Records
Labadie Collection, University of Michigan Special Collections, Ann Arbor, Mich.
George Carey Papers
Agnes Inglis Papers
Library of Congress, Washington, D.C.
Federal Writers' Project Manuscripts, 1936–1940
Henry A. Murray Research Center, Radcliffe College, Cambridge, Mass.
World of Our Mothers Oral History Project
National Archives I, Washington, D.C.
Immigration and Naturalization Service Records, RG 85
United States Customs Service Records, RG 36
National Archives II, College Park, Md.
Department of Justice Records, RG 60, RG 65, RG 204
Federal Home Loan Bank Board Records, RG 58
The New York Public Library, Manuscripts and Archives Division, Astor, Lenox and Tilden Founda-
tions, New York, N.Y.
Fiorello La Guardia Papers
Vito Marcantonio Papers

New York State Archives and Records Administration, Albany, N.Y.
 Bedford Hills Correctional Facility, Series 14610-77B
Sophia Smith Collection, Smith College, Northampton, Mass.
 Italian Immigrant Women in New York City's Garment Industry Oral Histories
Robert F. Wagner Labor Archives, Tamiment Library, New York University, New York, N.Y.
 American Labor Party Papers
 Elizabeth Gurley Flynn Papers
 New York City Immigrant Labor History Project
 Oral History of the American Left
 Rose Schneiderman Papers
 Mark Starr Papers
 Girolamo Valenti Papers

Government Publications

Atti della giunta parlamentare per l'inchiesta agraria. Rome: Forzani, 1881–86.
Commissariato Generale dell'Emigrazione. *Annuario statistico della emigrazione italiana dal 1876 al 1925*. Rome: L'Universale Tipografia Poliglotta, 1926.
———. Direzione Generale della Statistica. *Censimento alla popolazione del regno d'Italia al 31 dicembre 1881*. 4 vols. Rome: 1882–84.
———. *Censimento della popolazione del regno d'Italia al 10 febbraio 1901*. 5 vols. Rome: Tipografia Nazionale G. Bertero, 1902–4.
———. "L'emigrazione delle donne e dei fanciulli dalla provincia di Caserta." *Bollettino dell'emigrazione* 12 (1913): 1423–43.
Dillingham, William. *Report of the United States Immigration Commission*. Washington, D.C.: Government Printing Office, 1911.
Direzione Generale della Statistica. *Annuario statistica italiano*. Rome: Tip. Elzeviriana, 1878–1922.
———. *Censimento degli opifici e delle imprese industriali al 10 giugno 1911*. Rome: Bertero, 1913.
———. *Censimento della popolazione del regno d'Italia al 10 febbraio 1901*. Rome: Bertero, 1904.
———. *Movimento della popolazione 1913*. Rome: Tip. Ditta Ludovicho Cecchini, 1915.
———. *Statistica degli scioperi avvenuti in Italia*. Rome, 1913.
———. *Statistica della emigrazione italiana per l'estero*. Rome, 1891.
———. *Statistica della società cooperative, 1894–1895*. Rome, 1897.
———. *Statistica della società cooperative: Società cooperative di lavoro fra braccianti, muratori ed affini al 31 Dicembre 1894*. Rome, 1895.
Education Bureau. Americanization. "Training Teachers for Americanization, Course Study for Normal Schools and Teachers' Institutes," by John J. Mahoney. Bulletin 12. Washington, D.C.: Government Printing Office, 1920.
Ellena, V. "La statistica di alcune industrie italiane." *Annali di statistica*, ser. II, vol. 13. Rome, 1880.
Federal Writers Project. Works Progress Administration. *The Italians of New York*. New York: Random House, 1938.
Inchiesta parlamentare sulle condizioni dei contadini. Rome: Tipografia Nazionale di Giovanni Bertero, 1910.
Inchiesta parlamentare sulle condizioni dei contadini nelle provincia meridionale e nella Sicilia. Rome: Bertero, 1911.
Ministero degli affari esteri. Commissariato dell'Emigrazione. *Bollettino dell'emigrazione*. Rome: Tipografia Nazionale di Giovanni Bertero, 1904.
Ministero di agricoltura, industria e commercio. Generale della Statistica. *Censimento della popolazione del regno d'Italia al 10 febbraio 1901*. Vol. 5: *Relazione sul metodo di esecuzione e sui*

risultati del censimento raffrontati con quelli dei censimenti italiani precedenti e di censimenti esteri.
Rome, 1904.

———. Direzione Generale della Statistica e del Lavoro. Ufficio del lavoro. *Le organizzazioni operaie cattoliche in Italia.* Rome, 1911.

———. Direzione dell'Industria e del Commercio. "Sul lavoro dei fanciulli e delle donne. Riposte alla circolare n. 45 del 25 luglio 1879." *Annali dell'industria e del commercio* 15 (1880).

Municipio di Napoli. *Relazione sul V censimento generale della popolazione e sul i censimento industriale.* Naples, 1912.

Naturalization Bureau. Americanization. "How Women's Organizations May Help in Americanization Work." Washington, D.C.: Government Printing Office, 1923.

———. "Suggestions for Americanization Work among Foreign-Born Women." Washington, D.C.: Government Printing Office, 1921.

———. "Suggestions for How Women's Organizations May Help in Americanization Work." Washington, D.C.: Government Printing Office, 1921.

New York. Committee of Fourteen. *The Social Evil in New York City: A Study of Law Enforcement.* New York: A. H. Kellogg, 1910.

New York State. Department of Labor. *Annual Report of the Factory Inspectors of the State of New York.* Albany: Argus Company, 1886–1900.

———. *Annual Report of the Industrial Commission, 1918.* Albany: Argus Company, 1919.

———. *Fifth Annual Report of the Factory Inspectors of the State of New York.* Albany: James B. Lyon, State Printer, 1891.

———. *Homework in the Men's Clothing Industry in New York and Rochester.* New York: State Department of Labor Special Bulletin no. 147. Albany: Argus Company, 1926.

———. *Report of the Growth of Industry in New York.* Albany: Argus Company, 1904.

———. *Seventh Annual Report of the Factory Inspectors of the State of New York.* Albany: James B. Lyon, State Printer, 1893.

———. *Twentieth Annual Report of the Bureau of Labor Statistics.* Albany: Argus Company, 1903.

New York State. Factory Investigating Commission. *Preliminary Report of the Factory Investigating Commission, 1912.* Albany: Argus Company, 1912.

New York State Assembly. Tenement House Committee. *Report.* Albany: James Lyon, 1895.

New York State Welfare Conference. *Report of the Special Committee on the Standard of Living.* New York, 1907.

Social Security Death Index 151-32-9978 (1958–59), Social Security Administration, U.S. Department of Commerce, Springfield, Va.

Statistical Abstract of the United States. Washington, D.C.: Government Printing Office, 1929.

U.S. Commissioner of Immigration. "Immigration from Italy." *North American Review* 162:6 (June 1896).

U.S. Congress. Senate. *Investigation Activities of the Department of Justice,* 66th Cong., 1st sess., S. Doc. 153. Washington, D.C.: Government Printing Office, 1919.

———. *Report on Condition of Woman and Child Wage Earners.* Vol. 2: *Men's Ready-Made Clothing.* 61st Cong., 2nd sess., S. Doc. 645. Washington, D.C.: Government Printing Office, 1911.

———. *Reports of the Immigration Commission.* Vol. 26: *Immigrants in Cities,* 1:20. Washington, D.C.: Government Printing Office, 1910.

U.S. Department of Commerce. Bureau of Census. *Twelfth Census of the United States: 1900.* Washington, D.C.: Government Printing Office, 1904.

———. *Thirteenth Census of the United States: 1910.* Washington, D.C.: Government Printing Office, 1914.

———. *Fourteenth Census of the United States: 1920.* Washington, D.C.: Government Printing Office, 1922.

———. *Fifteenth Census of the United States: 1930*. Washington, D.C.: Government Printing Office, 1931.

———. *Sixteenth Census of the United States: 1940*. Washington, D.C.: Government Printing Office, 1941.

———. *Women in Gainful Occupations, 1870–1920*, by Joseph A. Hill, Census Monographs 9. Washington, D.C.: Government Printing Office, 1929.

U.S. Department of Commerce and Labor. Bureau of the Census. *Occupations at the Twelfth Census*. Washington, D.C.: Government Printing Office, 1904.

———. *Statistics of Women at Work*. Washington, D.C.: Government Printing Office, 1907.

U.S. Department of Labor. Bureau of Labor Statistics. *Regularity of Employment in the Women's Ready-to-Wear Garment Industries*. Bulletin 183. Washington, D.C.: Government Printing Office, 1916.

———. *Wages and Regularity of Employment and Standardization of Piece Rates in the Dress and Waist Industry: New York City*. Bulletin 146. Washington, D.C.: Government Printing Office, 1914.

———. *Woman and Child Wage Earners in the U.S.* Bulletin 175. Washington, D.C.: Government Printing Office, 1916.

U.S. Immigration Commission. *Abstracts of Reports of the Immigration Commission*. 61st Cong., 3rd sess. Washington, D.C.: Government Printing Office, 1911.

———. *Dictionary of Races or Peoples*. Washington, D.C.: Government Printing Office, 1911.

———. *Immigrants in Cities*. 61st Cong., 2nd sess., S. Doc. 338. Washington, D.C.: Government Printing Office, 1911.

———. *Immigrants in Industries*. 61st Cong., 1st sess., S. Doc. 633. Washington, D.C.: Government Printing Office, 1911.

Women's Bureau. "Immigrant Woman and Her Job," by Caroline Manning. Bulletin 74. Washington, D.C.: Government Printing Office, 1930.

Interviews

American Labor Museum, Botto House National Landmark, Haledon, N.J.

Sylvia Bochese, by Robert Kirkman, 19 March 1981

Bunny Kuiken, by Robert Kirkman, 19 March 1981

Henry A. Murray Center for Research on Women at Radcliffe College, Cambridge, Mass.

"World of Our Mothers Study of Jewish and Italian Immigrant Women": interviews with 39 Italian immigrant women by Ruth Coser, 1980–85

Sophia Smith Collection, Smith College, Northampton, Mass.

ITALIAN IMMIGRANT WOMEN IN NEW YORK CITY'S GARMENT INDUSTRY ORAL HISTORIES

Mary Cacchione and Vincenza Cracchiolo, by Colomba Furio, ca. 1977

Tina Catania, by Colomba Furio, 30 March 1978

Grace De Luise Natarelli, by Colomba Furio, 22 September 1978

Tina Gaeta, by Colomba Furio, 22 November 1976

Carolina Golzio, by Steve Golin, 13 June 1983

Ralph Iannanto, by Colomba Furio, ca. 1977

Antonetta Lazzaro, by Colomba Furio, 29 March 1977

Howard Molisani, by Colomba Furio, 23 February 1978

Pauline Newman, by Colomba Furio, 17 November 1976

Diane Romanik, by Colomba Furio, 1 April 1977
Rose Villano, by Steve Golin, 14 June 1983

Robert F. Wagner Labor Archives, Tamiment Library, New York University, New York, N.Y.

NEW YORK CITY IMMIGRANT LABOR HISTORY PROJECT
Lily Campanile, by Nina Cobb and Jay Facciolo, 16 May 1975
Carolina Cappallette, by Joan Granucci, 28 April 1973
Mario Cinisomo, by Leon Fink, 4 April 1973
Rose Cohen, interviewer unknown, 30 March 1973
Carolina Crupi, by Joan Granucci, 8 May 1974
Rose Davy (with Angela Saltalamacchina), by Nina Cobb, David Lightner, and Jay Facciolo, 14 May
    1975
Maria Fischetti, by Joan Granucci, 8 May 1974
Grace Gello, by Janice Albert, n.d., ca. 1973–76
Dominick Granato, by Martin Lesser and Joan Granucci, 4 April 1973
Shirley Harris, interviewer unknown, 11 April 1973
James Ippolito, by Joan Granucci, 12 April 1973
Rose Lapidus, by Frank Faragasso, 18 March 1975
Rebecca Leff, by Frank Faragasso, ca. 1975
Joseph Maglicano, by Joan Granucci, 27 March 1973
Agnes Mazza, by David Lightner, 1973–76
Mabel Mitchell, by Steven Holmes, 26 March 1973
Filomena Ognibone, by Karen Kearns, 12 April 1973
Tina Quartaroni, by N. Newman, ca. 1974–76
Evandi Richards, by Rhonda Weiss, 28 March 1973
Angela Saltalamacchia (with Rose Davy), by Nina Cobb, David Lightner, and Jay Facciolo, 14 May
    1975
Mary Sansone, by Joan Granucci, 9 April 1974
Alex Sirota, interviewer unknown, ca. 1974–76
Primo Tassio, by Howard Harris, 8 April 1975
Benny Terranova, by Martin Lesser and Joan Granucci, ca. 1974–76
Three Italian Women at Senior Citizen Center (Cristina Di Matteo, Angela Santamaria, and Anna
    Delgado), ca. 1974–75
Mrs. Vercellino, by John Salerno, 25 April 1973
Angela Wanderling, by Sante Cigliano, ca. 1973–76

ORAL HISTORY OF THE AMERICAN LEFT
Abner Berry, by Mark Naison, 1974–77
Fannie Borun, by Bea Lemisch, 6 January 1981
Alice Citron, by Bea Lemisch, 6 January 1981
Edigio Clemente, by Eugene Miller, 11 May 1981
Albina Delfino, by Ruth F. Prago, 8 January 1981
Esther Dolgoff, by Bea Lemisch, 27 January 1982
Mary Gale, by Ruth F. Prago, 29 January 1982
Alex and Faye Gardners, Abe Kantor and Hyman Hodes, by Paul Buhle, 29 January 1982
Mollie Goldstein, by Bea Lemisch, 7 November 1981
ILGWU, anonymous members, by David Gurowsky, 1974–77
Maud White Katz, by Ruth F. Prago, 18 October 1981

Vito Magli, by Paul Buhle, 15 March 1983
Anthony Martocchia and Philip Lamantia, by Paul Buhle, 31 October 1982
Mother Audley Moore, by Mark Naison, 1972
Louise Patterson, by Ruth F. Prago, 16 November 1981
Annette Rubenstein, by Richard Wormser and Bea Lemisch, 18 December 1980
Fred Thompson, by Paul Buhle, 26 July 1983

YM/YWHA, Charles Goldman Judaica Library, Wayne, N.J.

Helen Meadow, by Rita Isaacs and Jerry Nathans, 17 and 24 August 1982

Interviews and Correspondence with Author

Jennie Citarella, 27 March 1996
Bea Conte, 12 September 1996
Jane Gallo, 27 January 1996
Edvige Giunta, 12 June 2001
Jill Guabello and family, 20 August 2001
Athena Iris (Capraro) Warren, 5 December 2005
Nunzio Pernicone, 1 September 2007, 16 July 2008

Newspapers and Periodicals

L'Adunata dei Refrattari	La Follia di New York	New York Times
Alba Nuova	Giustizia	New York Tribune
American Journal of Sociology	La Guardia Rossa	Novatore
American Magazine	Il Grido della Stirpe	Il Nuovo Mondo
Amsterdam News	Harper's Weekly	Il Nuovo Vessillo
L'Araldo Italiano	L'Idea	L'Operaia
L'Asino	Industrial Worker	OSIA News
L'Aurora	L'Italia Nostra	La Parola del Popolo
L'Avvenire	Jewish Daily Forward	La Prensa
Bollettino della Sera	Justice	Primo Maggio
Bollettino dell'emigrazione	Il Lavoratore	Il Progresso Italo-Americano
Brooklyn Daily Eagle	Il Lavoro	Il Proletario
Il Carroccio	Life	Prometeo
Charities	La Lotta	La Questione Sociale
Il Cittadino	Lotta di Classe	Il Refrattario
Collier's	Il Martello	La Ricossa
Corriere d'America	Masses	Rinascimento
Corriere della Sera	Message	Saturday Evening Post
Cosmopolitan	Nation	Time
Cronaca Sovversiva	New Amsterdam	Il Traditore
Daily News	New York Age	L'Unità Operaia
Daily Worker	New York Call	L'Unità del Popolo
La Donna Italiana	New York Evening Post	Il Veltro
East Harlem News	New York Herald Tribune	Washington Post
L'Eco	New York Journal	Weekly Bulletin of
L'Era Nuova	New York Post	the Clothing Trades
Evening Sun	New York Sun	

Other Primary Sources

Anonymous. *Four Years in the Underbrush: Adventures as a Working Woman in New York*. New York: C. Scribner's Sons, 1921.

———. *Maria Nambrini*. Florence: Tipografia Salani, 1907.

Adams, Charlotte. "Italian Life in New York." *Harper's* 62:371 (April 1881): 676–85.

Addams, Jane. *Democracy and Social Ethics*. New York: Macmillan, 1902.

———. *A New Conscience and an Ancient Evil*. Urbana: University of Illinois Press, 2002 [1912].

Andrews. J. B. "Neapolitan Witchcraft." *Folk-Lore: Transactions of the Folk-Lore Society* 3:1 (March 1897).

Atlas of the City of Paterson, New Jersey. Philadelphia: A. H. Mueller, 1915.

Bakke, E. Wight. *Citizens without Work: A Study of the Effects of Unemployment upon the Workers' Social Relations and Practices*. New Haven: Yale University Press, 1940.

Baldwin, James. "On Being 'White' . . . and Other Lies." *Essence*, April 1984. Reprinted in David Roediger, ed., *Black on White: Black Writers on What It Means to Be White*. New York: Schocken, 1999.

———. *The Price of the Ticket: Collected Nonfiction, 1948–1985*. New York: St. Martin's Press, 1985.

Balzano, Vincenzo. *Abruzzi e Molise*. Turin: Unione Tipografia-Editrice Torinese, 1927.

Barnum, Gertrude. "At the Shirt Waist Factory." *Ladies' Garment Worker*, May 1910.

———. "The Children's Crusade: The New York Strikers are Winning Fights." *Ladies' Garment Worker*, February 1913.

Becchetti, Nena. *La figlia dell'anarchico. Dramma sociale in tre atti*. Jessup, Pa.: Gruppo Autonomo, 1928.

Bell, Ernest, ed. *Fighting the Traffic in Young Girls, or the War on the White Slave Trade*. Chicago, 1910.

Bennett, William S. "Immigrants and Crime." *Annals of the Academy of Political and Social Science* 34 (July 1909): 117–24.

Bernardy, Amy. "L'emigrazione delle donne e dei fanciulli italiane nella North Atlantic Division." *Bollettino dell'emigrazione* (1909).

Bertocci, Angelo P. "Memoir of My Mother." *Harper's Magazine* 175:2 (June 1937).

Betts, Lillian. "The Italian in New York." *University Settlement* 1:3–4 (1905–6).

———. "Italian Peasants in a New Law Tenement." *Harper's Bazaar* 38 (1904).

Bixio, Nino. *Epistolario*. Vol. 2 (1861–65). Rome: Vittoriano, 1942.

Bogardus, Emory S. *Essentials of Americanization*. Los Angeles: University of Southern California Press, 1923.

———. *Immigration and Race Attitudes*. New York: D. C. Heath, 1928.

Borghi, Armando. *Mezzo secolo di anarchia (1898–1945)*. Naples: Edizione Scientifiche Italiane, 1954.

Borosino, Victor. "Home Going Italians." *Survey* 28 (28 September 1912).

Botti, Ettore. *La delinquenza femminile a Napoli*. Naples: L. Pierro, 1904.

Boyd, Frederick, ed. *The Pageant of the Paterson Strike*. New York: Success Press, 1913.

Brace, Charles Loring. *The Dangerous Classes in New York City*. Montclair, N.J.: Patterson Smith, 1967 [1880].

Brandt, Lillian. "In Behalf of the Overcrowded and the Apathy That Arises from It." *Charities and the Commons* 12 (1904): 503.

Brissenden, Paul. *The IWW: A Study of American Syndicalism*. New York: Russell and Russell, 1957 [1919].

Brown, Claude. *Manchild in the Promised Land*. New York: Macmillan, 1965.

Browne, Henry J. "The 'Italian Problem' in the Catholic Church of the United States, 1880–1900." *United States Catholic Historical Society, Historical Records and Sketches* 35. New York: U.S. Catholic Historical Society, 1946.

Bruccoleri, Giuseppe. *La Sicilia di oggi: Appunti economici*. Rome: Athanaeum, 1913.

Calvino, Italo. *Italian Folktales*. New York: Pantheon Books, 1956.

Caminita, Ludovico. *Nell'isola delle lagrime: Ellis Island*. Paterson: Libreria Sociologica, 1924.

Cammareri-Scurti, Sebastiano. *La lotta di classe in Sicilia*. Milan: Ufficio della Critica Sociale, 1896.

Capotorto, Rosette. *Bronx Italian*. Hoboken: Pronto Press, 2003.

Carr, John Foster. "The Coming of the Italian." *Outlook* 82 (1906): 418–31.

Castiglione, G. E. di Palma. "Italian Immigration into the United States, 1901–4." *American Journal of Sociology* 11:2 (September 1905): 183–206.

Cavour, C. *Carteggi: La liberazione del mezzogiorno e la formazione del regno d'Italia*. Vol. 3 (October–November 1860). Bologna: Zanichelli, 1952.

Chambers, Bradford. "The Juvenile Gangs of New York." *American Mercury* 62 (1946): 480–86.

Chapin, Robert Coit. *The Standard of Living among Workingmen's Families in New York City*. New York: Charities Organization Society, 1909.

Chenault, Lawrence. *The Puerto Rican Migrant in New York City*. New York: Russell and Russell, 1970 [1938].

Chotzinoff, Samuel. *A Lost Paradise—Early Reminiscences of Samuel Chotzinoff*. New York: Alfred A. Knopf, 1955.

Ciccotosto, Emma, and Michal Bosworth. *Emma, a Translated Life*. Fremantle, Australia: Fremantle Press, 1990.

Claghorn, Kate Holladay. "Our Immigrants and Ourselves." *Atlantic Monthly* 85:516 (October 1900): 535–48.

Closson, Carlos C. "The Hierarchy of European Races." *American Journal of Sociology* 3:3 (November 1897): 314–27.

Cohn, Fannia. "The Uprising of the Sixty Thousand." *Justice*, 1 September 1933.

Colajanni, Napoleone. *Gli avvenimenti in Sicilia e le loro cause*. Palermo: Flaccovio, 1894.

———. *L'Italia nel 1898*. Milan: Universale Economica, 1898.

Coletti, Francesco. *La populazione rurale in Italia*. Piacenza: Federazione italiana dei consorzi agrari, 1925.

Conte, Gaetano. *Dieci anni in America*. Palermo: Tip. G. Spinnato, 1903.

Corsi, Edward. *In the Shadow of Liberty: The Chronicle of Ellis Island*. New York: Macmillan, 1935.

Coselschi, Eugenio. *Universalità del fascismo: raccolta di giudizi di personalità e della stampa di tutto il mondo, 1922–1932*. Florence: Vallecchi, 1933.

Covello, Leonard. "Building Democratic Ideals through a School-Community Program." *Library Journal* 65 (1 February 1940): 108.

———. *The Heart Is the Teacher*. New York: McGraw-Hill, 1958.

———. *The Social Background of the Italo-American School Child*. Leiden: E. J. Brill, 1967.

Crowell, F. Elizabeth. "The Midwives of New York." *Charities and the Commons* 17 (1907): 667–77.

D'Alesandre, John, Jr. *Occupational Trends of Italians in New York City*. Bulletin No. 8. New York: Casa Italiana Education Bureau, 1935.

D'Amato, Gaetano. "The 'Black Hand' Myth." *North American Review* 187 (January–June 1908).

———. "The Truth about the Italian Immigrant." *Appleton's Magazine* 9:4 (April 1907).

Damiani, Gigi. *I paesi nei quali non si deve emigrare: La questione sociale nel Brasile*. Milan: Umanità Nuova, 1920.

Daniel, Annie S. "The Wreck of the Home: How Wearing Apparel Is Fashioned in the Tenements." *Charities* 14:1 (1 April 1905): 624–29.

Davenport, William E. "The Italian Immigrant in America." *Outlook* 73 (1903).

Davis, Benjamin J. *Communist Councilman from Harlem*. New York: International Publishers, 1969.

De Biasi, A. "Il fascismo negli Stati Uniti." *La battaglia dell'Italia negli Stati Uniti*. New York, 1927.

De Bourcard, Francesco. *Use e costumi di Napoli e contorni descritti e dipinti*. Naples: Stab. Tip. Di G. Nobile, 1853–58.

De Forest, Robert, and Lawrence Veiller. *The Tenement House Problem*. New York: Macmillan, 1903.

De Lesser, Creuzé. *Voyage en Italie et en Sicile*. Paris: P. Didot l'Aîné, 1806.

Denison, Lindsay. "Black Hand." *Everybody's Magazine* 19 (Sept 1908): 543–49.

De Nobili, Irene De Bonis. *Per il voto alle donne*. Rome: Righetti, 1909.

De Nobili, Leonello. "L'emigrazione in Calabria. Effetti dell'emigrazione in generale." *Rivista di Emigrazione* 1:5 (July 1908).

De Raho, Francesco. *Il tarantolismo nella superstizione e nella scienza*. Rome: Sensibili alle foglie, 1994 [1908].

Diana, F. P. *Femminismo e anti-femminismo: Conferenza tenuta nel circolo degli impiegati il 6 Maggio 1904*. Agrigento: Montès, 1905.

Di Domenica, A. "Conditions among Italians in America." *Missionary Review of the World* 58 (February 1935): 71–71.

Di Prima, Diane. "Don't Solidify the Adversary!" In *Through the Looking Glass: Images of Italians and Italian Americans in the Media*, edited by Mary Jo Bona and Anthony Julian Tamburri. Chicago: American Italian Historical Association, 1994.

———. *Recollections of My Life as a Woman*. New York: Viking, 2001.

Dorso, Guido. *La rivoluzione meridionale*. Turin: Gobetti, 1924.

Douglas, Norman. *Old Calabria*. London: Century Publishing, 1915.

Drake, Leonard A., and Carrie Glasser. *Trends in the New York Clothing Industry*. New York: Institute of Public Administration, 1942.

Drake, St. Clair, and Horace R. Cayton. *Black Metropolis: A Study of Negro Life in a Northern City*. Chicago: University of Chicago Press, 1993 [1945].

Esteve, Pedro. *Memoria de la conferencia anarquista internacional cellebrada en Chicago en septiembre de 1893*. Paterson: El Despertar, 1900.

———. "La revolución en la practica." In *El problema politico de la revolución, por Gastón Leval*. N.p., 1958, Columbia University Microfilm.

———. *Vest-Pocket Essays for the Laborer*. Translated by M. H. Woolman. New York: Cultura Obrera, 1912.

Fabbri, Luigi. *Malatesta: L'uomo e il pensiero*. Naples: Edizioni RL, 1951.

Fenollosa, Mary. *Sunshine Beggars*. New York: Little, 1919.

Ferrari, Robert. "American Immigrant Autobiographies," microfilm pos. 4634, IHRC.

Ferri, Enrico. *Studi sulla criminalità*. Turin: Bocca, 1901.

Fiamingo, Giuseppe M. "Italian Anarchism." *Contemporary Review* 78 (September 1900): 339–43.

Fiaschetti, Michael. *You Gotta Be Rough: The Adventures of Detective Fiaschetti of the Italian Squad*. New York: Doubleday, Doran, 1930.

Flynn, Elizabeth Gurley. *Rebel Girl, an Autobiography: My First Life (1906–1926)*. New York: International Publishers, 1955.

———. *Words of Fire: The Life and Writing of Elizabeth Gurley Flynn*. Edited by Rosalyn Fraad Baxandall. New Brunswick: Rutgers University Press, 1987.

Foerster, Robert Franz. *The Italian Immigration of Our Times*. Cambridge, Mass.: Harvard University Press, 1919.

Forman, Allan. "Italians in New York." *American Magazine* 9 (1885): 46–52.

Fortunato, Giustino. *Il mezzogiorno e lo stato italiano*. Bari: Laterza, 1911.

Forzato Spezia, Bellalma. *Per le nuove generazioni*. New York: Nicoletti Brothers Press, 1911.

Franchetti, Leopoldo, and Sidney Sonnino. *La Sicilia nel 1876*. Florence: Valecchi, 1925.

Frankfurter, Felix. *The Case of Sacco and Vanzetti*. Boston: Little, Brown, 1927.

Ganz, Maria. *Rebels: Into Anarchy and Out Again*. New York: Dodd, Mead, 1919.

Gebhart, John C. *The Growth and Development of Italian Children in New York City*. New York: New York Association for Improving the Condition of the Poor, 1924.

Giacone, G. *Zabut; notizie storiche del Castello di Zabut e suo contiguo casale—oggi comune di Sicilia*. Sciacca: Guadagna, 1932.

Gillett, Lucy. *Adapting Nutrition Work to the Community*. New York: New York Association for Improving the Condition of the Poor, 1924.

Godkin, E. L. "Italian Trouble: Riots." *Nation* 66 (19 May 1898).

———. "Our Sweating System." *Nation* 50 (June 1890).

Goldman, Emma. *Emma Goldman: A Documentary History of the American Years*. Edited by Candace Falk. Berkeley: University of California Press, 2003.

———. *Living My Life*. New York: Dover Publications, 1970 [1931].

Grabo, Carl H. "Americanizing the Immigrants." *Dial* 66 (1919): 539–41.

Gramsci, Antonio. "Alcuni temi della questione meridionale" (1926). In *La costruzione del Partito Comunista (1923–1926)*, edited by Elsa Fubini. Turin: G. Einaudi, 1971.

———. *Folclore e senso comune*. Rome: Riuniti, 1992.

———. *La questione meridionale*. Rome: Edizioni Rinascità, 1953.

———. *Il risorgimento*. Rome: Riuniti, 1991 [1954].

———. *Selections from the Prison Notebooks*. New York: Columbia University Press, 1991.

———. *The Southern Question*. Translation and introduction by Pasquale Veridicchio. West Lafayette, Ind.: Bordighera, 1995.

Griel, Cecile L. *The Problems of the Mother in a New Country*. New York: National Board of the YWCA, 1919. Reprinted in *Italians in the United States: A Repository of Rare Tracts and Miscellanea*. New York: Arno Press, 1975.

Halstead, Murat. *The Illustrious Life of William McKinley*. Chicago: Murat Halstead, 1901.

Hapgood, Hutchins. *Types from City Streets*. New York: Funk & Wagnalls, 1910.

Hardman, Jacob Benjamin Salutsky. *The Amalgamated Today and Tomorrow*. New York: Amalgamated Clothing Workers of America, 1939.

Hardy, Jack. *The Clothing Workers: A Study of the Conditions and Struggles in the Needle Trades*. New York: International Publishers, 1935.

Harper's Magazine. *New York: A Collection from Harper's Magazine*. New York: Gallery Books, 1991.

Hartt, Rollin Lynde. "Made in Italy." *Independent*, 23 July 1921.

Haywood, William. *Bill Haywood's Book: The Autobiography of William D. Haywood*. New York: International Publishers, 1929.

———. "On the Paterson Picket Line." *International Socialist Review* 13 (June 1913).

———. "A Rip in the Silk Industry." *International Socialist Review* 13 (May 1913).

Herzfeld, Elsa. *Family Monographs: The History of Twenty-four Families Living in the Middle West Side of New York City*. New York: Kempster, 1905.

———. "Superstitions and Customs of the Tenement-House Mother." *Charities and Commons* 14 (1905): 983–86.

Hutchins, Grace. *Labor and Silk*. New York: International Publishers, 1929.

International Ladies' Garment Workers' Union. *ILGWU Illustrated: Pictorial Story of the ILGWU 23rd Convention, May 1937, Atlantic City, NJ* (New York, 1937).

———. *Proceedings of Convention*. 1910.

———. *Proceedings of Convention*. 1925.

———. *48 Libro Ricordo: XXV anniversario della unione dei cloak makers italiani, Local 48, 1916–1941*.

———. *Report and Proceedings to the 15th Biennial Convention* (1920).

———. Report of the Ladies' Waistmakers' Union Local 25 to the 16th Convention of the ILGWU, Cleveland, May 1922.

Irwin, Elisabeth A. "The Story of a Transplanted Industry: Lace Workers of the Italian Quarter of New York." *Craftsman* 12:4 (July 1907): 404–9.

Jones, Thomas Jesse. *Sociology of a New York City Block*. Studies in History, Economics and Public Law, vol. 21, no. 2. New York: Columbia University Press, 1904.

Kimball, Charlotte. "An Outline of Amusements among Italians in New York City." *Charities* 5 (18 August 1900).

King, H. Bolton, and Thomas Okey. *Italy Today*. London, 1909.

Kneeland, George J. *Commercialized Prostitution in New York City*. New York: Century, 1913.

Labriola, Teresa. *Per voto alla donna: Conferenza (24 marzo 1906)*. Rome: E. Loescher, 1906.

Lang, Harry. *"62": Biography of a Union*. New York: Astoria Press, 1940.

Lapolla, Garibaldi M. *The Fire in the Flesh*. New York: Vanguard Press, 1931.

——. *The Grand Gennaro*. New York: Vanguard Press, 1935.

Leland, Charles. *Etruscan Magic and Occult Remedies*. New York: University Books, 1963.

——. *Legends of Florence*. New York: Macmillan, 1895.

Leupp, Constance. "The Shirtwaist Makers' Strike." *Survey*, 18 December 1909.

Levi, Carlo. *Christ Stopped at Eboli*. New York: Farrar, Straus, and Co., 1986 [1947].

Levine, Louis. *The Women's Garment Workers Union: A History of the International Ladies' Garment Workers' Union*. New York: B. W. Huebsch, 1924.

Local 48-ILGWU. *"48" Libro Ricordo del XXV anniversario della unione dei cloakmakers italiani*. New York: International Newspaper Printing Co., 1941.

Lombroso, Cesare. "Criminal Anthropology: Its Origins and Applications." *Forum* 20 (1895).

——. *Criminal Man*. Translated with new introduction by Mary Gibson and Nicole Hahn Rafter. Durham: Duke University Press, 2006.

——. *In Calabria (1862–1897)*. Catania: Niccolò Giannotta, 1898.

——. "The Ultimate Triumph of the Boers." *North American Review* 171:524 (July 1900): 135–44.

——. *L'uomo bianco e l'uomo di colore: Lettere sull'origine e la varietà delle razze umane*. Padua: F. Sacchetto, 1871.

——. *L'uomo delinquente in rapporto all'antropologia, alla giurisprudenza ed alle discipline carcerarie*. Turin: Bocca, 1897–98.

——. "Why Homicide Has Increased in the United States—I." *North American Review* 165:493 (December 1897): 641–49.

——. "Why Homicide Has Increased in the United States—II." *North American Review* 166:494 (January 1898): 1–12.

Lombroso, Cesare, and Guglielmo Ferrero. *Criminal Woman, the Prostitute, and the Normal Woman*. Translated with a new introduction by Nicole Hahn Rafter and Mary Gibson. Durham: Duke University Press, 2004.

Lord, Eliot, and John J. D. Trenor, and Samuel Barrows. *The Italian in America*. New York: Buck, 1905.

Lorenzoni, Giovanni. *Inchiesta parlamentare sulle condizioni dei contadini nelle provincie meridionali e nella Sicilia*. Vol. 4. Rome: Bertero, 1910.

Lowenfels, Walter. "Frankie's Fight on Race Hatreds." *Daily Worker*, 25 November 1945.

Luhan, Mabel Dodge. *Intimate Memories*. Albuquerque: University of New Mexico Press, 1999 [1936].

Magee, Mabel A. *Trends in Location of the Women's Clothing Industry*. Chicago: University of Chicago Press, 1930.

Mailly, William. "The Working Girls' Strike." *Independent* 67 (1909): 1416–20.

Malatesta, Errico. *L'anarchia*. London: Biblioteca dell'Associazione, 1891. Reprint, London: Freedom Press, 1974.

Malcolm X. *Malcolm X on Afro-American History*. Expanded and illustrated edition. New York: Pathfinder Press, 1970.

Malkiel, Theresa. *The Diary of a Shirtwaist Striker*. Ithaca: Cornell University Press, 1990 [1910].

——. "Striking for the Right to Live." *Coming Nation* 1:124 (25 January 1913).

Mangano, Antonio. "Americanizing Italian Mothers." *Missions*, January 1919.

——. "The Associated Life of the Italians in New York City." *Charities* 12 (7 May 1904).

——. "The Effect of Emigration upon Italy." *Charities and the Commons* 20 (4 April 1908).

——. "The Effect of Emigration upon Italy." *Charities and the Commons* (2 May 1908).

——. *Sons of Italy: A Social and Religious Study of the Italians in America*. New York: Methodist Book Concern, 1917.

Mangione, Jerre. *Monte Allegro*. New York: Crown, 1972.

Mansueto, Anthony. "'Blessed are the Meek' . . . Religion and Socialism in Italian American History." In *The Melting Pot and Beyond: Italian Americans in the Year 2000*, edited by Jerome Krase and William Egelman. Staten Island: American Italian Historical Association, 1987.

Mariano, John Horace. *The Italian Contribution to American Democracy*. Boston: Christopher Publishing House, 1921.

Marot, Helen. "A Woman's Strike: An Appreciation." *Proceedings of the Academy of Political Science* 1 (October 1910): 119–28.

Marselli-Valli, Maria. *Donne e femminismo*. Florence: Rassegna Nazionale, 1908.

Massari, Angelo. *The Wonderful World of Angelo Massari*. Translated by Arthur D. Massolo. New York: Exposition Press, 1965.

McCabe, James, Jr. *Lights and Shadows of New York Life*. New York: Vintage Books, 1991.

McKay, Claude. *Harlem: Negro Metropolis*. New York: Harcourt, Brace, Jovanovich, 1968 [1940].

McKay, George. "The Effect upon the Health, Moral, and Mentality of Working People Employed in Overcrowded Work-Rooms." In *Fifth Annual Report of the Factory Inspectors of the State of New York*. Albany: James B. Lyon, State Printer, 1891.

McLaughlin, Allan. "Italians and Other Latin Immigrants." *Popular Science Monthly* 65 (August 1904): 341–47.

McLeod, Christian [Anna C. Ruddy]. *The Heart of the Stranger: A Story of Little Italy*. New York: Revell, 1908.

Merlino, S. "Camorra, Mafia and Brigandage." *Political Science Quarterly* 9:3 (September 1894): 466–86.

———. "Italian Immigrants and Their Enslavement." *Forum* 15 (April 1893): 183–90.

Messina, Maria. *Piccoli gorghi*. Palermo: Sellerio, 1988 [1911].

Miceli, F. Paul. *Pride of Sicily*. New York: Theo. Gaus Sons, 1950.

Michelangeli, Ernesta. *La vera missione della donna*. Bologna: Zanichelli, 1901.

Milone, A. "L'Emigrazione e una partita del suo bilancio morale passive." *Rivista di emigrazione* 1:7 (September 1908).

Mohr, Nicholasa. *Nilda*. New York: Harper and Row, 1973.

Monroe, William Seymour. *Sicily, the Garden of the Mediterranean: The History, People, Institutions and Geography of the Island*. Boston: L. C. Page, 1909.

Montana, Vanni. *Amorostico. Testimonianze euroamericane*. Livorno: U. Bastogi, 1975.

More, Louise Bolard. *Wage-Earners' Budgets: A Study of Standards and Cost of Living in New York City*. New York: Henry Holt, 1907.

Morgan, E. Strachan. "Secret Societies in the Two Sicilies." *Littell's Living Age* 175:2268 (17 December 1887).

Morgan, J. Appleton. "What Shall We Do with the Dago?" *Popular Science Monthly* 38 (December 1890).

Mosso, Angelo. *Vita moderna degli italiani*. Milan: Fratelli Treves Editori, 1906.

Mozzoni, Anna Maria. *Liberazione della donna*. Edited by Franca Pieroni Bortolotti. Milan: G. Mazzotta, 1975.

———. *Un passo avanti nella cultural femminile, tesi e progetto*. Milan: G. Mazzotta, 1975.

Munthe, Axel. *Letters from a Mourning City*. Translated by Maude Valerie White. London, 1887.

Navarro della Miraglia, Emmanuele. *La nana*. Bologna: Capelli, 1963.

———. *Storielle siciliane*. Palermo: Sellerio, 1974.

Nettlau, Max. *Bakunin e l'Internazionale in Italia dal 1864 al 1872*. Geneva: Edizione del "Risveglio," 1928.

———. *Breve storia dell'anarchismo*. Cesena: Edizioni L'Antistato, 1964.

———. *Errico Malatesta: Vita e pensieri*. New York: Casa Editrice "Il Martello," 1922.

———. *A Short History of Anarchism*. Edited by Heiner M. Becker. London: Freedom Press, 1996.

Newman, Pauline. "Our Women Workers." *Ladies' Garment Worker*, April 1914.

———. "Out of the Past—Into the Future." *Life and Labor*, June 1921.

———. "The White Goods workers' Strike." *Ladies' Garment Worker*, March 1913.

Niceforo, Alfredo. *La delinquenza in Sardegna*. Palermo: Sandron, 1897.

———. *L'Italia barbara contemporanea (Studi ed appunti)*. Milan and Palermo: Remo Sandron, 1898.

———. *Italiani del nord e italiani del sud*. Florence: Tip. Cooperativa, 1899.

Nicotri, Gaspare. *Rivoluzioni e rivolte in Sicilia*. Palermo: Reber, 1909.

Nievo, Ippolito. *Lettere garibaldine*. Edited by Andreina Ciceri. Turin: Edizioni della Fondazione Giovanni Agnelli, 1961.

Nitti, Francesco Saverio. "Italian Anarchists." *North American Review* 167 (November 1898): 598–608.

———. *Napoli e la questione meridionale*. Naples, 1900.

———. *Scritti sulla questione meridionale*. Bari: Laterza, 1958.

Noce, Teresa. *Gioventù senza sole*. Rome: Editori Riuniti, 1973.

Norr, William. *Stories of Chinatown*. New York, 1892.

Odencrantz, Louise. *Italian Women in Industry: A Study of Conditions in New York City*. New York: Russell Sage Foundation, 1919.

Padilla, Elena. *Up from Puerto Rico*. New York: Columbia University Press, 1958.

Pagano, Jo. *The Golden Wedding*. New York: Random House, 1943.

Panunzio, Constantine M. *The Deportation Cases of 1919–1920*. New York: Da Capo Press, 1921.

———. *Immigration Crossroads*. New York: Macmillan, 1927.

———. *The Soul of an Immigrant*. New York: Macmillan, 1921.

Park, Robert, and Herbert Miller. *Old World Traits Transplanted*. New York: Harper and Brothers, 1921.

Parker, Cornelia Stratton. *Working with the Working Woman*. New York: Harper and Brothers, 1922.

Pecorini, Alberto. "The Italians in the United States." *Forum* 45 (1911): 15–29.

Pellet, Marcellin. *Napoli contemporanea, 1888–1892*. Translated by Francesco D'Ascoli. Naples, 1898.

Perri, Francesco. *Enough of Dreams*. New York: Brentano, 1929.

Pesotta, Rose. *Bread upon the Waters*. New York: ILR Press, 1987 [1944].

Phillips, Russell. "The Strike at Little Falls." *International Socialist Review* 13 (December 1912): 453–60.

Pike, Violet. "New World Lessons for Old World Peoples. Lesson VI: Joining the Union." *Life and Labor* 2 (March 1912).

Pitrè, Giuseppe. *La famiglia, la casa, la vita del popolo siciliano*. Biblioteca delle Tradizioni Popolari Siciliane, vol. 25. Palermo: Libreria Internazionale A. Reber, 1913.

———. *Feste patronali nella Sicilia orientale*. Catania: Brancato Editore, 2000.

———. *Proverbi siciliani*. Palermo: Il Vespro, 1978 [1870].

———. *Sicilian Folk Medicine*. Translated by Phyllis H. Williams. Lawrence, Kans.: Coronado Press, 1971.

———. *Spettacoli popolari siciliani*. Catania: Brancato Editore, 2000.

———. *Usi e costumi del popolo siciliano*. Edited by Giuseppe Lisi. Bologna: Cappelli, 1961.

Pope, Jesse. *The Clothing Industry in New York*. Columbia, Mo.: E. W. Stephens, 1905.

Powell, Adam Clayton, Jr. *Marching Blacks*. New York: Dial Press, 1945.

Ragusa, Kym. *The Skin between Us: A Memoir of Race, Beauty, and Belonging*. New York: W. W. Norton, 2006.

Rampersad, Arnold, ed. *The Collected Poems of Langston Hughes*. New York: Knopf, 1995.

Razovki, Cecilia. "The Eternal Masculine." *Survey* 39 (1917): 117.

Reid, Sydney. "Death Sign." *Independent* 70 (6 April 1911).

Renda, Antonio. *La questione meridionale, Inchiesta*. Milan: Sandron, 1900.

Riis, Jacob A. "Feast-Days in Little Italy." *Century Magazine* 58:4 (August 1899): 491–99.

———. *How the Other Half Lives*. Boston: Bedford Books, 1996 [1890].

———. *Out of Mulberry Street: Stories of Tenement Life in New York City*. New York: Century. 1989.

Ripley, William Z. *The Races of Europe: A Sociological Study.* New York: D. Appleton, 1899.

Riviello, Raffaele. *Costumanze, vita e pregiudizi del popolo potentino.* Potenza: Garramone, 1893.

Roberts, Marjorie. "Italian Girls on American Soil." *Mental Hygiene* 13 (October 1929): 757–68.

Roche, Josephine. "The Italian Girl." In *The Neglected Girl.* New York: Russell Sage Foundation, Survey Associates, 1914.

———. *West Side Studies* 2 (1913).

Rogari, Sandro. *Mezzogiorno ed emigrazione. L'inchiesta Faina sulle condizioni dei contadini nelle province meridionali e nella Sicilia, 1906–1911.* Florence: Centro Editoriale Toscano, 2002.

Roseboro, Viola. "The Italians of New York." *Cosmopolitan: A Monthly Illustrated Magazine,* January 1888.

Ross, Edward A. *The Old World in the New: The Significance of Past and Present Immigration to the American People.* New York: Century, 1914.

Rossi, Adolfo. "La situazione in Sicilia." *La tribuna* (8 October 1893).

———. "Vantaggi e svantaggi dell'emigrazione dal mezzogiorno d'Italia." *Bollettino dell'emigrazione* 13 (1908): 1549–1645.

Rotolo, Suze. *A Freewheelin' Time: A Memoir of Greenwich Village in the Sixties.* New York: Broadway Books, 2008.

Russo, Nicholas J. "The Origin and Progress of Our Italian Mission in New York." *Woodstock Letters* 25 (1896): 135–43.

Rygier, Maria. *Il sindacalismo alla Sbarra.* Bologna: Libreria Scuola Moderna, 1911.

———. *Sulla soglia di un'epoca. La nostra Patria.* Rome: Liberia Politica Moderna, 1915.

Salomone-Marino, Salvatore. *Costumi e usanze dei contadini di Sicilia.* Palermo: Ando, 1968.

———. *Customs and Habits of the Sicilian Peasants.* Edited and translated by Rosalie N. Norris. Rutherford: Fairleigh Dickinson University Press, 1981.

———. *Lu vèspiru sicilianu storia popolare in poesia.* Palermo: L. P. Lauriel, 1882.

Salvemini, Gaetano. *Italian Fascist Activities in the United States.* Edited by Philip V. Cannistraro. New York: Center for Migration Studies, 1977 [1940].

———. *Scritti sulla questione meridionale, 1896–1955.* Turin: G. Einaudi, 1955.

Sargeant, Elizabeth Shipley. "Toilers of the Tenements: Where the Beautiful Things of the Great Shops Are Made." *McClure's Magazine* 35 (July 1910).

Satriani, Raffaele Lombardi, ed. *Canti popolari calabresi.* Naples: Editore De Simone, 1934.

Schlossberg, Joseph. *Problems of Labor Organization.* New York: Amalgamated Clothing Workers of America, 1921.

———. *The Rise of the Clothing Workers.* New York: Amalgamated Clothing Workers of America, 1921.

Seidman, Joel. *The Needle Trades.* New York: Farrar & Rinehart, 1942.

Selekman, Ben Morris, Henriette R. Walter, and W. J. Couper. *The Clothing and Textile Industries in New York and Its Environs.* New York: Regional Plan of New York and Its Environs, 1925.

Senner, Joseph H. "Immigration from Italy." *North American Review* 162:6 (June 1896).

Sergi, Giuseppe. *Arii e italici.* Turin: Bocca, 1898.

———. *The Varieties of the Human Species: Principles and Method of Classification.* Washington, D.C.: Smithsonian Institute, 1894.

Shedd, William B. "The Italian Population in New York City." *Casa Italiana Educational Bulletin,* no. 7. New York, 1936.

Simkhovitch, Mary Kingsbury. *The City Worker's World.* New York: Macmillan, 1917.

———. *Here Is God's Plenty: Reflections on American Social Advance.* New York: Harper and Brothers, 1949.

———. *Greenwich House, 26–28 Jones Street, Eighth Annual Report* (October 1909).

———. *Greenwich House, 26–28 Jones Street, Tenth Annual Report* (October 1911).

———. *Greenwich House, 26–28 Jones Street, Twelfth Annual Report* (January 1913).

———. *Greenwich House, 26–28 Jones Street, Fourteenth Annual Report* (January 1916).

————. *Neighborhood: My Story of Greenwich House*. New York: W. W. Norton, 1938.

Simons, Sarah E. "Social Assimilation. IV." *American Journal of Sociology* 7:3 (November 1901): 386–404.

————. "Social Assimilation. V." *American Journal of Sociology* 7:4 (January 1902): 539–56.

Sinatra, Nancy. *Frank Sinatra, My Father*. Garden City, N.Y.: Doubleday, 1985.

Smith, J. T. *The Catholic Church in New York*. New York: Locke and Hall, 1905.

Spadoni, Adriana. "The Italian Working Woman in New York." *Collier's*, 23 March 1912.

Speranza, Gino. "The Italians in Congested Districts." *Charities and Commons* 20 (1908): 56.

Sonnino, Sidney. *I contadini in Sicilia*. Florence: G. Barbèra, 1877.

Stella, Antonio. "From Italy's Fields to Manhattan's Sweatshops." *Survey* (7 May 1905).

Stolberg, Benjamin. *Tailor's Progress: The Story of a Famous Union and the Men Who Made It*. Garden City, N.Y.: Doubleday, Doran, 1944.

Teper, Lazare. *The Women's Garment Industry*. New York: ILGWU, 1937.

Testa, Rev. Stefano L. "'Strangers from Rome' in Greater New York." *Missionary Review of the World* 31 (March 1908): 216–18.

Tobenkin, Elias. "Anarchists and Immigrants in America." *World To-Day* 14 (May 1908): 482–85.

Tolino, John V. "The Priest in the Italian Problem." *Ecclesiastical Review* 109 (November 1943): 321.

Tosti, Gustavo. "The Financial and Industrial Outlook of Italy." *American Journal of Sociology* 8:1 (July 1902): 47–57.

Train, A. "Imported Crime." *McClure's Magazine* 39 (May 1912): 82–97.

Tresca, Carlo. *The Autobiography of Carlo Tresca*. Microfilm reel, IHRC.

Twain, Mark. *Innocents Abroad*. Hartford, Conn.: American Publishing, 1869.

Turner, George Kibbe. "The City of Chicago." *McClure's Magazine*, April 1907.

————. "The Daughters of the Poor: A Plain Story of the Development of New York City as a Leading Center of the White Slave Trade of the World, under Tammany Hall." *McClure's Magazine*, November 1909.

————. "'The Strange Woman.'" *McClure's Magazine*, May 1913.

————. "Tammany's Control of New York by Professional Criminals." *McClure's Magazine*, June 1909.

Van Kleeck, Mary. *Artificial Flower Makers*. New York: Russell Sage Foundation, Survey Associates, 1913.

————. "Child Labor in New York City Tenements." *Charities and the Commons* 18 (18 January 1908): 1–16.

————. *A Seasonal Industry: A Study of the Millinery Trade in New York*. New York: Russell Sage Foundation, 1917.

————. *Working Girls in Evening Schools: A Statistical Study*. New York: Russell Sage Foundation, 1914.

————. "Working Hours of Women in Factories." *Charities and Commons* 17 (1906–7): 13–21.

Van Vleck, William Cabell. *The Administrative Control of Aliens: A Study in Administrative Law and Procedure*. New York: Commonwealth Fund, 1932.

Van Vorst, Mrs. John, and Marie Van Vorst. *The Woman Who Toils*. New York: Doubleday, 1903.

Vega, Bernardo. *Memoirs of Bernardo Vega: A Contribution to the History of the Puerto Rican Community in New York*. Edited by Cesar Andreu Iglesias. Translated by Juan Flores. New York: Monthly Review Press, 1984.

Ventura, Gioacchino. *La donna cristiana*. Milan, 1867.

Verga, Giovanni. *Tutte le novelle*. Milan: Garzanti, 1940.

Vorse, Mary Heaton. *Labor's New Millions*. New York: Modern Age Books, 1938.

Wald, Lillian D. *The House on Henry Street*. New York: Holt, 1915.

Walsh, James J. "The Irish and the Italians." *Il Caroccio* 27 (January 1928): 114–16.

Warner, Arthur. "Amputating the Black Hand." *Survey* 22 (1 May 1909).

Warner, John De Witt. "Sweating System in New York City." *Harper's Weekly* 39 (9 February 1895).

Watchorn, Robert. "Black Hand and the Immigrant." *Outlook* 92 (31 July 1909): 794–97.

Watson, Elizabeth C. "Homework in the Tenements." *Survey* 25 (4 February 1911): 772–781.

White, Frank Marshall. "Against the Black Hand." *Colliers* 45 (3 September 1910).

———. "The Black Hand in Control in Italian New York." *Outlook* 104 (16 August 1913): 857–65.

———. "Fostering Foreign Criminals." *Harper's Weekly*, 8 May 1909.

———. "How the United States Fosters the Black Hand." *Outlook* 93 (30 October 1909).

———. "The Passing of the Black Hand." *Century Illustrated Monthly Magazine* 95 (November 1917– April 1918).

Willcox, Walter F. *International Migrations*. New York: National Bureau of Economic Research, 1931.

Willett, Mabel H. *The Employment of Women in the Clothing Trade*. New York: Columbia University, 1902. Reprint, New York: AMS Press, 1968.

Willemse, Cornelius W. *A Cop Remembers*. New York: E. P. Dutton, 1933.

Williams, Phyllis H. *South Italian Folkways in Europe and America*. New Haven: Yale University Press, 1938.

Women's Trade Union League of New York, *Annual Reports, 1910–13*.

Woods, Arthur. "Problem of the Black Hand." *McClure's Magazine* 33 (May 1909): 40–47.

Woods, Robert A., and Albert J. Kennedy. *Young Working Girls*. New York: Houghton Mifflin, 1913.

X, Malcolm. *Malcolm X on Afro-American History*. Expanded and illustrated edition. New York: Pathfinder Press, 1970.

Zema, Garbriel A. "The Italian Immigrant Problem." *America* 55 (16 May 1936): 129–30.

SECONDARY SOURCES

Books and Articles

Acosta-Belen, Edna, ed. *The Puerto Rican Woman: Perspectives on Culture, History, and Society*. Westport, Conn.: Praeger Press, 1986.

Adler, Jeffrey S. "'We've Got a Right to Fight; We're Married': Domestic Homicide in Chicago, 1875–1920." *Journal of Interdisciplinary History* 34:1 (Summer 2003): 27–48.

Alexander, M. Jacqui. *Pedagogies of Crossing: Meditations on Feminism, Sexual Politics, Memory, and the Sacred*. Durham: Duke University Press, 2005.

Alexander, Meena. *The Shock of Arrival: Reflections on Postcolonial Experience*. Boston: South End Press, 1996.

Alexander, Ruth. *The "Girl Problem": Female Sexual Delinquency in New York, 1900–1930*. Ithaca: Cornell University Press, 1995.

Aliano, David. "Brazil through Italian Eyes: The Debate over Emigration to São Paulo during the 1920s." *Altreitalie* 31 (July–December 2005): 87–107.

Allen, Theodore. *The Invention of the White Race*. 2 vols. London: Verso, 1994 and 1997.

Allende, Isabel. *Aphrodite: A Memoir of the Senses*. New York: HarperCollins, 1998.

Alloula, Malek. *The Colonial Harem*. Minneapolis: University of Minnesota Press, 1986.

Almaguer, Tomás. *Racial Fault Lines: The Historical Origins of White Supremacy in California*. Berkeley: University of California Press, 1994.

Alvim, Zuleika M. F. *Brava Gente! Os italianos em São Paulo, 1870–1920*. São Paulo: Editora Brasiliense, 1986.

American Social History Project. *Who Built America? Working People and the Nation's Economy, Politics, Culture, and Society*. Vol. 2: *1877 to the Present*. New York: Worth Publishers, 2000.

Anbinder, Tyler. *Five Points: The 19th-Century New York City Neighborhood That Invented Tap Dance, Stole Elections, and Became the World's Most Notorious Slum*. New York: Free Press, 2001.

Anderson, Benedict. *Imagined Communities: Reflections on the Origin and Spread of Nationalism*. Rev. ed. London: Verso, 1991.

Andreucci, Franco, and Tommaso Detti, eds. *Il movimento operaio italiano, dizionario biografico, 1853–1943*. 6 vols. Rome: Edizioni Riuniti, 1975–78.

Andrews, George Reid. "Black and White Workers, São Paulo, Brazil, 1888–1928." *Hispanic American Historical Review* 68:3 (August 1988): 491–524.

———. *Blacks and Whites in São Paulo, Brazil, 1888–1988*. Madison: University of Wisconsin Press, 1991.

———. "Race versus Class Association: The Afro-Argentines of Buenos Aires, 1850–1900." *Journal of Latin American Studies* 11:1 (May 1979): 19–39.

Appel, Willa. "The Myth of the *Jettatura*." In *The Evil Eye*, edited by Clarence Maloney. New York: Columbia University Press, 1976.

Ardizzone, Tony. *In the Garden of Papa Santuzzu*. New York: Picador, 1999.

Argersinger, Jo Ann E. *Making the Amalgamated: Gender, Ethnicity, and Class in the Baltimore Clothing Industry, 1899–1939*. Baltimore: Johns Hopkins University Press, 1999.

Arneson, Eric. "Up from Exclusion: Black and White Workers, Race, and the State of Labor History." *Reviews in American History* 26 (March 1998): 146–74.

———. "Whiteness and the Historians' Imagination." *International Labor and Working-Class History* 60 (Fall 2001): 3–32.

Arrighi, Giovanni. *The Long Twentieth Century: Money, Power, and the Origins of Our Times*. London: Verso, 1994.

Asher, Robert, and Charles Stephenson, eds. *Labor Divided: Race and Ethnicity in United States Labor Struggles, 1835–1960*. Albany: State University of New York Press, 1990.

Attanasio, Maria, and Giuseppe Leone. *Il divino e il meraviglioso. Feste religiose in Sicilia*. Palermo: Bruno Leopardi, 2002.

Audenino, Patrizia. "Le custodi della montagna: Donne e migrazioni stagionali in una comunità alpine." *Annali dell'Istituto Alcide Cervi* 12 (1990): 265–88.

———. *Un mestiere per partire. Tradizione migratoria, lavoro e communità in una vallata alpina*. Milan: Franco Angeli, 1990.

Audenino, Patrizia, Barbara Cancian, Silvana Crescio, Giuseppa Garzia, Enrica Rauso, and Aurora Zedda. "Storie di donne che partono e che arrivano nel Biellese." In *Fumne. Storie di donne. Storie di Biella*, edited by Paola Corti and Chiara Ottaviano. Turin: Cliomedia Edizioni, 1999.

Avrich, Paul. *Anarchist Portraits*. Princeton, N.J.: Princeton University Press, 1988.

———. *Anarchist Voices*. Princeton, N.J.: Princeton University Press, 1995.

———. *The Modern School Movement: Anarchism and Education in the United States*. Princeton, N.J.: Princeton University Press, 1980.

———. *Sacco and Vanzetti: The Anarchist Background*. Princeton, N.J.: Princeton University Press, 1991.

Babb, Valerie. *Whiteness Visible: The Meaning of Whiteness in American Literature*. New York: New York University Press, 1998.

Bacci, Massimo Livi. *L'immigrazione e l'assimilazione degli italiani negli Stati Uniti secondo le statistiche demografiche americane*. Milan: Giuffrè, 1961.

Baden, Naomi. "Developing an Agenda: Expanding the Role of Women in Unions." *Labor Studies Journal* 10 (1986): 229–49.

Baer, James A. "Tenant Mobilization and the 1907 Rent Strike in Buenos Aires." *Americas* 49:3 (January 1993): 343–68.

Baiamonte, John V., Jr. *Spirit of Vengeance: Nativism and Louisiana Justice, 1921–1924*. Baton Rouge: Louisiana State University, 1986.

———. "Who Killa da Chief Revisited: The Hennessy Assassination and Its Aftermath, 1890–1891." *Louisiana History* 33 (Spring 1992): 117–46.

Baily, Samuel L. *Immigrants in the Land of Promise: Italians in Buenos Aires and New York City, 1870–1914*. Ithaca: Cornell University Press, 1999.

———. "Italian Immigrants in Buenos Aires and New York City, 1870–1914: A Comparative Analysis of Adjustment." In *Mass Migration to Modern Latin America*, edited by Samuel L. Baily and Eduardo José Míguez. Wilmington, Del.: Scholarly Resources, 2003.

———. "The Italians and the Development of Organized Labor in the United States and Argentina, Brazil, and the United States, 1880–1914." *Journal of Social History* 3:2 (Winter 1969–1970): 123–34.

———. "The Italians and Organized Labor in the United States and Argentina." *International Migration Review* 1:3 (Summer 1967): 55–66.

Baily, Samuel L., and Franco Ramella. *One Family, Two Worlds: An Italian Family's Correspondence across the Atlantic, 1901–1922*. New Brunswick: Rutgers University Press, 1988.

Balce, Nerissa S. "The Filipina's Breast: Savagery, Docility, and the Erotics of the American Empire." *Social Text* 87 24:2 (Summer 2006): 89–110.

Ballantyne, Tony, and Antoinette Burton. *Bodies in Contact: Rethinking Colonial Encounters in World History*. Durham: Duke University Press, 2005.

Banfield, Edward. *The Moral Basis of a Backward Society*. Glencoe, Ill.: Free Press, 1958.

Bao, Xiaolan. *"Holding Up More Than Half the Sky": Chinese Women Garment Workers in New York City, 1948–92*. Urbana: University of Illinois Press, 2001.

Baron, Ava, ed. *Work Engendered: Toward a New History of American Labor*. Ithaca: Cornell University Press, 1991.

Barone, Ciano, and Romano Pagano. *Briganti e partigiani*. Rome: Campania Bella, 1997.

Barra, Francesco. *Cronache del brigantaggio meridionale, 1806–1815*. Naples: Società Editrice Meridionale, 1981.

Barrett, James R. *Work and Community in the Jungle: Chicago's Packinghouse Workers, 1894–1922*. Urbana: University of Illinois Press, 1987.

———. "Americanization from the Bottom Up: Immigration and the Remaking of the Working Class in the United States, 1880–1930." *Journal of American History* 79 (December 1992): 996–1020.

Barrett, James R., and David R. Roediger. "Inbetween Peoples: Race, Nationality and the 'New Immigrant' Working Class." *Journal of American Ethnic History* 16 (Spring 1997): 3–44.

Barton, Josef. *Peasants and Strangers: Italians, Rumanians and Slovaks in an American City, 1890–1950*. Cambridge, Mass.: Harvard University Press, 1975.

Barzman, Karen-Edis. "Sacred Imagery and the Religious Lives of Women, 1650–1850." In *Women and Faith: Catholic Religious Life in Italy from Late Antiquity to the Present*, edited by Lucetta Scaraffia and Gabriella Zarri. Cambridge, Mass.: Harvard University Press, 1999.

Battan, Jesse F. "'In the Marriage Bed Woman's Sex Has Been Enslaved and Abused': Defining and Exposing Marital Rape in Late Nineteenth-Century America." In *Sex without Consent: Rape and Sexual Coercion in America*, edited by Merril D. Smith. New York: New York University Press, 2001.

———. "The 'Rights' of Husbands and the 'Duties' of Wives: Power and Desire in the American Bedroom, 1850–1910." *Journal of Family History* 42:2 (April 1999): 165–86.

———. "'The Word Made Flesh': Language, Authority, and Sexual Desire in Late Nineteenth-Century America." *Journal of the History of Sexuality* 3:2 (1992): 223–44.

Bauman, John F. *Public Housing, Race, and Renewal: Urban Planning in Philadelphia, 1920–1974*. Philadelphia: Temple University Press, 1987.

Bayer, Osvaldo. "L'influenza dell'immigrazione italiana nel movimento anarchico argentino." In *Gli italiani fuori d'Italia, gli emigrati italiani nei movimenti operai dei paesi d'adozione 1880–1940*, edited by Bruno Bezza. Milan: Franco Angeli, 1983.

Bayor, Ronald H. *Neighbors in Conflict: The Irish, Germans, Jews, and Italians of New York City, 1929–1941*. Baltimore: Johns Hopkins University Press, 1978.

Becker, Peter, and Richard F. Wetzell, eds. *Criminals and Their Scientists: The History of Criminology in International Perspective*. New York: Cambridge University Press, 2006.

Bederman, Gail. *Manliness and Civilization: A Cultural History of Gender and Race in the United States, 1880–1917*. Chicago: University of Chicago Press, 1995.

Beer, Janet, and Katherine Joslin. "Diseases of the Body Politic: White Slavery in Jane Addams' *A New Conscience and an Ancient Evil* and Selected Short Stories by Charlotte Perkins Gilman." *Journal of American Studies* 33 (1999): 1–18.

Begg, Ean C. *The Cult of the Black Virgin*. New York: Penguin, 1997.

Bell, Rudolph. *Fate and Honor, Family and Village: Demographic and Cultural Change in Rural Italy since 1800*. Chicago: University of Chicago Press, 1985.

Bellucci, Mabel, and Cristina Camusso. *La huelga de inquilinos de 1907: El papel de las mujeres anarquistas en la lucha*. Buenos Aires: CICSO, 1987.

Bender, Daniel E. *Sweated Work, Weak Bodies: Anti-sweatshop Campaigns and Languages of Labor*. New Brunswick: Rutgers University Press, 2004.

———. "'Too Much of this Distasteful Masculinity': Historicizing Sexual Harassment in the Sweatshop." *Journal of Women's History* 15 (Winter 2004): 91–116.

Bender, Daniel E., and Richard A. Greenwald, eds. *Sweatshop USA: The American Sweatshop in Historical and Global Perspective*. New York: Routledge, 2003.

Bernstein, Irving. *The Lean Years: A History of the American Worker 1920–1933*. Baltimore: Penguin, 1966.

———. *The Turbulent Years: A History of the American Worker, 1933–1941*. Boston: Houghton Mifflin, 1970.

Bernstein, Lee. *The Greatest Menace: Organized Crime in Cold War America*. Amherst: University of Massachusetts Press, 2002.

Bertellini, Giorgio. "*Duce/Divo*: Masculinity, Racial Identity, and Politics among Italian Americans in 1920s New York City." *Journal of Urban History* 31:5 (2005): 685–726.

Bettini. *Bibliografia dell'anarchismo*. Florence: Crescita Pollitica Editrice, 1976.

Bevilacqua, Piero. *Breve storia dell'Italia meridionale dall'ottocento a oggi*. Rome: Donzelli Editore, 1993.

———. "Il Mezzogiorno nel mercato internazionale (secoli XVIII–XX)." *Meridiana* 1 (1987): 19–47.

Bezza, Bruno, ed. *Gli italiani fuori d'Italia, gli emigrati italiani nei movimenti operai dei paesi d'adozione 1880–1940*. Milan: Franco Angeli, 1983.

Bianco, Carla. *The Two Rosetos*. Bloomington: Indiana University Press, 1974.

Biondi, Martha. *To Stand and Fight: The Struggle for Civil Rights in Postwar New York City*. Cambridge, Mass.: Harvard University Press, 2003.

Birnbaum, Lucia Chiavola. *Black Madonnas: Feminism, Religion, and Politics in Italy*. Boston: Northeastern, 1993.

———. *Liberazione della donna/Feminism in Italy*. Middletown, Conn.: Wesleyan University Press, 1986.

Blackwelder, Julia Kirk. *Women of the Depression: Caste and Culture in San Antonio, 1929–1939*. College Station: Texas A&M University Press, 1984.

Blee, Kathleen. *No Middle Ground: Women and Radical Protest*. New York: New York University Press, 1998.

———. *Women of the Klan: Racism and Gender in the 1920s*. Berkeley: University of California Press, 1991.

Bodnar, John. *Immigration and Industrialization: Ethnicity in an American Mill Town, 1870–1940*. Pittsburgh: University of Pittsburgh Press, 1977.

———. *The Transplanted: A History of Immigrants in Urban America*. Bloomington: Indiana University Press, 1985.

———. *Workers' World: Kinship, Community, and Protest in an Industrial Society, 1900–1940*. Baltimore: Johns Hopkins University Press, 1982.

Boelhower, William, and Rocco Pallone, eds. *Adjusting Sites: New Essays in Italian American Studies*. Stony Brook: Forum Italicum, 1999.

Boelhower, William, and Anna Scacchi, eds. *Public Space, Private Lives: Race, Gender Class, and Citizenship in New York, 1890–1929*. Amsterdam: VU University Press, 2004.

Bongiovani, Bruno. "The Question of the South" and "Anthology of the Problem of the South." In *Modern Italy: Images and History of a National Identity*, edited by Carlo Pirovano. Milan: Electa Editrice, 1982.

Boris, Eileen. *Home to Work: Motherhood and the Politics of Industrial Homework in the United States*. New York: Cambridge University Press, 1994.

———. "Sexual Divisions, Gender Constructions: The Historical Meaning of Homework in Western Europe and the United States." In *Homeworkers in Global Perspective*, edited by Eileen Boris and Elisabeth Prügl. New York: Routledge, 1996.

Boris, Eileen, and Cynthia R. Daniels, eds. *Homework: Historical and Contemporary Perspectives on Paid Labor at Home*. Urbana: University of Illinois Press, 1989.

Bortolotti, Franca Pieroni. *Alle origini del movimento femminile in Italia, 1848–1892*. Turin: Einaudi, 1975.

———. *Le donne della resistenza antifascista e la questione femminile in Emilia Romagna, 1943–1945*. Milan: Vangelista Editore, 1978.

———. *Femminismo e partiti politici in Italia, 1919–1926*. Rome: Editori Riuniti, 1978.

———. *Socialismo e questione femminile in Italia*. Milan: G. Mazzotta, 1974.

———. *Sul movimento politico delle donne, Scritti inediti*. Rome: Cooperativa Utopia, 1987.

Botein, Barbara. "The Hennessy Case: An Episode in Anti-Italian Nativism." *Louisiana History* 20 (Summer 1979): 261–79.

Brancato, Francesco. "Femminismo politico e opinione pubblica in Sicilia tra otto e novecento." In *Donne e società*, edited by Janne Vibaek. Palermo: Arti Grafiche Siciliane, 1982.

Brecher, Jeremy. *Strike!* San Francisco: Straight Arrow Press, 1972.

Brennan, Timothy. "Antonio Gramsci and Postcolonial Theory: 'Southernism.'" *Diaspora* 10:2 (2001): 143–87.

Briggs, John. *An Italian Passage: Immigrants to Three American Cities, 1890–1930*. New Haven: Yale University Press, 1978.

Briggs, Laura. "The Race of Hysteria: 'Overcivilization' and the 'Savage' Woman in Late Nineteenth-Century Obstetrics and Gynecology." *American Quarterly* 52:2 (June 2000): 246–73.

———. *Reproducing Empire: Race, Sex, Science, and U.S. Imperialism in Puerto Rico*. Berkeley: University of California Press, 2002.

Bristow, Edward J. *Prostitution and Prejudice: The Jewish Fight against White Slavery 1870–1939*. New York: Schocken Books, 1983.

Brodkin, Karen. *How Jews Became White Folks and What That Says about Race in America*. New Brunswick: Rutgers University Press, 2000.

Brody, Jennifer DeVere. *Impossible Purities: Blackness, Femininity, and Victorian Culture*. Durham: Duke University Press, 1998.

Brophy, Alfred L. *Reconstructing the Dreamland: The Tulsa Race Riot of 1921, Race, Reparations, and Reconciliation*. New York: Oxford University Press, 2002.

Brown, Elsa Barkley. "Polyrhythms and Improvisation: Lessons for Women's History." *History Workshop* 31 (Spring 1991): 85–90.

Brown, Mary Elizabeth. *Churches, Communities, and Children: Italian Immigrants in the Archdiocese of New York, 1880–1945*. Staten Island: Center for Migration Studies, 1995.

———. *From Italian Villages to Greenwich Village: Our Lady of Pompeii, 1892–1992*. Staten Island: Center for Migration Studies, 1992.

———. "Italian-Americans and Their Saints: Historical Considerations." In *The Saints in the Lives of Italian-Americans*, edited by Joseph A. Varacalli et al. Stony Brook: Forum Italicum, 1999.

Brundage, Fitzhugh. *Lynching in the New South: Georgia and Virginia, 1880–1930*. Urbana: University of Illinois Press, 1993.

Brunetta, Gian Piero. "Il sogno e stelle e striscie di Mussolini." In *L'estetica della politica. Europa e America negli anni trenta*, edited by Maurizio Vaudagna. Bari: Laterza, 1989.

Buccellato, Pier Fausto, and Marina Iaccio. *Gli anarchici nell'Italia meridionale: La stampa (1869–1892)*. Rome: Bulzoni Editore, 1982.

Buhle, Mari Jo. *Women and American Socialism*. Urbana: University of Illinois Press, 1981.

Buhle, Mari Jo, Paul Buhle, and Dan Georgakas, eds. *Encyclopedia of the American Left*. New York: Garland, 1990.

Buhle, Paul. "Anarchism and American Labor." *International Labor and Working Class History* 23 (Spring 1983): 21–34.

Buhle, Paul, and Dan Georgakas, eds. *The Immigrant Left in the United States*. New York: State University of New York Press, 1996.

Bull, Anna Cento. "The Lombard Silk-Spinners in the Nineteenth Century: An Industrial Workforce in a Rural Setting." In *Women and Italy: Essays on Gender, Culture and History*, edited by Zygmunt G. Baraski and Shirley W. Vinall. New York: St. Martin's Press, 1991.

Burgaretta, Sebastiano. "Il ruolo della donna nel ciclo di raccolta e lavorazione della mandorala nel siracusano." In *Donne e società*, edited by Janne Vibaek. Palermo: Arti Grafiche Siciliane, 1982.

Burton, Antoinette. *Burdens of History: British Feminists, Indian Women, and Imperial Culture, 1896–1915*. Chapel Hill: University of North Carolina Press, 1994.

Butler, Judith. *The Psychic Life of Power: Theories in Subjection*. Stanford: Stanford University Press, 1997.

Butler, Judith, and Joan Scott, eds. *Feminists Theorize the Political*. New York: Routledge, 1992.

Byrne, Moyra. "Antonio Gramsci's Contribution to Italian Folklore Studies." *International Folklore Review* 2 (1982): 70–75.

Cacopardo, María Cristina, and José Luis Moreno. *La familia Italiana y meridonal en la emigración a la Argentina*. Naples: Edizioni Scientifiche Italiane, 1994.

Calapso, Jole. "La Donna in Sicilia e in Italia: La realta e la falsa coscienza nella statistica dal 1871 ad oggi." *Quaderni Siciliani* 2 (March–April 1973): 13–20.

———. *Una donna intransigente: Vita di Maria Giudice*. Palermo: Sellerio Editore, 1996.

———. *Donne Ribelli: Un secolo di lotte femminili in Sicilia*. Palermo: Flaccovio, 1980.

Calcagno, Giorgio, ed. *Bianco, rosso e verde: L'identità degli italiani*. Rome: Laterza, 1993.

Calzone, Nicolino. *Briganti o partigiani? La rivolta contro l'unità d'Italia nel Sannio e altre province del Sud (1860–1880)*. Benevento: Realtà sannita, 2001.

Cameron, Ardis. *Radicals of the Worst Sort: Laboring Women in Lawrence, Massachusetts, 1860–1912*. Urbana: University of Illinois Press, 1993.

Camp, Stephanie. *Closer to Freedom: Enslaved Women and Everyday Resistance in the Plantation South*. Chapel Hill: University of North Carolina Press, 2004.

Cannistraro, Philip V. *Blackshirts in Little Italy: Italian Americans and Fascism, 1921–1929*. West Lafayette, Ind.: Bordighera Press, 1999.

———. "Fascism and Italian-Americans." In *Perspectives in Italian Immigration and Ethnicity*, edited by S. M. Tomasi. New York: Center for Migration Studies, 1977.

———. "Luigi Antonini and the Italian Anti-Fascist Movement in the United States, 1940–1943." *Journal of American Ethnic History* 21 (Fall 1995): 21–40.

———. "Mussolini, Sacco-Vanzetti, and the Anarchists: The Transatlantic Context." *Journal of Modern History* 68:1 (March 1996): 31–62.

———, ed. *The Italians of New York*. New York: New York Historical Society, 1999.

Cannistraro, Philip V., and Gianfausto Rosoli, eds. "Fascist Emigration Policy in the 1920s." *International Migration Review* 13 (Winter 1979): 673–92.

Cannistraro, Philip V., and Gerald Meyer, eds. *The Lost World of Italian American Radicalism: Politics, Culture, History*. Westport, Conn.: Praeger, 2003.

Cannistraro, Philip V., and Elena Aga Rossi. "La politica e il dilemma dell'antifascismo italiano negli Stati Uniti: Il caso di Generoso Pope." *Storia contemporanea* 17 (April 1986): 217–43.

Canosa, Romano, and Amedeo Santosuosso. *Magistrati, anarchici e socialisti alla fine dell'Ottocento in Italia.* Milan: Feltrinelli, 1981.

Cantarow, Ellen, and Susan Gushee O'Malley. "Ella Baker: Organizing for Civil Rights." In *Moving the Mountain: Women Working for Social Change*, edited by Ellen Cantarow et al. New York: Feminist Press, 1980.

Cantor, Milton, and Bruce Laurie, eds. *Class, Sex and the Woman Worker.* Westport, Conn.: Greenwood Press, 1977.

Capeci, Dominic J. "Fiorello H. La Guardia and the Harlem 'Crime Wave' of 1941." *New York Historical Society Quarterly* 64 (January 1980): 7–29.

———. *The Harlem Riot of 1943.* Philadelphia: Temple University Press, 1977.

Cappannari, Stephen C., and Leonard W. Moss. "The Black Madonna: An Example of Culture Borrowing." *Scientific Monthly*, June 1953, 319–24.

———. "In Quest of the Black Virgin: She Is Black Because She Is Black." In *Mother Worship: Theme and Variations*, edited by James J. Preston. Chapel Hill: University of North Carolina Press, 1982.

Cappelli, Vito. "Le donne in Calabria nelle società di mutuo soccorso (1875–1900)." *Movimento Operaio e Socialista* 3:4 (1981): 287–97.

Cappello, Mary. *Night Bloom: An Italian-American Life.* Boston: Beacon, 1998.

Caracciolo, Alberto. *L'inchiesta agraria Jacini.* Turin: G. Einaudi, 1973.

Cara-Walker, Ana. "Cocoliche: The Art of Assimilation and Dissimulation among Italians and Argentines." *Latin American Research Review* 22:3 (1987): 37–67.

Carey, George. "'La Questione Sociale,' an Anarchist Newspaper in Paterson, N.J. (1895–1908)." In *Italian Americans: New Perspectives in Italian Immigration and Ethnicity*, edited by Lydio F. Tomasi. New York: Center for Migration Studies, 1985.

———. "The Vessel, the Deed, and the Idea: Anarchists in Paterson, 1895–1908." *Antipode* 10:3 (1979): 46–58.

Carnevale, Nancy C. "Culture of Work: Italian Immigrant Women Homeworkers in the New York City Garment Industry, 1890–1914." In *A Coat of Many Colors: Immigration, Globalization, and Reform in New York City's Garment Industry*, edited by Daniel Soyer. New York: Fordham University Press, 2005.

Caroli, Betty Boyd, et al., eds. *The Italian Immigrant Woman in North America.* Toronto: Multicultural History Society of Ontario, 1978.

———. *Italian Repatriation from the United States, 1900–1914.* New York: Center for Migration Studies, 1973.

Carr, John Foster, and Sarah G. Pomeroy. *Assimilation of the Italian Immigrant.* New York: Arno Press, 1975.

Carroll, Michael P. *Madonnas That Maim: Popular Catholicism in Italy since the Fifteenth Century.* Baltimore: Johns Hopkins University Press, 1992.

———. *Veiled Threats: The Logic of Popular Catholicism in Italy.* Baltimore: Johns Hopkins University Press, 1996.

Carson, Minna. *Settlement Folk: Social Thought and the American Settlement Movement, 1885–1930.* Chicago: University of Chicago Press, 1990.

Cartosio, Bruno. "Gli emigrati italiani e l'Industrial Workers of the World." In *Gli italiani fuori d'Italia, gli emigrati italiani nei movimenti operai dei paesi d'adozione 1880–1940*, edited by Bruno Bezzo. Milan: Franco Angeli, 1983.

———. "Italian Workers and Their Press in the United States, 1900–1920." In *The Press of Labor Migrants in Europe and North America, 1800s to 1930s*, edited by Christiane Harzig and Dirk Hoerder. Bremen: Universität Bremen, 1985.

Casarrubea, Giuseppe. *I fasci contadini e le orgini delle sezioni socialiste della provincia di Palermo*. Palermo: Flaccovio, 1978.

Castañeda, Antonia I. "Sexual Violence in the Politics of Conquest: Amerindian Women and the Spanish Conquest of Alta California." In *Building with Our Hands: New Directions in Chicana Studies*, edited by Adele de la Torre and Beatríz M. Pesquera. Berkeley: University of California Press, 1993.

———. "Women of Color and the Rewriting of Western Women's History: The Discourse, Politics, and Decolonization of History." *Pacific Historical Review* 61 (November 1992): 501–33.

Castiglia, Christopher. *Bound and Determined*. Chicago: University of Chicago Press, 1996.

Castillo, Ana. *Massacre of the Dreamers: Essays on Xicanisma*. New York: Plume, 1994.

Cenni, Franco. *Italianos no Brasil*. São Paulo: Martins Ed. Da Universidade de São Paulo, 1974.

Cerrito, Gino. *Radicalismo e socialismo in Sicilia (1860–1882)*. Messina and Florence: G. D'Anna, 1958.

———. "Sull'emigrazione anarchica italiana negli Stati Uniti d'America." *Volontà*, July–August 1969, 269–76.

Cetti, Luisa. "Donne italiane a New York e lavoro a domicilio (1910–1925)." *Movimento Operaio e Socialista* 7:3 (1984): 291–303.

———. "Work Experience among Italian Women in New York, 1900–1930." *Rivista di Studi Anglo Americani* 3:4–5 (1984–85): 493–505.

Chan, Sucheng, ed. *Social and Gender Boundaries in the United States*. Lewiston, N.Y.: E. Mellon Press, 1989.

———, ed. *Entry Denied: Exclusion and the Chinese Community in America, 1882–1943*. Philadelphia: Temple University Press, 1991.

Chapman, Charlotte Gower. *Milocca: A Sicilian Village*. Cambridge: Shenkman, 1971.

Charney, George. *A Long Journey*. New York: Quadrangle, 1968.

Chauncey, George. *Gay New York: Gender, Urban Culture, and the Making of the Gay Male World*. New York: Basic Books, 1994.

Cheng, Lucie, and Edna Bonacich, eds. *Labor Immigration under Capitalism: Asian Workers in the United States before World War II*. Berkeley: University of California Press, 1984.

Chin, Margaret H. "Expanding Spheres: Men and Women in the Late Twentieth-Century Garment Industry." In *A Coat of Many Colors: Immigration, Globalization, and Reform in New York City's Garment Industry*, edited by Daniel Soyer. New York: Fordham University Press, 2005.

———. *Sewing Women: Immigrants and the New York City Garment Industry*. New York: Columbia University Press, 2005.

Cinel, Dino. *From Italy to San Francisco: The Immigrant Experience*. Stanford: Stanford University Press, 1982.

———. "Land Tenure Systems, Return Migration and Militancy in Italy." *Journal of Ethnic Studies* 12:3 (Fall 1984): 55–75.

———. "Italians in the South: The Alabama Case." *Italian Americana* 9 (Fall–Winter 1990): 7–24.

———. *The National Integration of Return Migration, 1870–1929*. Cambridge: Cambridge University Press, 1991.

———. "The Seasonal Emigration of Italians in the Nineteenth Century: From Internal to International Destinations." *Journal of Ethnic Studies* 10:1 (1982): 43–68.

Cingari, Gaetano. *Brigantaggio, proprietari e contadini nel sud (1799–1900)*. Reggio Calabria: Meridionali, Riuniti, 1976.

Cinotto, Simone. "Leonard Covello, the Covello Papers, and the History of Eating Habits among Italian Immigrants in New York." *Journal of American History* 91:2 (September 2004): 497–521.

Clemente, Pietro, et al., eds. *Il dibattito sul folklore in Italia*. Milan: Edizioni di Cultura Popolare, 1976.

Cobble, Dorothy Sue. *The Other Women's Movement: Workplace Justice and Social Rights in Modern America*. Princeton, N.J.: Princeton University Press, 2005.

Cocchiara, G. *Il folklore siciliano*. 2 vols. Palermo: Flaccovio, 1957.

——. *Pitrè, la Sicilia e il folklore*. Messina: D'Anna, 1951.

——. *Storia del folklore in Europa*. Turin: Boringhieri, 1971 [1952].

Cohen, Cathy J., et al., eds. *Women Transforming Politics: An Alternative Reader*. New York: New York University Press, 1997.

Cohen, Lizabeth A. *Making a New Deal: Industrial Workers in Chicago, 1919–1939*. New York: Cambridge University Press, 1990.

Cohen, Miriam. "Changing Education Strategies among Immigrant Generations: New York Italians in Comparative Perspective." *Journal of Social History* 11:3 (Spring 1982): 443–66.

——. "Italian-American Women in New York City, 1900–1950: Work and School." In *Class, Sex and the Woman Worker*, edited by Bruce Laurie and Milton Cantor. Westport, Conn.: Greenwood Press, 1977.

——. *Workshop to Office: Two Generations of Italian Women in New York City, 1900–1950*. Ithaca: Cornell University Press, 1992.

Collins, Jane L. *Threads: Gender, Labor, and Power in the Global Apparel Industry*. Chicago: University of Chicago Press, 2003.

Collomp, Catherine, and Marianne Debouzy. "European Migrants and the U.S. Labor Movement 1880s–1920s." In *The Roots of the Transplanted*, vol. 2: *Plebian Culture, Class and Politics in the Life of Labor Migrants*, edited by Dirk Hoerder et al. New York: Columbia University Press, 1994.

Cometti, Elizabeth. "Trends in Italian Emigration." *Western Political Quarterly* 11:4 (December 1958): 820–34.

Connelly, Mark Thomas. *The Response to Prostitution in the Progressive Era*. Chapel Hill: University of North Carolina Press, 1980.

Connelly, Nathan. "Colored Caribbean and Condemned: Miami's Overtown District and the Cultural Expense of Progress, 1940–1970." *Caribbean Studies* 34:1 (January–June 2006): 3–60.

Cooper, Frederick. "Back to Work: Categories, Boundaries and Connections in the Study of Labour." In *Racializing Class, Classifying Race: Labour and Difference in Britain, the USA, and Africa*, edited by Peter Alexander and Rick Halpern. New York: St. Martin's Press, 2000.

Corbella, Nicolleta Pardi. "Storia di un sindacato operaio italiano a New York." In *Gli Italiani negli Stati Uniti*, edited by Francesco Cordasco. New York: Arno Press, 1975.

Cordasco, Francesco, and Eugene Bucchioni. *The Italians: Social Backgrounds of an American Group*. Clifton, N.J.: A. M. Kelley, 1974.

Cordasco, Francesco, and Michael Vaughn Cordasco. *The Italian Emigration to the United States, 1880–1930: A Bibliographical Register of Italian Views*. Fairview, N.J.: Junius-Vaughn Press, 1990.

Cordasco Francesco, and Rocco G. Galatioto. "Ethnic Displacement in the Interstitial Community: The East Harlem Experience." *Phylon* 31:3 (1970): 302–12.

Cornelisen, Ann. *Torregreca: Life, Death, and Miracles in a Southern Italian Village*. 2nd ed. South Royalton, Vt.: Steerforth Press, 2002.

——. *Women of the Shadows: The Wives and Mothers of Southern Italy*. New York: Dell, 1977.

Corti, Paola. "Donne che vanno, donne che restano; Emigrazione e comportamenti femminili." *Annali dell'Istituto Alcide Cervi* 12 (1990): 213–36

——. "Genere, emigrazione e territorio." In *Fumne. Storie di donne. Storie di Biella*, edited by Paola Corti and Chiara Ottaviano. Turin: Cliomedia Edizioni, 1999.

——. "Sociétés sans hommes et intégrations des femmes à l'étranger; Le cas de l'Italie." *Revue européenne des migrations internationales* 9:2 (1993): 113–28.

——. "Women Were Labour Migrants Too: Tracing Late-Nineteenth-Century Female Migration from Northern Italy to France." In *Women, Gender, and Transnational Lives: Italian Workers of the World*, edited by Donna Gabaccia and Franca Iacovetta. Toronto: University of Toronto Press, 2002.

——, ed. *Società rurale e ruoli femminili in Italia tra ottocento e novecento*. Bologna: Il Mulino, 1991.

Cosco, Joseph P. *Imagining Italians: The Clash of Romance and Race in American Perceptions, 1880–1910*. Albany: State University of New York Press, 2003.

Coser, Ruth Laub, et al. *Women of Courage: Jewish and Italian Immigrant Women in New York.* Westport, Conn.: Greenwood Press, 1999.

Cott, Nancy F. *The Grounding of Modern Feminism.* New Haven: Yale University Press, 1987.

Cott, Nancy F., Gerda Lerner, Kathryn Kish Sklar, Ellen DuBois, and Nancy Hewitt. "Considering the State of U.S. Women's History." *Journal of Women's History* 15 (Spring 2003): 145–71.

Couty, Louis. *O Brasil em 1884; Esboços sociológicos.* Rio de Janeiro: Senado Federal, 1984.

Covello, Leonard. *The Social Background of the Italo-American School Child.* Leiden: E. J. Brill, 1967.

———. *The Heart Is the Teacher.* New York: McGraw Hill, 1958.

Crawford, John S. *Luigi Antonini.* New York: Educational Department of the Italian Dressmakers' Union, 1950.

Crispino, James A. *The Assimilation of Ethnic Groups: The Italian Case.* New York: Center for Migration Studies, 1980.

Cunningham, George E. "The Italian: A Hindrance to White Solidarity in Louisiana, 1890–1898." *Journal of Negro History* 50 (January 1965): 23–35.

Cusumano, Camille. *The Last Cannoli.* Ottawa, Canada: Legas, 1999.

Dadà, Adriana. *L'Anarchismo in Italia, fra movimento e partito: Storia e documenti dell'anarchismo Italiano.* Milan: Teti, 1984.

———. "Contributo metodologico per una storia dell'emigrazione e dell'antifascismo italiani negli Stati Uniti." *Annali dell'istituto di storia.* Florence: Olschki, 1979: 203–22.

D'Agostino, Peter. "Craniums, Criminals, and the 'Cursed Race': Italian Anthropology in U.S. Racial Thought." *Comparative Studies of Society and History* 44:2 (April 2002): 319–43.

———. "The Religious Life of Italians in New York." In *The Italians of New York*, edited by Philip Cannistraro. New York: New York Historical Society, 1999.

———. "The Triad of Roman Authority: Fascism, the Vatican, and Italian Religious Clergy in the Italian Emigrant Church." *Journal of American Ethnic History* 17:13 (Spring 1998): 3–37.

Dal Lago, Enrico. *Agrarian Elites: American Slaveholders and Southern Italian Landowners, 1815–1861.* Baton Rouge: Louisiana State University Press, 2005.

Dal Lago, Enrico, and Rick Halpern, eds. *The American South and the Italian Mezzogiorno: Essays in Comparative History.* New York: Palgrave, 2002.

D'Ambrosio, Paul. *Ralph Fasanella's America.* Cooperstown: New York State Historical Association, 2001.

———. "Ralph Fasanella: The Making of a Working-Class Artist." *Folk Art* 20:2 (Summer 1995): 26–33.

Daniels, Cynthia. "Between Home and Factory: Homeworkers and the State." In *Homework: Historical and Contemporary Perspectives on Paid Labor at Home*, edited by Eileen Boris and Cynthia R. Daniels. Urbana: University of Illinois Press, 1989.

Daniels, Roger. *Coming to America: A History of Immigration and Ethnicity in American Life.* New York: Harper Collins, 1990.

Danish, Max D. *The World of David Dubinsky.* Cleveland: World Publishing, 1957.

Danzi, Angela D. *From Home to Hospital: Jewish and Italian American Women and Childbirth, 1920–1940.* Lanham: University Press of America, 1997.

D'Attilio, Robert. "Virgilia D'Andrea (1890–1933): Maestra, poetessa, anarchica." *Bollettino Archivio G. Pinelli* 3 (February 1994): 32–34.

Davies, Carole Boyce. *Left of Karl Marx: The Political Life of Black Communist Claudia Jones.* Durham: Duke University Press, 2007.

Davis, Allen F. *Spearheads for Reform: The Social Settlements and the Progressive Movement, 1890–1914.* New York: Oxford University Press, 1967.

Davis, John A. *Conflict and Control: Law and Order in Nineteenth-Century Italy.* London: Macmillan Education, 1988.

———. *Sacco and Vanzetti.* New York: Ocean Press, 2004.

Dawley, Alan. *Struggles for Justice: Social Responsibility and the Liberal State*. Cambridge, Mass.: Harvard University Press, 1991.

Debouzy, Marianne, ed. *In The Shadow of the Statue of Liberty: Immigrants, Workers, and Citizens in the American Republic, 1880–1920*. Champaign: University of Illinois Press, 1992.

De Ciampis, Mario. "Storia del movimento socialista rivoluzionario italiano." *La Parola del Popolo, cinquantesimo anniversario, 1908–1958* 9 (December 1958–January 1959): 136–63.

De Clementi, Andreina. "Gender Relations and Migration Strategies in the Rural Italian South: Land, Inheritance, and the Marriage Market." In *Women, Gender, and Transnational Lives: Italian Workers of the World*, edited by Donna Gabaccia and Franca Iacovetta. Toronto: University of Toronto Press, 2002.

———. "Madri e figlie nell'emigrazione americana." In *Storie delle donne in Italia. Il lavoro delle donne*, edited by Angela Groppi. Rome: Laterza, 1996.

DeConde, Alexander. *Half Bitter, Half Sweet: An Excursion into Italian-American History*. New York: Charles Scribner's Sons, 1971.

De Grand, Alexander. *The Italian Left in the Twentieth Century: A History of the Socialist and Communist Parties*. Bloomington: University of Indiana Press, 1989.

de Grazia, Victoria. *How Fascism Ruled Women, Italy, 1922–1945*. Berkeley: University of California Press, 1992.

De Jaco, Aldo, ed. *Il brigantaggio meridionale*. Rome: Editori Riuniti, 1979.

———. *Gli anarchici: Cronaca inedita dell'unità d'Italia*. Rome: Editori Riuniti, 1971.

Delamater, Jerome, and Mary Anne Trasciatti, eds. *Representing Sacco and Vanzetti*. New York: Palgrave, 2005.

de la Torre, Adele, and Beatríz M. Pesquera, eds. *Building with Our Hands: New Directions in Chicana Studies*. Berkeley: University of California Press, 1993.

Del Carria, Renzo. *Proletari senza rivoluzione: Storie delle classi subalterne italiane dal 1860 al 1950*. Milan: Edizioni Oriente, 1966.

Del Castillo, Adelaida R. "Malintzin Tenepal: A Preliminary Look into a New Perspective." In *Essays on La Mujer*, edited by Rosaura Sánchez and Rosa Martínez Cruz. Los Angeles: Chicano Studies Research Center Publications, University of California, 1977.

Del Guidice, Luisa. *Studies in Italian American Folklore*. Logan: Utah State University Press, 1993.

De Martino, Ernesto. *Future, simbolo, valore*. Milan: Il Saggiatore, 1962.

———. *Il mondo magico*. Turin: G. Einaudi, 1948.

———. *Sud e magia*. Milan: Il Saggiatore, 1961.

———. *La terra del rimorso*. Milan: Il Saggiatore, 1959. Reprint, Milan: Il Saggiatore, 1961.

De Matteo, Giovanni. *Brigantaggio e risorgimento—leggittimisti e briganti tra i Borbone e i Savoia*. Naples: Alfredo Guida Editore, 2000.

Denning, Michael. *The Cultural Front: The Laboring of American Culture in the Twentieth Century*. New York: Verso, 1996.

De Rosa, Gabriele. *Chiesa e religione popolare nel Mezzogiorno*. Bari: Laterza, 1979.

———. *Vescovi, popolo e magia nel Sud*. Naples: Guida editori, 1971.

De Ruggieri, Niccolò. "Indagine antropologica sulla personalità del brigante Giuseppe Nicola Summa, detto Ninco-Nanco." *Archivio storico per la Calabria e la Lucania* 42 (1975): 231–33.

DeSalvo, Louise. *Crazy in the Kitchen*. New York: Bloomsbury, 2004.

———. *Vertigo: A Memoir*. New York: Feminist Press, 2002.

DeSalvo, Louise, and Edvige Giunta, eds. *The Milk of Almonds: Italian American Women Writers on Food and Culture*. New York: Feminist Press, 2002.

De Simone, Roberto. *La Tarantella napoletana nelle due anime del Guarracino*. Naples: Edizioni Benincasa, 1992.

De Souza, Newton Stadler. *O anarquismo da Colônia Cecília*. Rio de Janeiro: Civilização Brasileira, 1970.

De Stefano, F., and F. L. Oddo. *Storia della Sicilia dal 1860 al 1910*. Bari: Laterza, 1963.

De Stefano, George. *An Offer We Can't Refuse: The Mafia in the Mind of America*. London: Faber & Faber, 2006.

Dickie, John. *Cosa Nostra: A History of the Sicilian Mafia*. New York: Palgrave, 2005.

———. *Darkest Italy: The Nation and Stereotypes of the Mezzogiorno, 1860–1900*. New York: St. Martin's Press, 1999.

———. "Imagined Italies." In *Italian Cultural Studies, An Introduction*, edited by David Forgacs and Robert Lumley. New York: Oxford University Press, 1996.

———. "Stereotypes of the Italian South, 1860–1900." In *The New History of the Italian South*, edited by Robert Lumley and Jonathan Morris. Devon: University of Exeter Press, 1997.

Diffee, Christopher. "Sex and the City: The White Slavery Scare and Social Governance in the Progressive Era." *American Quarterly* 57:2 (2005): 411–37.

Diggins, John P. "Mussolini and America: Hero Worship, Charisma and the Vulgar Talent." *Historian* 28:4 (August 1966): 559–85.

———. *Mussolini and Fascism: The View from America*. Princeton, N.J.: Princeton University Press, 1972.

Di Giacomo, Salvatore. *Per la storia del brigantaggio nel napoletano*. Venosa: Edizioni Osanna Venosa, 1990.

Di Lecce, Giorgio. *La danza della piccola taranta. Cronaca da Galatina: 1908–1993. A memoria d'uomo*. Rome: Sensibili alle foglie, 1994.

Di Leonardo, Micaela. "The Female World of Cards and Holidays: Women, Families, and the Work of Kinship." *Signs* 12:3 (1987): 440–53.

———. *The Varieties of Ethnic Experience: Kinship, Class and Gender among California's Italian Americans*. Ithaca: Cornell University Press, 1984.

Di Nola, Alfonso. *Lo specchio e l'olio: Le superstizioni italiane*. Bari: Laterza, 1993.

Di Scala, Spencer M. *Dilemmas of Italian Socialism: The Politics of Filippo Turati*. Amherst: University of Massachusetts Press, 1980.

———. *Italy, from Revolution to Republic, 1700 to the Present*. Boulder, Colo.: Westview Press, 1995.

Doezema, Jo. "Loose Women or Lost Women? The Re-emergence of the Myth of White Slavery in Contemporary Discourses of Trafficking in Women." *Gender Issues* 18:1 (Winter 2000): 23–50.

Doherty, Jonathan L., ed. *Women at Work: 153 Photographs by Lewis W. Hine*. New York: Dover, 1981.

Dolci, Danilo. *Sicilian Lives*. New York: Pantheon, 1981.

Dolgoff, Sam. *The Cuban Revolution: A Critical Perspective*. Montreal: Black Rose Books, 1976.

Donaldson, Laura E. "The Breasts of Columbus: A Political Anatomy of Postcolonialism and Feminist Religious Discourse." In *Postcolonialism, Feminism, and Religious Discourse*, edited by Laura E. Donaldson and Kwok Pui-lan. New York: Routledge, 2003.

Donovan, Brian. "The Sexual Basis of Racial Formation: Anti-vice Activism and the Creation of the Twentieth-Century 'Color Line.'" *Ethnic and Racial Studies* 26:4 (2003): 707–27.

———. *White Slave Crusades: Race, Gender, and Anti-vice Activism, 1887–1917*. Urbana: University of Illinois Press, 2006.

Doyle, Don Harrison. *Nations Divided: America, Italy, and the Southern Question*. Athens: University of Georgia Press, 2002.

Draper, Theodore. *The Roots of American Communism*. New York: Viking Press, 1963.

Drukman, Steven. "Suzan-Lori Parks and Liz Diamond: Doo-a-diddly-dit-dit." *Drama Review* 39:3 (1995): 56–75.

Dubinsky, David. *A Life With Labor*. New York: Simon and Schuster, 1977.

Dubofsky, Melvyn. *When Workers Organize: New York City in the Progressive Era*. Amherst: University of Massachusetts Press, 1968.

DuBois, Ellen Carol, and Vicki L. Ruiz, eds. *Unequal Sisters: A Multicultural Reader in U.S. Women's History*. New York: Routledge, 1990.

Du Bois, W. E. B. *Darkwater*. New York: Harcourt, Brace and Howe, 1920.

Dye, Nancy Schrom. *As Equals and as Sisters: Feminism, Unionism and the Women's Trade Union League of New York*. Columbia: University of Missouri Press, 1980.

Dyer, Thomas G. *Theodore Roosevelt and the Idea of Race*. Baton Rouge: Louisiana State University Press, 1980.

Ealham, Chris. *Class, Culture and Conflict in Barcelona, 1898–1937*. London: Routledge, 2005.

Ehrlich, Elizabeth. *Miriam's Kitchen, a Memoir*. New York: Viking, 1997.

Enstad, Nan. *Ladies of Labor, Girls of Adventure: Working Women, Popular Culture, and Labor Politics at the Turn of the Twentieth Century*. New York: Columbia University Press, 1999.

Esquivel, Laura. *Like Water for Chocolate*. New York: Doubleday, 1992.

Estés, Clarissa Pinkola. *The Gift of Story: A Wise Tale about What Is Enough*. New York: Ballantine Books, 1993.

Ets, Marie Hall. *Rosa: The Life of an Italian Immigrant*. Madison: University of Wisconsin Press, 1970.

Evans, Sara. *Personal Politics: The Roots of Women's Liberation in the Civil Rights and the New Left*. New York: Vintage, 1979.

Ewen, Elizabeth. "City Lights: Immigrant Women and the Rise of the Movies." *Signs* 5:3 (1980): 545–65.

———. *Immigrant Women in the Land of Dollars: Life and Culture on the Lower East Side, 1890–1925*. New York: Monthly Review Press, 1985.

Fabbri, Fabio, ed. *Il movimento cooperativo nella storia d'Italia*. Milan: Feltrinelli, 1979.

———, ed. *L'audacia insolente. La cooperazione femminile, 1886–1986*. Venice: Marsilio Editori, 1986.

Fabbri, Luigi. *Malatesta: L'uomo e il pensiero*. Naples: Edizioni RL, 1951.

Fagiani, Gil. "The Italian Identity of Frank Sinatra." *VIA: Voices in Italian Americana* 10 (Fall 1999): 19–32.

Falk, Candace. *Love, Anarchy, and Emma Goldman: A Biography*. New Brunswick: Rutgers University Press, 1990.

———, ed. *Emma Goldman: A Documentary History of the American Years*. Berkeley: University of California Press, 2003.

Faue, Elizabeth. *Community of Suffering and Struggle: Women, Men, and the Labor Movement in Minneapolis, 1915–1945*. Chapel Hill: University of North Carolina Press, 1991.

Fausto-Sterling, Anne. "Gender, Race, and Nation: The Comparative Anatomy of 'Hottentot' Women in Europe, 1815–1817." In *Deviant Bodies: Critical Perspectives on Difference in Science and Popular Culture*, edited by Jennifer Terry and Jacqueline Urla. Bloomington: Indiana University Press, 1995.

Favero, Luigi, and Graziano Tassello. "Cent'anni di emigrazione italiana." In *Un secolo di emigrazione italiana, 1876–1976*, edited by Gianfausto Rosoli. Rome: Centro Studi Emigrazione, 1978.

Fedeli, Ugo. *Giuseppe Ciancabilla*. Cesena: Edizione L'Antistato, 1956.

Feldman, Egal. "Prostitution, the Alien Woman and the Progressive Imagination, 1910–1915." *American Quarterly* 19:2 (Summer 1967): 192–206.

Felici, Isabelle. *La Cecilia: Histoire d'une communauté anarchiste et de son fondateur Giovanni Rossi*. Lyon: Atelier de Création Libertaire, 2001.

———. "Gli anarchici italiani di São Paolo e il problema dell'organizzazione operaia, 1898–1917." In *La riscoperta delle Americhe*, edited by Vanni Blengino et al. Milan: Nicola Teti Editore, 1992: 326–38.

Femia, Joseph V. *Gramsci's Political Thought: Hegemony, Consciousness, and the Revolutionary Process*. Oxford: Clarendon Press, 1981.

Femminella, Francis X., ed. *The Interaction of Italians and Irish in the United States*. Jamaica, N.Y.: St. Johns University, 1983.

Fenton, Edwin. *Immigrants and Unions: A Case Study, Italians and American Labor, 1870–1920*. New York: Arno Press, 1975.

Fernández, Bieito Alonso. "Migración y sindicalismo. Marineros y anarquistas españoles en Nueva York (1902–1930)." *Historia Social* 54 (April 2006): 113–56.

Fernández, Frank. *Cuban Anarchism: The History of a Movement*. Tucson: Sharp Press, 2001.

Ferrais, Luigi Vittorio. "L'assassinio de Umberto I e gli anarchici di Paterson." *Rassegna Storica del Risorgimento* 60:1 (January–March 1968): 47–64.

Ferraro, Thomas J. *Feeling Italian: The Art of Ethnicity in America.* New York: New York University Press, 2005.

Filippucci, Paola. "Anthropological Perspectives on Culture in Italy." In *Italian Cultural Studies*, edited by David Forgacs and Robert Lumley. New York: Oxford University Press, 1996.

Foner, Philip S. *History of the Labor Movement in the United States.* 10 vols. New York: International Publishers, 1964.

——. *The Industrial Workers of the World, 1905–1917.* New York: International Publishers, 1965.

——. *May Day: A Short History of the International Workers' Holiday, 1886–1986.* New York: International Publishers, 1986.

——. *Organized Labor and the Black Worker, 1619–1981.* 2nd ed. New York: International Publishers, 1981.

——. *Women and the American Labor Movement.* 2 vols. New York: Free Press, 1979.

Foner, Philip S., and Ronald L. Lewis. *The Black Worker: A Documentary History from Colonial Times to Present; The Era of Post-War Prosperity and the Great Depression, 1920–1936*, vol. 6. Philadelphia: Temple University Press, 1981.

Forgacs, David, ed. *An Antonio Gramsci Reader.* New York: Schocken Books, 1988.

Forgacs, David, and Robert Lumley, eds. *Italian Cultural Studies: An Introduction.* New York: Oxford University Press, 1996.

Frank, Dana. *Buy American: The Untold Story of Economic Nationalism.* Boston: Beacon Press, 1999.

——. "Housewives, Socialists, and the Politics of Food: The 1917 New York Cost-of-Living Protests." *Feminist Studies* 11:2 (Summer 1985): 355–85.

——. "Where Is the History of U.S. Labor and International Solidarity? Part I: A Moveable Feast." *Labor: Studies in Working-Class History of the Americas* 1:1 (Spring 2004): 95–119.

——. "White Working-Class Women and the Race Question." *International Labor and Working-Class History* 54 (Fall 1998): 80–102.

Frankel, Noralee, and Nancy S. Dye, eds. *Gender, Class, Race, and Reform in the Progressive Era.* Lexington: University Press of Kentucky, 1991.

Franzina, Emilio. *Gli italiani al nuovo mondo: L'emigrazione italiana in America, 1492–1942.* Milan: Arnoldo Mondadori Editore, 1995.

Fraser, Steve. "Dress Rehearsal for the New Deal: Shop Floor Insurgents, Political Elites, and Industrial Democracy in the Amalgamated Clothing Workers." In *Working-Class America: Essays on Labor, Community, and American Society*, edited by Michael H. Frisch and Daniel J. Walkowitz. Urbana: University of Illinois Press, 1983.

——. "From the 'New Unionism' to the New Deal." *Labor History* 25 (1984): 405–30.

——. "Landslayt and Paesani: Ethnic Conflict and Cooperation in the Amalgamated Clothing Workers of America." In *Struggle a Hard Battle: Essays on Working-Class Immigrants*, edited by Dirk Hoerder. DeKalb: Northern Illinois University Press, 1986.

Friedman-Kasaba, Kathie. *Memories of Migration: Gender, Ethnicity, and Work in the Lives of Jewish and Italian Women in New York, 1870–1924.* Albany: State University of New York Press, 1996.

Furio, Colomba M. "The Cultural Background of the Italian Immigrant Woman and Its Impact on Her Unionization in the New York City Garment Industry, 1880–1919." In *Pane e Lavoro: The Italian American Working Class*, edited by George E. Pozzetta. Toronto: Multicultural History Society of Ontario, 1980.

Fussell, Betty Harper. *My Kitchen Wars.* New York: North Point Press, 1999.

Gabaccia, Donna R. "America's Immigrant Women: A Review Essay." *Journal of Ethnic History* 8:2 (1989): 127–33.

——. *From Sicily to Elizabeth Street: Housing and Social Change among Italian Immigrants, 1880–1930.* Albany: State University of New York Press, 1984.

———. *From the Other Side: Women, Gender, and Immigrant Life in the U.S., 1820–1900*. Bloomington: Indiana University Press, 1994.

———. "Immigrant Women: Nowhere at Home?" *Journal of American Ethnic History* 10:4 (Summer 1991): 61–87.

———. "Inventing 'Little Italy.'" *Journal of the Gilded Age and Progressive Era* 6:1 (January 2007): 7–41.

———. "Is Everywhere Nowhere? Nomads, Nations, and the Immigrant Paradigm of United States History." *Journal of American History* 86 (December 1999): 1115–34.

———. "Italian History and gli italiani nel mondo, Part I." *Journal of Modern Italian Studies* 2:1 (1997): 45–66.

———. "Italian History and gli italiani nel mondo, Part II." *Journal of Modern Italian Studies* 3:1 (1998): 73–97.

———. "Italian Immigrant Women in Comparative Perspective." *Altreitalie* 9 (January–June 1993): 163–75.

———. *Italy's Many Diasporas*. Seattle: University of Washington Press, 2000.

———. "Kinship, Culture and Migration: A Sicilian Example." *Journal of American Ethnic History* 3 (1984): 39–53.

———. "Migration and Militancy among Italy's Laborers." In *Roots of the Transplanted*, ed. Dirk Hoerder, Horst Rössler, and Inge Blank. New York: Columbia University Press, 1994.

———. *Militants and Migrants: Rural Sicilians Become American Workers*. New Brunswick: Rutgers University Press, 1988.

———. "Neither Padrone Slaves or Primitive Rebels: Sicilians on Two Continents." In *"Struggle a Hard Battle": Essays on Working-Class Immigrants*, edited by Dirk Hoerder. DeKalb: Northern Illinois University Press, 1986.

———. "Peopling 'Little Italy.'" In *The Italians of New York: Five Centuries of Struggle and Achievement*, edited by Philip V. Cannistraro. New York: Mondadori and the New York Historical Society, 1999.

———. "Race, Nation, Hyphen: Italian-Americans and American Multiculturalism in Comparative Perspective." In *Are Italians White? How Race Is Made in America*, edited by Jennifer Guglielmo and Salvatore Salerno. New York: Routledge, 2003.

———. "Sicilians in Space: Environmental Change and Family Geography." *Journal of Social History* 16 (1982): 53–66.

———. *We Are What We Eat: Ethnic Food and the Making of Americans*. Cambridge, Mass.: Harvard University Press, 2000.

———. "Worker Internationalism and Italian Labor Migration, 1870–1914." *International Labor and Working-Class History* 45 (1994): 63–79.

———. "The 'Yellow Peril' and the 'Chinese of Europe': Global Perspectives on Race and Labor, 1815–1930." In *Migration, Migration History, History: Old Paradigms and New Perspectives*, edited by Jan Lucassen and Leo Lucassen. New York: Peter Lang, 1997.

———, ed. *Seeking Common Ground: Multidisciplinary Studies of Immigrant Women in the United States*. Westport, Conn.: Praeger, 1992.

Gabaccia, Donna, and Franca Iacovetta. "Women, Work, and Protest in the Italian Diaspora: An International Research Agenda." *Labour/Le Travail* 42 (Fall 1998): 161–81.

———, eds. *Women, Gender, and Transnational Lives: Italian Workers of the World*. Toronto: University of Toronto Press, 2002.

Gabaccia, Donna, and Fraser Ottanelli. "Diaspora or International Proletariat? Italian Labor, Labor Migration and the Making of Multiethnic States, 1815–1939." *Diaspora* 6:1 (Spring 1997): 61–84.

———, eds. *Italy's Workers of the World: Labor, Migration, and the Making of Multi-Ethnic Nations*. Urbana: University of Illinois Press, 2001.

Gabaccia, Donna, and Vicki L. Ruiz. *American Dreaming, Global Realities: Rethinking U.S. Immigration History*. Urbana: University of Illinois Press, 2006.

Gabin, Nancy. *Feminism in the Labor Movement: Women and the United Auto Workers, 1935–1970.* Ithaca: Cornell University Press, 1990.

Gallagher, Dorothy. *All the Right Enemies: The Life and Murder of Carlo Tresca.* New York: Penguin, 1988.

Galzerano, Giuseppe. *Gaetano Bresci: Vita, attentato, processo, carcere e morte dell'anarchico che "giustizio" Umberto I.* 2nd ed. Salerno: Galzerano Editore, 2001.

Gamber, Wendy. *The Female Economy: The Millinery and Dressmaking Trades, 1860–1930.* Urbana: University of Illinois Press, 1997.

Gambs, John S. *The Decline of the I.W.W.* New York: Russell & Russell, 1966.

Ganci, Massimo. *I fasci dei lavoratori.* Catania: S. Sciascia Editore, 1977.

Gandolfo, Romolo. "Las sociedades italianas de socorros mutuos de Buenos Aires: Cuestiones de clase y etnía dentro de una comunidad de inmigrantes (1880–1920)." In *Asociacionismo, trabajo e identidad étnica,* edited by Ferdinando J. Devoto and Eduardo J. Miguez. Buenos Aires: CEMLA-CSER-IEHS, 1992.

Gardner, Martha. *The Qualities of a Citizen: Women, Immigration, and Citizenship, 1870–1965.* Princeton, N.J.: Princeton University Press, 2005.

Gaudioso, Francesco. *Calabria ribelle: Brigantaggio e sistemi repressivi nel Cosentino (1860–1870).* Milan: Franco Angeli, 1987.

Gennari, John. "Mammissimo: Dolly and Frankie Sinatra and the Italian-American Mother/Son Thing." In *Frank Sinatra: History, Politics, and Italian American Culture,* edited by Stanislao Pugliese. Westport, Conn.: Greenwood Press, 2003.

Gerson, Simon W. *Pete: The Story of Peter V. Caccione, New York's First Communist Councilman.* New York: International Publishers, 1976.

Gerstle, Gary. "Working-Class Racism: Broaden the Focus." *International Labor and Working-Class History* 44 (Fall 1993): 33–40.

Giacobbe, Iolanda Crimi. *Donne siciliani nella resistenza.* Catania: Circolo Anna Frank, 1962.

Giallombardo, Fatima. "La donna nelle feste popolari siciliane." In *Donne e società,* edited by Janne Vibaek. Palermo: Arti Grafiche Siciliane, 1982.

Gibson, Mary. "Biology or Environment? Race and Southern 'Deviancy' in the Writings of Italian Criminologists, 1880–1920." In *Italy's "Southern Question": Orientalism in One Country,* edited by Jane Schneider. New York: Berg, 1998.

———. "The 'Female Offender' and the Italian School of Criminal Anthropology." *Journal of European Studies* 12 (1982): 155–65.

———. "On the Insensitivity of Women: Science and the Woman Question in Liberal Italy, 1890–1910." *Journal of Women's History* 2:2 (Fall 1990): 11–41.

———. "Prostitution and Feminism in Late Nineteenth-Century Italy." In *The Italian Immigrant Woman in North America,* edited by Betty Boyd Caroli et. al. Toronto: Multicultural History Society of Ontario, 1978.

———. *Prostitution and the State in Italy, 1860–1915.* 2nd ed. Columbus: Ohio State University Press, 2000.

———. "Romanticism and Crime: Comments on the Historical Panel." *Wordsworth Circle* 19:2 (Spring 1988): 82–84.

Gilfoyle, Timothy. *City of Eros: New York City, Prostitution, and the Commercialization of Sex, 1790–1920.* New York: Norton, 1992.

Gillan, Jennifer, Maria Mazziotti Gillan, and Edvige Giunta, eds. *Italian American Writers on New Jersey: An Anthology of Poetry and Prose.* New Brunswick: Rutgers University Press, 2003.

Gillian, Rose. *Feminism and Geography: The Limits of Geographical Knowledge.* Minneapolis: University of Minnesota Press, 1993.

Gilligan, Edmund. "The Wall Street Explosion Mystery." *American Mercury* 45 (September 1938): 63–67.

Gilman, Sander. "Black Bodies, White Bodies: Toward an Iconography of Female Sexuality in Late
Nineteenth-Century Art, Medicine, and Literature." *Critical Inquiry* 12:1 (Autumn 1985): 203–42.
———. *Difference and Pathology: Stereotypes of Sexuality, Race, and Madness*. Ithaca: Cornell
University Press, 1985.
Gilmore, Glenda Elizabeth. *Defying Dixie: The Radical Roots of Civil Rights, 1919–1950*. New York:
W. W. Norton, 2008.
Giron, Loraine Slomp. "L'immigrata in Brasile e il lavoro." *Altreitalie* 9 (January–June 1983): 102–15.
Giunta, Edvige. "The *Giara* of Memory." In *The Milk of Almonds: Italian American Women Writers on
Food and Culture*, edited by Louise DeSalvo and Edvige Giunta. New York: Feminist Press, 2002.
Glasser, Ruth. *My Music Is My Flag: Puerto Rican Musicians and Their New York Communities,
1917–1940*. Berkeley: University of California Press, 1995.
Glenn, Evelyn Nakano. *Issei, Nisei, War Bride: Three Generations of Japanese American Women in
Domestic Service*. Philadelphia: Temple University Press, 1986.
———. "Racial Ethnic Women's Labor: The Intersection of Race, Gender, and Class Oppression."
Review of Radical Political Economies 17:3 (Fall 1985): 86–108.
———. *Unequal Freedom: How Race and Gender Shaped American Citizenship and Labor*. Cambridge,
Mass.: Harvard University Press, 2002.
Glenn, Evelyn Nakano, et al., eds. *Mothering: Ideology, Experience, and Agency*. New York: Routledge,
1994.
Glenn, Susan Anita. *Daughters of the Shtetl: Life and Labor in the Immigrant Generation*. Ithaca:
Cornell University Press, 1990.
———. *Female Spectacle: The Theatrical Roots of Modern Feminism*. Cambridge, Mass.: Harvard
University Press, 2000.
Goglia, Luigi. *Il colonialismo italiano da Adua all'impero*. Rome: Laterza, 1993.
Goldberg, Barry, and Colin Greer. "American Visions, Ethnic Dreams: Public Ethnicity and the
Sociological Imagination." *Sage Race Relations Abstracts* 15:1 (1990): 5–60.
Goldberg, David J. *A Tale of Three Cities: Labor Organization and Protest in Paterson, Passaic, and
Lawrence, 1916–1921*. New Brunswick: Rutgers University Press, 1989.
Golin, Steve. "Defeat Becomes Disaster: The Paterson Strike of 1913 and the Decline of the IWW."
Labor History 24 (Spring 1983): 223–49.
———. *The Fragile Bridge: Paterson Silk Strike, 1913*. Philadelphia: Temple University Press, 1988.
González, Deena J. *Refusing the Favor: The Spanish-Mexican Women of Santa Fe, 1820–1880*. New
York: Oxford University Press, 1999.
Goodman, Cary. *Choosing Sides: Playground and Street Life on the Lower East Side*. New York:
Schocken, 1979.
Goodman, James E. *Stories of Scottsboro*. New York: Vintage, 1995.
Gordon, Linda. *Heroes of Their Own Lives: The Politics and History of Family Violence, Boston,
1880–1960*. New York: Viking, 1988.
———. *Pitied But Not Entitled: Single Mothers and the History of Welfare, 1890–1935*. New York: Free
Press, 1994.
Grant, Joanne. *Ella Baker: Freedom Bound*. New York: John Wiley and Sons, 1998.
Green, James. *Taking History to Heart: The Power of the Past in Building Social Movements*. Amherst:
University of Massachusetts Press, 2000.
———. *The World of the Worker: Labor in Twentieth-Century America*. New York: Hill and Wang,
1980.
Green, Martin. *New York 1913: The Armory Show and the Paterson Strike Pageant*. New York: Collier
Books, 1990.
Green, Nancy L. "From Downtown Tenements to Midtown Lofts: The Shifting Geography of an
Urban Industry." In *A Coat of Many Colors: Immigration, Globalization, and Reform in New York
City's Garment Industry*, edited by Daniel Soyer. New York: Fordham University Press, 2005.

————. *Ready-to-Wear and Ready-to-Work: A Century of Industry and Immigrants in Paris and New York*. Durham: Duke University Press, 1997.

Green, Venus. *Race on the Line: Gender, Labor, and Technology in the Bell System, 1880–1980*. Durham: Duke University Press, 2001.

Greenberg, Cheryl. *"Or Does It Explode?" Black Harlem in the Great Depression*. New York: Mifflin Houghton, 1991.

Greenwald, Richard A. "'More than a Strike': Ethnicity, Labor Relations, and the Origins of a Protocol of Peace in the New York Ladies' Garment Industry." *Business and Economic History* 27:2 (Winter 1998): 318–29.

————. *The Triangle Fire, the Protocols of Peace, and Industrial Democracy in Progressive Era New York*. Philadelphia: Temple University Press, 2005.

Gregory, Steven. *Black Corona: Race and the Politics of Place in an Urban Community*. Princeton, N.J.: Princeton University Press, 1999.

Gremmo, Roberto. *Gli anarchici che uccisero Umberto 1*. Biella: Storia Ribelle, 2000.

Gribaudi, Gabriella. "Images of the South: The *Mezzogiorno* as seen by Insiders and Outsiders." In *The New History of the Italian South: The Mezzogiorno Revisited*, edited by Robert Lumley and Jonathan Morris. Devon: Exeter Press, 1997.

Grittner, Frederick K. *White Slavery: Myth, Ideology and American Law*. New York: Garland Publishing, 1990.

Gross, Kali N. *Colored Amazons: Crime, Violence, and Black Women in the City of Brotherly Love, 1890–1910*. Durham: Duke University Press, 2006.

Guérin, Daniel. *No Gods, No Masters: An Anthology of Anarchism*. San Francisco: AK Press 1998.

Guglielmo, Jennifer. "*Donne Ribelli*: Recovering the History of Italian Women's Radicalism in the United States." In *The Lost World of Italian American Radicalism: Politics, Labor, Culture*, edited by Philip V. Cannistraro and Gerald Meyer. Westport, Conn.: Praeger, 2003.

————. "Italian Women's Proletarian Feminism in the New York City Garment Trades, 1890s–1940s." In *Women, Gender, and Transnational Lives: Italian Workers of the World*, edited by Donna Gabaccia and Franca Iacovetta. Toronto: University of Toronto Press, 2002.

————. "Sweatshop Feminism: Italian Women's Political Culture in New York City's Needle Trades, 1890–1919." In *Sweatshop, USA: The American Sweatshop in Historical and Global Perspective*, edited by Daniel E. Bender and Richard A. Greenwald. New York: Routledge, 2003.

Guglielmo, Jennifer, and Salvatore Salerno, eds. *Are Italians White? How Race Is Made in America*. New York: Routledge, 2003.

Guglielmo, Thomas A. "Encountering the Color Line in the Everyday: Italians in Interwar Chicago." 123 (Summer 2004): 45–77.

————. "Fighting for Caucasian Rights: Mexicans, Mexican Americans, and the Transnational Struggle for Civil Rights in World War II Texas." *Journal of American History* 92 (March 2006): 1212–37.

————. "The Forgotten Enemy: Wartime Representations of Italians in American Popular Culture, 1941–1945." *Italian Americana* 18 (Winter 2000): 5–22.

————. "Rethinking U.S. Whiteness Historiography." In *Whiteout: The Continuing Significance of Racism*, edited by Ashley Doane and Eduardo Bonilla-Silva. New York: Routledge, 2003.

————. "Toward Essentialism, Toward Difference: Gino Speranza and Conceptions of Race and Italian-American Racial Identity, 1900–1925." *Mid-America* 81 (Summer 1999): 169–213.

————. *White on Arrival: Italians, Race, Color, and Power in Chicago, 1890–1945*. New York: Oxford University Press, 2003.

Guglielmo, Thomas A., and Earl Lewis. "The Changing Meaning of Difference: Race, Color, and Ethnicity in America, 1930–1964." In *Race and Ethnicity in America: A Concise History*, edited by Ronald H. Bayor. New York: Columbia University Press, 2003.

Gurock, Jeffrey S. *When Harlem Was Jewish, 1870–1930*. New York: Columbia University Press, 1979.

Gutiérrez, David. *Walls and Mirrors: Mexican Americans, Mexican Immigrants, and the Politics of Ethnicity*. Berkeley: University of California Press, 1995.

Gutman, Herbert G. *Work, Culture, and Society in Industrializing America*. New York: Vintage-Random House, 1977.

Gutman, Judith Mara. *Lewis Hine and the American Social Conscience*. New York: Walker, 1967.

Guy, Donna J. *Sex and Danger in Buenos Aires: Prostitution, Family, and Nation in Argentina*. Lincoln: University of Nebraska Press, 1990.

———. *White Slavery and Mothers Alive and Dead: The Troubled Meeting of Sex Gender, Public Health, and Progress in Latin America*. Lincoln: University of Nebraska Press, 2000.

———. "Women, Peonage, and Industrialization: Argentina, 1810–1914." *Latin American Research Review* 16:3 (1981): 65–89.

Haas, Edward F. "Guns, Goats, and Italians: The Tallulah Lynching of 1899." *North Louisiana Historical Association Journal* 13 (1982): 45–58.

Hagedorn, Ann. *Savage Peace: Hope and Fear in America, 1919*. New York: Simon and Schuster, 2008.

Hale, Grace Elizabeth. *Making Whiteness: The Culture of Segregation in the South, 1890–1940*. New York: Pantheon, 1998.

Hall, Stuart. "Gramsci's Relevance for the Study of Race and Ethnicity." *Journal of Communication Inquiry* 10:2 (1986): 5–27.

Hamill, Pete. *Why Sinatra Matters*. Boston: Little, Brown, 1998.

Handlin, Oscar. *The Uprooted*. Boston: Little, Brown, 1951.

———. *Race and Nationality in American Life*. Garden City, N.Y.: Doubleday Anchor, 1950.

Haney Lopez, Ian. "The Social Construction of Race: Some Observations on Illusion, Fabrication, and Choice." *Harvard Civil Rights–Civil Liberties Law Review* 29 (Winter 1994): 1–62.

———. *White by Law: The Legal Construction of Race*. New York: New York University Press, 1996.

Harasym, Sarah, ed. *The Post-Colonial Critic: Interviews, Strategies, Dialogues. Gayatri Chakravorty Spivak*. New York: Routledge, 1990.

Harney, Robert F. "Men without Women: Italian Migrants in Canada, 1885–1930." In *The Italian Immigrant Woman in North America*, edited by Betty Boyd Caroli et al. Toronto: Multicultural History Society of Ontario, 1978.

Harney, Robert F., and J. Vincenza Scarpaci, eds. *Little Italies in North America*. Toronto: Multicultural History Society of Ontario, 1981.

Harris, Cheryl I. "Whiteness as Property." *Harvard Law Review* 106 (June 1993): 1707–91.

Harris, Joseph E. *African-American Reactions to War in Ethiopia, 1936–1941*. Baton Rouge: Louisiana State University Press, 1994.

Harrowitz, Nancy A. *Antisemitism, Misogyny and the Logic of Cultural Difference*. Lincoln: University of Nebraska Press, 1994.

Haywoode, Terry L., and Laura Polla Scanlon. "World of Our Mothers: College for Neighborhood Women." *Women's Studies Quarterly* 3–4 (1993): 133–41.

Helfgott, Roy B. "Puerto Rican Integration in the Skirt Industry in New York City." In *Discrimination and Low Incomes: Social and Economic Discrimination against Minority Groups in Relation to Low Incomes in New York State*. New York: Studies of New York State Commission against Discrimination, New School for Social Research, 1959.

———. "Trade Unionism among the Jewish Garment Workers of Britain and the United States." *Labor History* 2:2 (1961): 202–14.

———. "Women's and Children's Apparel." In *Made in New York: Case Studies in Metropolitan Manufacturing*, edited by Max Hall. Cambridge, Mass.: Harvard University Press, 1959.

Helmbold, Lois R. "Beyond the Family Economy: Black and White Working Class Women during the Great Depression." *Feminist Studies* 13 (Fall 1987): 629–56.

Herbst, John A., and Catherine Keene. *Life and Times in Silk City: A Photographic Essay of Paterson, New Jersey.* Haledon: American Labor Museum, 1984.

Hewitt, Nancy A. "In Pursuit of Power: The Political Economy of Women's Activism in Twentieth-Century Tampa." In *Visible Women: New Essays on American Activism,* edited by Nancy A. Hewitt and Suzanne Lebsock. Urbana: University of Illinois Press, 1993.

———. *Southern Discomfort: Women's Activism in Tampa, Florida, 1880s–1920s.* Urbana: University of Illinois Press, 2001.

———. "Varieties of Voluntarism: Class, Ethnicity, and Women's Activism in Tampa." In *Women, Politics, and Change,* edited by Louise A. Tilly and Patricia Gurin. New York: Russell Sage Foundation, 1990.

———. "'The Voice of Virile Labor': Labor Militancy, Community Solidarity, and Gender Identity among Tampa's Latin Workers." In *Work Engendered: Toward a New History of Men, Women, and Work,* edited by Ava Baron. Ithaca: Cornell University Press, 1991.

———. *Women's Activism and Social Change: Rochester, New York, 1822–1872.* Ithaca: Cornell University Press, 1984.

Higbie, Toby. "Crossing Class Boundaries: Tramp Ethnographers and Narratives of Class in Progressive Era America." *Social Science History* 21:4 (Winter 1997): 559–92.

Higginbotham, Evelyn Brooks. "African-American Women's History and the Metalanguage of Race." *Signs* 17:2 (1992): 251–74.

Higham, John. *Strangers in the Land: Patterns of American Nativism, 1860–1925.* New Brunswick: Rutgers University Press, 2002 [1963].

Hill, Herbert. "Guardians of the Sweatshops: The Trade Unions, Racism, and the Garment Industry." In *Puerto Rico and Puerto Ricans: Studies in History and Society,* edited by Adalberto López and James Petras. New York: Wiley, 1974.

———. "The ILGWU: Fact or Fiction." *New Politics* 2:2 (Winter 1963): 26–27.

Hirsch, Arnold. *Making the Second Ghetto: Race and Housing in Chicago, 1940–1960.* Chicago: University of Chicago Press, 1998.

———. "Massive Resistance in the Urban North: Trumbull Park, Chicago, 1953–1966." *Journal of American History* 82 (September 1995): 522–50.

History Task Force, Centro de Estudios Puertorriquenos. *Labor Migration under Capitalism: The Puerto Rican Experience.* New York: Monthly Review Press, 1979.

Hobsbawm, Eric J. *Bandits.* London: Pelican, 1972.

———. *Primitive Rebels.* New York: W. W. Norton, 1963.

Hobson, Barbara Meil. *Uneasy Virtue: The Politics of Prostitution and the American Reform Tradition.* New York: Basic Books, 1987.

Hoerder, Dirk, ed. *The Immigrant Labor Press in North America, 1840s–1970s: An Annotated Bibliography.* Vol. 3: *Migrants from Southern and Western Europe.* Westport, Conn.: Greenwood Press, 1987.

Holloway, Thomas. *Immigrants on the Land: Coffee and Society in São Paulo, 1886–1934.* Chapel Hill: University of North Carolina Press, 1980.

Hondagneu-Sotelo, Pierette. *Gendered Transitions: Mexican Experiences of Immigration.* Berkeley: University of California Press, 1994.

hooks, bell. *Black Looks: Race and Representation.* Boston: South End Press, 1992.

Horn, David G. *The Criminal Body: Lombroso and the Anatomy of Deviance.* New York: Routledge, 2003.

Horowitz, Daniel. *The Italian Labor Movement.* Cambridge, Mass.: Harvard University Press, 1963.

Hunter, Tera W. *To 'Joy My Freedom: Southern Black Women's Lives and Labors after the Civil War.* Cambridge, Mass.: Harvard University Press, 1997.

Hutchinson, Earl Ofari. *Blacks and Reds: Race and Class in Conflict, 1919–1990.* East Lansing: Michigan State University, 1995.

Hyman, Colette A. *Staging Strikes: Workers' Theatre and the American Labor Movement*. Philadelphia: Temple University Press, 1997.

Hyman, Paula. "Immigrant Women and Consumer Protest: The New York City Kosher Meat Boycott of 1902." *American Jewish History* 70 (September 1980), 91–105.

Iacovetta, Franca. *Such Hardworking People: Italian Immigrants in Postwar Toronto*. Montreal: McGill-Queen's University Press, 1992.

———. "Writing Women into Immigration History: The Italian Canadian Case." *Altreitalie* 9 (January–June 1993): 24–41.

Iacovetta, Franca, and Karen Dubinsky. "Murder, Womanly Virtue and Motherhood: The Case of Angelina Napolitano, 1911–22." *Canadian Historical Review* 72:4 (December 1991): 505–31.

Ichioka, Yuji. "Ameyuki-san: Japanese Prostitutes in Nineteenth-Century America." *Amerasia Journal* 4:1 (1977): 1–22.

———. *Issei: The World of the First Generation Japanese Immigrants, 1885–1924*. New York: Collier Macmillan, 1988.

Ignatiev, Noel. *How the Irish Became White*. New York: Routledge, 1995.

Irving, Katrina. *Immigrant Mothers: Narratives of Race and Maternity, 1890–1925*. Urbana: University of Illinois, 2000.

Jackson, Kenneth T. *Crabgrass Frontier: The Suburbanization of the United States*. New York: Oxford University Press, 1985.

Jacobson, Matthew Frye. *Barbarian Virtues: The United States Encounters Foreign Peoples at Home and Abroad, 1876–1917*. New York: Hill and Wang, 2000.

———. "More 'Trans-,' Less 'National.'" *Journal of American Ethnic History* 25:4 (Summer 2006): 74–84.

———. *Roots Too: White Ethnic Revival in Post–Civil Rights America*. Cambridge, Mass.: Harvard University Press, 2006.

———. *Special Sorrows: The Diasporic Imagination of Irish, Polish, and Jewish Immigrants in the United States*. Cambridge, Mass.: Harvard University Press, 1995.

———. *Whiteness of a Different Color: European Immigrants and the Alchemy of Race*. Cambridge, Mass.: Harvard University Press, 1998.

Jaffe, Julian F. *Crusade against Radicalism: New York during the Red Scare, 1914–1924*. Port Washington, N.Y.: Kennekat Press, 1972.

James, Winston. *Holding Aloft the Banner of Ethiopia: Caribbean Radicalism in Early Twentieth-Century America*. London: Verso, 1998.

Janiewski, Dolores E. *Sisterhood Denied: Race, Gender, and Class in a New South Community*. Philadelphia: Temple University Press, 1985.

Jenson, Joan M., and Sue Davidson, eds. *A Needle, a Bobbin, a Strike: Women Needleworkers in America*. Philadelphia: Temple University Press, 1984.

Jetter, Alexis, Annelise Orleck, and Diana Taylor, eds. *The Politics of Motherhood: Activist Voices from Left to Right*. Hanover: University Press of New England, 1997.

Johnson, Colleen Leahy. *Growing Up and Growing Old in Italian-American Families*. New Brunswick: Rutgers University Press, 1985.

Johnson, Val Marie. "'The Moral Aspects of Complex Problems': New York City Electoral Campaigns against Vice and the Incorporation of Immigrants, 1890–1901." *Journal of American Ethnic History* 25:2–3 (Winter–Spring 2006): 48–73.

———. "Protection, Virtue, and the 'Power to Detain': The Moral Citizenship of Jewish Women in New York City, 1890–1920." *Journal of Urban History* 31:5 (2005): 655–84.

———. "'The Rest Can Go to the Devil': Macy's Workers Negotiate Gender, Sex, and Class in the Progressive Era." *Journal of Women's History* 19:1 (Spring 2007): 32–57.

Jones, David A. *History of Criminology*. Westport, Conn.: Greenwood Press, 1986.

Juliani, Richard N. "The Settlement House and the Italian Family." In *The Italian Immigrant Woman in North America*, edited by Betty Boyd Caroli et al. Toronto: Multicultural History Society of Ontario, 1978.

Kadi, Joanna. *Food of Our Grandmothers: Writing by Arab-American and Arab-Canadian Feminists.* Boston: South End, 1994.

Kamel, Rachael and Anya Hoffman, eds. *The Maquila Reader: Cross Border Organizing since NAFTA.* Philadelphia: AFS Committee, 1999.

Kang, Laura Hyun Yi. *Compositional Subjects: Enfiguring Asian/American Women.* Durham: Duke University Press, 2002.

Kaplan, Amy. *The Anarchy of Empire in the Making of U.S. Culture.* Cambridge, Mass.: Harvard University Press, 2005.

Kaplan, Amy, and Donald E. Pease, eds. *Cultures of United States Imperialism.* Durham: Duke University Press, 1993.

Kaplan, Caren, Norma Alarcón, and Minoo Moallem, eds. *Between Woman and Nation: Nationalisms, Transnational Feminisms, and the State.* Durham: Duke University Press, 1999.

Kaplan, Temma. "Female Consciousness and Collective Action: The Case of Barcelona, 1910–1918." *Signs* 7:3 (1982): 546–66.

Karabel, Jerome. "Revolutionary Contradictions: Antonio Gramsci and the Problem of the Intellectuals." *Politics and Society* 6 (1976): 123–72.

Karim, Iman Benjamin, ed. *The End of White World Supremacy: Four Speeches by Malcolm X.* New York: Merlin House, 1971.

Karlin, J. Alexander. "The Italo-American Incident of 1891 and the Road to Reunion." *Journal of Southern History* 8:2 (May 1942): 242–46.

Katznelson, Ira. *When Affirmative Action Was White: An Untold History of Racial Inequality in Twentieth-Century America.* New York: W. W. Norton, 2005.

Kasinitz, Philip. *Caribbean New York: Black Immigrants and the Politics of Race.* Ithaca: Cornell University Press, 1992.

Keeran, Roger. "The Italian Section of the International Workers Order, 1930–1950." *Italian American Review* 7:1 (Winter–Spring 2000): 63–82.

Keire, Mara L. "The Vice Trust: A Reinterpretation of the White Slavery Scare in the United States, 1907–1917." *Journal of Social History* 35:1 (Fall 2001): 5–41.

Kelley, Robin D. G. "'But a Local Phase of a World Problem': Black History's Global Vision, 1883–1950." *Journal of American History* 86:3 (December 1999): 1045–77.

———. *Hammer and Hoe: Alabama Communists during the Great Depression.* Chapel Hill: University of North Carolina Press, 1990.

———. "How the West Was One: The African Diaspora and the Re-mapping of U.S. History." In *Rethinking American History in a Global Age*, edited by Thomas Bender. Berkeley: University of California Press, 2002.

———. "'We Are Not What We Seem': Rethinking Black Working-Class Opposition in the Jim Crow South." *Journal of American History* 80:1 (June 1993): 75–112.

Kessler-Harris, Alice. *Gendering Labor History.* Urbana: University of Illinois Press, 2007.

———. "Organizing the Unorganizable: Three Jewish Women and Their Union." *Labor History* 17 (1976): 5–23.

———. *Out to Work: A History of Wage-Earning Women in the United States.* New York: Oxford University Press, 1982.

———. "Problems of Coalition-Building: Women and Trade Unions in the 1920s." In *Women, Work and Protest: A Century of U.S. Women's Labor History*, edited by Ruth Milkman. Boston: Routledge and Kegan Paul, 1985.

———. "Treating the Male as 'Other': Redefining the Parameters of Labor History." *Labor History* 34:2–3 (1993): 190–204.

————. "Where are the Organized Women Workers?" *Feminist Studies* 3 (Fall 1975): 92–110.

Kessner, Thomas. *The Golden Door: Italian and Jewish Immigrant Mobility in New York City*. New York: Oxford University Press, 1977.

Kessner, Thomas, and Betty Boyd Caroli. "New Immigrant Women at Work: Italians and Jews in New York City, 1880–1905." *Journal of Ethnic Studies* 5 (Winter 1978): 19–31.

Kidwell, Claudia B., and Margaret C. Christman. *Suiting Everyone: The Democratization of Clothing in America*. Washington, D.C.: Smithsonian Institution Press for the National Museum of History and Technology, 1974.

Killinger, Charles L. *Gaetano Salvemini: A Biography*. Westport, Conn.: Praeger, 2002.

Kissack, Terence. *Free Comrades: Anarchism and Homosexuality in the United States, 1895–1917*. Oakland: AK Press, 2008.

Kisseloff, Jeff. *You Must Remember This: An Oral History of Manhattan from the 1890s to World War II*. Baltimore: Johns Hopkins University Press, 1989.

Kleinberg, S. J. *Widows and Orphans First: The Family Economy and Social Welfare Policy, 1880–1939*. Urbana: University of Illinois Press, 2006.

Klindienst, Patricia. *The Earth Knows My Name: Food, Culture, and Sustainability in the Gardens of Ethnic Americans*. Boston: Beacon Press, 2006.

Kornbluh, Joyce. *Rebel Voices—An IWW Anthology*. Chicago: Charles H. Kerr Press, 1988.

Kornweibel, Theodore, Jr. *"Investigate Everything": Federal Efforts to Compel Black Loyalty during World War I*. Bloomington: Indiana University Press, 2002.

————. *"Seeing Red": Federal Campaigns against Black Militancy, 1919–1925*. Bloomington: Indiana University Press, 1998.

Kosak, Hadassa. *Cultures of Opposition: Jewish Immigrant Workers, New York City, 1881–1905*. Albany: State University of New York Press, 2000.

Kozol, Wendy. "Madonnas of the Fields: Photography, Gender, and 1930s Farm Relief." *Genders* 2 (Summer 1988): 1–23.

Krause, Corinne Azen. *Grandmothers, Mothers, and Daughters: Oral Histories of Three Generations of Ethnic American Women*. Boston: Twayne Publishers, 1991.

Kunzel, Regina G. *Fallen Women, Problem Girls: Unmarried Mothers and the Professionalization of Social Work, 1890–1945*. New Haven: Yale University Press, 1993.

LaGumina, Salvatore J. "Reflections of an Italian-American Worker." *Journal of Ethnic Studies* 3:2 (1975): 65–77.

————. *Wop! A Documentary History of Anti-Italian Discrimination in the United States*. San Francisco: Straight Arrow Books, 1973.

Lahr, John. *Sinatra: The Artist and the Man*. New York: Random House, 1997.

Lamont, Michèle, ed. *The Cultural Territories of Race: Black and White Boundaries*. Chicago: University of Chicago Press, 1999.

Langum, David J. *Crossing over the Line: Legislating Morality and the Mann Act*. Chicago: University of Chicago Press, 1994.

Lasch-Quinn, Elisabeth. *Black Neighbors: Race and the Limits of Reform in the American Settlement House Movement, 1890–1945*. Chapel Hill: University of North Carolina Press, 1993.

Laudani, Simona. "Trasformazioni agricole e condizioni femminile in Sicilia." In *Società rurale e ruoli femminili in Italia tra ottocento e novecento*, edited by Paola Corti. Bologna: Il Mulino, 1991.

Laurino, Maria. *Were You Always an Italian? Ancestors and Other Icons of Italian America*. New York: Norton, 2000.

LaVigna, Claire. "The Marxist Ambivalence toward Women: Between Socialism and Feminism in the Italian Socialist Party." In *Socialist Women: European Socialist Feminism in the Nineteenth and Early Twentieth Centuries*, edited by Marilyn J. Boxer and Jean H. Quataert. New York: Elsevier, 1978.

Lawson, Ronald, and Stephen E. Barton. "Sex Roles and Social Movements: A Case Study of the Tenant Movement in New York City." *Signs* 6:2 (1980): 230–47.

Lawson, Ronald, and Mark Naison, eds. *The Tenant Movement in New York City, 1904–1984*. New Brunswick: Rutgers University Press, 1986.

Lee, Erika. *At America's Gates: Chinese Immigration during the Exclusion Era, 1882–1943*. Chapel Hill: University of North Carolina Press, 2003.

Leeder, Elaine. *The Gentle General: Rose Pesotta, Anarchist and Labor Organizer*. Albany: State University of New York Press, 1993.

Lentz-Smith, Adriane. *Freedom Struggles: African Americans and World War I*. Cambridge, Mass.: Harvard University Press, 2009.

Lesser, Jeff. *Negotiating National Identity: Immigrants, Minorities, and the Struggle for Ethnicity in Brazil*. Durham: Duke University Press, 1999.

Levi, Giovanni. "Regioni e cultura delle classi popolari." *Quaderni storici* 15:2 (1979): 720–73.

Levy, Carl. "Currents of Italian Syndicalism before 1926." *International Review of Social History* 45 (2000): 209–50.

———, ed. *Italian Regionalism: History, Identity, and Politics*. Oxford: Berg, 1996.

Lhamon, W. T., Jr. *Raising Cain: Blackface Performance from Jim Crow to Hip Hop*. Cambridge, Mass.: Harvard University Press, 1998.

Lipsitz, George. *The Possessive Investment in Whiteness: How White People Profit from Identity Politics*. Philadelphia: Temple, 1998.

Lissak, Rivka Shpak. *Pluralism and Progressives: Hull House and the New Immigrants, 1890–1919*. Chicago: University of Chicago Press, 1989.

Livi-Bacci, Massimo. *A History of Italian Fertility during the Last Two Centuries*. Princeton: Princeton University Press, 1977.

Lomas, Clara. "Transborder Discourse: The Articulation of Gender in the Borderlands in the Early Twentieth Century." *Frontiers* 24:2–3 (2003): 51–74.

Longo, Bartolo. *Storia del santuario di Pompeii*. Pompeii: Pontificio Santuario di Pompeii, 1981.

López, Adalberto, and James Petras, eds. *Puerto Rico and Puerto Ricans: Studies in History and Society*. New York: Wiley & Sons, 1974.

Louie, Miriam Ching Yoon. *Sweatshop Warriors: Immigrant Women Workers Take on the Global Factory*. Cambridge: South End Press, 2001.

Luconi, Stefano. *La "diplomazia parallela": Il regime fascista e la mobilizazione politica degli italo-americani*. Milan: Franco Angeli, 2000.

Lui, Mary Ting Yi. *The Chinatown Trunk Mystery: Murder, Miscegenation, and Other Dangerous Encounters in Turn-of-the-Century New York City*. Princeton, N.J.: Princeton University Press, 2005.

Lumley, Robert, and Jonathan Morris, eds. *The New History of the Italian South: The Mezzogiorno Revisited*. Devon: University of Exeter Press, 1997.

Lyttelton, Profe. *The Seizure of Power: Fascism in Italy, 1919–1929*. New York: Routledge, 2003.

Mackey, Thomas C. *Pursuing Johns: Criminal Law Reform, Defending Character, and New York City's Committee of Fourteen, 1920–1930*. Columbus: Ohio State University Press, 2005.

MacLean, Nancy. *Behind the Mask of Chivalry: The Making of the Second Ku Klux Klan*. New York: Oxford University Press, 1995.

———. "The Culture of Resistance": Female Institution-Building in the International Ladies' Garment Workers Union, 1905–1925. Ann Arbor: University of Michigan, 1982.

———. *Freedom Is Not Enough: The Opening of the American Workplace*. Cambridge, Mass.: Harvard University Press, 2006.

Magliocco, Sabina. *The Two Madonnas: The Politics of Festival in a Sardinian Community*. Long Grove, Ill.: Waveland Press, 2005.

———. *Witching Culture: Folklore and Neo-Paganism in America*. Philadelphia: University of Pennsylvania Press, 2004.

Maglione, Connie A., and Carmen Anthony Fiore. *Voices of the Daughters*. Princeton, N.J.: Townhouse, 1989.

Majorino, Tarquinio. *Storia e leggende di briganti e brigantesse*. Piemme: Casale Monferrato, 1997.

Malpezzi, Frances M. *Italian-American Folklore*. Little Rock: August House Publishers, 1992.

Mangione, Jerre, and Ben Morreale. *La Storia: Five Centuries of the Italian American Experience*. New York: HarperCollins, 1992.

Marazzi, Martino. *Voices of Italian America: A History of Early Italian American Literature*. Madison, N.J.: Fairleigh Dickinson University Press, 2004.

Marcuson, Lewis R. *The Stage Immigrant: The Irish, Italians, and Jews in American Drama, 1920–1960*. New York: Garland, 1990.

Marsh, Margaret S. *Anarchist Women, 1870–1920*. Philadelphia: Temple University Press, 1981.

Marshall, Peter. *Demanding the Impossible: A History of Anarchism*. London: HarperCollins, 1992.

Massa, Ann. "Black Women in the 'White City.'" *Journal of American Studies* 8 (December 1974): 319–37.

Massafra, Angelo, ed. *Il mezzogiorno preunitario*. Bari: Dedalo, 1988.

Mathias, Elizabeth, and Richard Raspa. *Italian Folktales in America: The Verbal Art of an Immigrant Women*. Detroit: Wayne State University Press, 1985.

Matos-Rodríguez, Félix V., and Pedro Juan Hernández, eds. *Pioneros: Puerto Ricans in New York City, 1896–1948*. New York: Center for Puerto Rican Studies, 2001.

Matthei, Linda Miller. "Gender and International Labor Migration: A Networks Approach." *Social Justice* 23:3 (Fall 1996): 38–54.

Maynes, Mary Jo. "Gender, Labor, and Globalization in Historical Perspective: European Spinsters in the International Textile Industry, 1750–1900." *Journal of Women's History* 15:4 (Winter 2004): 47–66.

McAlister, E. "The Madonna of 115th Street Revisited: Vodou and Haitian Catholicism in the Age of Transnationalism." In *Gatherings in Diaspora: Religious Communities and the New Immigration*, edited by R. S. Warner and J. G. Wittner. Philadelphia: Temple University Press, 1998.

McBride, Paul. "The Italian-Americans and the Catholic Church: Old and New Perspectives, A Review Essay." *Italian Americana* 1:2 (Spring 1975): 270–86.

McClintock, Anne. *Imperial Leather: Race, Gender and Sexuality in the Colonial Conquest*. New York: Routledge, 1995.

McClymer, John F. "The Federal Government and the Americanization Movement, 1915–1924." *Prologue: The Journal of the National Archives* 10 (Spring 1978): 22–41.

———. "Gender and the 'American Way of Life': Women and the Americanization Movement." *Journal of American Ethnic History* 10 (Spring 1991): 3–12.

McDowell, Linda. *Gender, Identity, and Place: Understanding Feminist Geographies*. Cambridge: Polity Press, 1999.

McGirr, Lisa. "The Passion of Sacco and Vanzetti: A Global History." *Journal of American History* 93:4 (March 2007): 1085–1115.

———. *Suburban Warriors: The Origins of the New American Right*. Princeton, N.J.: Princeton University Press, 2002.

McKibben, Carol Lynn. *Beyond Cannery Row: Sicilian Women, Immigration, and Community in Monterey, California, 1915–1999*. Urbana: University of Illinois Press, 2006.

Meazza, Renata, and Guido Bertolotti. "La macchina rituale: I gigli di Nola al Lorenteggo." In *Mondo popolare in Lombardia: Milano e il suo territorio*, edited by Franco Della Peruta et al. Milan: Silvana Editoriale, 1985.

Merithew, Caroline A. "Anarchist Motherhood: Toward the Making of a Revolutionary Proletariat in Illinois Coal Towns." In *Women, Gender, Transnational Lives: Italian Workers of the World*, edited by Donna Gabaccia and Franca Iacovetta. Toronto: University of Toronto, 2002.

———. "Making the Italian Other: Blacks, Whites, and the Inbetween in the 1895 Spring Valley, Illinois, Race Riot." In *Are Italians White? How Race Is Made in America*, edited by Jennifer Guglielmo and Salvatore Salerno. New York: Routledge, 2003.

Merli, Stefano. *Proletariato di fabbrica e capitalismo industriale. Il caso italiano, 1880–1900*. Florence: La Nuova Italia Editrice, 1972.

Meyer, Gerald. "Annette T. Rubinstein: 95th Birthday Celebration." *Monthly Review*, May 2005. <<www.monthlyreview.org/annetterubinstein.htm>>

———. "Frank Sinatra: The Popular Front and an American Icon." *Science & Society* 66:3 (Fall 2002): 311–35.

———. "Italian Americans and the American Communist Party." In *The Lost World of Italian American Radicalism*, edited by Philip V. Cannistraro and Gerald Meyer. Westport, Conn.: Praeger, 2003.

———. "Italian Harlem: America's Most Italian Little Italy." In *The Italians of New York: Five Centuries of Struggle and Achievement*, edited by Philip Cannistraro. Milan: Mondadori, 1999.

———. "Leonard Covello (1887–1982): An Italian American's Contribution to the Education of Minority-Culture Students." *Italian American Review* 5:1 (Fall 1996): 36–44.

———. "Leonard Covello: A Pioneer in Bilingual Education." *Bilingual Review* 12:1–2 (January–August 1985): 55–61.

———. "Leonard Covello and Vito Marcantonio: A Lifelong Collaboration for Progress." *Italica* 62:1 (Spring 1985): 54–66.

———. *Vito Marcantonio: Radical Politician, 1902–1954*. Albany: State University of New York Press, 1989.

———. "When Sinatra Came to Harlem: The 1945 'Race Riot' at Benjamin Franklin High School." In *Are Italians White? How Race Is Made in America*, edited by Jennifer Guglielmo and Salvatore Salerno. New York: Routledge, 2003.

Meyerowitz, Joanne J. *Women Adrift: Independent Wage-Earning Women in Chicago, 1880–1930*. Chicago: University of Chicago Press, 1988.

Michney, Todd M. "Race, Violence, and Urban Territoriality: Cleveland's Little Italy and the 1966 Hough Uprising." *Journal of Urban History* 32:3 (March 2006): 404–28.

Milkman, Ruth, ed. *Women, Work and Protest: A Century of U.S. Women's Labor History*. Boston: Routledge and Kegan Paul, 1985.

Miller, Sally M. *Race, Ethnicity, and Gender in Early Twentieth-Century American Socialism*. New York: Garland Publishing, 1996.

Minh-ha, Trinh T. *Woman, Native, Other: Writing Postcoloniality and Feminism*. Bloomington: Indiana University Press, 1989.

Mink, Gwendolyn. *Old Labor and New Immigrants in American Political Development: Union, Party, and State, 1875–1920*. Ithaca: Cornell University Press, 1986.

Mirabal, Nancy Raquel. "'No country but the one we must fight for': The Emergence of an Antillean Nation and Community in New York City, 1860–1901." In *Mambo Montage: The Latinization of New York*, edited by Agustín Laó-Montes and Arlene Dávila. New York: Columbia University Press, 2001.

Modell, John, and Tamara K. Hareven. "Urbanization and the Malleable Household: An Examination of Boarding and Lodging in American Families." *Journal of Marriage and the Family* 35 (1973): 467–79.

Moe, Nelson. "Altro che Italia! Il Sud dei piemontesi (1860–61)." *Meridiana; Revista di storia e scienze sociali* 15 (1992): 53–89.

———. "The Emergence of the Southern Question in Villari, Franchetti, and Sonnino." In *Italy's "Southern Question": Orientalism in One Country*, edited by Jane Schneider. New York: Berg, 1998.

———. "'This is Africa': Ruling and Representing Southern Italy, 1860–61." In *Making and Remaking Italy: The Cultivation of National Identity around the Risorgimento*, edited by Albert Russell Ascoli and Krystyna von Henneberg. New York: Oxford, 2001.

———. *The View from Vesuvius: Italian Culture and the Southern Question*. Berkeley: University of California Press, 2002.

Mohanty, Chandra Talpade. *Feminism without Borders: Decolonizing Theory, Practicing Solidarity.* Durham: Duke University Press, 2003.

Molfese, Franco. *Storia del brigantaggio dopo l'unità d'Italia.* Milan: Feltrinelli, 1964.

———. "Il brigantaggio nel Mezzogiorno dopo l'unità d'Italia." *Archivio storico per la Calabria e la Lucania* 47 (1975): 99–136.

———. "La repressione del brigantaggio post-unitario nel mezzogiorno continentale (1860–70)." *Archivio storico per le province napoletane* 101 (1983): 48–62.

Molyneux, Maxine. "No God, No Boss, No Husband: Anarchist Feminism in Nineteenth-Century Argentina." *Latin American Perspectives* 13:1 (Winter 1986): 119–45.

Montgomery, David. *Workers' Control in America: Studies in the History of Work, Technology, and Labor Struggles.* Cambridge: Cambridge University Press, 1979.

Moody, J. Carroll, and Alice Kessler-Harris, eds. *Perspectives on American Labor History: Toward a Synthesis.* DeKalb: Northern Illinois University Press, 1989.

Moore, Laurence R. "Flawed Fraternity: American Socialist Response to the Negro, 1901–1912." *Historian* 32 (November 1969): 1–18.

Morelli, Anne. "Nestore's Wife? Work, Family, and Militancy in Belgium." In *Women, Gender, and Transnational Lives: Italian Workers of the World,* edited by Donna Gabaccia and Franca Iacovetta. Toronto: University of Toronto Press, 2002.

Morgan, Jennifer L. "Male Travelers, Female Bodies, and the Gendering of Racial Ideology, 1500–1770." In *Bodies in Contact: Rethinking Colonial Encounters in World History,* edited by Tony Ballantyne and Antoinette Burton. Durham: Duke University Press, 2005.

Mormino, Gary, and George Pozzetta. "The Cradle of Mutual Aid: Immigrant Cooperative Societies in Ybor City." *Tampa Bay History* 7:2 (1985): 36–55.

———. "Immigrant Women in Tampa: The Italian Experience, 1890–1930." *Florida Historical Quarterly* 61 (July 1982): 296–312.

———. *The Immigrant World of Ybor City: Italians and Their Latin Neighbors in Tampa, 1885–1985.* Urbana: University of Illinois Press, 1987.

———. "Italian Immigrants and the American Catholic Church: A Parish Perspective." *Studi emigrazione* (1989): 95–108.

———. "The Reader Lights the Candle." *Labor's Heritage* 5:1 (Spring 1993): 4–27.

———. "Spanish Anarchism in Tampa, Florida, 1886–1931." In *"Struggle a Hard Battle": Essays on Working-Class Immigrants,* edited by Dirk Hoerder. DeKalb: Northern Illinois University Press, 1986.

Morokvasic, Mirjana. "Birds of Passage Are Also Women." *International Migration Review* 18:4 (1984): 886–907.

Morrison, Toni. *Playing in the Dark: Whiteness and the Literary Imagination.* Cambridge, Mass.: Harvard University Press, 1992.

Moss, Leonard, and Stephen C. Cappannari. "The Black Madonna: An Example of Cultural Borrowing." *Scientific Monthly* 73 (June 1953): 319–24.

———. "In Quest of the Black Virgin: She Is Black Because She Is Black." In *Mother Worship: Theme Variations,* edited by James J. Preston. Chapel Hill: University of North Carolina, 1982.

Moss, Pamela. *Feminisms in Geography: Rethinking Space, Place, and Knowledges.* Lanham, Md.: Rowman & Littlefield, 2007.

Moya, José. *Cousins and Strangers: Spanish Immigrants in Buenos Aires, 1850–1930.* Berkeley: University of California Press, 1998.

———. "Italians in Buenos Aires's Anarchist Movement: Gender Ideology and Women's Participation, 1890–1910." In *Women, Gender, and Transnational Lives: Italian Workers of the World,* edited by Donna Gabaccia and Franca Iacovetta. Toronto: University of Toronto Press, 2002.

Mumford, Kevin. *Interzones: Black/White Sex Districts in Chicago and New York in the Early Twentieth Century.* New York: Columbia University Press, 1997.

Munck, Ronaldo, with Ricardo Falcon and Bernardo Galitelli. *Argentina: From Anarchism to Peronism; Workers, Unions and Politics, 1855–1985*. London: Zed Books, 1987.

Muncy, Robyn. *Creating a Female Dominion in American Reform, 1890–1935*. New York: Oxford University Press, 1991.

Murphy, Paul L. *The Passaic Textile Strike of 1926*. Belmont, Calif.: Wadsworth, 1974.

Murray, Robert K. *Red Scare: A Study in National Hysteria, 1919–1920*. Minneapolis: University of Minnesota Press, 1955.

Nadel, Stanley. "Reds versus Pinks: A Civil War in the International Ladies' Garment Workers' Union." *New York History* 66 (January 1985): 48–72.

Nadell, Pamela S., ed. *American Jewish Women's History: A Reader*. New York: New York University Press, 2003.

Naison, Mark. *Communists in Harlem during the Depression*. New York: Grove Press, 1983.

———. "From Eviction Resistance to Rent Control: Tenant Activism in the Great Depression." In *The Tenant Movement in New York City, 1904–1984*, edited by Ronald Lawson. New Brunswick: Rutgers University Press, 1986.

Naples, Nancy A. *Grassroots Warriors: Activist Mothering, Community Work, and the War on Poverty*. New York: Routledge, 1998.

Nasaw, David. *Children of the City: At Work and at Play*. New York: Anchor/Doubleday, 1985.

Nelli, Humbert S. *The Business of Crime: Italians and Syndicate Crime in the United States*. Chicago: University of Chicago Press, 1981.

———. *From Immigrants to Ethnics: The Italian Americans*. New York: Oxford University Press, 1983.

———. "The Hennessy Murder and the Mafia in New Orleans." *Italian Quarterly* 19 (1975): 77–95.

Nelson, Bruce. "Class, Race, and Democracy in the CIO: The 'New' Labor History Meets the 'Wages of Whiteness.'" *International Review of Social History* 41 (1996): 351–74.

———. *Workers on the Waterfront: Seamen, Longshoremen, and Unionism in the 1930s*. Urbana: University of Illinois Press, 1988.

Newman, Louise Michele. *White Women's Rights: The Racial Origins of Feminism in the United States*. New York: Oxford University Press, 1999.

Ngai, Mae M. *Impossible Subjects: Illegal Aliens and the Making of Modern America*. Princeton, N.J.: Princeton University Press, 2004.

Nicolosi, Pietro. *50 anni di cronaca siciliana (1900–1950)*. Milan: Flaccovio, 1975.

Nicotri, Gaspare. *Storia della Sicilia nelle rivoluzioni e rivolte*. New York, 1934.

Nievo, Ippolito. *Lettere garibaldine*. Edited by Andreina Ciceri. Turin: Edizioni della Fondazione Giovanni Agnelli, 1961.

Noether, Emiliana P. "The Silent Half: Le Contadine del Sud before the First World War." In *The Italian Immigrant Woman in North America*, edited by Betty Boyd Caroli et al. Toronto: Multicultural History Society of Ontario, 1978.

Nord, Deborah Epstein. "The Social Explorer as Anthropologist: Victorian Travelers among the Urban Poor." In *Visions of the Modern City: Essays in History, Art, and Literature*, edited by William Sharpe and Leonard Wallock. Baltimore: Johns Hopkins University Press, 1987.

Norwood, Stephen H. "Bogalusa Burning: The War against Biracial Unionism in the Deep South, 1919." *Journal of Southern History* 63:3 (August 1977): 591–628.

Novelli, Cecilia Dau. "I vescovi e la questione femminile (1900–1917)." *Rivista di storia e letteratura religiosa* 30 (1984): 439–40.

Novotny, Ann. *Strangers at the Door: Ellis Island, Castle Garden, and the Great Migration to America*. Riverside, Conn.: Chatham Press, 1971.

Oboler, Suzanne. "History on the Move . . . Revisiting *The Suffering of the Immigrants* from the Latino/a Perspective." *Qualitative Sociology* 29:1 (March 2006): 117–26.

Odem, Mary. *Delinquent Daughters: Policing Adolescent Female Sexuality in the United States, 1885–1920*. Chapel Hill: University of North Carolina Press, 1997.

O'Farrell, Brigid. "A Stitch in Time: The New Deal, the International Ladies' Garment Workers' Union, and Mrs. Roosevelt." *Transatlantica* 1 (2006): 2–14.

O'Farrell, Brigid, and Joyce L. Kornbluh. *Rocking the Boat: Union Women's Voices, 1915–1975*. New Brunswick: Rutgers University Press, 1996.

Olive i Serret, Enric. "El movimiento anarquista catalan y la masoneria en el ultimo tercio del siglo XIX." In *La masoneria en la historia de España*, edited by José A. Ferrer Benimeli. Zaragoza: Gobierno de Aragón, 1985.

Omi, Michael, and Howard Winant. *Racial Formation in the United States from the 1960s to the 1980s*. New York: Routledge & Kegan Paul, 1986.

Ong, Aihwa. "The Gender and Labor Politics of Postmodernity." In *The Politics of Culture in the Shadow of Capital*, edited by Lisa Lowe and David Lloyd. Durham: Duke University Press, 1997.

Orleck, Annelise. *Common Sense and a Little Fire: Women and Working-Class Politics in the United States, 1900–1965*. Chapel Hill: University of North Carolina Press, 1995.

———. *Storming Caesar's Palace: How Black Mothers Fought Their Own War on Poverty*. Boston: Beacon Press, 2005.

———. "'We Are That Mythical Thing Called the Public': Militant Housewives during the Great Depression." *Feminist Studies* 10:1 (Spring 1993): 147–72.

Orsi, Robert A. *Between Heaven and Earth: The Religious Worlds People Make and the Scholars Who Study Them*. Princeton: Princeton University Press, 2005.

———. "The Fault of Memory: 'Southern Italy' in the Imagination of Immigrants and the Lives of Their Children in Italian Harlem, 1920–1945." *Journal of Family History* 15:2 (1990): 133–47.

———. *The Madonna of 115th Street: Faith and Community in Italian Harlem, 1880–1950*. New Haven: Yale University Press, 1985.

———. "The Religious Boundaries of an 'Inbetween' People: Street *Feste* and the Problem of the Dark-Skinned Other in Italian Harlem." *American Quarterly* 44:3 (September 1992): 313–47.

———. *Thank You, St. Jude: Women's Devotion to the Patron Saint of Hopeless Causes*. New Haven: Yale University Press, 1996.

Ortíz, Altagracia. "'En la aguja y el pedal eché la hiel': Puerto Rican Women in the Garment Industry of New York City, 1920–1980." In *Puerto Rican Women and Work: Bridges in Transnational Labor*, edited by Altagracia Ortíz. Philadelphia: Temple University Press, 1996.

———. "Puerto Rican Workers in the Garment Industry of New York City, 1920–1960." In *Labor Divided: Race and Ethnicity in United States Labor Struggles, 1835–1960*, edited by Robert Asher and Charles Stephenson. Albany: State University of New York Press, 1990.

Osborne, James D. "Italian Immigrants and the Working Class in Paterson: The Strike of 1913 in Ethnic Perspective." In *New Jersey's Ethnic Heritage*, edited by Paul Stellhorn. Trenton: New Jersey Historical Commission, 1978.

———. "Paterson: Immigrant Strikers and the War of 1913." In *At the Point of Production: The Local History of the IWW*, edited by Joseph R. Conlin. Westport, Conn.: Greenwood Press, 1981.

Osofsky, Gilbert. *Harlem: The Making of a Ghetto; Negro New York, 1890–1930*. New York: Harper and Row, Harper Torchbooks, 1971.

Ottanelli, Fraser M. "'If Fascism Comes to America We Will Push It Back into the Ocean': Italian American Anti-Fascism in the 1920s and 1930s." In *Italian Workers of the World: Labor Migration and the Formation of Multiethnic States*, edited by Donna R. Gabaccia and Fraser M. Ottanelli. Urbana: University of Illinois Press, 2001.

Painter, Nell Irvin. *Standing at Armageddon: The United States, 1877–1919*. New York: W. W. Norton, 1987.

Palazzi, Maura. *Donne sole. Storie dell'altra faccia dell'Italia tra antico regime e società contemporanea*. Milan: Bruno Mondadori, 1997.

———. "Famiglia, lavoro e proprietà: Le donne nella società contadina fra continuità e trasformazione." In *Società rurale e ruoli femminili in Italia tra ottocento e novecento*, edited by Paola Corti. Bologna: Il Mulino, 1991.

Palombo, Fabio. *Camillo Di Sciullo anarchico e tipografo di Chieti*. Chieti: Biblioteca del *Pensiero*, 1996.

Panaccione, Andrea, ed. *Sappi che oggi è la tua festa . . . per la storia del 1 maggio*. Venice: Marsilio Editori, 1986.

Panettieri, José. "Modelli ideologici: Immigrazione, lavoro e ciclo economico nelle origini dei movimento operaio in Argentina." In *La riscoperta delle Americhe*, edited by Vanni Blengino et al. Milan: Nicola Teti Editore, 1992.

Panizza, Letizia, and Sharon Wood, eds. *A History of Women's Writing in Italy*. New York: Cambridge University Press, 2000.

Panofsky, Gianna S. "A View of Two Major Centers of Italian Anarchism in the United States: Spring Valley and Chicago, Illinois." In *Italian Ethnics: Their Languages, Literature, and Lives*, edited by Dominic Candeloro, Fred L. Gardaphé, and Paolo A. Giordano. Staten Island: American Italian Historical Association, 1990.

Papa, Emilio R., ed. *Il positivismo e la cultura italiana*. Milan: Franco Angeli, 1985.

Park, Robert E., and Herbert A. Miller. *Old World Traits Transplanted*. New York: Harper and Bros., 1921.

Parkhurst, Helen. *Undertow: The Story of a Boy Called Tony*. New York: Farrar, Straus, 1963.

Parreñas, Rhacel Salazar. *Servants of Globalization: Women, Migration and Domestic Work*. Stanford: Stanford University Press, 2001.

Parrino, Maria. "Breaking the Silence: Autobiographies of Italian Immigrant Women." *Storia Nord Americana* 5:1 (1988): 81–98.

Pasquinelli, Carla, ed. *Antropologia culturale e questione meridionale: Ernesto De Martino e il dibattito sul mondo popolare subalterno negli anni 1948–1955*. Florence: La nuova Italia, 1977.

Passerini, Luisa. "Storia delle donne, storia di genere: Contributi di merito e problemi aperti." In *Società rurale e ruoli femminili in Italia tra ottocento e novecento*, edited by Paola Corti. Bologna: Il Mulino, 1991.

Patriarca, Silvana. "How Many Italies? Representing the South in Official Statistics." In *Italy's "Southern Question": Orientalism in One Country*, edited by Jane Schneider. New York: Berg, 1998.

———. *Numbers and Nationhood: Writing Statistics in Nineteenth-Century Italy*. New York: Cambridge University Press, 1996.

Pautasso, Luigi. "La donna italiana durante il periodo fascista in Toronto." In *The Italian Immigrant Woman in North America*, edited by Betty Boyd Caroli et al. Toronto: Multicultural History Society of Ontario, 1978.

Payne, Charles. *I've Got the Light of Freedom: The Organizing Tradition and the Mississippi Freedom Struggle*. Berkeley: University of California Press, 1996.

Pearce, Roy Harvey. *Savagism and Civilization: A Study of the Indian and the American Mind*. Baltimore: Johns Hopkins University Press, 1965.

Peck, Gunther. *Reinventing Free Labor: Padrones and Immigrant Workers in the North American West, 1880–1930*. New York: Cambridge University Press, 2000.

———. "White Slavery and Whiteness: A Transnational View of the Sources of Working-Class Radicalism and Racism." *Labor Studies in Working-Class History of the Americas* 1:2 (2004): 41–63.

Peiss, Kathy. *Cheap Amusements: Working Women and Leisure in Turn-of-the-Century New York*. Philadelphia: Temple University Press, 1986.

Pérez, Emma. *The Decolonial Imaginary: Writing Chicanas into History*. Bloomington: Indiana University Press, 1999.

Perlmann, Joel. *Ethnic Differences: Schooling and Social Structure among the Irish, Italians, Jews and Blacks in an American City, 1880–1935*. Cambridge: Cambridge University Press, 1988.

Pernicone, Nunzio. "Anarchism in Italy, 1872–1900." In *Italian American Radicalism*, edited by Rudolph J. Vecoli. New York: American Italian Historical Association, 1973.

———. "Carlo Tresca and the Sacco-Vanzetti Case." *Journal of American History* 66:3 (December 1979): 535–47.

———. *Carlo Tresca: Portrait of a Rebel*. New York: Palgrave, 2005.

———. *Italian Anarchism, 1864–1892*. Princeton, N.J.: Princeton University Press, 1993.

———. "Italian Immigrant Radicalism in New York." In *The Italians of New York: Five Centuries of Struggle and Achievement*, edited by Philip V. Cannistraro. New York: New York Historical Society, 1999.

———. "The Italian Labor Movement." In *Modern Italy: A Topical History Since 1861*, edited by Edward R. Tannenbaum and Emiliana P. Noether. New York: New York University Press, 1974.

———. "Luigi Galleani and the Italian Anarchist Terrorism in the United States." *Studi emigrazione* 30:111 (September 1993): 469–89.

Petkov, Steven, and Leonard Mustazza, eds. *The Frank Sinatra Reader*. New York: Oxford University Press, 1995.

Petrusewicz, Marta. *Latifundum: Moral Economy and Material Life in a Nineteenth-Century Periphery*. Ann Arbor: University of Michigan, 1996.

Petry, Ann. *The Street*. Boston: Houghton Mifflin, 1946.

Pick, Daniel. "The Faces of Anarchy: Lombroso and the Politics of Criminal Science in Post-Unification Italy." *History Workshop* 21 (1986): 60–86.

———. *Faces of Degeneration: A European Disorder, 1848–1918*. New York: Cambridge University Press, 1989.

Pickering-Iazzi, Robin W. *Unspeakable Women: Selected Short Stories Written by Italian Women during Fascism*. New York: Feminist Press, 1993.

———, ed. *Mothers of Invention: Women, Italian Fascism, and Culture*. Minneapolis: University of Minnesota Press, 1995.

Pignone, Charles. *The Sinatra Treasures*. New York: Bulfinch Press, 2004.

Pirovano, Carlo, ed. *Modern Italy: Images and History of a National Identity*. Milan: Electa Editrice, 1982.

Pitkin, Thomas Monroe, and Francesco Cordaso. *The Black Hand: A Chapter in Ethnic Crime*. Totowa, N.J.: Littlefield, Adams, 1977.

Pittenger, Mark. "'What's on the Worker's Mind': Class Passing and the Study of the Industrial Workplace in the 1920s." *Journal of the History of the Behavioral Sciences* 39:2 (April 2003): 143–61.

———. "A World of Difference: Constructing the 'Underclass' in Progressive America." *American Quarterly* 49:1 (1997): 26–65.

Piven, Frances Fox, and Richard Cloward. *Poor People's Movements: Why They Succeed, How They Fail*. New York: Vintage, 1977.

Pozzetta, George E. "Immigrants and Craft Arts: Scuole d'Industrie Italiane." In *The Italian Immigrant Woman in North America*, edited by Betty Boyd Caroli et al. Toronto: Multicultural History Society of Ontario, 1978.

———. "Italians and the General Strike of 1910." In *Pane e Lavoro: The Italian American Working Class*, edited by George Pozzetta. Staten Island: American Italian Historical Association, 1980.

———. "The Italian Immigrant Press of New York City: The Early Years, 1880–1915." *Journal of Ethnic History* 1:3 (Fall 1973): 32–46.

———. "The Mulberry District of New York City: The Years before World War One." In *Little Italies in North America*, edited by Robert F. Harney and J. Vincenza Scarpaci. Toronto: Multicultural History Society of Ontario, 1981.

———, ed. *Pane e Lavoro: The Italian American Working Class*. Staten Island: American Italian Historical Association, 1978.

Pozzetta, George E., and Bruno Ramirez, eds. *The Italian Diaspora across the Globe: Essays in Honor of Robert F. Harney (1939–1989)*. Toronto: Multicultural History Society of Ontario, 1992.

Prandi, Carlo. *La religione popolare, fra potere e tradizione*. Milan: Franco Angeli, 1983.

Preston, William, Jr. *Aliens and Dissenters: Federal Suppression of Radicals, 1903–1933*. New York: Harper and Row, 1963.

Primeggia, Salvatore, and Joseph A. Varacalli. "The Sacred and the Profane among Italian-American Catholics: The Giglio Feast." *International Journal of Politics, Culture, and Society* 9:3 (Spring 1996): 423–49.

Principe, Angelo. "Glimpses of Lives in Canada's Shadow: Insiders, Outsiders, and Female Activism in the Fascist Era." In *Women, Gender, and Transnational Lives: Italian Workers of the World*, edited by Donna Gabaccia and Franca Iacovetta. Toronto: University of Toronto Press, 2002.

Procacci, Giovanna. "State Coercion and Worker Solidarity in Italy (1915–1918): The Moral and Political Content of Social Unrest." *Annali Fondazione Feltrinelli* 27 (1990–91): 145–77.

Pucci, Idanna. *The Trials of Maria Barbella*. New York: Random House, 1996.

Pugliese, Stanislao. *Fascism, Antifascism, and the Resistance in Italy: 1919 to the Present*. Lanham: Rowman & Littlefield, 2004.

———, ed. *Frank Sinatra: History, Identity, and Italian American Culture*. New York: Palgrave Macmillan, 2004.

———, ed. *Italian Fascism and Antifascism: A Critical Anthology*. Manchester: Manchester University Press, 2001.

Qureshi, Sadiah. "Displaying Sara Baartman, the 'Hottentot Venus.'" *History of Science* 42 (2004): 233–57.

Rafter, Nicole Hahn. *Creating Born Criminals*. Urbana: University of Illinois Press, 1997.

———. "Criminal Anthropology in the United States." *Criminology* 30 (November 1992): 525–45.

Rafter, Nicole Hahn, and Mary Gibson, eds. *Criminal Woman, the Prostitute, and the Normal Woman*, by Cesare Lombroso and Guglielmo Ferrero. Durham: Duke University Press, 2004.

Ragionieri, Ernesto. "Italiani all'estero ed emigrazione di lavoratori italiani: Un tema di storia del movimento operaio." *Belfagor* 17 (November 1962): 641–69.

Ragusa, Kym. *The Skin between Us: A Memoir of Race, Beauty, and Belonging*. New York: W. W. Norton, 2006.

Ramella, Franco. "In fabbrica e in famiglia: Le operaie italiane a Paterson, New Jersey." *Quaderni storici* 33:2 (August 1998): 383–414.

———. "Reti sociali e mercato del lavoro in un caso di emigrazione. Gli operai italiani e gli altri a Paterson, New Jersey." *Annali Fondazione Feltrinelli* (1997): 741–75.

Ramirez, Bruno. "Immigration, Ethnicity, and Political Militance: Patterns of Radicalism in the Italian-American Left, 1880–1930." In *From the "Melting Pot" to Multiculturalism: The Evolution of Ethnic Relations in the United States and Canada*, edited by Valeria Gennaro Lerda. Rome: Bulzoni Editore, 1990.

———. *On the Move: French-Canadians and Italian Migrants in the North Atlantic Economy, 1860–1914*. Toronto: University of Toronto Press, 1990.

Randall, Margaret. *Hunger's Table*. Watsonville, Calif.: Papier-Mache Press, 1997.

Ransby, Barbara. *Ella Baker and the Black Freedom Movement*. Chapel Hill: University of North Carolina Press, 2003.

Ravera, Camilla. *Breve storia del movimento femminile in Italia*. Rome: Editori Riuniti, 1978.

Reeder, Linda. "When the Men left Sutera: Sicilian Women and Mass Migration 1880–1920." In *Women, Gender, and Transnational Lives: Italian Workers of the World*, edited by Donna Gabaccia and Franca Iacovetta. Toronto: University of Toronto Press, 2002.

———. *Widows in White: Migration and the Transformation of Rural Italian Women, Sicily, 1880–1920*. Toronto: University of Toronto Press, 2003.

Reichl, Ruth. *Tender at the Bone*. New York: Random House, 1998.

Reimer, Eleanor S., and John C. Fout. *European Women: A Documentary History, 1789–1945*. Brighton: Harvester Press, 1983.

Renda, Francesco. *I fasci siciliani (1892–94)*. Turin: Einaudi, 1977.

————. *Socialisti e cattolici in Sicilia*. Rome: Sciascia, 1972.

Reppetto, Thomas A. *American Mafia: A History of Its Rise to Power*. New York: H. Holt, 2004.

Revelli, Nuto. *L'anello forte. La Donna: Storie di vita contadina*. Turin: Giulio Einaudi, 1985.

Richards, David A. J. *Italian American: The Racializing of an Ethnic Identity*. New York: New York University Press, 1999.

Richards, Vernon. *Errico Malatesta, His Life and Ideas*. London: Freedom Press, 1965.

Rieder, Jonathan. *Canarsie: The Jews and Italians of Brooklyn against Liberalism*. Cambridge, Mass.: Harvard University Press, 1985.

Rigazio, Francesco. "Alberto Guabello, Firmino Gallo e altri anarchici di Mongrando nella catena migratoria dal Biellese a Paterson, N.J." *Archivi e storia* 23–24 (2004): 143–258.

Rimanelli, Marco, and Sheryl L. Postman, eds. *The 1891 New Orleans Lynching and U.S.-Italian Relations: A Look Back*. New York: Peter Lang, 1992.

Rodrigues, Edgar, and Andrea Chersi, eds. *Lavoratori italiani in Brasile: Un secolo di storia sociale dell'altra Italia*. Casalvelino Scalo, Salerno: Galzerano, 1985.

Rodríguez, Clara E. "Puerto Ricans: Between Black and White." In *The Puerto Rican Struggle: Essays on Survival in the U.S.*, edited by Clara E. Rodríguez, Virginia Sánchez Korrol, and José Oscar Alers. Maplewood, N.J.: Waterfront Press, 1980.

Rodríguez-Morazzani, Roberto P. "Beyond the Rainbow: Mapping the Discourse on Puerto Ricans and 'Race.'" *Centro: Journal of the Center for Puerto Rican Studies* 8:1–2 (1996): 151–69.

————. "Puerto Rican Political Generations in New York: Pioneros, Young Turks, and Radicals." *Centro: Journal of the Center for Puerto Rican Studies* 4:1 (1991–92): 96–116.

Roediger, David R. *Black on White: Black Writers on What It Means to Be White*. New York: Schocken Books, 1998.

————. *Colored White: Transcending the Racial Past*. Berkeley: University of California Press, 2002.

————. *Towards the Abolition of Whiteness: Essays on Race, Politics, and Working Class History*. New York: Verso, 1994.

————. *The Wages of Whiteness: Race and the Making of the American Working-Class*. New York: Verso, 1991.

————. *Working toward Whiteness: How America's Immigrants Became White*. New York: Basic Books, 2005.

Rogin, Michael. *Blackface, White Noise: Jewish Immigrants in the Hollywood Melting Pot*. Berkeley: University of California Press, 1996.

Romano, Salvatore Francesco. *La Sicilia nell'ultimo ventennio del secolo XIX*. Palermo: Flaccovio, 1958.

————. *Storia dei fasci siciliani*. Bari: Giuseppe Laterza e Figli, 1959.

Rosen, Ruth. *The Lost Sisterhood: Prostitution in America, 1900–1918*. Baltimore: Johns Hopkins University Press, 1982.

Rosenblum, Walter, et al. *America and Lewis Hine: Photographs 1904–1940*. New York: Aperture, 1977.

Rosoli, Gianfausto. "Le popolazioni di origine italiana oltreoceano." *Altreitalie* 2 (November 1989): 3–35.

Rosoli, Gianfausto, et al., eds. *Un secolo di emigrazione italiana: 1876–1976*. Rome: Centro Studi Emigrazione, 1978.

Rudwick, Elliott M., and August Meier. "Black Man in the 'White City': Negroes and the Columbian Exposition, 1893." *Phylon* 26 (Winter 1965): 354–61.

Ruiz, Vicki L. *Cannery Women, Cannery Lives: Mexican Women, Unionization, and the California Food Processing Industry, 1930–1950*. Albuquerque: University of New Mexico Press, 1987.

————. *From Out of the Shadows: Mexican Women in Twentieth Century America*. New York: Oxford University Press, 1987.

Rupp, Leila. *Worlds of Women: The Making of an International Women's Movement*. Princeton, N.J.: Princeton University Press, 1997.

Rydell, Robert W. *All the World's a Fair: Visions of Empire at American International Expositions, 1876–1916*. Chicago: University of Chicago Press, 1984.

Said, Edward. *Orientalism*. New York: Vintage Books, 1978.

Salerno, Salvatore. "'No God, No Master': Italian Anarchists and the IWW." In *The Lost World of Italian American Radicalism: Culture, Politics, History*, edited by Philip V. Cannistraro and Gerald Meyer. Westport, Conn.: Praeger, 2003.

———. "'I Delitti della Razza Bianca' (The Crimes of the White Race): Italian Immigrant Anarchists' Racial Discourse as Crime." In *Are Italians White? How Race Is Made in America*, edited by Jennifer Guglielmo and Salvatore Salerno. New York: Routledge, 2003.

———. "Paterson's Italian Anarchist Silk Workers and the Politics of Race." *Working USA: The Journal of Labor and Society* 8:5 (September 2005): 611–25.

———. *Red November, Black November: Culture and Community in the Industrial Workers of the World*. New York: State University of New York Press, 1989.

———, ed. *Direct Action and Sabotage: Three Classic IWW Pamphlets from the 1910s*. Chicago: Charles H. Kerr Press, 1997.

Salomone-Marino, Salvatore. *Customs and Habits of the Sicilian Peasants*. East Brunswick: Associated University Presses, 1981.

Salvatore, Nick. "Lest We Forget: The Paintings of Ralph Fasanella." *Labor's Heritage* 1:4 (October 1989): 25–26.

Salvatore, Ricardo D. "Criminology, Prison Reform, and the Buenos Aires Working Class." *Journal of Interdisciplinary History* 23:2 (Autumn 1992): 279–99.

Sánchez, George J. "'Go After the Women': Americanization and the Mexican Immigrant Woman, 1915–1929." In *Unequal Sisters: A Multicultural Reader in U.S. Women's History*, edited by Ellen Carol DuBois and Vicki L. Ruiz. New York: Routledge, 1990.

Sánchez-González, Lisa. *Boricua Literature: A Literary History of the Puerto Rican Diaspora*. New York: New York University Press, 2001.

Sánchez-Korrol, Virginia. *From Colonia to Community: The History of Puerto Ricans in New York City, 1917–1948*. Westport, Conn.: Greenwood Press, 1983.

Sangiuolo, Luisa. *Il brigantaggio nella provincia di Benevento, 1860–1880*. Benevento: De Martino, 1975.

Sanjek, Roger. *The Future of Us All: Race and Neighborhood Politics in New York City*. Ithaca: Cornell University Press, 1998.

Santarelli, Enzo. *Il socialismo anarchico in Italia*. Milan: Feltrinelli, 1959.

Sante, Luc. *Low Life: Lures and Snares of Old New York*. New York: Farrar, Straus and Giroux, 2003.

Santomauro, Angelica M., and Evelyn M. Hershey. *Around Haledon: Immigration and Labor*. Mount Pleasant, S.C.: Arcadia Publishing, 2008.

Sapelli, Giulio, ed. *Il movimento cooperativo in Italia. Storia e problemi*. Torino: Einaudi, 1981.

Sassen, Saskia. "Strategic Instantiations of Gendering in the Global Economy." In *Gender and U.S. Immigration: Contemporary Trends*, edited by Pierrette Hondagneu-Sotelo. Berkeley: University of California Press, 1999.

Satriani, Luigi M. Lombardi. *Il folklore come cultura di contestazione*. Messina: Peloritana, 1968.

Saunders, George. "The Magic of the South: Popular Religion and Elite Catholicism in Italian Ethnology." In *Italy's "Southern Question": Orientalism in One Country*, edited by Jane Schneider. Oxford: Berg, 1998.

Scaraffia, Lucetta. "'Christianity Has Liberated Her and Placed Her alongside Man in the Family': From 1850 to 1988 (Mulieris Dignitatem)." In *Women and Faith: Catholic Religious Life in Italy from Late Antiquity to the Present*, edited by Lucetta Scaraffia and Gabriella Zarri. Cambridge, Mass.: Harvard University Press, 1999.

Scarpaci, Jean A. (Vincenza). "Angela Bambace and the International Ladies' Garment Workers'

Union: The Search for an Elusive Activist." In *Pane e Lavoro: The Italian American Working Class*, edited by George E. Pozzetta. Staten Island: American Italian Historical Association, 1978.

———. "La Contadina: The Plaything of the Middle Class Woman Historian." *Journal of Ethnic History* 9 (Summer 1981): 21–38.

———. "Walking the Color Line: Italian Immigrants in Rural Louisiana, 1880–1910." In *Are Italians White? How Race Is Made in America*, edited by Jennifer Guglielmo and Salvatore Salerno. New York: Routledge, 2003.

———, ed. *The Interaction of Italians and Jews in America*. Baltimore: Towson State College, 1974.

Schacter, Gustav. *The Italian South: Economic Development in Mediterranean Europe*. New York: Random House, 1965.

Schiller, Nina Glick, Linda Basch, and Cristina Blanc-Szanton, eds. *Nations Unbound: Transnational Projects, Postcolonial Predicaments, and Deterritorialized Nation-States*. New York: Gordon & Breach, 1994.

———, eds. *Towards a Transnational Perspective on Migration: Race, Class, Ethnicity and Nationalism Reconsidered*. New York: Academic Press, 1992.

Schneider, Eric C. *Vampires, Dragons, and Egyptian Kings: Youth Gangs in Postwar New York*. Princeton, N.J.: Princeton University Press, 1999.

Schneider, Jane C. "Of Vigilance and Virgins: Honor, Shame, and Access to Resources in Mediterranean Societies." *Ethnology* 9:1 (1971): 1–24.

———. "Trousseau as Treasure: Some Contradictions in Late Nineteenth-Century Change in Sicily." In *Beyond the Myths of Culture: Essays in Cultural Materialism*, edited by Eric B. Ross. New York: Academic Press, 1980.

———, ed. *Italy's "Southern Question": Orientalism in One Country*. New York: Berg, 1998.

Schneider, Jane C., and Peter T. Schneider. *Culture and Political Economy in Western Sicily*. New York: Academic Press, Inc., 1976.

———. *Festival of the Poor: Fertility Decline and the Ideology of Class in Sicily, 1860–1980*. Tucson: University of Arizona Press, 1996.

Schoener, Allen. *New York: An Illustrated History of the People*. New York: W. W. Norton, 1998.

Schofield, Ann. "Rebel Girls and Union Maids: The Woman Question in the Journals of the AFL and IWW, 1905–1920." *Feminist Studies* 9:2 (Summer 1983): 335–58.

———. "The Uprising of the 20,000: The Making of a Labor Legend." In *A Needle, a Bobbin, a Strike: Women Needleworkers in America*, edited by Joan M. Jenson and Sue Davidson. Philadelphia: Temple University Press, 1984.

Schwartz, Joel. *The New York Approach: Robert Moses, Urban Liberals, and Redevelopment of the Inner City*. Columbus: Ohio State University Press, 1993.

Schwarz, Judith. *Radical Feminists of Heterodoxy: Greenwich Village, 1912–1940*. Lebanon, N.H.: New Victoria Publishers, 1982.

Sciascia, Leonardo. "Le zie di Sicilia," Interview with Franca Leosini. *L'Espresso* (Rome), 27 January 1974, 10.

Scott, James C. *Domination and the Arts of Resistance: Hidden Transcripts*. New Haven: Yale University Press, 1990.

———. *Weapons of the Weak: Everyday Forms of Peasant Resistance*. New Haven: Yale University Press, 1985.

Scott, Joan W. "Experience." In *Feminists Theorize the Political*, edited by Judith Butler and Joan W. Scott. New York: Routledge, 1992.

———. *Gender and the Politics of History*. New York: Columbia University Press, 1988.

Scuro, Jennifer. "Exploring Personal History: A Case Study of an Italian Immigrant Woman." *Oral History Review* 31:1 (Winter–Spring 2004): 43–69.

Seixas, Peter. "Lewis Hine: From 'Social' to 'Interpretive' Photographer." *American Quarterly* 39:3 (Autumn 1987): 381–409.

Seller, Maxine Schwartz. "The Uprising of Twenty Thousand: Sex, Class, and Ethnicity in the Shirtwaist Makers' Strike of 1909." In *"Struggle a Hard Battle": Essays on Working-Class Immigrants*, edited by Dick Hoerder. DeKalb: Northern Illinois University Press, 1986.

Shange, Ntozake. *If I Can Cook/You Know God Can*. Boston: Beacon Press, 1999.

———. *Sassafras, Cypress and Indigo*. New York: St. Martin's Press, 1982.

Shankman, Arnold. "The Image of the Italian in the Afro-American Press, 1886–1936." *Italian Americana* 4:1 (1978): 30–49.

Sharpley-Whiting, T. Denean. *Black Venus: Sexualized Savages, Primal Fears, and Primitive Narratives in French*. Durham: Duke University Press, 1992.

Shohat, Ella, and Robert Stam. *Unthinking Eurocentrism: Multiculturalism and the Media*. New York: Routledge, 1994.

Shor, Francis. "The IWW and Oppositional Politics in World War I: Pushing the System beyond the Limits." *Radical History Review* 46 (Winter 1996): 74–94.

———. "'Virile Syndicalism' in Comparative Perspective: A Gender Analysis of the IWW in the United States and Australia." *Radical History Review* 56 (Fall 1999): 65–77.

Siebert, Renate. *Cenerentola non abita più qui: Uno sguardo di donne sulla realtà meridionale*. Turin: Rosenberg & Sellier, 1999.

———. *"È femmina, però è bella": Tre generazioni di donne al sud*. Turin: Rosenberg & Sellier, 1991.

Silberstein, Carina Frid de. "Immigrants and Female Work in Argentina: Questioning Gender Stereotypes and Constructing Images—The Case of the Italians, 1879–1900." In *Mass Migration to Modern Latin America*, edited by Samuel L. Baily and Eduardo José Míguez. Wilmington, Del.: Scholarly Resources, 2003.

———. "Immigrantes y trabajo en Argentina: Discutiendo estereotipos y construyendo imagenes. El caso de las italianas (1870–1900)." In *As idéias e os números do gênero: Argentina, Brasil e Chile no século XIX*, ed. Eni Mesquita de Samara. São Paulo: Editora Hucitec, 1997.

———. "Mas allá del crisol: Matrimonios, estrategias familiares y redes sociales en dos generaciones de italianos y españoles (Rosario, 1895–1925)." *Estudios migratorios latinoamericanos* 28 (1994): 481–520.

———. "Migrants, Farmers, and Workers: Italians in the Land of Ceres." In *Italy's Workers of the World: Labor, Migration, and the Making of Multi-Ethnic Nations*, edited by Donna R. Gabaccia and Fraser M. Ottanelli. Urbana: University of Illinois Press, 2001.

Silverman, Sydel. *Three Bells of Civilization: The Life of an Italian Hill Town*. New York: Columbia University Press, 1975.

Sitkoff, Harvard. *A New Deal for Blacks*. Oxford: Oxford University Press, 1981.

Skidmore, Thomas E. *Black into White: Race and Nationality in Brazilian Thought*. New York: Oxford University Press, 1974.

Sklar, Kathryn Kish. *Florence Kelley and the Nation's Work: The Rise of Women's Political Culture, 1830–1900*. New Haven: Yale University Press, 1995.

Slaughter, Jane. *Women and the Italian Resistance, 1943–1945*. Denver: Arden Press, 1997.

Slotkin, Richard. *Regeneration through Violence: The Mythology of the American Frontier, 1600–1860*. Middletown: Wesleyan University Press, 1983.

Smith, Denis Mack. *Modern Italy: A Political History*. Ann Arbor: University of Michigan Press, 1997.

———. *Mussolini's Roman Empire*. New York: Penguin Books, 1976.

———. "The Peasants Revolt in Sicily, 1860." In *Victor Emanuel Cavour and the Risorgimento*. New York: Oxford University Press, 1971.

———. "Regionalism." In *Modern Italy*, edited by Edward R. Tannenbaum and Emiliana P. Noether. New York: New York University Press, 1974.

Smith, Judith E. *Family Connections: A History of Italian and Jewish Lives in Providence, Rhode Island, 1900–1940*. Albany: State University of New York Press, 1985.

———. "Italian Mothers, American Daughters: Changes in Work and Family Roles." In *The Italian

Immigrant Woman in North America, edited by Betty Boyd Caroli et al. Toronto: Multicultural History Society of Ontario, 1978.

———. "Our Own Kind: Family and Community Networks." *Radical History Review* 17 (1978): 99–120.

Smith, Robert Courtney. *Mexican New York: Transnational Lives of New Immigrants*. Berkeley: University of California Press, 2006.

Smith, Timothy L. "Immigrant Social Aspirations and American Education, 1880–1930." *American Quarterly* 21:3 (Autumn 1969): 523–43.

Smith-Rosenberg, Carroll. *Disorderly Conduct: Visions of Gender in Victorian America*. New York: Knopf, 1985.

Snowden, Frank M. *Naples in the Time of Cholera, 1884–1911*. Cambridge: Cambridge University Press, 1995.

———. *Violence and the Great Estates in the South of Italy: Apulia, 1900–1922*. Cambridge: Cambridge University Press, 1986.

Snyder, Robert E. "Women, Wobblies, and Workers' Rights: The 1912 Textile Strike in Little Falls, New York." *New York History* 60 (January 1979): 29–57.

Soderlund, Gretchen. "Covering Urban Vice: The *New York Times*, 'White Slavery,' and the Construction of Journalistic Knowledge." *Critical Studies in Media Communication* 19:4 (December 2002): 438–60.

Solomon, Mark. *My Cry Was Unity: Communists and African Americans, 1917–1936*. Jackson: University Press of Mississippi, 1998.

Soyer, Daniel, ed. *A Coat of Many Colors: Immigration, Globalization, and Reform in New York City's Garment Industry*. New York: Fordham University Press, 2005.

Spackman, Barbara. *Fascist Virilities: Rhetoric, Ideology, and Social Fantasy in Italy*. Minneapolis: University of Minnesota Press, 1996.

———. "Fascist Women and the Rhetoric of Virility." In *Mothers of Invention: Women, Italian Fascism, and Culture*, edited by Robin Pickering-Iazzi. Minneapolis: University of Minnesota Press, 1995.

Spergel, Irving. *Racketville, Slumtown, Haulburg: An Exploratory Study of Delinquent Subcultures*. Chicago: University of Chicago Press, 1964.

Stange, Maren. *Symbols of Ideal Life: Social Documentary Photography in America, 1890–1950*. New York: Cambridge University Press, 1989.

Stange, Margit. *Personal Property: Wives, White Slaves, and the Market in Women*. Baltimore: Johns Hopkins University Press, 1998.

Stansall, Christine. "The Origins of the Sweatshop: Women and Early Industrialization in New York City." In *Working-Class America: Essays on Labor, Community, and American Society*, edited by Michael E. Frisch and Daniel J. Walkowitz. Urbana: University of Illinois Press, 1983.

Starr, Dennis J. *The Italians of New Jersey: A Historical Introduction and Bibliography*. Newark: New Jersey Historical Society, 1985.

Stave, Bruce M. *From the Old Country: An Oral History of the European Migration to America*. New York: Twayne, 1994.

Stein, Leon. *Out of the Sweatshop: The Struggle for Industrial Democracy*. New York: Quadrangle/New York Times Book Co., 1977.

———. *The Triangle Fire*. Philadelphia: J. B. Lippincott, 1962.

Stenning, Alison. "For Working Class Geographies." *Antipode* 40:1 (2008): 9–14.

Stepan, Nany Leys. *The Hour of Eugenics: Race, Gender, and Nation in Latin America*. Ithaca: Cornell University Press, 1991.

Stepan, Nancy Leys, and Sander L. Gilman. "Appropriating the Idioms of Science: The Rejection of Scientific Racism." In *The Bounds of Race: Perspectives on Hegemony and Resistance*, edited by Dominick La Capra. Ithaca: Cornell University Press, 1991.

Stewart, Donald. *A Short History of East Harlem*. New York: Museum of the City of New York, 1972.

Stocking, George W., Jr. *Race, Culture, and Evolution*. New York: Free Press, 1968.

Stolberg, Benjamin. *Tailor's Progress*. New York: Doubleday, Doran, 1944.

Stoler, Ann Laura. "Carnal Knowledge and Imperial Power: Gender, Race, and Morality in Colonial Asia." In *Gender and the Crossroads of Knowledge: Feminist Anthropology in the Postmodern Era*, edited by Micaela di Leonardo. Berkeley: University of California Press, 1991.

———, ed. *Haunted by Empire: Geographies of Intimacy in North American History*. Durham: Duke University Press, 2006.

Strom, Susan Hartman. "Challenging 'Woman's Place': Feminism, the Left and Industrial Unionism in the 1930s." *Feminist Studies* 9 (Summer 1983): 359–86.

Sugrue, Thomas J. *The Origins of the Urban Crisis: Race and Inequality in Postwar Detroit*. Princeton, N.J.: Princeton University Press, 1996.

Swanton, Philip S., ed. *Silk City: Studies on the Paterson Silk Industry, 1860–1940*. Newark: New Jersey Historical Society, 1985.

Szasz, Ferenc M., and Ralph F. Bogardus. "The Camera and the American Social Conscience: The Documentary Photography of Jacob A. Riis." *New York History* 55:4 (1974): 409–36.

Tax, Meredith. *The Rising of the Women: Feminist Solidarity and Class Conflict, 1880–1917*. New York: Monthly Review Press, 1980.

Terborg-Penn, Rosalyn. "Discontented Black Feminists: Prelude and Postscript to the Passage of the Nineteenth Amendment." In *Decades of Discontent: The Women's Movement, 1920–1940*, edited by Lois Scharf and Joan M. Jensen. Westport, Conn.: Greenwood Press, 1983.

Terkel, Studs. *"The Good War": An Oral History of World War Two*. New York: Pantheon Books, 1984.

Teti, Vito. "Noti sul comportamenti delle donne sole degli 'americani' durante la prima emigrazione in Calabria." *Studi emigrazione* 24 (1987): 13–46.

———. *La razza maledetta: Origini del pregiudizio antimeridionale*. Rome: Manifesto, 1993.

Thomas, Piri. *Down These Mean Streets*. New York: Vintage, 1967.

Thompson, Fred, and Patrick Murfin. *The IWW — Its First Seventy Years — 1905–1975*. Chicago: IWW, 1976.

Till, Antonia. *Loaves and Wishes*. New York: Random House, 1992.

Tilly, Louise A. "I Fatti di Maggio: The Working Class of Milan and the Rebellion of 1898." In *Modern European Social History*, edited by Robert J. Bezucha. Lexington, Mass.: D. C. Heath, 1972.

———. "Paths of Proletarianization: Organization of Production, Sexual Division of Labor and Women's Collective Action." *Signs* 7:2 (1981): 400–17.

———. *Politics and Class in Milan, 1881–1901*. New York: Oxford University Press, 1992.

Tilly, Louise A., and Joan W. Scott. *Women, Work, and Family*. New York: Holt, Rinehart & Winston, 1978.

Tirabassi, Maddalena. "Bringing Life to History: Italian Ethnic Women in the United States." In *The Italian Diaspora, Migration across the Globe*, edited by George Pozzetta and Bruno Ramirez. Toronto: Multicultural History Society of Ontario, 1992.

———. "Italiane ed emigrate." *Altreitalie* 9 (January–June 1993): 139–51.

Tomasi, Silvano M. *Piety and Power: The Role of the Italian Parishes in the New York Metropolitan Area, 1890–1930*. New York: Center for Migration Studies, 1975.

Tomasi, Silvano M., and Edward C. Stabili. *Italian Americans and Religion: An Annotated Bibliography*. 2nd ed. New York: Center for Migration Studies, 1992.

Topp, Michael Miller. "The Italian-American Left: Transnationalism and the Quest for Unity." In *The Immigrant Left in the United States*, edited by Paul Buhle and Dan Georgakas. New York: State University of New York Press, 1996.

———. "'It is Providential that There Are Foreigners Here': Whiteness and Masculinity in the Making of Italian American Syndicalist Idenitity." In *Are Italians White? How Race Is Made in America*, edited by Jennifer Guglielmo and Salvatore Salerno. New York: Routledge, 2003.

———. *The Sacco and Vanzetti Case: A Brief History with Documents*. Boston: Bedford/St. Martin's, 2005.

———. *Those without a Country: The Political Culture of Italian American Syndicalists*. Minneapolis: University of Minnesota, 2001.

Trapani, Franca. *Le brigantesse*. Rome: Editrice Nanni Canesi, 1968.

Trento, Angelo. "'Wherever We Work, That Land Is Ours': The Italian Anarchist Press and Working-Class Solidarity in São Paulo." In *Italy's Workers of the World: Labor, Migration, and the Making of Multi-ethnic Nations*, edited by Donna R. Gabaccia and Fraser M. Ottanelli. Urbana: University of Illinois Press, 2001.

Tricarico, Donald. *The Italians of Greenwich Village: The Social Structure and Transformation of an Ethnic Community*. New York: Center for Migration Studies, 1984.

Tripp, Anne Huber. *The IWW and the Paterson Silk Strike of 1913*. Urbana: University of Illinois Press, 1987.

Trupia, Jole Scavone. "La donna e gli studi siciliani di folklore dell'800." In *Donne e società*, edited by Janne Vibaek. Palermo: Arti Grafiche Siciliane, 1982.

Turcato, Davide. "Italian Anarchism as a Transnational Movement, 1885–1915." *International Review of Social History* 52 (December 2007): 407–44.

Turner, Kay. *Beautiful Necessity: The Art and Meaning of Women's Altars*. New York: Thames & Hudson, 1999.

Tuttle, William M. *Race Riot: Chicago in the Red Summer of 1919*. New York: Antheneum, 1970.

Tyler, Gus. *"Look for the Union Label": A History of the International Ladies' Garment Workers' Union*. Armonk, N.Y.: Sharpe, 1995.

Valle Ferrer, Norma. *The Story of Luisa Capetillo: A Pioneer Puerto Rican Feminist*. New York: Peter Lang, 2006.

Vanek, Wilda M. "Piero Gobetti and the Crisis of the 'Primo Dopoguerra.'" *Journal of Modern History* 37:1 (March 1965): 1–17.

Varacalli, Joseph A. "The Changing Nature of the 'Italian Problem' in the Catholic Church of the United States." *Faith and Reason* 12:1 (Spring 1986): 28–73.

———. *Models and Images of Catholicism in Italian Americana*. Stony Brook, N.Y.: Forum Italicum, 2004.

Varacalli, Joseph A., et al., eds. *The Saints in the Lives of Italian-Americans*. Stony Brook: Forum Italicum, 1999.

Vecchio, Diane C. *Merchants, Midwives and Laboring Women: Italian Immigrants in Urban America*. Urbana: University of Illinois Press, 2006.

Veccia, Theresa R. "'My Duty as a Woman': Gender Ideology, Work, and Working-Class Women's Lives in São Paulo, Brazil, 1900–1950." In *The Gendered Worlds of Latin American Women Workers*, edited by John D. French and Daniel James. Durham: Duke University Press, 1997.

Vecoli, Rudolph J. "Anthony Capraro and the Lawrence Strike of 1919." In *Pane e Lavoro: The Italian American Working Class*, edited by George E. Pozzetta. Staten Island: American Italian Historical Association, 1978.

———. "Cult and Occult in Italian-American Culture: The Persistence of a Religious Heritage." In *Immigrants and Religion in Urban America*, edited by Randall Miller and Thomas Marzik. Philadelphia: Temple University Press, 1977.

———. "'Free Country': The American Republic Viewed by the Italian Left, 1880–1920." In *In the Shadow of the Statue of Liberty: Immigrants, Workers, and Citizens in the American Republic*, edited by Marianne Debouzy. Saint Denis: Presses Universitaires de Vincennes, 1988.

———. *The Go Betweens: The Lives of Immigrant Children*. Minneapolis: University of Minnesota, University Art Museum, 1986.

———. "The Italian Diaspora, 1876–1976." In *The Cambridge Survey of World Migration*, edited by Robin Cohen. Cambridge: Cambridge University Press, 1995.

―――. "The Italian Immigrant Press and the Construction of Social Reality, 1850–1920." In *Print Culture in a Diverse America*, edited by James P. Danky and Wayne A. Wiegand. Urbana: University of Illinois Press, 1998.

―――. "Italian Immigrants in the United States Labor Movement from 1880–1929." In *Gli italiani fuori d'Italia, gli emigrati italiani nei movimenti operai dei paesi d'adozione 1880–1940*, edited by Bruno Bezzo. Milan: Franco Angeli, 1983.

―――. "The Making and Un-making of an Italian Working Class in the United States, 1915–1945." In *The Lost World of Italian American Radicalism: Politics, Culture, History*, edited by Philip V. Cannistraro and Gerald Meyer. Westport, Conn.: Praeger, 2003.

―――. "Pane e giustizia." *La Parola del Popolo* 26 (September–October 1976): 58–59.

―――. *The People of New Jersey*. Princeton, N.J.: D. Van Nostrand, 1965.

―――. "Prelates and Peasants: Italian Immigrants and the Catholic Church." *Journal of Social History* 2 (Spring 1969): 217–68.

―――. "Primo Maggio in the United States: An Invented Tradition of the Italian Anarchists." In *May Day Celebration*, edited by Andrea Panaccione. Venice: Marsilio Editore, 1988.

―――, ed. *Italian American Radicalism: Old World Origins and New World Developments*. Staten Island: American Italian Historical Association, 1972.

Ventresca, Robert A., and Franca Iacovetta. "Virgilia D'Andrea: The Politics of Protest and the Poetry of Exile." In *Women, Gender, and Transnational Lives: Italian Workers of the World*, edited by Donna Gabaccia and Franca Iacovetta. Toronto: University of Toronto Press, 2002.

Ventresco, Fiorello B. "Crises and Unity: The Italian Radicals in America in the 1920s." *Ethnic Forum* 15:1–2 (1995): 12–34.

―――. "Italian-Americans and the Ethiopian Crisis." *Italian Americana* 6:1 (Fall–Winter 1980): 4–27.

―――. "The Struggle of the Italian Anti-Fascist Movement in America." *Ethnic Forum* 6:1–2 (1986): 17–48.

Venturini, Nadia. "Leonard Covello and Intercultural Education at Benjamin Franklin High School in the 1930s." *Italian American Review* 9:1 (Spring–Summer 2002): 73–110.

―――. "Nascita di un complesso di edilizia popolare a New York: East River Houses." *Storia urbana* 75 (1996): 53–83.

―――. *Neri e Italiani ad Harlem. Gli anni trenta e la guerra d'Etiopia*. Rome: Edizioni Lavoro, 1990.

―――. "'Over the Years People Don't Know': Italian Americans and African Americans in Harlem in the 1930s." In *Italian Workers of the World: Labor Migration and the Formation of Multiethnic States*, edited by Donna R. Gabaccia and Fraser M. Ottanelli. Urbana: University of Illinois Press, 2001.

Verdicchio, Pasquale. *Bound by Distance: Rethinking Italian Nationalism through the Diaspora*. Madison, N.J.: Fairleigh Dickinson University Press, 1997.

Vezzosi, Elisabetta. "Class, Ethnicity, and Acculturation in *Il Proletario*: The World War One Years." In *The Press of Labor Migrants in Europe and North America, 1880s to 1930s*, edited by Christiane Harzig and Dirk Hoerder. Bremen: Labor Newspaper Preservation Project, 1985.

―――. "La Federazione Socialista Italiana del Nord America tra autonomia e scioglimento nel sindacato industriale, 1911–1921." *Studi emigrazione* 73 (March 1984): 81–110.

―――. "Radical Ethnic Brokers: Immigrant Socialist Leaders in the United States between Ethnic Community and the Larger Society." In *Italian Workers of the World: Labor Migration and the Formation of Multiethnic States*, edited by Donna R. Gabaccia and Fraser M. Ottanelli. Urbana: University of Illinois Press, 2001.

Vibaek, Janne, ed. *Donne e società*. Palermo: Arti Grafiche Siciliane, 1982

Viviano, Frank. *Blood Washes Blood: The True Story of Love, Murder, and Redemption under the Sicilian Sun*. New York: Pocket Books, 2001.

Wakefield, Dan. *Island in the City: The World of Spanish Harlem*. Boston: Houghton Mifflin, 1959.

Waldinger, Roger. "Another Look at the International Ladies' Garment Workers' Union: Women, Industry Structure, and Collective Action." In *Women, Work and Protest: A Century of U.S. Women's Labor History*, edited by Ruth Milkman. Boston: Routledge and Kegan Paul, 1985.

———. *Through the Eye of the Needle: Immigrants and Enterprise in New York's Garment Trades.* New York University Press, 1986.

Ware, Caroline. *Greenwich Village, 1920–1930.* New York: Harper and Row, 1965.

Warner, Marina. *Alone of All Her Sex: The Myth and Cult of the Virgin Mary.* New York: Knopf and Random House, 1976.

Watkins-Owens, Irma. *Blood Relations: Caribbean Immigrants and the Harlem Community, 1900–1930.* Bloomington: Indiana University Press, 1996.

Watson, Patrick. *Fasanella's City.* New York: Alfred A. Knopf, 1973.

Webb, Clive. "The Lynching of Sicilian Immigrants in the American South, 1886 to 1910." *American Nineteenth Century History* 3:1 (Spring 2002): 45–76.

Weigand, Kate. *Red Feminism: American Communism and the Making of Women's Liberation.* Baltimore: Johns Hopkins University Press, 2002.

Weinberg, Sydney Stahl. *The World of Our Mothers: The Lives of Jewish Immigrant Women.* New York: Schocken Books, 1988.

Wertheimer, Barbara Mayer. *We Were There: The Story of Working Women in America.* New York: Pantheon Books, 1977.

Wexler, Laura. *Tender Violence: Domestic Visions in an Age of U.S. Imperialism.* Chapel Hill: University of North Carolina Press, 2000.

Wilder, Craig Steven. *A Covenant with Color: Race and Social Power in Brooklyn.* New York: Columbia University Press, 2000.

Willcox, Walter F. *International Migrations.* New York: National Bureau of Economic Research, 1931.

Williams, Patricia J. "The Ethnic Scarring of American Whiteness." In *The House That Race Built: Black Americans, U.S. Terrain,* edited by Wahneema Lubiano. New York: Pantheon Books, 1997.

Williams, Phyllis H. *South Italian Folkways in Europe and America.* New Haven: Yale University Press, 1938.

Wills, Jane. "Mapping Class and Its Political Possibilities." *Antipode* 40:1 (2008): 25–30.

Wing, Adrien Katherine, ed. *Global Critical Race Feminism: An International Reader.* New York: New York University Press, 2000.

Wolfe, Joel. "Anarchist Ideology, Worker Practice: The 1917 General Strike and the Formation of São Paulo's Working Class." *Hispanic American Historical Review* 71:4 (November 1991): 809–46.

———. "There Should Be Dignity: São Paulo's Women Textile Workers and the Strike of the 300,000." In *Workers' Control in Latin America,* edited by Jonathan Brown. Chapel Hill: University of North Carolina Press, 1997.

———. *Working Women, Working Men: São Paulo and the Rise of Brazil's Industrial Working Class, 1900–1955.* Durham: Duke University Press, 1993.

Wong, Elaine Gale. *The Negro in the Apparel Industry.* Philadelphia: University of Pennsylvania Press, 1974.

X, Malcolm. *Malcolm X on Afro-American History.* Expanded and illustrated edition. New York: Pathfinder Press, 1970.

Yans-McLaughlin, Virginia. *Family and Community: Italian Immigrants in Buffalo, 1880–1930.* Ithaca: Cornell University Press, 1971.

———, ed. *Immigration Reconsidered: History, Sociology, and Politics.* New York: Oxford University Press, 1990.

Yu, Renqiu. *To Save China, to Save Ourselves: The Chinese Hand Laundry Alliance of New York.* Philadelphia: Temple University Press, 1992.

Yung, Judy. "The Social Awakening of Chinese American Women as Reported in *Chung Sai Yat Po,* 1900–1911." In *Unequal Sisters,* edited by Ellen Carol DuBois and Vicki Ruiz. New York: Routledge, 1990.

———. *Unbound Feet: A Social History of Chinese Women in San Francisco.* Berkeley: University of California, 1995.

Zane, Marcello. "Anarchia e nostalgia: La diaspora degli anarchici in Brasile dopo l'esperienza della colonia sperientale Cecilia di Giovanni Rossi, 1890–1907." In *L'America degli italiani*, edited by Vanni Blengino. Rome: Bulzoni, 1986.

Zaninelli, Sergio, ed. *Le lotte nelle campagne dalla grande crisi agricola primo dopoguerra, 1880–1921.* Milan: Celuc, 1971.

Zappi, Elda Gentili. *If Eight Hours Seem Too Few: Mobilization of Women Workers in the Italian Rice Fields.* Albany: State University of New York Press, 1991.

Zappia, Charles. "Unionism and the Italian American Worker: The Politics of Anti-Communism in the International Ladies' Garment Workers' Union." In *Italian Americans through the Generations*, edited by Rocco Caporale. Staten Island: American Italian Historical Association, 1986.

Zaretz, Charles E. *The Amalgamated Clothing Workers of America: A Study in Progressive Trades Unionism.* New York: Ancon, 1934.

Zedner, Lucia. "Women, Crime, and Penal Responses: A Historical Account." In *Crime and Justice: A Review of Research*, edited by Michael Tonry. Chicago: University of Chicago Press, 1991.

Zolberg, Aristide R. *A Nation by Design: Immigration Policy in the Fashioning of America.* Cambridge, Mass.: Harvard University Press, 2006.

Dissertations, Theses, and Unpublished Papers

Altarelli, Carlo. "History and Present Conditions of the Italian Colony of Paterson, New Jersey." M.A. thesis, Columbia University, 1911.

Anderson, Nels. "The Social Antecedents of a Slum: A Study of the East Harlem Area of Manhattan Island, New York City." Ph.D. diss., New York University, 1930.

Bencivenni, Marcella. "Italian American Radical Culture in New York City: The Politics and Arts of the Sovversivi, 1890–1940." Ph.D. diss., City University of New York, 2003.

———. "Writing from the Left: The Voices of Italian Immigrant Radical Women in the United States, 1890s–1930s." Paper presented at "History/Gender/Migration" Conference, École Normale Supérieure and Université Paris, 27–29 March, 2006.

Berkowitz, Michael. "Americanization and Ethnicity in an Italian Community: Immigrants, Education, and Politics in East Harlem, 1920–1941." Senior thesis, Princeton University, 1987.

Caponetto, Rosetta Giuliani. "'Going Out of Stock': Mulattoes and Levantines in Italian Literature and Cinema of the Fascist Period." Ph.D. diss., University of Connecticut, 2008.

Carroll, Tamar. "Grassroots Feminism: Direct Action Organizing and Coalition Building in New York City, 1955–1995." Ph.D. diss., University of Michigan, 2007.

Carter, Robert Frederick, "Pressure from the Left: The American Labor Party, 1936–1944." Ph.D. diss., Syracuse University, 1965.

Cimilluca, Salvatore. "The Natural History of East Harlem from Eighteen Eighty to the Present Day." M.A. thesis, New York University of Education, 1931.

D'Ambrosio, Paul S. "Ralph Fasanella (1914–1997): The Making of a Working-Class Artist." Ph.D. diss., Boston University, 2001.

De Gregorio, Michele. "'This Is Not Your Union until You Speak Our Language': Language Locals and the Exclusion of African American and Puerto Rican Workers in the New York City Garment Industry." Unpublished paper, 2007.

Dodyk, Delight. "Winder, Warpers, and Girls on the Loom: A Study of Women in the Paterson Silk Industry and their Participation in the General Strike of 1913." M.A. thesis, Sarah Lawrence College, 1979.

Ealham, Chris. "Parallel Lives and Clashing Iberian Identities in the 'Capital of the World': Pedro Esteve's Anarchist Internationalism versus Francisco Jose Navarro's Colonialist-Entrepreneurialism,

1855–1925." Paper presented at "Rethinking the Iberian Atlantic," University of Liverpool, 20–22 April 2007.

Elwood, Sophie L. Frignoca. "The Roots and Results of Radicalism among Piedmontese Silk Workers, 1848–1913." Certificate of Advanced Study Thesis, Wesleyan University, 1988, American Labor Museum/Botto House.

Furio, Colomba M. "Immigrant Women and Industry: A Case Study; The Italian Immigrant Women and the Garment Industry, 1880–1950." Ph.D. diss., New York University, 1979.

Gabaccia, Donna R. "Italians Everywhere, Gender, and American Whiteness." Paper presented at "Defining Whiteness: Race, Class and Gender Perspectives in North American History" Symposium, University of Toronto, 13–15 October 2000.

Gore, Dayo Folayan. "To Light a Candle in a Gale Wind: Black Women Radicals and Post-War Politics." Ph.D. diss., New York University, 2003.

Guglielmo, Grace. "My Antonia." Unpublished essay, 1988.

Gurowsky, David. "Factional Disputes within the ILGWU, 1919–1928." Ph.D. diss., State University of New York at Binghamton, 1978.

Johnson, Val Marie. "Defining 'Social Evil': Moral Citizenship and Governance in New York City, 1890–1920." Ph.D. diss., New School for Social Research, 2002.

Laurentz, Robert. "Racial/Ethnic Conflict in the New York Garment Industry, 1933–1980." Ph.D. diss., State University of New York at Binghamton, 1980.

Lenzi, Richard. "'Saturated with Anarchy': The Galleanist Movement in New Britain, Connecticut, 1910–1919." Unpublished paper, 1999.

Mapelli, Mario. "Giuseppe Ciancabilla, uno sguardo sull'anarchismo italoamericano di inizio novecento." Tesi di Lauria in Storia. Università Statale di Milano, 1999.

Montalto, Nicholas. "The Forgotten Dream: A History of the Intercultural Education Movement, 1924–1941." Ph.D. diss., University of Minnesota, 1977.

Pozzetta, George Enrico. "The Italians of New York City, 1890–1914." Ph.D. diss., University of North Carolina, 1974.

Quaggiotto, Pamela. "Altars of Food to St. Joseph: Women's Ritual in Sicily." Ph.D. diss., Columbia University, 1988.

Salerno, Salvatore. "B. Emilio." Unpublished paper, 2001.

———. "The Black Madonna and Italian American Identity." Unpublished paper, 1985.

Shell-Weiss, Melanie R. "'I washed, I ironed, I cooked, and I done everything.' A Comparative Study of Female Migrant Silk Workers in Saint Chamond, France and Paterson, New Jersey, 1865–1914." Paper presented at the Social Science History Association annual meeting, Washington, D.C., 16–19 October 1997.

Sione, Patrizia. "Industrial Work, Militancy, and Migrations of Northern Italian Workers in Europe and Paterson, New Jersey, 1880–1913." Ph.D. diss., State University of New York, Binghamton, 1992.

Veccia, Theresa Rita. "Family and Factory: Textile Work and Women's Lives in São Paulo, Brazil, 1880–1940." Ph.D. diss., University of Wisconsin–Madison, 1995.

Vecoli, Rudolph J. "The African Connection: Italian Americans and Race." Paper presented at the American Italian Historical Association annual meeting, Cleveland, Ohio, 13–15 November 1997, IHRC Print Collection.

———. "The Go-Betweens: An Historical Perspective on Immigrant Children." Keynote address, National Advisory Panel, Immigrant Students Project, National Coalition of Advocates for Students, 12 March 1987, Cambridge, Mass., IHRC Print Collection.

———. "Giuseppe Ciancabilla." Unpublished paper, n.d., IHRC Print Collection.

Vellon, Peter. "A Darker Past: The Development of Italian American Racial Consciousness, 1886–1920." Ph.D. diss., City University of New York, 2003.

Waltzer, Kenneth Alan. "The American Labor Party: Third Party Politics in New Deal–Cold War New York, 1936–1954." Ph.D. diss., Harvard University, 1977.

Zappia, Charles. "Unionism and the Italian American Worker: A History of the New York City 'Italian Local' in the International Ladies' Garment Workers' Union, 1900–1933." Ph.D. diss., University of California, Berkeley, 1994.

Videorecordings

Linciati: Lynchings of Italians in America, DVD, 51 min., 2004, directed by Heather M. Hartley. Distributed by National Film Network.

Metropolitan Avenue. VHS, 16 mm, 56 min. 1985, directed by Christine Noschese. Distributed by New Day Films, Harriman, N.Y.

Nine Good Teeth. DVD, 80 min., 2004, directed by Alex Halpern. Distributed by Pickled Punk Pictures.

The Sixth Section/La Sexta Sección, DVD, 27 min., 2003, directed by Alex Rivera.

Acknowledgments

The inspiration for this project began in a graduate course on Chicana feminisms with historian Deena J. González well over a decade ago. My immense thanks to Deena and everyone in that course, for helping me to realize the power of telling our own community histories: Alicia Gaspar de Alba, Dana Flores, Aurora Morcillo, and Cynthia Gomez. The support and guidance of Jane Slaughter, Sandrea Gonzales, Teresa Córdova, Victoria C. González-Rivera, Kintree Whitecloud, and Craze, at that time, was also fundamental. Since then, Donna Gabaccia has been this project's most treasured adviser. I am deeply thankful for her friendship, wisdom, and encouragement throughout the entire journey. David Roediger has also been a cherished adviser, and I am grateful for his many insights, leads, and support.

My deepest gratitude also extends to Melchia Crowne, mentor and wise woman extraordinaire. The wisdom that she and Ana Lups have bestowed upon me has greatly enriched my life and this book in the process. Rachel Maxine Koch has been there from the very beginning, offering her limitless wisdom and love. My heartfelt thanks also to my other sister writers: Kym Ragusa, Edvige Giunta, Caterina Romeo, Phyllis Capello, Rosette Capotorto, Ronnie Mae Painter, Nancy Carnevale, and Loryn Lipari. Their friendship and that of my many other New York–New Jersey *compagne*—including Louise DeSalvo, Nicole Lanzillotto, Annie Lanzillotto, Mary Ciuffitelli, Franca Barchiesi, Monica Calabritto, B. Amore, Flavia Alaya, Arlene Holpp Scala, Stephanie Romeo, Maria Lisella, Michela Musolino, Jenna Capeci, Chiara Montalto, and my many other *sorelle* in the Malìa Collective—provided me with a sense of solidarity when I needed it most.

In addition, this project benefited immensely from the advice of two great historians: Nan Enstad and Annelise Orleck each read the entire manuscript several times, offering detailed, thoughtful, and rigorous suggestions, and I am forever thankful for their close and considered readings. I am also indebted to my dear friend Salvatore Salerno. It was he who brought Maria Roda and the Paterson anarchists to my attention, and his friendship, intellectual insights, and generosity, greatly enriched this project. Franca Iacovetta, Joseph Sciorra, and Nunzio Pernicone also read drafts along the way and graciously helped me to strengthen my analysis. Peter McGovern's warm spirit and generous reading of the final draft helped me to cross the finish line.

My thanks also to Majdi Abu-Sharar, Stefano Albertini, Federica Anichini, Vivek Bald,

Marcella Bencivenni, Lori J. Berman and John Collins, Emily Bernard, Giorgio Bertellini, Marianne Buehler, Darcy Buerkle, Philip Cannistraro, Rosetta Giuliani Caponetto, Becca Carchman, Miriam Cohen, Brian De Boer, Chris Ealham, Leslie English, Caitlin Ewing, Candace Falk, Dana Frank, John Gennari, Steve Golin, Nancy Hewitt, Catherine Hondorp, Karin Isaacson, Matthew Frye Jacobson, Ingrid Johnson, Val Marie Johnson, David Lester, Terza Lima-Neves, Shaun T. Lopez, Nancy Raquel Mirabal, Caroline Merithew, Gerald Meyer, Allison Levine, Franco Montalto, Mee-Ja Moore, Gary Mormino, José Moya, Michelle Muniz, John Nieto-Phillips, Fraser Ottanelli, Goffredo Plastino, Sujani Reddy, Mary Renda, Katey Robinson, Mérida Rua, Onorio Ruotolo, Mateo L. Sánchez, Nadya Sbaiti, Jane Schneider, Judith E. Smith, Eeva Sointu, Michael Miller Topp, Wilson Valentín-Escobar, Fiorello Ventresco, Amanda Webb, Joel Wolfe, Kenyon Zimmer, Andrew Zinn, and everyone up on Isle-au-Haut. Mark Naison in particular met with me as a beginning graduate student and uttered the phrase that ultimately led me to take my work more seriously: "You are the person to write this book." I am deeply grateful for his encouragement.

I am also very thankful to the many brilliant scholars I worked alongside as a doctoral student in History at the University of Minnesota: Marjorie Bryer, Gaye Theresa Johnson, Jean O'Brien-Kehoe, Erika Lee, Sara Evans, Catherine Ceniza Choy, Todd Michney, Margot Canaday, Adam Pagán, Adrian Gaskins, Yuichiro Onishi, Deirdre Murphy, Steve Garabedian, May Fu, Lisa Kellmeyer, Angela Dillard, and Rudolph J. Vecoli. The early support and mentoring of Jeanne Boydston, Joyce Follet, Marie Laberge, Maureen Fitzgerald, Leisa Meyer, Laura McEnaney, Nancy MacLean, Roger Horowitz, Jennifer Frost, Susan L. Smith, Florencia Mallon, Gerda Lerner, Linda Gordon, Ada Deer, Stanlie James, and Bonnie Blustein, when I was an undergraduate at the University of Wisconsin–Madison, made it possible for me to imagine becoming a historian.

I hope this book reflects the community of gifted scholars that I am fortunate to work alongside at Smith College. I am especially thankful to my beloved writing group: Elisabeth Armstrong, Ginetta Candelario, Daphne Lamothe, Michelle Joffroy, and Adriane Lentz-Smith. Special thanks to all of my colleagues in the History Department, American Studies Program, and the Program for the Study of Women and Gender. My thanks also extends to the many students who challenged me to think in new ways, some of whom read and commented on early drafts of the manuscript: Faron Levesque, Corinne Guest, Jenna Raffaela McKean Randall, Melissa MacDonald, Candace Gibson, Adrian Comly, Jacqueline Batten, Xiomara Iraheta, Tamara Llosa-Sandor, Emma Malbon, Darcy Rendón, Marilyn Flores, Kailie Larkin, Meara Heubach, Melissa Peña, Allison Pilatsky, Olivia Cummings, and Elizabeth Crews.

This project was made possible by a whole host of institutional support. Smith College provided generous research grants and time off from teaching to write. The Immigration History Research Center (IHRC) at the University of Minnesota, with funding from the Order of the Sons of Italy in America, provided the dream of a lifetime: the chance to spend four years immersed in this invaluable archive as a graduate research assistant. My thanks also to the University of Minnesota's Department of History, Modena–St. Paul Sister Cities Project, American Italian Historical Association, the Immigration and Ethnic History Society, the University of New Mexico Graduate School, and the Mellon Foundation for financial support. I am especially thankful to the American Association of University Women, the Social Science Research Council, and the Samuel Deinard Memorial Fund, for their generosity in the early stages of this project. My thanks as well to the many archivists, librarians, and administrators who made my research easier and more enjoyable, especially Joel Wurl, Timo Rippa, and Daniel Necas at the IHRC; Pam Skinner at Smith College; and Evelyn M. Hershey at the American Labor Museum/Botto House National Landmark. Many thanks also to the Guabello family for sitting down to talk with me about their anarchist roots in Paterson; to Athena Warren for kindly sharing her memories of her parents Nino and Marie Capraro; to Philip Camponeschi for graciously sharing materials on his mother Angela Bambace; and to the Romeo, Marazzi, and Valzania families for taking such good care of me while I did research in Italy. I am tremendously thankful to my editor Kate Torrey, as well as Dino Battista, Paul Betz, and Michael Donatelli at the University of North Carolina Press, for their enthusiasm.

And finally, my heartfelt thanks to my massive and beautiful family, which includes a long line of storytellers. My grandparents Grace and Angelo, my father Tom, my brothers Tommy and Mark, and my dozens of uncles, aunts, and cousins in Queens and beyond, have all spent their lives weaving mystery, drama, and struggle into magnificent tales, mostly around kitchen tables, but also in music, theater, film, photography, poetry, painting, sculpture, sermons, rap, and scholarship. I am thankful to all of you, for your love and for teaching me the transformative power of a good story. Special thanks to both of my brothers, who enrich my every day with their loving kindness and brilliance; and my father for his steadfast encouragement and support. This book is for my entire family, in memory of my mother Maryloretta and my great grandmothers Antonia Zullo and Josephine DeMeo.

Index

Abbatista, Antoinette, 118
Abruzzo, 100, 116, 154, 172, 209, 225
Abuse. *See* Violence
Abyssinian War. *See* Italian-Ethiopian War
Accurso, Carmela, 115, 116
Adams, Charlotte, 92
Addams, Jane, 104
L'Adunata dei Refrattari (The Gathering of the Disobedient), 224, 228
AFANA. *See* Alleanza Anti-Fascista di Nord America
Africa, 82, 83, 87, 88–89, 90, 108, 165, 215, 253
African Americans, 76, 99, 121, 159, 214, 265, 267, 269; anarchist movement and, 204–5, 217; fascism and, 217–18; in Harlem, 1930s to 1940s, 230, 234–40, 241, 242, 255, 257–58, 260, 263–64; racism against, 1910s to 1920s, 93, 95, 97, 106, 107; racism against, 1930s to 1940s, 204–5, 233, 234, 236–37, 240, 251, 252, 254, 258; southern Italian immigrants as "racially superior" to, 5, 6, 93, 97; women compared with Italian women, 93, 96, 105, 106; women in garment industry, 242, 250–51, 252, 254–55
Africans, 83, 86, 87, 88–89, 90
Afro-Brazilians, 65, 66
Agricultural labor, 36, 37, 39; Argentine Italian immigrants and, 60–61; Brazilian Italian immigrants and, 64; in New Jersey, 74; of women in southern Italy, 15–16, 48–51, 54
Alagna, Rose, 185
Alba, 156, 166
Albino, Theresa, 72–73
Alexander, M. Jacqui, 7, 128
Alleanza Anti-Fascista di Nord America (Anti-Fascist Alliance of North America; AFANA), 209
Allessandrina, Mary, 118

Alleva, Aurora, 150
Altars, 30–31, 129, 131
Amalgamated Clothing Workers of America (ACWA), 155, 210, 214, 223; Local 63, 198
American-born generation, 127, 202, 205, 208; fascism and, 216, 218, 220; in Harlem, 1930s to 1940s, 234, 235, 237; unions and, 177, 191, 201, 210, 242
American Federation of Labor (AFL), 181, 186, 187, 193–94, 206, 214
American Federation of Teachers, 260
Americanization movement, 102–8, 124, 133, 237
American Labor Party (ALP), 261, 262
Amore libero (free love), 168, 170, 171–72, 173, 225
L'Anarchia (Malatesta), 144
Anarchist movement, 6, 98; antifascism and, 209, 221–22, 223, 224, 228; antiracism and, 204–5, 217, 254, 256–57; Virgilia D'Andrea and, 225–27; Immigration Act of 1918 and, 203, 311 (n. 18); Industrial Workers of the World and, 177, 186, 187, 194, 204, 210; Italian immigrants and, 105, 142–55, 191, 292 (n. 161), 299 (nn. 13, 15); in Italy, 11, 12, 32, 36–39, 82, 87–88, 139, 156–57, 158, 225; in Latin America, 63, 64, 66; legacy of, 266–67; Palmer raids of 1920 and, 199–200, 201–3, 204, 209, 266; in Paterson, N.J., 87, 98, 139, 142, 143, 144–46, 147, 148, 149–50, 151–54, 158, 160–61, 194, 199–205; Sacco and Vanzetti and, 6, 137, 138, 148, 200, 203, 228; women's participation in, 2, 3, 134, 139–41, 147–48, 150–51, 154–56. *See also* Antiorganizationalist anarchists; Bombings; Circoli politici; Individualist anarchists; Italian-language newspapers; *Organizzatori*; Socialism

Anarchist women's groups, 2, 3; antifascism and, 228, 229; in Argentina, 62–64; in Brazil, 65; Catholic Church and, 164, 169–71; feminism and, 63, 139–41, 160, 162–75, 224–25; in Italy, 12, 36; labor strikes of women and, 187–88, 195, 198; in New York, N.Y., 160; in Paterson, N.J., 1, 139–41, 155–57, 159–62, 163, 171; theater and, 172–75

Anarcho-syndicalists, 65, 148, 151, 155, 169, 170, 175, 198, 207, 210, 223, 225

Anglo-Saxon Protestant women, 7, 90, 95, 103, 105, 201

Anticlericalism, 32, 128–29

Antifascism, 209, 215, 217–18, 221–29, 239, 241, 267; women participants, 222–25, 256, 257. See also Fascism

Antifascist Alliance of North America (AFANA), 148, 223

Antiorganizationalist anarchists, 147, 162, 203, 304 (n. 119). See also Individualist anarchists

Antiracist politics, 204–5, 217, 241, 254, 256–57

Anti-sweatshop movement, 91, 93, 97

Antonini, Luigi, 252

Apulia, 25, 33, 36, 88, 100, 155, 173; Bari, 39, 51, 100, 173. See also Puglia

Arabs, 85, 87

Argentina: Italian immigrants in, 4, 59–64, 66, 141, 149; Italian women immigrant activists in, 2–3, 62–64

Artificial flowers, 68, 69, 70, 72, 74, 76, 91–92

Artisans, 13, 18, 35–36, 39, 47, 51–53, 54, 68, 71

Ascoli Piceno, 150

Assimilation, 89, 94, 101–2, 106, 132–33, 206, 232, 239. See also Americanization movement

Astoria, Queens, 181

L'Avanti, 39, 66

Avellino, 219, 224

Avezzano, Abruzzo, 225

Avrich, Paul, 143, 150, 170

Badami, Minnie, 244

Baker, Ella, 241

Bakunin, Mikhail, 144

Baldisserotto, Anna, 202

Baldisserotto, Pietro, 199

Baldwin, James, 6, 217, 231–32, 236, 240

Bambace, Angela, 1, 185, 312 (n. 46); as antifascist, 223; early life, 57–58, 207; as union organizer, 133, 155, 184, 189, 197, 207–9, 211, 213, 214, 245, 270, 313 (n. 65)

Bambace, Antonio, 57, 58

Bambace, Giuseppina, 57, 58, 155, 184, 185, 207

Bambace, Maria, 155, 184, 189, 197, 198, 207, 270

Bandits. See Brigandage

Barbera, Antonetta, 248

Barbieri, Maria, 1, 2, 164, 167, 172, 208

Barcelona, 158, 163

Baronio, Ninfa, 1, 151–54, 159–60, 163, 172, 173–74, 194, 195, 202, 208, 270

Barrozo, Delia, 63

Barruso, Emma, 21, 117

Basilicata: Avigliano, 23, 114; class consciousness in, 18; immigrants from, in New York, 52, 56, 68, 100, 114, 256; fasci of, 36; Pisticci, 34; Potenza, 26, 51; Spinoza, 52, 68; witches of, 29; women, in absence of migrating men in, 13, 14, 22, 23; women agricultural laborers of, 50; women brigands of, 34

Bassano, Mary, 260, 261

Battan, Jesse, 168

Battini, Silvio, 258

Becchetti, Nena, 173

Belgians, 76, 145

Belgium, 141, 162, 165

Benjamin Franklin High School (East Harlem), 234, 237, 238, 261

Benuto, Nina, 118

Bertocci, Angelo, 118

Betts, Lillian, 120

Biella, 124, 148, 149, 171

Bilbo, Theodore, 238

"Black Hand," 94–95

Blondi, Zappira, 57

Boffa, Pierina, 173–74

Il Bolletino della Sera, 161, 180

Bologna, 11, 36, 162, 225

Bombings, 87, 95, 158, 199, 201; of Wall Street in 1920, 203, 311 (n. 22)

Borghi, Armando, 225, 226

Boston, 1, 61, 140, 153, 173, 201, 214

Botto, Maria, 195, 196, 208

Botto family, 195–96

Bourgeoisie, 226; feminism and, 4, 7, 84, 141, 164; in Italy, 13, 27, 32, 82, 221; in United States, 104–5

Brady, Edward, 158

Brandt, Lillian, 119

Brazil: Italian immigrants in, 4, 57, 59–60, 61, 64–66; Italian women immigrant activists in, 2–3, 65

Bresci, Gaetano, 144, 148, 161

Brigandage, 33, 34, 87–88, 94

Bronx, 137, 205, 220, 235; anarchist movement and, 142, 154

Brooklyn, 50, 53, 103, 136, 161, 172, 205, 231; anarchist movement and, 142, 143, 144, 145, 155, 159, 225, 226, 228, 299 (n. 15); fascism and, 220; strikes in, 176, 180, 194, 197; Williamsburg, 122, 129–30, 269
Bruno, Angelina, 193
Bruno, Paolina, 248
Buenos Aires, 1, 3, 13, 55, 59, 61–63, 64, 87, 140, 149, 163
Buhle, Paul, 134, 187
Buongiorno, Virginia, 164

Cacici, Tina, 155
Cagliari, Carmela, 22, 125, 128, 274 (n. 62)
Calabria, 9, 25, 26, 33, 56, 94; Cannitello, 57, 58; Cosenza, 19; immigrants from, in Latin America, 60, 64; immigrants from, in New York, 100, 207, 218; labor unions of women in, 36, 39; labor unrest in, 11, 83; Madonna in, 29–30; Reggio Calabria, 25; San Giovanni, 42; witches of, 28–29; women, in absence of migrating men, 13, 14, 16, 41, 42, 48–50; women migrants to cities and, 55
Calapso, Jole, 35
California laws against Chinese, 95–96
Calvino, Italo, 20
Caminita, Ludovico, 98, 147, 199, 202
Caminita, Mary, 98
Cammarata, Maria, 36
Cammarota, Mary, 260, 261
Camorra, 94, 97, 171
Campanalismo (regionalism), 121, 206
Campania, 16, 33, 36, 53, 56, 137; Avellino, 219, 224; Caserta, 13, 54–55; immigrants from, in Latin America, 60, 64; women agricultural laborers of, 50, 54
Camponeschi, Romolo, 207
Canno, Anna, 187
Canvassing, 227, 228, 260
Capitalism, 1, 7, 15, 209, 211, 229; activist struggle against, 36, 63, 102, 147, 149, 167, 172, 186, 190, 197, 198, 200, 203, 241; industrial, 14, 23, 44, 45, 47, 49, 51, 72, 77, 109, 164, 165, 267
Caporaleti, Teresa, 63
Capraro, Antonino, 133, 207, 208
Caribbean immigrants, 121, 235, 242, 258
Carnevale, Nancy, 182
Carnot, Sadi, 157
Caroti, Arturo, 180, 187, 188
Carroll, James F., 98
Caruso, Maria, 224
Caruso, Michelangelo, 38

Casa Italiana (Columbia University), 216
Caserio, Sante, 157
Cassado, Donna, 118
Cassio, Anna, 189
Castellucci, Almerinda, 189
Catalan anarchists, 149, 153, 158
Catania, 30, 38, 39, 51, 54
Catania, Tina, 246–48, 249, 250
Catastini, Ida Merini, 166
Catello, Elvira, 173, 208
"Catherine the Wise," 20
Catholic Church, 27, 62, 119; anarchist women's groups and, 164, 169–71; fascism and, 216, 220; folk healing and, 28, 29; ideal of women from, 23, 49, 85–86; Italian and Irish immigrants and, 121, 129; Italian immigrant women and, 127–32; women of Southern Italy and, 29–32. See also Madonna
Cavalleri, Rosa, 24, 25, 30, 88
Cavedagni, Ersilia, 162, 165, 167, 172
Cement and Concrete Workers' Union, 258, 262
Census records: in Italy, 48, 51–52, 54; in United States, 67–69, 89, 91, 123
Centro Feminista Anarquista, 62
Century, 94
Cerantonio, Concettina, 155
Cereida, Rosie, 193
Chapman, Charlotte Gower, 29
Chicago, 1, 3, 13, 61, 140, 192, 204, 210
Child labor, 37–38, 50, 51, 53, 54, 62, 64, 68, 70–73, 139, 184, 245
Chinese, 67, 93, 95–96, 97, 99, 106, 145, 235, 251, 269; California laws against, 95–96; living conditions of, 102
Chinese Exclusion Act of 1882, 96
Ciancabilla, Giuseppe, 162, 304 (n. 119)
Cicio, Lillian, 122, 123–24
Cigar making, 51, 56, 59, 62, 67, 76, 92, 141, 145, 159, 180
Cimma, Romea, 32
Cioffari, Philomena, 78
Cioffi, Marie, 123
Circoli politici, 142–43, 144, 145, 149, 150, 170, 191, 207, 256; radical theater and, 173; women's participation in, 151, 154–56, 160, 162, 164, 172, 188. See also Anarchist movement
Circoli di studi sociali, 142
"Civilization work," 103, 106, 109
Civil rights, 231, 241
Claflin, Tennessee, 105
Class, 5, 40, 80, 95, 225, 239, 263, 267; class struggle, 36, 42, 55, 91, 150, 186, 206; cross-class relation-

Class (*continued*)
    ships, 4, 104–5, 179; fascism and, 216, 218, 220; in Italy, 12, 17–19, 32, 33; race and, 7, 84, 87, 88, 103. *See also* Bourgeoisie; Middle-class women
Class consciousness, 12, 18, 33, 119, 240
Cleveland, 3, 201, 244
Cloakmakers, 187–88, 190, 212, 243
Clothing manufacture. *See* Garment industry
Club Avanti, 145, 300 (n. 31)
Club Femminile di Musica di Canto (Women's Club for Music and Song), 172–73
Cobianci, Teresa, 195
Cocozzelli, Philamina, 15, 117–18
Collazo, Maria, 63
Cololito, Marguerite, 193
Colombo, Caroline, 126–27, 133
Colônia Cecília, 64
Colonialism, 1, 121, 165, 217; racism and, 87, 88
Comari, 17
Comitato Italiano Pro Vittime Politiche (Italian Committee for Political Victims), 209
Commons, John, 75
Communist Party, 212, 214, 227, 243, 256, 257; American, 241; fascism and, 217
Communist Party's International Workers' Order, 256
Communists, 201, 202, 209, 210, 211, 212, 214, 221, 223, 225, 228, 229, 236, 251
Como, 139, 148, 156–57
Concistre, Marie, 121
Conforti, Rosalia, 189
Construction work, 44, 58, 65, 107, 136, 143, 149, 186, 235
Contadina. See Peasant women
Contemporary Barbarian Italy (Niceforo), 84
Cooperative movement, 37, 39
Cooper Union, 176, 193, 196, 227
Corleone, 35, 36, 37, 38, 39
Cornelisen, Ann, 26
Corsi, Edward, 116, 258
Cortile, 18, 19–21, 24, 30, 43, 100, 120
Costanzo, Caterina, 9
Covello, Leonard, 258, 263; early life, 23, 26, 105, 114–15, 116, 217; as educator, 237, 238, 256, 261; folk healing and, 135; Sicilian life described by, 20, 27, 29, 101, 118, 130
Cravello, Antonio, 160
Cravello, Ernestina, 1, 160–62, 172, 173, 208, 270
Cravello, Vittorio, 160, 162
Crime, 5; organized, 1890s, 93–95, 98; organized, Harlem, 1930s, 248; in southern Italian neighborhoods of New York, 93–98, 100

Criminology: anarchism and, 64, 87–88, 144–45; criminal woman and, 41, 85–87; southern Italy racism and, 82–90, 93–98; women's sexual deviance and, 83, 84–85, 86–87
Criscuolo, Luigi, 238
Crispi, Francesco, 11, 38
Crivello, Antonino, 170, 188, 191
Crivello, Francesca, 170, 191
Cubans, 67, 121, 145, 158, 159, 230, 235, 236
Cultural Front, The (Denning), 241
Cultura Obrera, 159
Cuoco, Adoneta, 260, 261
Custom-made clothes, 48, 52, 68, 69, 77
Czolgosz, Leon, 144

D'Agnese, Peggy, 248
Daily Worker, 243
Damiani, Gigi, 65
D'Amico, Caterina, 144
Dancing, 27, 28
D'Andrea, Virgilia, 225–27, 228
d'Aza, Zo, 158
De Biasi, Agostino, 219
DeCaro, Silvia, 248
De Felice, Giuffrida, 38
De Felice, Marietta, 38
De Gigli, Anna, 169
de Grazia, Victoria, 218, 228
De Gregorio, Aurora, 257
Delfino, Albina, 214, 227, 245
De Luca, Maria, 52, 68
De Luise, Grace, 189–90, 198, 213, 246, 247, 248–49, 250
De Martino, Ernesto, 27
Denning, Michael, 241
De Nobili, Irene De Bonis, 21
Depew, Chauncey, 92
DeSalvo, Louise, 132
El Despertar, 159
De Stefano, George, 95
Dialects, 20, 21, 32–33, 39, 121
Diasporic radicalism, 4, 63, 67, 141, 145, 158, 159
Di Geronimo, Rose, 260
Di Guglielmo, Laura, 198
di Leonardo, Micaela, 117
Dillingham Report, 68, 69, 73, 89, 94, 101
Di Maddi, Pietro, 223
Di Maggio, Margaret, 189–90, 198, 222–23, 244–45, 246–47, 248, 250
Di Meo, Concetta, 58
Di Neri, Pasquale, 206
di Prima, Diane, 231

Di Sciullo, Camillo, 154, 165
Di Silvestro, Giovanni, 219
Dolci, Danilo, 24
Domestic violence. *See* Violence
La donna delinquente. *See* Criminology
Dorsey, George, 90
Douglas, Norman, 13, 28, 30, 42, 50
Douglass, Laura, 211
Dowries, 49, 59. *See also* Trousseaus
Drago, Dorothy, 244
Dressmakers, 254; African Americans as, 252;
    Italian immigrant women as, 45, 47–48,
    52–53, 58, 61, 67, 68, 183, 190, 198, 211, 212,
    213–14; strike, New York City, 1913, 176, 177;
    strike, New York City, 1933–34, 242–44. *See
    also* Garment industry; International Ladies'
    Garment Workers Union; Italian Dressmak-
    ers' Local 89
Dutch immigrants, 76, 145

Eastern European immigrants, 106
Eastern European Jews. *See* Jewish immigrants;
    Jewish women
East Harlem, 58, 99, 100, 101, 114–15, 116, 119, 123,
    219; activism in, 134, 184, 207; African Ameri-
    cans in Harlem and, 230, 234–40, 241, 242,
    255, 257–58, 260, 263–64; anarchist movement
    and, 105, 145, 155, 173; folk healing in, 135–36;
    Italian Dressmakers' Local 89 in, 243–50, 319
    (nn. 92–93); Puerto Ricans in, 251–52, 254,
    255, 263; racism in, 1930s to 1940s, 230–31, 232,
    233–40; radical theater and, 173; religion in,
    128, 129, 130, 131–32. *See also* Harlem; Italian
    Harlem
East Harlem Housing Committee, 258–63, 264;
    tenement fires and, 261–63, 322 (n. 156)
Editrice Lux, 173
Einaudi, Maria, 22, 23
El France Dress Company, 254
Elizabeth Street, 91, 100, 128
Ellis Island, 67, 109, 114, 199, 202
Ellison, Ralph, 107
Elmhurst-Corona, Queens, 269
Elwood, Sophie, 266
Emancipata, 172
Emancipazione, 4, 139, 141, 154, 155, 159–62, 165,
    172, 225. *See also* Feminism; *Femminismo*
Emanuele, Fannie, 248
Embroidery, 30, 52, 53, 62, 68, 70, 76, 92, 103
Emigration: from Basilicata, 52, 56, 68, 100, 114,
    256; from Calabria, 60, 64, 100, 207, 218; from
    Campania, 60, 64; from Italy to Argentina, 4,

60–64; from Italy to Brazil, 64–66; from Italy
to New York City, 55, 66–69; mass emigration from Italy, 11, 12, 13–14, 15–16, 19, 23–24,
40–43, 47–57, 279 (n. 68); from Naples, 55, 70,
99, 100, 114, 173; from Naples to New York, 70,
99, 100, 128, 129, 132, 173; from northern Italy,
13, 60, 64, 88, 89, 110, 124, 139, 148, 155, 160,
161; from Sicily, 35, 36, 60; from Sicily to New
York, 100, 101, 107, 108, 110, 150, 170, 207, 219,
222, 227, 231, 243, 244; of women from Sicily to
New York, 52–54, 56–59, 77, 102, 118, 124, 128,
129, 144, 155, 246; of women to Italian cities,
48, 55, 58. *See also* Immigration
Emilio, B. *See* Mello, Gemma
England, 141
English workers, 76, 145
Enstad, Nan, 189
L'Era Nuova, 147, 148, 149, 150, 163, 190, 204
Eritrea, 87
Espi, Severo, 199
Esteve, Pedro, 140, 149, 158–59, 163, 303–4 (n. 106)
Esteve, Sirio, 159, 170
Ethiopia, 88, 215, 217–18, 219, 221
Ethnic nationalism, 198, 201, 205–6, 233
Evil eye (*mal'occhio*), 130, 132

Factory labor: in Italy, 36, 39, 45, 47–48, 51–52,
54–55, 56; in Latin America, 61, 65; in New
York City, 52–53, 56, 58–59, 68–69, 70, 72–78,
91–92, 103. *See also* Garment industry; Labor
strikes; Labor unions
Faina, Eugenio, 82
Fair Labor Standards Act, 239
Fama, Anna, 198
La famiglia (family), 17
Farruggia, Angelina, 244
Fasanella, Ralph, 183
Fasci, 10–11, 35–40
Fascio delle lavaratrici (union of women's
groups), 10
Fascism, 215–21, 234, 244, 253; women partici-
pants, 6, 218–21, 237, 314 (nn. 95–96). *See also*
Antifascism
Fascist League of North America (FLNA), 216
La fatica (exhausting labor), 15–16
Fatti di maggio, 11, 40
Federación Obrera Regional Argentina
(FORA), 62
Federal Bureau of Investigation (FBI), 204
Federal Housing Act, 239
Federal Housing Authority (FHA), 263
Federazione Socialista Italiana (FSI), 148, 181

Feminism, 49, 117, 128, 134; anarchist movement and, 63, 139–41, 160, 162–75, 224–25; bourgeois women and, 4, 7, 84, 141, 164; criminology and, 86; fascism and, 221; Italian women immigrant activists and, 1, 3, 4, 7–8, 160, 162–72, 191; labor unions and, 179, 187–92; theater and, 172–75; transnational nature of, 6–7, 163, 191

Femminismo, 1, 4, 141, 191

Ferrari, Cecilia, 15

Ferre, Paolo, 160

Ferrer, Francisco, 153

Ferrero, Guglielmo, 82, 85

Ferrer schools, 153, 199

Ferri, Enrico, 83, 87

Festa (feast), 127–28, 162

Festa della Frutta, 145–46, 174

La Figlia dell'Anarchico (The Anarchist's Daughter), 173

Filipino men, 97

Filodrammatica (theater group), 173

Five Points district, 99, 100

Florence, 11, 121

Flynn, Elizabeth Gurley, 3, 134, 150, 152, 187, 195, 196

Folk healing, 27, 28–29, 135–36

Food, 132–38

Ford, Henry, 209

Forgnene, Rosalia, 174

Forte, Maria, 115–16, 136

Forte, Millie, 248

France, 13, 141, 149, 157, 162

Frank, Dana, 78

Free love (*amore libero*), 168, 170, 171–72, 173, 225

French workers, 62, 76, 145, 251

Frignoca, Angelina, 108, 124, 170–71

Fuorusciti (refugees), 225

Gabaccia, Donna, 2, 57, 102

Gaeta, Lucia, 44–45, 46, 47, 132

Gaeta, Tina, 44, 45, 46, 47, 132, 191, 245, 249–50

Galleani, Luigi, 143, 144, 147, 191, 201, 301 (n. 40)

Galleanisti, 147, 148, 199, 203

Gallo, Firmino, 151–54, 199, 203

Gallo, Grace, 126

Gallo, Lena, 154

Gallo, William, 151, 153, 302 (n. 73)

Gangsters, 190, 210, 247, 248. *See also* Mafia

Garavente, Natalia. *See* Sinatra, Dolly

Gardening, 15, 18, 49, 51, 54, 65, 134–38

Garment industry, 235; antifascism and, 222, 223, 229; everyday resistance and, 183–85; "Great

Revolt" of 1910, 187–88; homework, 91–92, 182, 191; Italian American women in, 1930s to 1940s, 241–55; Italian women immigrants in, 15, 44–45, 52–53, 56–60, 67–78, 79–80, 91–93, 176–98, 204–6, 244, 293–94 (n. 13); in Italy, 51, 52, 54; labor unions of women in, 145, 148, 170, 177, 188–92, 206, 208–9, 210–12, 213–14, 241–50; Popular Front and, 241; ready-made garments and, 48, 69; schools for women working in, 103; strike, 1909, 179–83, 187, 192; strike, 1913, 175, 176–77, 192–97, 206; strike, 1919, 155, 197–98, 202, 204, 207, 211–12; strike, 1926, 210–12; strike, 1933, 241–44; women's networks in, 119. *See also* African Americans; International Ladies' Garment Workers Union; Jewish women; Puerto Ricans

Gasperano, Mary, 194

Gattuso, Maria, 57

Gender: anarchist movement and, 168, 172, 174; emigration ratios and, 56; fascism and, 221; industrialization and, 47, 49, 72, 79, 86, 127; Italian patriarchy and, 23, 141, 151, 154, 214, 248; migration affecting ideals of, 42, 53, 86, 89; race and class and, 80, 84, 96; unions and, 241, 243, 248–49, 250; Victorian-era norms of, 103

Genisio, Alba, 164

Gennari, John, 112

Genoa, 11, 51, 89, 110

Germans, 67, 69, 76, 101, 110, 145, 176, 180, 235, 251

Giallombardo, Fatima, 31

Gilman, Sander, 85

Giornale di Sicilia, 36

Giovannitti, Arturo, 188, 252, 253

Giuliani, Carolina, 248

Giunta, Edvige, 19, 132

Giustizia, 148

Glenn, Susan, 174

Globalization, 6–7, 45, 47, 77, 102

Goddesses, 130–31

Goldman, Emma, 157–58, 161, 172

Goletto, Andrea, 81

Goletto, Maria, 81

Golin, Steve, 194, 196

Golzio, Carrie, 75, 184, 195

Gorgoni, Rose, 77

Gori, Pietro, 143, 149, 191

Gossip, 20–21, 22, 108, 120, 126

Government repression: in Argentina, 63; in Italy, 9, 11, 32, 33–34, 35, 38, 39–40, 87; in United States, 145, 149, 150, 152, 199–200, 202–4, 209, 233

Gramsci, Antonio, 27, 83, 84
Grandi, Fiorina, 202
Grandi, Serafino, 199
Grassa, Rose, 189
Grass-roots activism, 12, 138, 142, 210, 231, 257, 269
Graziano, Andre, 204
Graziano, Rosa, 97
Great Depression, 4, 61, 102, 130, 177, 231; housing conditions during, 258–59, 264; neighborhood movements during, 138, 240–50, 255–65, 267–69; racism during, 230–31, 233, 234; socialism and, 236, 241
Great Revolt of 1910, 187–88
Greeks: immigrants, 145, 176, 251, 269; influence in Italy, 29, 83, 94
Greenwich House, 79–80, 103, 104, 119
Greenwich Village, 52, 70, 92, 99, 107, 119, 191, 223, 240
Gruppo di Propaganda Femminile (Women's Propaganda Group), 160
Gruppo Diritto all'Esistenza (Right to an Existence Group), 139, 145, 147, 148, 149, 150, 151, 152, 160, 199, 201
Gruppo Emancipazione della Donna (Women's Emancipation Group), 139, 159–60
Gruppo Gli Insorti (The Insurgents), 199, 203
Gruppo Il Risveglio (The Awakening Group), 145, 300 (n. 32)
Gruppo I Risorti (Resurrected Group), 151
Gruppo L'Era Nuova (The New Era Group). See Gruppo Diritto all'Esistenza (Right to an Existence Group)
Gruppo Pensiero e Azione (Thought and Action Group), 152
Gruppo Verità (Truth Group), 152
Guabello, Adalgisa, 152, 153, 154
Guabello, Alberto, 152, 153, 154, 199
Guabello, Paolo, 154, 194, 199
Guabello, Spartaco, 151, 153, 154
Guabello family, 152, 153–54
Guglielmo, Thomas A., 90, 219
Guida, Lucy, 189
Gustavo, Soledad, 163, 304 (n. 126)

Haarlem House, 219, 262
Hackensack, N.J., 149, 180, 194, 216
Haledon, N.J., 108, 124, 146, 152, 195, 266
Harding, Sandra, 86
Harlem, 176, 181; American-born generation in, 234, 235, 237; anarchist movement and, 142; antifascism and, 217; community organizing, 1930s to 1940s, 240–50; neighborhood coalitions, 1930s to 1940s, 255–65; Puerto Ricans in, 235–40, 256, 257, 263–64. See also African Americans; East Harlem; Italian Harlem
Harlem Legislative Conference (HLC), 255–57, 262, 263, 264
Harlem Youth Congress, 256
Harper's Magazine, 92
Harris, Helen, 258
Harrison, Barbara Grizzuti, 111
Haywood, William "Big Bill," 187, 196
Healing practices. See Folk healing
Hell's Kitchen, 101
Henry Street Settlement, 119
Hewitt, Nancy, 7
"Hidden transcript," 25, 26, 124. See also "Public transcript"
Hine, Lewis Wickes, 79, 80, 108
Hoboken, N.J., 1, 2, 3, 110–11, 139, 144, 149, 161, 167, 174; fascism and, 216; labor strikes in, 180, 187, 187–88, 194. See also West Hoboken, N.J.
Hodes, Martha, 90
Hoover, J. Edgar, 204
Household budget, 16
Household labor, 15, 21, 40, 50, 59, 118, 120, 166, 195–96
Housewives, 48, 49, 54, 56
How the Other Half Lives (Riis), 93, 99
Hungarian workers, 76, 145, 176, 193, 251
Hunter, Elsie, 254
Hyman, Colette, 174

Iacovetta, Franca, 2, 225
Iandoli, Carmelo, 246
Illustrazione Italiana, 83
Immigration: invisibility of Italian women activists and, 3, 4–5, 61; invisibility of Italian women laborers and, 45–46, 77; Italian women and, early twentieth century, 15–16, 21, 66–69, 79–80, 98–114; Italian women activists and, 1–3, 11–12, 36, 63, 139–41; Italian women seamstresses and, 15, 44–47, 52–53, 56–60, 67–78, 128; mass, from Italy, 2, 36, 56, 58–60, 61, 94; mass, from Italy, of men at first, 13–16, 41, 47, 49; restrictions on, 145, 200–201, 203, 205; southern Italian immigrants as "racially inferior" and, 5–6, 81, 82–98, 234, 238; southern Italian immigrants as "racially superior" to other groups and, 5, 6, 66, 78, 90–91, 93, 95, 97. See also Emigration; New York City
Immigration Act of 1918, 203, 311 (n. 18)
Imola, 11, 36

Imperialism, 165, 201, 204, 221, 226, 252
Individualist anarchists, 147, 158. *See also* Anti-organizationalist anarchists
Industrial capitalism. *See* Capitalism: industrial
Industrialization, 33, 51, 60
Industrial labor unions. *See* Labor unions
Industrial Workers of the World (IWW), 142, 154, 159, 188, 202, 207; antifascism and, 222; founding of, 185–86; raids against, 200, 204; strike, New York City, 1909 and, 180, 181, 186–87; strike, New York City, 1913, and, 176, 177, 193; strike, New York City, 1919, and, 155; strike, Paterson, N.J., 1913 and, 152, 194–97; after World War I, 209–10
International Ladies' Garment Workers Union (ILGWU), 180; antifascism and, 222–23; "civil war" in, 211, 223; Cloak and Skirt Makers' Union, 190; "Great Revolt" of 1910 and, 187–88; Italian Branch of Local 25, 181, 189, 211–12; Italian Cloakmakers' Local 48, 198, 243; Italian Dressmakers' Local 89, 198, 213–14, 222, 243–50, 253–54, 319 (n. 92); Italian immigrant women and, 70, 133, 181, 182, 184, 187–98; Italian-language locals, 148, 190, 206, 227, 251, 252; strike, 1909, 179–83, 187; strike, 1913, 176–77, 192–97, 206; strike, 1919, 197–98; strikes, 1926, 210–12; strike, 1933, 241–42, 243; after World War I, 210
International Workers' Order, 256
Irish immigrants, 3, 28, 69, 76, 99, 100, 101, 107, 110, 111, 176, 194; Catholic Church and, 121, 129; versus Italians, 235
Isca, Valerio, 226
Italian American Labor Council, 247
Italian American Left, 148, 169
Italian Branch of Local 25 (ILGWU), 181, 189, 211–12
Italian census. *See* Census records: in Italy
Italian Chamber of Commerce, 216
Italian Chamber of Labor, 148
Italian Cloakmakers' Local 48 (ILGWU), 198, 243
Italian Dressmakers' Local 89 (ILGWU), 198, 213–14, 222, 243–50, 253–54, 319 (n. 92)
Italian Emigration Commission, 54
Italian-Ethiopian War, 88, 215, 217–19, 221
Italian Harlem, 92, 105, 227, 235, 236, 237, 238, 255, 260, 263. *See also* East Harlem
Italian-language locals (IGLWU), 148, 190, 206, 227, 251, 252; Italian Branch of Local 25, 181, 189, 211–12; Italian Cloakmakers' Local 48,

198, 243; Italian Dressmakers' Local 89, 198, 213–14, 222, 243–50, 253–54, 319 (n. 92)
Italian-language newspapers, 36, 38, 39, 66, 107, 134, 141, 142, 257; anarchist movement and, 3, 139, 146–50, 152, 154, 155–56, 159, 163, 169–70, 202–5, 224–25, 299 (nn. 13, 15), 301 (n. 51), 304 (n. 119); antifascism and, 209, 222, 223–24; in Argentina, 64, 163; fascism and, 216, 220; of ILGWU, 190–91; labor strikes of women and, 179, 180–81, 185, 193; reformist unions and, 206
Italian Socialist Federation, 253
Italian Socialist Party, 11, 35, 36, 40, 225
Italian Social Workers Association, 256, 262
Italian unification, 32–33, 82, 88, 94
Italian Women's Mutual Benefit Society, 188

Jacobson, Matthew Frye, 109
Jamaicans, 67, 145, 235, 269
Japanese, 67, 97, 106, 251
Jersey City, N.J., 149, 174, 180, 216, 217
Jewish immigrants, 91, 95, 96, 99, 257; Eastern European, 67, 69; in garment industry, 69, 76–77, 181, 214, 251, 253; versus Italians, 153, 235–36; Russian, 67, 252
Jewish women, 4; activism, 1950s to 1960s, 269; Eastern European Jews and, 3, 76, 122; in garment industry, 177, 178, 179, 181–82, 187, 188, 192, 193, 194, 210, 213, 242, 250, 251, 252; versus Italian women, 92, 102, 104, 105, 181, 182; Italian women immigrants and, 76–77, 119, 121, 122, 124, 188, 242, 269; Russian Jews and, 3, 76, 122
Johnson Act of 1921, 89
Johnson-Reed Act of 1924, 89
Joyce, Emmet, 246
Joyce, Thomas, 203

Kessler-Harris, Alice, 212
King, Bolton, 50
Kin work, 113, 117–18, 134, 245
Kitchens, 120, 133–34; as sweatshops, 45, 69–72
Klindienst, Patricia, 137, 138
Ku Klux Klan, 198, 207, 208, 217, 234

Labor strikes, 2, 3, 178, 185; "Great Revolt" of 1910, 187–88; in Latin America, 62–63, 65–66; Lawrence textile, 1912, 192, 193, 196, 253; Lawrence textile, 1919, 155, 192, 193, 207, 208; New Jersey, 1909–13, 180, 187–88, 192; New Jersey, 1926, 210–12; New York City, 1909, 179–83,

186–87, 192; New York City, 1913, 175, 176–77, 192–97, 206; New York City, 1919, 155, 197–98, 202, 204, 207, 211–12; New York City, 1933–34, 241–44; New York City and New Jersey, 1890s to 1900s, 180–81; northern Italy, 1898 to 1914, 36, 39–40, 149; in Sicily, late nineteenth century, 9–11, 12–13, 32–40, 85, 87; silk mill, in Paterson, N.J., 152, 174, 175, 180–81, 184, 186, 192, 193–97, 210–12, 242

Labor unions, 105; American-born generation and, 177, 191, 201, 210, 242; antifascism and, 222, 223, 229; in Argentina, 62, 63; in Brazil, 65–66; for children, 37–38; feminism and, 179, 187–92; Italian American women and, 1930s to 1940s, 213, 231, 241–50; Italian immigrants and, 141–42, 147, 148; Italian immigrant women and, 3, 78, 185–87; Italian women in Sicily and, 9–11, 35–39; National Industrial Recovery Act and, 242; racism and, 239, 250, 253–54; after Red Scare, 206, 210, 212, 222, 241; in silk mills and factories, 75, 180; after World War I, 209–15. *See also* Garment industry; International Ladies' Garment Workers Union

Labriola, Arturo, 253–54
Lacemaking, 30, 38, 52, 53, 54, 56, 68, 70, 92, 103
La Guardia Club, 262
Lamantia, Mary, 189
Lane, Layle, 260
La Porta, Sadie, 187
Laundresses, 54, 61, 62
Il Lavoro, 148
Lawrence textile strikes: in 1912, 192, 193, 196, 253; in 1919, 155, 192, 193, 207, 208
Lazzaro, Antonetta, 246, 247–48, 249
Lectures, 38, 145, 154–55, 167, 172, 226
Leland, Charles, 28
Lemasson, Margherita, 23
Lemlich, Clara, 179
Leopold (king of Belgium), 165
Lero, Minnie, 189
Lesbians, 85, 168
Levi, Carlo, 13, 17, 18, 19, 22, 29, 34, 41, 42
Liberti, Frank, 243, 244
La Libreria Elvira Catello, 173, 306 (n. 185)
Libreria Sociologica, 151–52
Liguori, Yolanda, 244
Liguria, 21, 85
Limanti, Angelina, 198
Little Italy, 100, 121, 234. *See also* East Harlem; Italian Harlem
Lizza, Carmela, 52

Lodi, N.J., 76, 194, 210, 217
Loiacono, Itala, 220
Lombardy, 64, 88, 149
Lombroso, Cesare, 82, 83, 85, 86, 87–88, 90
Long Island Railroad, 44
Longo, Bartolo, 28
López, Luisa, 254
Lo Pizzo, Anna, 190
Lotta di Classe (Class Struggle), 148, 190
Lower East Side, 93, 119, 120; anarchist movement and, 142, 145, 170, 191
Lower Manhattan, 91, 110, 176, 193. *See also* Manhattan
Low-wage labor, 1, 51, 77, 78; in Italy, 34, 45, 46, 47, 49, 59; in United States, 68, 73, 92–93, 141, 177, 180, 182, 197, 251
Lurie, Willie, 190
Lynching, 107, 204, 234, 255, 257

Macaluso, Annunziata, 127
Macari, Filomena, 76
Madonna, 23, 29–30, 85, 97, 127–28, 130–32, 170; Black Madonna (*la madonna nera*), 30
Madres Unidas, 263
Mafia, 33, 94–95
Magic. *See* Sorcery
Magli, Vito, 134
Malatesta, Errico, 143, 144, 147, 149, 159, 162, 224, 301 (n. 40)
Malcolm X, 107
Mal'occhio (evil eye), 130, 132
Manetta, Lina, 198
Mangano, Antonio, 50
Manhattan, 58, 73, 99, 101, 103, 119, 128, 162, 172, 174, 244; anarchist movement and, 149, 156, 157, 160, 203; fascism in, 220; labor unions of women in, 196, 198, 227; Lower Manhattan and, 91, 110, 176, 193; strikes in, 180, 194, 197
Mann Act. *See* White Slave Traffic Act of 1910
Manufacturing, 45, 59, 60, 61, 65, 68–69, 73, 76, 91, 93, 122, 147, 194; in Italy, 51, 54, 56. *See also* Factory labor; Garment industry; Silk mills; Textile industry
Marandi, Betty, 211
Maraviglia, Osvaldo, 224
Marcantonio, Vito, 134, 238, 255–56, 257, 258, 261, 263, 264
Marchesi, Mary, 248
Marchisio, Teresa, 63
March on Washington movement, 260
Maresca, Giuseppa, 190

Marinelli, Marino, 96
Marriage, 41, 154, 168–69, 208, 245. *See also* Free love
Marseilles, 13, 23, 226
Il Martello, 209
Matyas, Jennie, 247
May Day (*Primo Maggio*), 145–46, 178
McClintock, Anne, 84
McClure's Magazine, 92, 93, 96
McKinley, William, 144
Medicinal practices. *See* Folk healing
Melli, Elena, 224
Mello, Gemma, 172, 203
Mellone, Viola, 237–38
Melone, Cristina, 171
Memoirs, 19, 114, 119, 134, 151, 157, 202, 235
Memories, 14, 22, 132, 150; collective, 79, 267
Mercado, Fausta, 257, 260, 263
Messia, Agatuzza, 20
Messina, 17, 39, 51, 54
Mexican Revolution, 145, 147
Mexican women, 5, 107
Mexico, 147, 149, 153
Meyer, Gerald, 256
Miceli, Paul, 205
Michel, Louise, 63
Middle-class women, 4, 5, 7, 72, 218; in Italy, 18, 19, 32, 33, 49; in United States, 80–81, 89, 92, 103–5, 179
Midwives, 49, 54, 59, 110, 111, 117, 122
Miele, Stefano, 220
Milan, 1, 11, 40, 51, 139, 140, 144, 157, 158, 159, 171
Mining, 1, 13, 66, 140, 186
Miracles, 29, 30, 130
Mirandola, Modena, 155
Mirenda, Josephine, 223
Molisani, Howard, 247
Molly Yahn's Brook, 266
Montgomery, David, 210
Moraga, Cherríe, 266
More, Louise Bolard, 107
Morrison, Toni, 7
Motherhood, 26, 31, 100, 104, 106, 111–13, 121–27, 166–67, 192, 237; fascism and, 218, 220
Mott Street, 91, 100
Moya, José, 63
Mozzoni, Anna Maria, 163, 167
Mulberry district, 99–100, 119, 142, 235
Mulberry Street, 91, 99–100, 104, 130
Multiethnic communities, 66, 99–100, 145, 165, 198, 235, 253
Mumford, Kevin J., 96

Mussolini, Benito, 88, 217; Italian American resistance against, 222–23, 224, 226, 228; Italian American support for, 6, 155, 215–16, 218–19, 220–21. *See also* Antifascism; Fascism
Mutual aid societies, 117, 129, 141–42, 181, 182, 188, 193, 219, 236; anarchist movement and, 63, 145, 149; in Italy, 35–36, 37, 148–49
Mysticism, 26–32, 170. *See also* Madonna

Nambrini, Maria, 34
Naples, 15, 19, 28, 30, 39, 82, 84, 87, 94, 97, 105–6, 136, 144; immigrants from, in New York, 70, 99, 100, 128, 129, 132, 173; as emigration center, 55, 114; factories of, 51, 55; in late nineteenth century, 55–56; uprisings of 1892–94 and, 11, 36
Napolitana, Margaret, 123
National Industrial Recovery Act (NIRA), 242, 244, 261
Nationalism, 4, 6, 46, 63, 145, 165; Italians, in United States, 191, 198, 201, 205–6, 218–19, 253
National Youth Administration (NYA), 257
Naturalization, 4, 89, 90, 93, 101–2
Natural world, 27, 116, 134, 136
Navarro della Miraglia, Emmanuele, 19
Neapolitan Camorra. See *Camorra*
Needle Trades' Workers' Industrial Union, 214
Needlework, 53, 69, 103. *See also* Embroidery; Lacemaking; Seamstresses
Negri, Ada, 157
Negro Labor Committee, 252
Nehama, Saby, 252
Neighborhood coalitions, 138, 240–50, 255–65, 267–69
Neighborhood tensions, 217–19, 230–40
Newark, N.J., 3, 142, 149, 155, 174, 216, 217, 224
New Deal, 239, 258–59, 261
New Jersey: agricultural labor in, 74; Atlantic City, 142, 247; Camden, 149, 216; Clifton, 142, 174, 210; Elizabeth, 149, 214; Garfield, 76, 210, 216; Hackensack, 149, 180, 194, 216; labor strikes, 180–81, 187–88, 192, 210–12; Lodi, 76, 194, 210, 217; Montclair, 216; North Bergen, 194; North Hudson, 180; Nutley, 216; Orange Valley, 142; Phillipsburg, 194; Plainfield, 181; Pompton Lakes, 194; Stirling, 194; Summit, 194; Trenton, 76, 149, 216, 217; Union City, 76, 149; Union Hill, 142, 194; Weehawken, 159, 194; West New York, 180, 194, 216. *See also* Haledon, N.J.; Hoboken, N.J.; Jersey City, N.J.; Newark, N.J.; Passaic, N.J.; Paterson, N.J.; West Hoboken, N.J.

New London, Conn., 162, 172, 173, 194

Newman, Louise, 80

New York Archdiocese, 129

New York Association for Improving the Condition of the Poor, 104

New York Call, 193

New York Central Railroad, 92

New York City: anarchist movement and, 87, 142–55, 199–200, 201, 202, 203–4, 209, 228; anarchist women's groups and, 1, 155, 160, 163, 165, 172–74, 225–26; antifascism and, 221–29; factory labor in, 52–53, 56, 58–59, 68–69, 70, 72–78, 91–92, 103; fascism and, 215–21; garment industry, 57, 58, 59, 67–69, 91–93, 178, 188, 190, 210, 245, 250–55; garment industry strike, 1909, 179–83, 186–87, 192; garment industry strike, 1913, 175, 176–77, 192–97, 206; garment industry strike, 1919, 155, 197–98, 202, 204, 207, 211–12; garment industry strike, 1933, 241–44; Italian American women in, and housing activism, 1930s to 1940s, 256–65; Italian American women in, 1950s to 1960s, 269; Italian immigrants in, 13, 21, 23, 55, 61, 66–69, 79–80, 81; Italian women immigrant activists in, 3, 11, 139, 155, 160, 162, 167, 170, 172, 214; Italian women immigrant networks, 114–24; Italian women immigrants' Americanization and, 102–8, 124; Italian women immigrants' food and, 132–38; Italian women immigrants' spiritual lives in, 127–32; Italian women immigrants with men, 124–27; Italian women seamstresses in, 15, 44–47, 52–53, 62, 67–72, 128; racial violence, 1920s to 1940s, 204, 217, 230–31, 232, 233, 237, 238, 257; racism against southern Italians in, crime reports, 93–98, 100; racism against southern Italians in, living conditions, 98–102. *See also* East Harlem; Emigration; Harlem; Immigration; Lower East Side; Lower Manhattan; Manhattan; Sicilians

New York Housing Authority, 258, 261

New York Post, 215

New York Public Library, 256

New York State Commission against Discrimination, 254

New York Times, 94, 96, 97, 99, 130, 157, 176, 199, 215, 243

Niceforo, Alfredo, 82, 83, 84, 89, 94

Nievo, Ippolito, 84

Ninco-Nanco, 34

Ninfo, Salvatore, 187

Northern Italy, 13, 48, 49, 56, 60, 64, 81, 121, 124, 155, 160, 161; elites of, 5, 12, 33, 50, 82–83;

industrialization in, 51–52, 139, 148; people compared with southern Italians, 82–89, 90, 107–8, 110; strikes, 1898 to 1914, 36, 39–40, 149; uprisings of 1892–94 and, 11, 33, 36, 87

Norwalk, Conn., 194

Noschese, Christine, 269

Nosotras, 256

Novara, 203

Il Nuovo Mondo, 223

O'Brien, Marty, 110–12

Odencrantz, Louise, 76

Okey, Thomas, 50

L'Operaia (The Woman Worker), 148, 190

Oral tradition / histories, 15, 20, 24, 29, 52, 114, 117, 122, 125, 128, 134, 169, 184, 222

Order of the Sons of Italy (OSIA), 216, 219–20, 221

Organizzatori, 147–49

Orlando, Filomena, 121, 126

Orleck, Annelise, 188

Orsi, Robert, 116, 127, 129, 234, 236, 264

Ortíz, Altagracia, 214, 252

Our Lady of Loreto (church), 128

Our Lady of Mount Carmel (church), 128, 131–32

Pacelli, Tito, 107

Padrone system, 95

Paesani (countrymen/women), 33, 113, 115, 116, 118, 121, 125, 142

Paese (homeland), 16, 57, 129, 183

Pagano, Cammilla, 260

Page Law (1875), 96

La Pagina della Donna (ILGWU newspaper page), 190

Paglia, Jenny, 172

Palermo, 9, 19, 20, 30, 39, 51, 52, 58, 87, 100, 121, 128, 129, 170, 244

Palmer, A. Mitchell, 199–200, 201

Palmer raids, 199–200, 201–3, 209, 266

Pancini, Concetta, 15, 118

Pappa, Mary, 125

Parades, 62, 174, 178, 186, 217, 258, 263

Paragon Silk Mill, 161

Paris, 1, 140, 157, 158, 226

Parker, Cornelia Stratton, 104

Park Palace Casino, 241, 255

Parola, Anna, 14

Partido Liberal Mexicana, 147

Passaic, N.J., 3, 76, 142, 149, 180, 181, 197, 210

Pastora, Maria'a, 34

Paterson, N.J., 3, 135, 214, 228; anarchist movement and, 87, 98, 139, 142, 143, 144–46, 147, 148, 149–50, 151–54, 158, 160–61, 194, 199–205; anarchist women's groups and, 1, 139–41, 155–57, 159–62, 163, 171; Palmer raids in, 199–200, 201–3, 204, 266; radical theater and, 172–75; silk mills of, 73–75, 76, 144, 145, 151, 161, 172, 201, 203, 266; silk mill strikes in, 152, 174, 175, 180–81, 184, 186, 192, 193–97, 210–12, 242; strike, 1913, 152, 174, 175, 180, 193–97, 242; strikes, 1926, 210–12

Patriarchal culture, 47, 89, 105, 117, 124–27, 148, 163, 165, 168, 255; fascism and, 221, 224; in Italy, 13, 23–24, 30, 49, 85

Peasant women (*contadina*), 5, 6, 9–14, 16, 18–19, 21, 23, 27, 48; stereotypes of, 41–43, 50, 81; uprisings of 1892–94 and, 11, 32–40, 83, 87

Pelizzari, Armando, 142, 299 (n. 11)

Pellitteri, Elena, 38

Pergola, Salvatore, 234, 238

Pernicone, Nunzio, 143, 146

Perrini, Paolo, 173

Perrone, Angelina, 260

Pesotta, Rose, 247

Petitions, 258, 260, 261

Philadelphia, 1, 13, 15, 61, 140, 150, 153, 201, 213, 224

Piana dei Greci, 9, 11, 35, 36, 37, 38, 39, 40

Piazzas, 9, 12, 18, 24, 32, 34, 35, 38, 40

Picnics, 143, 144, 145, 146, 151, 191, 195, 228

Piecework, 45, 46, 58, 59, 62, 68, 70, 79–80, 132, 180, 251. *See also* Garment industry

Piedmont, 21, 60, 149

Pingaro, Esta, 256–57, 260

Pirozzi, Nicola, 205

Pirrone, Sarah, 248

Piscitello, Joseph, 248, 251–52

Pisicano, Paul, 218–19

Pitrè, Giuseppe, 17, 20, 23, 88

Pizzo Di Lorenzo, Felicia, 9

Polcari, Emma, 211

Political prisoners, 145, 157, 162, 209, 223

Pope, Generoso, 216, 224

Popular Front, 241, 255, 256, 264, 267

Porcelli, Francesco Paolo, 137

Positivist anthropologists, 82–89

Poverty, 13–14, 27, 28, 32, 41, 42, 55, 79, 83, 91

Powell, Adam Clayton, Jr., 255

Prato, 148

Prestianni, Maria, 198

Priests, 11, 22, 30, 32, 37, 129, 130, 171, 192. *See also* Catholic Church

Primo Maggio (May Day), 145–46, 178

Processions, 37, 131–32

Profascist. *See* Fascism

Progressive Era, 103, 109, 179

Il Progresso Italo-Americano, 146, 180, 216

Prohibition, 111

Il Proletario, 142, 148, 180, 253

Prominenti, 182, 192, 216, 219

Prosetto, Rose, 248

Prostitution, 29, 30, 41, 49, 56, 61, 62; criminology and, 85–86; white slavery and, 95–97

La Protesta, 62

Protestant values, 7, 103, 105, 179

Provenzano, Mamie, 96–97

Proverbs, 17, 18, 22–23, 42, 46, 88, 132

Providence, R.I., 3, 214

Public housing, 239, 260–61, 263–64

"Public transcript," 25, 131. *See also* "Hidden transcript"

Public Works Administration (PWA) Housing Division, 261

Puerto Ricans, 5, 67, 121, 145, 158, 159, 265; in Harlem, 1930s to 1940s, 230, 233, 234, 235–40, 251–52, 254, 255, 256, 257, 263–64; women in garment industry, 250–52, 254–55

Puglia, 11, 53. *See also* Apulia

Queens, 194, 205, 207, 220, 235; Astoria, 181; Elmhurst-Corona, 269

La questione meridionale (The Southern Question; Gramsci), 83

La Question Sociale, 148, 149–50, 154, 158; antiracism and, 204; garment industry strikes and, 180; women's participation in, 139, 155, 156, 159, 162, 163, 165–67, 170, 171–72, 190

Quintiliano, Luigi, 209, 223

Racial ideologies, 182, 239, 253–54; in Argentina, 63; in Brazil, 64; criminology and, 82–90, 93–98

Racialization: of Italian immigrant women, 81–82, 84, 85–87, 88, 90–91; between northern and southern Italian immigrants, 82–89, 90, 107–8, 110. *See also* Whiteness

Racism: against African Americans, 1910s to 1920s, 93, 95, 97, 106, 107; against African Americans, 1930s to 1940s, 204–5, 233, 234, 236–37, 240, 251, 252, 254, 258; in Brazil, 65–66; class and, 7, 84, 87, 88, 103; ethnic conflict and, 75, 121–22, 233, 239, 250; fascism and, 217–18; 220, 221; Italian, 1930s to 1940s, 230–31, 233–40; southern Italian immigrants as "racially superior" to other groups, 5, 6, 66, 78, 81, 90–91, 93, 95, 97; against southern Italians, 5–6, 81, 82–98, 234, 238; against southern Italians, in assimilation movement, 106–8; against southern Italians, in slums, 98–102; violence and, 107, 204, 217, 230–31, 232, 233, 237, 238, 257. *See also* Antiracist politics; Segregation

Radicalism, 3, 5, 35, 40, 46, 63, 66, 105, 107, 133, 134, 138, 181, 184, 198; of Maria Roda and other women, 155–75, 190–97, 208–9, 211–12, 225–26, 227; subculture of, 4, 6, 78, 141–55, 165, 170, 175, 187, 188, 190, 197, 206, 210, 218, 222, 231, 236. *See also* Anarchist movement; Anarchist women's groups; Diasporic radicalism; Palmer raids; Red Scare

Radical press. *See* Italian-language newspapers

Radical theater, 172–75

Rafanelli, Leda, 190–91

Raffuzzi, Louis, 160

Raffuzzi, Maria, 160

Ragusa, Kym, 135

Raitano, Lillie, 223, 250

Rallies, 38, 39, 65, 145, 174, 195, 217, 222, 224, 256, 260, 262, 263

Ramella, Remilda, 143

Randolph, A. Philip, 260

Razza (race), 88

Red Scare, 6, 149, 150, 198, 201–7; antifascism and, 224; fascism and, 216, 218, 221, 234; labor unions after, 206, 210, 212, 222, 241

Reeder, Linda, 41, 48

Regeneración, 147

Reisch, Sadie, 247

Remittances, 14, 49, 53

Repatriation, 4, 57, 101

Revelli, Nuto, 30

Revolutionary industrial unionism, 1–2, 3, 4–5, 6. *See also* Labor strikes; Labor unions

Revolutionary socialism. *See* Socialism

Reynolds, Minnie J., 97

Ribaudo, Frances, 214, 215, 227

Il Ribelle (The Rebel), 173

Rigola, Rinaldo, 149

Riis, Jacob, 79, 93, 99

Rinaldi, Josefina, 62

Rivera, Oscar García, 258

Rivetti Mill, 149

Rockefeller, John D., 96

Rocky Mountain News, 97

Roda, Cesare, 156–57

Roda, Maria, 1, 139–40, 148, 155–60, 163, 165, 166, 167, 168, 170, 173, 208, 270, 303–4 (n. 106)

Rodríguez, Carlotta, 252

Rodríguez, Johnny, 230

Rolón, Catalino, 235

Roman Empire, 82, 83, 88

Romanik, Diane, 244

Rome, 1, 11, 36, 37, 38, 58, 82, 140, 207, 224, 226

Romualdi, Lucia, 223, 250

Roosevelt, Eleanor, 244

Roosevelt, Franklin Delano, 242, 258

Roosevelt, Theodore, 145

Rosario, Argentina, 60, 61

Rosario, Maria, 70

Rose, Aida, 247

Ross, Edward A., 94

Rossi, Adolfo, 11, 37, 38

The Rubicon, 238

Rubinstein, Annette, 255–56

Russian immigrants, 62, 69, 145, 176, 180, 235, 251

Russian Jews. *See* Jewish immigrants; Jewish women

Russian Revolution, 197, 202, 206, 211

Russo, Anna, 260, 261

Russo, Nicholas, 128

Rygier, Maria, 155

Sabotage, 147, 186, 210

Sacco, Nicola, 6, 136–38, 148, 200, 203, 223, 226, 228

Saints, 28, 29–30, 31, 127, 129, 130, 132

Salandra, Nettie, 248

Salemme, Jenny, 173

Salerno, 44, 51, 55

Salerno, Salvatore, 204

Sallitto, Dominick, 150

Salvemini, Gaetano, 215

Sanfilippo, Mary, 189

San Francisco, 61

San Gennaro, 129

San Giovanni Batista, 130

San Giuseppe in Salemi, 31

Sanjek, Roger, 270

Sant'Agata of Catania, 30, 31, 129

Santa Lucia, 30, 129

Santa Rosalia, 30, 129

Santoro, Maria, 53

Santos, Brazil, 57

Santucci, Agnes, 57

São Paulo, 3, 13, 57, 61, 64–66, 87, 163

Sardinia, 10, 82, 90, 143

Sarmiento, Domingo, 63

La Sartina. See Seamstresses

La Sartina (pseudonym), 156

Saturday Evening Post, 215
Saverio Merlino, Francesco, 143
Schneider, Eric, 233
Scott, James, 24–25, 26
Scottsboro "boys," 257
Scuola d'Industrie Italiane, 103–4
Seamstresses: in Argentina, 62; from Italy to New York City, 15, 44–47, 52–53, 56–60, 62, 67–78, 128; in southern Italy, 44, 46, 47–48, 52
Section for Factory and Home Workers (SOLD), 218
Segregation, 102, 106, 138, 238, 239, 240, 254, 260, 264, 269
Selassie, Haile, 217
Sergeant, Elizabeth Shipley, 92
Sergi, Giuseppe, 82, 83, 89, 90
Settlement houses, 103–4, 107, 120, 126, 188, 255, 261; Greenwich House, 79–80, 103, 104, 119; Haarlem House, 219, 262; Henry Street Settlement, 119; Union Settlement, 105, 258, 262, 292 (n. 161)
Sevirole, Lucy, 21, 118
Sexual abuse, 24–25, 65, 75
Sexuality, 95–96; sewing and, 53; southern Italian women as "deviant," 83, 84–85, 86–87, 93, 200; of women in southern Italy, 24–25, 27, 41–42. *See also* Free love
Sharecropping, 16, 18
Sicilians: anarchism and, 87, 143, 145, 147, 207; as immigrants in Argentina, 60; language, 121, 124; mafia and, 33, 94–95; as New York immigrants, 100, 101, 107, 108, 110, 150, 170, 207, 219, 222, 227, 231, 243; as "racially inferior," 82, 84, 88, 90, 94, 106–7; seamstresses, 46, 52–53; women agricultural laborers, 48–49, 50, 54; women immigrants, in New York, 52–54, 56–59, 77, 102, 118, 124, 128, 129, 144, 155, 244, 246; women's labor strikes in Sicily and, 9–11, 12–13, 32–40, 85, 87; women's lives in Sicily and, 16–32, 40–43, 46, 55, 171
Sicily: Agrigento, 40; Bagheria, 35; Balestrate, 9; Belmonte, 9, 38; Belmonte Mezzagno, 36, 38; Campofiorito, 36; Cinisi, 101; Leonforte, 57; Messina, 17, 39, 51, 54; Milocca, 29; Misterbianco, 35, 38; Molise, 33; Monreale, 9; Sambuca di Sicilia, 39, 48; San Giuseppe Jato, 36, 37, 38; Sciacca, 40; Siracusa, 30, 39; Sutera, 18, 38; Trapani, 31, 38, 39, 51; Villafrati, 9. *See also* Catania; Corleone; Palermo; Piana dei Greci
Siebert, Renate, 14, 17, 21, 22, 24, 30
Sigman, Morris, 212–13

Silk mills, 67, 108, 124; in Italy, 39, 51, 55, 56; labor strikes of women in, 152, 154, 174–75, 180–81, 184, 186, 192, 193–97, 210–12, 242; of Paterson, N.J., 73–75, 76, 144, 145, 151, 161, 172, 186, 201, 203, 266
Silvestrini, Concetta, 169, 172
Simkhovitch, Mary Kingsbury, 79–80, 103
Sinatra, Anthony. *See* O'Brien, Marty
Sinatra, Dolly, 110–13, 114
Sinatra, Frank, 111–12
Socialism, 60, 66, 150, 225, 254, 255, 267; antifascism and, 221–23; Great Depression and, 236, 241; in Italy, 9, 32, 36, 37–40; labor unions and, 105, 124, 179, 186, 187, 189, 198, 206, 211, 214, 223, 235, 249, 252, 253; reformists and, 206, 223; revolutionary, 142, 143, 145, 177, 186, 190, 198, 201, 211; women and, 3, 134, 139, 142, 155, 156, 170, 207, 256. *See also* Anarchist movement; Italian Socialist Party
Socialist Party, 124, 181
Social Security Act, 239
Songs, 9, 20, 26, 27, 29, 39, 42, 88, 139, 157, 172, 183, 186, 231
Sorcery, 28–29
Southern Italy: people compared with northern Italians, 82–89, 90, 107–8, 110; poverty, turn of twentieth century, 13–14, 27, 28, 32, 41, 42, 55; "primitive" nature of people from, 7, 12, 50, 81, 82–83, 86–87, 210; racial inferiority beliefs about people from, 5–6, 81, 82–98, 234, 238; seamstresses of, 44, 46, 47–48, 52; women, in absence of migrating men, 23–24, 40–43, 44, 48; women laborers of, 15–16, 47–56; women's lives in, 16–43, 46, 55, 171. *See also* Apulia; Basilicata; Calabria; Campania; Emigration; Immigration; Sicilians; Sicily
Sovversivi, 142, 148, 153, 173, 187, 205
Spada, Joseph, 237
Spagnoletti, Ginevra, 122, 183, 191, 223
Spain, 90, 141, 149, 159, 227
Spanish Civil War (1936–39), 227
Spanish Harlem, 235. *See also* East Harlem; Harlem; Italian Harlem
Spanish Left Opposition Group, 252
Spanish workers, 63, 145, 235
Spezia, Bellalma Forzato, 155, 167, 302 (n. 81)
Spinelli, Grace Billotti, 126
Spinners, 23, 38, 39, 48, 51
Spirituality. *See* Catholic Church; Madonna; Mysticism
Spring Valley, Ill., 160
Squillante, Anna, 198

La Stampa Libera, 223
State County and Municipal Employees of America, 261
Staten Island, 205, 217, 248
Stone, Frank, 204
Storytelling, 20, 34, 46–47, 88, 170
Strikes. *See* Labor strikes
Sulmona, Abruzzo, 116, 225
Sweatshops, 91–93, 103, 242; anti-sweatshop movement and, 91, 93, 97; homework and, 70–72, 73, 286 (n. 73); Italian women seamstresses in, 45, 69–72
Switzerland, 13, 142, 162
Syrian workers, 76, 251

Tampa, 3, 159, 163, 192
Tarantino, Millie, 189
Tax protests, 9, 14, 16, 33, 35, 37, 38–39
Teatro Sociale, 172
Tenements, 70, 71, 72, 76, 108, 117, 120, 127, 129–30; in East Harlem, 114, 115–16, 119, 207, 258, 259, 260, 261–63; fires in, 261–63, 322 (n. 156)
Textile industry, 45, 59, 159, 167; in Italy, 48, 51–52, 56, 139, 148–49, 161; in Latin America, 62, 65; Lawrence textile strike, 1912, 192, 193, 196, 253; Lawrence textile strike, 1919, 155, 192, 193, 207, 208; strike, 1909, 180, 181; strike, 1913, 175, 194; strike, 1919, 197, 204; strikes, 1926, 210–12; unions and, 141, 145, 186, 187; work conditions, 73–74, 76. *See also* Silk mills
Thomas, Piri, 230
Time magazine, 234
Tirreno, Millie, 198
Titì, 156, 165, 166, 167–69
Tomasi, Maria, 228
Topp, Michael Miller, 148
Transatlantic migration, 2, 14–16, 42, 55, 60. *See also* Emigration
Transnationalism, 3, 4, 5, 13, 15, 40, 66, 101–2, 206; anarchist movement and, 87, 163, 177, 267; antifascism and, 201, 224; family economy and, 53, 57, 59; fascism and, 201, 215; feminism and, 6–7, 191; labor migration and, 45–46, 56
Trenton, N.J., 76, 149, 216, 217
Tresca, Carlo, 3, 134, 142, 187, 196, 209
Triangle Shirtwaist Factory Fire (1911), 192
La Tribuna, 11
Tropiano, Mary, 21
Trousseaus, 53
Turati, Filippo, 11

Turin, 51
Turkish immigrants, 62, 145, 251, 269
Turner, George Kibbe, 96

Umberto I (king of Italy), 144, 161
Union Local Hispana, 252
Union Settlement, 105, 258, 262, 292 (n. 161)
L'Unita del Popolo, 134, 257
United Council of Working Class Women, 256
United Garment Workers of America (UGW), 210
United Mine Workers of America, 142
U.S. Bureau of Immigration, 89
U.S. Housing Authority (USHA), 261
U.S. Immigration Commission, 52, 89
Unity, Nobility, and Ambition Society (UNA), 220–21
Urban renewal, 264, 268

Valdinoci, Carlo, 201
Valenti, Anna, 122, 132, 183–84
Valenti, Catherine, 187
Valle Superiore, 161
Vanzetti, Bartolomeo, 6, 137, 148, 200, 203, 223, 226, 228
Varanelli, Alma, 189
Vásquez, Helen, 256, 257, 260
Vecoli, Rudolph, 27, 128, 143, 205, 206
Vedove bianche (widows in white), 40–43
Vega, Bernardo, 235, 241
Velasco, Beatrice, 263
Veneto, 13, 64
Ventresca, Robert, 225
Vercelli, 148
Verga, Giovanni, 50
Verro, Bernardino, 37
Violence: domestic abuse, 24–25, 26; racial violence, early twentieth century, 107; racial violence, 1920s, 217; racial violence, 1930s to 1940s, 204, 230–31, 232, 233, 237, 238, 257
Von Gloeden, Wilhelm, 84
La Voz de la Mujer, 63

Wage work. *See* Low-wage labor
Wagner Act, 239
Wald, Lillian, 119
Wall Street bombing (1920), 203, 311 (n. 22)
Washington, D.C., 201, 226, 242, 244, 261
Weavers, 47, 49, 51, 54, 74, 75, 149, 156, 172, 181, 195; silk, 73, 139, 144, 194, 203
Welfare programs, 209, 239, 261
Welfare Workers Federation of America, 261

West Hoboken, N.J., 76, 142, 155, 181, 186, 228; fascism and, 216, 224. *See also* Hoboken, N.J.

Whiteness, 5, 66, 90–91, 109; Italian Americans identifying with, 6, 81–82, 91, 108, 201, 217, 230–32, 233–34, 236–40, 254, 255, 264

"White slavery," 95–97

White Slave Traffic Act of 1910, 96

White supremacy, 6, 83, 106, 150, 200, 207, 233, 234, 237, 238

Willett, Mabel Hurd, 119

Williams, John, 257

Williams, Phyllis H., 135, 136

Williamsburg, Brooklyn, 122, 129–30, 269

Witches, 28–29, 85

"Wobblies." *See* Industrial Workers of the World

Wolfe, Joel, 65

Women's Trade Union League (WTUL), 179, 180, 181

Woodhull, Victoria, 105

World War I, 39, 209, 268; anarchist movement and, 6, 147, 150, 153, 199; antiwar demonstrations by southern Italian women, 40; emigration from Italy and, 56

World War II, 231, 233, 237, 239, 251, 268

Zaccari, Maria, 228

Zannotti, Susanna, 171

Zara, Clara, 189, 191

Zimmerman, Charles, 252

Zullo, Antonia, 137